Forensic Aspects of Vision and Highway Safety

Revised and updated

Merrill J. Allen, O.D., Ph.D.
Bernard S. Abrams, O.D.
Arthur P. Ginsburg, Ph.D.
Leslie Weintraub, O.D.

Lawyers & Judges Publishing Company, Inc.

Lawyers & Judges Publishing Company, Inc.

P.O. Box 30040 • Tucson, AZ 85751-0040
(800) 209-7109 • FAX (800) 330-8795
Website: http://www.lawyersandjudges.com
E-mail: sales@lawyersandjudges.com

Forensic aspects of vision and highway safety / Merrill J. Allen ... [et al.].
Revised and updated.
p. cm.
Includes bibliographical references and index.
ISBN:1-930056-03-6
1. Automobile medicine. 2. Automobile driving. 3. Traffic accident investigation.
I. Allen, Merrill J., 1918–
RA1062.5 .F67 2000
614/.1 21

C.I.P.

ISBN 1-930056-03-6
Printed in the United States of America
10 9 8 7 6 5 4 3 2 1

Table of Contents

Acknowledgments

Many people have assisted me in conducting the research and publishing the many documents leading to this book.

I particularly wish to thank Joan, my lovely wife, for her support throughout my research career. She did the typing and editing of my first book, *Vision and Highway Safety*, published by the Chilton Book Company, 1970. That book provides the basics for this book, *Forensic Aspects of Vision and Highway Safety.*

I appreciate the long term support provided by Henry W. Hofstetter, O.D., Ph.D., Director of the Division of Optometry of Indiana University, retired 1993. One of his staff, Jacque Edgar Kubley, M.S. Ed., provided photographs and drawings for most of the figures. Mrs. Ritsuko Noda, R.N., currently a staff member of the School of Optometry, provided the very important color figures using the latest computer technology. James V. Redding, P.E. formerly of the Indiana University Electronics Department, helped design and build the mechanical and electronic equipment used in the multiple research experiments which support this book.

—Merril J. Allen

Foreword

Professor Merrill Allen has been in the forefront of technical and policy concern over the visual environment provided by the contemporary motor vehicle. His findings in the past have stimulated legislative, motor vehicle manufacturer, and repair and maintenance action. In this book he brings together his and other experts' research and analyses to encourage the motor vehicle industries to continue to improve the driver's visual environment by removing the many known defects in visual design, such as windshield and dash panel glare; dark, camouflaging vehicle colors; and the absence of standard, vertically power adjustable driver's seats in all vehicles to help the short driver see to drive. His goal is to assist the driver to cope with an ever more demanding highway environment. He informs drivers of the myths and commercial banalities that impair and hinder their visual perception.

Will the manufacturers and the U.S. Department of Transportation finally listen and act?

—Ralph Nader

Preface

This book is intended to provide optometrists, highway engineers, legislators, manufacturers, law enforcement personnel, attorneys, and others with information on the visual aspects of driving a motor vehicle. The optometrist will find valuable information for examining eyes, for prescribing driving glasses and for better understanding of the vision requirements of the driving task, all of which will be helpful should it be necessary to serve as an expert witness in a court of law or to help shape legislation to improve highway safety, and so forth. Careful vision testing for a driver's license and better standards for those tests will ensure that the driver is fully prepared visually.

Improving the visual driving environment, both in the vehicle and on the streets and highways, *will eliminate at least half of the deaths, injuries and the costs associated with motor vehicle accidents.*

Today alcohol is involved in less than 50 percent of the accidents, and over half of those are single-car "ran off the road" accidents. Surprisingly, when analyzed objectively and unemotionally, the alcohol-associated accidents point out the deficiencies in our transportation system. In many alcohol-related accidents, the accident was *not* caused by the presence of alcohol. In others, the alcohol simply delayed recognition time and contributed to the accident as if the driver were older or distracted by smoking, car phones, map reading, adjusting the radio, and so forth.

Half of all accidents could be prevented if there was 0.75 second of earlier awareness of the danger (Eneke). This earlier awareness can be provided by improvements in the visibility of the driving scene, even when some drivers are intoxicated or have their attention on something other than driving.

At least 50 percent of all motor vehicle related fatalities can be prevented by proper vision design. Bureaucratic indifference is killing at least 20,000 people per year. Our present blaming of alcohol and the driver serves to divert our attention from the designed-in vehicle and roadway killers. Alcohol reduces the driver's ability to compensate, thus pointing out the designed-in problems.

The news media coverage has been of help in the past. However, because many of the causes of accidents have been published for at least thirty years without any industry or governmental response, it appears that law suits against NHTSA, the SAE, the designers of motor vehicles, and the motor vehicle manufacturers, will be the most effective way to get the attention of these agencies that are ignoring the carnage that they are responsible for in America.

The following are most of the easily fixed, built-in, safety hazards that must be corrected: black bumpers; black mud guards; black paint; black tires; factory-installed window tint; add-on window tint; failure to put a dull black finish (often seen on bumpers) on dash panels; large windshield corner posts that obstruct vision; large and high-mounted, vision-obstructing outside rear view mirrors; inadequate and nonstandard, vertically adjustable power seats needed by short drivers; excess eye height of truck drivers which destroys the effectiveness of retroreflective road signs and pavement markings; wide variations in headlight and tail light height and spacing; the absence of white shape-coding of red tail lights, red brake lights and red stop and go signal lights which is needed by 2 percent of the male population who can't see red; the absence of safe side and rear truck under-run protection; the absence of side and rear lights near the pavement (18") on commercial vehicles; the absence of energy-absorbing bumpers (such as air bag bumpers) on cars, trucks or trains; the absence of automatic dirt removal (or mandatory hand cleaning) of windows, tail lights, sidelights, headlights and reflectors on trucks and other vehicles; the absence on motorcycles of flashing identification headlights or of triangular shape-coding, using three headlights day and night on low as well as high beams; the absence of side lights on trains; the absence of multiple, low, wide-angle, headlights on all locomotives, and so forth.

Most fatal motorcycle accidents occur because an oncoming vehicle turns into the path of the motorcycle. While not standard, some motorcycles do have accessory three headlights that give a triangular shape coding. Unfortunately, the three headlights are displayed only on high beam and thus do not prevent the cycle's low beam headlight from looking like a headlight on the oncoming car behind the motorcycle. Rapidly flashing headlights are available on some motorcycles to distinguish them from cars and trucks.

To start saving lives, the first, cheapest and easiest safety step is to provide a flat-black for the top of the dash panel. Except for the black needed on the dash panel, the second step is to totally eliminate all black and dark colors on all motor vehicles and pedestrians. The third step is to provide powered, vertically adjustable seats on all motor vehicles to help the many small, short drivers. I believe these three steps alone will reduce accidents and deaths 50 percent.

This book will provide most of the information needed to improve all visual aspects of the driving task. The student interested in pursuing the details of the massive literature on the visual aspects of driving will find assistance in the bibliography and in library computer services.

—Merril J. Allen, 1 September 2000.

Forensic Aspects of Vision and Highway Safety

Chapter 1

Introduction

Merrill J. Allen, O.D., Ph.D.

In view of the growth of the human population, the number of motor vehicles that we have, and the miles driven, it is amazing that we have as few accidents as we do! However, we do have a serious problem of deaths and injuries caused by motor vehicle accidents. Accident statistics indicate the magnitude of the problem and help us understand that we must do our best to reduce the carnage.

It is reported that in 1899 the first automobile accident death was Henry H. Bliss, struck by an automobile in New York City. From 1900 to 1964 motor vehicle deaths in the United States totaled 1,510,000, while military deaths totaled only 605,000 from 1775 to 1964 (American Trial Lawyers' Association, 1966).

Deaths among battle casualties in World War I were 8 percent of those reaching the hospital or medical installation. In World War II these deaths dropped to 4.5 percent, in the Korean War they were 2.5 percent, and in Vietnam, about 2 percent. Of automobile deaths, 33 percent die at the scene, in the ambulance, or within minutes of arriving at the hospital (NAS, June 1969). Since 67 percent of the crash victims in 1969 died in the civilian hospital, could it be that motor vehicle injuries are more devastating than war injuries?

The number of drivers in 1967 was 103 million, of whom 13.5 million were involved in accidents. The number whose injuries caused at least a day of restricted activity or medical care was 3,535,000 or nearly 10,000 per day (DOT, 1969). Forty percent of all fatal accidents involve two or more motor vehicles. One out of three cars will cause an injury or death, and three out of four cars will be in an accident. In 1968 injuries, deaths, and property damage cost over 14.24 billion dollars and 55,500 deaths. (Assuming 5 percent per year increase in the cost of living, the cost in 2000 will be 67.8 billion dollars.)

I am pleased to report that the number of vehicle accident deaths in 1999 declined to fewer than 40,000. The deaths per 100 million miles declined from 5.5 in 1966 to 1.8 in 1992. (*Am. J. Pub. Health*, Jan. 1996).

The first automobile safety standards were imposed by the General Services Administration in 1966 on cars purchased for the government fleet. I was a member of the Advisory Panel. Standards began to be imposed on all new cars in 1968. Federal Standards lead to crash worthiness tests, high mounted brake lights, seat belts and air bags. Unfortunately, starting in the 1990s, NHTSA has been eliminating many vehicle safety standards, including the maximum allowable size for the windshield corner posts. This is truly a disaster. Go take a look at new cars. There is an unbelievable disregard for vision and accident prevention in the industries.

Daytime running lights are not required in the USA, but are legal. My data, plus a quarter century of over the road experience with daytime running lights in Europe and Canada, indicate that we Americans can expect a 12 to 15 percent reduction in all accidents, once all vehicles have daytime running lights.

In the fall of 1995, General Motors began installing daytime running lights on new automobiles. This means all manufacturers soon will be installing them. Thanks to GM for this most significant step forward to improve motor vehicle safety!

Based on my study of thousands of accident reports, my research, and my experience in the courtroom, I predict that along with daytime running lights, *we can prevent 90 percent of all motor vehicle accidents, deaths and injuries* by improving the visual aspects of vehicles, highways, signals and lighting! We can cut our accidents, casualties, and costs at little expense. Here are examples: Ban black on all motor vehicles including cars, trains, bicycles, motorcycles, busses, trucks, utility vehicles and even pedestrians. Require black on the top of all instrument panels. Make all bumpers on all vehicles white. Put white side panels on all vehicles. Make white tires standard on all motor vehicles including trucks. Make white mud guards standard. Ban tinted glass in windshields. Ban all tint added to windows and lights.

"The Nut Behind the Wheel" has been blamed long enough for the problems caused by the "Bureaucrat Behind the Desk!"

To what extent is the vision of the nut behind the wheel involved in accidents? Analysis of accidents to determine the role played by visual acuity, peripheral vision, color vision and dark adaptation, have been disappointing. The most reliable early studies are from the Institute of Transportation and Traffic Engineering of the Department of Engineering of the University of California, Los Angeles, in cooperation with the California Department of Motor Vehicles. Starting in 1962, 17,500 test subjects were studied in depth. Burg summarized these studies in 1967:

> Among the vision variables studied, dynamic visual acuity shows the strongest and most consistent relationships with driving record. There is substantial but not conclusive evidence that static visual acuity, glare recovery and visual fields also are related to driving record.

> The data suggest differential vision driving relationships as a function of age; however, at the present stage of analysis, the precise nature and extent of these differential relationships cannot be determined.

> The data strongly suggest differential vision driving relationships as a function of sex. More definitive information will be provided by planned analyses involving specific accident types and qualitative exposure.

As to predicting a person's driving record, Burg, in the same report, states:

> Among vision variables, the results support the original research hypothesis by showing that dynamic visual acuity is by far the most consistent contributor to prediction, followed by static acuity, glare recovery, and visual field. The two remaining vision variables (glarimeter threshold and phoria) do not contribute consistently to prediction of a driving record variable; this does not imply that they might not contribute significantly in prediction of specific accident types, a possibility that future analyses will examine.

That alcohol was responsible for over 50 percent of the fatal accidents (Haddon et al., 1964); that mechanical failures have contributed significantly to accident causation (Moseley et al., 1961–62 and 1962–63); that a significant number of "accidents" are murders, suicides, or both (Ford and Moseley, 1963); that a significant number are true accidents with no one at fault; that there is a high percentage of innocent victim involvement; and that there are many factors beside vision that determine driving success, make Burg's accomplishment of relating vision to accidents all the more remarkable.

More recent researchers have also found it difficult to relate driver vision to accident causation. In addition to alcohol, other hazards to safe driving such as carbon monoxide, tranquilizers, antihistamines and so forth, act in part by destroying visual acuteness, eye movement control, body coordination, and perceptual alertness. Any compensatable visual anomaly becomes progressively less compensatable under the influence of these agents. Darkness alone, for example, reduces the ability to fuse the eye images, to focus the eyes, and, for the cross eyed driver, to suppress double vision. In addition, the reaction time is increased, space judgments are altered, and alertness is reduced. One could expect that heavy smokers, all of whom have higher levels of carbon monoxide in their blood (McFarland and Moseley, 1954), would have more visual discomfort and more problems with binocular vision and focus than persons not exposed to carbon monoxide; and that carbon monoxide symptoms would increase at higher elevations above sea level (McFarland et al., 1944). The harmful effects of carbon monoxide on driving are increased by alcohol, darkness, fatigue, and elevation.

The magnitude of the visual problems in America has been shown in several studies. It is reported that glaucoma exists in 2 percent of all over the age of forty; strabismus (eye turn) exists in from 2 to 7 percent of the population; more than 8 percent of drivers have some form of color vision anomaly; about 17 percent of the drivers have anisocoria (a difference in size of the left and right eye's pupil) to an extent which may be hazardous, and 0.5 to 4 percent have amblyopia (poor acuity, usually in only one eye). At grade school levels, 20 percent have visual anomalies sufficient to merit correction; and everyone by the age of sixty needs a visual correction of some type.

A study of the population visiting the state fair in Indiana (Allen, 1964) showed that visual deterioration with age was extensive. Field defects, retinal pathology, and visual inadequacy at far or near increased with age. Most people tested were capable of normal vision but had not taken steps to obtain it. Probably these statistics were colored by self-selection. People in poor health may have come to the test booth in higher numbers than those who believed their vision was corrected.

In the interests of retaining driving privileges, almost everyone would seek vision care. Knowledgeable optometrists are available to cooperate with and monitor the license bureau test stations to ensure effective visual screening. Unfortunately, ensuring adequate vision of our drivers will provide only a small reduction in the number of deaths and injuries.

Automobile manufacturers need to be reminded that they contribute to accidents with improper vehicle design. Examples are as follows: (1) glare from the windshield and dash panel; (2) seats that cannot be adjusted to suit all drivers; (3) huge corner post and rearview mirror obstructions; (4) black bumpers which make you less visible by day and invisible at night; (5) truck headlights mounted above passenger car driver eye height thus causing excessive glare; (6) window tinting and add-on window tinting which reduce the candle power of street and headlights; and 7) the use of black mud guards and black tires when white mud guards and white tires would be seen much better at night.

We must not tolerate less than optimum vision design features of the products offered for sale, because of expediency in manufacture, the influence of marketing factors unrelated to visual efficiency, and the fact that next year's vehicle has already been designed and "cannot be changed." When the manufacturer asks for proof that the visually correct way is better, we should ask in turn to be shown justification for the hazardous approach being used.

This applies not only to manufacturers of automobiles, trucks, buses, motor cycles and bicycles but also to manufacturers of spectacle frames and lenses. Frames can obstruct vision. Lens colors can impair signal light detection. The wearer may be led to believe that tinted lenses will improve vision!

That the need for a pair of glasses might cause an accident is a simplification of the multiple visual factors entering into safe driving. Certainly, without vision there can be no driving of today's automobiles. No other sense modality holds such a veto power. Yet good vision alone is not enough to drive a motor vehicle. It is the myriad of other factors that makes the job of the scientist so difficult when he tries to prove the degree to which vision affects driving. This book will give the reader a greater appreciation of the complexities of the problem as well as some recommendations about what can be done to reduce accidents.

Chapter 2

The Driving Task

Merrill J. Allen, O.D., Ph.D.

What is the nature of the problem facing the driver? What does he have to do and what information is available to him? Aside from the simplicity of the statement that the driving task is the task of operating a motor vehicle from point A to point B without an accident, the Servo System analysis is much more informative.

The eye is the only source of driver information about the distance, size, course, speed, and possibly hazardous nature of objects on the roadway and about signal lights and roadway signs. In addition, it is the most important feedback source of information on the effects of the steering, accelerating, and braking actions of the driver. Auditory, vestibular, and pressure sensors at various points in the body, also supply information to the brain during steering, braking, and accelerating.

Figure 2.1 is a diagram of the Closed Loop Servo System composed of the driver, the motor vehicle, and the roadway. Turning the steering wheel changes the visual input to the brain, which modifies the signals to the muscles, which turn the steering wheel, which then changes the visual input to the brain, and so forth.

If a system involving a roadway, a driver, and a vehicle is to work properly, the driver must have proper knowledge, memory and experience, the motor vehicle must be responsive and predictable, and there must be feedback from the environment by way of several sense modalities. That these ideal conditions do not always exist in the present day driving situation is little appreciated. There are numerous sources of interference (noise) in the information supplied to the driver. Noise is indicated by lightning streaks in Figure 2.1.

Power brakes provide *positive feedback* to the driver. First, the driver presses his/her foot on the brake pedal. For one-half to two inches of pedal travel no braking effect occurs, and the pedal force is very low. Then a modest pedal force in a short distance is enough to lock all four wheels. When braking commences, the tires gripping the road pull back on the axles, which transmit the force to the frame, and the automobile body starts to slow down. Later, the driver begins to slow down when the padding in the seat has been put under tension by the slow-

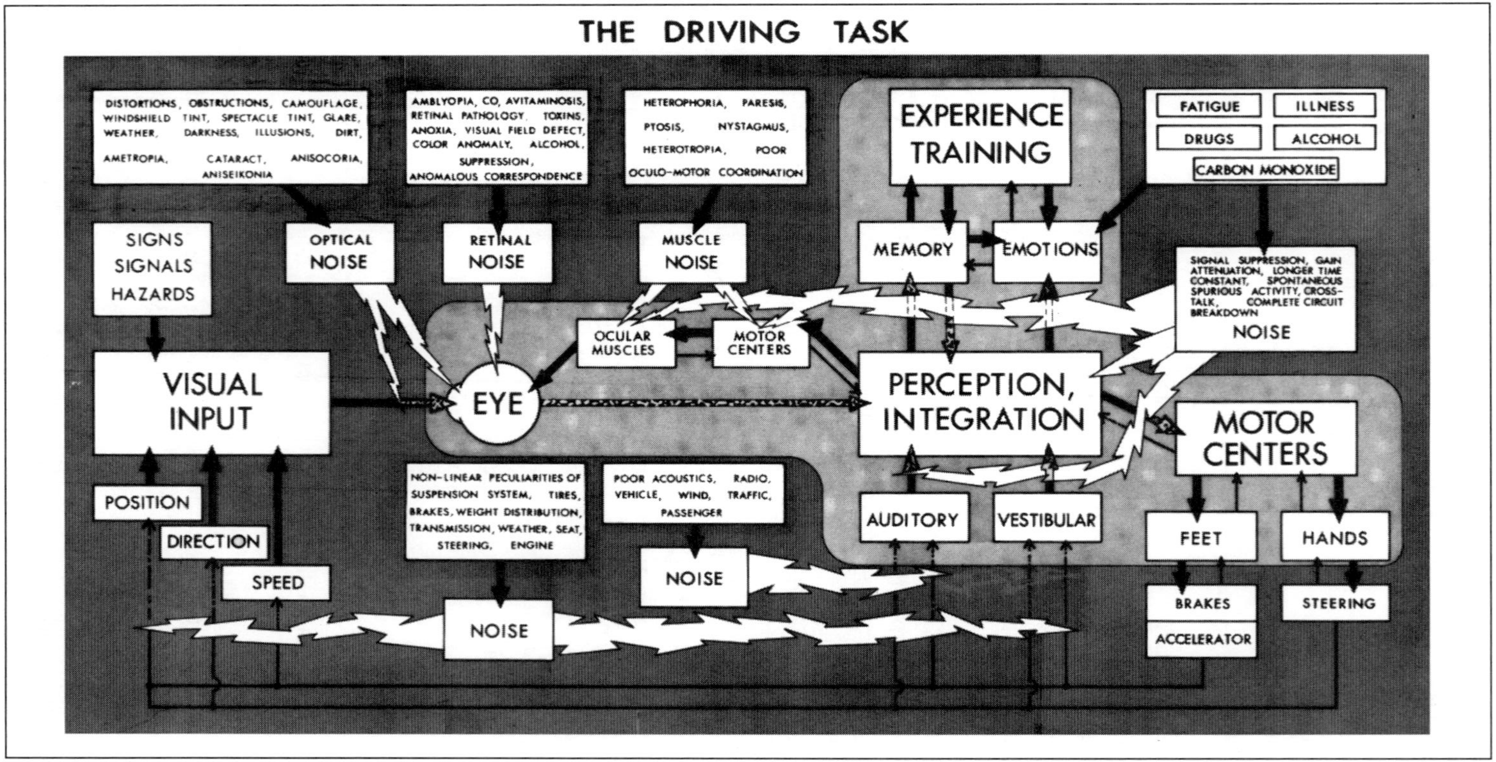

Figure 2.1 *The driving task closed loop servo system. The light input into the eyes is the beginning of the loop. The eye sends information to the perception centers, to the integration centers and to the motor control centers of the brain. The brain then sends signals to the hands and feet to operate the vehicle controls which modify the position on the road, and modify the visual input. The lightning streaks represent potential interferences (noise) which can reduce the efficiency of the driver. The main arrows show interference by being drawn as spotty. Note that the brain can filter out much of the noise and obtain surprisingly accurate information. Because of the brain's ability to compensate, few realize that the hazards, present in every day driving, can become serious if the brain's ability is compromised by fatigue, illness, lack of training, overloading, alcohol, etc.*

ing of the car. Thus, the driver tends to slide forward when the brakes are applied. Positive feedback is this increased pressure on the brake due to the forward movement of the driver. The increased brake action causes the driver to slide forward still more, putting on still more brake. To avoid locking the wheels, the driver must reduce foot pressure on the brake pedal to control the stopping rate. Practice and good coordination are necessary to make a smooth stop by releasing brake pressure enough to compensate for positive feedback. This is an almost impossible feat in a crisis. Resting your shoe heel on the floor will reduce this positive feedback.

There is little doubt that this positive feedback can result in the loss of vehicle control, as in rear-end accidents and skids on wet or icy streets. No doubt accidents have been averted by having such sensitive brakes, but the loss of steering and the reduction of braking efficiency resulting when wheels are locked must also be viewed as accident-producing characteristics.

In about 75 percent of the rear-end accidents there is enough time to release the brakes and steer around the hazard. Braking to a stop at 60 miles per hour

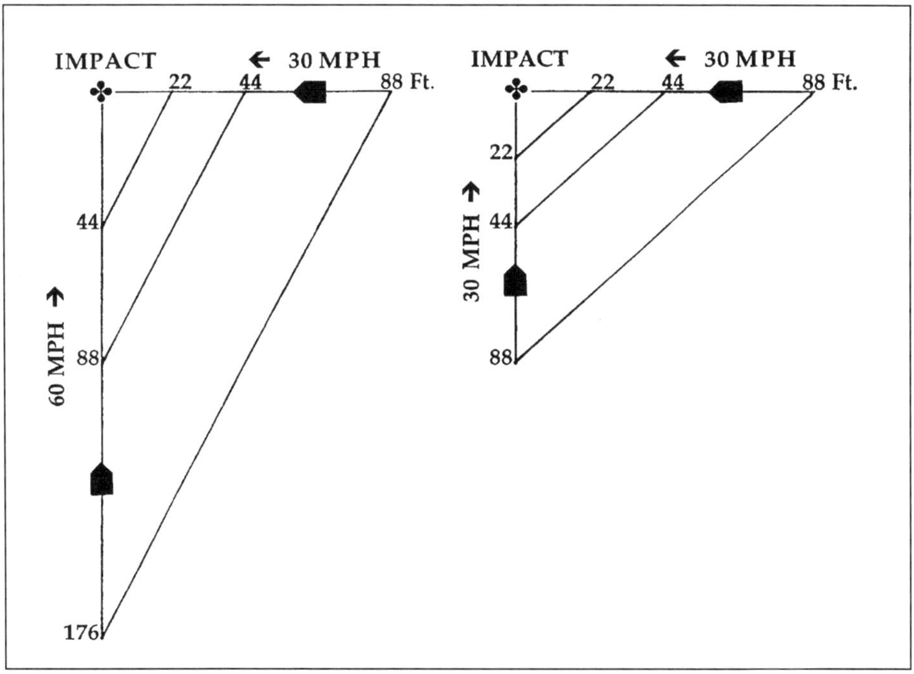

Figure 2.2 *The collision course. Two vehicles that arrive at the same point in time and space are on a collision course. The drawings show roads at right angles. Similar drawings for other angles and for curved roads are easily made. Note that with constant velocity each vehicle will be seen by the driver of the other vehicle at the same position in the field of view. Some of these positions will be obstructed by the rear view mirror, or by the windshield corner posts.*

takes 4 seconds. Swerving 8 feet to the side takes only one second! *Antilock brakes* can preserve steering control and prevent many accidents.

A smoothly operating, self-limiting *negative feedback* control system is the automobile accelerator. Pressure on the pedal causes the automobile to accelerate, which in effect pulls the accelerator pedal away from the foot and reduces the engine power. While it could cause a galloping acceleration in a car with excessive power and loose body and seat springing, it usually provides smooth, proportional, self-limiting control that the driver can moderate predictably.

The mechanical problems in steering are no less serious than those in braking. A prime example is the discontinued Corvair models with severe steering problems which contributed to many deaths and injuries. (Nader, 1965). The hazard of a tire failure is the loss of predictable steering ability. The driver might not be able to compensate soon enough for the unexpected change in vehicle characteristics to avert an accident, especially if the tire failure occurred in a turn or on wet pavement. A small, short vehicle will have a spin speed faster than that of a longer heavier machine, thus the spin due to tire failure may occur too quickly for an average driver to compensate. Pickup trucks, Jeep-styled vehicles and the

***Figure 2.3** A 1996 automobile with excessive obstruction of vision that can lead to accidents (also see Figure 2.4). The camera is low and pointed to the left to simulate the view of a short driver. Young, female and older drivers tend to be short. Vertically adjustable power seats must be made standard on all vehicles. That power seats are not standard, combined with the obstructions to vision shown in these photos, indicate that NHTSA and the automobile industry minimize the importance of drivers being able to see out of a motor vehicle. This was an overcast day so windshield glare was minimal.*

many vehicles with big wheels and elevated springs are likely to roll over.

The above examples illustrate the nature of negative and positive feedback that can affect a driver's perception of what the machine is doing. We see in Figure 2.1 that perception is modified by a certain amount of interference entering with the desired information. This is called *noise*. The information that comes back to the driver from the machine should help the driver to know how well it is responding and what it can do.

Using a stick to reach a wasp's nest is analogous to driving an automobile. Once the stick user gets the feel of the characteristics of the stick, it becomes part of the user's body. The experienced automobile driver knows where each wheel is on the road, what to expect for a certain steering wheel twist or brake push, what a low tire feels like, how much room it takes to turn around, where the bumpers are, etc., just as if these parts of the vehicle were parts of the driver's own body.

Now let us look at the visual inputs that every driver must have. The wide assortment of sources and types of visual information needed and used in driving is indicated in Figure 2.1.

Figure 2.4 *Same as Figure 2.3 except the camera is aimed to the right. It shows that the large corner post structures can hide an approaching vehicle on a collision course. As in Figure 2.3 the door upholstery just below the side window is not glossy, while the plastic dash panel in front of the driver is. An upholstery like finish is under the rear window of all 1996 new and used vehicles, but it is not on the dash panel of any! When applied to the dash panel, this velvet like finish must be black. In 2000, industry is still not using the ideal dull black flock cloth finish.*

Obstruction of visual input by structural components of the vehicle reduces the information that would be available to the motorist. Roof support structures, the rearview mirror, the hood and the fenders are the principal obstructors of useful visual information from the driver's seat. Figure 2.2 shows examples of collision courses. The collision course is unique because the oncoming vehicle does not move left or right but just gets bigger. When near to the windshield posts or the rearview mirror, an object on a collision course may not be seen by the driver in time to avoid a collision. An object that does not move in peripheral vision, as when on a collision course, is likely to be overlooked until too late.

In the case of the hood and fenders, some benefit is provided by giving useful visual clues as to the vehicle's size, location and direction of movement; information that is not supplied in the case of flat nosed trucks, buses, and vans. The mere presence of a windshield increases the visual noise level. Reflections, dirt and surface scratches reduce image contrast.

A modern windshield set at an angle of 60 degrees from the vertical reflects about 20 percent of the visible light, see Figure 8.5, and provides a location for dust, water droplets, and bugs to collect. The tint in the windshields in most automobiles cause an additional signal attenuation which raises the visual noise level. According to the Society of Automotive Engineers specifications (SAE 1981), a windshield is permitted to lose 30 percent of the visible light at normal incidence, i.e. the windshield is vertical and the light strikes the glass at 90 degrees. The windshield, installed in the vehicle at 60 degrees from the vertical, will lose about 39 percent of the visible light due to absorption and reflection.

The loss of red light is even greater. When tested vertically in the laboratory, the tinted windshield will transmit about 58 percent of the red light. At the 60 degree angle in the automobile, only 48 percent of the red light is transmitted (see Figure 8.9). Thus the windshield reduces the candle power of red signal lights by more than 50 percent.

The windshield becomes a one-way mirror when viewed from the outside. When you try to look into a car with a tinted windshield, the image of the sky, mirrored by the glass is usually brighter than the light coming from inside the car. Similarly, when trying to see out of the windshield, reflections from the top of the dash panel, or from papers on it, will be superimposed on the roadway ahead. If these reflections are brighter than the pedestrians or cars ahead, the motorist will find it difficult or impossible to see these hazards (see Figures 2.5 through 2.7).

A source of noise typical of automobiles manufactured prior to 1968 was the sunlight reflected from chromium surfaces. That noise reduced the amount of useful information. Lower intensity but large area sources, such as a light colored shiny hood or the open sky, can also cause performance losses. (Allen, Spring 1968); see Figure 2.8. Plastic is widely used in today's motor vehicles in place of chromium. Our next step is to convince the industry that all *plastic bumpers should be white* to improve conspicuity.

The driver is the most important component in the Servo Loop. The driver must see and process the information, eliminate the unimportant, and compensate for the several interferences that occur even under the best conditions. To do this the driver behaves like a sophisticated computer, with a memory bank of experience and training, entering into each decision. If impaired by alcohol, illness, or other physiologically detrimental factors, the number of events per second that can be processed through the computer brain will be proportionately reduced.

Heavy traffic and high speed increase the number of decisions to be made and the amount of information that has to be processed. Safe performance with an increasing perceptual load can be expected only up to a point. Beyond that point, our computer brain breaks down from perceptual overload, performance becomes erratic, and an accident may occur.

A person required to carry on an exciting conversation while driving may become perceptually overloaded even at 20 miles per hour; thus, it is difficult to say categorically when overload begins or whether a given situation constitutes a safe perceptual load. The amount of visual noise, the condition of the driver and

Figure 2.5 *Photo taken from outside a vehicle in a dealer's parking lot to show that windows act as mirrors. In addition to the bright glare coming off the dash and reflected by the windshield, the lower right area shows a pole, light and wires reflected by the side window.*

Figure 2.6 *This photograph was taken in 1969 to show the view when dash panel glare is controlled with a dull black cloth. Figure 2.7 shows the glare without the cloth.*

Figure 2.7 *About 1960, as the Director of the American Optometric Foundation, Night Vision Research Project, I was driving a Chevrolet from the Indiana University car pool, when I encountered this glare problem. I couldn't see in the daytime! I immediately expanded the study to include day time visual problems. In spite of our studies, reports and news releases, the situation today is the same as it was 40 years ago!*

Figure 2.8a *About 9 a.m., looking west. All cars, buildings and the pavement show up in good detail. In Figure 2.8b, the camera car will be located in front of the building in the center of this photo.*

Figure 2.8b *Camera car is now facing east at 9 a.m. Cars, poles, street detail, and pedestrians (none shown) are difficult to see because shadows are viewed against shadows and the pavement and sky are glaring. The camera car has a black cloth covering the dash panel to eliminate dash panel glare which would have made a tough seeing situation worse.*

of the vehicle, the speed, the traffic density, and the diversions facing the driver, must all be considered to determine whether a driver is likely to lose safe control of the vehicle. Fortunately AASHTO 1985 (American Association of State Highway and Transportation Officials) has evaluated the data and come up with some reasonable estimates of driver responses under assorted conditions. The average driver can respond in 1.64 seconds, and 90 percent of the drivers can respond in 2.5 seconds to a clearly visible, unexpected hazard.

The driving task, then, is one of monitoring roadway information visually in the presence of noise. This noisy information is then analyzed against a background of experience, knowledge and expectancy that is more or less available, depending upon the physiological state and the training of the driver. The noise in the visual information is thus analyzed out, and the driver usually perceives a fairly true picture of roadway events, but at a later time.

Decisions are made and nerve impulses to the body muscles control the vehicle. The extent to which the vehicle responds is then monitored visually, vestibularly, auditorialy and kinesthetically. The detection time, perception time, the driver's reaction time, and the time characteristics of the vehicle provide the potential for Servo System oscillation. Such oscillations occur when, for example, an intoxicated person tries to drive. A sign of alcohol, age and inexperience is the difficulty in keeping the vehicle going straight, and in making smooth stops, starts and turns.

Chapter 3

Vision Requirements for Driving

Merrill J. Allen, O.D., Ph.D.

Synopsis

3.1 Visual Acuity

Good visual acuity is the ability to see the fine details of an object at a distance. For a given object, say a person's face, good acuity will allow the recognition of friends, of their facial expressions, and even of their direction of gaze from a great distance. Poorer acuity will be manifest as the need to be closer to an object to recognize its details. In driving, the ability to resolve fine detail permits the reading of signs and signals at a greater distance, thus providing more time in which to change lanes, change speed, or make other maneuvers.

Thus, good acuity, 20/20 or better, permits the detection of hazardous situations earlier and provides more time for study and action. This in effect, slows down the action and permits the driver to be more relaxed. An acuity of 20/10 would permit twice as much time to act as an acuity of 20/20; with 20/40, only one-fourth as much time would be available compared to the excellent 20/10 acuity. For large objects like trucks and cars, and for pavement with bright center and edge lines, good acuity is not so important.

Good acuity implies an optical system that is functioning at top efficiency. Night driving visual performance, and the detection of small objects on the roadway, both at night and in the daytime, is quickest when good acuity exists. All aspects of vision are usually best when acuity is best; hence, the ability of drivers with good acuity should be better than for drivers with poor acuity, all else being equal. Visual acuity is the most easily and frequently measured visual function. It is related to contrast, illumination, and exposure duration. If any of the three is reduced, a larger acuity test letter size is needed. In the automobile, visual acuity is but a small part of the visual requirements for safe driving. It is a central retinal function. The fovea (0.5 degrees) inside the macula (5 degrees) requires peripheral vision (90 degrees to either side) to detect objects that need to be inspected by the good acuity in the fovea and macula.

3.2 Peripheral Vision

Peripheral vision lies outside the central 5-degree macular area. The photo receptors in the peripheral retina have fewer neurons connecting to the brain per unit of retinal area than is the case for the central retina. We use the peripheral retina for the majority of our defensive seeing. Any movement or change in movement of an above-threshold object within the normal peripheral field will be quickly detected, and if it is of interest or hazard to us, we will turn our eyes to study the details of the object that moved. All of us have been startled by a sudden movement in the "corner of our eye" of an unnoticed object such as a mouse. We may jump or scream involuntarily without having had time to fixate the object.

It is little realized that accurate information on the spatial direction and distance of objects is obtained from peripheral vision and that a person's own orientation in space is largely a function of the peripheral retina.

The importance of the peripheral retina to driving can be appreciated from the following. We know from eye movement studies that about 0.25 seconds are required per fixation. At 60 miles per hour we are moving at 88 feet per second. With one-quarter second fixations, we can inspect the pavement with central vision every 22 feet. The remainder of the scene, with its many details and spatial relationships, must be sensed by peripheral vision. We simply do not have time to inspect with foveal vision, every inch of roadway, every taillight, every oncoming car, every street sign, pretty girl, etc., with foveal vision.

Without peripheral vision to keep us informed of the big picture and our position within it, and to let us know what merits our careful inspection, we would be badly handicapped even for walking around in our own home. Thus, good acuity alone is not enough for driving safety.

Normal peripheral vision is good, but not perfect. For example, in each eye there is a blind area starting about 12 degrees temporal-ward from the fixation point and covering an oval area about 6 degrees wide and 8 degrees high. There are also some sizable blood vessels onto which traffic lights, chuck holes, and even people could be imaged, and would not be seen. Such blind areas are largely compensated for by frequent eye movements and by overlap with the normal areas in the other eye.

A modern driver cannot afford to be handicapped by defective peripheral vision or by obstructions that might interfere with peripheral vision such as rear-view mirrors, large windshield corner posts, low seat height, spectacle frames, clothing, hair and hats. Good peripheral vision provides a maximum of information with a minimum of eye movements and, hence, speeds the detection of hazards in driving. This increased perceptual efficiency allows more time for decision and action by the driver. Good peripheral vision, like good visual acuity, also effectively slows the action in the scene and permits more comfortable and relaxed driving. Freedom from confusion and complete awareness of the driving scene are accompaniments of good peripheral vision.

3.3 Color Vision

Color vision and visual acuity are primarily central retinal functions. In the modern driving environment red is said to mean stop, yellow to mean danger or caution, and green to mean go. Red meaning STOP is confused by the use of red for advertising, driveway markers, taillights, turn signals, motor vehicle paint, and the fact that one out of fifty men can't see red. For normal color vision, both red and green are strong signal colors, and traditional usage recommends them for this purpose. However, their use is not without ambiguity and confusion on occasion (Lavender, 1968). The words STOP, CAUTION, and GO in large letters could serve less ambiguously, but the advantage of smaller size and perhaps greater economy lies with the colored signal.

Color coding offers certain real advantages for drivers with abnormal color vision. About 0.5 percent of the women and 8 percent of the men have some color vision abnormality. Since aging interferes with color perception because of reduced optical transmission, increased scatter of shorter wavelengths, and neurological deterioration, a higher percentage of abnormal color vision is to be expected from older people.

Persons with deuteranopia or deuteranomaly can identify green and red, particularly if the green is bluish. Persons with protanopia or protanomaly cannot recognize red except as a light of low intensity.

Cole et al. (1965) have shown that the color defective driver requires about twice as much time as a normal driver to act upon colored signals, and the incidence of errors in the recognition of the color is higher. The normal person makes virtually 100 percent correct judgments on red, yellow, and green discriminations. Thus, the possession of good color vision ensures that practically no mistakes will be made in reading the meaning of red, yellow, and green traffic signals. Good color vision, therefore, provides more time in which to make decisions and, in effect, reduces the perceptual load on the driver. Poor color vision, on the other hand, finds the driver using other clues to try to learn the meaning of a light and, hence, the driver's decisions will always be delayed and uncertain, a circumstance which leads to reduced perceptual capacity, to fatigue, and to accidents.

Color defective drivers must be advised of the nature of their handicap and the circumstances that must be avoided whenever possible. This presupposes that we know what type of color vision defect is present in a given case. To help these otherwise highly qualified people to drive safely, our signal systems must provide the information in some way other than by color. Shape coding of signal lights offers an inexpensive solution (see Appendix A, Figure A.1).

3.4 Dark Adaptation

Dark adaptation is the ability of the retina in the eye to increase its sensitivity so that tiny amounts of light are effective in causing visual responses. The measure of the ability to adapt to the dark is the time required to see at a given light level. The time in total darkness required to develop maximum retinal sensitivity is about thirty minutes, although gains in sensitivity may continue to occur over a twenty-four-hour period of total darkness. Sensitivity can rise to such levels that starlight can provide enough light to walk about at night in the open. After five minutes in the dark, the rods in the retina become more sensitive than the cones. Rod vision is scotopic vision and cone vision is photopic vision. Cones give good acuity and are necessary for color vision. At full moonlight luminance levels, the cones are beginning to operate. At the luminance levels on the highways at night, the cones are operating. Adaptation to night highway luminance levels is reasonably complete within five minutes in the dark, and adaptation to the fluctuations in luminance of objects on the roadway, such as headlights, street lights and so forth, occurs within a few seconds.

Most people adapt quickly to the levels of nighttime highway luminance. Individual differences show up best only after dark adaptation for twenty-five to thirty minutes, a condition never encountered on the modern highway. However, older drivers with small pupils, and cataract symptoms, have reduced ocular transmission and their retinal luminance levels may be one-fifth to one-twentieth of normal. They will require much longer to dark adapt because the retina is receiving less light. Night road luminance levels would be too low for such people to use photopic vision. Their overall nighttime visual performance will be significantly inferior to that of younger drivers. Drivers with retinal pathology or with neurological involvements are also likely to suffer from abnormal loss of visual performance at night.

Testing for impaired ability to see at night should be done routinely, especially on those persons of advanced age and with known retinal pathology. A test with low luminance background and low contrast letters, such as the Night Vision Performance Tester (Allen and Lyle, Nov. 1963) would give an indication of the person's ability to see when driving at night.

3.5 Glare Resistance

The ability to recognize useful information in a visual display in the presence of a bright source of light is called glare resistance. The ability to resist glare is an individual characteristic dependent upon a variety of factors, almost all of which degrade the quality of the optical image falling on the photoreceptors. The clearer the optical system is, the better it will behave in the presence of glare. Sometimes, neurological and retinal factors, usually pathological, can be such that glare (over excitation) at some point in the field of view will cause reduction in visual performance. Whatever the factors, the better the visual system behaves in the presence of a glare source, the greater is said to be its glare resistance.

At night on the highway facing approaching headlights, a driver is required to see roadway details well enough to avoid hazards and remain in the lane of travel. This is the classic concept of why a driver needs good glare resistance and why he should be tested for glare resistance. While glare is often thought of in terms of distress caused by oncoming headlights at night, it also enters into a normal daytime scene where no glare sources in the accepted sense are present (Allen, Spring 1968). When an optical system scatters light, the scattered light reduces the contrast of all images on the retina and reduces visual performance. It is common experience that glare sensitivity is reduced when a lens correction is supplied to sharpen the retinal image. Thus, the eye with poor glare resistance may also be an eye with poor image quality.

At high luminance levels with good contrast details, no difficulties in operating a motor vehicle would be expected even though glare resistance is low. At low luminances, such as at twilight, at night or on dull days when no shadows are present to accentuate objects, the driver's visual performance will be impaired if glare resistance is low. At night the ability to see the roadway will be impaired if glare resistance is low.

The average automobile windshield adds so much stray light, due to scratches, pits, internal reflections, and dirt, both in the daytime and at night, that the driving glare resistance of even the most glare resistant individual, as tested in the license bureau, may be inadequate to permit safe operation of the vehicle at night and under some day time conditions. Thus, it is probably academic to worry about the glare resistance of the driver when the glare from smoke stained, pitted, scratched, dirty, fog on the inside of the windshield, rain on the outside, etc., is so prevalent and so devastating to vision. Fortunately, it seems that those mostly older drivers who have poor glare resistance and poor dark adaptation tend to limit themselves to drive only during the hours of daylight. Unfortunately, at present, there is no way to ensure that the automobiles on the roads at night have clean, new, untinted windshields.

3.6 Reaction Time

The simple reaction time can be measured by a person quickly pushing a switch in response to a flash of light. It involves photochemical, neurological, and perhaps psychological delays on the sensory side. On the motor side it involves neurological, muscular, and mechanical movement delays. Classically the fastest one can respond to a visual stimulus after a lot of practice is about 0.18 second. Complex situations cause longer reaction times. The usual reaction time to a red brake or stop light in *controlled experiments on the highway* is about 0.55 second in alert responsive subjects. Color defectives will need about twice as long. When weaker stimuli are used, still more time is needed. When a clearly visible, unexpected hazard is presented on the highway, half of the drivers can respond in 1.64 seconds while 90 percent can respond in 2.5 seconds (AASHTO).

The factors affecting reaction times are both optical and physiological. A person whose central nervous system is depressed by alcohol, barbiturates, carbon monoxide, or lipemia (a high blood cholesterol level), will have a longer reaction time. A person receiving weak stimuli will take longer to react; hence, those with small pupils, an absorptive or a scattering optical media, or wearing a pair of dark tinted sun glasses will show a significantly longer reaction time. A person who has been training doing reaction time experiments, will continue to shorten the reaction time for that stimulus even after weeks and many thousands of responses. Hence it is important that an experiment designed around reaction times be set up so that the reaction time learning curve is averaged over all tests of the experimental variables.

A person driving at today's speeds and traffic densities must be able to make decisions quickly and accurately. Slow response often means slow thinking and inadequate understanding of the hazards. One really ought not to laugh at such jokes as the one defining a split second as the time between the light change and the honking of the horn of the car behind you. There are significant differences in driver alertness and ability to react to a hazardous situation.

A visual reaction time test should be given to drivers applying for license and license renewal because of its ability to measure the performance of the whole driver. In fact, incorporating a visual reaction time tester into every automobile dash panel would be an excellent means of warning a motorist when overall functional ability is impaired. The driver may need to get off the road if driving for too long, or if exposed to noxious fumes or to alcohol.

Since we know it is difficult to change the driver, we must change the system to reduce the perceptual load.

3.7 Ocular Muscle Imbalance

Ocular muscle imbalance, currently largely ignored in driver tests, probably is an important contributor to driver inefficiency. In, out, or up turning tendencies (eso, exo, or hyperphorias) are usually more or less easily compensated for by a driver at normal daytime levels of illumination, although the effort to compensate may take its toll in fatigue and discomfort. However, at night, a small day time imbalance may become unmanageable, especially if the driver is fatigued, overfed or drugged as by alcohol, carbon monoxide, or medications. When a tendency to turn the eyes is uncompensated, double vision results. Double vision of sudden onset without warning can be catastrophic, especially to a naive driver. (At a safe, low speed on an empty street, try crossing your eyes while you are driving!) I believe that a large proportion of the one car accidents late at night result from misjudgments by young drivers who have 0.75 diopter or more of uncorrected hyperopia and who are fatigued. Upon loss of the lights of other cars, as happens late at night their eyes may cross, and they become confused, frightened and run off the road. Such youngsters typically have 20/20 vision or better in the daytime. About 50 percent of alcohol-related deaths are single car "ran off the road" accidents late at night.

Darkness tends to cause night myopia and a turning in of the eyes (esophoria) to about the plane of the windshield, even in normal eyes. In many situations windshield dirt or water can be a stronger fusion stimulus than the highway proper, thus, causing the eyes to turn in and the road to be seen double. Certainly a test for hyperopia and muscle imbalance should be a mandatory part of a license bureau eye test, and some information about the hazards of driving late at night should be given to the farsighted youngster with good daytime acuity.

The Substance Abuse Alcohol Simulator (SAAS), invented and patented by Sydney Slavin, O.D. (P.O. Box 29757, Richmond, VA 23242-0757, Ph 804-360-1442), is an important example of how to help drivers understand what can go wrong after consuming alcohol.

Dr. Slavin has published the effect of shifting the images for each eye in the same direction using yoked prisms (the same power and direction for each eye). This shift of the visual images can cause symptoms resembling alcohol intoxication. Alcohol modifies the neurones of the visual sensory, visual motor, vestibular mechanism, the spinal column and the neurons of the brain itself, so that vision may no longer agree with the other sense modalities just as Slavin's SAAS invention does.

Dr. Slavin reports the following regarding his studies of the effects of yoked prisms:

> Among the 20 or more intoxicating effects that can be easily induced are: loss of balance, posture and gait; loss of fine movement skills; reduction or loss of side vision; diminished depth perception; loss of coordination in eye-hand, eye-foot, and eye-body skills; slowing down of some problem solving and thinking capability; reduction in the speed of perception and information processing; distorted figure-ground (foreground-background) spatial interrelationships; slowing down of reaction time; distorting of body image and schemes; loss of focusing speed and binocular (two eye integrated) fusion skills; double vision, the ultimate vision loss, can also be created.

Figure 2.1 in Chapter 2 shows the many places that alcohol can interfere with a driver's judgment and performance. Thus Slavin's glasses do realistically produce symptoms similar to the adverse effects of alcohol.

Chapter 4

Space Perception and Driving

Merrill J. Allen, O.D., Ph.D.

Synopsis

4.1 The Problem

Good visual acuity, good color vision, good dark adaptation, and good fields of vision are not enough to permit safe driving when space perception is abnormal. It is believed that the development of space perception is largely learned and requires a long time of dynamic interaction with one's environment. Those human beings who, at an early age, have done the normal amounts of running, jumping, throwing, climbing and chasing, will have a reasonably good appreciation of space.

If these early experiences were not normal because of such things as illness, congenital cataracts, paralysis, etc., the appreciation of spatial relationships will not be as good, and would cause a degree of handicap for driving. Those, for example, who "couldn't hit the side of a barn" when throwing a ball are probably not muscularly defective, as often believed, but are perceptually defective, being unable to accurately localize objects in the space around them. The person who cannot park without occasionally creasing a fender, or who parks two feet away from the curb, or who strikes the curb hard in angle parking, or who hugs the center line in driving, or who bumps the garage door, probably is a person with a space perception problem. Such little problems become critical problems when high speeds and long distance judgments are involved.

Alcohol is an example of a judgment impairing and spatially disorienting agent, and alcohol has been credited with being involved in over 50 percent of all fatal accidents (Selzer and Weiss, 1966). More recent data indicate a lower percentage. New drivers who have not developed good spatial judgment in the driving task and who are not as tall, have the highest accident rates of all drivers. Deceptive arrangement of some of the clues to space perception have been demonstrated to have marked effects upon the judgment and stopping distances of drivers (Allen and Crosley, May 1967). Thus, the evidence grows that adequate clues to space perception and adequate skill in interpreting those clues are essential to safe motoring.

Space perception is almost entirely relative, which accounts for the ease with which we can be fooled in our judgments of speed, location, and direction of movement of vehicles, including our own. There are both monocular and binocular clues available to the driver, which he uses unconsciously. The following discussion will show the complexity of the information supplied to the driver and will clarify the need for the driver to be in good health, sober, and possessed of extensive experience in making highway space judgments.

4.2 Perspective Clues

Railroad tracks appear to diminish to a point on the horizon because of the diminishing angular size of an object at greater distances. The object/image relationship in cameras and eyes is such that, for a given focus setting, the image size is inversely proportional to the object distance. Hence, the farther away the railroad track, the smaller is its image. Equal-sized objects will be imaged equally in size, only if they are at equal distances from the observer.

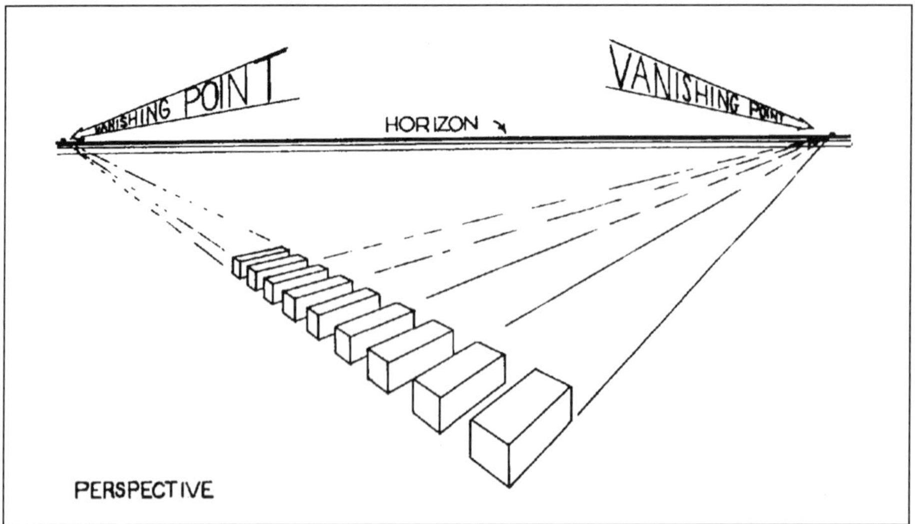

Figure 4.1 *The visual angle of an object becomes smaller with increasing distance. This is unconsciously interpreted as a distance change and not a size change. Thus, we see objects as if they were of the same angular size, but at different distances. This drawing shows how vanishing points may be used in drawing a scene.*

The human brain does not interpret different retinal image sizes of similar objects as different-sized objects, but rather as equal-sized objects at different distances. This is possible by judging the object relative to other objects in the field of view, using perspective clues.

Figure 4.1 shows a simple scene with vanishing points for the main lines in the drawing. Figure 4.2 shows the effect of ignoring perspective clues in part of the drawing. Size constancy is the ability of a person to judge that a distant object is the same size as a nearby one, or the ability to relate loss in image size to increased distance and not to an object's shrinkage. Without relative positioning in a scene, such as against the pavement, errors of size and position judgment are common.

A normally proportioned, but small object will be interpreted as farther away than it really is, even though the position within the scene should accurately locate it. Figures 4.3 and 4.4 illustrate that, when placed high, near the horizon, the toy car looks big and far away. When placed lower in the scene, its diminished size is apparent because it is localized nearby. One of the principal perspective clues is that more distant objects are usually nearer to the horizon. When an object is exactly at eye level (horizon height), this location clue is lost. Then, only its image size and the memory of its true size are of help in localizing it.

Figure 4.2 *When objects of identical sizes are drawn into a scene which makes some of them appear farther away, the conflict in size and distance is resolved by interpreting the distance about right and the size as increasing with greater distance. The block house at the left is, of course, identical in measured size to the one at the right. This illusion is based upon the fact that an object is judged to be further away if it is higher in the scene; that is, nearer to the horizon.*

A useful indicator of relative distance on the highway is overlay, or the obliteration of part of one object by a nearer object.

4.3 Atmospheric Clues

Atmospheric boil, attenuation, and scatter provide clues to distance. Their action, singly or in combination, reduces contrast, reduces border sharpness, attenuates and shifts colors toward the red, and makes blues look black. Superimposed over these effects is additional scattered blue light, which increases with distance until the object cannot be seen, and only a blue haze remains.

Atmospheric boil results when air is heated, becomes turbulent, and, thus, presents multiple and varying refractive index irregularities throughout its volume; this makes distant objects shimmer. Shimmering is usually so rapid that it blurs the borders of objects. The amount of shimmer increases with distance.

Atmospheric attenuation and scatter increase with distance. Objects that appear to be less bright are thus associated with being farther away. Loss of color of familiar objects and the presence of a veiling blue haze are associated with great distance.

Figure 4.3 *Two automobiles appear to be on a collision course. However, one subtle clue is the absence of a shadow under the Mustang. See Figure 4.4.*

4.4 Illumination Clues

Brightness, especially at night, is a major clue to distance, partly because there are few others. When an object is far enough away that it subtends about 1 minute of arc (3.5 inches at 1,000 feet), further increase in its distance causes no change in point image size but, rather, causes a loss in retinal image illumination per unit area in compliance with the inverse square law; that is, twice the distance reduces the light on the retina to one-fourth. For people with 20/40 acuity, the critical size is 2 minutes or 3.5 inches at 500 feet. Thus, past experience leads us to believe that dim points of light are farther away than bright ones, though they are at exactly the same distance. Errors in judgment are regularly made when judging small lights at a distance; for example, in one test, red taillights at 270 feet were judged to be much farther away than bright white lights at 750 feet.

Larger sources such as automobile surfaces or road signs do not lose bright-

Figure 4.4 *When the Mustang is removed from its wire frame atop the tripod and placed at the foot of the tripod, its true size becomes apparent. Or, put another way, its actual size has not changed much but the judgment of its distance has been greatly modified by lowering it to the surface of the ground. The lesson is clear. For an object to be accurately localized and correctly judged for size and shape, it must be visibly attached to or rest upon the ground or pavement. (The measured small decrease in physical size in this photograph compared to Figure 4.3 is owing to the increased distance from the lens of the camera when the model sits on the ground.)*

ness with ordinary driving distances, except for atmospheric losses. They must be very far away to subtend 1 minute of angle or less at the observer's eye.

4.5 Stereopsis or Binocular Parallax

Stereopsis is considered to be the highest skill of a person with binocular vision. It is the relative judgment of spatial relationships dependent only upon the subtle differences in view provided by the separation of the two eyes. If the eyes are properly oriented, split-second exposures of the two eyes simultaneously is enough to provide stereo awareness of spatial relationships. Stereopsis is relative and depends upon a framework of known objects for accurate localization. Stereoscopic range finders have great accuracy, but the observer is asked merely to equate the distances of a fixed reticle and the target in question. The accuracy of the instrument depends upon how accurately it projects the fixed reticle into the scene.

Stereopsis is a powerful help in localization of objects within a person's immediate environment, such as at the work bench. Since all space judgments are relative, it is important that the observer know exactly where some of the objects in the environment are at all times. By touching or handling nearby objects, an absolute reference for judging more remote objects by stereopsis and other clues is provided. A person who must attempt several times to grasp a pencil or a control knob has faulty stereopsis and cannot be expected to perform well on tasks where monocular clues to space perception are largely absent, as in driving a car at night. One-eyed people have a real handicap in spatial perception, as they are dependent entirely upon the several monocular clues, which may sometimes be absent and at best will require more time to interpret. A person without stereopsis is essentially one-eyed and is as handicapped in space perception as the one-eyed person.

4.6 Monocular Parallax

When a person's head moves, visual objects shift their relative positions within the scene. This shift due to head movement is called monocular parallax. Moving the head, body or being in a moving vehicle produces the same effect. The term monocular is used to differentiate it from binocular parallax, which is stereopsis, or a simultaneous comparison of the different views from the two eyes. Monocular parallax causes near objects to appear to move against the movement of the observer while remote objects move with the observer. The relative speed of object movement is related to the distance of the object from a reference object, the speed of observer movement, and the distance of the observer from the reference object. The ability to make parallactic judgments is very good. Movement of a sizable object within a scene can be detected when it moves more than 6 minutes of arc when viewing conditions are good. This requires an object of good contrast in a detailed environment and a movement that is completed in a short period of time. Hazard exists when no monocular parallax occurs as a result of real movement of the object itself. When an object is on a collision course with a car, it grows in size and does not change its direction from the driver. Hence, a collision course with its disastrous termination is devoid of monocular parallax clues and as a result is the most difficult to detect.

4.7 Velocity Judgments

In collision situations, the only clue to the hazard is the increasing size of the object. If seen early, an intuitive guess by the driver that a collision is imminent may be made. The ability to judge an increase in size is a function of the distance and the object. Halving the distance doubles the size. A car traveling at 60 miles per hour covers a half-mile in thirty seconds. It doubles its size in thirty seconds if it is first noted one mile away. Assuming it is about 7.25 feet wide, its angular size will have increased from 5 minutes to 10 minutes of arc. For comparison, a 20/20 letter subtends 5 minutes of arc at 20 feet. Imagine it requiring thirty seconds to grow to a 20/40 letter size! Such slow size changes at great distances cannot mean much. On the other hand, it takes only fifteen seconds for the size to double again as the car travels from 0.5 to 0.25 mile away. As the car approaches, doubling in apparent size occurs at increasingly shorter intervals and the angular size rapidly increases. For example, in traveling from 200 feet to 100 feet the size will double in just 1.13 seconds. The angular increase will be from 125 to 250 minutes of arc, while the area increase would be proportional to the square of these numbers. Thus, it is difficult to judge the speed of an approaching automobile until the rate of its angular size change exceeds the threshold value for a given individual.

Judgment of closing speed is a function of vehicle size, distance and rate of travel. Trucks would seem to approach faster than regular cars, which would seem faster than compact or sports cars or motorcycles. A motorist will usually not pass the car ahead when faced by an approaching truck, even though there is adequate time. On the other hand, the motorist may elect to pass when faced by a motorcycle or low-slung sports car even when inadequate passing time exists.

On the highway we expect vehicles to be moving at normal speeds. Thus overtaking a slow moving vehicle on the highway, day or night, is extremely hazardous. Emergency flashing lights of the slow-moving vehicle are imperative to try to protect it from being rear ended. Day or night, a stopped vehicle on the highway in the lane of travel is even more hazardous. Whenever possible, flares, triangles and/or a person signaling traffic should be provided. The blockage of the highway should be cleared away as quickly as possible.

Chapter 5

Vision Tests

Merrill J. Allen, O.D., Ph.D.

Synopsis

5.1 Introduction

The complete optometric examination will be outlined, and those areas of particular concern in vision tests for drivers will be discussed in detail. It is assumed that the reader of this chapter has a basic proficiency in making the tests so that the remarks can be directed to refinements in clinical testing and special precautions that may not be generally understood. This chapter is not directed toward the needs of the license bureau tester or legislator, although certain portions could be of general informational value. The visual and ocular examination (the "21 point" examination) is outlined as follows:

A. Case history:
   1. Chief complaint of patient
   2. Nature of work, lighting, distances etc., associated with patient's activities
   3. Patient's statement of symptoms or history of ocular and systemic disease
   4. Medications, internal and external, currently being taken by patient
   5. Extent of use of alcohol and tobacco by the patient
   6. Patient's exposure to chemicals, both at home and work
   7. Scintillating scotoma, migraine and other headaches
B. Preliminary examination: A search for pathology or abnormality
   1. Visual acuity tests at distance and near, old R_X
   2. Motility of the eyes
   3. Visual fields test of peripheral vision
   4. Pupil dynamics and the condition of the iris
   5. Lids and corneal health
   6. Lens and vitreous clarity
   7. Fundus study, inspection of retina and blood vessels
   8. Intraocular pressure measurements
   9. Photo myoclonic, photo convulsive, and photo phobic tendencies
C. Refraction
   1. Objective tests for lens prescription
   2. Subjective tests for lens prescription
D. Five fundamental variables of ocular muscle coordination
   1. Distance phoria (position of the eyes relaxed)
   2. Positive fusional convergence
   3. Negative fusional convergence
   4. Amplitude of accommodation
   5. A.C.A. (accommodative convergence divided by accommodation) ratio
E. Special tests
   1. Aniseikonia (difference in size of right and left eye images)
   2. Color vision
   3. Stereopsis
   4. Night visual performance

5. Visual fields
6. Reaction time
7. Glaucoma (field defects, abnormal intraocular pressure)

5.2 Case History

If given the opportunity, the patient will tell what his major symptoms are and what he wants done. Through careful sympathetic questioning, most of the information needed about health, medication, diet, and intoxicants becomes readily available. Specific questions about driving should be asked, including what make and model automobile, the color of the hood and dash-panel top, and the location of chromium surfaces that can reflect the sky. Ask about seeing double at night, such as occurs by double reflection within the windshield. Ask if he wears sunglasses to drive; if so, take a look at them. They should not be clip-over glasses and should not be green or made of wavy glass or plastic. Ideally, they should be gray polarizing with prescription incorporated, with large lenses that tend to "wrap around" and with thin frames and high temples.

Ask if he wears night-driving glasses of any kind; if so, inspect them. They should not be tinted any color including yellow, except for the lightest shades of cosmetic pink. Green sunglasses, tinted windshields, and Thermanon all absorb red excessively and are not recommended for any driving day or night.

Does the patient have trouble seeing street signs at night; seeing against headlight glare; seeing with normal amounts of light in the home, in the yard at night, and so forth? Problems here can indicate increasing ocular scatter, as in a beginning cataract; the steamy cornea of glaucoma; increased light absorption; or pinhole pupils, all of which reduce the light available on the retina; or they may indicate a systemic problem which interferes with retinal metabolism, such as a vitamin deficiency or the presence of toxic agents harmful to the retina or neural pathways. Common toxic agents, carbon monoxide and alcohol, interfere with dark adaptation, accommodation, and fusion. Chronic alcoholism or inadequate diet may cause nutritional deficiencies.

Drugs of interest to inquire about are those that cause pupil constriction and accommodative activity (parasympathomimetic), paralysis of accommodation and dilation of the pupil (parasympatholytic), or dilation of the pupil alone (sympathomimetic). The *Physicians' Desk Reference* or equivalent will provide needed information on the effects of a particular drug the patient is using. The *Merck Manual* will provide information on what drugs are commonly used for what diseases. This will assist whenever the patient is unaware of what medication he is taking but knows the name of his disease.

Information on smoking is of two-fold interest. If the patient is a smoker of cigarettes about which he/she has repeatedly been warned, you know he/she has little regard for self or safety, and is also apt to be a less safe driver because of attitude (Adams and Williams). The second reason for interest in smoking is that tobacco smoke contains carbon monoxide. The street and highway atmospheres have significant levels of carbon monoxide as well. The adverse effects of carbon monoxide are exaggerated by altitude and alcohol, and consist of anoxia at the tissue level. Anoxia causes "red-out" and, finally, "black-out," just as positive G-forces cause these same symptoms in an aircraft pilot. Focusing ability is impaired, esophoria occurs, fusional amplitudes fall, and 0.50 to 1.50 diopters of accommodative myopia may occur. Asthenopia, diplopia, blurring, headache, and drowsiness can all result from smoking, or smoking combined with high levels of atmospheric carbon monoxide. In addition, the dark adaptation ability is impaired and the recovery from bright headlights will be delayed. These all produce a longer response time to driving hazards.

The need to know about environmental intoxicants is of importance for similar reasons. Many people do not realize that lead absorbed from food, drink, and from air amounts to 30 micrograms a day in the city for an average nonsmoker and 40 for a smoker. This can lead to symptoms of lead poisoning. Similarly paint solvents, gasoline, carbon tetrachloride, and many other chemical vapors common around the house and job can be detrimental to health. Hair sprays, hair dyes, perfumes, tooth paste, and other "harmless" items can cause trouble for some people. Symptoms often mimic eye disorders or cause eye changes.

Two classical examples are naphthalene (moth balls) and insecticides. Ingestion or long exposure to the vapors can cause cataract and accommodative spasms as well as wide systemic problems. Moth crystals, toilet and room deodorizers, isopropyl alcohol, insecticides, and cleaning solvents are common in many homes, with little thought being given to their hazardous nature. There are many other cataractogenic and systematically toxic chemicals that a workman may encounter on his job or to which a do-it-yourself artist may expose himself. They are all the more hazardous in spray form. Some researchers (Clark, 1993b) argue that toxic agents around the home and job can cause cancer, diabetes, AIDS, etc., by stimulating the growth of intestinal parasites (e.g., fluke worms, etc.) normally present in the body. Supposedly these parasites then invade the thymus gland causing AIDS, the pancreas then causing diabetes, the liver causing cancer, etc. Perhaps other conditions, like migraine headaches, can have a similar etiology.

The use of atropine and related drugs is common. Atropine and alkaloids are poisons that have some medicinal value. They have a parasympatholytic action, their effects are cumulative, and they require about two weeks to wear off. These alkaloids are available without a prescription in cold remedies (such as Contac), laxatives (Alophen Pills), rectal suppositories (Wyanoids), and asthma powders (Asthamador), among others. They and related compounds are regularly and freely prescribed for intestinal, digestive, and ulcer symptoms and to dry up mucous secretions. The effect of small doses over prolonged periods of time by self-medication or by prescription will most assuredly be worse than the illness it was intended to treat.

Typical symptoms are blurring of vision because of enlarged pupils and a paralysis of accommodation, dryness of the eyes, and asthenopia (visual discomfort) due to a higher than normal A.C.A. (convergence caused by focusing the eyes) ratio. Vague symptoms of eye distress, pain, and headache may be due to atropine-caused elevated intraocular pressure. Certainly, it is well known that atropine is a provocative test for glaucoma, yet apparently it is little realized that atropine anywhere in the body affects the eyes if ingested long enough. One interesting clue to atropine poisoning is male impotence!

Extensive use of alcohol is harmful to the liver, which is the important reservoir of vitamin A needed by the eyes. Tobacco-alcohol amblyopia appears to be due almost entirely to vitamin deficiencies. Night blindness and dry skin (xerophthalmia) with eventual corneal opacification, is the result of prolonged vitamin A deficiency. The effects of alcohol in some ways resemble carbon monoxide poisoning. The ability of alcohol to remove social inhibitions also seems to parallel losses of inhibitory behavior of visual pathways. Border contrasts, successive contrasts, and hence acuity and threshold visibilities are degraded. The increased reaction times and general disorientation of the "drunk," especially at night, make him, as statistics have shown, a poor risk on the highway, either as a driver or a pedestrian.

A record of a person's visual symptoms without pertinent questions about poisons, drugs, intoxicants, and nutrients is apt to prove misleading when one attempts to determine whether or not spectacles will relieve the symptoms.

Scintillating scotomas and migraine headaches have been the subjects of many papers and studies. Generally they are considered to be of little importance, and treatment is often only symptomatic. On the assumption that these phenomena are the result of vascular disturbances, the author has found experimental evidence that chewing niacin, vitamin B_3 in a 50 to 100 mg. dose at the first, prodromal visual symptom, will, in a high percentage of cases, halt the development of the scintillating scotoma and avert the headache that normally follows the visual disturbances. Recent medical evidence indicates that natural and induced migraine attacks can be aborted by increasing the level of serotonin in the system. During the height of the untreated scintillation phenomena, the retina has very poor sensitivity in the portions of the visual field affected, and may become completely blind for a short time. Since the scintillation effect usually starts as a small area in the periphery and grows over a ten or fifteen minute period to include a major portion of the field, often sparing the fovea, the patient has adequate warning of the impending headache. *Please note that niacin will cause a facial reddening, skin itching and a feeling of fever which lasts about 20 minutes and is a normal and harmless response to niacin.*

If relief medication is not at hand, the driver with a scintillating scotoma should not continue driving until after the scotomas have entirely disappeared. Even then, the migraine headache that usually follows would probably make driving unwise. A person with a history of migraine or scintillating scotoma should be studied carefully to determine whether a refractive error, aniseikonia, muscle imbalance or incoordination, or environmental chemicals could be contributing factors. Since many migraine patients have all but given up hope of obtaining relief from their malady, they may not know that relief can sometimes be dramatic. They should be referred, when indicated, for further medical consideration and treatment.

5.3 Preliminary Examinations

A. Visual acuity

This portion of the optometric examination is a search for pathology and for hereditary, traumatic, or functional anomalies. The first test is visual acuity. While there are many factors that affect visual acuity, the test does give an indication of the general visual efficiency of the person at the test distance and for the test illumination.

A valuable aid to visual acuity testing would be an acuity chart with luminance variable from 150 down to 0.5 apparent foot candles. The Night Vision Performance Tester (Allen and Lyle, 1963) provides a suitably wide range of luminances, in addition to providing low contrast visual acuity targets which simplify the assessment of reductions in visual performance due to refractive error, abnormal pupil size, ocular scatter, and absorption in the ocular media.

It is certain that an acuity of 20/40 at high luminances will deteriorate, perhaps to less than 20/200, at night roadway luminances (Allen and Lyle, 1963; Richards, May 1966). Adjustment of luminance on a specific target, from too low upward until the target is just readable, provides a sensitive test for evaluating the effects of small lens-power changes or small changes in cataract density. Note: The Night Vision Performance Test was never marketed. Several other tests involving low contrast letters are available (see Chapter 12).

B. Ocular motility

Ocular motility needs to be tested in all quadrants of the fixation field to determine whether a paresis or paralysis exists. Equally important is to watch the eyes track a moving target. Eye movement records may be taken with the Ober 2:Visagraph from Taylor and Associates, 200-2 East Second Street, Huntington Station, NY, 11746. A special pair of spectacles comfortably and quickly monitors eye movements while the patient watches a moving object, reads, etc., and it provides a computer print out for the record. A significant percentage of people are visually poorly coordinated. The result of general or ocular incoordination is easy disorientation, frequent errors of judgment, and ease of confusion, none of which is desirable while climbing stairs, walking across a street, or driving an automobile.

The value of testing for gross visual incoordination is that something can and should be done for it. The beauty of using an eye movement recording device is that the improvement in coordination can be shown to the patient, who will probably also have noticed a favorable difference in visual comfort and confidence. Gross motor coordination tests also give information about the visuomotor coordination and should be included whenever case history, examination results, or recent accident experience indicates a need. High degrees of esophoria or exophoria at distance are unusual. They should not be accepted as unchangeable. They should not be allowed to go untreated when the patient is likely to drive at night. Prism correction may work, provided ghost images from lens internal reflections do not negate their benefit. I do not recommend the use of prisms. Visual training is the best and can modify phorias favorably. When combined with spectacles (if needed), visual training can make a comfortable and safer nighttime driver.

If paresis (partial paralysis) is present, much improvement or even complete compensation can be achieved with visual therapy. If a paralysis exists, often enough rehabilitation work can be done to provide comfortable binocular vision in at least a portion of the visual field. An eye that has had muscle surgery will almost always show abnormalities of coordination and of muscle fields. Such eyes have been injured, and visual rehabilitation is needed just as surely as it is needed after facial and ocular injuries in an automobile crash. Such people should be studied carefully to see if it is safe or can be made safe for them to operate a motor vehicle at night. *Vision training is the ultimate therapy.*

C. Visual fields

A number of authors have shown that glaucoma symptoms will appear in the central visual fields (tangent screen test) virtually every time there is a peripheral field restriction; hence, peripheral fields would not seem to be more valuable than central fields for glaucoma study. For this reason, it is desirable that a multiple-pattern visual field screening device be used on every patient regardless of age. The confrontation test is crude but often quite adequate to pick up extreme peripheral field lesions.

For drivers, the horizontal limits to the visual field should be tested on a perimeter or a screening device similar to those used in some driver licensing bureaus and driver training schools. Any loss in visual fields to less than 180 degrees is abnormal and is cause for suspicion of pathology. The driving limitation in some states of not less than 140 degrees of horizontal visual field is purely an arbitrary cutoff point for driver testing. A person with only 140 degrees of visual field has some kind of abnormality which may be in the retina, central neurology, or optics of the eye (usually lenticular). It may also be due to the field limitations due to high power lenses or even standard spectacles!

Since peripheral vision is essential to safe driving, any field anomaly should be evaluated as to its possible effects on driving. Even a reduction in the color fields for red and amber may be sufficient grounds for restricting driving. Fields are of little value unless taken through an adequate correction lens. The newer testing machines make testing and recording of visual field defects both easy and fast and are highly recommended.

D. Pupil dynamics

The pupil can be a useful source of information to the examiner. A large pupil will provide a higher retinal illuminations, and the pupils of younger people open wide at night. Since the pupil musculature is both sympathetically and parasympathetically innervated, it can show the systemic effects of sympathomimetic and parasympathomimetic agents. It also mirrors the effects of emotions, accommodation, convergence, light, mental activity, glaucoma, iritis, and neurological lesions. It even appears that abnormal binocular vision may cause an abnormal pupil size of one or both pupils.

An anisocoria which produces a two-to-one difference in image intensity between the two eyes will cause significant visual space perception anomalies (Lit, 1966). Greater differences can occur as, for example, in the early stages of monocular cataract formation with increased light absorption in the lens in one eye. Patients with image intensity differences between the two eyes will be confused by rapidly moving objects in the field of view. This is called the *Pulfrich stereo phenomenon.*

E. Equating retinal illumination

Measurements of pupil size may not reveal the existence of a Pulfrich stereo anomaly because light loss may be due to absorption in the lens, to different focal lengths of each eye, to the presence of a neurological anomaly, or even to a blurred uniocular image which then behaves like a reduced intensity image. When any doubt exists, it is wise to test for the anomaly. Testing, of course, is unnecessary if the patient does not have good binocular vision with stereopsis.

Figure 5.1 shows a white pendulum which will move in a plane and be seen correctly by the normal patient. It will be seen to move in an ellipse by the person with unequal optical image intensities, with a lowered monocular border

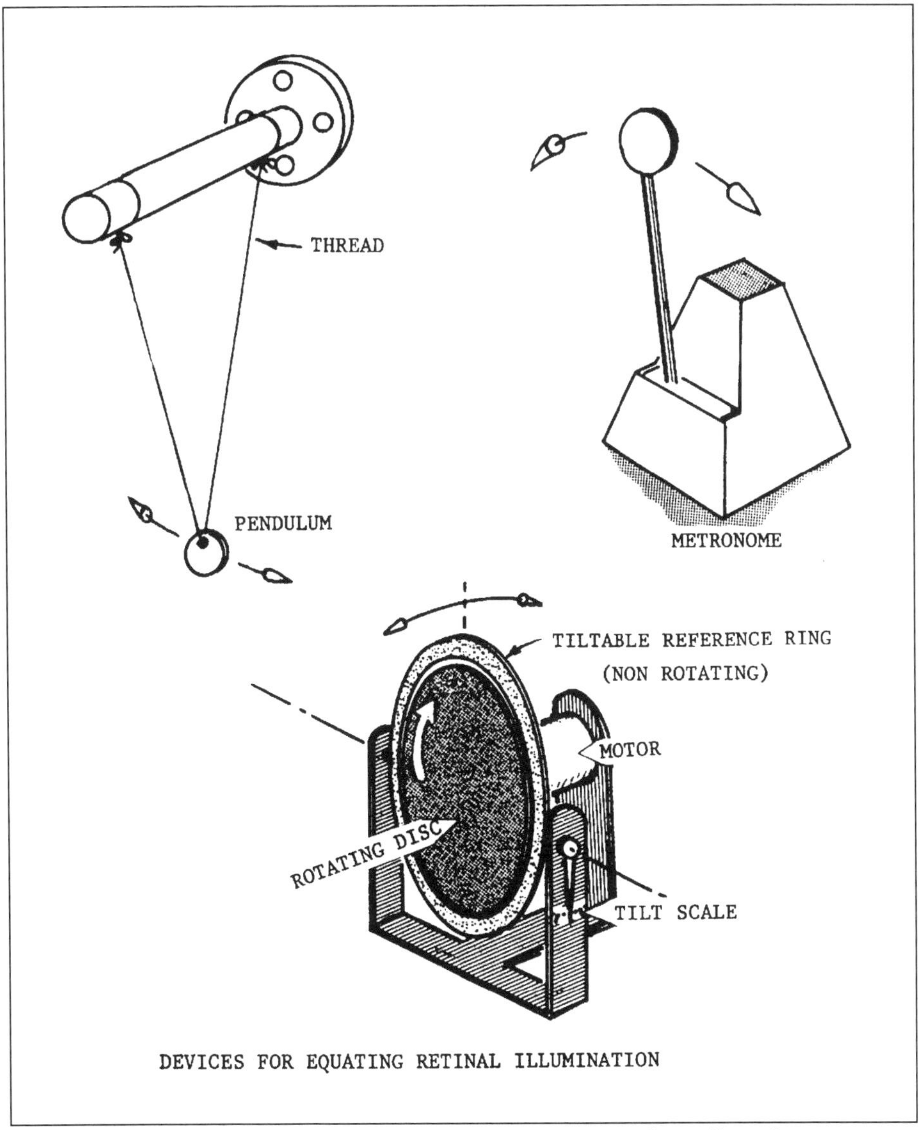

Figure 5.1 *Three methods for demonstrating the Pulfrich stereo effect. All involve a moving target and a difference in luminance levels at the two retinas, as by a filter before one eye.*

gradient due to ametropia or ocular scatter, or even with a difference in image size.

Figure 5.1 also shows the use of a metronome for testing the relative luminances of the retinas of the two eyes. A larger excursion can be obtained by casting a shadow of the moving disc on a translucent screen or on a large projection screen. The third device, a tiltable ring, rotating disc apparatus, offers a precise means of measuring the Pulfrich stereo phenomenon (Walker, 1968) or of balancing the two eyes with lenses or filters to eliminate the tilt of the moving disc.

F. Lids and cornea

Lids, cilia, and the palpebral conjunctiva should be healthy and in normal relationship to the eyes. Evidences of chronic or acute inflammation should be treated or referred. Corneal hazing, epithelial edema, or purulent material in the tear fluid, are all contributory to increased ocular scatter and to poor night vision. In addition, such inflammation of the lids and conjunctiva may be symptomatic of vitamin A deficiency, which is important in nighttime vision. The cilia in an older person may turn in toward the cornea and account for photophobic symptoms, tearing, and asthenopia. The cilia may be absent, or not dense and dark enough to form a sun shade to help reduce sky glare, thus contributing to photophobia. On the other hand, the lids may droop so low that the cilia split the pupil into multiple pinholes, thus causing all manner of weird symptoms.

There is some evidence that eyelash cosmetics flake off and enter the eye, causing corneal abrasions similar to those from wearing contact lenses, thus producing photophobic symptoms. Hair sprays can also be a problem, especially for contact lens wearers. Exposure to ultraviolet light, as in snow fields, at high altitudes, in welding, over the water, in the laboratory, or under a sun lamp, may cause a painful burn of the corneal epithelium which, when severe, is called snow blindness. An ultraviolet burn is characterized by extreme photophobia. Iritis and uveitis are also characterized by photophobic symptoms. The post surgical cataract patient with an ultra violet absorbing artificial lens implant, is not likely to suffer excessively from photophobia. Cataract surgery requiring strong spectacle lenses, will cause photophobia because of the increased ocular transmission, and an increase in the effective aperture size of the eye due to the strong spectacle lenses.

G. Lens and vitreous

The lens and vitreous contribute much of interest to the patient's symptoms. Excessive scattering and losses in transmission are usually lenticular in origin. Sometimes the cornea or vitreous or even the retina itself may be implicated in the intraocular scatter of light. The healthy cornea seems never to cloud up (Allen and Vos, 1967) even up to age eighty. Corneal clouding is usually indicative of glaucoma, vitamin deficiency, or interstitial keratitis.

The lens, on the other hand, shows progressive deterioration of optical clarity beginning in children. Vitamin C, the B vitamins, zinc, and antioxidants, along with good nutrition, offer hope of delaying or reversing the aging of the crystalline lens. Some encouraging results have been observed in improving ocular transmission and reducing lens opacity in selected cases using proteolytic enzymes. Since excessive amounts of proteolytic enzymes may have some hazard, studies should proceed cautiously.

The vitreous remains clear, unless uveitis or retinitis exists. Vitreous floaters, however, accompany liquefaction of the vitreous and are generally thought to be untreatable. Three points of interest are (1) the floaters are more conspicuous when a small pupil exists, (2) the floaters may pose less of a problem or disappear altogether after the patient improves nutrition and health, and (3) quick and large eye movements can often displace a large floater away from the fovea. Liquefaction of the vitreous is frequently found among those being treated for glaucoma with a miotic drug, such as pilocarpine. Iris nodules and other adverse symptoms may also appear in addition to the severe impairment of night vision by direct effects upon retinal sensitivity and by the extreme reduction of retinal illumination due to a small pupil.

H. Fundus study

The fundus, the vascular and neural tissue lining the inside of the eye, offers clues to retinal health as well as neurological and systemic health. Retinopathies or other evidences of active ocular pathology usually must be referred for medical attention. Visual symptoms would be reduced acuity, reduced contrast sensitivity, excessive vitreous floaters, poor night vision, distorted retinal images, and so on. Patients with evidences of untreated hypertension, arterio or athero sclerosis, or diabetes should be referred for medical attention. A driver's license should not be permitted until cleared by a physician who is cognizant of the hazards of modern day driving and the probable risk involved of a cardiac crisis occurring during driving. Patients showing physical signs of liability to episodes that could render them incapable of operating a motor vehicle should be told of the seriousness of attempting to drive. Notification should be sent to the driver licensing agency if the physical or ocular conditions noted seem to contraindicate safe driving. Recent research (Michael and Allen 1994; Allen and Lowry 1998; Allen, Jarding and Zehner 1998) shows that nutrition and electrical stimulation of the eye can slow or reverse the symptoms of macular degeneration and even retinitis pigmentosa.

I. Intraocular pressure

Intraocular pressure must be measured on all patients where symptoms or signs of glaucoma exist and on all patients forty years of age or older. Early glaucoma is not a basis for restricting driving day or night, provided the patient is not being treated with pilocarpine or some other miotic. However, when visual fields fall below 60 degrees to either side of the line of sight, the person usually should not be allowed to drive. Acute attacks of glaucoma (high pressure in the eye) cause increased ocular scatter similar to that seen through a lycopodium powdered plate[1] and will definitely be a hazard to attempted night or even daytime driving. In addition, the headache and nausea that often accompany acute glaucoma attacks would probably discourage a person from continuing to drive. Nutrition and general health should be evaluated.

J. Photo convulsive behavior

High intensity light flashing at 15 to 18 cycles per second produce widespread abnormal central nervous system responses in a few especially sensitive people (Allen and Courtney, 1967). It is believed that one out of about 250 epileptic patients will have a tendency to grandmal or petitmal epilepsy when exposed to a strong natural photic environment such as picket fences, dashed highway stripes, or tree shadows, viewed while riding in an automobile or while walking. Helicopters at slow blade speeds may be a hazard to the pilot with photo convulsive sensitivity. Usually the person has no noticeable warning, loses consciousness and falls. The attack may last from a few minutes to twenty minutes or longer.

If the case history reveals any unexplained episodes of unconsciousness or other suspicious signs, patients who drive or whose occupations are potentially hazardous to themselves or others should be tested (Bickford 1948). A bright light viewed through a sectored disc chopping the light about 18 times per second should induce symptoms of an attack. Prodromal signs are a twitching of the eyelids and an interference in speech. In stroboscopic light, the lid twitching might be noted only by palpation. It may take less than ten seconds to induce an attack. Ask the patient to count as long as he can while he faces the flickering light. If he falters he may be nearing unconsciousness. The Translid Binocular Interaction Trainer which provides stimulation rates alternately to the eyes at 7 to 9 cycles per second is too slow and is not intense enough to produce seizures.

For therapy, treatments may be given consisting of a flashing light into both eyes while monitoring brain waves. Upon the first signs of epileptiform brain waves, the flashing light is turned off. When the brain rhythms have returned to normal, the flashing stimulus is again applied. Tolerance to flashing lights is thus built up in a few training periods. Without electroencephalograph equipment, the same effects could probably be obtained by a cautious treatment program starting with one to five seconds of low intensity light stimulation at 15 to 18 cycles per second followed by 30 to 60 seconds of no stimulation. An increase should be made in the length of time of stimulation or in the intensity of the flashing light at each succeeding visit. When the patient can withstand several minutes of high-intensity flickering light, he/she is probably beginning to be safe for driving.

There is also some evidence that red-free (green) light will not cause photo convulsions. There are cases in the literature of epileptics, uncontrolled by drugs, becoming symptom free after wearing red free filter glasses. The use of such green lenses should be tried. The hazard, of course, is the insensitivity to red signal lights while wearing green lenses. *No one should wear green colored glasses while driving.*

5.4 Refraction

A. Objective tests

Retinoscopy with the patient looking at a distant wall chart, still is the foundation in refraction, even though a number of objective, automatic machines are available. The problem with these objective tests is the phenomenon called "awareness of nearness." The patient looks into a "box" which tends to induce accommodation (the near reflex) and is expected to relax the focus of the eyes. The usual error of these devices is too much minus lens power. Excess minus causes the further development of myopia.

For improved reflex brightness and a larger patient pupil, a blue free (yellow) filter (such as Corning's 3-67, glass no. 3482) could be placed over the retinoscope source. The older patient with excessive ocular scattering of blue light will be easier to scope with the yellow filter. There should be less than a quarter diopter difference between the scope findings with and without the filter.

A second item of importance to accurate retinoscopy is a spectacle made especially for the older optometrist to wear during retinoscopy. This spectacle should contain in the upper portion of the lens the examiner's distance prescription increased by the value of the usual retinoscopy working distance. A bifocal near add will be needed for writing. Such a bifocal prescription provides an unobstructed view of the phoropter and an in-focus view of the patient's pupil through the upper portion of the spectacle lens. The examiner must focus on the reflex in the plane of the patient's pupil for accurate retinoscopy. This retinoscopy spectacle will improve accuracy, and make the reflex easier to see.

If the pupil size is small, retinoscopy cannot be done accurately at the usual distance. By scoping at 33 or 25 cm. and by wearing the correct retinoscopy lenses as a fit-over to allow a clear view of the patient's pupil, the difficulties of scoping a small pupil may be circumvented. However, since ophthalmoscopy also is difficult with a small pupil, it is wise in such cases to dilate the pupils, using one or two drops of 10 percent ophthalmic Neosynephrine in each eye. Dilation should begin to occur within twenty minutes and be complete in thirty minutes. The effects should wear off in two to four hours. Visual fields should be taken as well as ophthalmoscopy and retinoscopy while the pupils are dilated. This will give a truer measure of field defects and, hence, of retinal health. However, for a driver's visual field test, the pupils should be at their normal size.

Another objective test, keratometry, can reveal evidences of elevated intraocular pressure because the cornea becomes irregular or bumpy at elevated pressures. This will cause the mires to look distorted or irregular and may cause corneal power readings to be different from time to time. A hazy corneal stroma or an irregular corneal surface precludes good visual acuity and suggests glaucoma.

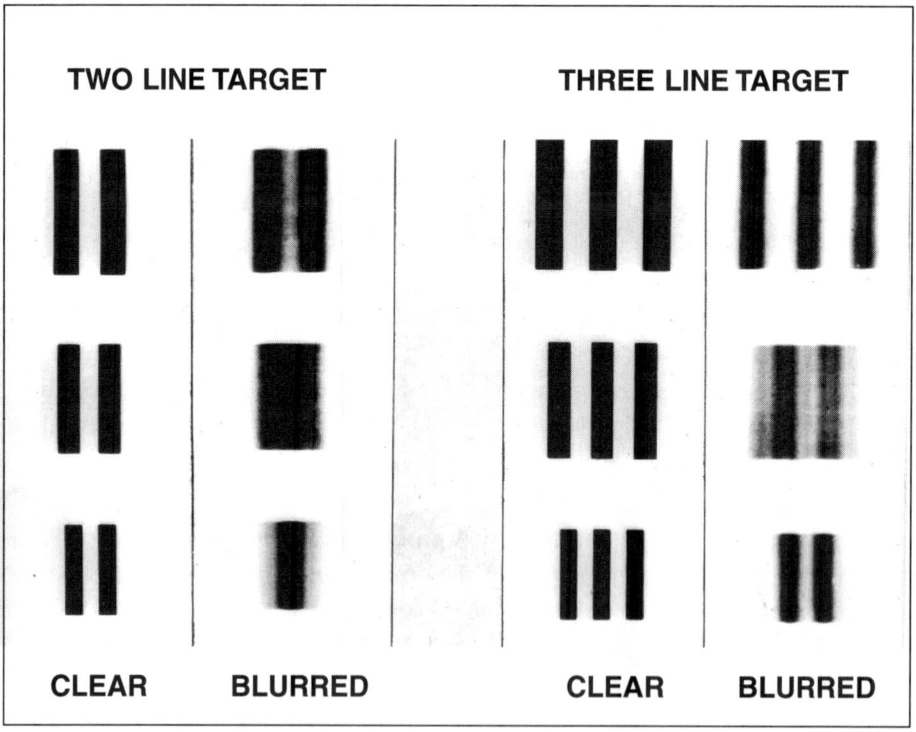

Figure 5.2 *One test for astigmatism uses a clock dial pattern of three lines at each hour position. The effect of blur on two and three line targets is shown.* ***Constant blur with different line spacings, as shown,*** *is like the effect of different amounts of blur on fixed line spacing, such as used in the astigmatic dial test. More intricate patterns can occur in a person's eye because the blur circle image for a point object is more complex than the image from a camera lens. A blurred image of three lines could look like a clear image of two lines.*

B. Subjective tests

1. Monocular

A patient with a small pupil cannot easily make the clarity judgments asked of him because of the large depth of focus and because of a reduced light level at the retina. Dilation of the pupil with 10 percent neosynephrine is helpful just as it is in retinoscopy. Raising light levels on the test screen and on the walls of the refracting room will also help. The refraction might be done with a cardboard letter test chart illuminated by about 250 watts of reflector flood lighting instead of the regular projector test chart. It should be apparent to doctor and patient that night driving should be avoided.

The generally useful red green test requires some care. The filters are subject to fading, which reduces the sensitivity of the test. In addition many filters, even when new, are not properly balanced both as to wavelength and total transmission. If the filters are a bright blue green and a bright orange red of equal brightness, you can be assured of good performance on the test. The red should actually appear brighter to a normal person, so that it will help the protanopic

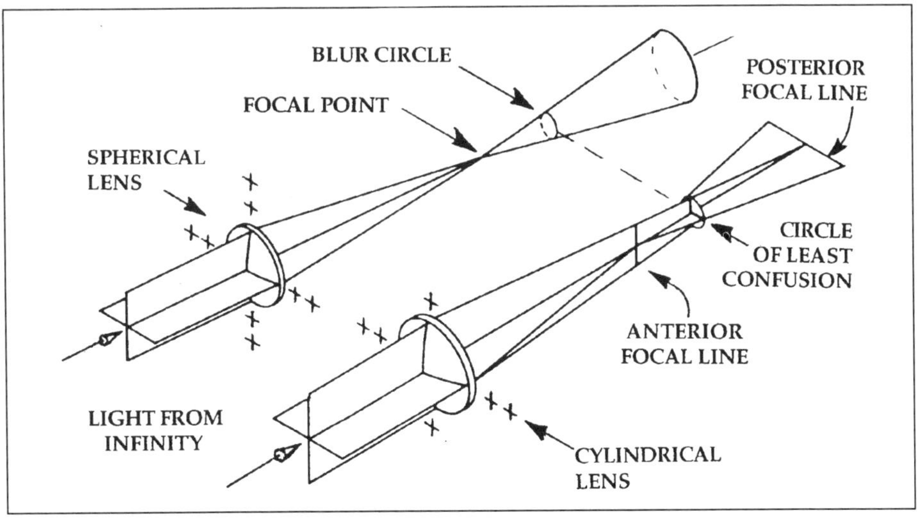

Figure 5.3 *The diagram on the left represents the focusing of a bundle of light rays by a spherical lens. If the rays intercept a surface such as the retina at the position labeled BLUR CIRCLE, the light will be distributed in the circular area shown. In the diagram on the right the bundle of light rays is refracted by a cylindrical lens to produce an astigmatic focus. There is a position between the two focal lines which is called the CIRCLE OF LEAST CONFUSION and resembles the spherical blur circle in the left diagram. The crossed cylinder test, properly applied, alternately increases and reduces the distance between the two focal lines and thus makes the Circle of Least Confusion larger or smaller. This gives the patient an easy choice of which position of the crossed cylinder gives the clearest focus (smallest Blur Circle). People with astigmatism see things blurred but not slanted, as popularly depicted. The slant or distortion occurs when spectacles are used to correct the astigmatism. Contact lenses produce virtually no distortion.*

and protanomalous color defectives who are much less sensitive to red light. *High test chart brightness* will reduce the adverse effects of protanopia, and of the small pupils and greater media absorption in the older patient.

For the red green test, the projector's aluminized screen must appear dark when the projector is off, though the room should have 2 to 15 foot candles of illumination on the walls. The aluminized screen should be adjusted to reflect directly toward the patient. The projector lenses and targets should be clean and aligned to provide a high screen illumination. A higher wattage bulb in the projector will be beneficial. Caution: Some projectors cannot keep a high wattage bulb cool, and the optics may be damaged by heat. A change from 50 to 100 watts is a safe change and will give more than a two fold increase in screen luminance. Higher screen luminances as seen by the patient will speed up a subjective refraction and make it more accurate.

The fan dial test for astigmatism should be conducted under the right amount of blur, that is, the least amount to ensure control of the test. If a three line pattern and progressively more blur is used, the patient may first see three out of focus lines, then two clear lines, then multiple clear fine lines, and finally only a uniform gray area (see Figure 5.2).

Hence, upon asking which lines are clearest, one must also *ask how many lines the patient sees.* It is possible for the patient to pick out as clearest a pattern of two lines 90 degrees away, instead of correctly choosing the less blurred three line pattern which does not appear to be as clear. If a single line pattern is used in the sun burst or clock dial, then often two clear lines are seen instead of a blurred single line.

Similarly, locating the middle of the astigmatic interval upon the retina (see Figure 5.3) is critical to the success of the Jackson cross cylinder test. The standard procedure is to add +0.25 diopter of plus sphere for every –0.50 diopter of cylinder to keep the proper condition of "no blur." Similarly, if the patient keeps rejecting minus cylinder, add an 0.25 diopter of plus sphere and retest. If he keeps asking for more minus cylinder, give an 0.25 diopter of minus sphere and retest. Usually, this is enough to reverse the patient's pattern of answers and to bring them back into agreement with the objectively determined cylinder.

2. Binocular

The blur balance test is acceptable if the patient has good acuity in each eye, has equal pupil sizes and is binocular. If acuities are not the same, then a balance by blurring should not be used. The red green test chart used binocularly with vertical dissociation is a good test. If acuities are too poor for this test (20/40 or poorer), the retinoscope finding or the monocular subjective maximum plus sphere should be used to establish the balance.

The Turville infinity balance test is excellent as a means of determining the subjective and for checking aniseikonia, vertical phoria, and lateral phoria tendencies. In this test, an occluder about the width of the patient's interpupillary distance is placed halfway between the test chart screen and the patient. This gives the patient a view of the right half of the test chart by the right eye and the left half by the left eye. Polarizing techniques are available and the principles of testing are much the same. Though polarizing techniques simplify alignment, a serious light loss occurs which interferes with its use for older patients unless luminances are increased per the discussion in the section on Monocular Subjective Tests.

An effective "binocular" test may be performed with both eyes open, but with one blurred by about +1.00 diopter. The best subjective refraction of the clearer eye is determined; then the one diopter blur is moved from one eye to the other, and the best refraction of the second eye is determined

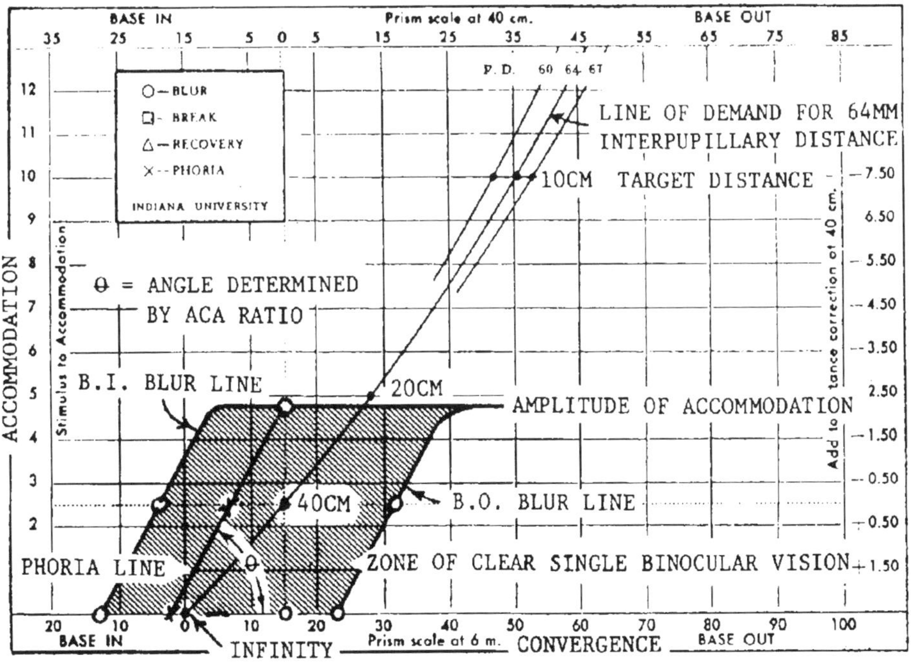

Figure 5.4 *The zone of clear single binocular vision is indicated by the cross hatched area. The hypothetical patient whose data are diagrammed here has a 2 exophoria, a base out blur of 23 prism diopters, and a base in blur of 13 prism diopters all at distance (infinity). At 40 centimeters, he has 8 exophoria, a base out blur of 16 prism diopters, a base in blur of 19 prism diopters, a plus lens to blur of +2.50 diopters, and a minus lens to blur of –2.25 diopters. The amplitude of accommodation is 4.75 diopters, and the A.C.A. ratio is about 3.33. The line of demand is curved because accommodation and convergence are not measured from a common point.*

5.5 Five Fundamental Variables of Ocular Muscle Coordination

A. Distance phoria

The phoria at distance is the position of rest of the lines of sight of the two eyes in the absence of fusional and accommodative innervation. The classical distance phoria provides the starting point in building and understanding the relationship between accommodation and convergence. Using the phoria as a starting position, the amount of fusional innervation needed for a given target will be proportional to the amount and direction of the distance phoria from ortho (eyes approximately parallel). The distance phoria, in turn, is somewhat affected by the direction, duration, and amount of fusional innervation as well as by classical considerations such as orbital fat, extraocular muscle size and strength, check ligaments, orbital shape, and compensatory tonicity innervation as from reading a book or driving a car before the test.

The distance phoria test involves zero stimulus to accommodation and to fusion. If a large distance phoria exists, or an intermittent tropia is present, the patient should be warned of the hazards in driving late at night where the conditions may approach a phoria test, that is, no stimulus to fusion. In many squinters, it is typical that the ability to maintain single vision depends upon keeping their eyes at their normal squint angle. Night driving removes many of the important visual orientation clues, and, hence, a squinter cannot be relied upon to remain fully compensated at night or in fog. A person who has crossed or out-turning eyes needs to have at least some vision training. For exotropia and esotropia the cause usually is esophoria due to uncorrected hyperopia or to a high A.C.A. ratio. Thus the exotrope needs a plus R_X for near, *usually with dramatic therapeutic success*, while the esotrope will require antisuppression and eye-straightening vision training, again with sensational normalcy resulting (see Figure 5.4).

B. Positive fusional convergence

The ability to increase convergence from the phoria position without increasing accommodation is called positive fusional convergence. It is needed to align the eyes when an exophoria (out-turning tendency) exists. It appears to be impossible to induce fusional convergence by any means other than with a binocular fusional stimulus. It is a relatively slow posture adjustment, which is easier to induce gradually with variable power prisms than to induce suddenly with a quick change in prism. With the lids closed, the eyes tend to revert to the phoria position. Upon opening the eyes, a double image is seen until a fusional movement has occurred. Recovery findings in the blur, break and recovery prism tests, give some idea of the ability to recover fusion. For example, a high exophoria and a low positive fusional amplitude, as measured with the base out prism-to-blur test, indicates a need for a spectacle prescription, and/or visual therapy, and advice to avoid night driving until the condition is corrected.

C. Negative fusional convergence

The ability to decrease convergence from the phoria position without a change in accommodation is called negative fusional convergence. Negative fusional convergence is the opposite of positive fusional convergence, and becomes important in visual analysis when an esophoria (tendency to turn inward) exists. A weak negative fusional convergence ability or a high esophoria or both indicates a susceptibility to seeing double under adverse conditions, because most adverse conditions, such as blur, fog, darkness, fatigue, or alcohol, tend to increase the esophoria. Visual therapy and abstinence from night driving are indicated.

D. Amplitude of accommodation

The accommodative amplitude is an indication of the flexibility of seeing clearly at all distances. The amplitude is determined by how close an object can be and still be seen clearly. The lower the amplitude, the longer it takes to change accommodation and the more difficult it is to see objects nearby, such as the instrument panel. In some ways a reduced amplitude is favorable for driving, because it precludes the effects of accommodative spasms (night myopia), which may occur in an empty field, at low levels of illumination, after drinking alcohol, and after exposure to hypoxia or to carbon monoxide. Multifocals for dash panel and map reading are essential for safe driving when a low amplitude is present. They make an older driver able to read the dash panel quicker than a younger driver not wearing bifocals.

E. A.C.A. ratio

The A.C.A. (accommodative convergence divided by accommodation) ratio is the amount of convergence change induced by a one-diopter change of accommodation. We know a great deal about the A.C.A. ratio, but we do not know how to make permanent changes in it. Pathological or pharmaceutical attacks on the accommodative mechanism can cause the A.C.A. ratio to rise. Similarly, impairments of the convergence mechanism will cause it to fall. Many factors are contributory, such as the strength and attachment of the medial recti muscles, the ciliary muscle size, the zonular fiber strength and arrangement, and the age of the lens in the eye. Even so, the A.C.A. ratio is surprisingly constant for a given individual year after year. (It does slowly increase with age because the lens in the eye grows larger and is less flexible).

Whatever the causative factors, an A.C.A. ratio outside the limits of four to six prism diopters of convergence per each diopter of accommodation is abnormal, and can contribute to discomfort in reading and driving, to learning disabilities, to myopia, and may even contribute to diplopia and crossed eyes under certain conditions. If the abnormal A.C.A. is of a transient nature, as for example resulting from atropine in medications for colds or ulcers, it is only necessary to wait a few weeks after cessation of medication for it to return to normal. If the abnormal A.C.A. ratio is a "natural" condition for the patient, appropriate lenses should be provided which may include a bifocal.

If a hazard of diplopia due to crossed eyes exists under low levels of illumination, visual therapy should be given to ensure that diplopia will not occur. Such therapy would include stress prisms or lenses, large excursion rotations, and eye-hand coordination training using a rotating pegboard and a training occluder (Oppenheimer, 1968) (see Figure 5.5). Stress prisms would be base in for a high A.C.A. ratio and base out for a low A.C.A. ratio. Stress lenses would be minus for a high A.C.A. ratio; but for an A.C.A. ratio of less than 3/1, stress lenses are of little value.

A "new" and little understood concept is to use the patient's own tonicity reflexes to straighten the eyes as if surgery had been done. Once the eyes are straight (behind occluders), antisuppression and fusional training will permit normal binocularity to take over.

Eye straightening should be done as the first step in vision therapy before amblyopia or antisuppression treatment is given. By putting on increasing amounts of prism in the direction you want the eyes to go, and by letting the person interact with the environment for a few days or weeks, the eyes will adapt to the prisms. When the eyes are physically straight, put on binasal occluders for regular wear while you do the antisuppression and fusion training. You will have

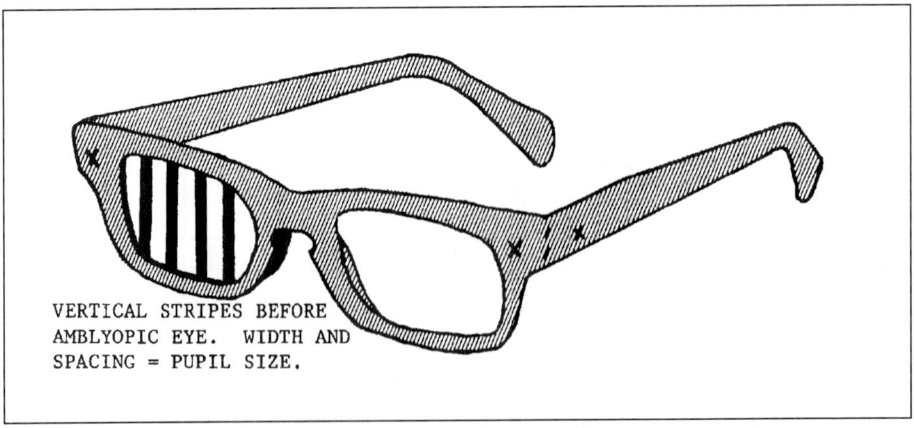

Figure 5.5 *Vertical stripes applied to a spectacle lens provide a unique stimulus to an amblyopic eye or a means of increasing binocular interaction. No serious interference with the field of view occurs when such a partial occluder is worn in contrast with complete uniocular occlusion. (Adapted from Oppenheimer, 1968.)*

straightened the patient's eyes naturally without drugs or surgery. When fusion is reactivated by antisuppression treatment (the TBI), just remove the binasals.

5.6 Special Tests

A. Aniseikonia

Aniseikonia is a perceived difference in the image sizes of the two eyes. It can be meridional, or overall, and can be a serious problem in spatial orientation. Aniseikonia is usually considered to be induced by spectacle differences, or differences in the lengths of the two eyes. However, photoreceptor distribution and cortical representations from the two eyes are equally important factors in aniseikonia. Indeed, like refractive errors and phorias, the wonder is that there are so few people with a significant amount of aniseikonia (5 percent or more). People adapt to their environment. Adaptation to a new pair of glasses is usually strangely distressing for a few minutes, hours, or days, but within two weeks it is usually complete. If a person has an appreciable natural aniseikonia, it is possible that binocular abilities have never been fully developed and that a program of building normal binocular function will permit a successful adaptation to the aniseikonia. Heavy emphasis should be placed on the maintenance of binocular vision while the patient does spatial orientation training, such as baseball, table tennis, or inserting golf tees in a rotating pegboard disc, etc.

In any event, aniseikonic spatial distortions, like chromeostereopsis errors, usually show up only when normal perspective clues are missing or are unreliable. This occurs in the leaf room[2] or behind the wheel of an automobile late at night, when other automobiles are seldom encountered, and when fatigue has reduced the driver's compensating ability. The symptoms of aniseikonia then will be illusions of going up or down hills, or being on a roadway that slopes to the right or left, or a combination of these effects. A sudden loss of normal perspective and overlay spatial clues could create a dangerous illusion for the aniseikonic patient when driving; this could result in disorientation, confusion, and perhaps an accident.

Aniseikonia is suspected when refractive and muscle balance corrections have been supplied and headaches or asthenopia persist. Further evidence is supplied if monocular occlusion for a few days eliminates the symptoms. The aniseikonia would then have to be differentiated from cyclophoria, lateral phoria, or vertical phoria anomalies, which can cause the same symptom complex.

It is never safe to rely upon assumptions about aniseikonia based upon refractive considerations alone, except where a person of known good binocularity has been comfortable and we are contemplating a change in base curves or thickness, as in safety glasses, or strong lenses after old fashioned cataract surgery. Then, we can use the present base curves, thicknesses, prescription powers, and vertex distances to determine intelligently these variables in the new prescription. Otherwise, the only safe procedure is to measure the amount of aniseikonia with an Eikonometer through the new prescription and to redesign one or both lenses as needed to bring the Eikonometer reading to zero.

Eikonometry can only be done if normal binocular vision with stereopsis is present. Binocular anomalies of suppression, anomalous correspondence, amblyopia, and strabismus can result from aniseikonia. But, persons with such anomalies cannot be tested with an Eikonometer because they do not have stereopsis. A technique based upon afterimages has been recommended by William Ludlam, O.D., Ph.D., Pacific University, College of Optometry. Have the person view a pair of parallel, lighted showcase lamps on a wall to induce an after image in the nonamblyopic eye. Turn off the lights. Occlude the after image eye and have the patient walk toward or away from the wall until the afterimages appears to be the same size as the unlighted bulbs. The ratio of the distance used to induce the afterimage, to the distance needed to make the second eye image the same size as the afterimage in the first eye, is the measure of aniseikonia in the meridian at right angles to the bulbs. At 10 feet, a one-foot difference between the viewing distances of the two eyes gives a 10 percent size difference; hence distances must be carefully measured and the test repeated on several different office visits if any question of accuracy exists.

The formula for computing the magnification (*M*) of a spectacle lens is as follows: M = shape magnification × power magnification

$$M = \left(\frac{1}{1-\frac{t}{n}F_1}\right)\times\left(\frac{1}{1-aF'_v}\right)$$

where F_1 = Front surface power

t = Center thickness of the lens

a = Distance of entrance pupil from back vertex of lens

F'_v = Back vertex power of the lens

n = Refractive Index.

The ratio of the magnification of each spectacle lens should be the same as the aniseikonia ratio to be corrected, but opposite in sign; that is, the larger imaged eye would need the smaller spectacle magnification.

B. Color vision

Dalton in 1798 wrote about his own color vision defect as follows:

> I found that persons in general distinguish six kinds of colour in the solar image, namely red, orange, yellow, green, blue, and

> purple. Newton, indeed, divides the purple into indigo and violet; but the difference between him and others is merely nominal. To me it is quite otherwise. I see only two, or at most three distinctions. These I should call yellow and blue, or yellow, blue and purple. My yellow comprehends the red, orange, yellow and green of others; my blue and purple coincide with theirs (Judd, 1943).

This lucid description of a visual problem clearly indicates the futility of designing a traffic-control signal system, based entirely on color. About 10 percent of the male population has a permanent color vision defect of some sort. One out of fifty can't see red light. It looks black! Very few females have any color blind problems. Acquired color vision defects from injury, disease and age also occur.

Color defective people tend to confuse red, green, and yellow signals, and the color vision defect may be slight or severe. Some tests for diagnosing the several types of color vision defects follow.

The anomaloscope is an instrument for mixing red and green to match yellow. The yellow is adjustable in brightness. An extra amount of red in the match indicates protanopia; of green, deuteranopia; and the ability to match any color combination of red plus green with yellow indicates absolute color blindness. Protanomaly and deuteranomaly are less severe degrees of protanopia and deuteranopia. The Nagel Anomaloscope[3] is the best known example of such instruments.

The Farnsworth 100 Hue Test[4] consists of eighty-five plastic caps containing a series of graded Munsell papers that the patient arranges in a sequence of look alike or matching colors. Errors in placing the colors in proper order give clues to the anomaly.

The Farnsworth Dichomatous Test[5] is less time-consuming than the 100 Hue Test because it has only fifteen caps that must be arranged in a sequence of similar colors. It gives a clear indication in most cases of the type of defect present.

The American Optical Company Hardy, Rand, and Rittler[6] (A.O.H.R.R.) Pseudoisochromatic test plates are perhaps the best of the book tests for color vision defects. Some indication of the type of defect can be obtained from this test, but this and other book tests, such as the Dvorine and Ishihara Tests, are primarily intended as pass-fail tests.

The lantern test in which the person is asked to name the color displayed, has also been used. It is possible that a color defective person could pass such a test by guessing.

In all tests, one must maintain rigorous adherence to brightness levels and the quality of light used to illuminate the test colors. The recommended lamp source should be used at the prescribed distance. Color vision defects should be noted and the patient warned of the hazards in driving. Color defectives take longer and make many errors compared to normal sighted persons. If the optometrist is called upon to evaluate a person's ability to drive in the face of a color vision defect, a driving test is perhaps the only way to evaluate the ability of such a person to use the other factors that contribute information and make driving relatively safe in spite of color vision defects. Even so, night driving for color defectives might need to be restricted to well-lighted streets and freeways. A protanopic or protanomalous color defective is very insensitive to red light and will be handicapped when approaching an unfamiliar intersection or an obstacle like a car or truck showing only a red light.

The color defective may be able to analyze a signal light in the day time because the red light is placed above the yellow light. If yellow or green cannot be seen then the signal probably is red, or is not working. At night, when a person can't see the light's position, the primary clue would be the behavior of other traffic.

A person with a color vision defect cannot be licensed to drive a truck in interstate commerce. Japan has long discriminated against the color vision defective citizen in all walks of life starting in grade school (Tagayanagi). Only recently have the multiple, discriminatory restrictions begun to be removed in Japan as a result of Tagayanagi's work. The worldwide use of the Ishihara Color Vision Test indicates Japan's leadership in color vision testing.

Why should we continue to use a system that make second class citizens out of otherwise normal people? It is clear that as soon as possible we need to shape code our red lights used in transportation by adding a white horizontal band across every red signal. This will reduce the driving hazards for all of us.

C. Stereopsis

Stereopsis is the three-dimensional depth sense mediated through the simultaneous use of two eyes. Stereopsis gives the relative distance of one object compared to another. Perspective and overlay clues are also very important spatial clues which work well for everyone, including people with one eye. Beyond about 3,000 feet, stereopsis is not helpful in judging which object is nearer because of the small separation of the two eyes and the stereo acuity limit of about 12 seconds of arc. In fact, one would expect that objects at infinity would be just noticeably farther away than objects at 3,000 feet.

Chromatic aberration in the eyes coupled with a displaced pupil can create the illusion that lights of different colors are displaced in front of or behind their true position. (For example, a vertical red line between two vertical green lines on a piece of paper, probably will appear to be closer or farther away than the green lines.) That chrome stereopsis is real, is another argument for adding white shape coding to red lights used in our transportation system. White is not subject to a chrome stereopsis error.

Normal stereopsis is highly desirable for maneuvering or driving a bus, truck or automobile when parking, loading or driving in closely spaced traffic. In such situations, the absence of stereopsis means that a driver must obtain spatial information from the perspective clues, from monocular parallax caused by vehicle movements and perhaps by head bobbing. Like color vision, a lack of stereopsis may be evaluated as to its interference with safe driving by a performance test in the vehicle under realistic or actual operating conditions. Stereopsis for high speed highway travel probably is not very important because viewing distances are usually great. Conversely, stereopsis errors in the judgment of the distances of red versus white or green can be very harmful at highway speeds.

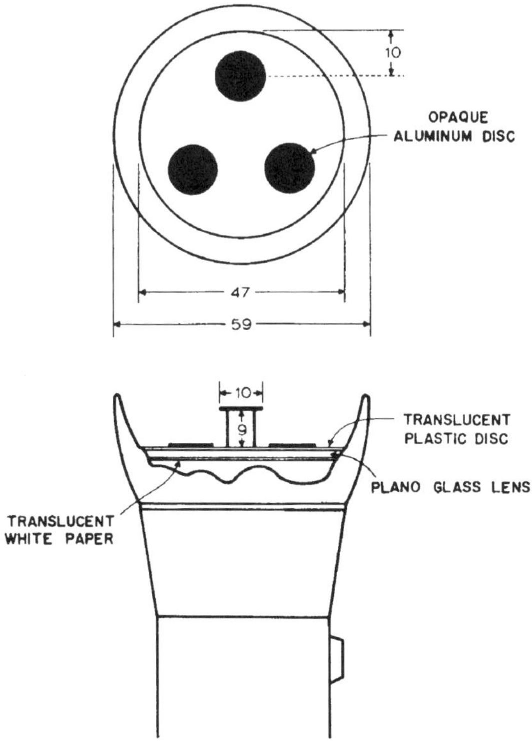

Figure 5.6 *Cutaway showing the diastereo test flashlight (the dimensions given are in millimeters). The top view is that seen by the subject, who must select the black spot that appears nearest. A criterion of at least three correct responses out of four presentations at different positions seems adequate to eliminate the chance guess factor, which could give a passing score in the absence of stereopsis.*

Stereopsis testing can be carried out with the classical peg test operated from twenty feet by the subject pulling on a string to bring a movable peg into side-by-side relationship with a fixed peg. The clever ways in which air cadets have defeated this test are legend. It is argued that stereopsis is an all or none phenomenon and that, if you have stereopsis, its excellence depends upon such factors as the accuracy of the binocular vision correction. On this basis, a simple test like the stereo fly or the diastereo test (Hofstetter, 1968) is ample (see Figure 5.6). The latter is a flashlight with a frosted plastic face bearing three spots, one of which is elevated toward the observer. The test criterion may be a simple four correct out of six different presentations at different positions, since, by guessing, one would expect only two out of six correct answers. Hofstetter's studies indicate that those who failed this test, though otherwise normal in superficial appearance, later turned out to be squinters (crossed, or out turning eyes) who had been overlooked in the routine clinic examination.

D. Night visual performance

Driving performance at night may be significantly handicapped by the lack of light. This impairment comes about because of the following factors:

(a) Reduction in illumination levels at night reduces the visual information available to the driver.

(b) Lowered retinal illumination permits pupil dilation, which increases the optical aberrations and reduces the depth of focus.

(c) Visual acuity falls with lowered light levels so that 20/20 by day will be considerably poorer under night seeing conditions. Acuity deteriorates more with some observers than with others, depending upon the condition of their eyes.

(d) Brightness contrast sensitivity is reduced at low levels of illumination; hence easily seen objects of 5 percent contrast at room lighting levels become invisible at roadway illumination levels.

(e) Photochemical dark adaptation makes seeing possible at the low levels of night driving. This process is adversely affected by pre-exposure to bright light even up to twelve or more hours beforehand. Hence, it is desirable to protect the driver's eyes from excessive daylight if good performance is desired at night.

(f) High altitudes provide lowered oxygen partial pressures in the atmosphere, lowered oxygen tension at the individual body cell, and impaired dark adaptation.

Dark adaptation test performance is adversely affected by vitamin A deficiency, a small pupil, absorption and scatter in the crystalline lens, and the refractive error.

The test performance usually can be improved by eating blueberries, taking taurine, taking a zinc supplement as well as vitamin A and other vitamins.

Since night driving requires many facets of vision besides the absolute light sensitivity threshold, called scotopic vision, and since nighttime driving is done at mesopic and low photopic levels rather than at the scotopic levels, a performance test at the levels of night driving, or a predictor of performance at such levels, is needed.

The Night Vision Performance Tester is one such test for predicting night vision performance. Figure 5.7 shows the details of this apparatus, which in essence is a low contrast 20/40 test letter viewed against a background of variable luminance and protected from room illumination by a layer of filters. The normally encountered room reflections from the filter surfaces are eliminated by angling the filters so that they reflect only from a black surface. Two instruments using this principle have been designed. One has a large luminance range and is suitable for office use in measuring age deterioration effects upon vision and in measuring subtle improvements in vision performance due to refractive refinements, diet, or medical treatments. The second instrument is a pass-fail instrument

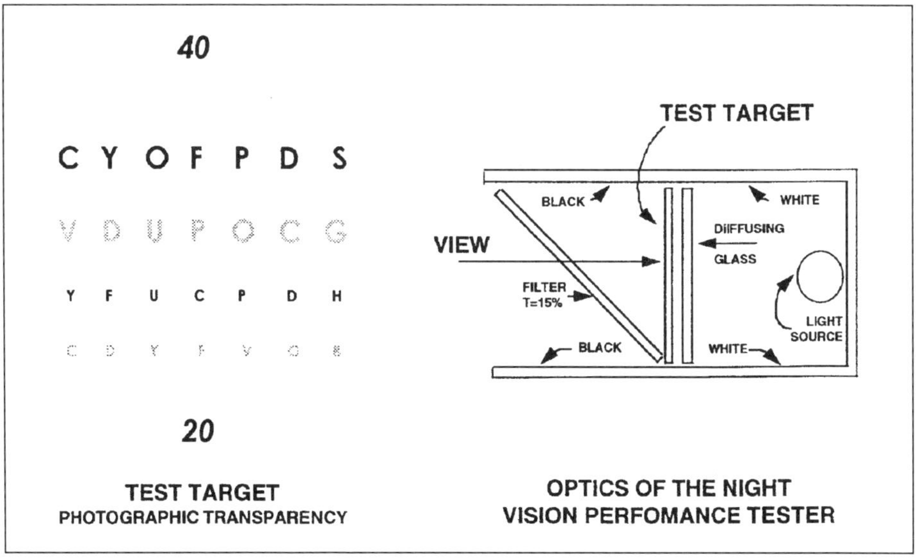

Figure 5.7 *The Night Vision Performance Tester provides high and low contrast test letters against a variable luminance background. By covering the chart with a filter, the influence of the room illumination is reduced. By increasing the lamp's light output from zero, the high contrast larger letters will be the first to be readable. More light will be needed to see the smaller letters and those of lower contrast. Similarly when the eye image is reduced in contrast because of cataract, blur, glare light, etc., more light will be required. If the pupil is small, or if excess light absorption occurs in the optical media (cataract), more light will be required. Low contrast test letters and adjustable brightness make this test highly predictable of night driving performance.*

with brightness adjust ability sufficient only to compensate for light source aging. Both instruments contain photosensitive equipment for ensuring specified brightness levels.

Figures 5.8 and 5.9 show the deterioration of visual performance when tested with the Night Vision Performance Tester using lenses to simulate ametropia. Figure 5.10 shows the effect of refractive error upon nighttime visual performance in detecting a black or white obstacle the size of an automobile. Figure 5.11 shows the effect on the test scores of wearing filters.

The Night Vision Performance Tester yields a score in terms of the illumination needed to see a given target; hence, it provides a real indication of the light levels that will be needed for nighttime driving. The tester measures overall visual performance, whatever the factors: these factors are pupil size, ocular transmission, ocular scatter, retinal pathologies, physiological abnormalities, and refractive errors.

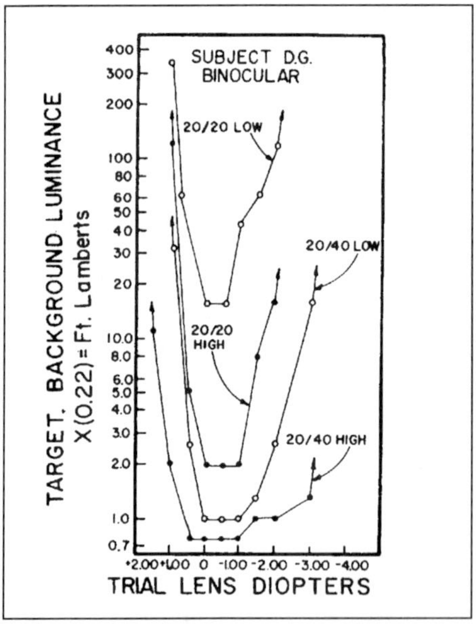

Figure 5.8 The effect of simulated myopia (+ lenses) and simulated hyperopia (– lenses) upon the night vision performance tester back ground luminance for a twenty-year-old binocular subject reading 20/20 high and 20/40 low contrast letters.

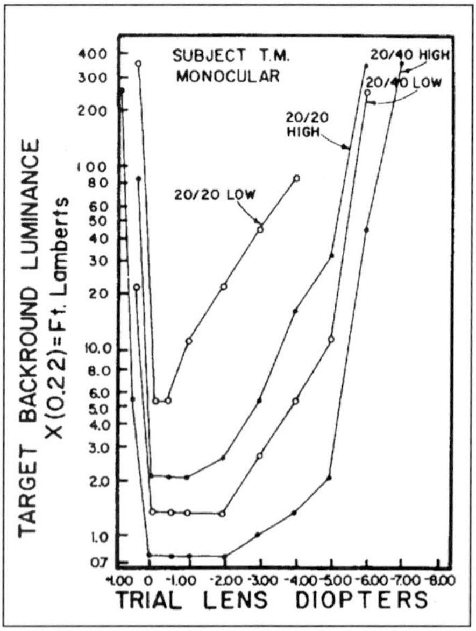

Figure 5.9 The effect of simulated myopia (+ lenses) and simulated hyperopia (– lenses) upon the night vision performance tester background luminance for a forty-year-old subject tested monocularly. Figures 5.8 and 5.9 show the dependence of acuity upon contrast and luminance levels as classically shown in Figure 9.2. In addition, the devastating effect upon visual performance of blur due to refractive errors is shown as a need for more light.

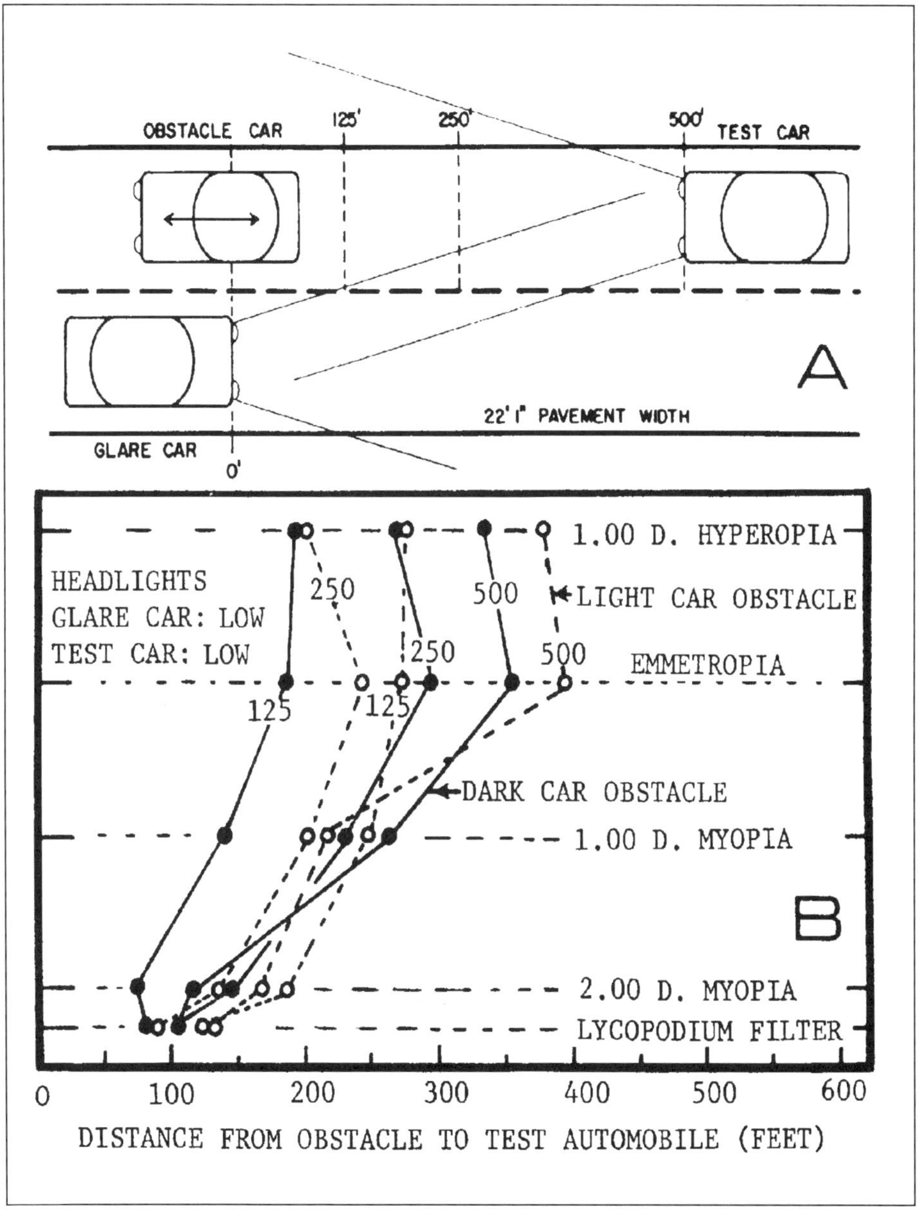

Figure 5.10 *Part A shows the experimental arrangement of vehicles used to gather the data in part B. The rear of the obstacle car faced the observer in the test car. A white compact car covered with a white cloth was the light car obstacle. A black compact car covered with a black cloth was the dark car obstacle. The test car was placed at 125, 250, and 500 feet from the glare car. The obstacle car was moved toward the test car until detected. Part B shows that myopia and simulated glaucoma and cataract (lycopodium filter) caused startling losses in the detection distance of an obstacle as large as an automobile. Even the presence of hyperopia reduced performance somewhat in this twenty-six-year-old subject.*

The American Automobile Association Glareometer contains a pair of lights simulating headlights and a series of target patterns to be identified. The lower the illumination level on the targets needed to recognize them, the better the performance on the test.

None of the above three tests has been evaluated against the actual driving performance of drivers at night, and, hence, it is not known whether one is superior to another. It is conceivable that they are measuring different things and that one may correlate better with driving performance than another. From the optometric standpoint, the Night Vision Performance Tester or equivalent would seem to be the choice for office use.

E. Visual fields

All patients, young or old, should have a visual fields check at each eye examination. There is a good correlation between visual field defects and poor health. The mapping of a visual field is analogous to the neurologist mapping the pain and temperature sensitive areas on the skin and studying sensory motor reflexes.

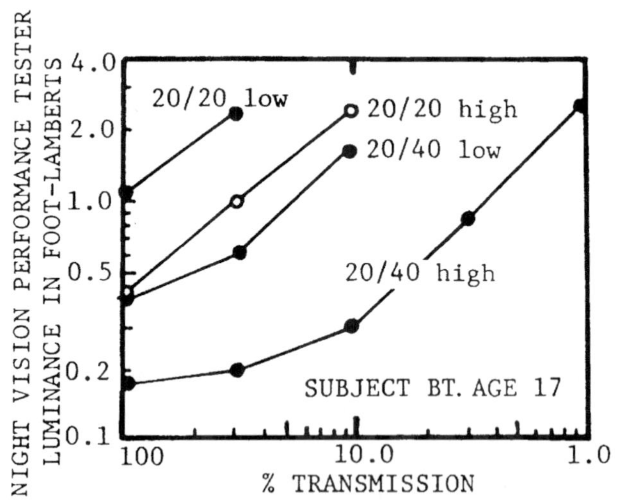

__Figure 5.11__ The effect of a reduced ocular transmission with age is simulated with neutral density filters before the eyes of a seventeen-year-old subject. One possible reason that a straight line relationship was not obtained is that the pupil tends to compensate for the lowered retinal luminance occurring with the filters. Increased ocular absorption should thus be detected with this instrument. Since about twice as much light is needed to perform the same visual task for each thirteen-year increase in age, a lifetime can cause a need for over 50 times more light compared to a thirteen-year-old. Yet Figure 7.5 shows that the actual transmission change of the eye between a two-year-old and a seventy-five-year-old is not likely to exceed 2.5 times. Probably a degradation in optical image quality and retinal function and a change in pupil size accounts for needing twice the amount of light for every thirteen years of age.

Such information permits the expert to pinpoint the location and the probable kind of lesion affecting the nerve pathways. With visual field mapping and checking for other neurological symptoms, brain tumors, abscesses, aneurysms, infarcts, and hemorrhages can be located or ocular pathology revealed. Because visual fields testing is so easy, few realize its tremendous practical value. For example, if "Glaucoma Day" screening efforts were centered around a tangent screen instead of a tonometer, the yield would include nearly three times more actual glaucoma victims than are now detected; and, in addition, brain tumors, retinopathies, cataracts, and such blinding systemic diseases as diabetes would be detected. Another bonus would be a drop in the overreferral rate for glaucoma from such screening.

Projection, self recording, tangent screens; projection photographic recording screens; and pantographic self recording screens are now available to simplify and speed the tangent screen test.

The driver licensing requirement is usually 140 degrees of visual field. Optometric examination can establish the amount of the field defect, its significance for treatment and the possible need to stop driving.

F. Reaction time

A reaction time test gives information on the total performance potential of an individual. If a sharp, bright retinal image is received and if the neurological components between the eye and the responding skeletal muscles are operating at optimum efficiency, the patient will have a fast reaction time. On the other hand, a blurred, low contrast, low intensity retinal image reduces the strength of the input signal and the reaction time will be longer. Similarly alcohol, drugs, fatigue, and cortical ischemia due to arteriosclerosis or atherosclerosis, will cause a longer reaction time. If, in addition, there is neurological damage or loss of tissue, the reaction time will be further lengthened. Normal young active people have simple visual reaction times, after some practice, of between 0.18 and 0.20 second. If a sound signal is present, the reaction time may become primarily auditory and speed up to 0.15 second. In experimental situations on the highway, visual reaction times from signal change to brake application exceeds 0.5 second. In normal highway traffic, the average reaction time to a clearly visible hazard is 1.64 seconds. 90 percent of all drivers will respond in 2.5 seconds.

Since the reaction time cuts across so many functional systems and gives a measure of performance which can reflect on driving ability, it seems reasonable that licensing agencies should begin testing visual reaction times. Police doing accident investigation could measure driver reaction times as well as blood alcohol levels. It is a simple test, and it will undoubtedly rise to a position of importance in license bureau testing and in optometric offices.

All detrimental factors in driving, e.g. rain, darkness, excess traffic, poor acuity, defective color vision, etc., can be thought of in terms of an increased reaction time!

G. Glaucoma

Optometric testing for glaucoma should include the case history, the optometric examination, the use of some test for visual fields, and the use of a tonometer. Reputable authorities classify chronic simple glaucoma as a symptom and not a disease in its own right. Authorities also agree that it is not clear whether increased intraocular pressure causes the visual field defects, or whether the process causing the field defects is also causing the elevated pressures, which are often, but not always, observed.

Since so little agreement exists on the association of a markedly elevated pressure in the eye with peripheral vision loss, it is essential that a glaucoma detection procedure, or a blindness prevention program, rely upon the case history, fundus examination, central vision, and visual field studies as important prognosticators of health. The tonometer must also be used, for it may indicate an abnormality not noted by any of the other procedures.

The presence of glaucoma presupposes visual field defects, either partial or total. Field defects can make driving hazardous. The larger the defect, and the more it involves both eyes, the more handicapping it is. Glaucoma, using the word to mean elevated pressure, is associated with increased light glare, mostly from the cornea. Stressing the cornea causes a distortion of stromal fibers, reduces corneal transparency and increases the amount of scattered light. The increase in scatter is proportional to the increase in pressure within the eye; hence, a slit lamp or ophthalmoscopic view showing increased corneal scatter, should suggest increased intraocular pressure. Except in an active inflammatory process (or residual clouding from an old one) almost no other cause for increased corneal clouding is commonly encountered. When the pressure reverts to normal ranges, the clouding usually clears up.

Glaucoma affects driving ability by causing visual field defects, by increased ocular scatter, and by reduced night vision capability. The patient treated for glaucoma with pilocarpine has a small pupil which reduces retinal illumination to about 11 percent, assuming a pilocarpine pupil of 2 millimeters compared to the 6 millimeter pupil which is normal under night driving conditions. There is also some evidence that pilocarpine has an adverse effect upon the retina itself. This will further interfere with night vision. One-eyed treatment with pilocarpine will cause severe spatial distortions both by day and night due to the difference in brightness of the right eye, left eye images (the Pulfrich effect).

The treatment of glaucoma by a sympathomimetic drug such as

neosynephrine causes a large pupil, so there is no handicap for night driving. Combination drugs are available which keep a fairly normal pupil size. Diamox given by mouth will hold pressures in line for long periods, while glycerin given by mouth or intravenously is useful in lowering intraocular pressure in a crisis. *All such treatments are treatments of the symptoms of glaucoma.* For a cure, it appears that other health factors must be evaluated and improved as needed. Improved nutrition and exercise have been shown to favorably affect intraocular pressure.

End Notes

1. Made by dusting lycopodium powder over a clean plate of glass bearing a thin film of petroleum jelly and then covering it with a clean cover glass. Lycopodium powder should be available from a pharmacist.
2. The leaf room is a test room whose square corners and flat surfaces have been covered over with leaves hanging by their stems so that the normal appearance of the room is obliterated. Under such conditions, space distortions often become apparent, because the subject does not know what the room is supposed to look like.
3. Distributed in U.S. by Alfred P. Poll, 410 West 55th Street, New York, N.Y., 10019. A similar instrument has been manufactured by Bausch and Lomb Optical Company, Ophthalmic Division, 635 St. Paul Street, Rochester, N.Y., 14602.
4. Munsell Color Corporation Inc., 2441 North Calvert Street, Baltimore, Md., 21218.
5. The Psychological Corporation, 304 East 45th Street, New York, N.Y., 10017.
6. The American Optical Company, Instrument Division, Buffalo, N.Y., 14215.

Chapter 6

Prescribing for Driving

Merrill J. Allen, O.D., Ph.D.

Synopsis

6.1 Daytime

A. Lens power

The proper prescription for daytime driving has not been extensively studied. However, certain indications help us to make a rational decision. Outdoor people do not like to wear a full plus prescription, preferring to have up to 0.50 diopter of accommodation in play at distance. Indoor people, on the other hand, easily accept full plus at distance, apparently to obtain the relief of reduced strain on their accommodative mechanism at near.

Luckiesh et al. (1940, 1941, 1943, 1949), using the Sensitometric Method of refraction, concluded that the best prescription at distance was up to 1.00 diopter less plus than normally prescribed.

For young adults, night myopia, empty field myopia, and blurred or fogged vision myopia all indicate that accommodation of about 1.00 diopter is natural when no stimuli are present. Myopes tend to show less accommodative tonicity and hyperopes to show more. Night myopia includes both spherical aberration, due to an enlarged pupil, and a shift in spectral sensitivity toward the blue end of the spectrum caused by shifting to rod vision. This accounts for up to 1.00 diopter of myopia, while accommodation may increase the myopia above 1.50 diopters.

For the normal clinical determination of the best distance prescription for daytime driving, the duochrome test is recommended as the test of choice. When testing binocularly in a twenty foot room, leave the presbyopic patient clearer for black letters on the green background.

For the prepresbyope, the amount to under correct at distance would be determined by the following considerations:

A patient with a high A.C.A. ratio will probably accept full plus. An uncorrected hyperope receiving his first glasses will not accept the full plus and should not be given full plus. *Undercorrection of hyperopia will encourage growth toward emmetropia.* The less plus acceptance occurs with younger drivers and with the greater amount of previously uncorrected hyperopia.

The uncorrected myope is likely to accept the maximum plus, red equals green, prescription without complaint, although a higher minus might give better vision. The flexibility of accommodation demanded by the hyperope may actually be the cause of discomfort for many myopes. The reason is that virtually all myopes have a higher than normal A.C.A. ratio and do extensive near work which would be benefited by plus instead of minus lenses. For beginning myopia the best prescription should be a pair of reading glasses to be worn for all close work. Within a week or so the distance vision will clear without the help of glasses.

Astigmatism should be slightly undercorrected for cylinder axes at or near the 90 or 180 degree meridian. For oblique axes, the cylinder lens power should be reduced, and the axes shifted toward vertical or horizontal to reduce image distortions. For best visual acuity, a full prescription is recommended. However, for oblique axis astigmatism, the spectacle lens distortion problems can be severe, and contact lenses would be the better choice.

An alternative to glasses and contact lenses is now being promoted. It uses surgery or laser beams on the cornea to correct nearsightedness. Results after several years indicate that the correction is not permanent. This is just like when myopia is corrected with glasses, the correction is not permanent.

Like glasses, the surgery is treating the symptom and not the cause. The cause of the myopia is the need for plus at near to relieve esophoria. If plus is provided both at distance and near to relieve the esophoria, most myopia will reduce or disappear. When testing, one should not rely on the near phoria alone, but on the difference between the far and near phorias to determine that a high A.C.A. ratio exists.

If the patient was reading in the waiting room before the eye exam, orthophoria or exophoria will be manifest at near. If the patient was driving for an hour or more and came right into the examination without any waiting, esophoria probably will be present during the near tests. *People adapt to what they are doing! Myopia itself is an adaptation to relieve esophoria during near work.*

B. Spectacle frames

It is unfortunately true that at the same time that automotive vision experts extol the virtues of unlimited visibility without obstructions or distortions, the ophthalmic practitioners provide both obstructions and distortions in the eye wear they dispense (Bewley, 1969). Frames with heavy eye wires and bulky temples are commonplace. Visually superior frames and mountings are not usually recommended by the eye doctors. They seem to prefer the easier approach of letting fashion dictate eyewear styles. That these are poor choices is well known to everyone who dispenses and has to adjust, repair, straighten, or put lenses in many of the more popular styles.

A pair of lenses is a visual aid, and should permit unrestricted vision throughout the visual field, both with the fovea and the peripheral retina. The edges of high plus lenses cause a blind zone which is a function of the power of the prescription, the diameter of the lens, and the distance from the eye. High minus lenses, on the other hand, even with thick edges, provide a field overlap and, hence, no blind area. There is, however, a discontinuity in space perception at the edge of the minus lenses. To put the plus lens blind area as far in the periphery as possible requires large lenses of high base curve and a fit that is close to the eyes. Many wraparound sunglasses achieve this effect reasonably well, but prescription lenses cannot usually be made this way.

The steeper the base curve, the less distortion produced by a spectacle lens. However, a minus power, corrected curve lens with good marginal performance is flatter as the minus power increases. Hence, distortion may become a problem even though edge to edge visual acuity may be quite good. By using globular lenses (Wollaston portion of the Tscherning ellipse) both astigmatism and distortion are minimized. This is a reasonable approach mechanically for low power minus lenses, but for high powers the curves are not practical to manufacture by the laboratory. Even if they were, the lenses would be of very small overall diameter. Hence, to correct a high myope properly, because of distortions, contact lenses are indicated. For high hyperopes and aphakics, the blind zone at the edge of the lens dictates contact lenses, or very large spectacle lenses fitted as close to the eyes as feasible.

The proper spectacle frame is one that accurately and reliably places the lenses at their design distance and angle with an absolute minimum of obstruction in the field of view, with one important exception. Overhead lights and the open sky cause considerable distress and eyebrow lowering. Hence, spectacle frames that add to the shading effect of the eyebrows can be beneficial. The use of nylon bands and/or thin metal for the eye wires provides an attractive, practi-

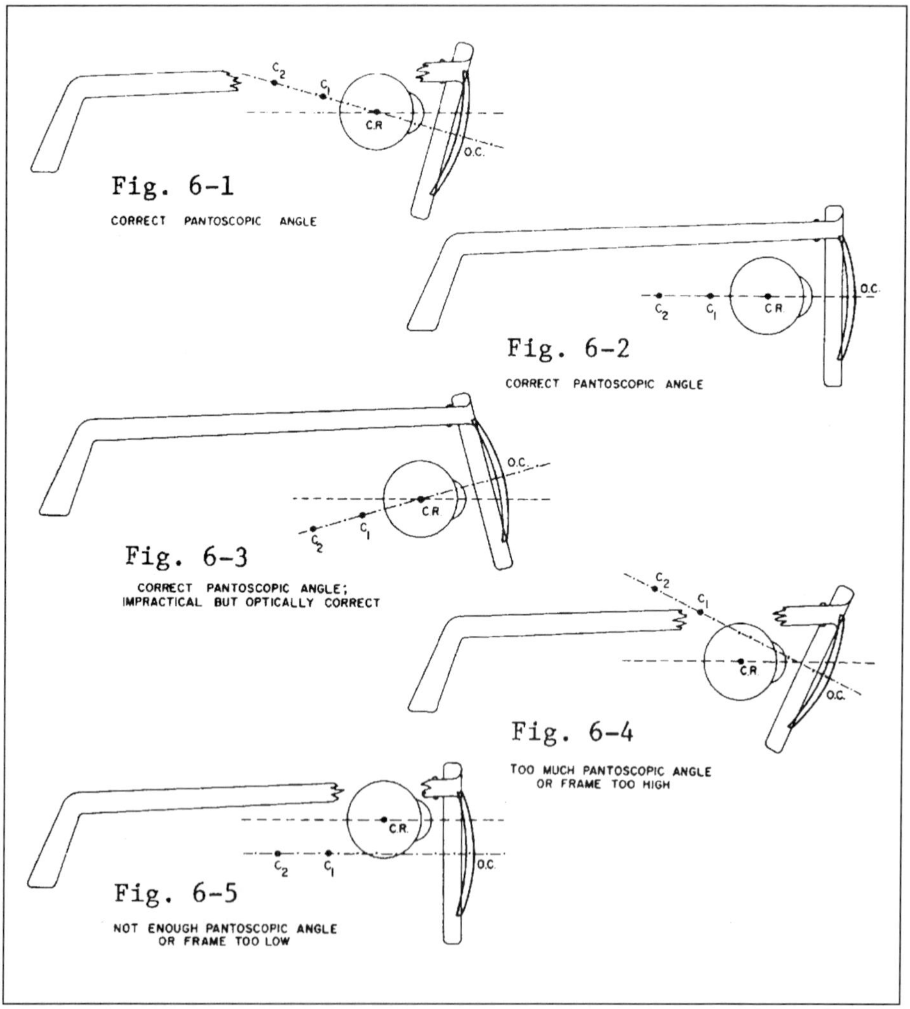

Figures 6.1 through 6.5 *Placement of spectacle lenses. Figures 6.1, 6.2, and 6.3 show optically correct placement, while Figures 6.4 and 6.5 are incorrect. Corrected curve lenses are designed for an eye whose center of rotation (C.R.) is located on the optic axis of the lens. The optic axis is the line joining* C_2, C_1 *and O.C. The pantoscopic or spectacle tilt angle is thus interrelated with the vertical position of the lenses before the eyes. Frames that do not maintain the desired lens placement thus impair the performance of the lens prescription, adding errors and distortions of their own.*

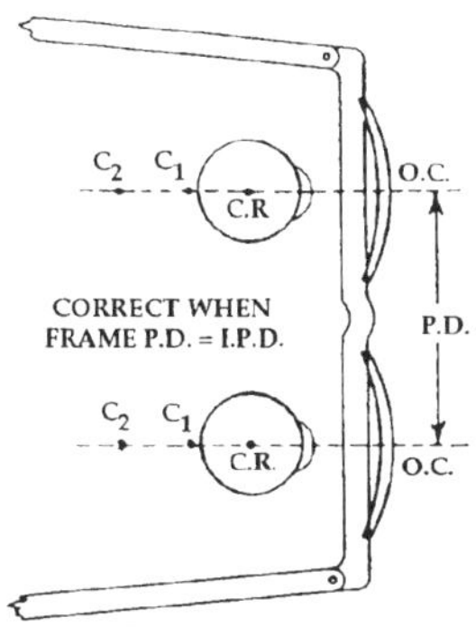

FIGURE 6-6

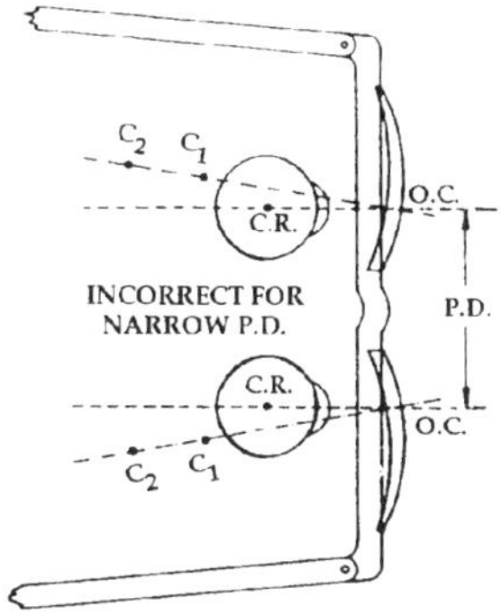

FIGURE 6-7

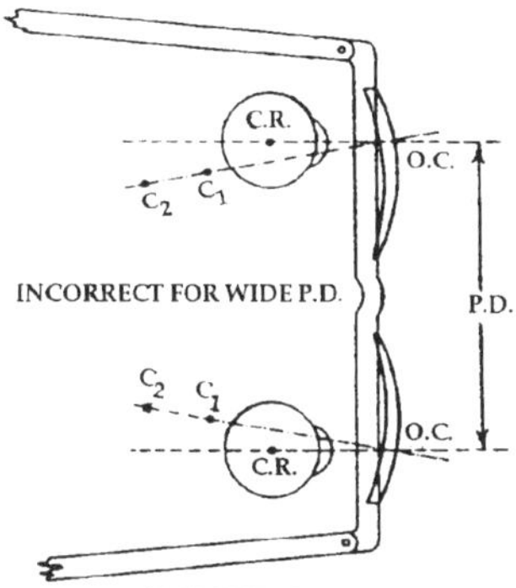

FIGURE 6-8

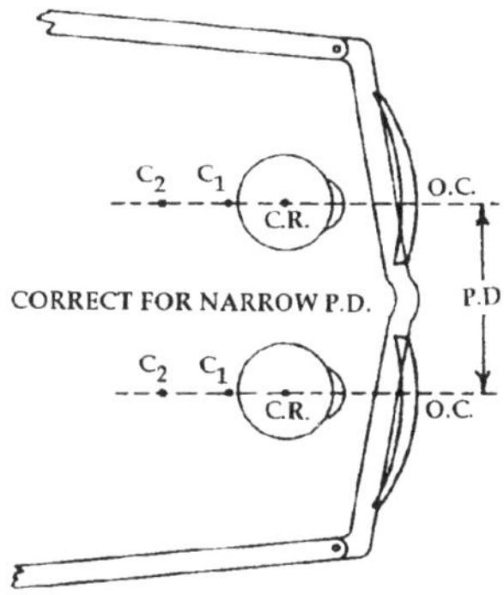

FIGURE 6-9

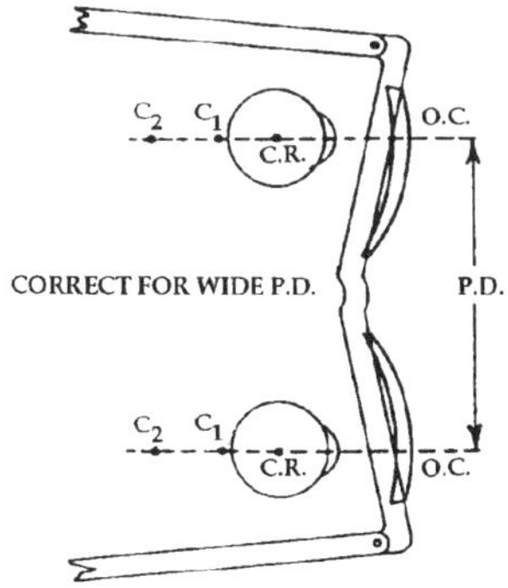

FIGURE 6-10

Figures 6.6 through 6.10 *The relationship between patient interpupillary distance (P.D.) and the optical axes of the spectacle lenses is shown. Figure 6.6 is the normal situation in which the optical center (O.C.) of the lenses and the patient's P.D. agree. Spectacle lenses are customarily aligned in the frame so the back surfaces lie in a plane as shown. Figures 6.7 and 6.8 show the complication of maintaining a flat spectacle plane when the patient's P.D. does not agree with the spectacle P.D. The lens O.C.s agree with the P.D., but the optical axes of the lenses do not pass through the C.R. of the eyes as required for optimum lens performance. Figures 6.9 and 6.10 show the remedy that may be obtained by bending the frame at the center or by special edge treatment of the lenses so that they are properly angled when inserted in a flat frame.*

cal, nonobstructive spectacle frame. Temples that are high, at eyebrow level, and are less than one-quarter inch wide are acceptable.

After a pair of glasses has been placed on the patient's face, the accuracy of the height and pantoscopic tilt must be checked to ensure optimum performance of the lenses. A retinoscope, ophthalmoscope, or penlight held close to the fitter's eye can be used as a source to show the optic axis of the lens and the line of sight of the patient's eye (Allen, April 1962). While the patient is fixating the source, the fitter moves around until the reflections from the two surfaces of the lens coincide. If they are also centered in the patient's pupil, the lens is properly aligned (see Figures 6.1 through 6.5). If the lens reflections and the center of the pupil do not coincide, tilting the lenses or raising or lowering them will correct the error. Sometimes it is necessary to change the plane of the frame by bending it back or forward at the bridge to correct a lateral misalignment (see Figures 6.6 through 6.10).

If prism is present, optimum corrected curve lens performance can be obtained if the optic axis passes through the sighting center (C.R.) of the eye as indicated in the figures, even though this means that the frame needs to be bent back at the bridge to angle the temporal edge of the lenses nearer to the face, or vice versa. In any event, the optic axes of the lenses need not be parallel for optimum corrected curve performance on a given patient.

This problem is important in all cases where spectacles are used for vision correction and it becomes extremely important when lens powers of 1.50 diopters and over are required. Failure to observe proper alignment causes distortion of familiar surroundings, as well as a loss in acuity due to aberration powers (sphere and cylinder) which are not found in the lens when it is properly positioned. Greater attention to spectacle optics will improve the patient's acceptance

Table 6.1

Ophthalmic Filter	*No Coating* **% Transmission**	*Uniform Coating* **% Transmission**		*Gradient Coating* **% Transmission**	
			Top	**Center**	**Bottom**
White	92.0%	10.2	1.5%	8.0%	91.5%
Azurlite	40%	10.0%	.6%	2.4%	38.7%
Calobar	25.8%	Defective coating	.2%	13.1%	24.7%
G-15	16.3%	Defective coating	.3%	14.0%	16.0%
Smoke Rose	21.8%	Defective coating	.2%	12.2%	22.2%
Kalichrome	81.0%	13.8%	1.0%	7.4%	73.0%

of a new pair of glasses and should materially shorten the time needed to adapt to them. It will also reduce the complications of confusion and dizziness that spectacle distortions induce in dynamic situations such as driving.

C. Sunglasses

There are two kinds of data available on sunglasses. The one type evaluates the visual performance through the sunglass, while the other considers its protective aspects. A study of visual performance through sunglass filters was made by the author, using a high-intensity room under various degrees of clear and fog atmosphere. Fog was controlled at 0, 50, and 75 percent scattered light for room wall luminances of 470 to 7,000 foot lamberts. The filters used are shown in Table 6.1.

The uniform and gradient coatings were supplied by American Metal Lux (now a subsidiary of the American Optical Corporation). The coating material had uniform absorption for all wavelengths across the visible spectrum varying from 11 percent to 12.5 percent transmission on the sample tested. All filter coated lenses were also antireflection coated, which reduced the mirror-like reflections enough to resemble the reflections from ordinary glass. The coating was on the side nearest the eye and was kept free of oil and water, which would have caused an increase in surface reflections. Fifteen pairs of sunglasses, all in identical Air Force frames, were used on each of six subjects, who made threshold brightness measurements at twenty feet and reaction time responses to a near target on the dash panel. Measurements were made of the time required to recognize the position of the gap in a Landolt C target presented at random and in either of two windows on an aircraft instrument panel.

The results at 400 foot lamberts, which is about the average luminance under an overcast sky, showed that no sunglasses gave the best visual performance. At 7,000 foot lamberts, which is about as bright as the sky ever gets except very near the sun, both the performance and comfort were improved with sunglasses. The darker sunglasses gave the better performances. The yellow (Kalichrome) sunglasses were especially disliked by all subjects when room intensities went above 400 foot lamberts.

Since normally bright days will give an average scene luminance of about 900 foot lamberts, the wearing of sunglasses probably will not improve visual performance much if any at all. In fact, dash panel readability tests in different automobiles using two subjects who compared no sunglasses with fit over sun glasses of good quality, and who made over two thousand reaction time measurements each, showed a 12 percent reduction in performance using the sun glasses. (Allen, October 1964) Measurements were made on bright summer days.

Performance would have been poorer on overcast days, according to the fog room studies just reported.

If glare surfaces of chromium or glossy, light colored paint are in the field of view of a driver, the sunglasses may be necessary to achieve comfort, but in the seeing task itself, which is never so bright as glossy metal or paints, no improvement in visual performance is to be expected with sunglasses, and on dull days sun glasses will surely be a visual handicap.

While flying, the sky luminances approach and may exceed the 7,000 foot lamberts used in the fog room experiment, and relief is needed. At such luminances, sunglasses bring a measurable though small increase in visual performance for both far and near tasks, and will increase comfort. For flying, by far the best performance in quickly recognizing the instrument panel numbers was obtained with a gradient density filter that had about 1 percent transmission at the top and 100 percent transmission in the lower 12 millimeter zone of the lens. There is some indication that this lens might be useful in driving. However, such an extreme gradation might be distracting to an earthbound wearer, especially a pedestrian, where less extreme gradients might be more acceptable.

An important source of visual degradation due to wearing sunglasses as opposed to clear glasses is the face reflection from the back surface of the dark glass. The glass will continue to reflect about 4 percent at each surface even though transmission may be very low. Hence, reducing the lens transmission is like increasing its surface reflectance. At 4 percent transmission, the surface reflection from the back surface will equal the light transmitted, and we have the ingredients for a one-way mirror. For sunglass wear, an antireflection coating and dark-colored face skin are distinct visual advantages; they will permit haze free vision. In military situations, it may be beneficial to blacken the skin near the eyes to avoid these reflections. Wraparound lenses or transparent filter side shields will also help by shading the face near the eyes.

D. Yellow lenses

An important but little known feature of yellow sunglasses or shooting glasses, is that they fluoresce in daylight (ultraviolet) and scatter a yellow haze over the scene. The haze effect of blue scattered in the atmosphere, and of ultraviolet fluorescence in the crystalline lens, is replaced by a yellow haze from fluorescing of the glass itself. This undoubtedly accounts in part for the failure of yellow glass to provide the theoretically expected better acuity and performance scores. Generally the scores are the same or worse through such glasses. Some plastics of the Armorlite variety, contain an ultraviolet absorbing agent which does not fluoresce (Bailey and Hofstetter, 1959) and should give better vision in daylight than the usual yellow shooting or driving glasses. Fluorescent lights may emit up to

20 percent of their energy in ultraviolet. Hence, a nonfluorescing ultraviolet filter may be desirable for general wear. Fluorescence of spectacle lenses can be detected with the standard Burton ultraviolet lamp used to view fluorescene patterns in contact lens fitting. The ability of a lens to absorb ultraviolet can be judged by the amount of shading it causes when interposed between the ultraviolet source and a lens or mineral that fluoresces. If the light from the Burton lamp, after passing through a lens to be tested, fails to fluoresce a substance like fluorescene, little if any ultraviolet gets through that lens.

Ultraviolet is of concern because the protein substances in the human eye fluoresce energetically. The visible light thus produced is scattered over the retinal surface and reduces the visibility, especially of small, critical, or poorly illuminated objects.

E. Cosmetic tint

The use of the first shade of pink as a cosmetic tint is justified when prescribing rimless eye wear, or the nylon thread rimmed lenses. It also can be used to reduce the sometimes serious internal multiple reflections, especially in lenses of minus power, without appreciably affecting transmission in the very thin central portion of the lens. For lenses in frames and for plus lenses in general, there seems to be little justification for a cosmetic tint, except for low minus powers, to help control internal reflections. Most pink tints in glass absorb ultraviolet efficiently, although some fluoresce. If high intensities of ultraviolet exist in the patient's environment, as out of doors, perhaps pink is justified; otherwise not enough absorption of other wavelengths occurs to make it worthwhile by any other criterion. If the glass fluoresces, the protective absorption of ultraviolet will cause a loss in visual contrast due to the veil of visible light produced by fluorescence.

While little justification can be found for cosmetic tints, there is little harm done by prescribing them for general wear or for day or night driving. The losses in light are only about 5 percent more than the 8 percent loss due to surface reflections. Hence a first shade of pink tint in an average prescription power will transmit about 87 percent of the light. If the surfaces are coated, the transmission should rise to about 93 percent.

Ott (April 1965) has recommended on the basis of a group of plant and animal experiments that ultraviolet is desirable and healthful, and that even window glass as well as spectacles should be made of quartz to pass the ultraviolet. Other researchers cite the proven carcinogenic powers of excessive doses of ultraviolet and its proven ability to age the skin. At the same time, it is to be noted that its action upon the skin produces vitamin D, which is necessary for proper calcium metabolism and bone formation.

Little appears to be gained by exposing the eye to ultraviolet, since the cornea stops virtually all of the shorter wavelengths and the lens absorbs, or fluoresces the remainder, up to 400 nanometers wavelength. None of the ultraviolet penetrates to the retina in an adult, and any beneficial effects of ultraviolet must come from its action elsewhere on the body. Certainly the known effects on the eye to date are harmful. *For infants ultraviolet penetrates to the retina with a high potential for retinal injury.*

Thermanon, a pale greenish-blue tinted glass similar to ordinary window glass, has been used as a cataract preventing lens. Thermanon absorbs both infrared and ultraviolet light energy, and its appearance on the average person is what might be called anticosmetic. It is advertised as a heat-absorbing glass. A modern glass company found no evidence of the so-called glass blower's cataract among its workers for the past thirty years. It was noted that the employees, exposed to the red hot glass, often wore no protective eye wear, while the executives and visitors did. Apparently glass blower's cataract must be from some other hazard, perhaps furnace fumes, or poisoning from chemicals. Thus the suggested ability of Thermanon to affect the course of a developing cataract is highly speculative.

There are no extensive sources of infrared that the ordinary person could be exposed to that might call for a heat-absorbing glass such as Thermanon. On the other hand, Thermanon absorbs visible red light just as a tinted automobile windshield does and reduces the sensitivity of the wearer to red signals. Combined with a tinted windshield, a Thermanon prescription, especially in plus, would make even the normal driver protanopic. Thus Thermanon or other blue or green glasses should not be prescribed for a driver, pilot, or industrial worker who might depend upon the ability to recognize red quickly for his safety or the safety of others.

F. Windshield tint

Windshield tint conceivably could be a prescription item after the fashion of the fabled Texan who had his spectacle prescription ground into his Cadillac windshield. Windshield tint seems to be considered by the automobile dealers to be essential for all owners of expensive cars and cars with air conditioners; dealer stocks in Bloomington, Indiana, in 1969 were over 95 percent tinted for Oldsmobiles, Pontiacs, Buicks, and Cadillacs. Other manufacturers also used a high percentage of tinted windshields, but not as high as General Motors. In 2000, the provision of tinted windshields is virtually standard.

The efficiency of the tint for absorbing the invisible heat rays can never exceed 50 percent, because visible light supplies 50 percent of the heating effect. Once absorbed by the glass, the energy elevates the temperature of the glass, which in turn heats the air on both sides of the glass and the glass radiates heat. At best only about 25 percent of the energy hitting the glass can actually be kept out of the car. Since the window area contributes less than 30 percent of the solar heat pickup of the car, and since at best only 25 percent of that, or 7.5 percent, is diverted by the tint in the glass, tint seems an impractical and dangerous way to control radiation heat uptake, because it interferes with vision. A better approach would be to use roof, door, and floor insulation and light colored exterior paints. A white roof paint plus roof insulation would eliminate at least 44 percent of the solar radiation heat uptake.

Manufacturers insist that tint serves to cut discomfort from sitting in the hot sun and that probably this is more important to driver safety than the "small losses" in visibility caused by the tint. Tinted windshield and tinted side windows are extra cost items.

If comfort contributes to safety, why is tinting an extra cost item? The evidence seen in the dealer's inventory stock, in the salesmen's arguments, and in the facts about the low efficiency of tint, indicate that tint is more a sales gimmick than a safety or comfort feature. It is not necessary for effective operation of today's adequate air conditioners with local air control, nor is it effective in keeping passengers comfortable in the direct rays of the sun. Heat-absorbing glass is, in effect, clear glass contaminated with iron and is probably cheaper to manufacture than high-quality clear glass.

Tint might conceivably be prescribed to reduce "glare" in the daytime. However, there is not enough tint to make any comfort difference when 2,000 to 5,000 foot lamberts of scene brightness needs to be reduced to about 500 foot lamberts for comfort and maximum seeing efficiency. On the other hand, since the windshield is biased to absorb infrared, it also excessively absorbs the red light from signals and brake lights. This situation is depicted in Figure 8.6. On a bright day where background luminances are high, the feeble red signal lights, which are barely adequate at night are further selectively reduced by the tinted windshield. Windshield tint creates a significant color vision problem for normal drivers.

A plate of glass loses light in proportion to its angle to the beam of light (see Figure 8.5). At a 60 degree tilt angle, which is approximately the windshield angle used in American passenger cars, the 70 percent minimum transmission standard for tinted windshields recommended by the Society of Automotive Engineers becomes less than 65 percent. Since a clear windshield at these angles will transmit about 78 percent of the visible light, manufacturers barely pass the SAE code when they use the best clear glass they now make and tilt it to a 60 degree angle. (As far as solar heat and sky light are concerned, these come in nearly normal to the surface of the glass, as shown in Figure 8.1.) In this position, heat-absorbing glass will have the least effect in blocking out the harmful or uncomfortable radiation.

One would correctly conclude that the best windshield tint is no tint and the better windshield position is more nearly vertical. One can at least prescribe that the windshield shall not be tinted and shall be kept clean inside and out. If it were possible to order a band of infrared and light-absorbing material in the upper part of the windshield, no lower than 10 degrees above the line of sight of the 90th percentile driver, this would be desirable. As of the writing of this book there is a hint of possible future government regulation to prevent tint in the lower part of the windshield. At this moment a tinted upper area is automatically accompanied by undesirable uniform tinting over the remainder of the windshield. Since plastic add-on window tinting is widely promoted, it is possible to put a sky band near the top of a clear windshield. This is the only place on a motor vehicle that I approve of the addition of window tint.

G. Contact lenses

Contact lenses offer both a benefit and a potential handicap to the driver. Usually visual acuity is not as good with spherical contact lenses as with the best spectacle corrections, because of residual astigmatism. Nevertheless, many contact lens patients report they see better than with spectacles, apparently because an unrestricted field of view is provided. Contact lenses stay cleaner and transmit more light without lens reflections. Cylindrical contact lenses with a spherical back surface and a prism ballast appear to be easy to fit, are comfortable, and provide acuities as good as when spectacles are used.

The spectacle frame is a limiting factor in vision and its removal is a welcome improvement in awareness of everything in the visual field. However, its removal may result in photophobic reactions because the spectacle frame is also a good sun shade. Space distortions from spectacles practically vanish when contact lenses are substituted and the cosmetic improvement for many patients is a benefit worthy of the increased care and patience that the use of contact lenses requires.

6.2 Night Driving

A. Optimum prescription lenses

At night we may have need for a different distance prescription than for the daytime. Night myopia occurs at low levels of illumination at or below that provided by a full moon. There are three components to this phenomenon. First, when the pupil dilates, peripheral zones of the cornea and lens are brought into use. Typically these peripheral zones are spherically aberrated positively. Second, at such low levels of illumination the output of the retina seems to be inadequate to hold accommodation accurately on a distant target, and the eyes tend to focus for near. Third, due to the low level of illumination, the cones in the retina are dominated by the rods. Since the maximum sensitivity of the rods is about 505 nanometers and that of the cones about 555 nanometers, a shift in the maximum sensitivity toward the blue end of the spectrum occurs, the so-called Purkinje shift. Because the refractive index of the eye increases with shorter wavelengths, the refractive power of the eye increases about 0.50 diopter. These three factors together total about 1.50 diopters increase in refractive power of the eye; that is, about 1.50 diopters of myopia is induced.

A concomitant of night myopia is night presbyopia, which is manifest as a lower measurable amplitude of accommodation as the illumination drops to full night myopia levels. For patients with low amplitudes of accommodation, say 2.00 diopters or less, only the spherical aberration and chromatic aberration components contribute much to night myopia. For night driving, the level of pavement illumination usually exceeds the mesopic vision levels (Richards, August 1967); hence rods never dominate cones. For many patients the pupil size, when on the highway at night, does not bring in the peripheral zones enough to have a significant effect on refraction. Hence, classical night myopia is not present in most driving situations. However, as indicated under the Sensitometric Method of refraction, the eyes of younger people accept less plus than is normally prescribed for optimum distance seeing. Thus, one cannot decide for a given patient whether he needs more minus lens power until after he has been tested under actual or simulated night driving conditions.

Because lighting levels fluctuate, one has to have vision commensurate with the dominant type of environment encountered. Unless otherwise indicated, the best daytime driving prescription (not sunglasses) is most likely to be the best at night, especially for older persons. The same considerations for youth, uncorrected hyperopia, A.C.A. ratio, etc., as detailed at the beginning of this chapter, apply for nighttime driving as well and may indicate a need for somewhat less plus at night.

B. Lens reflections

Certain powers of spectacle lenses (about +.5 to –2 diopters) are subject to the production of spurious images that are seen clearly by the driver. These images, formed by reflections between the front and back surfaces of the lens, are characteristic of all lenses, but are only clearly focused on the retina in lenses near zero power, especially on the minus side. For these few, it is virtually mandatory that the lenses be antireflection coated. A cosmetic tint is of some help, but the antireflection coating is the procedure of choice. These reflections will not be a problem in sunglasses. Sometimes the corneal reflex itself is mirrored by a lens surface so as to be clearly focused on the retina. This can be corrected easily by changing the lens distance from the eye, changing the height of the lens, or tilting it.

C. Yellow lenses

"Night driving" lenses have been shown to provide no benefit in seeing ability at night (Richards 1964). They are even hazardous, because they give the driver a feeling of seeing better, which no one has yet been able to explain (Septon, 1968). Studies have shown that they actually impair visual performance and retard glare recovery. Many promoters have made unfounded claims for the ability of amber to improve night vision. They have employed mass solicitation, usually by mail. The Federal Trade Commission has correctly ruled that such practices are illegal since the lenses do not perform as claimed.

D. Contact lenses

Contact lenses have some problems for drivers at night. Corneal contact lenses are about 8 millimeters in diameter and float on a film of tears near the center of the cornea. The optical zone is usually about 6 millimeters in diameter. Often the edge and peripheral transition zone near the edge of these lenses can cause a ring of light or a circular shadow to be seen around objects. At night the pupil may enlarge to 7 millimeters, which is larger than the optical zone of the contact lens, and lights will appear to have a flare or blur around them from the edge of the contact lens.

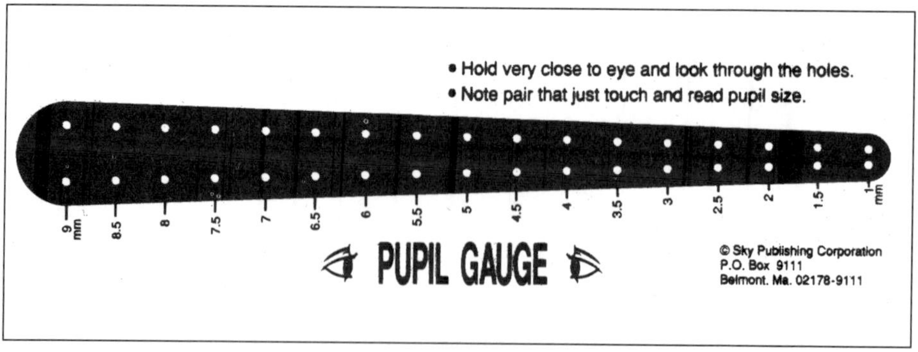

Figure 6.11 *Pupil size gauge for measuring your own pupil size, for example under low light conditions. This illustration is not full size. The pattern is printed on clear plastic. Hold the gauge close to the eye and look at a uniform surface such as the open sky. Choose the pair of holes that appear to just touch. The number on the scale is the size of your pupil in millimeters. The principle is that a small aperture at the anterior focal point of the eye (14.7 millimeters from the cornea) will produce a circular pattern on the retina equal to the size of the pupil. The spacing of the apertures that create patterns that appear to just touch will be the diameter of the pupil.*

To be sure that the lenses are large enough for night as well as day wear, a diurnal study of the pupil size should be run. This can be done with a subjective pupil gauge (see Figure 6.11) with which the patient can measure his own pupil at several times during the twenty four hour period and report the results. The contact lens optical zone should be at least the same size as the largest pupil encountered. Hence, if the patient reports a 7 millimeter pupil on the highway at night, the optical zone diameter should be at least 7 millimeters. This will ensure that the edge blur is well outside the central field of view under most driving conditions.

Contact lenses must be kept free of oily deposits, which will degrade the retinal image and lower visual performance, especially when driving at night. If a suitably large lens, that remains clean and wetted throughout the wearing period, cannot be found, the patient should not wear contact lenses for night driving. Of course, there may be serious spectacle problems at night as well, in which case it may be prudent to recommend no driving at night.

Bifocal contact lenses should be evaluated for the degree of interference occurring with the larger pupil usually found with night driving. A simple test consists of a bare flashlight bulb, without a reflector, viewed by the patient at twenty feet, in a dark room. Allow three minutes for the pupil to achieve approximately its full size. Glare, haze, or halo problems will be seen as an excessive amount of streaking, halo or hazing around the point of light. The type of light scatter displayed will vary with the design and placement of the segment and with the pupil size. It is wise to have the subject move his/her eyes, as in driving, to determine the effect of lens lag upon the scattered light.

E. Cosmetic tint

For night use a cosmetic tint, such as Cruxite A or Soft Lite #l, does not seem to present a significant hazard. The 5 percent loss due to the tint provides some benefit by reducing the ghost images produced by reflections between the lens surfaces. Antireflection coating on a cosmetic tint would provide an overall transmission somewhat greater than that of uncoated clear glass. Thermanon and similar lens filters, cannot be recommended because of the reduced transmission, especially of red light, and because its red light absorption adds to the red light absorption in tinted windshields.

F. Windshield tint

If you prescribe a tinted windshield for night driving to reduce glare, consider what happens if we carry this to the ultimate limit with darker and darker windshield tints. The last thing you will be able to see as the tint darkens will be the glare sources themselves. Let's go the other way instead and remove all tint and start adding more light to the environment (which your own headlights do). The ultimate would be full daytime brightness, where we have the lowest accident rate, and where headlights are no longer glaring, even when we look directly at them. Thus the tinted windshield offers no benefit, and increases the hazard, both day and night.

Perhaps the greatest hazard posed by the tinted windshield is to pedestrians. Every driver with tinted windows knows that when he's looking for a house number at night, he rolls down his side window to see better. Pedestrians are noted for wearing dark clothing and may unexpectedly appear as if out of nowhere. Unfortunately, windshields cannot be rolled down to permit greater visibility. The typical driver statement in nighttime pedestrian accidents is, "I didn't see him" or, "I didn't see him until he was right in front of my car and I couldn't stop." Most victims at night are adults; in the daytime they also include children. The typical daytime comment is "He darted into the street." Since more than 10,000 pedestrians are killed each year and most of these deaths occur at night, one wonders about the argument that the daytime benefits of tinted windshields outweigh their increased hazard at night.

A tinted windshield cannot be sold safely as a prescription item for a given person because it is likely that the car will be driven by others. A tinted windshield should be labeled as hazardous for driving at night and for seeing red signal lights.

G. Windshield reflections

One of the most annoying windshield defects shows up at night as doubled lights, due to internal reflections in the glass. These are also present in the daytime and serve to reduce contrast and to increase glare. The doubling effect can be seen in the daytime by looking through the windshield at the glare reflected from chromium. At night approaching automobiles typically will have an accompanying line of ghost headlights nearby. Red taillights will have an ethereal red ghost floating near them. Multiple internal reflections of the windshield will not produce visible ghost images if the flat glass surfaces are parallel, and if the bent glass is properly wedged. A driver patient reporting double vision might have a monocular refractive, or a binocular fusional, problem, a set of in-focus reflections from his own glasses, a poor quality windshield, or even images produced by a highly polished hood.

H. Windshield age

A review of the literature reveals virtually no evidence that windshield aging studies have been carried out on motor vehicles on the highway. When the plastic layer in the middle of the windshield sandwich was chosen it was investigated for aging, but the aging of the glass itself seems not to have been considered. That glass deteriorates is reported by drivers in desert regions where sandstorms occur and where wipers act on a layer of abrasive dust during window washer operation. Little attention has been paid to the deterioration caused by energetic cleaning methods, or just by grinding the road dust into the glass with a paper towel as is done in below freezing weather.

Windshield deterioration first came to the author's attention when I found that I could not clean a three-year-old windshield. After trying several solvents I inspected the glass itself by focusing on it while headlights approached at night. A series of circular rings appeared centered about the lights and extended across virtually the entire windshield. These scratches were not concentric with the wiper arm axle but with the light itself. This indicated a random series of microscopic scratches in the glass, probably caused by the circular movements used in hand cleaning the glass. A most dramatic improvement in the ability to see against the oncoming headlights occurred by leaning out the side window and looking around the windshield. Instantly there was no glare. The roadway ahead was seen easily and the approaching headlights caused no difficulties or discomfort. *This same test at night will show how much vision is lost by windshield tinting.*

A new windshield did not cause the glare problem. By looking at the image of the sun produced by many windshields, as in a parking lot on a bright day, one can see these scratches. A new windshield produces a sharp image of the sun, while an old windshield has a concentric ring pattern around the sun, and windshield wiper scratches leading from the sun's image toward the hub of the wiper blade. Of course, a dirty windshield causes a haze effect, but without the bright circular hairline scratches, or wiper blade oriented scratches.

The optometrist whose patient complains of glare or annoyance in driving, even after he has received a new pair of glasses, *should arrange to inspect the windshield and headlights of the patient's car* (see Figure 6.12). If any vehicular problems exist, it should be easy to demonstrate to the owner the wisdom of a new or resurfaced windshield, better headlight aim, and greater cleanliness of head lamps, tail lamps and windows. (Don't forget to recommend black velvet cloth on the top of the dash panel.)

I. Headlight aim

The percentage of cars with a burned out headlight, with headlights improperly aimed, with headlights covered by a generous layer of dirt, or with filters or sleepy eye shields attached (see Figure 8.14), is very great. It is to be hoped that mandatory vehicle inspection adopted in some states will make it clear to the driving public that headlights are an important part of safer night driving. The usual argument against driving with one headlight out is that other drivers cannot determine whether they are approaching a car or a motorcycle. A more serious problem is the loss in roadway illumination that accompanies the loss of a headlight.

Glare is a problem in contrast. If you try to look into the window of a house in the daytime you find it impossible, because the amount of light reflected from the outside is greater than that from inside the house. Yet, that same amount of inside light is quite adequate for vision as soon as you enter the house.

At night there is little light from the outside of the house, and it is easy to see into the house. Similarly, at night, approaching automobile headlights would reduce vision like the bright outside wall of the house. By adding some light to the night scene from your own automobile headlights, the contrast of the approaching lights is reduced and vision is improved! Headlights must be aimed to avoid glare to others, and they must also provide as much illumination on the roadway, and as far forward as possible. Properly aimed headlights that are dirty become glaring to others, and because of a reduced ability to light the roadway, dirt on your own headlights makes oncoming headlights seem more glaring. Cleaning

Figure 6.12 *Windshield deterioration. A windshield removed and photographed after 102,349 miles of driving in the Toledo, Ohio region. The radial pattern is from the wipers while the zigzag patterns are from scraping the surface with a hard substance such as metal. The effect of the glare from oncoming headlights will be increased by such windshield damage.*

lights and windows can save lives!

The optometrist should recommend headlight alignment, and the maintenance of clean headlights, free of filters, half shields, or other gimmickry that reduce the light output or spoil the distribution. Next to a good prescription to provide clear, comfortable vision, *good headlight aim, clean lights, and clean windows are the most important solutions to glare at night.* It may prove desirable to recommend auxiliary driving lights to increase the lighting on the road ahead. If all automobiles had more low beam headlight power, the highways would be safer at night.

Chapter 7

Drivers with Special Visual Problems

Merrill J. Allen, O.D., Ph.D.

Synopsis

7.1 Squint

Squint is an outturning, upturning or a crossing of one eye. The incidence of squint in the population is from 2 to 7 percent. Some authorities consider a squinter to be the equivalent of a one-eyed person. The squinting eye is relied upon for peripheral vision and in some cases it alternates, taking turns with the other eye for "normal" seeing. Thus a squinter is not one-eyed in performance.

The abnormal eye position of a squinter almost always is a result of perceptual adaptation to live with double vision. Under anesthesia half of all squinters are straight (Reinecke and Miller, 1966). Under stress situations, the squint angle can change radically, which would displace the retinal image from its usual squint position. By having the patient stand and spin around, the vestibular mechanism will cause nystagmus. If the muscles are normal, this test will show normal ocular motility, and that the eyes are no longer crossed! This is an excellent way to cause a squinter to see double. At low levels of illumination under stress such as fatigue, alcohol, carbon monoxide, and ill health, the adaptations that protect the squinter from double vision and confusion may be lost. Hence no squinter should be assumed to be a completely safe driver until it is demonstrated that he cannot be easily induced to see double under any condition.

The majority of *unoperated* squinters are well adapted to their condition and do not often become visually confused, but this does not preclude the possibility that they might behave like a binocular person with a misaligned eye under certain conditions. The postsurgical squinter has a more serious problem which will affect his or her ability to drive safely. He or she is probably still a squinter but one whose perceptual adaptation has been destroyed by surgical changes in eye position. The success of surgery in restoring normal binocular vision, even with the aid of medical orthoptics as currently practiced, is less than one out of every seven patients.

Most squint treatment by surgery is intended to achieve at least a cosmetic cure, which is achieved in about 80 percent of the patients. Because 98 percent of all squinters do not have a muscle problem (Adler, 1965, p. 524), the patient's eyes usually do not stay where the muscle surgery places them. A series of operations is thus scheduled, each on a different muscle (Reinicke et al, 1964) until the eyes remain within 15 prism diopters of straight. While this is a cosmetic cure, it is a perceptual disaster. New scar tissue and adhesions are formed with each surgical intervention, motility is impaired, and the patient (usually a child) is left with diplopia, limited ocular motility, and a squint angle that varies with the direction of gaze, a terrible situation. Should we give the victim of eye muscle surgery a driver's license?

In the Indiana University Optometry Clinic, I treated an eighteen-year-old college student, who had been through seven eye surgeries, and was still cross-eyed. She thought she was crazy, because she was so confused. Her doctors typically said, "You have had the best treatment there is! You are doing just fine!" Her doctors had no idea of what was causing her problems.

When I told her the symptoms that I believed she had after seven surgeries, namely: confusion, bumping, spilling, stumbling, can't believe her eyes, etc., she went home and cried. These *were* her symptoms! With simple vision training we straightened her eyes and changed her life!

One comment she made is especially pertinent, *"No one ever told me that when you change the position of the eye (by surgery) everything in the world changes position. I felt that I was being punished. Five nurses held me down for anesthesia! I had to endure the surgery and distress over and over again. When people call you cross-eyed, clumsy, etc., it is terrible."*

The following quotation by Ruedeman (1953), a well known American ophthalmologist, will give us an indication of what we can expect of citizens who have been "cured" of squint by surgery.

> Over a period of years, keeping very accurate studies of the end results of ocular muscle surgery, I have been embarrassed and

chagrined many times by the tendency of the foveas to revert to their previous positions. The central vision in the operated eye is not maintained and, although the youngster is somewhat improved, many are unable to carry on in school at an intelligence level equal to their age and normal social group.

There has been, and is, something drastically missing in our handling of the normal so called muscle problem. Over a period of years, the records of these cases have been reported visually in a photographic way without records as to their fusional end results, not taken at periods long enough after the surgery has been instituted, to warrant listing them as cures. From this study of my own statistics, for the sake of the record, I might say that I have cosmetically straightened 80%, of my cases, at least giving them a good anatomic correction. This is truly a cosmetic result and has little to do with the physiological, psychological intellectual level of the individual upon whom this operation has been performed. By chance, and with some orthoptic treatment, about 10%, of this group has been held in 2nd grade fusion and less than 10%, in 3rd grade fusion. It was my contention as long as 20 years ago that, unless we carried these patients completely to 3rd grade fusion and unless they could hold this fusion over long enough periods of time with good fusional amplitude, we were developing our own group of neurotics, our own group of people who had nervous breakdowns, and people with inferior intellectual abilities.

The key to successful reeducation is to build an individual's use of the foveas, which means an early diagnosis and reeducation to precede and follow the muscle surgery, if that is necessary, which in reality is only a means of interrupting the faulty eye brain pattern.

An *untreated* squinter of driving age usually is visually well adapted and, except to the extent that society has ridiculed and made fun of him, he will be competent in most situations. Squinters of long duration are usually so well adapted to their condition that, without the help of vision training they have great difficulty accepting normal binocular vision even when the surgeon provides them with reasonably straight eyes.

Unfortunately the more hazardous, surgically treated group will not be obvious to the motor vehicle driver license examiner, while the safer untreated squinter will usually be easy to detect. The examiner, upon noting a deviating eye or learning of eye surgery for a deviation of the eyes, should restrict driving to daytime low stress situations, unless the applicant has been certified by an optometrist or ophthalmologist as being safe to drive without restriction.

Squinters cured by vision training can be considered normal. In work at the Optometric Center of New York, William Ludlam (1961) found that the cure rate was 73 percent for squinters who had not had surgery. The criteria of cure (Flom, 1958) were so rigid that these former squinters could not be identified, upon routine optometric examination, if the case history was omitted!

7.2 Suppression

Suppression of vision in one eye, when both eyes are open, is an adaptive mechanism to some binocular problem. By itself suppression is not dangerous although the subject will not have stereopsis. He or she probably will be somewhat handicapped in close situations such as required of school bus drivers, truckers, crane operators, fork lift operators, or operators of road building equipment. However, ordinary high-speed highway driving probably relies very little on stereopsis except when traffic densities are high on multiple lane highways.

The treatment of suppression is the basic treatment needed in amblyopia, tropia, anomalous retinal correspondence, and eccentric fixation. Fortunately it is very easy to treat. A light flashing at 9 cycles per second, properly applied, will cure suppression in minutes or hours.

7.3 Amblyopia

Amblyopia is a condition of reduced acuity in one eye and it may or may not be associated with a squint. Like suppression, it is an adaptation and poses no special problem so long as a squint does not exist and peripheral fusion is present. The remarks above on the lack of stereopsis associated with suppression pertain also to amblyopia. Treatment of suppression will cure amblyopia.

7.4 Anisocoria

A difference in pupil size between the two eyes of a clinically significant amount occurs in about 17 percent of the population. Pathology should always be suspected in anisocoria. The anisocoria may disappear as the patient recovers from the pathology. If the anisocoria is permanent, it may be desirable to prescribe the following: a compensating spectacle or contact lens filter before one eye, a contact lens with an artificial pupil, or eye drops to make the pupils more equal.

A difference in pupil size will cause a difference in retinal illumination which will cause a stereoscopic judgment error for moving targets. This stereoscopic effect, the Pulfrich stereo phenomenon (Lit, 1966), can also be produced by glare

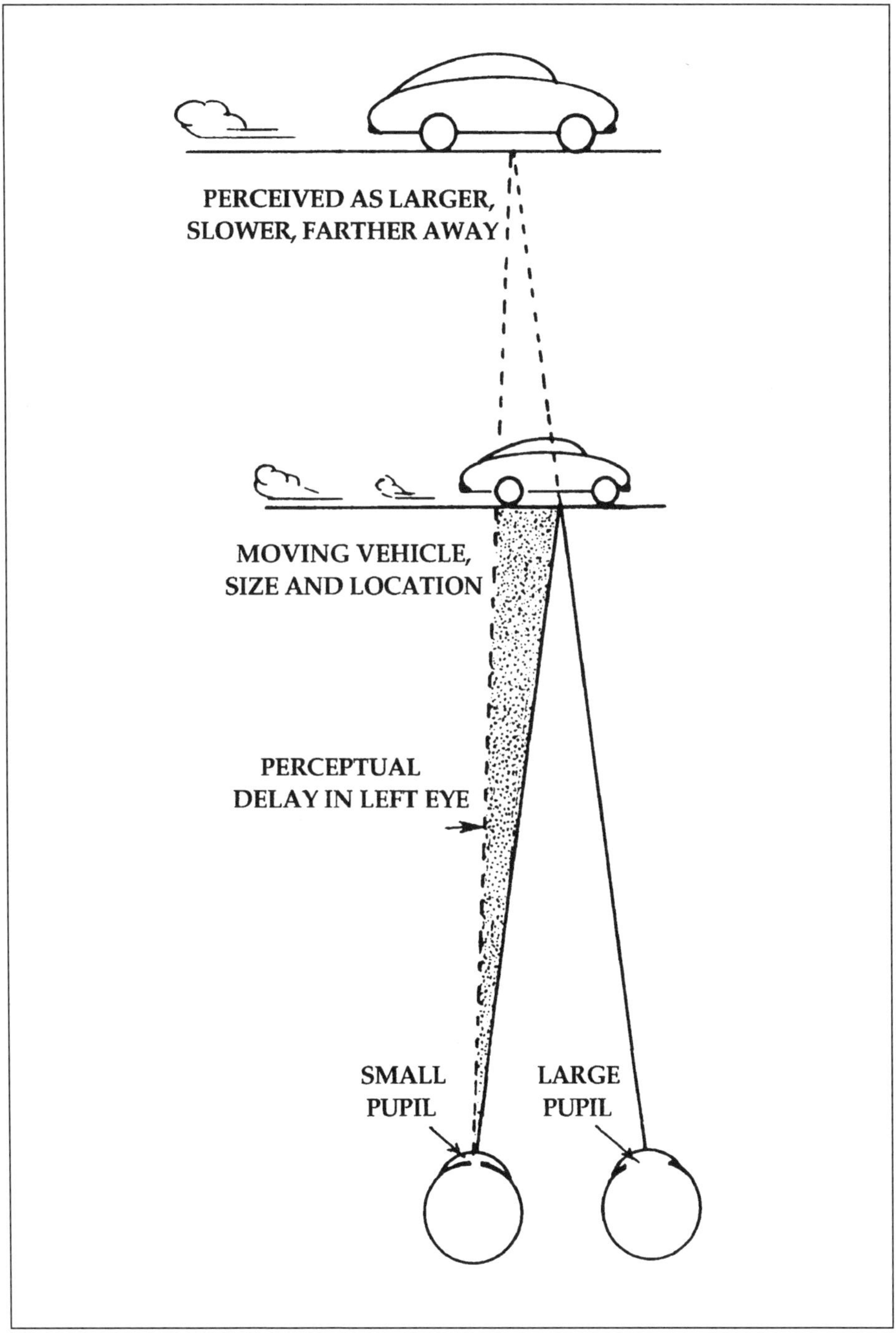

Figure 7.1 *Schematic representation of the effect of reducing the illumination in the left eye. The small pupil in the left eye reduces the retinal illumination and causes a delayed perception for the left eye.*

entering only one eye, by an uncorrected difference in refraction, or by a difference in retinal image size. Other sources of differences leading to Pulfrich stereo effects are uniocular beginning cataract, a cloudy vitreous, vitreous or aqueous floaters, and retinal abnormalities.

The Pulfrich stereo phenomenon causes illusions affecting the apparent location, speed of movement, and size of objects seen while driving and could lead to collision situations. Figure 7.1 shows that the perceptual delay caused by reduced retinal illumination in the left eye will cause an automobile moving to the right across the highway to be seen farther away. Of course, objects moving to the left would appear closer.

While driving, objects on either side of the roadway appear to move farther to the side as we move past them. The images of the objects move across the retina at their proper velocities and proper sizes, but because of the image brightness differences, the output of the retina from the darker retinal image is delayed. An observer with anisocoria as illustrated in Figure 7.1, reports the following: objects on the right appear to be larger than normal and to move at a slower rate; those on the left appear to be smaller and to zip by at an alarming rate. When rounding a curve, the speed and distance distortions are rather startling and lead to a feeling of insecurity. *In fact, all five drivers who wore a gray 20 percent transmission filter over one eye on a winding rural Indiana road for thirty minutes became car sick.*

To see the effect of the Pulfrich phenomenon upon normal driving, take a tour slowly through the local neighborhood and then at normal speeds on the highway. Wear a pair of dark sunglasses (about 20 percent transmission) with one lens removed. In the first five minutes or so there probably will be little noticeable effect of the brightness imbalance between the eyes. Slowly the awareness of the difference in speed between the right and left sides of the street will develop, followed closely by marked size differences and finally by road slant. If worn long enough, a feeling of insecurity and even nausea will probably develop.

A most fascinating illusion occurs when wearing a unilateral filter while walking or riding very slowly. For example, sit in your automobile in your driveway and look out your side window at the ground. Drive the car forward very slowly for a few feet, stop gently, and reverse direction for a few feet. Depending on the eye that is covered with the filter, the ground will appear close or far away, and vegetation along the driveway will shrink or enlarge to surprising proportions. A hedge becomes a forest of trees or becomes tiny as if viewed from the top of the house.

It seems unlikely that adaptation can occur to these aberrations of space.

Since the illusions depend upon both the velocity and direction of motion across the retina, the adaptation, if it could occur, would require a long time and probably would never be complete. Both the spatial distortion effects and the nausea observed during our studies indicate that differential retinal image brightness should be of concern in tending the visual needs of the motoring public. One method of handling involves the prescription of a filter over the eye with the brighter image. This filter is chosen by viewing at five meters, a swinging pendulum or a rotating disc as described in Chapter 5. Any falsely perceived circular pendulum motion or tilt of the rotating disc can be neutralized by filters placed before the eye with the greater transmission.

To equate the retinal luminances, sunglass filters of about 50 percent transmission, used singly or in combination, will provide fine enough increments to permit useful measurements. One must keep in mind that a daytime correction may become a nighttime error, because the pupils may become equal (or unequal) upon dilation in the dark. Thus, it may be necessary to wear a different balancing filter, one for day and one for night use. Because of the cosmetic problem created by a uniocular filter, the use of Neosynephrine to dilate the smaller pupil or eserine to constrict the larger pupil might be a method of choice. Since the drug actions cannot be precisely controlled and since there may be contraindications to the use of drugs over prolonged periods of time, only large pupil size differences may be suited for this approach.

The use of an 0.50 to 0.75 diopter fogging lens over the weaker eye, may be sufficient to destroy stereopsis, and eliminate the space-distorting effects of the differences in pupil size. Since this has not been clinically reported as a successful method, and since there are important contraindications, it should be approached with caution.

Contact lenses of differing transmission appear to be acceptable, both cosmetically and functionally, to correct a transmission difference between the eyes, whatever may be the cause of that difference. Of course, the Pulfrich stereo phenomenon requires good binocular vision with stereopsis, and, if stereopsis is not present, it is not necessary to consider a correction for brightness differences between the eyes.

7.5 Aniseikonia

Differences in retinal image size up to 5 percent appear to be clinically unimportant for most people. For differences of over 5 percent, patients may suffer significant space distortions, double vision, tropias, headaches, nausea, and disorientation. Aniseikonia causes space distortions only for people who have good binocular vision with stereopsis. Large amounts of aniseikonia (over approximately 15 percent), preclude binocular vision, leading to suppression, amblyopia, or even squint.

During daytime hours, multiple clues to space help uncorrected aniseikonic patients maintain proper orientation. However, when only points of light and limited roadway illumination are present, as at night, the effects of aniseikonia may become serious. Aniseikonia can cause stereo displacements for objects moving across the retina just as does a filter placed before one eye. It also causes effects such as ground tilt to the left or right or an uphill or downhill tilt, depending on the type of aniseikonia. The patient may compensate adequately when he is fully rested, but he will have increasing difficulty under conditions of low illumination, fatigue, alcohol, carbon monoxide, or other physiological stressors.

It appears that the small aniseikonic differences between old and new spectacles are the source of new spectacle annoyance which may require up to two weeks for patient adaptation. That patients can adapt is of interest, for it implies a functional shifting of corresponding points on the two retinas. Furthermore, the surprisingly small percentage of aniseikonic patients found in the average practice indicates *a high degree of neurological adaptability* of humans to optical differences, both natural and induced by spectacles. This suggests that aniseikonic patients, and patients receiving new eye wear, might adapt more quickly if training of binocular vision, stereoscopic vision, ocular motility, antisuppression, etc., were prescribed. Such procedures will quickly restructure the neurological connections to make the person's eyes and brain match the real world.

A serious consequence of prescribing large aniseikonic corrections is an increase in spectacle distortion. This should encourage a vision training approach. Size difference corrections are obtained by steepening or flattening the base curves on one lens, by increasing the thickness of one lens, and by changing the distance of one of the lenses in front of the eyes relative to the other lens. As a result the optimum prescription correction from edge to center is lost, and increasing distortions are noticed. Distortions themselves are, in effect, nonlinear aniseikonic errors which, like the Pulfrich Stereo phenomenon, are not easy to adapt to. Whenever a choice exists, base curves should be steepened rather than flattened to reduce distortions. Eyewear that provides secure placement of the lenses should be chosen to prevent abnormal pantoscopic angles or downward displacement due to mishandling by the patient. Alignment of spectacles to the face should be done by aligning the line of sight and the lens surface reflections as indicated in Figures 6.1 through 6.10.

7.6 Cyclophoria

The measurement of cyclophoria is often neglected because most practitioners feel that nothing can be done about it. Very few clinic cases are reported in the literature except in association with squint, and its importance in driver's vision is little understood. Cyclophoria tends to cause a vertical doubling on either side of the fovea, and stereopsis errors for objects above and below the fovea.

The average person has about 1 degree of excyclophoria at distance. If only 2 minutes of excyclo disparity angle exists during binocular vision, a street light 100 meters away and 6 meters above the roadway will appear to be 6 meters nearer than the point on the roadway immediately beneath the light. If, under low levels of illumination, the excyclo disparity increases, the error in localizing the street light will increase alarmingly.

Though there are no spectacle or contact lenses to correct cyclophoria, One can confidently undertake ocular motility training to reduce or eliminate cyclophoria. Training of ocular motility and of lateral fusional amplitudes will, in general, strengthen vertical and cycloduction abilities. Cyclofusional training can be given in a synoptophore, stereoscope, or other form of haploscope where the targets can be rotated separately. Cyclofusion will improve with antisuppression training. It will also improve if rotation training is given throughout the range of normal ocular motility.

A simple trainer is a hand-held piece of string viewed against a uniform background. View the vertical string binocularly at about 13 inches. Incyclofusion is stimulated when the string is tilted top toward your eyes, while excyclofusion is stimulated when the top is tilted away from your eyes. Cyclofusional movements are like vertical fusional movements in that they occur very slowly. Thus, cyclofusional doubling will occur sooner if the string tilt is increased rapidly.

7.7 Color Blindness

Normal color vision is called trichromatism because three primary colors can be mixed to match every possible color. Color "blindness" commonly includes the anomalous trichromats as well as the dichromats and monochromats. An excellent analysis of color vision types and characteristics is given in Table 7.1 (Judd, 1943).

An important consideration in color vision is the sensitivity of the eye to various wavelengths of light. Protanomaly and protanopia are both clearly different from the normal in this respect, while most other color vision defects have wavelength sensitivities which are more or less normal. See Figure 7.2.

Color vision may be further classified as acquired or inherited. Acquired color vision defects may accompany diseases affecting the retina, nerve pathways, or

Table 7.1
Color Vision Systems, Classification & Characteristics

				Designations			
		Maximum	Neutral	Nontheoretical	Theoretical		
Type	Discrimination possible	luminosity, nm	points, nm	v. Kries	Young Helmholtz	Hering	G.E. Muller
TRICHROMATISM	Light-dark Yellow-blue Red-green	555	None	Normal System	Normal System	Normal System	Normal System
TRICHROMATISM	Light-dark Yellow-blue Red-green (weak)	540	None	Protanomaly[1]	Abnormal red function	–	Alteration[4] system
TRICHROMATISM	Light-dark Yellow-blue Red-green (weak)	560	None	Deuter-anomaly[1]	Abnormal green function	Red-green weakness	Alteration[4] system
TRICHROMATISM	Light-dark Red-green Yellow-blue (weak)	560	None	Tritanomaly[2]	Abnormal violet function	Yellow blue weakness	Alteration[4] system
DICHROMATISM	Light-dark Yellow-blue	540	493	Protanopia[6]	Red blindness	–	Outer red-green blindness
DICHROMATISM	Light-dark Red-green	560	497	Deuteranopia[6]	Green blindness	Red-green blindness	Inner red-green blindness
DICHROMATISM	Light-dark Red-green	560	572	Tritanopia	Violet blindness	–	Outer yellow-blue blindness
DICHROMATISM	Light-dark Red-green	560	470	Tetartanopia[3]	–	Yellow blue blindness	Inner yellow-blue blindness
MONOCHROMATISM	Light-dark	510	All	Congenital total color blindness[7]			Cone blindness[5]
MONOCHROMATISM	Light-dark	560	All	Acquired total color blindness		Total color blindness	Inner Total color blind-ness Type I
MONOCHROMATISM	Light-dark	540	All				Inner total color blind-ness Type II

[1] Konig proposed the designation *anamalous trichromatism* for the classes later designated separately by Nagel in an extension of the v. Kries terminology.
[2] This extension of the v. Kries terminology was proposed by Engelking.
[3] This extension of the v. Kries terminology was proposed by Muller.
[4] The term *alteration system* was proposed especially by v. Kries; Muller also uses Nagel's terminology.
[5] The term *cone blindness* is based upon the duplicity theory of v. Kries and Parinaud, now widely accepted.
[6] Protanopic observers are sometimes called *scoterythrous*; and deuteranopic, *photerythrous*.
[7] Total color blindness is often called *achromatopsia* or *achromatopia*.

Table 7.2
Frequency of Occurrence of Inherited Visual Systems

Designation		Percentage of the Population	
No. of Components	**Nontheoretical**	**Male**	**Female**
Anomalous	Protanomaly	1.0	0.02
Trichromatism	Deuteranomaly	4.9	0.38
	Tritanomaly	0.0001	0.0000
		5.9	0.40
Dichromatism	Protanopia	1.0	0.02
	Deuteranopia	1.1	0.01
	Tritanopia	0.0001	0.0000
	Tetartanopia	0.0001	0.0000
		2.1	0.03
Monochromatism	Total Color Blind	0.003	0.002
	Total Abnormal	8.0	0.43
	Total Normal	92.0	99.57

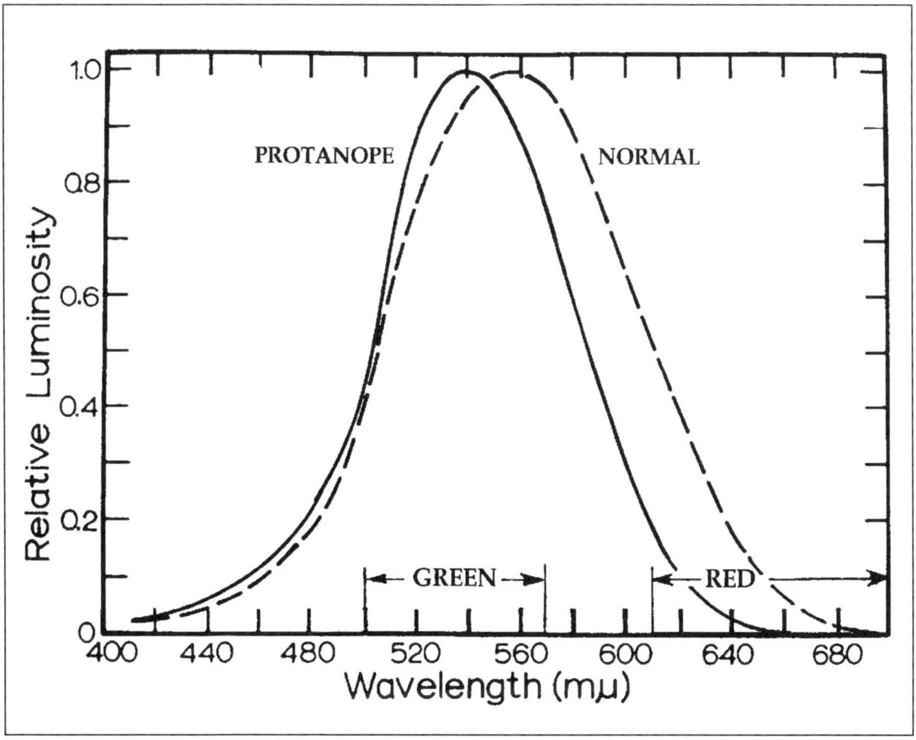

Figure 7.2 *Relative sensitivities of protanopic color blind and normal color vision persons. Those wavelengths that could be called green or red are indicated by the bars along the abscissa.*

visual cortex. Significant among these are multiple sclerosis, optic neuritis, pernicious anemia, leukemia, vitamin deficiency, diabetes, and retinopathies. Toxic amblyopia has an accompanying color defect. Among the causes of toxic amblyopia are carbon disulfide, lead, certain of the antibiotics, iodoform, thallium (rat poison and depilatory), alcohol, and tobacco (including snuff). Older people suffer from abnormal color vision as the crystalline lens changes with age.

Inherited color vision defects are believed to account for the bulk of color vision problems. Retinal photopigment differences appear to be the primary factor in defective color vision. However "normal" color vision is only normal under the right conditions. For example, parafoveal vision resembles deuteranomaly, intermediate peripheral vision resembles deuteranopia, while the extreme peripheral vision resembles monochromatism. In the parafoveal region it is possible to see small lights whose areas are insufficient to elicit a color sensation, thus resembling monochromatism.

At low luminance levels (mesopic and scotopic) the normal eye behaves as if it were totally color blind. Also during short or repetitive flashes of light, the normal color sensation may not develop, or it develops in an abnormal manner dependent upon the color of the flash, the frequency, the light-dark interval, and the surround. A temporary color perception aberration occurs following preadaptation to a given color, or exposure of a color in an extensive colored surround.

Evidence exists that some anomalous trichromats are not defective at all but are somehow different from normals. The dichromats and monochromats are currently thought to be defectives in one way or another. Though there is strong evidence that photo pigments can be defective or abnormal, there is also increasing evidence of an important neurological aspect to color vision.

A review of current electrophysiological research indicates that some color vision anomalies, especially of the anomalous trichromatic type, might better be named color amblyopias and that training techniques appropriate to amblyopia might be successfully applied. During World War II many attempts were made to train color defectives. No systematic studies using anomaloscopes or colorimeters were run on the majority of those trained; hence claims of success were generally unsubstantiated. Efforts at training were simple and usually without the benefit of knowledge of what type of anomaly was being treated.

I predict that the deuteranomalous group, 2.62 percent of the population, will show the greatest response to training while the protanopic and monochromatic groups will be the least responsive, if at all, to training. Ball and Bartley (1967) showed that color perception can be changed temporarily from normal to anomalous and vice versa, indicating a strong neurological aspect to the perception of color.

If the driver with a color vision defect knows the nature of the hazard it creates, he/she will be more careful. Color vision tests and counseling for those who are defective, should be routine for all drivers using our present traffic signals, and motor vehicle tail and brake lighting.

From the above, it is apparent that the present colored signals and vehicle lights are not safe for all drivers, and shape coding with white light is absolutely essential for red lights.

7.8 Glaucoma

Glaucoma is characterized by depression of visual function and progressing field defects. When treated with miotics to lower the intraocular pressure, a reduced retinal illumination and a reduction in retinal sensitivity results, due to direct action of the miotic on the pupil and the retina. Iris nodules and a predisposition toward cataract have been noted to accompany prolonged use of miotics. Both the visual field defects, the reduction of light transmission, and the reduction of retinal sensitivity contraindicate driving at night. Windshield tint is especially contraindicated for glaucoma patients receiving daily eye drops. Headlights should be kept clean and properly aimed and have their light output boosted with auxiliary lights to improve night vision.

If glaucoma can be controlled with diet or medications other than miotics, there should be little problem driving at night so long as the visual fields remain normal. Uniocular, miotic treatment for glaucoma can cause serious space distortions due to the Pulfrich stereo effect, and should be avoided whenever alternatives are possible.

7.9 Albinism

A true albino has no retinal or iris pigment and has a very poor contrast sensitivity, has poor visual acuity, and is color blind. However, complete albinism is rare. An albino probably can not demonstrate the needed acuity to drive an automobile but, if he or she did pass the vision test, he or she should drive only with extreme caution. A scleral contact lens that shades the sclera and the iris should markedly improve contrast sensitivity and glare resistance and make some albinos into safe drivers in bright daylight. An albino should be given a performance test under typical driving conditions before being allowed full driving freedom.

Visual treatment for albinism should begin within a few days or weeks following birth to avoid the permanent neurological deficit that makes adult vision so poor. Treatment consists of supplying a clear high-contrast retinal image for at least an hour each day in infancy and childhood. This can be done by means of a pinhole 8 millimeters in diameter for each eye in occluder glasses. When the infant is old enough, scleral contact lenses with dark portions covering the sclera and iris simulating normal ocular pigmentation should be provided. While I have not had such a patient, it is clear to me that providing a normal ocular image in a young albino will permit the visual neurons to develop normally and guarantee reasonably normal vision later in life.

7.10 Retinitis and Uveitis

Acute inflammatory processes will be characterized by abnormalities in color perception, dark adaptation, critical fusion frequency, visual acuity, visual fields, and contrast sensitivity. Vitreous floaters and blood in the aqueous can quickly reduce vision to finger counting. Sometimes a person may not be fully aware of the dangers of driving. In addition to treatment, people with retinal pathology should be advised to not drive until given permission to do so.

Macular degeneration is a problem for many older citizens. It is my belief that it has a nutritional etiology. A deficiency of taurine due to limited diet, or to intestinal pathogens, will lead to loss of retinal function. In Australia about 30 years ago, cats went blind with retinal degeneration similar to macular degeneration and retinitis pigmentosa. They were being fed dog food labeled cat food. Taurine was shown to be the missing ingredient in dog food. Taurine is now known to be critical to retinal health, and to normal growth and development in babies. It appears that the "hereditary" and devastating disease called retinitis pigmentosa is benefited by daily multiple vitamins and minerals plus 50 milligrams of zinc; 500 milligrams of taurine; lutein in spinach or other greens; bilberry capsules or grocery store blueberries; and ginko biloba. Micro amperage electrical stimulation of the eyes along with nutritional supplements have been shown to have benefits in reversing or slowing macular degeneration. Some intestinal pathogens may threaten retinal health (Michael, Allen, 1993; Allen, Lowry, 1998; Allen, Jarding, Zehner 1998.).

Chronic internal ocular disease may or may not produce marked abnormalities of perception. Visual field defects, or reduced acuity, may be enough to prevent the patient from holding a driver's license. Some patients may be able to drive safely by day, but few will be safe at night. For some patients a small telescopic element at the upper corner of one spectacle lens can be used to help in reading road signs.

7.11 Photophobia

Unusual sensitivity to light, or photophobia, varies from vague discomfort to copious tearing and blepharospasm. Uncorrected refractive errors, aphakia, albinism, dilated pupils and nutritional problems are common causes of photophobia. Sun burning of the cornea or conjunctiva, or the presence of an iritis, will produce a photophobia. Abnormalities in the central nervous system or the eye due to disease, angiospasm, or to nutritional deficiencies, are often accompanied by photophobia. Cataracts may produce photophobic symptoms in the early stages due to light scattered within the eye and to fluorescence of the lens in blue light.

Some protection from the discomfort of photophobia is provided by sunglasses, which should transmit about 30 percent and should be neutral gray in color. Losses in the red end of the spectrum occur when green lenses are worn, and such green and blue lenses make the wearer effectively protanopic (insensitive to red light). Yellow or amber lenses heighten the photophobic reaction of most people.

Photophobia induced by headlights at night *must not* be treated with sunglasses or a tinted windshield. First, the optometrist should suspect that the person's car has a scratched and dirty windshield. Second, the headlights are likely to be misaligned, partially inoperative and dirty. It is reasonable to inspect the patient's automobile for such defects.

When photophobia appears to be unusually acute, a nutritional, toxic, or pathological condition might be the cause. A health and nutritional evaluation is appropriate. This may also result in stopping or reversing early cataract formation. The Alpascope (Hofstetter, January 1968) may be helpful in assessing the normalcy of a patient's reaction to high intensity glare sources and for evaluating improvements which may occur with treatment.

7.12 Cataract

"Nearly everyone over 55 has peripheral spokes or opacities in the lens, yet even in the age group having the highest rate of cataract extraction (women of over 75 years of age), only 0.3 percent per year do in fact have a cataract of sufficient severity to need removal." (Pirie, 1968).

From Table 7.3 we may infer that 45 percent of all beginning cataracts are

Table 7.3
Classification of Extracted Human Cataracts (Pirie, 1968)

Group	Characteristics of Lens	Percent
I	Uniform pale yellow	45
II	Pale cortex with visible nucleus	42
III	Pale cortex with hazel brown nucleus	11
IV	Pale cortex with deep brown nucleus	2

apt to be of the diffuse type without central nucleus involvement, and that presumably such a cataract would grow mostly in from the periphery. Thus roughly one-half of the cataracts will give good daytime vision (peripheral cataract and a small pupil) and the other half good nighttime vision (central cataract and a large pupil) in the early stages. Figure 7.3 shows the incidence of first cataract surgery per 10,000 population per year in England. Presumably cataract surgery would be delayed until acuities below 20/40 had developed and were handicapping the patient in driving, reading, and other activities.

Figure 7.4 shows the number of drivers by age and sex in the United States in 1994. About 44 million drivers were 55 and older. Because cataract surgery is widely used and very successful, there cannot be many drivers with serious cataract involvement in the United States.

People undergoing cataract extractions presumably had failing vision and had surgery performed. Presumably in the age groups of 60 and beyond, job retention is not a factor but automobile driving might be. The person may have undergone eye surgery because of failure of a drivers vision test or the driver may have been shaken by discovering that driving on a busy highway at night with cataracts simply is not safe. Usually they proceed to have cataract surgery or they retire from driving.

In the early stages of diffuse cataracts, visual acuity by day is often no different from normal, but at night the visual performance suffers enormously. In

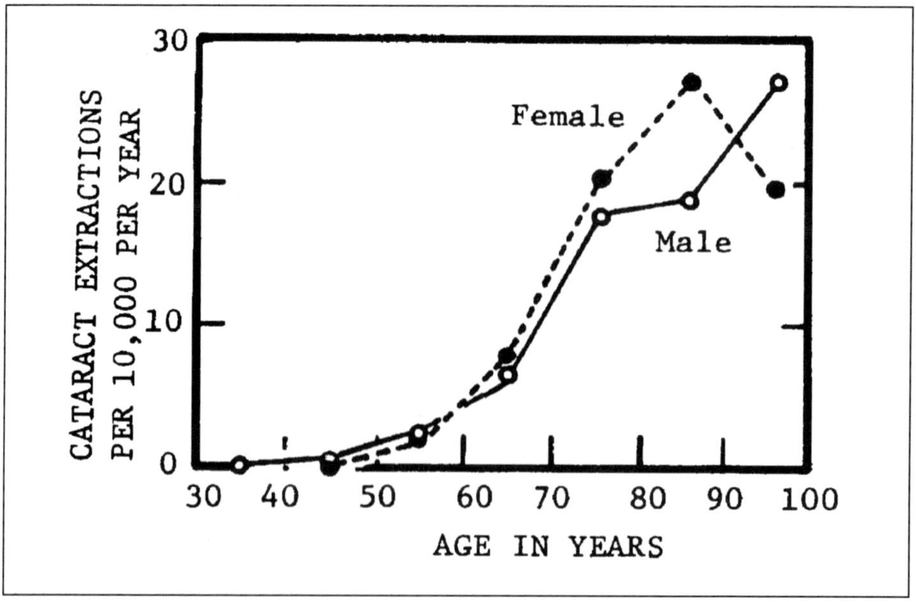

Figure 7.3 *Age of first extraction of a cataract per 10,000 at risk per year (Pirie, 1968).*

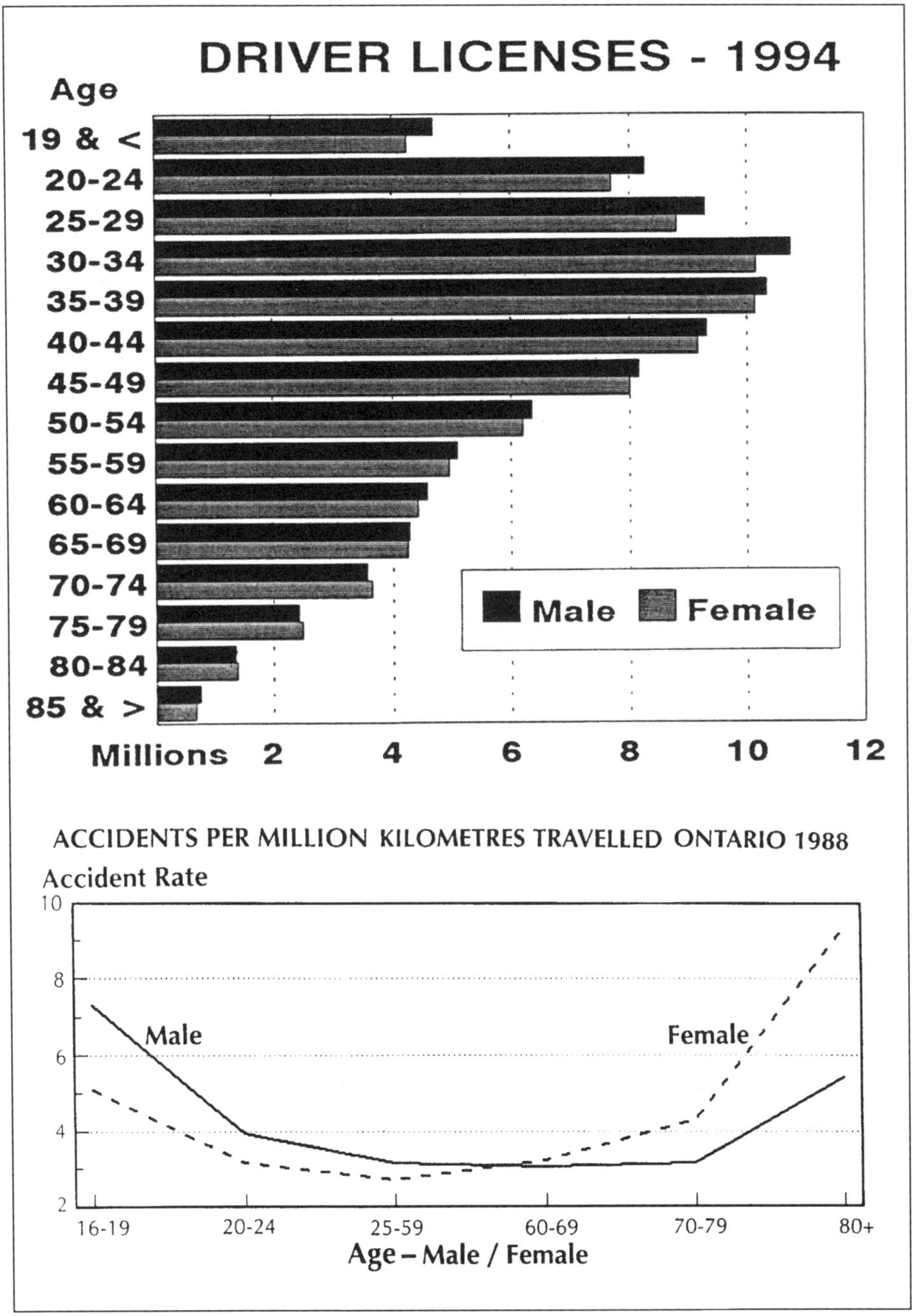

Figure 7.4 *The top chart (DOT, Office of Highway Information Management) shows the number of drivers per age and sex in 1994. The bottom chart shows the accident rate per age and sex in Ontario, Canada in 1988. The female curve is explainable by the fact that older women lose height with age faster than older men. Power adjustable seats should be standard on all vehicles!*

nuclear cataracts just the reverse is true. The greatest problem by day usually is the increased scattering of light by the cloudy lens. Since night driving is accompanied by an enlarged pupil, the peripheral spokes in the lens from a cortical cataract would be uncovered, making night driving more difficult.

Increased absorption of light in the eye with age is normal; see Figure 7.5. (Boettner and Wolter, 1962). By the time a cataract begins to interfere with measured acuity it has usually already become a serious hazard for nighttime driving. We find greater light absorption and scatter with age, irregularities in refraction, shifting cylinder powers and streaking of lights due to zonal defects in the lens. These defects may be due to variations in index and/or irregular bulging of the lens.

Distress caused by headlight glare at night may be unrelated to ordinary daytime acuity test scores. The Night Vision Performance Tester described in Chapter 5, was developed to predict nighttime performance. Many researchers have recognized the interrelationship between contrast, luminance levels, and letter size in vision testing and have made equipment, gathered data, and advocated procedures for such testing.

The effects of age have been studied, and in some cases, also the effects of refractive errors. The following are representative of such studies: Luckiesh, 1937,

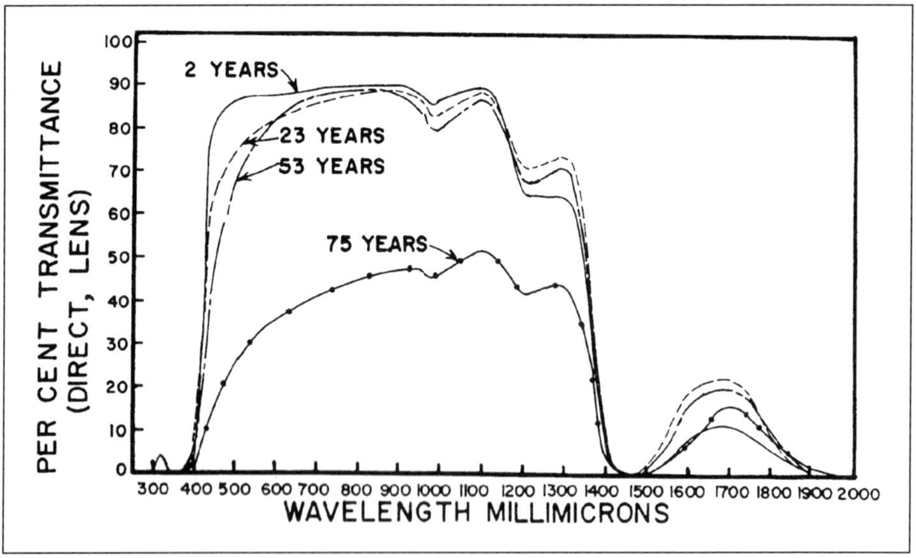

Figure 7.5 *The influence of age and wavelength upon the transmission of the crystalline lens in the eye. The visible spectrum extends from 460 to 700 millimicrons. Comparison of curves two years and seventy five years indicates that the older lens transmits only about 40 percent as much light as the younger lens. Since the lens is the element most affected by age in the eye, the age effect upon total ocular transmission can be assumed to be almost identical to these curves for the crystalline lens (Boettner and Wolter, 1962).*

Table 7.4

A REGIMEN FOR BETTER HEALTH

The measures that you take to improve your health and prolong your life should not be so burdensome and disagreeable as to interfere seriously with the quality of your life and make it difficult for you to continue with the regimen day after day, year after year. Compliance is very important. The regimen described in the following paragraphs is of such a nature that you should be able to adhere to it rigorously, day after day, for the rest of your life. The steps of the regimen are as follows:

1. Take vitamin C every day, 6 grams (g) to 18 g (6,000 to 18,000 milligrams [mg]) or more. Do not miss a single day.
2. Take vitamin E every day, 400 IU, 800 IU, or 1600 IU.
3. Take one or two Super-B tablets every day, to provide good amounts of the B vitamins.

One Tablet Contains:

B-1 (Thiamine Mononitrate)	50 mg.	**Folic Acid**	400 mcg.
B-2 (Riboflavin)	50 mg.	**Biotin**	400 mcg.
B-6 (Pyridoxine Hydrochloride)	50 mg.	**Pantothenic Acid** (D-Calcium Pantothenate)	100 mg.
B-12 (Cyanocobalamin)	100 mcg.	**Niacinamide**	300 mg.

4. Take a 25,000 IU vitamin A or a 15 mg. beta-carotene tablet every day.
5. Take a mineral supplement every day, such as one tablet of the Bronson Vitamin-Mineral Formula.

One Tablet Contains:

		B-12 (Cobalamin Concentrate)	6 mcg.	**Iodine** (as Potassium Iodide)	0.15 mg.
		Niacinamide	25 mg.	**Copper** (as Sulfate)	1 mg.
A (Palmitate)	5,000 I.U.	**Pantothenic Acid** (D-Calcium Pantothenate)	15 mg.	**Magnesium** (as Oxide)	75 mg.
D (Cholecalciferol)	400 I.U.	**Folic Acid**	400 mcg.	**Manganese** (as Sulfate)	3 mg.
C (Ascorbic Acid)	100 mg.	**Biotin**	150 mcg.	**Zinc** (as Sulfate)	15 mg.
B-1 (Thiamine Mononitrate)	3 mg.	E. Alpha Tocopherol (as DL-Alpha Tocopheryl Acetate)	30 I.U.	**Molybdenum** (Sodium Molybdate)	15 mcg.
B-2 (Riboflavin)	3 mg.	**Calcium** (as Carbonate)	100 mg.	**Chromium** (Chromium Chloride)	15 mcg.
B-6 (Pyridoxine Hydrochloride)	5 mg.	**Iron** (as Ferrous Fumarate)	18 mg.	**Selenium** (Sodium Selenate)	15 mcg.

6. Keep your intake of ordinary sugar (sucrose, raw sugar, brown sugar, honey) to 50 pounds per year, which is half the present U.S. average. Do not add sugar to tea or coffee. Do not eat high-sugar foods. Avoid sweet desserts. Do not drink soft drinks.
7. Except for avoiding sugar, eat what you like—but not too much of any one food. Eggs and meat are good foods. Also, you should eat some vegetables and fruits. Do not eat so much food as to become obese.
8. Drink plenty of water every day.
9. Keep active; take some exercise. Do not at any time exert yourself physically to an extent far beyond what you are accustomed to.
10. Drink alcoholic beverages only in moderation.
11. DO NOT SMOKE CIGARETTES.
12. Avoid stress. Work at a job that you like. Be happy with your family.

The great advantage of this regimen over other proposed methods of prolonging life and improving health is that it is firmly based on the new science of nutrition that has been developed only during recent years. Additional benefits may result from changes made in response to biochemical individuality.

From Chapter 2 of ***How to Live Longer and Feel Better*** by Linus Pauling, W.H. Freeman and Co., New York (1986).

Environmentally LPI Considerate

1939, 1942, 1944; Fortuin, 1951; Guth, 1954, 1957; Allen and Lyle, 1963; Eastman et al, 1963; Richards, 1966; Forbes et al, 1967; Allen and Vos, 1967. All of the above studies have shown that it is easy to measure visual performance deteriorations with age. These deteriorations are basically a reduction in contrast in the retinal image, a reduction in brightness of the retinal image, and possibly a reduction in physiological health of the retina and the nervous elements of vision.

Early advice to the patient to improve his health may stop or even reverse the trend toward cataracts, even at an advanced age. Cataract development should not be assumed to be inevitable and untreatable. Cataracts are a sign of the patient's physical condition and may serve as an index to the success or failure of efforts to improve overall health. No single drug, nutrient, or vitamin seems to offer the specific treatment for clearing a cloudy lens. (I have demonstrated that bromelain, the proteolytic enzyme in raw pineapple, can reverse dog cataracts.) Research into general nutrition and health is continuing. Linus Pauling's research and dedication lead to the information in Table 7.4. The reader will find it to be very informative and helpful.

In full sunshine, daytime comfort and slightly improved visual performance can result from wearing eye shades such as hats, sun visors and good sunglasses.

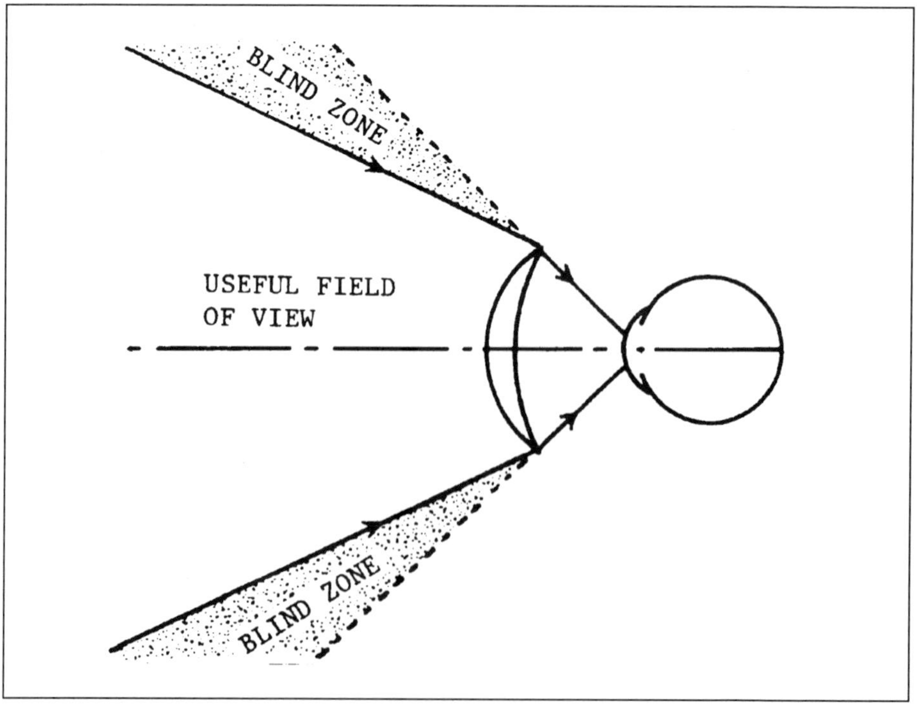

Figure 7.6 Blind zones created by a positive spectacle lens due to its magnifying properties.

7.13 Aphakia

Upon removal of the cloudy lens from the eye of the cataract patient, and replacing it with an intraocular lens implant, normal vision is usually restored. It is possible that spectacles or contact lenses will not be needed. For those who do not receive a lens implant during cataract surgery, thick spectacles lenses are usually required. The best corrections with the least spatial distortions result with contact lenses. Because vision is nearly natural with contact lenses, the aphake will easily adapt to them. Provided the optical zone is large enough, the aphake's vision, while wearing the contact lens, will be good both for day and night driving. In fact, the properly corrected aphake will have excellent night vision because of the improvement in overall light transmission following removal of the cataract. If retinal deteriorations have occurred causing losses in the visual fields, driving a motor vehicle is inadvisable.

The thick spectacle corrections for patients who have had surgery without a lens implant usually give good acuity. However, spatial distortions and blind areas at the margins of the lenses make driving hazardous and unwise when traffic is dense or swift. Aspheric spectacle lenses eliminate much of the spatial distortions and increase acuity in the marginal zones of the lenses, but they cannot relieve the blind zone at the edge of these strong plus lenses (see Figure 7.6). However, because of the improved optical qualities of the aspherics, they can be prescribed in larger diameters, which moves the blind areas farther into the periphery and thus increases the visual field. Because of the overall spectacle magnification in aphakia, it is questionable whether even aspherics can make the spectacle correction for aphakia safe enough for driving a motor vehicle in dense

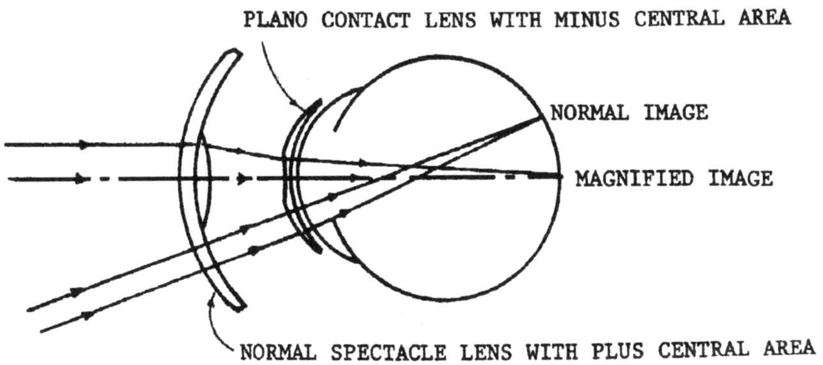

Figure 7.7 Telecon magnifying system. A contact lens with a small central area of high minus power is combined with a spectacle lens having a central zone of high plus power, thus constituting a Galilean telescope. The normally powered marginal regions of the contact lens and spectacle lens permit a wide field of view (Filderman, 1959).

traffic. Fortunately, most cataract surgery includes lens implants which avoid the above complications.

7.14 Low Vision

Because of losses in the peripheral field of view due to magnification of the central field, and due to their size and structure, ordinary telescopic devices are not safe for driving even though they improve acuity. However, if the patient has normal peripheral fields, and a telescopic unit is used that obstructs only a very small portion of the central field of view, it may be possible for the wearer to perform safely under most traffic conditions.

There will always be a small blind zone between the telescopic field of view and the normal spectacle lens. The extent of this blind area depends upon the amount of magnification, the size of the device and the pupil size. Figure 7.6 illustrates the optical problem involved. The hardware for holding a telescopic unit before the eyes may contribute to an increase in the extent of the blind area

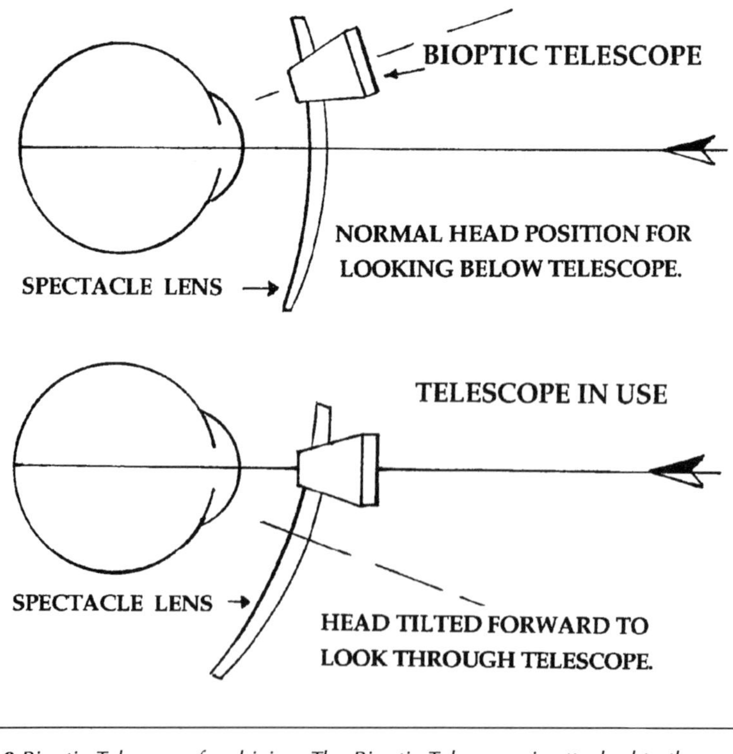

Figure 7.8 *Bioptic Telescope for driving. The Bioptic Telescope is attached to the upper and outer portion of one spectacle lens so that a clear view of the normal driving scene is provided with normal head position. To read signs, etc., the telescope is brought into position quickly, by tilting the head forward. (Feinbloom, W.; Fonda, G.; Vogel, G. L.)*

caused by the optical magnification.

The combination of contact lenses and spectacles to achieve telescopic effects, usually provides a visual field with distortions and blind zones like those found in thick spectacles to correct aphakia. A noteworthy exception is the Telecon lens system designed by Filderman (1959); see Figure 7.7. The Telecon system allows a magnified view straight ahead with normal vision laterally. The system works well on selected patients. If the patient can achieve acceptable central visual acuity, adapts to contact lenses and to the telescope system, he can be trained to drive safely.

An outgrowth of Filderman's work (shown in Figure 7.7) is the Bioptic Telescopic Spectacles by Feinbloom, Fonda and Vogel. It is shown in Figure 7.8. This clever design permits a normal, unrestricted view of the driving environment without magnification, distortions or blur. When reading road signs or seeing small objects is indicated, the telescope can be brought into play, virtually instantly, by tilting the head down to position the telescope in front of one eye.

Chapter 8

Visual Problems in the Automobile

Merrill J. Allen, O.D., Ph.D.

Synopsis

8.1 Eye Position on the Highway

The trend of automobile design is toward a lower silhouette. Few cars can provide an eye height of 48 inches even for above average height drivers. The low frontal area of an automobile is desirable for high speeds to reduce wind resistance, and the associated lowering of the center of gravity provides a greater resistance to rollover. On the present highways and at the present highway speeds, however, it does not seem to be necessary to lower the vehicle profile for safety from rollover, and therefore current trends appear to be almost entirely based upon styling, to build a sports car image, and to reduce wind resistance to save fuel.

Practical considerations of passenger comfort and safety require that the size of the passenger automobile be about that of the New York Safety Sedan (Hildebrand and Wakeland, 1966), whose dimensions are as follows: wheel base, 123 inches; tread, 62 inches; overall length, 220 inches; overall width, 80 inches; overall height loaded, 58 inches; weight loaded, 5100 pounds; engine, 260 horsepower.

These dimensions provide room for an average family plus room for thick, energy absorbing doors, for interior padding, for energy-absorbing sheet metal in front and behind the passenger compartment, and for excellent roll over protection. The eye height would be about 48 inches, depending on the driver and the seat adjustment. No American or foreign automobiles are as large as the New York Safety Sedan.

Complications of rakish styling and lowered height are the loss of driver's eye height and problems of head lighting the roadway. The horizon of a six foot man is almost three miles away. When he sits in any of the low American and European cars, he loses about a mile in seeing distance. For safety, a greater seeing range is needed with increasing speed; hence the eye height in automobiles should go up!

Distance judgments depend upon perspective clues, which are improved with increasing height. The time available for a motorist to recognize a hazard and react to it is less as speed increases. Similarly, the ability to determine whether a situation is hazardous is reduced as the eye height is lowered. No one likes to be of short stature at a sports event or on a crowded sidewalk.

Headlight performance is dependent upon height. The higher the headlight, the greater its range. On the other hand, the nearer the headlight is to the driver's eye level, the greater the atmospheric back scatter from dust, smoke, rain, snow,

Table 8.1

Eye Height	Horizon	
Feet	Feet	Miles
1	6,499	1.23
2	9,191	1.74
3	11,257	2.13
4	12,998	2.45
5	14,533	2.75
6	15,920	3.02
7	17,195	3.26
8	18,383	3.48
9	19,498	3.69
10	20,552	3.89

fog, and haze. Hence, the light must be both as far below the line of sight as possible and yet be as high above the roadway as possible.

The headlight system requires careful aiming to avoid glare in the eyes of the oncoming driver and yet provide illumination far ahead along the roadway. When the driver's eyes, the headlights and the roadway are all very nearly in the same plane, rain, snow and fog glare cannot be avoided.

On level ground, the effect of eye height upon the distance to the horizon, is as shown in Table 8.1.

If the drivers' eyes are 42 inches, and headlights are 24 inches above the pavement, and aimed down 1.5 degrees and to the right 1.5 degrees, a change in vehicle load enough to tilt the front up by more than 1.5 degrees will place the headlight beam in the oncoming driver's eyes. High speed and low eye height are not a safe combination for the American highway.

It is essential that the aim of the headlights be independent of vehicle load. This can be done by stabilizing the headlights themselves or by stabilizing the level of the vehicle. The driver's seat needs to be raised in future production, and/or a mirror system installed which effectively raises the eyes two or three feet.

8.2 Glare

The Dictionary of Visual Science (Schapero et al., 1968) lists ten kinds of glare which may be condensed to three principal types: sensory overload, optical image degradation, and psychological annoyance.

Sensory overload begins to occur when the average luminance level exceeds 1,000 foot lamberts. By 7,000 to 10,000 foot lamberts, tearing and eye spasms occur, and visual performance falls. Optically, the image quality is the same or somewhat better at the higher luminances because of the smaller pupil.

Optical image degradation, veiling glare, can occur via a uniform "film" of light scattered across the retina from a single bright glare source, or from every point of the white portion of this printed page. Multiple glare sources, such as chromium, mirrors, window glass, etc., cause a "veiling glare" which reduces the contrast in the retinal image and reduces visual performance, perhaps even to zero. The image degradation is known to be worsened by pathology, refractive errors, and age; what may be a compensatable glare to some may be incapacitating to others.

Psychological annoyance glare is also called *discomfort glare*. This is typified by the western sky in the late afternoon, which brightens as the sun comes down toward the horizon. A driver traveling west will ultimately find that the increasing sky brightness becomes uncomfortable. It is generally felt that discomfort glare has little relationship to veiling glare, although veiling glare also occurs in all such situations. Discomfort glare tolerance can be very low in certain refractive and pathological conditions.

Each of the foregoing three types of glare results in reduced visual performance. Only for sensory overload can ordinary nonpolarizing sunglasses be helpful. For best vision the optimum scene luminance should average about 400 foot lamberts. An improvement in performance occurs if luminances of several thousand foot lamberts are reduced to about 400.

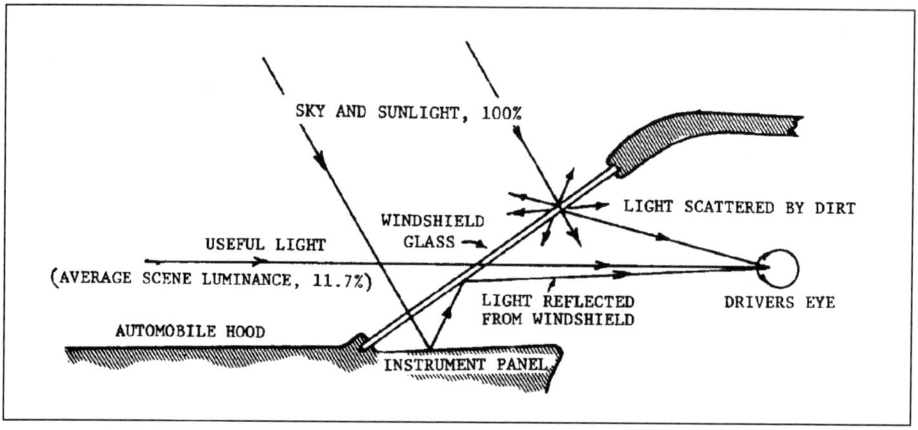

Figure 8.1 Sources of glare from the windshield and related structures. Note that average useful light from the scene is 11.7 percent. Dirt in full sunshine and/or the instrument panel top and windshield may easily direct enough light toward the eyes to be greater than the useful light.

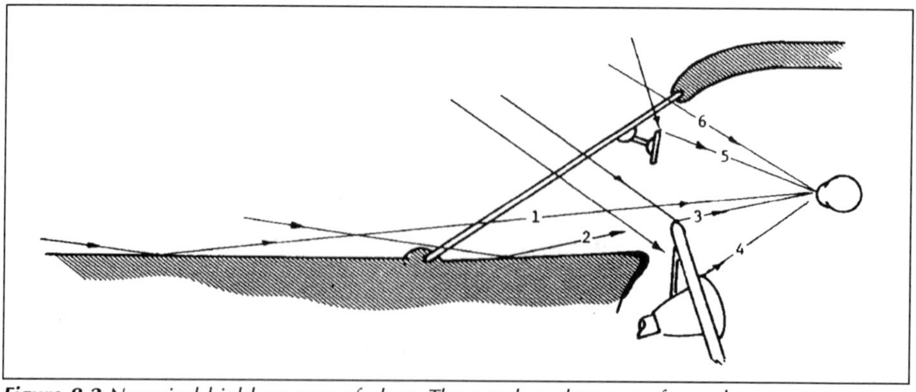

Figure 8.2 Nonwindshield sources of glare. The numbered rays are from glare sources as follows: (1) from the glossy hood paint, hood chromium, and fender chromium; (2) from the windshield trim, wiper hardware, speaker grille, and glossy dash panel top (especially pre-1967 automobiles); (3) glossy reflections from the rim of some steering wheels; (4) reflections from bright steering wheel hardware; (5) reflection from mirror hardware and pillar post (windshield corner post); and (6) glare light directly from the sun and/or sky.

Veiling glare reduces performance proportionally according to the equation:

$$B_v = \frac{KB_0}{\phi^n}$$

where B_0 is the illuminance falling on the pupil from the glare source, ϕ is the distance of the glare source away from the line of sight in degrees, and constants K and n are approximately equal to 10 and 2 respectively. Differences in the formulas reported in the literature, are largely due to age differences, and to other ocular conditions of the subjects, as well as to the different methods of specifying the amount of glare light entering the eye.

Discomfort glare reduces performance three ways, see Figure 8.1. Often there is an element of sensory overload when discomfort is experienced. The glare source scatters a veil of light throughout the eye. Deterioration in performance can be expected by sensory overload and image contrast reduction. The discomfort itself reduces performance by providing a perceptual interference that may even reach the emotional level of anger or crying.

The driver's glare resistance is enhanced by a clean windshield, clean glasses, clean and properly aimed headlights, an optimum correction for refractive errors, no vertical and lateral imbalances, and by the driver's optimum state of health and minimal perceptual load. Experiments indicate that the effects of glare on performance will be about five times worse on the highway than in an experimental situation. Either the perceptual load is increased, or attention to driving is reduced, or both.

Table 8.2
Average Scene Reflectivity

Sky Ft. Lamberts	Scene Ft. Lamberts	% Scene Reflective	Terraine Measured
6900	1080	15.65	Concrete Road
7000	880	12.57	Dirt
7100	500	7.04	Green Field
7200	900	12.50	Blacktop
7200	1380	19.17	Gravel parking
7300	1040	14.25	Concrete
7400	950	12.84	Dirt
7700	380	4.93	Green Field
7800	1280	16.41	Gravel Road
8000	570	7.41	Blacktop
8150	830	10.18	City Street
7850	680	8.66	City Street
Av. 7466	872	11.7	Av. scene

Glare light entering the driver's eyes comes from several sources, of which the windshield is the most important (Allen, Aug. 1969). Figure 8.1 shows that the primary source of glare light is the windshield.

In Table 8.2, the average scene reflectivity of 11.7 percent was determined by using a light meter pointed upward to measure the illumination falling on a horizontal plane on the earth, and by directing the meter horizontally to measure the light from the trees, houses, fields, etc.. When measuring the light from the environment, a flat black shield was placed on top of the light meter to block out the light from the sky. Because the shield obstructed half of the receptive field of the photocell, its readings were doubled to get the values tabulated.

Figure 8.2 shows the other factors involved in automobile glare in addition to those of the windshield. Ray 1 is reflected from the hood paint and hood or fender ornaments. Ray 2 is reflected from the dash panel, windshield trim, and wiper hardware. Ray 3 is reflected from the steering wheel structure. Ray 4 is reflected from the trim of the horn rim and steering wheel hub. Ray 5 is reflected from the mirror hardware, and Ray 6 is directly from the sun or from the open sky.

Figure 8.3 *Test automobile for the study of vehicle glare. The windshield has been removed and the sun visors enlarged. The hood is being covered with a flat black material. Roadside targets were triggered by the vehicle 325 feet in advance and the reaction times needed for their detection by each of three observers in the front seat were recorded. The device on the bumper tripped a string across the road to raise the target.*

Table 8.3
Equivalent Sky Luminance in Foot Lamberts—Clear Days*

	December 21					March and September 21					June 21				
Latitude	8 a.m.	10 a.m.	Noon	2 p.m.	4 p.m.	8 a.m.	10 a.m.	Noon	2 p.m.	4 p.m.	8 a.m.	10 a.m.	Noon	2 p.m.	4 p.m.
North															
30° N	450	600	600	600	450	700	1000	1050	1000	700	1550	1400	1000	1400	1550
34° N	350	550	550	550	350	800	800	900	800	800	1350	1400	950	1400	1350
38° N	300	550	550	550	300	750	800	900	800	750	1350	1300	950	1300	1350
42° N	250	500	500	500	250	700	750	800	750	700	1300	1300	950	1300	1350
46° N	150	450	500	450	150	700	750	750	750	700	1300	1250	950	1250	1300
South															
30° N	1100	1950	2250	1950	1100	1700	2300	2800	2300	1700	1200	1600	2400	1600	1200
34° N	1100	1900	2200	1900	1100	1700	2650	2900	2650	1700	1350	1650	2300	1650	1350
38° N	900	2300	2200	2300	900	1700	2700	2950	2700	1700	1350	1650	2300	1659	1350
42° N	600	2100	2150	2100	600	1700	2700	2450	2700	1700	1350	2000	2500	2000	1350
46° N	400	1900	2100	1900	400	1700	2700	2900	2710	1700	1350	2100	2700	2100	1350
East															
30° N	1550	1500	1000	700	400	2000	2500	1500	900	700	2800	2650	1400	1000	700
34° N	1350	1400	950	700	400	2400	2600	1600	950	650	2800	2700	1450	1000	700
38° N	1200	1300	900	650	350	2500	2600	1500	900	600	2800	2700	1400	1050	700
42° N	750	1200	850	600	250	2400	2400	1450	800	600	2900	2600	1400	1000	700
46° N	500	1100	800	500	150	2300	2100	1400	700	600	2850	2600	1400	1000	700
West															
30° N	400	700	1000	1500	1550	700	900	1500	2500	2000	700	1000	1440	2650	2800
34° N	400	700	950	1400	1350	650	900	1600	2500	2400	700	1000	1400	2700	2800
38° N	350	650	900	1300	1200	600	900	1500	2600	2500	700	1050	1400	2700	2800
42° N	250	600	850	1200	750	600	800	1450	2400	2400	700	1000	1000	2600	2800
46° N	150	500	800	1100	500	600	700	1400	2100	2300	700	1000	1400	2600	2850

* Average values, direct sunlight excluded.

Figure 8.3 shows an instrumented vehicle with a detachable windshield used to evaluate the effect of glare encountered in typical daytime driving. A study of forty-five drivers of all ages (Allen, Spring 1968) revealed that the most comfortable and efficient daytime driving occurred when all possible sources of glare had been removed. The windshield generally afforded the most predictable and important glare of all sources tested. At times, sky glare, hood glare, and chro-

Table 8.4
Equivalent Sky Luminance in Foot Lamberts
Average Overcast Day

Latitude	8 a.m. 4 p.m.	9 a.m. 3 p.m.	10 a.m. 2 p.m.	11 a.m. 1 p.m.	Noon
		December 21			
30° N	420	740	1020	1210	1270
32	350	700	960	1150	1200
34	320	650	910	1100	1140
36	260	600	840	1020	1070
38	230	550	790	940	1000
40	190	500	740	900	930
42	150	450	660	820	860
44	100	380	600	760	790
46	60	340	550	680	730
48	40	290	470	630	650
50	0	240	420	560	580
		March 21 or September 21			
30° N	910	1320	1710	2010	2140
32	880	1290	1650	1940	2070
34	860	1250	1600	1870	1980
36	840	1220	1560	1800	1900
38	800	1200	1500	1740	1840
40	790	1140	1460	1670	1760
42	760	1120	1410	1600	1690
44	740	1080	1340	1540	1620
46	710	1030	1290	1470	1550
48	690	990	1240	1410	1480
50	650	940	1180	1330	1400
		June 21			
30° N	1270	1730	2250		
32	1280	1730	2240		
34	1290	1730	2220		
36	1290	1730	2200	2960	
38	1290	1720	2160	2840	
40	1290	1700	2120	2650	3060
42	1300	1690	2080	2540	2860
44	1290	1670	2050	2430	2660
46	1290	1640	2010	2330	2520
48	1290	1620	1960	2250	2400
50	1260	1590	1900	2160	2280

mium glare were serious. When all sources gave maximum glare at the same time, the driver's performance was the most adversely affected.

Tables 8.3 and 8.4 give the variations in sky luminance with the earth's latitude, the time of year, and the time of day, for a clear, and for an overcast sky. In Table 8.3 the values are taken so that the area around the sun and the sun itself are not measured. Note that on June 21 at 8 a.m., looking east, and at 4 p.m., looking west, the sky is very bright. In March and September at 10 a.m., and at noon looking south, the sky is also very bright.

In Table 8.4 when the sky is overcast, the luminances of the sky are more uniform so that directional effects are not significant. Because sky luminances are low, the illumination at ground level is likely to be much lower than when the sun is visible. Furthermore, the loss of shadows when the sky is overcast causes a loss of contrast which increases the visual handicap imposed by sky glare. Thus, overcast days are more annoying to a motorist than a day of full sunshine. Motorists will turn on their headlights earlier at the end of an overcast day compared to a clear day. The new automatic daytime running lights will ensure adequate daytime vehicle conspicuity.

To summarize, daytime glare is of multiple types and causation. Excessive overall illumination can be reduced with sunglasses, and visual performance will be increased. Specific glare objects that are excessively bright, such as chromium, hood paint, sky, and sun adjacent to the normal visual task, cannot be toned down very much with sunglasses without a loss in visual performance. Sunglasses may actually reduce visual performance, because they may reduce the useful light below optimum values, still leaving the proportion of glare to useful light unchanged. They also add a veiling glare of their own from dirt and surface reflections. Discomfort glare is a function of total luminance, differential luminance, area, and distance from the visual task. Glare from the windshield and dash panel is apt to approach the discomfort level even on overcast days in the daytime. For this type of discomfort, sunglasses may be helpful, but visual performance may not improve.

Sky glare, road glare, water droplets, and dirt on the windshield all contribute significant amounts of glare, the total of which may be over powering. Sun visors are a simple and effective means to control the sky glare. Some glare control comes from the color band at the top of the windshield. The windshield washer is an excellent means for reducing glare in bright sunshine by removing dust and dirt.

Polarizing sunglasses will protect the motorist against the sun glare reflected from the roadway and the top of the hood. They will also reduce the windshield glare from the top of the dash panel. The better solution for the dash panel is a piece of *black velvet cloth* laid on top of it. (Be sure to cut openings for the hot air ducts that defrost the windshield.)

Automobile stylists are beginning to learn that the top of the dash panel is optically a part of the windshield and should be strictly off limits to decorators, painters, and artists. In this case, as in many others, doing it right will lend beauty as well as safety.

The author had a research car with a modified dash panel covered with black nylon flock. The nylon fibers were electrostatically propelled onto the wet epoxy adhesive. Each nylon fiber was at right angles to the surface and produced a durable equivalent of velveteen cloth. This surface treatment was truly dead black, looked nice, and did not show dirt. This finish was also applied to the hood. After twenty-four months the dash panel was still perfect, but the sun had bleached the nylon flock on the top of the hood.

The process seems ideal for dash panels and, if the material can be made sun resistant, its application to hoods is nothing short of a stylist's dream. *No other feature on Indiana University's research automobiles ever attracted so much attention as the black nylon flock on the hood of that white Coronet!*

On visiting new and used car lots in 1999, no dash panels were flock coated or painted black. However, to my surprise, I discovered that **flock finishes,** similar to the one above, but not in black, have been put *under the rear window of all passenger cars, new and used! All manufacturers know how but none are install-*

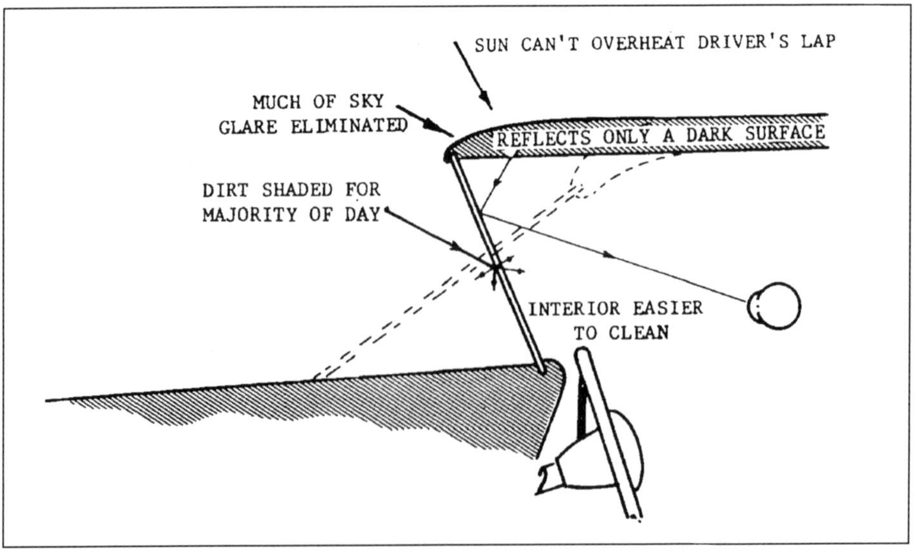

Figure 8.4 *Characteristics of a windshield with a reverse tilt. Air cushion crash protection will keep passengers away from the windshield during a crash; hence the only design considerations are optical and aerodynamic. This design is optically superior.*

ing it on the dash panel. The omission of this important safety feature indicates extreme bureaucratic indifference to safety. As a result of news items, and, television shows (KGO-TV News, San Francisco, Nov. 1995 and 20/20 News, Feb. 1999) which discussed and demonstrated the seriousness of the problem, it seems reasonable that antiglare dash panel finishes will soon become standard and motor vehicle safety will be significantly improved.

8.3 Dirt and Scratches on the Windshield

One solution to some of the more serious windshield problems is to tilt the windshield top forward, or opposite to its present tilt (Figure 8.4). The glass would then reflect the shaded portions of the inside of the roof structure instead of the sun-illuminated dash-panel top. Such a tilt would also eliminate much of the problem of the dirty windshield by shading the dirt. Dirt absorbs useful light, and reflects glare light toward the driver. The present windshield tilt exposes the dirt to full sunshine for over two-thirds of the day.

The reverse tilt of the windshield would make it easier to get to the inside surface to keep it clean, an often neglected consideration. Outside cleaning would be somewhat more difficult, but the windshield would be inherently cleaner than it is now since it would not frost or collect dew at night as readily, or trap air borne dust and dirt.

The only contraindication to such a design is aerodynamic. However, since vehicle stability at high speed is a serious problem, an air foil like upper contour of the automobile produces lift and can be dangerous. A number of land and water race drivers have died in vehicles that became airborne without ailerons, rudder, or horizontal stabilizer. An unknown number of passenger vehicle occupants have been injured or killed when they became airborne when caught in a strong wind at high speed in a lightweight vehicle. Since conventional automobile configurations do not assure ground hugging at high speeds, a windshield redesign could be the lift spoiler needed to help maintain vehicle stability. Lift spoilers are already in use on production automobiles as well as on racing cars.

Glare at night is mostly a problem of windshield dirt and scratches (see Figure 8.4). Allen (August 1969) has shown that the number of miles driven correlates with the number and severity of windshield scratches resulting from windshield wiper operation. At roughly 50,000 miles the windshield should be replaced or repolished to restore optimum vision at night against headlight glare.

Some cleaning procedures and some environmental factors, such as sandstorms, abrasive air pollutants, sand used in winter on ice and snow, etc., can quickly cause severe windshield damage. A test for scratch deterioration can be made by observing the reflection of the sun in the windshield (see Figure 8.19).

New glass will show a bright sun image on a clear sky background. An older glass will show bright scratch rings around the sun's image. These will extend out several inches from the edge of the solar image. Driving an old car and a new car against headlights at night will illustrate the greater spread of headlight glare and the greater difficulty of seeing when looking through the older glass. Resurfacing is able to restore new windshield performance.

8.4 Windshield Tint

The popular misconception that a tinted windshield reduces glare at night may stem from comparing the old, scratched, nontinted windshield with the new unscratched tinted windshield at the time of buying a new car. When new untinted glass is compared with new tinted glass, however, the untinted glass gives a superior performance at night (Blackwell, 1954; Haber, 1955; McFarland and Domey, October 1958).

It is often argued that daytime comfort offered by the tinted windshield offsets the extra nighttime hazard. Such arguments do not hold up. (1) There is evidence that comfort leads to inattention and, in the proper circumstances, to sleep. (2) The question of comfort is relative because tinted automobile glass removes less than 50 percent of the direct solar heat energy. (3) The nighttime hazard due to losing about 40 percent of the visible light is greater than usually claimed. *The experimental method used to show that tinted windshields do not reduce seeing at night was improper. On my testimony, the research report was withdrawn.*

Many studies on tinted windshields have been conducted on the detectability of objects on the roadway as illuminated by low-beam headlights. Low-beam headlights are aimed down 1.5 degrees and give a sharp cutoff in light pattern on the roadway ahead. An object is not likely to be seen until it is close enough to enter the bright portion of the headlight pattern. At the forward edge of the headlight pattern the inverse square law does not hold, and a few feet of change in distance of the automobile from the object can dramatically change the illumination on that object at pavement level. Hence the reduction in seeing of a tinted windshield, which reduces light at the eye about 40 percent, compared to a clear windshield would be compensated for by allowing the object to move a few feet nearer into the headlight pattern. Thus, promoters of tinted windshields are able to say that only a 1 to 3 percent loss in seeing distance occurs due to a tinted windshield.

If an object on the highway is not seen considerably prior to entering the low beam headlight pattern, it will probably be struck when traveling at 60 miles per hour. We are overdriving our low beam headlights from 40 miles per hour up!

Windshield tint interferes most with the detection of unlighted vehicles or pedestrians on or near city streets, on country roads, and on highways. Obstacles in front and to the left will not come into the bright portion of the low-beam headlight pattern as soon and will be rendered even less visible by a tinted windshield.

As retinal luminance levels are reduced toward the absolute threshold, for example, by old age and by windshield tint, the ability of the eye to discriminate subtle brightness differences falls off precipitously. At high levels a 1 percent brightness difference can be detected, whereas at the absolute threshold an object exhibiting a brightness difference from its background of 100 percent might not be detected.

A plate of glass loses light by surface reflection. Figure 8.5, Curve B, shows how the loss is dependent upon the angle of incidence of the light for a single

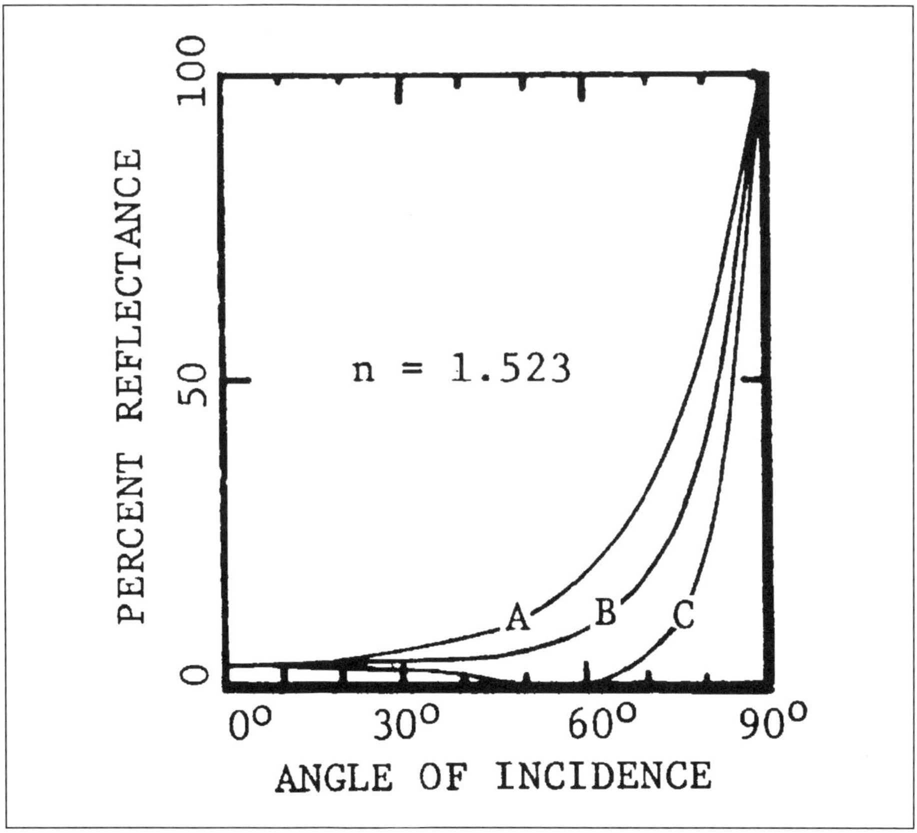

Figure 8.5 *Effect of angle of incidence of light striking a single glass surface upon percent of light reflected. Curve B is the average reflectance of the ordinary and extraordinary rays striking the surface. On Curve C the reflectance drops to zero near 55 degrees; thus only the A curve component of the light is reflected. In other words, the reflected light is completely polarized.*

surface. For two surfaces the loss is nearly doubled. Modern windshields are tilted to about 60 degrees from vertical. Figure 8.5 shows that a loss of about 20 percent due to reflection alone will occur with an untinted glass. Further inspection of Figure 8.5 reveals that the present windshield angle of American cars polarizes almost 100 percent of the light which it reflects. The amount reflected by a plate of clear glass at 60 degree incidence angle is about 20 percent; hence 80 percent is transmitted. This 80 percent is composed of 60 percent of the original amount of light which is unpolarized and 20 percent which is polarized. Hence, 25 percent of the light is polarized. Light reflected into the driver's eyes from the street, hood, etc., is partially polarized in the same plane as the light reflected from the windshield. In the daytime the angled windshield filters out some of the polarized component of specular glare from the pavement. However, by night, street lighting engineers rely on specular glare from the pavement to give efficient silhouette seeing with minimum wattage sources. The 60-degree angled windshield unfortunately removes a portion of the polarized component of that light also.

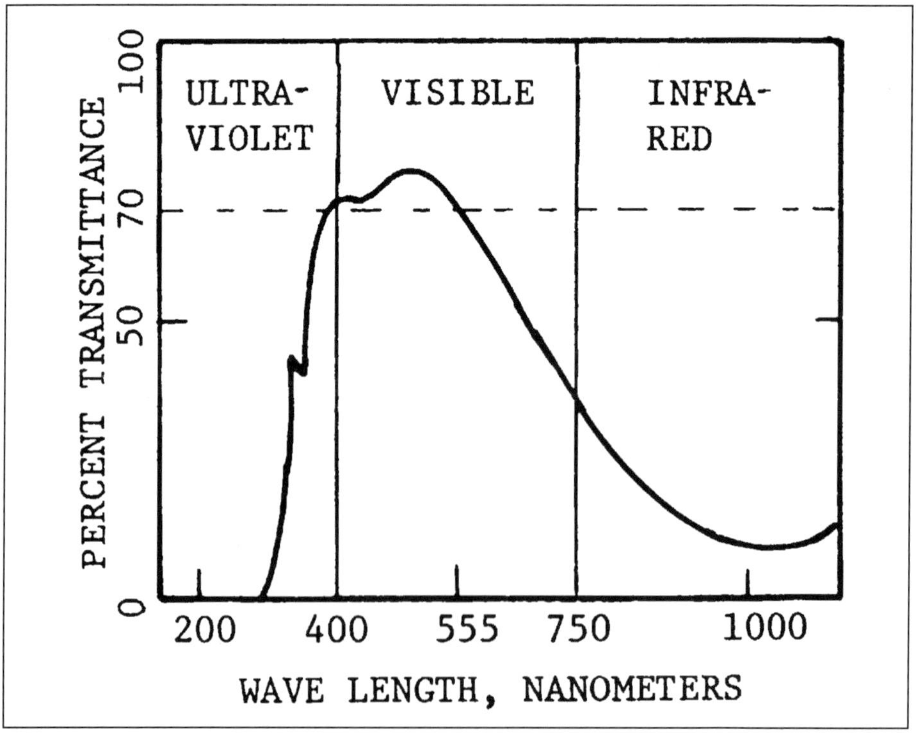

Figure 8.6 *The transmission curve of a modern heat absorbing automotive windshield (Whittemore, 1965). The bluish green color of this glass results from the lowered red light. Visible light lies between 400 and 750 nanometers (millimicrons).*

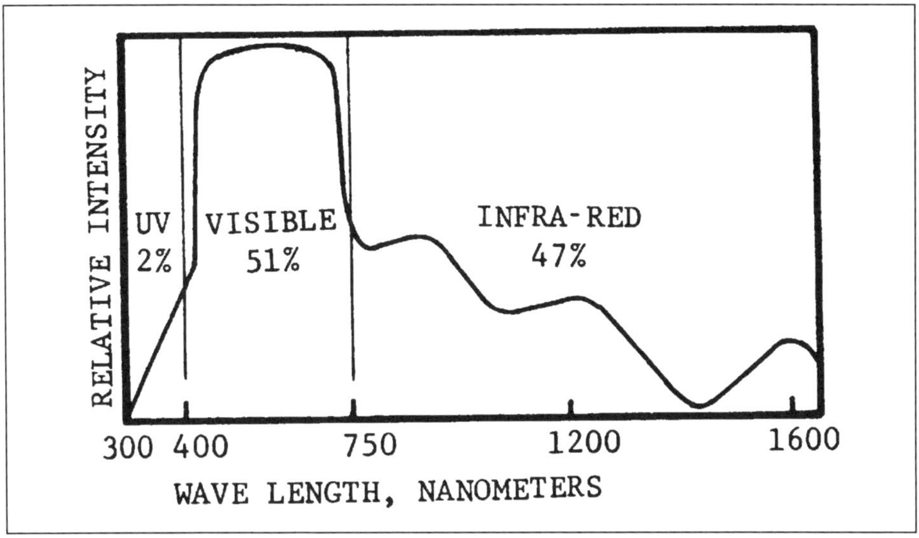

Figure 8.7 *The relative intensity of solar radiation at each wavelength (Whittemore, 1965). The heat content of the visible portion of solar radiation is 51 percent, while for infrared (the "heat" radiation) only 47 percent is present.*

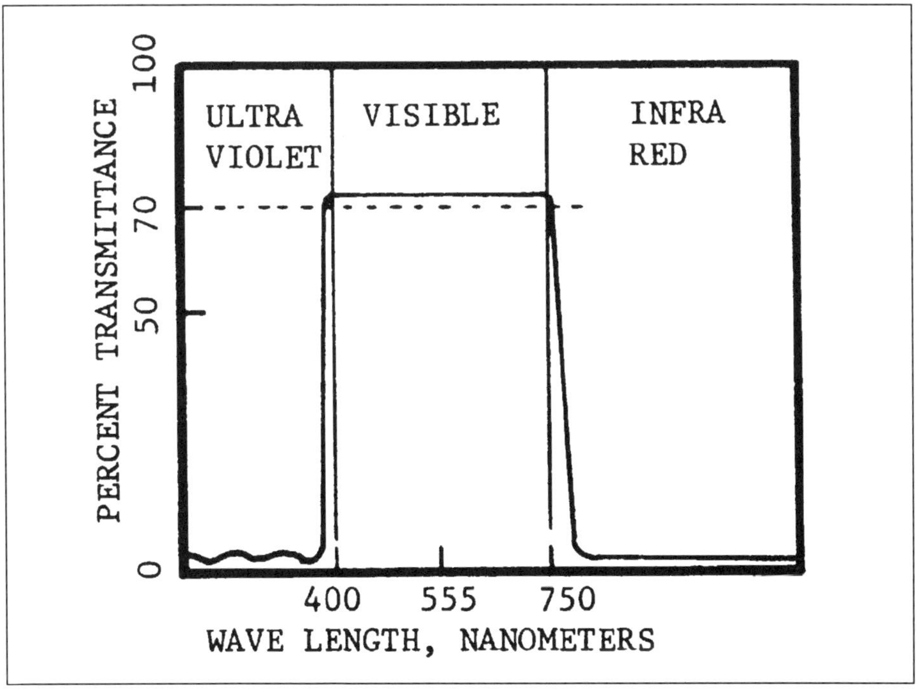

Figure 8.8 *An "ideal" automotive glass (Whittemore, 1965) would absorb all of the infrared and ultraviolet and only 70 percent across the spectrum of visible radiation's. Such a glass would absorb about 64.3 percent of the solar energy. In practice only about 50 percent is absorbed. The arbitrary choice of 70 percent transmission across the visible spectrum is challenged in this book as hazardous at night and inadequate during the day.*

The transmission curve of a tinted windshield shows the relative efficiency of the windshield in removing heat radiation compared to visible light (see Figure 8.6). Solar energy is distributed about equally between visible and invisible radiation (see Figure 8.7); hence a windshield that absorbs all of the infrared and ultraviolet energy still transmits 50 percent of the solar energy. From Figure 8.7 it is apparent that the infrared and ultraviolet energy absorption is not perfect, nor is visible light transmission perfect. Figure 8.8 gives the ideal windshield tint, which would transmit all of the visible light available and remove all of the solar energy that does not contribute to vision. Only uncolored glass can come near the 100 percent transmission ideal in the visible portion.

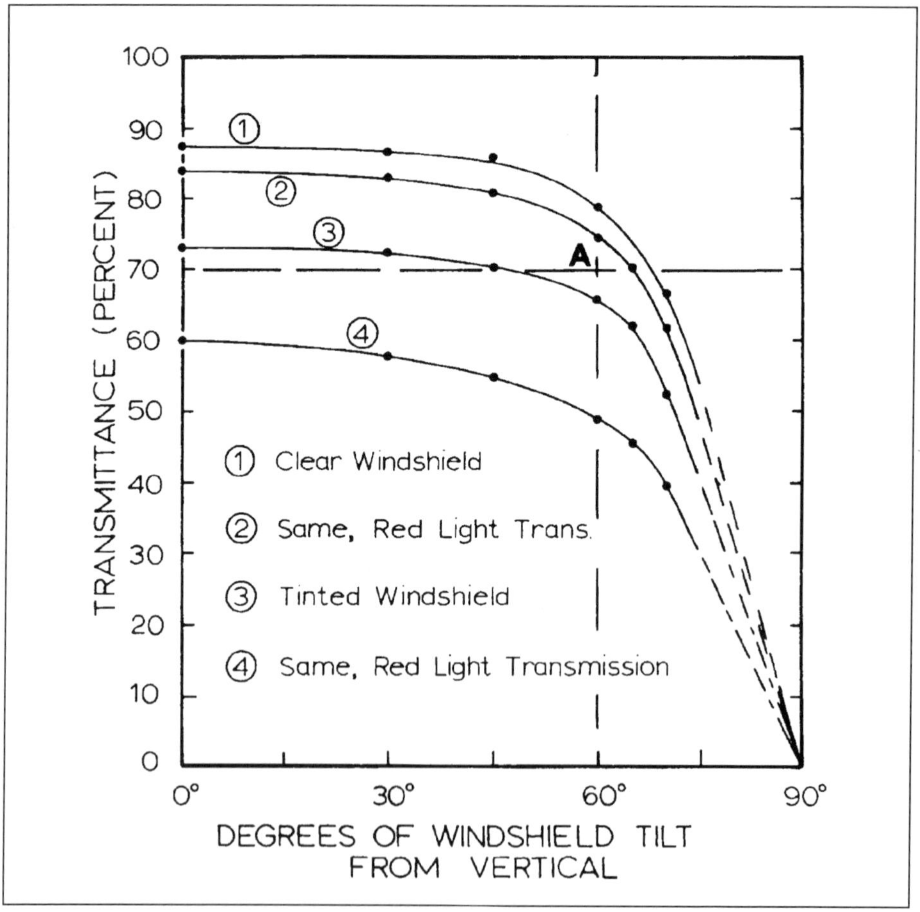

Figure 8.9 *Plot of transmission of a clear and tinted (heat absorbing) windshield for various tilt angles, and for red and white light transmission. Note that point A, the intersection between the tilt angle of 60 degrees and the Society of Automotive Engineers' lower limit of transmission, is above both the white light and the red transmission curves for a tinted windshield. These measurements were made on new one-foot-square samples.*

When windshield tint is present, angling the glass will increase the distance that the light has to travel in the glass; hence the absorptive effect of the tint on the light will be increased. Figure 8.9 gives the results of measurements with a Pritchard Spectra Photometer on samples of clear and tinted windshield glass supplied by the Ford Motor Company.

At 60 degrees tilt angle, the clear windshield sample transmitted 79 percent while the tinted windshield sample transmitted 65 percent of the white light from a tungsten source. At 60 degrees, when the red filter in the photometer was used, the clear windshield transmitted 75 percent, whereas the tinted windshield transmits only 49 percent of the red light from a tungsten source. The red filter in the Pritchard Spectra Photometer is tristimulus red, and will not necessarily match the red filter in a given taillight or stop signal. A deeper red (longer wavelength), will be attenuated below the 49-percent measurement obtained, see the windshield transmission curve, Figure 8.6.

From these data it is clear that the Society of Automotive Engineers' specification that a tinted windshield shall transmit not less than 70 percent visible light is misleading. The SAE specification holds for vertical windshields and not for windshields in automobiles, and ignores the selective absorption of tinted windshields for red light. If we are to hold to a 70 percent minimum allowable transmission, which most authorities have agreed to, it is apparent from Figure 8.9 that, even vertically, a tinted windshield cannot pass when tested for red light transmission! Furthermore, when installed in an automobile, the sample tested indicates that only 65 percent overall transmission for visible light is possible.

It is not possible to meet the minimum SAE specification of 70 percent transmission with the present tinted glass. Hence all American automobiles with tinted windshields violate the intent of this specification!

A protanopic or protanomalous color-defective person is insensitive to red light (see Figure 8.10). A normal person looking through a tinted windshield has a reduction in red sensitivity similar to being a protanope. A protanope who is already insensitive to red, will suffer even greater handicap viewing red lights through a tinted windshield (see Figure 8.10).

The curves in Figure 8.10 are for a vertical windshield. To determine the effects of tilting the windshield, the data in Figure 8.9 should prove useful. The selectively greater loss of red light by a tilted and tinted windshield is evidence that it is hazardous in the daytime, since red signal and brake lights may not be bright enough at best to be seen quickly in full daylight. The effect of the tint is to make the daylight relatively still brighter than the red signal light.

Another undesirable aspect of tinted window glass is that it reduces the chances of seeing the occupants of another automobile, thus further reducing the chances for social interactions. Social interactions are known to discourage anti-social behavior. I feel that a person's bad driving manners would improve if other drivers could talk about him or to him, as with a bull horn or a radio communications system. Driving mistakes could be discussed, and a sort of an on-the-job training would result. Since we do not have this, the eye-to-eye contact of drivers on occasion can be very useful.

Another adverse feature of tinted automobile glass is the inability to see through two or more cars if their windows are tinted. In regard to tilt angle, heat absorbing efficiency goes down the more nearly the glass faces the sun. At the same time the amount of glare light reflected from the sky toward other drivers increases. This increased sky or sun reflection from the windshield tends to obscure the view of the people in the car, accentuating the obscuration due to tint.

8.5 Distortions

Distortions may exist in front, rear, and side windows. Orange peel like irregularities, show up as blurred vision, while major surface defects produce gross displacements and distortions of objects from their true location and shape. Mi-

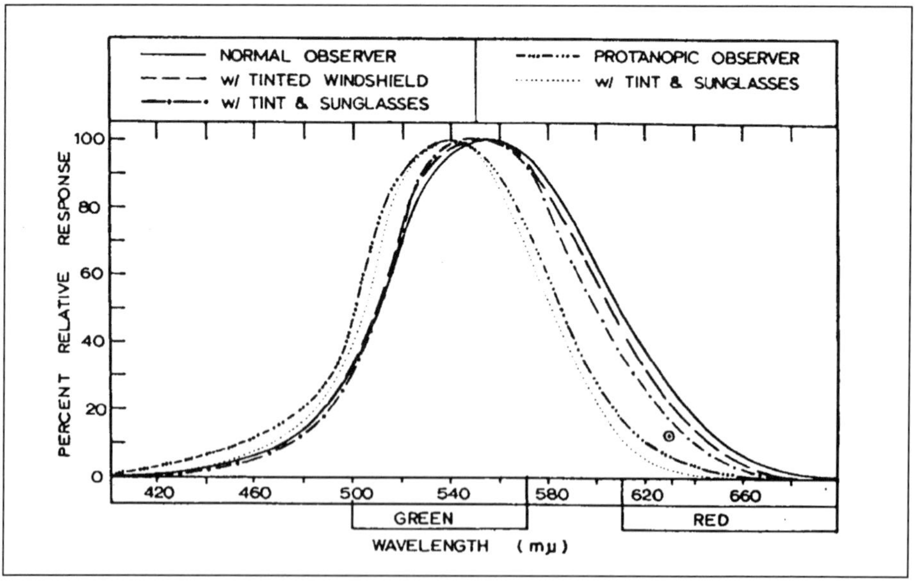

Figure 8.10 *The effect of windshield tint and green sunglasses upon normal and protanopic (red insensitive) luminosity curves when the windshield is vertical. Tilt of the windshield to 60 degrees from the vertical will reduce the red end of the tinted windshield curves by about 26 percent (see Figure 8.9). The encircled dot at 639 millimicrons indicates the effect of tilting a tinted windshield to 60 degrees when green sunglasses are worn by a normal observer. This figure shows that if a protanopic driver wears green sunglasses and peers through a tinted windshield it will be virtually impossible for him to see any red light!*

croscopic defects, such as inadequate surface polish or metallic deposits can cause light scatter and blurred vision.

The major surface defects are most serious when trying to see through the vehicle ahead. The combination of rear window and front window distortions may be considerably greater than the simple sum of the two distortions; hence rear window distortions as well as windshield distortions need to be minimized.

Quality control of gross distortions is improving. Most cars have reasonably good see through ability. Windshield distortions of vision can occur and are found to some degree among each manufacturer's products. Variations in sheet glass production, in heat forming, in lamination procedures, and in materials, combine to produce one windshield of reject quality while the next one will be acceptable. Whether the rejects are rejected is a matter of company quality control standards.

Distortions near the right side of the windshield, in effect, enlarge the corner post obstruction. When entering a roadway, vehicles approaching from the right and viewed through even slight distortion can be misjudged both as to speed and distance, and the distortion may cause driver behavior similar to that of not having seen the approaching vehicle at all. Major distortions near the straight ahead position can cause double images, eye fatigue, headache, and nausea. These symptoms may or may not interfere with driving efficiency, depending upon the person and the severity of the distortion. Distortions near the left corner post are especially hazardous when turning left and in detecting pedestrian and vehicle traffic approaching from the left. In effect the left corner post is enlarged by glass distortions.

Side window distortions do not seem to be as hazardous to the driving operation. However, these distortions do impair see through ability by other drivers in numerous instances, and generally a car is labeled as low quality if obvious distortions are present. It is probable that children and other passengers are more likely to have car sickness when side and rear windows are distorted.

Often we hear that the curved windshield is the cause of all manner of distortions and that a flat windshield would be better. Actually a curved windshield with the eye at the center of curvature is the more ideal arrangement (see Figure 8.11). Viewing through a flat plate of glass at an oblique angle, reduces transmission and exaggerates any irregularities in the surface and optical media, as well as creating an astigmatic like blur of the object viewed. The gentle curvature of the modern windshield is a reasonable compromise. However, the slope angle of 60 degrees backward tilt away from the vertical is a major source of light loss, dirt deposits, internal reflections, glare, heat build up, optical distortions and reflections from the dash panel. *Our present windshields are not ideal.*

8.6 Obstructions and the Rear-View Mirror

The largest single obstruction in the driver's forward field of view is usually the inside rear-view mirror. The placement of this mirror seems not to be determined by the eye height of the 95th-percentile driver but by the position of the rear window. As a result, most hard tops and almost all sedans have a serious obstruction to forward view due to the low position of the rear-view mirror. A survey of 1960 to 1962 automobiles (Allen, December 1962) showed that the rear view mirror occupied 14 to 18 degrees of the field of view and was between 32 to 53 degrees to the right side of straight ahead. In comparison the left windshield corner post varied between 5 and 17 degrees in lateral dimension and was located between 10 and 26 degrees to the left of straight ahead of the driver's eyes. The right windshield corner post was about 5 degrees in thickness and was about 75 degrees away from straight ahead.

The styling trends in 1996 have made these visual obstructions worse. In addition, designers have cramped the driver and passengers.

The outside rear-view mirror is improperly located on some vehicles. Federal standards first required in 1967 that outside rear-view mirrors be installed on all automobiles.

Outside rear-view mirrors in many 1996 automobiles, occupy most of the area that used to be the vent window in the front door glass (see Figures 2.3, 2.4). For short drivers, these obstructions are very serious. The seating height must be raised and the corner-post obstruction reduced.

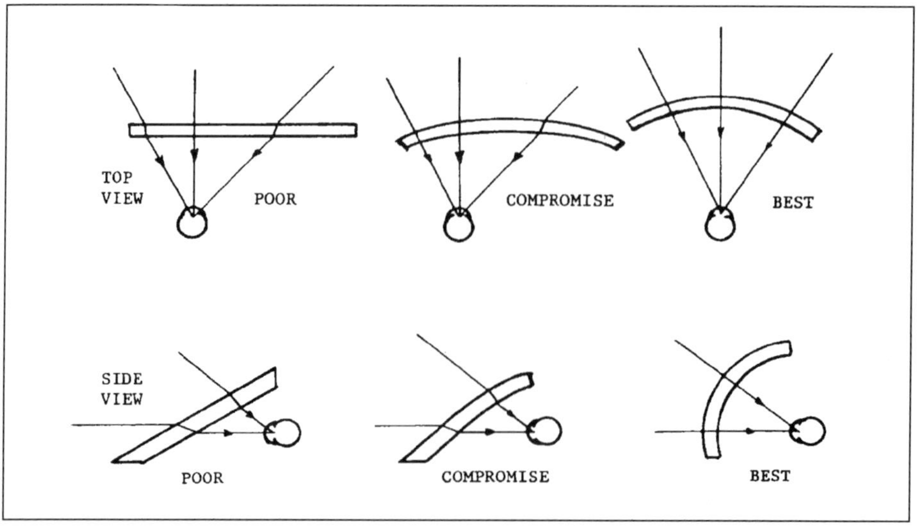

Figure 8.11 *Schematic diagram of some possible windshield designs. In general a concentric design would give zero distortion and negligible refractive power if the thickness were small.*

A properly designed periscopic rear view mirror could eliminate the need for the outside mirror and reduce obstructions to the drivers side vision. Periscopic and other exotic rear view mirror designs have been around for 50 years or more. They range from the simple convex single mirror through complex lens-reflector designs using astigmatic elements. Experimental systems include television displays, radar detectors, and laser ranging devices.

Flat mirror systems are more desirable than other systems because they are inexpensive; they are not subject to distortion; they give no inherent enlargement or reduction in the image viewed, and space perception is normal. They permit a wide range of head and eye movements. If properly arranged, they permit rearward view by looking upward slightly, thus not interfering seriously with forward vision.

All other systems suffer from disadvantages. For example, the television display of rearward scenery must of necessity be confined to a small area on the dash or elsewhere. This means that size and distance information are grossly distorted and resolution is reduced by the amount of the size reduction needed to get a large field of view. Being a near task, the driver must focus the eyes when looking at the miniature display. Those drivers over 45 years of age may not be able to focus on the display. This is not to say it cannot be done, but at present a television rear view display loses more than it gains. Training would be needed to get the most out of the information provided.

It is not possible to interpret accurately what is "out there" by what you see in that little TV window. Almost the same problems exist with the convex rear view mirror which is commonly placed adjacent to a flat mirror to help compensate for its limitations.

Principles to be observed in the construction of periscopic systems with flat mirrors are as follows: (1) an even number of reflections is needed for forward vision, (2) an odd number of reflections is needed for rearward vision, (3) the system should be as short as possible from the eye to the exit aperture to ensure the largest field of view, (4) filters should be avoided and as few optical elements used as possible because of light losses, (5) direct sun on components, and sky glare in the field of view should be avoided, and (6) the mirror should be placed directly ahead and above the line of sight of the driver to avoid obstructions in the field of view.

A windshield tilted forward at the top would provide space for the rearward and forward periscopic components. Figures 8.12 and 8.13 give the essentials of two designs of periscopes for automobile use. These combine forward and rearward visibility, with selection of view being based upon a simple movement of the eyes, or a forward movement of the head to look forward.

8.7 Instrument Panel Visibility

The major factors contributing to the speed and accuracy of instrument panel readability in the daytime are: the illumination on the display compared to the illumination on the road, the size of the numerals or letters, the contrast of the numerals or letters with their background, the accommodative ability of the eyes of the driver, and the placement of the seat and the steering wheel.

The speed of recognition of the critical dial or gauge is increased with larger sizes, greater illumination, greater contrast, and a younger driver who can focus his eyes more quickly.

A study on 1960, 1961 and 1962 automobiles (Allen, February 1963) showed that the average eye-to-dash-panel distance was 72 centimeters in fifty-six auto-

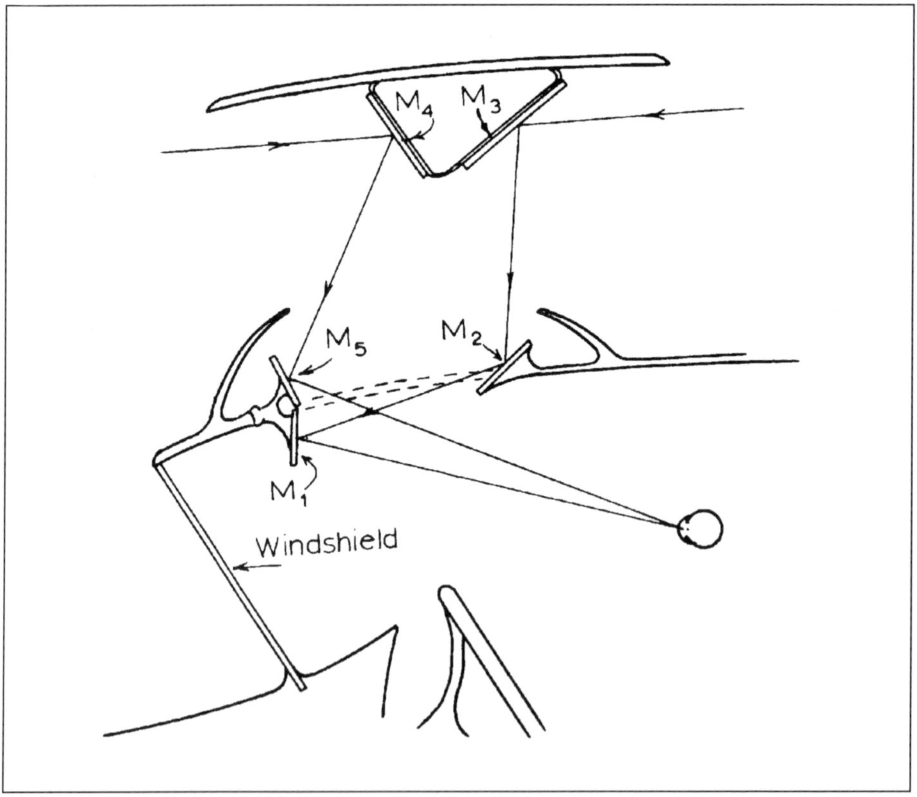

Figure 8.12 *Periscopic combination forward and rear view mirror systems for simultaneous viewing from one eye position.*

M_1 Mirror is adjustable about horizontal axis for rear view.

M_2 Mirror is fixed for rear view.

M_3 Mirror is fixed for rear view.

M_4 Mirror is fixed for forward view.

M_5 Mirror is adjustable for forward view.

mobiles with the seat in the position in which it was found. The height of each of the numbers on the speedometer averaged 1 degree 16 minutes, and each odometer numeral averaged 20 minutes in height. (A 20/20 letter is 5 minutes high.) At that time the illumination on the dash panel ranged from 46 to 1,640 foot candles. In average daytime conditions.

A study (Allen, October 1964) of 50 new 1963 automobiles in dealer stocks measured the time required to look from the sun lighted exterior scene to the dash panel and recognize a speedometer numeral. The two observers were seventeen years of age and pretrained for five days to build up their reaction time skills, The average time of these **practiced** subjects to clear the dash panel without sunglasses was 0.717 seconds, while the same task required 0.781 seconds with fit over sun glasses. In addition to this first recognition time a driver would still have to search until he found the speedometer needle or other gauge of importance. Following this he must return his eyes to the outside scene. It may be conservatively estimated that a normal driver of 35 to 40 years of age will re-

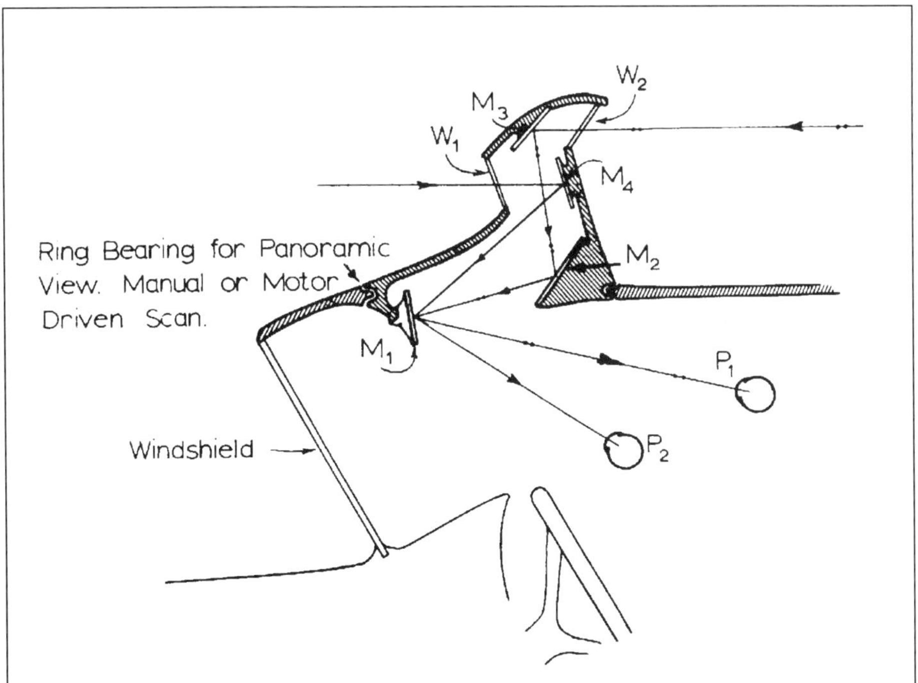

Figure 8.13 *Periscopic combination forward and rear view mirror systems requiring two position viewing. The normal eye position, P_1, would permit a periscopic rearward view, whereas movement of the head forward to P_2 would provide a periscopic forward view. Mirror M_1 is adjustable to allow for driver height. Fixed mirrors M_2 and M_3 provide a rearward view through window W_2, while fixed Mirror M_4 provides a forward view through Window W_1.*

quire more than two seconds to inspect the average dash panel and return attention to the highway. Some panels and some conditions would greatly lengthen this time.

Improvements have been made in dash panel design in general, but daytime illumination is a problem in some automobiles and displays are not standardized. A pair of glasses tinted in the upper portions and clear in the lower portions, combined with a properly powered bifocal for older drivers, makes a significant improvement in the speed of inspecting the dash panel and returning vision to the highway.

Dash panel visibility at night depends upon the same factors as for daytime visibility, except that panel lighting is supplied artificially. The best color depends upon the nature of the driver's refractive error. Because of chromatic aberration in the eyes, a hyperope and an emmetrope would see the instrument panel best with green or blue light, whereas a myope or a bifocal wearer, might see it better with red light, assuming normal color vision. At night the loss of surround lighting can contribute to disorientation, double vision, and drowsiness. This effect can be reduced by increasing the instrument panel illumination, and by turning on the inside overhead light.

Vision and Human Factors experts should optimize and standardize the information, location, size, brightness and color to be displayed on all motor vehicle dash panels. They should also standardize the location of control levers, buttons, etc. that control the seats, windows, door locks, door handles, turn indicator, gear shift lever, steering wheel controls, emergency signals, etc.

8.8 Headlights

A. Aim

Improper headlight aim, because of lamp replacement, bent fenders, broken or sagging springs, or unusual vehicle load, is a major cause of glare at night, but for a reason different from what most people think. Improper headlight aim reduces the illumination pattern in front of the automobile to less than optimum. This means that for a low beam aimed too low, the seeing distance is reduced, and the brightness of the illuminated road surface is higher than normal. If the low beam is aimed too high, a greater seeing range is provided, but the illumination on the pavement needed for vehicle guidance will be lowered. Within limits, in either case, there is not much difference in glare to oncoming motorists on a straight highway, because of the shape of the low beam pattern of American headlights. However the loss in head lighting range with a beam that is too low, and the loss in pavement illumination when the beam is too high, renders the driver with *poorly aimed headlights more susceptible to ordinary glare light from other cars* (see Table 9.12).

Glare at night is more a matter of the difference in luminance levels between the glare source and the visual task than of the intensity of the glare source alone. Anything which destroys the headlight aim or distribution built into the lamp will seem to increase oncoming headlight glare at night. Dirt and scratches on the headlight lens also produce important degradations in headlight efficiency. The light that is diverted from the roadway is scattered in part toward the oncoming driver's eyes, at the same time the losses of light on the roadway make oncoming headlights appear brighter or more glaring.

Gadgets sold to be attached to headlights are almost always harmful. For example, yellow filters absorb blue light as well as lose about 8 percent of the white light by reflection. "Sleepy-eye" chromium covers used over the top half of the head lamp lens are especially detrimental since they destroy the headlight pattern, thereby increasing the glare into oncoming drivers' eyes and reducing the useful illumination. Dark filters to fit over the headlights are for sale in auto supply stores! All of these should be banned along with add-on window tint. They can kill!

Improving the light pattern and increasing the headlight light output will definitely be of benefit for night time driving. The importance of headlight aim should be emphasized in new car literature and in automotive magazines. Warnings should be clearly stated about the hazards of covering the head lamp with anything, including dirt.

Many automobiles are so sensitive to load that two male adults in the rear seat are enough to require reaiming of the headlights. In 1969, manufacturers made it possible to reach headlight adjustment screws without removing chromium trim. This was an important improvement because it speeded up headlight adjustments and permitted the motorist to adjust head lamps to correct for an overload of his vehicle.

The new headlight designs make adjusting the headlight aim more difficult. The next step needed is to provide headlight adjustment from the driver's seat to match the load, or to provide a load stabilized vehicle that maintains the same headlight level whether loaded or empty. Improved head lighting means less highway glare and fewer accidents.

B. Filament shields

High beam head lamps used in four headlight arrays do not have filament shields to prevent upward scatter into rain, snow, and fog, whereas low beams do. These shields are the result of an invention by Orville Stamm who, personally, for seventeen years extolled their virtues and attempted to interest the automobile industry and the several large manufacturers of lamps. In 1955, the year that his patent expired, the lamp manufacturers began to advertise an improved fog penetrating head lamp incorporating his shield. All low beam headlights use similar shields. Certainly, the United States Patent Office protects the inventor, but it has, on occasions such as this, deprived the public of safety advancements for seventeen years while the inventor wastes his time, effort, and money trying to find a manufacturer willing to pay a royalty on a patent.

C. Sleepy eye shields

Headlight sleepy eye shields (see Figure 8.14), seen occasionally in 1996, were not adopted or endorsed by automobile manufacturers, nor did the manufacturers strongly oppose them, or dozens of other "sucker trade" accessory items offered for sale on the "after market." The sleepy eye shield increased glare and reduced roadway illumination because it destroyed the SAE standard headlight beam pattern (Allen, January 1967). They are especially dangerous in snow, rain and fog. The results of the study of these shields were sent to the Federal Trade Commission. The FTC completely ignored this study. Sleepy eye shields are no longer readily available in stores. Apparently, this headlight problem is about to disappear.

Figure 8.14 *Sleepy eye shields have long been improperly promoted as reducing glare and improving visibility. They have virtually disappeared because of new headlamp designs. Unbelievably, dark filters covering the headlights are now being sold. All such gimmicks should be illegal because they violate the headlight aim and brightness standards.*

D. Disappearing headlights

Headlights that are covered when not in operation are a true salesman's gimmick which has hazardous complications. Being mechanical, they are subject to failure and wearing out. Thus interferences with aim as well as the chances for mechanical failure exist. Such headlights are absolutely contraindicated when air flow streamlining, and fuel economy are important.

Complications occur even when they are operating properly. The lamps are exposed only when hot and road splatter dries on them. When the lights are turned off they are automatically stored, hot and dirty. When they would be washed in the rain or in the service station, they are covered. The dirt builds up and destroys the headlight distribution pattern and reduces the light output, thereby increasing the glare to oncoming motorists. (I asked a salesman of a used car dealer to open the headlights of a beautiful, clean used car. The headlights had a one-eighth-inch deposit of road dirt on them!) Less light where it belongs on the pavement, makes approaching headlights seem more glaring.

Disappearing headlights cannot be used in the daytime to signal an approaching driver. The lights are allowed up to three seconds to open (U.S. Department of Transportation, 1968). Let us assume two seconds. Two automobiles approaching each other at 60 miles per hour, will travel 352 feet closer in two seconds! Hence disappearing headlights are as useless for signaling in the daytime as the horn is for warning oncoming drivers on the highway.

There appears to be no justification for covering the headlights. We have few gravel roads and we are not a nation of race drivers. The only advantage seems to be styling. Styling also can be hazardous because the front and rear of the automobile now look almost identical when the headlights are covered. The disappearing headlight was put on the market at a time when great resistance was shown by the manufacturers to such things as energy-absorbing steering columns and dual brakes. The development cost for disappearing headlight designs probably equaled or exceeded the cost of each of the safety features that the industry was required to install and to which they objected so loudly, at least in the beginning.

Starting in 1995, all automobiles in the USA came equipped with daytime running lights. Low beam headlights, or half voltage high beam headlights are reasonably well suited for use as daytime running lights (Allen, September 1965). Disappearing headlights seemingly will have no place in future car production, thus *disappearing headlights will disappear.*

E. All weather head lighting system

An ideal all weather system installed in self leveling automobiles would be one that puts no light at all into a zone between three and five feet above the road (see Figure 8.15). There would be very little back scatter from fog, rain, or snow and the seeing range would be increased. Since such a headlight cannot light signs overhead. Headlights mounted above eye level are needed. These would be aimed so that no light drops below five feet. Because they would be nearer to the driver's eyes than conventional headlights, they could be less powerful and still provide adequate illumination for seeing overhead retroreflectorized signs.

In addition, such roof-mounted headlights, one at each side, would shape code the front of the automobile with a rectangular pattern of white lights which would not be confused with present taillight patterns or with the compatible proposed future taillighting system described in the next section.

8.9 Signal Visibility

A. Front signals

American automobiles suffer from a poorly designed signal system. For instance, front turn signals are not visible to adjacent cars in multilane traffic because they are placed too low and are aimed only in the forward direction. Except for being in a desirably shaded location, all other evidence indicates that turn signals should be raised to the top of the fender. This would permit visibility of the signal from all angles, front and side.

A desirable feature is that the parking lights in front are illuminated when the headlights are on. When one headlight is burned out, the parking light identifies the vehicle as an automobile and not a motor cycle. Recent surveys indicate the number of defective headlights to be about one out of seventy-five motor

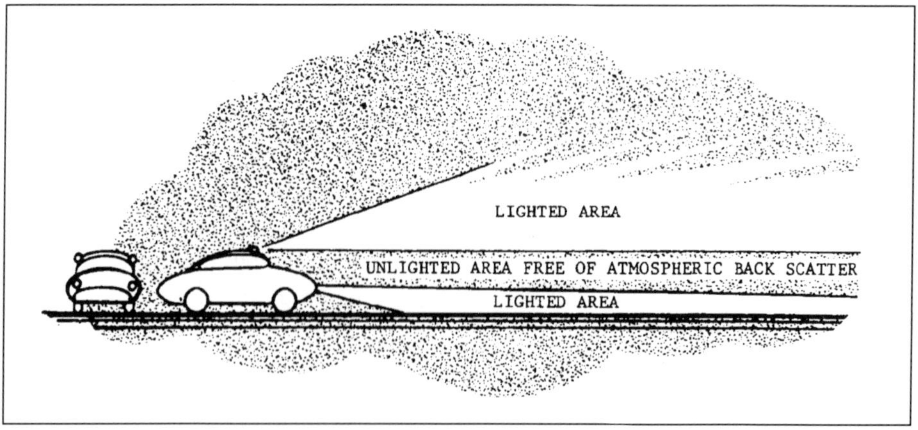

Figure 8.15 *Recommended vehicle lighting for forward vision. Regular headlights would be designed to have a limited upward component to prevent lighting particulate matter in the atmosphere before the driver's eyes. To permit reading freeway signs and stop signs, which are usually above eye level, the smaller top-mounted lights would be used.*

vehicles. Counts in Bloomington, Indiana, a college town, show about one out of 25 passenger cars has only one headlight!

Unfortunately, having the parking lights on reduces the signal value of the turn signal, which usually has its filament within the same bulb. Amber has been used both on the front and rear for turn signals. Among color defectives as well as normal people, amber is often confused with red (Heath and Schmidt, 1959).

Of the signal colors red, green and yellow (amber), the yellow is the weakest and produces the most mistakes in color recognition. It is sometimes called white, red, or green. In the daytime, body styling confuses the front and rear appearance of automobiles. The use of amber on the front may add to this confusion. At night when only the parking lights are on, the use of amber on the front also confuses the front and rear of an automobile.

The use of new lighting technology can provide signal lights operating at five to ten flashes per second. Such flash rates are very powerful in getting a driver's attention in a very short time. Normal flash rates are clearly inadequate.

B. Rear signals

1. Color

Rear lighting suffers significant deficiencies. Two percent of male drivers have a reduced sensitivity to red light of 20 percent or less (depending upon the wavelength composition of the red light), compared to a color-normal individual. Furthermore, tinted windshields, which are estimated to be in more than half of American automobiles, further reduce the transmission of red light compared to white or green light. To correct for these losses, taillights would need to be five times brighter or of a color other than red. The sensitivity to green is not adversely affected by windshield tint, by any of the common color vision defects, or by space perception aberrations (Allen, December 1964); hence its use for a rear running light is highly recommended.

The front turn signals should be amber but with a high flash rate. The brake light needs to be red, but shape coded with a white bar so that we do not discriminate against color blind drivers.

2. Position

For an open highway with low traffic density, taillights and brake lights need to be low for maximum appearance of nearness. When traffic becomes heavy, a high position for taillights and brake lights at the roof line of a passenger car is needed to permit them to be seen through other cars and to reduce the chances of a multiple rear end collision. Thus these lights need to be at both low and high positions on each motor vehicle.

When automobiles are traveling close behind one another on a straight, level stretch of roadway, a slight change in velocity of the lead car can cause a touch of the brake for the second and third cars, a panic braking for the fourth and fifth, and a rear end collision for most of the rest. Thus is born the spectacular freeway pile-up.

If the second driver could signal the fifth driver behind him that he had touched his brake, that driver would know of the hazard just as soon as the drivers who are nearer. By thus increasing the range of brake lights by five cars, the first rear end accident would not occur until the twenty-fifth car back instead of the fifth, a saving of twenty cars! Furthermore, the severity of the collisions that did occur would not peak as quickly, and more vehicles would escape with light damage.

In a study (Allen et al., February 1967) using auxiliary taillights mounted near the top of the rear window of a station wagon, the signal was found to penetrate to at least the third driver behind the lead car without time attenuation, whereas ordinary taillights required that each driver see the brake light ahead of him and put on his brakes to signal the man behind him to put on his brakes.

Figures 8.16 and 8.17 show the improvements in performance obtained in following behavior when the taillights were raised, and when a switch was put on the accelerator which lighted the taillights before the foot could get to the brake pedal. It is apparent that performance is best when the driver can see through the car ahead. It is also improved by accelerator switching of the brake light. In this experiment three drivers and a timer operator had to react when the lead vehicle applied its brakes. By subtracting a simple reaction time of 0.2 second for the timer operator, the average driver reaction time using the stock brakes was 0.58 second. With the high positioned accelerator switched brake light system, the individual driver reaction time averaged 0.25 second. In other words, high placement of brake lights can transmit information to *closely following* drivers much quicker than the stock brake lights can.

While there is a clear superiority of placing the brake light at eye level when cars are traveling close together, as on freeways, it is not proper to assume that the present taillights should be replaced with roof mounted lights. The taillight function is best located below eye level, to localize the position of the vehicle with respect to the pavement and the horizon. The high position brake light should be in addition to the stock brake lights and not a substitute for them. Since roof heights vary among vehicles, the high signal light placement should be at a standardized height above the pavement; for example, 60 inches.

In keeping with space perception cues it is desirable to make the car ahead of you appear as close as possible. This is done by lowering the regular tail (presence) lights and by increasing their luminance, their size, and their lateral separation. When brakes are applied it is desirable to increase still more the apparent nearness of the stopping vehicle. This is done by increasing the spacing and the intensity and by reducing the height of the brake lights compared to the taillights. Thus, brake lights should be outside of the taillights and should be larger, brighter, and lower. Appendix A, Figure A.2, shows the brake lights at the same level as the presence lights, because the presence lights have been placed as low as practicable to enhance their location fixing value.

3. Shape coding

As indicated in the preceding section, higher placed lights also must be added to help prevent freeway collisions. These are in effect high placed repeater lights, but they could serve another most valuable function. They would increase the apparent size of the rear end of a vehicle and would provide the means for effective shape coding (see Appendix A, Figure A.2). For example, a midline green light at the top of a passenger automobile would form the apex of a green triangle for taillights. A red brake light at each outer edge of the top, combined with the regular brake lights, would form a distinctive square (see Appendix A,

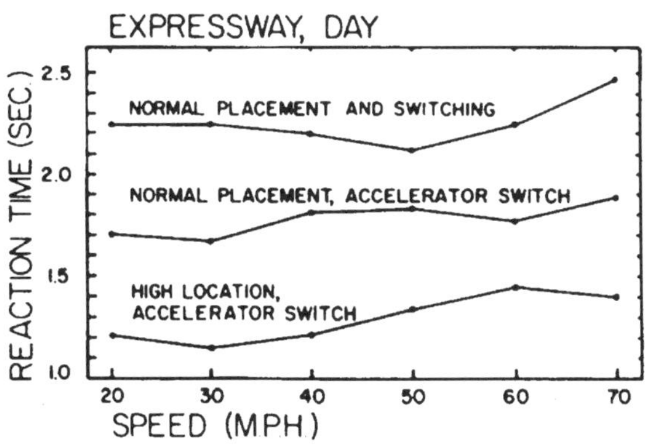

Figure 8.16 Drivers' reaction times at various speeds on the daytime expressway following test vehicles with two rear lighting arrangements and with brake and accelerator switching.

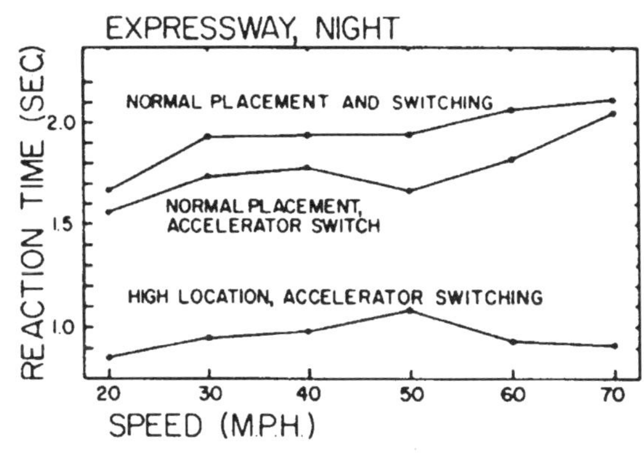

Figure 8.17 Same as Figure 8.16 except data were taken at night.

Figure 8.18a *GM's Silhouette has tail, turn and brake lights placed on either side of the rear window. The only lights near the pavement are the back up lights near the license plate. This photo is of a white van which compensates partially for the poor taillighting design. With dark bumpers and dark body colors, this taillight design is hazardous.*

Figure 8.18b *Black add-on filters over the headlights combined with the dark colored shield across the front of the hood, reduce the visibility of this vehicle and reduces headlight brightness about 50 percent. Every 13 years, we need twice as much light to do the same task as we did before. A 50 percent filter makes us 13 years older!*

Figure A.2). The separate turn signal lamp in the conventional lower location should be supplemented by a lamp adjacent to the high-mounted red brake light.

By shape coding the red lights with a horizontal white bar, the brake lights would be easily seen and recognized by all drivers including those with a color vision defect.

4. Dual intensity

Other deficiencies in present day taillighting are the use of the same intensity for daytime brake and turn signaling as is used at night, and the use of bright trim surrounding and covering over the taillights. Even the use of bright red paint for automobile colors makes an already inadequate daytime brake light virtually useless. In the daytime, a red brake light surrounded by red paint of an equal or greater intensity, becomes a flashing black signal and doesn't have any attraction or warning value unless one is looking directly at it. Tail and brake lights that brighten as the daylight increases are the answer and are easy to manufacture.

C. Flash rate

Special attention must be directed toward signal lights that now flash at pleasant frequencies rather than efficient frequencies. Flash rates of 120 per minute or less are recommended by the Society of Automotive Engineers. Old flashers and bulbs often combine to give flash rates of ten to fifteen per minute. Such a slow rate gives the light an on and an off phase of about 2.5 seconds each. Since a visual fixation takes only 0.20 to 0.25 second, a person could look at a light four or five times, always catch it in the dark or light phase, and thus not be sure it was flashing. Preliminary study indicates that a light that flashes five to ten times per second, gives a signal that is far more effective than the current system. Solid state lights perform very well at high flash rates.

D. Dirt

A major defect in modern automobile lighting is dirt. Styling dictates changes in lamp housing details, but changes to reduce dirt pickup and moisture penetration are not notable. The collection of dust and road mud is a function of position and air flow past the light (see Figure 8.19). Attention to air flow patterns should be a part of lighting design as well as a factor in wind resistance and effective lateral body area distribution. Until such is the case, the motorist and the trucker must make a lamp cleaning tour around the car or truck at each stop.

Head and taillights have been observed to have water in them! Even slight water and dust penetration spoils the efficiency of the retroreflector prism faces on the inside of the plastic lens. Paint and plastic materials deposited on the inside of the plastic lens from the heat of the lamp further destroy the retroreflector efficiency. Moisture damage to painted or aluminized reflective surfaces and

Figure 8.18c *Two truck trailers. The one on the right is relatively clean and has the new multiple strips of reflective tape to improve its visibility. It shows the newer, lower and stronger rear bumper with reflectors on it close to the pavement. In contrast, the trailer at the left is dirty and has none of the new safety features. Even though the trailer on the right has a new lower bumper, it needs to be still lower because it is higher than passenger vehicle bumpers.*

Figure 8.18d *A pickup truck's bumper is at the height of the bottom of the side window of a full size passenger vehicle. This pickup's headlights are at or above the eye level of most motorists. This causes excess glare at night. In addition, this pickup has glare producing sleepy eye shields on the headlights.*

Figure 8.19 *A simple test for windshield condition. Look at the reflected image of the sun as you view the windshields in a parking lot on a clear, bright day. There will be a few new, unscratched windshields and there will be some seriously scratched windshields as shown above. Light from damaged windshields added to light scattered from dirt and light reflected by the windshield from the top of the dash panel can cause an accident by preventing seeing a pedestrian, cyclist, automobile, bus, truck or train in time. (The circular object on the glass was intended but failed to block out the main image of the sun for the camera.)*

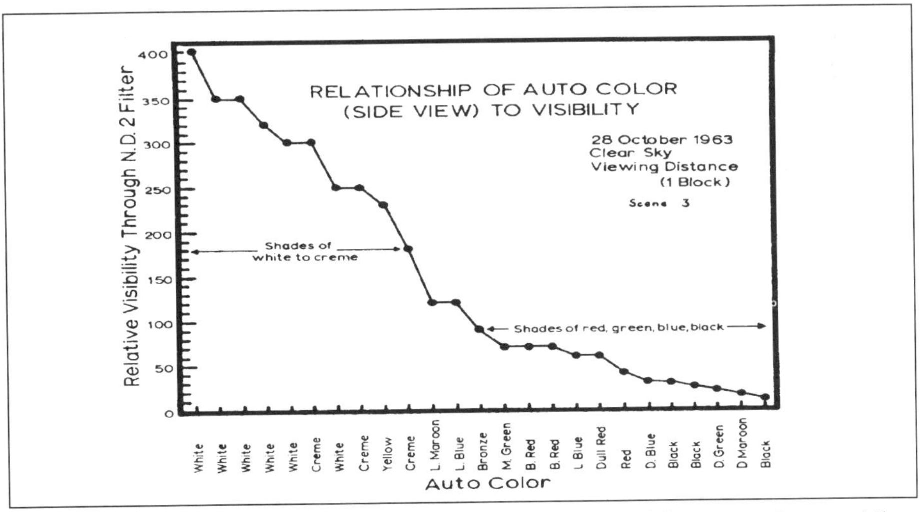

Figure 8.20 *Actual field measurements with a Luckiesh-Moss visibility meter of automobile color visibility. Automobiles were observed from a position in front about 45 degrees off the line of travel, much as would be the case in a developing intersection collision. Without question the shades of red, green, blue, and black were more camouflaged than the shades of yellow, cream, and white.*

moisture caused corrosion on electrical contacts are of importance because they reduce lamp light output. Old style sealed beam headlights did not have these problems.

8.10 Vehicle Visibility

After over fifty years of manufacturing automobiles in all conceivable colors, the automobile manufacturers still produce car colors in terms of what will sell, not what is safe. Studies have shown that up to ten times as many accidents happen to black cars as to white. Other data indicate white cars are up to forty times more visible than black (see Figure 8.20). Still other data indicate that greater visibility means fewer and less severe accidents. Red and black have the lowest visibility of all colors. Cream, yellow, and white are the most visible.

Along with statistics on color, it is known that the small, powerful sports car has the highest accident rate and greatest death rate compared to full sized automobiles. The higher death rate is no surprise because of the small amount of protective metal surrounding the passengers. The higher accident rate could be due to speed alone, but indications are that speed is only an indirect factor.

The most probable causes of more sports car accidents are the use of dark

Figure 8.21 *If it had white side wall tires, this van would be the perfect example of the Ban Black safety concept for all motor vehicles. Even so, this photo shows elements of camouflage. The main body, which is black with tinted windows, matches the trees while the top of the white lower portion lines up with the bottom of the trees and looks like the pavement! All white and no window tint would be best.*

colors, including red, and their small size (see Figure 8.21). We recognize an object's nearness in part by its size, and we recognize its approach speed almost entirely by the rate of increase in size. Therefore, a small vehicle is judged to be farther away and its approach speed is judged to be slower than it really is. The driver of a sports car cannot rely upon the help of those other drivers who reduce the overall number of accidents by compensating for the mistakes of others. The sports car driver, with his low vantage position, excessive speed potential, low visibility, and reduction of the amount of Good Samaritan Protection from other drivers, must rely almost entirely upon his own skills to avoid accidents. Obviously, from the accident statistics and insurance rates, his own skills alone are not always enough.

It is hoped that the automobile manufacturers will find it expedient to protect the motoring public from the misfit sports cars by at least improving their conspicuity.

It is hoped that manufacturers will adopt white bumpers, white tires, white mud guards, white lower side panels, etc., as standard equipment for all production vehicles, including passenger cars, sports cars, trucks, buses and construction equipment. This would eliminate about 70 percent of the accidents.

Chapter 9

Visual Hazards on Streets and Highways

Merrill J. Allen, O.D., Ph.D.

Synopsis

9.1 Nighttime Hazards

A. Inadequate illumination and blacktop pavements

The human eye is capable of an extreme range of adaptation to changes in the ambient light level. However, such flexibility does not tell the whole story. A major part of this adaptability comes from the ability to change the "grain" of the retina; that is, to group photoreceptors and bipolar, ganglion, and other cells into larger functional units as the light level falls, and into smaller units as the light level rises. The result is a dependency of visual acuity upon light level. See Figure 9.1.

Other important visual functions such as color vision, speed of perception reaction time, binocular fusion, and stereopsis are adversely affected by the increasing retinal grain at lower luminance levels. The contrast sensitivity also is degraded and is of importance in detecting objects as distinct from their background. The greater the contrast sensitivity, the easier it is to detect an object. Figure 9.2 shows the minimum contrast of an object which will make it perceptible at each luminance level. Contrast is defined by the equation:

$$C = (B_1 - B_2) \div B_1$$

where C is the contrast, B_1 is the background luminance, and B_2 is the test object luminance. Contrast sensitivity is the reciprocal of contrast. Increasing illumination increases the sensitivity to contrast and makes object detection easier. Conversely, Figure 9.2 shows that at nighttime roadway luminance levels of one foot lambert or less, an object must be considerably brighter or darker than its background to be seen. Thus reading road signs, and the detection of an object such as a pedestrian becomes more difficult. Also the times for detection, recognition, and response increase.

Since the amount of light present is the distinguishing difference between night and day, the problems of night driving would be reduced if more light were available. It has been shown that visibility even in the daytime is improved by adding lights to vehicles (Allen, May 1964, March 1965; Port of New York Authority, 1968). That more light at night is beneficial, using the same system of automobile and highway head lighting as we now have, is predicted from the behavior of the human eye with changing light levels (see Figures 9.1 and 9.2). This has been verified by a number of studies (Roper and Meese, 1964; Christie, 1968) involving accident experience vs. highway lighting and field testing of vehicles with increased headlight output.

Because of the need for more light at night, the blacktop (asphalt) highway, due to its low reflectance, is an uninspired design. The amount of light returned

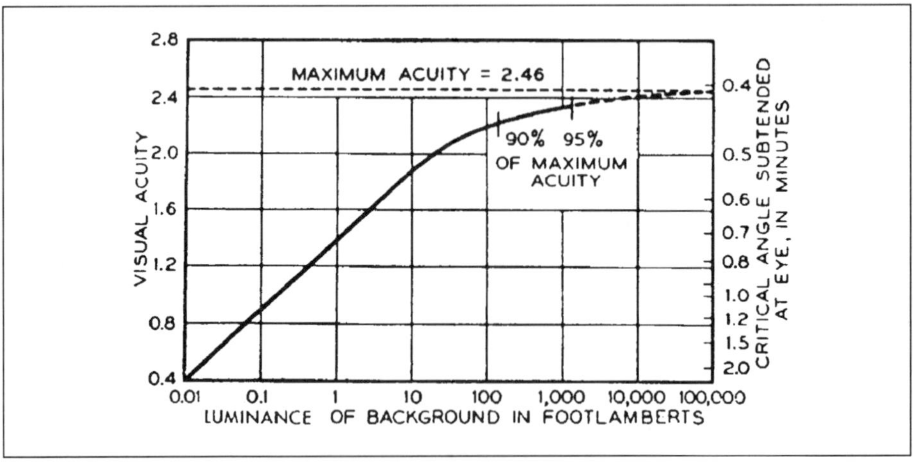

Figure 9.1 *The effect of illumination on visual acuity. A high contrast black Landolt ring was displayed on a variable luminance background and was observed with normal pupils and binocular vision. (From* IES Lighting Handbook, *4th ed., Figure 2.14, pp. 2–8.) (Note: The dotted extension of the curve is somewhat misleading as the acuity does not rise past about 900 foot lamberts, and 20,000 foot lamberts is reported to be intolerable to the eye.)*

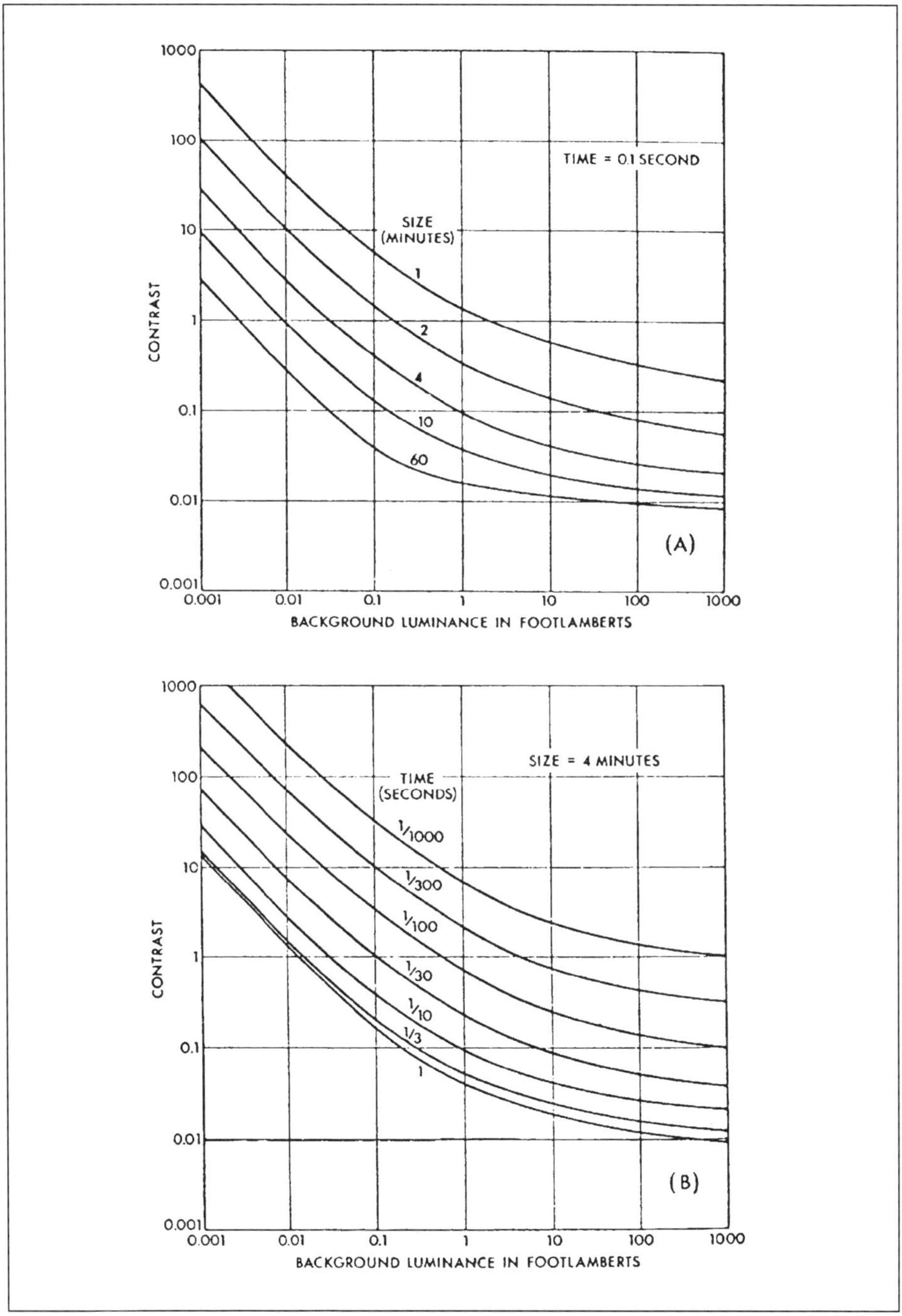

Figure 9.2 *The relationship between size, contrast, background luminance, and exposure duration for threshold seeing. Contrast is ΔL/L, where* L *is the luminance of the background and* ΔL *is the difference between the luminance of the target and the background. Contrasts above 100 are possible when the test object is brighter than the background. (From* IES Lighting Handbook, *4th ed., Figure 2.16, pp. 2–8.)*

from headlight beams depends upon the composition and aging of the blacktop surface and may vary from virtually zero when the pavement is new or wet to nearly the same as Portland concrete when the blacktop mixture includes a large proportion of light colored stone and the asphaltic cement has been worn away. Much of seeing at night is by silhouette or back lighting; that is, a dark object is seen against a light background. Portland cement gives good visibility because it provides a light background for objects. Pedestrians usually wear dark clothing and are best seen in silhouette; hence blacktopped roadways impair the seeing of pedestrians. Any light colored object will stand out better on black, but unfortunately not many roadway hazards are light in color, and few are as important as the pedestrian.

A person's alertness depends upon the amount of stimulation he receives. When alone on a highway at night, the lowered light level, especially from a new blacktop road, reduces alertness and increases the risk of falling asleep.

On the positive side, for dry blacktop pavements, reflectorized center and edge lines stand out more clearly. These reflectorized lines greatly assist night driving because they make the task of staying on the road in the proper lane easier. In addition, continuous edge marking could help reveal a pedestrian near the edge of the pavement at a greater than normal distance.

With the onset of rain the advantage of blacktop disappears in supplying contrast to edge and center reflectorized paint lines. Wet blacktop pavement becomes even blacker, and the currently used reflectorized paint loses most of its unique properties. The film of water prevents rays, which approach at grazing incidence, from penetrating to the pavement. The water defocuses the glass beads used in the reflectorized paint destroying their reflective ability. Hence at the time when headlight output is less due to dirt and rain drops, and cause more glare to oncoming motorists, the blacktop itself and its markings are significantly less visible.

On the other hand, the glossy surface reflectance when pavements are wet effectively extends the headlight range! Objects placed in the roadway may be illuminated at greater than dry weather conditions due to the pavement reflecting light like a mirror. Water reflectance is demonstrated by the red light reflected from the pavement as you approach a reflectorized stop sign at night!

Your headlights are reflected up to the sign, and the sign sends the light back in the direction from which it came. Thus the pavement glows red.

The motorist's ability to localize his own vehicle properly in his own lane is seriously impaired because of the loss of wet pavement edge detail, and because of the rain droplets in the atmosphere. The amount of obscuration is not dependent on the size of the droplets, but on the number falling on a unit of area in one second (Middleton, 1958). Thus obscuration depends upon the number of drops per unit volume of air at any given instant.

The combination effect on vision of drop obscuration in the atmosphere, water splatter on the windshield, and back scatter of light from the headlights by water drops in the air, results in a seeing condition that is unusually poor and hazardous in the rain at night.

B. Improper use of reflectors

The retroreflector, composed of internally reflecting cube corner prisms is an efficient practical means for alerting a motorist to its presence. Placed on automobiles, bicycles, trucks, trains, and pedestrians, these reflectors can be seen three to ten times farther away than unreflectorized objects. However, a retroreflector is just a spot of light in a field of blackness until the motorist is near enough to have his headlights reveal the nature of the object supporting the reflector. To aid in quick identification, reflectors placed on the rear of vehicles are red (except for reflectorized license plates) and those near the front are amber. To identify the type of vehicle or even where it is, requires the motorist to approach close enough for head lighting to reveal the details. The goal of marking a vehicle by reflectors is to provide a passive system at night that always reveals its presence and location.

Unfortunately, things do not work so well in practice because of a general lack of understanding of and how to use them. For example, nonhazardous driveways along a roadway are often marked with red reflectors, while bridge abutments within inches of high-speed traffic, even on new interstate highways, may not be reflectorized. A person may wish to identify his own driveway, and he should be permitted to do so, but not with red, which is supposed to mean danger.

Another example are the highway delineators, retroreflectors on top of four foot posts parallel to the edge of the roadway. The retroreflector color is normally white, with amber being used to mark exit ramps on divided highways, thus duplicating the reflector color on the front of an automobile or truck. Since the eye level of the driver of a modern automobile rarely exceeds forty-eight inches, most motorists must look up to see these reflectors.

If the road curves, the motorist can see the curve only by the apparent changes in reflector spacing and by the fact that the reflectors that are the farthest away are the dimmest. The normally powerful perspective cues to space are completely missing, or are reversed, if the reflectors are at or above the driver's eye level. At 48 inches in height the reflectors are in a less intense portion of the headlight beam pattern and hence cannot reflect much light.

The ideal location for such reflectors is attached to the pavement surface at the edge of the highway. If they must be moved back into the grass they should be placed within twelve inches of the ground. Perhaps the four-foot post is needed to prevent a mower from striking it, but the reflectors should be near the bottom. The presence of these delineator posts is an unnecessary obstruction. They are often struck, generally provide no useful information, and the reflectors divert the eyes from the road and are often deceptive. To ensure their low visibility, the posts themselves are usually painted a camouflaging green!

Reflectors placed on trucks and on slow moving vehicles are too high for accurate localization on the highway by perspective clues. In fact, on trucks the high placement and the narrow spacing of lights and reflectors, plus the dirt may deceive even the sophisticated motorist into believing that a slow moving truck is far away when in reality a collision may be imminent. Many rear-end accident drivers show little or no effort to brake prior to collision, and in many instances the motorist has actually left the highway, following the lights of a parked vehicle to collide with it.

One early morning on a four-lane divided highway, I saw two cars side by side about 600 feet ahead of me. I wondered which one I should get behind as I was gaining on them. Several seconds later I asked myself again which one I should follow. I was now about 300 feet behind them. As I studied these cars, I began to see something in the upper part of my windshield. It was the back of an unreflectorized truck about 90 feet away (instead of 300 feet away) and moving slowly. I only had time to swerve! I shook for 15 minutes! There were two taillights on the left of the truck and two on the right. Each pair appeared to me to be a car far down the highway! White mud guards and strip reflectors outlining the back of the truck would have solved this perceptual problem.

There are two classes of retroreflectors used on automotive equipment. Class A retroreflectors are defined by their light output distribution and intensity, which are given in Table 9.1

The *entrance angle* is the angle formed by the incident light beam with the normal to the surface of the reflective device, e.g., a sign or license plate; or from

Table 9.1

Minimum Candlepower per Incident Foot Candle for Class A Red Reflex Reflector

Observation	Entrance Angles, Degrees				
Angle, Degrees	0	10 Up	10 Down	20 left	20 Right
0.2	4.5	3.0	3.0	1.5	1.5
1.5	0.07	0.05	0.05	0.03	0.06

the optic axis, e.g., a taillight lens with integral retroreflector.

The *observation (divergence)* angle is the angle formed by the observer's line of sight and the illuminating beam where these two lines intersect at the reflector.

A Class B retroreflector must meet the requirements shown in Table 9.2.

The usual size for the Class A and B reflectors is four inches in diameter. Thus, the candlepower per square foot of reflector surface is quite high (12.6 times greater than the values given for the four-inch size). Even though the Class A reflector has a very high light returning ability, it does this only along the axis or normal to the surface. At 20 degrees off axis the light returned is down to one-third. Hence for wide angle usage as on the sides of automobiles the Class A reflector must be redesigned. Reflective sheeting, on the other hand, is composed of imbedded glass spheres instead of internally reflecting prisms and has as its great virtue a high efficiency at a large entrance angle.

Table 9.3 permits comparisons of reflective sheeting of various colors and efficiencies with cube corner Class A reflectors. In Table 9.3, candle power per foot candle per square foot is a measure of the efficiency of the reflector under certain standard conditions such as a divergence angle of 0.5 degree with an incidence angle of −4 degrees or +30 degrees, as used in retroreflective license plate testing.

The following formula gives the essential relationships:

$$CP_R = \frac{I_R d^2}{I_E A}$$

CP_R is the candle power of the reflector, I_R is the illumination falling on the plane of the reflector in foot candles, d is the distance between the source of illumination and the reflector, I_E is the illumination falling on the eye or the photo detector in foot candles returned from the reflector, and A is the area of the reflector in square feet.

The Federal Motor Vehicle Safety Standards (U.S. Department of Transportation, 1968) called for Class A retroreflectors for rear application and Class A

Table 9.2

Minimum Candlepower per Incident Foot Candle for Class B Red Reflex Reflector

Observation	Entrance Angles, Degrees				
Angle, Degrees	0	10 Up	10 Down	20 left	20 Right
0.2	0.50	0.40	0.40	0.20	0.20
1.5	0.01	0.01	0.01	0.01	0.01

TABLE 9-3
COMPARATIVE BRIGHTNESS OF 3M SCOTCHLITE BRAND SHEETING AND CUBE-CORNER REFLECTORS
(candle power per foot-candle per square foot)

Incidence Angle Degree	*Divergence Angle Degree*	*3070 (3M) White*	*3170 (3M) White*	*3270 (3M) Silver*	*3870 (3M) Silver*	*3M Signal Del. Silver*	*SAE Class A Cube Corner (White)*	*3171 (3M) Yellow*	*3271 (3M) Yellow*	*3274 (3M) Orange*	*3870 Type Amber (3M)*	*3M Signal Del. Amber*	*SAE Class B Cube Corner (Amber)*	*3272 (3M) Red*	*3870 Type Red (3M)*	*3M Signal Red*	*SAE Class A Cube Corner (Red)*
−4	0.2	30	45	60	155	187	224	25	30	16	60	112	140	12.5	30	56	56
+10	0.2			55		180	144		25	15		108	90	11.5		54	36
+15	0.2			50	100				25	13.5	42			10.5	21		
+20	0.2			40		173	72		20	11		104	45	8.5		52	18
+30	0.2			25	50	144			15	7	17	86		5.5	8.5	43	
+40	0.2	7.0	7.5	12.5	25	72		5.5	6.0	2.8		43		1.9		21	
+45	0.2			5.0	10				4.0	2.5	6			1.5	3.0		
+50	0.2			3.5					2.5	1.2				0.9			
−4	0.5	18	23	25	65	72		12.5	15	8	20	43		6.5	10	21	
+10	0.5			25		72			14	7.5		43		6.0		21	
+15	0.5			25	50				12	6.5	17			5.5	8.5		
+20	0.5			20		65			10	5.5		39		4.5		19	
+30	0.5			15	25	50			8	3.5	10	30		3.0	5.0	15	
+40	0.5	4.5	5.0	7.5	15	29		3.0	4	2.0		17		1.2		8.5	
+45	0.5			3.5	5.0				2.8	1.2	2.5			1.0	1.2		
+50	0.5			3.0					1.5	0.5				0.4			
−4	1.5	2.5	3.0	4.0	8		3.4	2.0	2.5	1.2			2.1	1.0			.84
+10	1.5			3.5			2.4		2.5	1.1			1.5	0.9			.60
+15	1.5			3.0					2.5	1.0				0.8			
+20	1.5			2.5			1.4		2.3	0.8			0.9	0.7			.36
+30	1.5			2.0					1.8	0.5				0.5			
+40	1.5	1.5	1.5	1.6	2.0			0.8	0.9	0.4				0.4			
+45	1.5			1.1					0.8	0.2				0.1			
+50	1.5			1.1					0.5	0.1				0.1			

retroreflectors or reflective sheeting for side markers. More recent standards require that truck trailers be outline reflectorized both on the sides and the rear. This is important safety improvement is beginning to be seen on trucks.

Highway reflectorized paint is a different problem, as will be seen in Figure 9.3. This figure details the role played by the left and right headlights in the typical automobile at the upper limit of the low beam head lamps. Since the 300 feet is not to scale with the height and spacing of the lamps, the angles are not true;

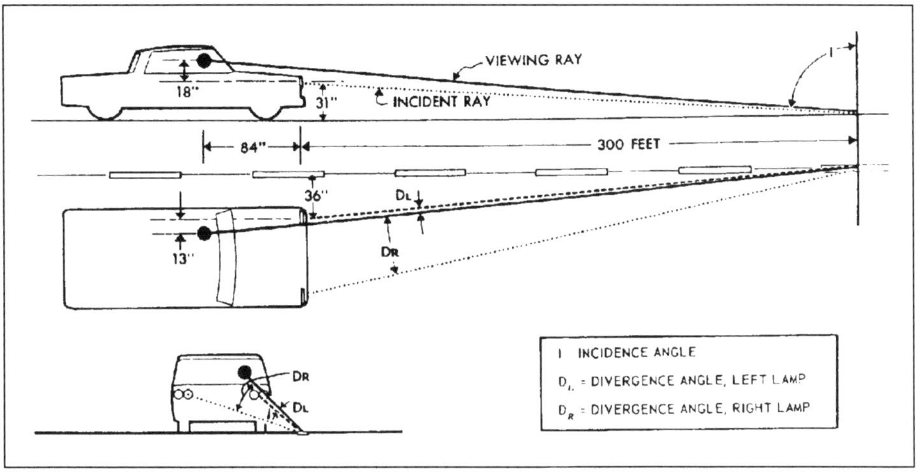

Figure 9.3 *Relationship between driver, head lamps, and pavement marking. Geometry involved in reflectivity from center line point at 300 feet distance, using representative dimensions for a dual head lamp vehicle. (From Harrington et al., 1962.)*

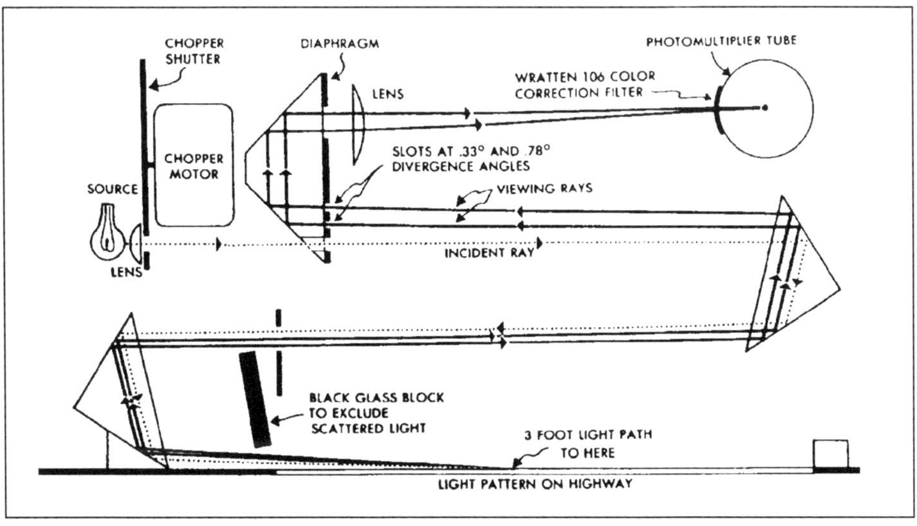

Figure 9.4 *Principal components of pavement marking photometer optical system. (From Harrington et al., 1962.)*

however, they do indicate the grazing nature of the illuminating and viewing rays. Such tiny angles make the measurement especially difficult.

Figure 9.4 shows the optics of a portable pavement-marking photometer built by the 3M Company. Note the folded light path needed to make the optical path long enough to permit reasonable aperture spacing to provide the 0.35 degree and 0.78 degree angles between the incident and view rays.

Figure 9.5 gives the aging characteristics of three different beaded paint stripes exposed to highway traffic as measured by the 3M instrument and the Hunter Night Visibility Meter, a fairly widely used instrument. Paint reflectance varies as beads wear away and new beads are exposed, which is not necessarily a linear effect.

A different device has been employed by the author to make paint stripe measurements. It uses the highly versatile Pritchard Spectrophotometer (Photo Research Corporation) as a photo detector and an automobile bulb as a light source. The optics are similar to those in a retinoscope. They are cheap, rugged, and self-aligning.

C. Pedestrians: A double hazard and a double right

A pedestrian has the right to be protected from careless motorists. Similarly, a motorist has a right to be protected from careless pedestrians. That headlights at

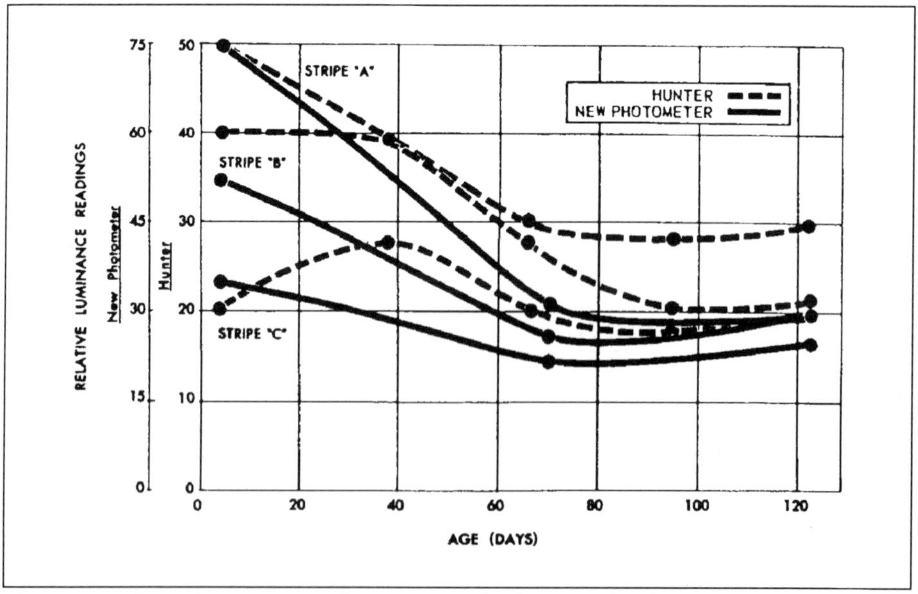

Figure 9.5 *Relative luminance readings vs. age of reflectorized highway paint. Comparison of reflectorized transverse test stripes for three representative 1.5 index beaded markings as measured by the Hunter and the new photometer. (Wisconsin Highway Department annual performance test stripes.) (From Harrington et al., 1962.)*

night do provide the pedestrian with warning of an approaching automobile as well as helping the motorist is indicated by the report of a 14.1 percent drop in pedestrian vehicle accidents after the change over was made to low beam headlights instead of parking lights within the New York City limits on February 4, 1952.

Unfortunately, the motorist usually has no warning of the presence of a pedestrian because of the normal low reflectivity of clothing. An illustration of the difficulty is the following incident which occurred early in our testing of pedestrian visibility. The experimenters found that cardboard boxes, spray painted black, were visible at considerable distances because of surface reflections.

To evaluate quickly the visibility of cloth, one of the graduate students volunteered to stand in the roadway, while a second student approached in an automobile at 20 miles per hour. The plan was to stop as soon as the driver saw the pedestrian's dark clothing. The pedestrian stood in line with the driver's side of the approaching car and waited, anticipating the driver's stop. It finally became necessary to leap out of the way as the car continued down the road at 20 miles per hour. When the driver returned to the pedestrian's location, he asked, "Where were you?" A simple question indeed, but one of great significance. Keep in mind the slow speed, the motorist's sure knowledge that a pedestrian was out there, the absence of glare, and the driver's ready to stop attitude.

In the nighttime pedestrian accident reports on record in the Indiana Department of Motor Vehicles for 1966, 87 percent of the drivers whose automobile struck a pedestrian at night claimed difficulty in seeing the pedestrian, while only 11.8 percent made the same claim during the daytime. Furthermore, 23.4 percent of the drivers at night claimed they heard the impact before they saw the pedestrian!

Since the percentage of blood alcohol is higher among dead pedestrians than among the population at risk at the same location as the accident (Haddon et al., 1961; Indiana University, 1964), pedestrians obviously are not always able to avoid an automobile even though headlights do offer a warning. The motorist

Table 9.4

Miles Per Hour	Critical Visibility Distance (ft.)
20	45
30	72
40	123
50	185
60	261
70	349
80	450

also deserves some warning sign to help protect the pedestrian and to protect himself. There are signs that announce a curve ahead, road repairs in progress, a dead end, or a stop sign, but the sign that flashes only when a pedestrian is present has not yet been invented.

Table 9.4 gives the reaction distance plus the stopping distance, called critical visibility distance, for an automobile with safe tires and brakes, traveling on dry pavement and driven by an individual with an assumed reaction time of 0.75 seconds.

Table 9.5 indicates the percentage of pedestrians that were detected by four sober researchers at distances equal to or greater than the critical visibility distance based on a 0.75 second response time instead of the 1.64 to 2.5 seconds needed for 50 to 90 percent of the people actually driving on our streets and highways (AASHTO). The pedestrian was a tall cardboard box, 1 foot by 1 foot by 4 feet, covered with cloth. The cloth reflectances were: black 9 percent; gray 16 percent; white 75 percent; and reflectorized tape, 1 inch by 12 inches, reflecting 50 candles per square foot per foot candle of illumination. The black cloth pedestrian was the least visible while the reflectorized pedestrian was the most visible.

Table 9.6 shows the adverse effect of alcohol (.06 percent to 0.10 percent) on the driver's ability to detect these targets. Except for the black cloth pedestrian at 20 miles per hour, the detection of all pedestrian targets was reduced by

Table 9.5

Percent Targets Detected Sober

	Miles per hour						
	20	**30**	**40**	**50**	**60**	**70**	**80**
Black P	86.4%	68.2%	45.4%	15.9%	0%	0%	0%
Gray P	100	100	47.2	13.9	5.5	5.5	0
White P	100	100	100	100	97.2	91.7	52.7
Reflectorized P	100	100	100	100	100	100	100

Table 9.6

Percent Targets Detected Alcohol

	Miles per hour						
	20	**30**	**40**	**50**	**60**	**70**	**80**
Black P	90.8%	63.6%	15.2%	0%	0%	0%	0%
Gray P	97.2	73.2	14.2	2.7	0	0	0
White P	100	100	94.4	88.9	80.5	61.1	25
Reflectorized P	100	100	100	100	100	100	94.5

alcohol. If AASHTO's 1.64 or 2.5 seconds response times had been used instead of 0.75, the ability to detect all targets would have dropped dramatically, sober or intoxicated. Had there been oncoming headlight glare, the detection rate would have been still further reduced. Keep in mind that a 97 percent probability of seeing 100 pedestrians still leaves 3 that were not.

The message is clear. The pedestrian must never depend on the oncoming driver to see him/her. White clothes, reflective material and a flash light should be standard for night time wear on streets and roadways. The pedestrian should always walk facing oncoming traffic to improve self protection.

Since men traditionally wear dark clothing, and since twice as many men are killed as women, who tend to dress more colorful, clothing appears to be a factor in accident statistics. However, more men are at risk than women, and such a conclusion is somewhat speculative. Certainly the pedestrian should be on guard at all times, and avoid trusting the oncoming driver to stop or turn.

Tables 9.5 and 9.6 show the remarkable benefit from a 1 by 12-inch piece of cloth, factory treated with reflective beads. The cloth appears silver gray to a driver until lighted by his headlights, then it appears to glow brightly. Pedestrian protection also could be provided by using reflectorized buttons, shoes and dangle tags.

Though not available, the motorist who has just been demoted to pedestrian status by a flat tire, could obtain increased visibility at night by using a side lamp directed to light the ground around the vehicle. About 1928, L. D. Bridge was issued a patent on a Safety Side Light to assist people entering and leaving an automobile. It provided considerable light for tire repairs, for illuminating the pedestrian, for localization of the vehicle, for entering driveways, and even was of some benefit in fogs. These lights were not adopted for passenger automobiles, though some manufacturers have a turn light that resembles the original Bridge light.

In 1928, Charles A. Sims invented the Sims Side Lamp (see Figure 9.6). His announcement began, "The Sims Side Lamp. At Last! After thousands have sacrificed their lives, after science has dug deep, and industry spent fortunes, a simple idea solves the glaring headlight trouble." His idea was never taken up by the auto industry, either. Decisions about head lighting were made, but they were for the high low beam headlight system we have today.

Without knowledge of the work of these early inventors, the author proposed a side light system (Allen, October 1962) to light the way for the oncoming driver. This involved lights in a number of positions, including the top of the car. The most efficient was at bumper height, aimed backward to light the pavement adjacent to the test vehicle. Figure 9.7 shows lights mounted on the front bumper on each side. The rear fender behind the rear wheel is probably the optimum place

Figure 9.6 *Side lamps for aiding oncoming motorist, patented by Charles Sims, January 10, 1928. Mr. Sims described the intended method of operation as follows: "As shown above when two cars approach each other the operators switch off their front lights entirely, and automatically switch on the side lights which illuminates the roadway for each other. Instead of shooting the light at each other, you reverse it and shoot it from each other. It's done instantly without vibration or flickering, no refocusing of the eyes to penetrate a different degree of light or darkness. You are still looking after the light and not into it." (Taken from materials describing the Sims patent, with permission.)*

to set the light into the body work. The light on the right side is of some benefit, but practical considerations might limit the system only to the lights at the left rear. Figures 9.8 and 9.9 show the benefits of the system in overcoming the glare of oncoming automobiles.

The idea for such a system came from using the light spilled laterally across the road by automobile headlights. Earlier headlight design and wrap around fenders eliminated this weak but valuable clue. In fact, the shielding of head and taillights from side view prompted the General Services Administration and later the Department of Transportation to require both side marker lights and reflectors on all new passenger cars, trucks, and buses by 1970.

Considerable experience was gained using the side light system shown in Figure 9.7. Twenty automobiles were equipped and sent out on a quiet highway in a caravan. Motion pictures were taken of the effects of meeting, passing, and following such vehicles. The results were considered to be highly favorable. The system was recommended as a means of providing glare free illumination on the

Figure 9.7 *Backward aimed headlights to aid the oncoming driver. A 5.5-inch sealed-beam headlight was mounted on the front bumper at each side. These lights were aimed backward as shown. The lower and more nearly straight back they were placed, the better they lighted the pavement for the oncoming driver.*

Figure 9.8 *Unseen pedestrians stand on the pavement beside four approaching cars on low beams. The camera car's low beams do not reveal the presence of the hazard.*

Figure 9.9 *Silhouette and direct lighting provided by side lights. The three pedestrians now become visible. Note the increased size of the field of view compared to Figure 9.8. The driver of a side-lighted automobile finds the increase in peripheral field of view a help in maintaining orientation and alertness.*

streets and highways which increases as traffic increases and does not require the cost and upkeep of extensive stationary highway lighting.

This is not a proposal to do away with conventional highway lighting or the very high mounted lighting advocated by the Texas Transportation Institute, but such lighting can never be everywhere or enough. The side lighting would provide ambient light when needed to reveal pedestrians and other road hazards. It would be turned off automatically when no cars were present. The lone motorist operating on high beams would be reasonably able to see hazards if speeds were not excessive. As soon as the driver dropped to low beams because of other automobiles, the side lights would come on to help oncoming motorists; at the same time the approaching motorists' side lights would come on when they dimmed their lights.

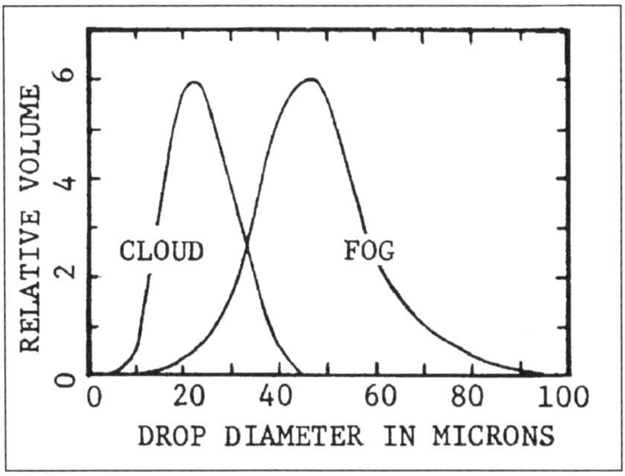

Figure 9.10 Typical drop size distributions for a coastal fog and for a cloud (mountain fog). The curves are plotted to show how the liquid water is distributed (by volume) among the various drop sizes. (After Houghton [1939], from Middleton [1958], Figure 3.18.)

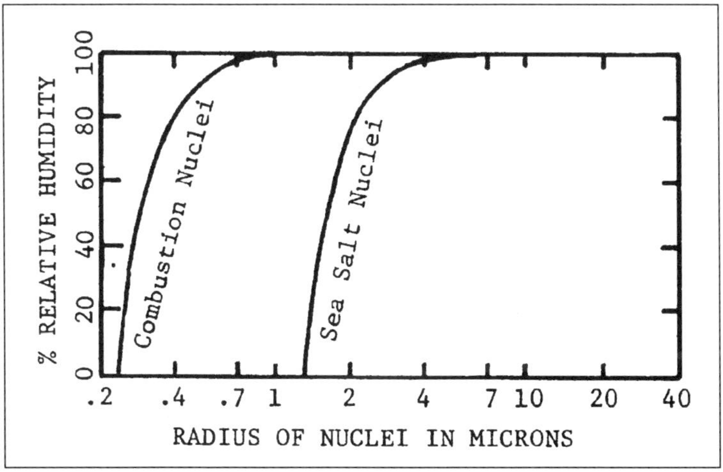

Figure 9.11 Variations in the radius of combustion nuclei and sea salt nuclei with relative humidity. (After Wright [1939], from Middleton, [1958], Figure 3.1)

D. Rain and fog hazards

Water particles between 2 and 100 microns are found in fog. Figure 9.10 shows that for practical purposes fog is not found with particle sizes less than about 10 microns, and this only in clouds. Particles below 2 microns produce haze. Water particles do not exist below about 0.2 microns, as seen in Figure 9.11.

Fog and cloud particles scatter visible light uniformly without regard to wavelength. Even haze does not scatter blue and green much more than red. Rayleigh's theory of light scatter leads to the following equation, where S is the total scattered light from a unit of illumination of wavelength λ, n is the refractive index, and V is the volume of the particle.

$$S = 24\pi^2\left[\left(\frac{n^2 - 1}{n^2 + 2}\right)\frac{V^2}{\lambda^4}\right]$$

Table 9.7, derived from Rayleigh's theory, gives the relative amounts of scattering by clean dry air at 1013.2 millibar pressure and 0 degrees Centigrade temperature for each wavelength in nanometers.

Rayleigh scatter holds for spherical particles up to 0.1 wavelength. As the particle sizes increase, the scattering function becomes more complex; and for certain particle sizes it is possible to have even more red scatter than blue. However, in general, clean atmospheric transmission favors the longer wavelengths. The table above shows that for automobile travel this is probably of no significance because the range usually involved is less than a half mile (800 meters).

The smallest cloud particles are encountered in stratus clouds which average 4 microns, with cumulus clouds averaging 5 microns and nimbostratus 10 microns, (Middleton, 1958). These sizes are significantly larger than the 0.55 micron wavelength of visible light; hence selective absorption of various wavelengths is practically non existent. Certainly, the average ground fog with particle sizes from 15 to 100 microns will act impartially upon all visible wavelengths.

Thus, automobile fog light color has no scientific basis, and the superior performance claimed for fog lights must result from secondary factors such as the narrow beam spread and remote location of the beam away from the line of sight. Similarly, arguments as to the benefits or disadvantages of one color over another in penetrating fog or rain have no substance for automobile signal sys-

Table 9.7

λ wavelength	400	500	600	700
Relative scatter	4.358	1.750	0.833	0.466
Loss at 800 meters	3.2%	1.4%	0.67%	0.361%

tems. A proper signal system can be chosen only after evaluating the physiological, psychological, and systems aspects of the driving problem.

Daytime fog is dangerous for driving because it scatters, or attenuates the useful light coming from the object, and substitutes random light from elsewhere. This reduces the contrast of the object without changing the sharpness of its borders. Increasing distance increases the attenuation of the useful light and increases the veiling light added. The attenuation function is that of any filter; that is, a percentage is lost per unit of distance the light travels. The veiling effect, however, makes the daytime seeing evaluation somewhat more complex, while the nighttime situation involving headlights is even more complex.

Without nearby headlights, an automobile's headlights or taillights can be seen at a considerable distance in fog, because, no matter how dense the fog, theoretically some light will get through to the observer.

If the intervening fog is illuminated by one's own headlights, the amount of light coming through the fog from the oncoming automobile must exceed the just noticeable brightness difference at the level of illumination caused by one's own lights. Of course, as fog density goes up, the greater is the nearby fog illumination from one's own lights and the smaller is the amount of light penetrating through the fog from the oncoming car.

Table 9.8
Atmospheric Transmission

Code No.	Weather	Maximum Daylight Visual Range (ft.)	Maximum % Transmission at Ranges Indicated. 3280 Ft	1640 Ft	820 Ft	410 Ft	205 Ft	102 Ft
0	Dense fog	164				1×10^{-6}	0.1	3
1	Thick fog	658	32×10^{-8}	.005	.71	8.41	29	54
2	Moderate fog	1640	.004	0.63	7.9	28	53	72
3	Light fog	3280	2	14	37.5	61	78	88
4	Thin fog	6560	14	37.5	61	78	88	94
5	Haze	26,240	37	61	78	88	94	96
6	Light Haze	32,800	68	82	91	95	98	
7	Clear	65,600	82	91	95	98		
8	Very clear	164,000	93	96	98			
9	Extra clear	164,000+	93+					

Data adapted from *Illuminating Engineering Society Hanbook*, 1952, pp. 9–44.

The classification of fog is difficult, but Table 9.8 provides an operational definition of the several subjective terms that are often used. The daylight visual range is for the detection of dark objects about the size of an automobile as seen against a light background. The atmospheric transmission is given for each type of fog for various distances and would be useful in calculating the range at which a light could be seen through fog, assuming that the minimum contrast for detection between the light and its background needs to be 4 percent or more.

The visibility of roadway details falls off more quickly than is the case for light sources. The following analogy will illustrate the principles involved. If one looks through a handkerchief held very near to the eyes he/she will be able to see large objects, but will have lost the ability to see detail. The white cloth transmits some light from the objects, but it also is itself an object, brightly illuminated by the ambient light. Now consider that the room is dark and that the objects you are trying to see are illuminated only by the light that has penetrated the handkerchief from a flashlight you hold in your hand. The handkerchief is equivalent to an impenetrable "fog" and you must change it to something like a nylon stocking of loose mesh, to pass enough light to be able to see through to the objects. If you hold the flashlight beyond the handkerchief or stocking so it illuminates the objects directly, without illuminating the cloth, visibility will be improved.

Thus, a fog light should illuminate no fog between the driver's eye and the object viewed. However, in practice, secondary scattering from fog particle to fog particle, and limitations as to where lights can be placed on the car, limit the performance of fog lights. To achieve the best possible vision in fog, the fog lamp should be low and to the extreme right corner of the vehicle away from the driver. The lamp should produce a concentrated beam with no upward scatter above the horizontal. In effect, it should be in a tube about two feet long to eliminate all spill light that could illuminate the fog particles in front of the driver's eyes.

E. Railroad crossings

Railroad crossings are a significant hazard. The Department of Transportation (DOT, 1968) reports as follows:

> Of the 3,932 crossing accidents of all kinds in 1967, 3,733 involved collisions between railroad movements and motor vehicles and resulted in 1520 deaths and 3,726 injuries. In 2,456 collisions, 65.79 percent, trains struck motor vehicles, resulting in 1,158, or 76.18 percent, of the deaths and in 2, 218, or 59.53 percent, of the injuries. In the other 1,277 collisions, 34.21 percent, motor vehicles struck the sides of train movements, resulting in 362, or 23.82 percent, of the deaths and in 1,508, or 40.47 percent, of the injuries.

> Of the 3,733 collisions, 1,617, or 43.32 percent, occurred at crossings which were especially protected by one of the following: lowered gates, train man, watchman, audible and visual signals, audible signals, or visible signals. The other 2,116, or 56.68 percent, occurred at crossings protected by signals or signs that did not indicate the approach of trains.
>
> The latest available statistics show a total of 214,417 rail highway crossings at grade. Of these crossings, 44,432 or 20.72 percent, were specially protected; 169,985, or 79.28 percent, were not specially protected.
>
> Of the 3,733 crossing collisions, 2,273, or 60.89 percent, occurred in daylight, and 1,460, or 39.11 percent, took place at night. There were 2,564 collisions, or 68.68 percent, in clear weather, and 1,169, or 31.32 percent, under cloudy or inclement weather conditions.
>
> Of the 3,733 collisions between trains and motor vehicles, automobiles were involved in 2,906, or 77.85 percent; busses in 11, or 0.29 percent; motor trucks in 780, or 20.89 percent, and motorcycles in 36, or 0.96 percent.

Very little modern technology has crept into railroading if the signals at 79.28 percent of the intersections are any criterion. At most crossings the only signal present is the typical railroad cross buck. Often only one is present and in design, color, and size of lettering is just as it was years ago. Nevertheless about $190 million per year was spent on railway crossings from 1963 to 1967 (Insurance Institute for Highway Safety, 1970).

In the past the railroads have lost few lawsuits and have been slow to make improvements. This is partly because accidents at a particular crossing are infrequent, and partly because it is difficult to convince a jury that a train can be unnecessarily difficult to see and hear. Of course, failure to provide locomotives and rolling stock with maximum visibility paints, reflectors, and lights, as well as failure to keep signs and signals in top condition, can be considered to be contributory negligence in many accidents. Because families and friends of motorists who have died in train accidents have not been able to organize effectively to loudly express their righteous indignation, we continue to live with the hazard.

A law suit in Kalamazoo, Michigan in which the railroad lost, and in which I testified, resulted in an increase in brightness of all railroad red signal lights across America.

Some railroads are incorporating lights mounted low on the front of the locomotive to help the engineer see land slides across the tracks. These improve locomotive visibility to motorists. The 275,000 candle power high mounted headlight on locomotives is used as a defense in court by the railroads. It is little realized that such brightness is only in the central ±5 degrees of the beam which is high above the driver and aimed to light the tracks.

The problem is manifold. (1) On the average the accident probability at a crossing is one every ten years (Schoppert et al., 1968), or so infrequently that it does not seem to be a problem to the local citizens. (2) A fast train on a collision course with an automobile must be looked for at angles ranging from 45 to 90 degrees from straight ahead or, for the most part, must be looked for through the side windows. (3) Trains provide their bulk above the line of sight, so that for a slow or stopped train it is often possible to view a seemingly unobstructed roadway beneath a railroad car, especially at night. (4) Trains are usually not painted in bright colors, are not reflectorized, are not lighted, and are not clean. (5) The active as well as the passive railroad crossing signals are archaic and hence not ideally designed to use all the clues of spatial localization, attention getting, maximum visibility, and signal information free of ambiguity.

Every railroad crossing could be signalized by using a strobe light on the locomotive and freight cars. They would greatly increase the conspicuity of the train and would light the trees and houses to alert the motorist. Strobes were being used for several years but were abandoned by the railroads in spite of strong supportive data. Apparently the Union Workers objected.

The evidence is that modern technology is ignored by the railroads. The railroad bureaucrats seem to believe that all accidents are due to the "nut behind the wheel." Abandoning the strobe flasher widely used elsewhere, is but one example. A second is that laser technology seems to have escaped them. A laser beam in each locomotive aimed at reflectors placed at each crossing would signalize all intersections across America with high intensity, high conspicuity flashing light, that would come on only when a train was coming. This laser system would cost only a tiny fraction of the archaic signal system now in use by the railroads.

We need the railroads! Let's help them figure out how to stop killing people. When an accident occurs, talk to the news media about it. This will help attract the attention of local citizens and of the railroad.

F. Trucks

Trucks on the streets and highways represent a special hazard to passenger automobile drivers because of their poor visibility. This is another instance of virtual protection or immunity being extended to trucks because of their economic importance and legislative lobbying ability. No lobby of the relatives of the dead is present in the legislative halls to counter truck lobbies. Part of their immunity comes from law. It is a fact that the vehicle striking the rear of another vehicle is held to be at fault automatically unless partially relieved of that fault by contributory negligence on the part of the struck vehicle. So long as the inadequate Interstate Commerce Commission requirements for lights and reflectors on trucks are adhered to, the stopped or slow moving truck is not held to be contributory, and hence there is little incentive to improve the visibility of trucks. Such protection also leads to inadequate under run protection, which leads to a high fatality rate for car truck collisions. Since there are fewer survivors of collisions with the rear or side of a truck compared to other types of collisions, because the passenger vehicle runs under the frame of the truck and shears off the top, the insurance or court proceedings are simpler and the amount of damages claimed are usually less.

Truckers operate their vehicles under the rules of the Interstate Commerce Commission, which seems to work closely with industry to set so called "realistic" standards, including those for vehicle lighting. That these standards might pose a hazard to passenger vehicles is difficult to prove in a court of law trying to assess who is to blame in a particular accident. Judges and juries are not naturally aware of highway and vehicle design deficiencies and are likely to assume that meeting federal regulations provides the best that there is. Though federal

Table 9.9

Originals from National Highway Traffic Safety Administration, DOT 49 CFR Ch. V (10–1–98 Edition)

TABLE I—REQUIRED MOTOR VEHICLE LIGHTING EQUIPMENT OTHER THAN HEADLAMPS

Multipurpose Passenger Vehicles, Trucks, Trailers, and Buses, of 80 or More Inches Overall Width

Item	Multipurpose passenger vehicles, trucks, and buses	Trailers	Applicable SAE standard or recommended practice (See S5 for subreferenced SAE materials)
Taillamps	2 red	2 red	J585e, September 1977.
Stoplamps	2 red	2 red	SAE J1398, May 1985.
License plate lamp	1 white	1 white	J587 October 1981.
Reflex reflectors	4 red; 2 amber	4 red; 2 amber	J594f, January 1977.
Side marker lamps	2 red; 2 amber	2 red; 2 amber	J592e, July 1972.
Backup lamp	1 white	None	J593c, February 1968.
Turn signal lamps	2 red or amber; 2 amber	2 red or amber	SAE J1395, April 1985.
Turn signal operating unit	1	None	J589, April 1964.
Turn signal flasher	1	None	J590b, October 1965.
Vehicular hazard warning signal operating unit.	1	None	J910, January 1966.
Vehicular hazard warning signal flasher..	1	None	J945, February 1966.
Identification lamps	3 amber; 3 red	3 red	J592e, July 1972.
Clearance lamps	2 amber; 2 red	2 amber, 2 red	J592e, July 1972.
Intermediate side marker lamps.	2 amber	2 amber	J592e, July 1972.
Intermediate side reflex reflectors.	2 amber	2 amber	J594f, January 1977.
Conspicuity	See S5.7	See S5.7	See S5.7

Table 9.10

Originals from National Highway Traffic Safety Administration, DOT 49 CFR Ch. V (10–1–98 Edition)

Table II—Location of Required Equipment

Multipurpose Passenger Vehicles, Trucks, Trailers, and Buses, of 80 or More Inches Overall Width

Item	Location on—		Height above road surface measured from center of item on vehicle at curb weight
	Multipurpose passenger vehicles, trucks, and buses	Trailers	
Headlamps	On the front, each headlamp providing the upper beam, at the same height, 1 on each side of the vertical centerline, each headlamp providing the lower beam, at the same height, 1 on each side of the vertical centerline, as far apart as practicable. See also S7.	Not required	Not less than 22 inches (55.9 cm) nor more than 54 inches (137.2 cm).
Taillamps	On the rear, 1 on each side of the vertical centerline, at the same height, and as far apart as practicable.	On the rear, 1 on each side of the vertical centerline, at the same height, and as far apart as practicable.	Not less than 15 inches, nor more than 72 inches.
Stop lamps	......do	......do	Do.
License plate lamp	At rear license plate, to illuminate the plate from the top or sides.	At rear license plate, to illuminate the plate from the top or sides.	No requirement.
Backup lamp	On the rear	Not required	Do.
Turn signal lamps	At or near the front—1 amber on each side of the vertical centerline, at the same height, and as far apart as practicable. On the rear—1 red or amber on each side of the vertical centerline, at the same height, and as far apart as practicable.	On the rear—1 red or amber on each side of the vertical centerline, at the same height, and as far apart as practicable.	Not less than 15 inches, nor more than 83 inches.
Identification lamps	On the front and rear—3 lamps, amber in front, red in rear, as close as practicable to the top of the vehicle, at the same height, as close as practicable to the vertical centerline, with lamp centers spaced not less than 6 inches or more than 12 inches apart. Alternatively, the front lamps may be located as close as practicable to the top of the cab.	On the rear—3 lamps as close as practicable to the top of the vehicle at the same height, as close as practicable to the vertical centerline, with lamp centers spaced not less than 6 inches or more than 12 inches apart.	No requirement.
Clearance lamps	On the front and rear—2 amber lamps on front, 2 red lamps on rear, to indicate the overall width of the vehicle, one on each side of the vertical centerline, at the same height, and as near the top as practicable.	On the front and rear—2 amber lamps on front, 2 red lamps on rear, to indicate the overall width of the vehicle, one on each side of the vertical centerline, at the same height, and as near the top thereof as practicable[2, 3, 4].	Do.
Intermediate side marker lamps.	On each side—1 amber lamp located at or near the midpoint between the front and rear side marker lamps.	On each side—1 amber lamp located at or near the midpoint between the front and rear side marker lamps.	Not less than 15 inches.
Intermediate side reflex reflectors.	On each side—1 amber located at or near the midpoint between the front and rear side reflex reflectors.	On each side—1 amber located at or near the midpoint between the front and rear side reflex reflectors.	Not less than 15 inches nor more than 60 inches.
Conspicuity	See S5.7	See S5.7	See S5.7
Reflex reflectors	On the rear—1 red on each side of the vertical centerline, as far apart as practicable, and at the same height. On each side—1 red as far to the rear as practicable, and 1 amber as far to the front as practicable.	On the rear—1 red on each side of the vertical centerline, as far apart as practicable, and at the same height. On each side—1 red as far to the rear as practicable, and 1 amber as far to the front as practicable.	Do.
Side marker lamps	......do	......do	Not less than 15 inches, and on the rear of trailers not more than 60 inches.

regulations are intended to represent the minimum, they often end up being the maximum in practice.

Federal lighting requirements for 1998 for trucks and trailers of 80 inches or wider are shown in Tables 9.9 through 9.12 (U.S. Department of Transportation, 1998). These standards offer some improvements. For example, two taillights and turn signals are now required on truck tractors instead of the previous one and none respectively. However, significant inconsistencies persist, such as, the amber brake, turn, and hazard warning signals permitted on the rear along with amber park, turn, and hazard warning signals on the front. Retention of other hazardous specifications indicate that more revisions are needed.

Such hazardous specifications include permitting headlights to be as high as 54 inches, when the average eye height of an automobile driver is below 48

Table 9.11

Originals from National Highway Traffic Safety Administration, DOT 49 CFR Ch. V (10–1–98 Edition)

TABLE III—REQUIRED MOTOR VEHICLE LIGHTING EQUIPMENT

All Passenger Cars and Motorcycles, and Multipurpose Passenger Vehicles, Trucks, and Buses, of Less Than 80 Inches Overall Width

Item	Passenger cars, multipurpose passenger vehicles, trucks, and buses	Trailers	Motorcycles	Applicable SAE standard or recommended practice (See S5 for subreferenced SAE materials)
Headlamps	See S7		1 white	For motorcycles only, J584, April 1964, J566, January 1960.
Taillamps	2 red	2 red	1 red	J585e, September 1977.
Stoplamps	2 red	2 red	1 red	SAE J586, February 1984.
High-mounted stoplamp.	1 red	Not required	Not required	J186a, September 1977.
License plate lamp.	1 white	1 white	1 white	J587, October 1981.
Parking lamps	2 amber or white	None	None	J222, December 1970.
Reflex reflectors	4 red; 2 amber	4 red; 2 amber	3 red; 2 amber	J594f, January 1977.
Intermediate side reflex reflectors.	2 amber	2 amber	None	J594f, January 1977.
Intermediate side marker lamps.	2 amber	2 amber	None	J592e, July 1972.
Side marker lamps	2 red; 2 amber	2 red; 2 amber	None	J592e, July 1972.
Backup lamp	1 white	None	None	J593c, February 1968.
Turn signal lamps	2 red or amber; 2 amber	2 red or amber	2 amber; 2 red or amber.	SAE J588, November 1984.
Turn signal operating unit.[3,4]	1	None	1	J589, April 1964.
Turn signal flasher	1	None	1	J590b, October 1965.
Vehicular hazard warning signal operating unit.	1	None	None	J910, January 1966.
Vehicular hazard warning signal flasher.	1	None	None	J945, February 1966.

Table 9.12

Originals from National Highway Traffic Safety Administration, DOT 49 CFR Ch. V (10–1–98 Edition)

TABLE IV—LOCATION OF REQUIRED EQUIPMENT

All Passenger Cars and Motorcycles, and Multipurpose Passenger Vehicles, Trucks, Trailers, and Buses of Less Than 80 Inches Overall Width

Item	Location on—		Height above road surface measured from center of item on vehicle at curb weight
	Passenger cars, multipurpose passenger vehicles, trucks, trailers, and buses	Motorcycles	
Headlamps	On the front, each headlamp providing the upper beam, at the same height, 1 on each side of the vertical centerline, each headlamp providing the lower beam, at the same height, 1 on each side of the vertical centerline, as far apart as practicable. See also S7..	On the front, on the vertical centerline, except that if two are used they shall be symmetrically disposed about the vertical centerline.	Not less than 22 inches (55.9 cm) nor more than 54 inches (137.2 cm).
Taillamps	On the rear—1 on each side of the vertical centerline, at the same height, and as far apart as practicable.	On the rear—on the vertical centerline except that if two are used, they shall be symmetrically disposed about the vertical centerline.	Not less than 15 inches, nor more than 72 inches.
Stoplamps	On the rear—1 on each side of the vertical centerline, at the same height, and as far apart as practicable.	On the rear—on the vertical centerline except that if two are used, they shall be symmetrically disposed about the vertical centerline.	Not less than 15 inches, nor more than 72 inches.
High-mounted stoplamp.	On the rear, on the vertical centerline [See S5.1.1.27, S5.3.1.8, and Table III], effective September 1, 1985, for passenger cars only.	Not required	See S5.3.1.8 for passenger cars. Not less than 34 inches for multipurpose passenger vehicles, trucks, and buses.
License plate lamp	At rear license plate, to illuminate the plate from the top or sides.	At rear license plate	No requirement.
Parking lamps	On the front—1 on each side of the vertical centerline, at the same height, and as far apart as practicable.	Not required	Not less than 15 inches, nor more than 72 inches.
Reflex reflectors	On the rear—1 red on each side of the vertical centerline, at the same height, and as far apart as practicable. On each side—1 red as far to the rear as practicable, and 1 amber as far to the front as practicable.	On the rear—1 red on the vertical centerline except that, if two are used on the rear, they shall be symmetrically disposed about the vertical centerline. On each side—1 red as far to the rear as practicable, and 1 amber as far to the front as practicable.	Not less than 15 inches, nor more than 60 inches.
Backup lamp	On the rear	Not required	No requirement.
Turn signal lamps	At or near the front—1 amber on each side of the vertical centerline, at the same height, and as far apart as practicable. On the rear—1 red or amber on each side of the vertical centerline, at the same height, and as far apart as practicable.	At or near the front—1 amber on each side of the vertical centerline at the same height, and having a minimum horizontal separation distance (centerline of lamps) of 16 inches. Minimum edge to edge separation distance between lamp and headlamp is 4 inches. At or near the rear—1 red or amber on each side of the vertical centerline, at the same height and having a minimum horizontal separation distance (centerline to centerline of lamps) of 9 inches. Minimum edge to edge separation distance between lamp and tail or stop lamp is 4-inches, when a single stop and taillamp is installed on the vertical centerline and the turn signal lamps are red..	No requirement. Not less than 15 inches, nor more than 83 inches.
Side marker lamps	On each side—1 red as far to the rear as practicable, and 1 amber as far to the front as practicable.	Not required	Not less than 15 inches.
Intermediate side marker lamps.	On each side—1 amber located at or near the midpoint between the front and rear side marker lamps.	Not required	Not less than 15 inches.
Intermediate side marker reflectors.	On each side—1 amber located at or near the midpoint between the front and rear side marker reflectors.	Not required	Not less than 15 inches, nor more than 60 inches.

inches; permission to place taillights and stop lights as high as 72 inches above the road; permission to place reflex reflectors as high as 60 inches when automobile head lamps are about 28 inches high and aimed downward; permission to place side marker lamps and turn signal lamps anywhere above 15 inches; and the continued use of identification and clearance lights whose respective purposes have little if anything to contribute to safe operation of the trucking equipment in traffic.

The nature of the remaining hazards becomes clear if one encounters a truck trailer crossing an intersection. The lights at the top are of no value in locating the truck; they might seem to be, for example, on a television antenna tower miles away. The reflectors on the sides are usually dirty and are above the beams of the standard automobile headlight and most truck headlights as well. The side marker lamps have no specified height above 15 inches and most usually are mounted high; hence they are of little utility in localizing the vehicle. Most truck trailers have a high bed permitting unobstructed vision beneath it, especially for those seated in an automobile. Upon seeing the roadway unobstructed, and with the weak ambiguous side lights mounted high overhead, the motorist may be lured into a side collision which will have a high probability of being fatal.

From the rear view the hazard is similar. Closely spaced taillights, as sometimes used, covered with dirt and mounted high, appear to be significantly farther away than they actually are and tend to lure the unwary motorist in too close. If the speed difference is great enough, a collision will result. With his lights on and reflectors in place, the trucker is not legally negligent, but the motorist who died is, even though he couldn't see the truck or misjudged its location and speed. Keeping one's vehicle under control as required by law is one thing, and having a fighting chance to know of the hazard one faces from the low visibility and deceptiveness of modern trucks is another. Motorists should not have to continue to pay with their lives to keep the trucks rolling in their present design condition and thus to save the owners and manufacturers a few dollars. There should be under run guards at passenger vehicle bumper height, and side and rear lights and reflectors at no higher than 15 inches above the pavement, where they can be seen and localized on the roadway. Truck and trailer wheels should be better shielded to reduce road spray and dirt collection. Mud guards as now used are only partially effective.

New regulations require retroreflective materials to outline the side and rear of trucks. This is a step forward. The next step is to move the reflective material down 15 inches above the pavement!

Black should be banned. White tires, white mud guards and a white painted under run protection panel all around the truck should be standard.

G. Black versus white tires

One possible improvement in visibility at very little if any cost would be the use of tires made of white rubber throughout. If this were done, the tire tread against the pavement would provide a gleaming white surface for easy seeing by the motorist as he approaches from the rear. Although the side walls would get dirty, they would be better reflectors than the current black tires now in use.

The benefits in increased visibility for all vehicles would be worthwhile, and especially for trucks. White tire treads would provide localization clues superior to anything we have available today, and their visibility would improve with adverse weather because of their self cleaning properties. So far the tire industry has ignored this safety feature.

H. One to four a.m.

The incidence of fatal one car accidents is extremely high in the early morning hours. The confirmed explanation of this phenomenon is not at hand; however, a look at some of the factors is in order. First is the matter of fatigue and the need for sleep.

One should never drive after his normal bedtime, because about 2 hours after normal bedtime it becomes difficult if not impossible to stay awake. By about two o'clock in the morning one enters a sleep producing driving environment. The traffic on the highway is sparse; therefore the bright points of light from tail and headlights are missing most of the time. All that remains is the dark of the night, with a gradual brightening in the lower field of view as the pavement comes nearer to the headlights. Neither vegetation nor the surface of the pavement can be clearly focused upon because of the low illumination and their steady "movement" as the automobile proceeds. Darkness allows pupil dilation, which tends to cause blurring due to aberrations. Darkness may also allow accommodation to increase, sometimes as much as 1.5 diopters, further blurring the limited detail available. The rapidly reducing strength of the visual stimulation because of increased blurring and lowered illumination is similar to that encountered with the eyes closed, when sleep readily occurs.

A hypnotic effect at night is undoubtedly involved; however, the distinction between a hypnotic trance and real sleep is difficult to make when a subject is unduly fatigued past his bedtime. Alcohol, carbon monoxide (cigarettes and automobile exhaust), and a full stomach are all predisposing factors. Each or all may team up with fatigue, the absence of detail in the roadway scene, and the hypnotic nature of the driving task, and can overcome even the best driver.

The loss of visual control is real. It appears that a nystagmus develops which lowers acuity. This is accompanied by a loss of fusion and an extreme urge to close the eyes. Such danger signs cannot be ignored! On the highway, one should open the window, turn up the radio, turn on the dome light, turn up the dash light, and indulge in singing and isometrics, and stop at the nearest stopping point.

The use of the interior lighting of the vehicle, including brightening the dash panel, is most comforting when driving for long periods at night. Fusion recovers, acuity improves, and the darkness seems literally to be pushed away when it had been in danger of engulfing the tired driver. The fear of destroying dark adaptation by having extra light in the car should be overbalanced by the fear of the complete loss of orientation which occurs with fatigue under low levels of illumination. Actually, dark adaptation to levels lower than the roadway will not occur, and normal interior lighting can have very little effect on the level of adaptation needed for the external scene. The only precaution is to be sure that the dash panel does not reflect into the windshield and that the windshield is clean. Observations indicate a very slight loss of visual range with interior lighting. At the same time vision seems clearer, probably due to a smaller pupil.

A number of ideas to add detail in the outside scene at night have been proposed. Small points of light on posts at the front edges of the hood would provide an ocular focus and would help maintain vehicle and driver orientation. A bright reticule or cross hair, as used in military gun sights, could be optically projected into the roadway, perhaps off the windshield's back surface. Such a target would be excellent for keeping convergence and accommodation under control. However, it would have to have a large aperture of perhaps twelve inches to permit freedom of head movement, and it would be both difficult to install and expensive to build. Nevertheless, plastic Fresnel lens components might provide the breakthrough needed.

The ultimate goal for night driving is more light. Both the Sims side light and the proposed side lighting (see Figure 9.7) supply surround light with a noticeable increase in comfort. Increasing headlight brightness will improve night driving safety.

Of course, the ideal admonition is to avoid driving during the early morning hours if one normally sleeps then. Avoid large meals, alcohol, and smoking (Adams and Belvin, 1966; MacFarland and Moseley, September 1954). Keep lights on bright as much as traffic will allow. If drowsiness seems to be occurring, change body position, change temperature in the car, turn on the radio and the dome light, and slow down five or ten miles per hour; at least do not go faster "to get there sooner." If out of control of your body physiology, stop well off the pavement, at a service station, roadside park, or other protected location. If you stop along the highway, move at least ten feet off the pavement, turn off your headlights, set your emergency four-way flasher into operation, turn off your engine, and take a nap.

The hazard of roadside stopping without the four way flasher is that your normal red taillights may lure another sleepy driver to follow you right off the pavement and collide with you. Above all, do not take a walk on the pavement, because few drivers will be looking out for a pedestrian. Even if they were, the chances are against the pedestrian being seen in time. If the shoulders are muddy, or if the roadway is not wide enough to pull off at least 10 feet, drive carefully until you find a service station or other safe location.

I. Headlight laws

A driver will have trouble seeing oncoming cars against the setting or rising sun, while oncoming drivers will be able to see perfectly well with the sun behind them. However, they should have their headlights on to help them to be seen. Many states require headlights to be turned on by 30 minutes after sunset to thirty 30 before sunrise. Such legislation should be changed to ensure that headlights must be turned on at least one hour before sunset and not turned off sooner than one hour after sunrise, if then. This would require headlights to be on any time the sun is lower than 15 degrees from the horizon. It is hoped that legislators would require headlights to be on all day long.

The use of daytime running lights now being installed in new cars will solve this problem. The only negative is that older cars without daytime headlights will be at still greater risk among the lighted cars.

Certainly, the rule of headlights on 30 minutes after the sun sets and off 30 minutes before the sun rises is archaic and unrealistic for today's driving. Figure 9.10 indicates that motorists themselves find driving without lights after sunset unacceptable. The far north, as in Alaska, has a poorly defined sunset and prolonged poor seeing, hence a safer rule for all states is to have headlights on anytime the engine is running. Since accidents are more frequent in the late afternoon hours and since this time is very difficult for drivers, especially on two-lane free access roads and highways, the motorist would be wise to stop and have a light supper and, if necessary, continue the trip after the sun has set.

9.2 Daytime Hazards

A. Sun and sky glare

On a bright sunny day who would think visibility could be a problem? Yet, as discussed in Chapters 2 and 8, numerous factors degrade vision in the daytime. Accident statistics show clear dry days to be especially hazardous. The most disabling circumstance in the daytime occurs when the sun is in the driver's forward field of view. The nearer it is to the line of sight of the driver, the more disabling. The eye becomes adapted to the high luminance levels. It is hampered by the stray light in the eye and the fact that all hazardous objects on the ground are viewed from their dark or shadowed side. Polished concrete or asphalt pavement may gleam like a ribbon of fire from a low-hanging sun. Seeing people, cars, or even trucks becomes impossible under certain situations and difficult under virtually all situations with a low sun. Nonpolarizing sunglasses make the seeing situation against the sun worse because they reduce the visibility of the already inadequately lighted objects in the field of view. Polarizing sunglasses will reduce pavement glare and windshield reflections and should improve vision.

Sky glare and sun glare usually are efficiently controlled with the sun visor provided in most cars. This has proven to be the most useful device in glare experiments for improving visual performance. Among the many sources of glare, sky glare seems to be as serious or more serious than any other. Reflection from the top of the hood can be distressing if the hood is of light color and highly polished. There are paints which remove the gloss without changing the appearance of the paint. They might be helpful, especially among police and fleet owners.

Reflections from the top of the dash panel off the back side of the windshield are still excessive in all new automobiles. As mentioned before, an adequate solution is a piece of black velveteen cloth draped over the top of the dash. Dirt on the windshield or on spectacles provides an amount of glare proportional to the amount of dirt and direction of the sun. The solution is to clean the spectacles and operate the windshield washer. Don't forget to clean the inside of the windshield.

B. Atmospheric boil

This condition is seen on hot days as a shimmering and unsteadiness of objects at a great distance. The effect is due to shifting of the optical density of the air due to wind and temperature differences. This phenomenon reduces the visual acuity for objects seen outdoors through several hundred feet of atmosphere compared to clinical acuity. The reduction in acuity depends upon the amount of atmosphere between the eyes and the target and the thermal discontinuities in the atmosphere. Under most conditions where highway signs are involved, acuity should not fall very much. However, conditions can vary widely in the atmosphere, and if one needs to know the acuity possible in a given circumstance, his best approach is to measure it. Atmospheric boil is at a minimum right after sunrise and just before sunset. It is maximum when the solar radiation is greatest. It is at a constant second maximum during the night hours. The effect is present winter or summer and is least on overcast days.

Atmospheric attenuation and sky light also tend to reduce the contrast of distant objects; hence for optimum visibility a sign or an object must have a high contrast with its background. With increasing speeds we need some signs to be legible from 2,000 feet or more. Certainly, this kind of visibility, cannot be provided in every kind of weather, no matter how big we make the sign. The freeway sign that slips by in the fog without being seen in time to read it, is a case in point.

Thus, it seems that a series of advance warning information signs, in addition to the main sign, are imperative to ensure that the motorist is informed of decisions to be made or actions to take. Visibility through short sections of the atmosphere will always be superior to that through longer sections, and perhaps the ideal sign system would be that placed nearby on the pavement itself. Color coding of lanes or of lane marking paint stripes has been shown to be of great value, at least in the daytime. Reflectorized paint colors would be necessary at night to permit enough light to be returned to the eyes to make seeing of the colors. Pavement rumble strips are highly desirable especially prior to signalized crossings on a highway.

C. Mirage effects

Mirages occur regularly on the highways. While typically seen in the daytime as shimmering white light resembling water on the distant pavement surface, mirages also are seen for several hours after sunset. Then they behave like a base up prism, refracting part of the rays from oncoming headlights to make them appear double as if two cars were approaching, one above the other. In the early morning hours, after the pavement has cooled more than the air, the surface air works like a base down prism, bending light downward, thus somewhat increasing visibility over hills.

Probably the most significant hazard from daytime mirages is the delayed appearance of a vehicle approaching on the crest of a hill. The heated air near the pavement surface bends light upward so that the rays of light from an oncoming automobile do not travel in a straight line. Hence the automobile beyond the crest of a hill must come closer, so that the bent light rays from it will arrive at our eyes, instead of going over our heads.

The heated air near the pavement also causes distant vehicles to disappear or to be so poorly defined that they cannot be accurately located or judged for speed. Sometimes a vehicle may be completely covered over by the bright sky light appearing to come from the boundary layer of air over the pavement. Others may lose some of their parts, such as their lower half or a portion in the middle.

Since the mirage of water on the highway is really a refracted image of the sky, a most unbearable glare from the pavement occurs when the part of the sky seen on the roadway contains the sun! Such a situation cannot be remedied effectively by any sunglasses, and the luminance level may become so high that the motorist will be forced, in the interest of safety, to pull into a rest area and wait 15 or 20 minutes until the condition subsides before continuing to drive.

D. Camouflage effects

The difference in luminance between an object and its background is a clue to an excellent camouflage technique. The smaller the luminance difference between an object and its background, the less likely will be the detection of the object. For example, when viewed from the air at low altitude, the highways are full of cars. As altitude increases, fewer cars are seen, and they are the lighter colored ones only. The lightest colors are the last to disappear at very great altitude. When earth scenery is viewed from a car, its average luminance is about the same as a well-worn highway. Against this average background, measurements with a Luckiesh Moss Visibility Meter show that light colored automobiles are significantly more visible. Thus, gray or dark colored automobiles have an element of camouflage built in. The fact that 21 candle power running lights or 4 candle power parking lights reduce the number and the severity of daytime accidents proves that such camouflage effects really do exist and do contribute to accidents.

A spotted Dalmatian dog sitting in the spotty shade of a tree will be camouflaged. This illustrates a second principle in camouflage: namely, the characteristic shape of an object can be disguised by adding meaningless spots, areas, and lines that could easily be confused with the background. Measurements on aircraft visibility both in the air and on the surface of the earth have shown that when an airplane was a single solid color it was the most detectable. When various patterns were used, the detectability was reduced in proportion to the amount of variegation, even for uniform sky viewing. Thus, two tone paint patterns on automobiles are likely to be less visible than a single color, especially a light one.

Automobile surfaces are already composed of large areas of glass, which average about the same luminance as the background. The popular vinyl top and black bumpers, used with all conceivable paint colors, adds to the two-toning effect provided by the windows and is not a wise color choice because of a severe reduction in the visibility of the car and an increase in the heat uptake inside the car in the summer.

Chromium reflects about 50 percent of the light falling on it. Because it is usually highly polished, it sparkles and brightly images the sun. Under many conditions the reflections from chromium make a car very visible. However, since chromium behaves like a mirror, there may be reflections from dark-colored objects at a given moment, whereupon the chromium looks dark or even black.

Chromium, therefore, cannot be relied upon to provide the visibility that a dark-colored automobile needs. On the other hand, bright metal surfaces on one's own car that reflect the sun tend to interfere with vision and to increase the effectiveness of camouflage on streets and highways.

The most effective camouflage technique is to hide the object rather than to disguise it. The automobile discovered in front of the truck one is passing, was hidden from view. An automobile in a fog is hidden. The pedestrian or vehicle partially or completely covered by the windshield corner posts or the rearview mirror is hidden. Even the dirt spots on the windshield and the dangling toys in some cars will hide or partially obscure an object on a collision course. As shown earlier, *an object on a collision course does not change its position in the field of view of the driver.* It just gets larger. Since objects attached to the car, such as windshield dirt spots, do not change their position either, they interfere with detecting the outside object.

Hiding tail and headlights from oblique view by forward and rearward jutting fenders led the government to require reflectors and/or side marker lights beginning with the 1968 models. Darkness is itself great camouflage.

Modern styling modifies the estimate of speed and direction of an object. Strong slanting lines will confuse the real size and shape of an object. Styling has thinned the roof line, which reduces the apparent height of a passenger automobile and makes it appear farther away and thus to be going slower. Window, fender, and grill lines are slanted in various directions and give the illusion of motion. The prevalence in accident reports of the statement, "I didn't see!" indicates the effectiveness with which camouflage operates in driving a motor vehicle.

E. Rain, mist, snow, and fog

Daytime rain, mist, snow, and fog serve to reduce the contrast of objects seen from a motor vehicle, They increase the already existing effects described above. Windshield dirt and water droplets tend to increase the detrimental effects which occur during rain due to the absence of shadows, atmospheric scattering, and dirt on roadway objects.

An especially significant hazard in adverse weather is the pedestrian. When getting wet, a human being becomes preoccupied. They will cover their head and run or walk in front of an automobile. Pedestrians seem to picture the motorist as an inconsiderate person, sitting dry and comfortable in the car, watching the poor pedestrian getting wet. The pedestrian believes the motorist can see him, can stop, and will stop if there is any question about the pedestrian getting hurt.

The motorist, on the other hand, has his/her own problems. The windshield wipers do not sweep all of the windshield area; the vision through what is wiped is not good; side windows, rear windows, and major parts of the windshield often are fogged. The motorist feels closed in. Because traffic moves slowly, he may become annoyed. Because pedestrians are taking unusual risks, the driver may feel that they are being "pushy" and are imposing, since the driver has so many other problems, many of them due to the weather. The confusion and poor visibility may be so adverse that the pedestrian may not be seen at all and an accident occurs.

Under adverse weather conditions, it is imperative that vehicles have their lights on so that pedestrians and motorists can see them. Umbrellas should be transparent so the pedestrian can see approaching automobiles. Each person must be taught that, in the final analysis, he/she is the only person to be depended upon for personal safety. Never walk with your back to oncoming traffic, be convinced of the difficulties of being seen, and act intelligently and safely. Understand that hair, hats, glasses, clothing, and anything else that interferes with side vision, can cost you your life.

The growing use of daytime headlights will reduce the dangers described above.

Chapter 10

Desirable Practices

Merrill J. Allen, O.D., Ph.D.

Synopsis

10.1 Street Lighting As a Supplement to Head Lighting

Numerous before and after studies in the United States have shown that increasing street lighting reduces accidents. Similar reductions in accidents have been observed in industry among factory workers. Few studies have been made of the effect on accidents of raising the highway illumination level by means of headlights alone. In England and Europe it was common practice to drive without headlights, because an extensive system of street lighting exists. Studies in England requiring motorists to change traditional "parking lights," as we would call them, to low-beam headlights in the city produced conflicting results, due partly to partial compliance and the mixing of the two types of lighting. Lighted automobiles mixed with unlighted automobiles puts the unlighted automobile at a visibility disadvantage.

A similar difficulty arises in the daytime between automobiles using headlights and those not using headlights. In states where holiday "lights on" campaigns have been held, more than half of the motorists failed to cooperate. Hence mass statistics do not clearly support the thesis that daytime headlights increase safety and they may actually increase the hazard to the driver who fails to participate.

Changing vehicles to daytime running lights as initiated by GM in 1996 will put unlighted cars at greater risk. Fortunately, retrofit kits are available, and earlier models can be easily converted to daytime running lights.

There is a conflict between head lighting and street lighting such that a pedestrian seen in silhouette by light from distant street lights reflected off the polished pavement, will lose some visibility at a critical distance from the automobile headlights. At that point part of the clothing blends into the background pavement. This could only occur within a limited zone in front of the automobile, depending upon the reflectance of the clothing, the aim of the headlights, and the intensity of street light reflected from the roadway. Also, since pedestrians are relatively tall compared to automobile headlights, and since the headlight distribution varies with elevation above the road, especially on low beams, it is unlikely that all parts of the pedestrian will be invisible at once. Only a part of the pedestrian would be of the same luminance as the pavement, the parts above being darker and the parts below being brighter than the background pavement. The lower the intensity of the street lighting and the dirtier the headlights, the more serious becomes the tendency for the headlights and street lights to cancel one another at certain distances. At low levels of lighting the eye is not as sensitive to brightness differences. Conversely, the higher the levels of illumination, the more efficient is the eye and the better will be the visual performance with head lighting and street lighting.

For those who would emphasize street lighting and exclude automobile head lighting, it is well to keep in mind that even *full natural daytime* street lighting shows an additional reduction in accidents when headlights and other running lights are used. We need both types of lighting and as much of both as we can afford. There is no one best way to light our highways and streets!

Street lighting is most efficient for seeing something on the pavement when it provides silhouette lighting, but objects off the pavement would probably not be seen with such lighting. The Texas Transportation Institute has been experimenting with 150-foot high "artificial moonlight" sources. These have been used as street lighting in Austin Texas since 1894. Large clusters of lamps with direction controlling reflectors are mounted on poles 200 to 300 feet high (see Figure 10.1) near cloverleaf interchanges on important highways, and in the city. They report both economy in installation and better seeing. The overall effect is comfortable because one can see the highway and the lighted countryside without the feeling of confinement by the limits of the headlight pattern.

Low (10 to 30 inch) street lighting with no upward component, has met with considerable acceptance in fog. The lights are directed across the road from either side and have been used on a number of bridges as a designed-in feature.

A. Edge and center line markings

Studies have shown that pavement paint markings are among the most effective means of controlling traffic flow and imparting information to the driver. Marking the edge of the pavement causes the traffic to move away from the edge. This is beneficial because dropping a wheel off the edge of the pavement is a frequent cause of losing vehicle control and skidding across the road into oncoming traffic, or overturning. Center line marking serves to stabilize traffic at a safer distance away from the center of the highway. Reflectorization of these lines using beaded paint is a major help at night.

Plastic or glass retroreflectors glued to the pavement, serve about the same purpose as reflectorized paint, and they are more rain proof. However, snow plows destroy them. Their use is largely confined to southern states. Should the snowplow problem be solved by a change over to plastic or rubber plow blades or by an improved plow-resistant reflector design, the "waterproof" reflectors could be put into more widespread use. It is possible to improve the performance of beaded paints in the rain. However, if water inundates them, even the plastic units will become useless.

Figure 10.1 *Tower lighting for freeway interchange. These towers are 200 to 300 feet high. Note that guard rails are used around the base of the tower to reduce the likelihood of a fatal crash into the tower structure. (Photograph supplied by the Texas Transportation Institute, Texas A & M College.)*

B. Reflectorization

Reflectorization of hazards at night serves to increase their visibility by making more efficient use of available light. Reflectorization is desirable for pavement paint, license plates, highway safety signs, street signs, pedestrians, bicycles, slow-moving vehicles, trucks, trains, buses and automobiles. Reflectorization of fence posts, driveways, business signs, and so on is not always desirable. Reflectors must be functional; that is, they must locate and identify an obstacle, sign, or edge of the highway. They must not appear to hang in space, seemingly unattached to the ground or to an object.

A pedestrian carrying a dangling reflector or reflectors attached to his shoes or clothes may be identified as a pedestrian by the walking motion. When standing still, the reflections might be construed to be from a fence post, a cat, or a beverage can.

Outline reflectorization of motorcycles, bicycles, buses, trucks, or trains clarifies the nature of the hazard, where it is, and how fast it is being overtaken. In an ocean of point reflectors the driver can be easily confused. If substance is added by changing points to outlines that tie the lights and point reflectors together, confusion will be eliminated. Thus wide spaced taillights may not appear to be on the same vehicle unless joined together by some structure that is lighted or reflectorized. *The side lights could be joined together by simultaneously and rapidly flashing them.*

The 3M Company has developed a reflectorized side wall material for tires. It is hoped that greater use of reflective materials on tires and other parts of trucks, buses, motorcycles, bicycles, passenger cars, and on pedestrians, will develop in the near future. Quicker detection, localization and identification will be the assured result. *In addition, the rapid flashing of all side, roof, front and rear outline lights will tie them all together and help identify the vehicle and its location.*

10.2 Fluorescent Materials

Fluorescence is the physical process by which short ultraviolet wavelength high energy radiation is absorbed and reradiated at a longer visible wavelength. The outdoor environment at sunset and twilight contains mostly this shorter, relatively invisible solar radiation. Fluorescent materials convert this energy into light in the visible spectrum and appear to be very bright. By choosing fluorescent materials that radiate energy at or near 555 nanometers, the peak sensitivity wave length for the eye, a remarkable brightness increase is possible. It has been found that an orange color is most attention getting at dusk, partly because of color contrast and partly because the performance of the fluorescent materials currently available is very good in this region.

At night fluorescent colors are without value because there is no ultra violet light energy available to operate them. In the daytime the fluorescence phenomenon occurs at such a high intensity and temperature that chemical bonds are broken and the life of the material is reduced. Even the more durable materials used on school zone signs, on school buses and on slow moving vehicle signs, have a useful life of no more than three years, losing about 50 percent of their brightness per year.

Fluorescent materials are excellent hazard markers on dreary days, in late afternoon, early morning, and during twilight. As a daytime warning of highway construction and other hazards, fluorescent materials are significantly brighter than red signal lights and may be detected up to a mile away in the daytime.

Signs using fluorescent materials are easily spotted and read in the daytime under adverse weather conditions. The fluorescent layer is applied over a bright base coat, so that normal bleaching of the fluorescent color with exposure to weather and ultraviolet light, leaves the sign with normal visibility. Thus, it is safe to use florescent materials on such signs, even though the effectiveness slowly reduces back to that of a normal sign.

10.3 Vehicle Visibility

A school bus that has a six-inch-wide strip of reflective material and a six-inch strip of fluorescent material outlining it on the front, rear, and sides, and has a strobe light, will have the degree of conspicuity needed when stops are unexpectedly made on the highway.

Police, fire, and ambulance vehicles also need to be as conspicuous as possible. Their daytime conspicuity is enhanced when they are coated with fluorescent material or at night when they are outlined with lights and reflectorized material. Emergency vehicles need to be as large as possible to make their speed and direction of movement apparent. Outlining a vehicle with fluorescent and reflectorized material will be almost as effective as solid coverage. A less effective use of fluorescent material would be to spot it here and there, which, in effect tends to camouflage the vehicle.

Red paint for fire trucks is improper and should be replaced with fluorescent yellow paint. Studies have shown that yellow fire trucks have fewer accidents (Solomon, Stephen S., James G. King, "Influence of Color on Fire Vehicle Accidents," *Journal of Safety Research*, Vol. 26, No. 1, pp. 41–48, 1995).

A motorcycle has such a small frontal area that a headlight is now required to be displayed in day as well as at night time to ensure that it will be seen. Because a single headlight can be camouflaged by headlights on cars, and become invisible as to the presence and location of the motorcycle, a triangle formed by three headlights is essential for motorcycle safety. The standard headlight would be supplemented by two lower headlights, one on each side of the front wheel. The taillight on the rear should also be shape coded by two extra lights to prevent the motorcycle being camouflaged by taillights on other vehicles. The side of the cycle should be protected by light from the head and taillights, and by fluorescent and reflectorized panels. The cyclist needs fluorescent and reflective materials on the helmet, jacket, slacks and shoes to ensure visibility from all directions.

A bicycle is a low visibility object of great vulnerability. Its proneness to accidents is increased because bicyclists often ignore stop signs and other traffic rules. Their visibility is handicapped by lack of adequate structure to provide a good visual target. At night some visibility is provided if the frame, fenders, and wheel rims are reflectorized. It is very important that the rider wear a reflectorized and fluorescent helmet and clothes. By day and night a bicycle headlight comparable to that of a motorcycle would be of assistance but is not available; hence a reflective and fluorescent waist band, jacket, helmet, clothing and shoes are highly desirable for all bicycle riders.

Bike riders should be encouraged to stay on the sidewalks as much as possible. Most sidewalks stand idle, and bicyclists are prohibited by law in most states from riding on them. The most effective way to prevent bicyclist automobile accidents is to remove the bicycles from the streets. In Europe virtually every highway or road has a paved bicycle path paralleling it at a safe distance. The pedestrians, bicycles, and motorized bicycles can mingle with much greater safety than when exposed to motor vehicles on the street or highway itself. In the cities and towns, separate cycle paths and sidewalks should parallel the streets.

For trains, a fluorescent panel and a retroreflective panel, each at least one foot square, placed every ten feet along the sides of each railroad car, would be helpful in preventing daytime and nighttime side crash accidents. While daytime accidents are not frequent, 786 in 1967 (U.S. Department of Transportation, 1968), they still account for two-thirds as many as the nighttime side impact accidents of highway vehicles into trains. In the daytime, highway traffic is four times greater than at night, while railway traffic is the same as at night. Since only two-thirds as many side impact accidents happen between car and train in the daytime, one may conclude that trains are considerably less visible at night than they are in the daytime.

In the daytime the train runs into the automobile three times as often as the automobile runs into the side of the train. At night, the automobile runs into the side of the train about 3 percent more frequently. Nighttime as well as daytime visibility of the locomotive is obviously inadequate. The maximum candle power of the high-placed locomotive headlight is within 5 degrees of straight ahead. That puts the beam over the head of pedestrians and motor vehicle drivers. Thus the locomotive headlight is a utility device and not a conspicuity device for alerting motorists.

At one time locomotives had oscillating headlights or strobe flashers to make them more visible. The unexplained bureaucratic decision to stop using them has cost us many lives. Outlining the locomotive, both front and side, with 12 inch wide fluorescent strips would reduce the number of daytime accidents. Extrapolating from experiences with running lights indicates that between a 35 percent and 50 percent reduction in daytime train accidents would occur if the entire train were protected with fluorescent materials, and if strobe and flashing lights were displayed on the locomotive in the daytime as well as at night.

The placement of automobile headlights on the front and sides of the locomotive near ground level, would greatly enhance the visibility of the locomotive. Eight high beam automobile headlights placed with two aimed forward, and three on each side of the locomotive aimed at 45, 90 and at 135 degrees from the side of the locomotive would ensure visibility to a motorist at all approach angles. By simultaneously flashing these lights at 1 to 2 cycles per second, they would be effective in getting a driver's attention, day or night.

These lights and the main headlight of the locomotive should be on at any time of the night or day that the train is in operation and when it obstructs a crossing. Such lighting would eliminate about 75 percent or more of the locomotive collisions.

10.4 Highway Signs

Much study has been directed toward the best way to inform a driver about hazards and routes. The American system of signs has been under study for a considerable time and improvements have been made (Forbes et al., 1968). There are indications that still further improvements are needed. Figures A.3a and A.3b, in Appendix A, show the principal highway signs as detailed in the 1995 *Indiana Driver's Licensing Information Manual.* It can be seen that there are five principal types of signs: round for railroad, octagonal for stop, diamond for hazard warning, triangular for yield, and rectangular for information.

It is apparent from research that for distinctiveness, the octagonal and circular signs are the poorest, while the triangular and long rectangular shapes are the best. This combined with well known color vision defects in the population, indicate that reliance on red color and an octagonal shape for stop signs is unwise. In the U.S.A., the STOP AHEAD warning signs are being replaced with an octagonal symbol without the word stop. *The one reliable shape code is the word STOP*. We know STOP can be read by everyone. Bureaucracy at work again?

In Europe, the difficulty of a multiplicity of languages has led to the development of a pictorial sign system. The European system is based on the Protocol on Road Signs and Signals as agreed upon by the United Nations Conference on Road and Motor Transports in Geneva in 1949 and revised in Vienna in 1968 (United Nations, 1969). Some of the mandatory signs, found in Appendix A, are shown in Figure A.4, some of the prohibitory signs in Figure A.5, and some of the warning signs in Figure A.6.

Note in Figure A.5 (see Appendix A) that prohibitory signs are round and red with a white bar, or round and white with a red rim and a red bar across various instruction symbols displayed on the white. All such signs should be taken as negative; i.e., no entry, no speed greater than, no turn, no pedestrians.

10.5 Signal Lights

One out of fifty male drivers have a color vision problem that makes red appear to be black or the signal appears to not be turned on. Among the older population, color recognition is impaired (Whillans) due in part to changes in the lens in the eye and due to reduced pupil size. Because of this major problem, the Colour Blind Committee recommends that all red signal lights, red taillights, red traffic signs, etc., be marked with a white horizontal bar as shown in Appendix A, Figure A.5. Such a modified signal would be helpful to all drivers, as well as solving the color blind driver's problem, and would be inexpensive to install and maintain.

Chapter 11

Some Popular Misconceptions

Merrill J. Allen, O.D., Ph.D.

Synopsis

11.1 Sunglasses

Glare and sunglasses are inseparably associated in the public mind, even to the extent that occasionally a person will try to use sunglasses for night driving to reduce headlight glare. In one fatal accident the driver was slated for trial on manslaughter charges because it was believed he should have seen a child running to catch a school bus. The children and the driver of the school bus could see the oncoming driver with the sun shining in his face. He was wearing sunglasses! He was driving against the morning sun 10 degrees above the horizon, and 25,000 foot lamberts of pavement brightness. The shaded side of the child was toward the driver. The child was running from the deep shadows among a long row of mailboxes under large trees on the right. Probably the child could not have been seen until she stepped out onto the shiny pavement.

The driver would have been able to see better without the sunglasses. In this case, the conditions were so severe that it is doubtful if the driver could have avoided hitting the child, even if not wearing sunglasses. For example, the flashing red school bus warning lights at the top of the bus were adjacent to the silver bus top, which was reflecting high intensity sunlight at grazing incidence toward the driver, so he probably could not have seen the flashing red lights. Furthermore, the school bus was in front of two 75-foot-long house trailers and two tractor trailer trucks, which camouflaged the bus!

Some people believe that camouflage does not occur on the highway because they have never seen it. If the driver in the above example had not struck the child, whom he said he did not see until after the impact, he would never have recognized that she was there! She was camouflaged by veiling glare from bright sources and by standing among mailboxes. Many times a passenger will comment about some event along the roadway that the driver has failed to see. Perhaps it was behind a corner post or the rear view mirror adjacent to hood or chromium glare, or his attention was directed to another point in the scene.

Often, even after being directed to the object or event, a driver cannot find it. Thus it is easy to understand that many things, in fact, most things are camouflaged and not seen at all, or perhaps seen with amazement after months of traveling the same routes!

Sunglasses transmit less useful light as well as less glare, and when useful light levels are reduced to below 400 foot lamberts, vision begins to decline because of a decrease in visual efficiency. When the sunglasses reduce critical objects significantly below this level, seeing is impaired. Hence seeing detail under shade trees is improved by removal of sunglasses. The light from the back surface of the lenses reflected from the face is more noticeable when useful light coming through the lenses is low. Dirt on the lenses further reduces seeing performance.

The quality of ready made sunglasses often is not ideal, because of irregular surfaces. Many are made of plastic and performance deteriorates due to scratches from cleaning and wiping the lenses. Comparison between clean glass and clean Plexiglas windshields, as found in military aircraft, shows that twice the loss in visual range occurs when looking through the Plexiglas compared to the plate glass.

11.2 Tinted Windshields

The tinted windshield controversy has at present been won by the manufacturers, who are supplying 100 percent of some of their passenger vehicles with this extra cost item. The controversy has been between those who claim that tint impairs night seeing and those who argue that night seeing is not as important as comfort in the day time for preventing accidents.

Until 1969, tinted windshields were a separate option from tint in the remaining window glass. In this year the Chevrolet Division of General Motors began supplying all or no windows tinted. Tinted windshields alone are not available. This policy made it easier for the manufacturer to defend his logic that heat absorbing windshields contribute to the comfort and hence to the safety of motoring.

The heat argument is transparent when one notes the extra cost of this feature, the fact that the majority of cars on the highway, and virtually all of those produced by General Motors at that time, had no heat insulation overhead, and that iron polluted (tinted) glass is cheaper to manufacture than clear glass. Thus, it appears that tinted windshields are a sales gimmick.

11.3 The Automobile Horn

The horn is a great device for awakening people who may be daydreaming at a traffic light. It has other "uses," such as calling the waitress at a drive-in, letting one's girl friend know he is driving by, and expressing annoyance with another motorist. For safety its use is limited to those few occasions when, out of control, with wheels locked and tires skidding, a driver wants to tell a pedestrian, dog, or motorist to get braced or to run. The horn is usually listed as a safety device as, for example, in vehicle inspection laws. It probably was a safety device fifty years ago when vehicles traveled less than 30 mile per hour!

The placement of the horn in many vehicles traps the sound in the engine compartment, where it is best heard by the driver. Few horns are directed ahead. Direct emission of the sound from the horn to the outside air is not available!

Safety experts advise us to use our horn when we see someone encroaching into our lane of travel on the highway. Analysis shows that this merely gives us something to do while we await the crash! Sound travels at 1,100 feet per second in calm air. Its intensity falls as the inverse square of the distance it travels. Thus if the sound has to travel 600 feet, its intensity will be about 1/360,000 of its intensity at one foot from the horn. If the oncoming car has its windows closed, the sound will lose 20 decibels or more penetrating the glass, metal, and rubber of the automobile. Even if the windows were open, the wind noises would mask the weakened horn sound. To be easily detected in a motor vehicle, the horn must be 10 decibels louder than the background noise, which, without radio or music, is about 70 decibels. A major problem with the horn is location. We cannot determine the source of the sound by hearing alone.

Rarely mentioned in any safety literature is the use of headlights instead of the horn for highway communication. With light there is no loss of time in transmission, and the location of the signaling vehicle is instantly established. The brightness of the headlight is not reduced, even up to 1,700 feet away, at which distance its angular size becomes about 1 minute of arc. Beyond 1,700 feet the inverse square law holds; i.e., at 3,400 feet, brightness of the headlight on the retina will be one-fourth of what it was at 1,700 feet. The probability of seeing a headlight in the highway situation just described is much greater than hearing the horn. Effective visual warning can be given from distances approaching a mile in good weather.

Safety literature, laws, and driver education courses should include the procedure of flashing headlights off and on, in rapid succession when it is necessary to warn oncoming traffic of your presence or of other hazards. The flashing of headlights with the horn button has been suggested by one inventor.

Please remember that, at night, flashing from low to high beams provides excessive glare and may prevent the oncoming driver from seeing an obstacle blocking the highway. Flashing the headlights on and off (not low beam to high beam) will improve the oncoming driver's vision of the danger ahead.

11.4 Watching for Turn of Front Wheels

Another favorite instruction by safety experts is to watch the front wheel of the oncoming car to detect when it first turns out of line. When a car is sitting at the curb, a turning of the steering wheel causes the front wheels to show the direction of travel before movement starts. As the car begins to move the effect of turning the wheel is more and more pronounced, so that at high speeds only a very slight movement of the steering wheel is required to move the car quickly from one side of the road to the other. In other words, the one or two degree movement of the front wheels would never be noticeable, although the displacement of the entire vehicle caused by it would. Only for very slow city driving can one rely on watching the front wheels.

On the highway one has many more things to watch. Thus, gross displacements of vehicles are much easier to detect and are more reliable indices of hazard than front wheel aim. In fact, drivers can depend upon central vision only for a detailed analysis of objects brought to attention by peripheral vision. A search procedure of the entire scene is helpful, but without peripheral vision the totality and interrelationships of the perception could not be maintained. In short, attention should be paid to the car and its position on the pavement, to its speed and direction with respect to the whole scene, and to whether its general behavior foretells some unusual maneuver.

11.5 Central versus Peripheral Acuity

The only test universally required by those states having driving licensing vision tests is central acuity. Peripheral acuity is not usually tested. Burg (1968) has shown that peripheral acuity correlates, although weakly, with driving performance. Its importance in driving can not be denied because it allows the inspection and interrelating of all the important objects in the field of view and allows the safe movement of the vehicle along the road. To test central vision alone may pass a person with dangerous restrictions in his visual fields. A person with 180 degrees of horizontal visual field is normal. Reductions of field from 180 to 140 degrees or less begins to be hazardous.

Similarly 20/40 vision is not enough for the safe operation of a motor vehicle at high speeds. For night driving, daytime 20/40 vision may become as poor as 20/200, depending upon the contrast of the target and the illuminance available. When we are being perceptually loaded more and more by increasing speeds and greater traffic density, we cannot afford to accept a daytime acuity to 20/40 when 20/20 or better is possible. The ultimate goal is the achievement of maximum visual performance for all drivers. The way to accomplish this is to upgrade the driving environment as discussed in the introduction. An acuity of 20/70 or worse should pass with restrictions to daytime driving. A review committee composed of optometrists, physicians, and Department of Motor Vehicle personnel should be called upon to study all aspects of an unsuccessful applicant's condition and situation if the applicant is dissatisfied with the results of the vision and other tests he received.

11.6 Young Drivers

By and large young drivers are inexperienced drivers. After World War II many Germans, thirty years of age and older, began to drive for the first time. Their accident experience curve looked much like that of the young drivers in the United States. The combination of inexperience on the highway and inexperience with alcohol accounts for part of young drivers' problems. Also, most young drivers drive more miles than older drivers, and the strongest correlation with driver accidents is the number of miles driven. Young drivers often are driving old, used cars. After you and I have used the safe miles in our cars, we despair of fixing all those little things like the worn brakes, worn tires, scratched windshield, misaligned front end, and worn shock absorbers, so we trade it in. Then, or after another owner or two, the kids get what's left over. Eager to prove they can drive like a pro, they push equipment to its limit. They learn what a motor vehicle can and cannot do. Unfortunately, some lose their lives or suffer permanent injury when a critical part like a brake line, a tie rod, a tire, a drive shaft, or a wheel bearing fails. Many survive because of skillful handling in the emergency, because of quick reactions, and because injuries are not as likely to be fatal for a young person.

The policy of insurance companies of dumping extra premium loads onto young nonvocal drivers is an added injustice to our potentially most useful citizens. It is also an indication of the indifference and selfishness of the adult population for allowing this to happen. In one college town, I observed the police stop a car full of college students for a minor infringement and ignore townspeople doing the same thing. Upon identifying a driver as a nonstudent, arresting officers have been known to fold up their ticket books, issuing only a verbal warning. Such discrimination against our youth is indeed unfair.

Drivers above the age of about fifty-five show a steady increase in accident rate. At age 55, women, whose careful driving has kept their accident rate per mile driven below that of men, begin to have more accidents than men! Older drivers are often deprived citizens, driving an older car that gets serviced and cleaned less often. After retirement, money and new cars do not come easily for many older people. The pace of the highway and city driving is increasing faster than they are prepared for, their reaction time is longer, their vision, hearing, and strength are impaired, and they are easily confused. That they have so few accidents is a result of their extra caution and small number compared to the larger numbers now driving at younger ages.

Could the young and older driver's increased accident rate be due to a vehicle design problem? What about driver eye height? Older women lose height faster than men. Teen age drivers are shorter than adult drivers! Is it possible that by *making adjustable seats standard on all cars,* we would level out the age versus accident curve?

11.7 Looking at Oncoming Headlights

For the most part, the admonition to avoid looking at oncoming headlights for fear of being blinded for a few seconds is of no practical importance and may in fact be hazardous! Suppose a long line of cars approaches with lights dimmed, as is most usually the case. Their lights, and your own, light the highway reasonably well, better than your lights alone would do. Now suppose there is a drunk driver behaving erratically in that line. If one watches only the right edge of the pavement, he may never see the collision developing, but if he watches the oncoming cars, he will be able to pick out those few cars that might cause trouble. With paint stripes on the edge of the pavement, and with modern headlights, one can easily drive by peripheral vision while studying the oncoming headlights.

As to being blinded by such headlights, one can only blind the area where the bright image falls on the retina; all other areas are reasonably protected from the high intensities of direct headlight beams. Such localized bleaching of photo pigment does not impair the ability to remain oriented by peripheral vision, since 98 percent of the rest of the retina is not bleached. Of some concern is the dirt on the outside of the windshield and the cigarette or pipe smoke deposits on the inside of the windshield. When a bright headlight beam strikes such a windshield, it appears to light up all over and provide a significant bleaching effect over the entire retina which may require a few seconds for recovery. This is not an ocular deficiency but a windshield problem, and the solution is simple and obvious, i.e., clean or replace the windshield.

To watch the oncoming automobiles and maintain position on the highway a driver tends to ignore pedestrians. However, pedestrians are not often encountered on open highways. When they are they are usually not seen, whether one looks for them or not. Experiments show, as do accident statistics, that the chance of seeing a pedestrian in time to stop, falls off markedly as speeds increase above 20 miles per hour. By 60 miles per hour, when driving with low headlights, on unlighted highways, and when meeting traffic, one might as well stop looking for pedestrians. If they are in the roadway the driver using low beam headlights cannot see them in time. It is up to pedestrians to protect themselves. Reflectorized, white, or light colored clothing, and increased headlight power will solve this problem.

11.8 High Beam Glare

In 1967 the Truckers of America felt the most hazardous thing a motorist could do at night was to drive with high beams. This point of view must have been reached from hearsay, because truck drivers as a rule sit so high, that automobile high beam headlights can scarcely interfere with their ability to see. In a series of driving tests made on interstate highways it was the truck driver in the oncoming lane located 100 feet or more across the median, who most often asked that lights be dimmed, even though only about 3 percent of all drivers felt bothered enough to signal the experimenter to dim.

Rarely does one see truckers driving with high beam headlights on, even on interstate highways. That the following facts are not safe has apparently missed truck drivers, legislators, or anyone, except for a few researchers. These facts are: 70 miles per hour is 103 feet per second, and the low beam headlight range is about 120 feet. 90 percent of the driving population needs 2.5 seconds, or 255 feet, to respond to a clearly visible unexpected hazard. The braking distance at 70 miles per hour is over 260 feet for a car, and still more for a truck. These figures total over 500 feet! Compared to 120 feet of low beam headlight range, it is clear that driving at night on low beams is extremely dangerous. Unfortunately, everyone is fearful of blinding with high beams, and law enforcement officers will arrest you if you use high beams when there are oncoming vehicles.

On wide open straight stretches of highway, one can see that high beams are safer than low. If two automobiles approach a mile or more apart with high beams, the roadway and shoulders between the two cars will be revealed. Soon, according to present law, the two drivers dim their lights. Suddenly areas of the road ahead are cloaked in darkness and visibility is worse. Now, unless obstacles, such as pedestrians, carry a light or retroreflective material, or unless the automobiles are equipped with special lighting, unlighted objects on or entering the pavement between the two cars will not be seen in time.

Most states admonish all drivers to dim their headlights on interstate highways when meeting another car. That such dimming does not improve vision but impairs it, does not improve safety, but causes a serious and obvious hazard, must somehow be made clear to the nation. On divided highways, high beams should not be optional but mandatory. The word of the trucker who literally sits above it all, cannot be taken as the guideline for traffic safety.

The facts are that low beams are inadequate even for 40 miles per hour. Even when overtaking, high beams should be permitted, since all cars have inside mirrors that can be tilted to reduce their brightness, and rear view mirrors that darken when the following lights are too bright are available at extra cost. Less distress would occur to the passed driver if he were also driving with high beams as here recommended. If the all-weather headlighting system recommended in Figure 8.15 were adopted, there would be practically no problems with glare, either from the front or rear, since the eye level zone of headlighting would be free of light.

Chapter 12

Forensic Aspects of Visual Perception

Arthur P. Ginsburg, Ph.D.

Synopsis

A little girl crossing the street is hit by a car. Why didn't the driver see the child in time to avoid the accident? Could the driver see the speed limit and the cross-walk signs from appropriate distances? Was the contrast of the words and symbols on the signs high enough to be seen? Should the driver have been able to see the child? Did the lighting conditions help or hurt the driver's ability to see the signs or child? Was there sufficient contrast to single out the child against the background? Did the driver have sufficient visual capability in terms of visual acuity and contrast sensitivity to see the child? Was the driver distracted by other objects or events in the scene? What were the driver's visual expectations along the road?

These are just some of the questions that may be asked concerning the visual perception of the driver. Similar kinds of questions could be asked of the pedestrian who is hit by a vehicle, or the witness who "saw the speeding car run the light and hit the pedestrian." Forensic visual perception deals with answering these kinds of questions, about whether someone has the visual capability to see a sign, person or event at certain distances under given lighting and visibility conditions.

In most accident situations, vision plays a key role in providing information to guide behavior and performance. Understanding the limitations and capabilities of human vision within a framework of perceptual analysis is important to help answer those kinds of questions in order to determine fault in an accident.

In this chapter we will review visual perceptual analysis in terms of visibility of the scene, as well as personal visual capabilities and perception. The importance of contrast and size in determining the visibility of objects such as signs, vehicles and pedestrians is discussed. Visual capability measured and understood in terms of contrast sensitivity, which overcomes the limitations of visual acuity, are also examined. Different methods of measuring contrast sensitivity are compared, in addition to examples of visual problems such as refractive surgery and cataract. These are used to illustrate the effects of poor contrast perception on the visibility of street scenes and reduced detection and identification distances of seeing road signs and pedestrians using a night driving simulator.

Examples of accidents due to low contrast sensitivity from eye disease, normal limitations of resolution in the visual field and visual illusions are discussed. Sections on visual perceptual analysis methodologies discuss scene documentation, consideration of human factors issues such as perception/reaction time and light adaptation. Issues are raised concerning documenting scene visibility and the limitation and capabilities of photos, film and video presentations with a caution about the how the visual capability of the judge and jury can affect their evaluation of visual information.

12.1 Visual Perceptual Analysis and Its Relation to Accidents

Visual perceptual analysis involves an understanding of three major aspects: visibility, visual function and perception. Visibility refers to what can be seen in a scene—what visual information is available to the observer in terms of contrast and conspicuity. Visual function refers to the capability of the observer's visual system, the physiological abilities, in terms of physiological limits and visual health. Perception refers to the observer's mental set and the interpretation by the observer of what is desired to be seen in a given scene and that information necessary to perform visually guided tasks. Although these aspects of vision are typically treated as separate entities in accidents, the integration of all three is key to providing the most comprehensive understanding of visually related accidents.

A. Visibility

Once visual obstructions are ruled out as a primary cause of an accident, the visibility of the object then becomes the primary concern. The degree of visibility of an object is based primarily on size and contrast. A greater degree of visual stimulation occurs when objects are larger and have a greater degree of contrast, making them more easily seen.

Contrast is the difference in lightness and darkness, or shading between an object and its background. Low contrast objects are more difficult to see than higher contrast objects because they provide less visual stimulation. A person easily seen in the sunlight can disappear in the shadow of a tree, in the glare of the sun, car headlights, in the dim illumination of a nighttime roadway, in smoke, fog, rain or snow. Visibility of objects can be quantified using luminance measures for the determination of object contrast and size.

Contrast determines conspicuity, i.e., the ability of an object to stand out or be noticed as separate from its background. Conspicuity is a primary determinant of whether or not an object in the periphery attracts attention, resulting in head or eye movements to place the object in the central retina for further examination. High contrast objects, such as a child in a dark snow suit, are more conspicuous than low contrast objects, a white snow suit seen against the snow bank. However, that child in the same dark clothing seen against a blacktop road is less conspicuous. Other scene features such as movement, flashing lights, light intensity and color add to the conspicuity of objects in the scene because they provide additional information to the visual system.

B. Visual function

A highly visible object to one observer may be virtually invisible to another, depending upon their visual function. Obvious questions such as whether the observer was wearing properly prescribed lenses correcting him or her to good acuity levels during the accident are answered first. Too often, positive answers to those questions stop any further examination of the observer. This stops short of understanding key visibility and visual issues of many accidents. Other less obvious questions about visual function need to be answered in order to ensure that the visual capability of the observer was not a key factor in the cause of the accident.

Just because an observer has good visual acuity it does not mean that they can see well. Twenty/twenty is not enough. There are many reasons why a person having good visual acuity can have poor visual performance. Many important components of vision are not measured by testing for acuity. Visual capabilities such as parafoveal and peripheral vision, light adaptation and depth perception are also integral components of visual performance.

C. Perception

Perception refers to the mental integration of the visibility of the scene information that is acted on by visual function to result in visually guided behavior. The visual system most always has a mental set concerning what is expected to be seen at any given time, which guides perception of objects. Mental sets come from past experience and can result in visual illusions such as a raised curb being perceived as a flat lane marker, or the solitary red light on the rear of a tractor being seen as rear red light of a motorcycle. A visual surprise results from a conspicuous feature in the scene that interferes with expectation, such as that experienced by a driver first seeing a pedestrian, stopped vehicle or animal in the middle of the road at night.

Visual surprises result in two factors that create accidents: increased perception/reaction time and visual attention directed away from sometimes more important tasks. For example, the driver, watching the flashing lights of a truck backing up into a roadway at night. His attention, directed away from a person in the middle of the street directing the truck is not seen, hence the driver runs over that person.

Perception is driven by mental set and the visibility of the scene. However, perception is only as good as visual function allows the visibility of the scene to be perceived. Therefore, the concept of how to measure reasonable visual capability becomes an important element in accident visibility analysis.

12.2 Measuring Visual Function

A. Limitations of visual acuity

Vision is usually evaluated using the Snellen visual acuity eye chart. This chart is designed to measure a person's ability to see black letters on a white background. Because visual acuity tests the resolution ability of the eye (how well the eye can focus on a small, high contrast image) visual acuity measures the quantity rather than the quality of vision. Although Snellen acuity has been used as the primary measure of visual capability since 1862 and eye doctors use the visual acuity chart for many clinical matters, it has not related well to complex visual performance tasks such as driving vehicles safely. A primary reason for this defect is that Snellen acuity measures vision under ideal high-contrast black target on white background test conditions. However, outside the physician's examination room, real-world objects are rarely black on an extended white background.

Real-world objects have many different sizes, shapes and levels of contrast. Most objects are viewed under less than ideal conditions such as twilight and dusk, nighttime, rain, snow, fog and smoke, all of which create low contrast visual environments. Other visibility conditions drivers frequently experience such as headlight glare and sun through a dirty or pitted windshield also affect a driver's ability to detect and identify road signs, pedestrians and other vehicles. Although the eye chart is used in many useful ways by the clinician, Snellen visual acuity simply cannot measure how well a person is able to see the wide range of objects and the wide range of visibility conditions we experience every day. Therefore, it is not surprising that Henderson and Burg[1] and Kinney[2] found low correlation between visual acuity under high and low illumination levels and that Shinar[3] found a poor relationship between visual acuity and driving.

Understanding visual function helps us understand the limitations of visual acuity measurements. The standard Snellen eye chart presents letters having only one high level of black and white contrast. However, the visual world contains a wide variety of objects that come in a wide range of sizes and contrast levels. The visual system has a range of independent mechanisms tuned to see different sizes.[4] Furthermore, visual acuity is limited to foveal vision, the center of the retina, whereas everyday objects must be detected and identified across the whole retina. The functioning of the cells in the fovea that provide letter identification have little to do with the functioning of the cells in other parts of the retina peripheral to the fovea that provide vehicle guidance.

Finally, standard eye charts have a contrast reserve. The contrast of a standard eye chart can be significantly reduced by improper or poor corrective lenses and/or eye disease and visual disorders, yet still have sufficient contrast for the letters to be identified.

However, when a real-world scene has the same amount of contrast reduced, important information is often lost. Consequently, standard visual acuity measurements provide little indication of visual function of complex scenes.

Contrast loss can be more visually debilitating than optical blur as the simple demonstrations in Figure 12.1 illustrate. The Snellen-type letter chart and street

ORIGINAL

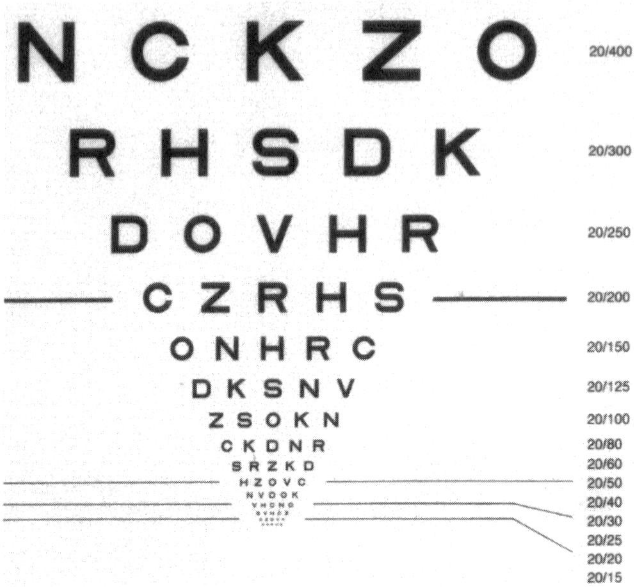

ORIGINAL

Figure 12.1 *(continued on next two pages)*

Blur filtered to 20/40

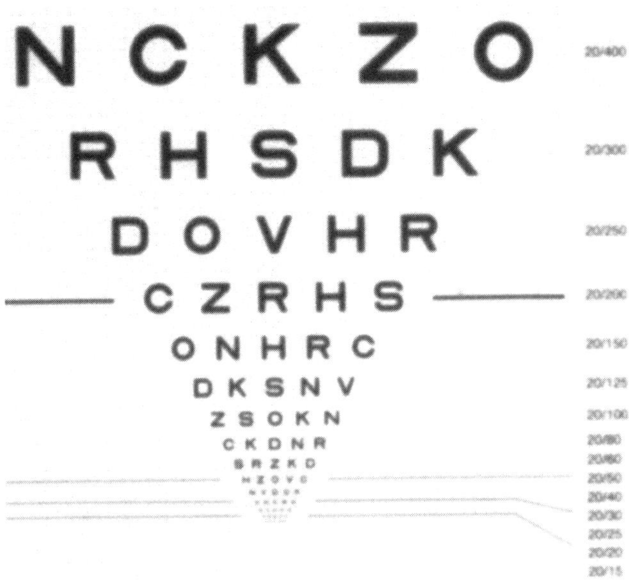

Blur filtered to 20/40

Figure 12.1 *(continued from previous page)*

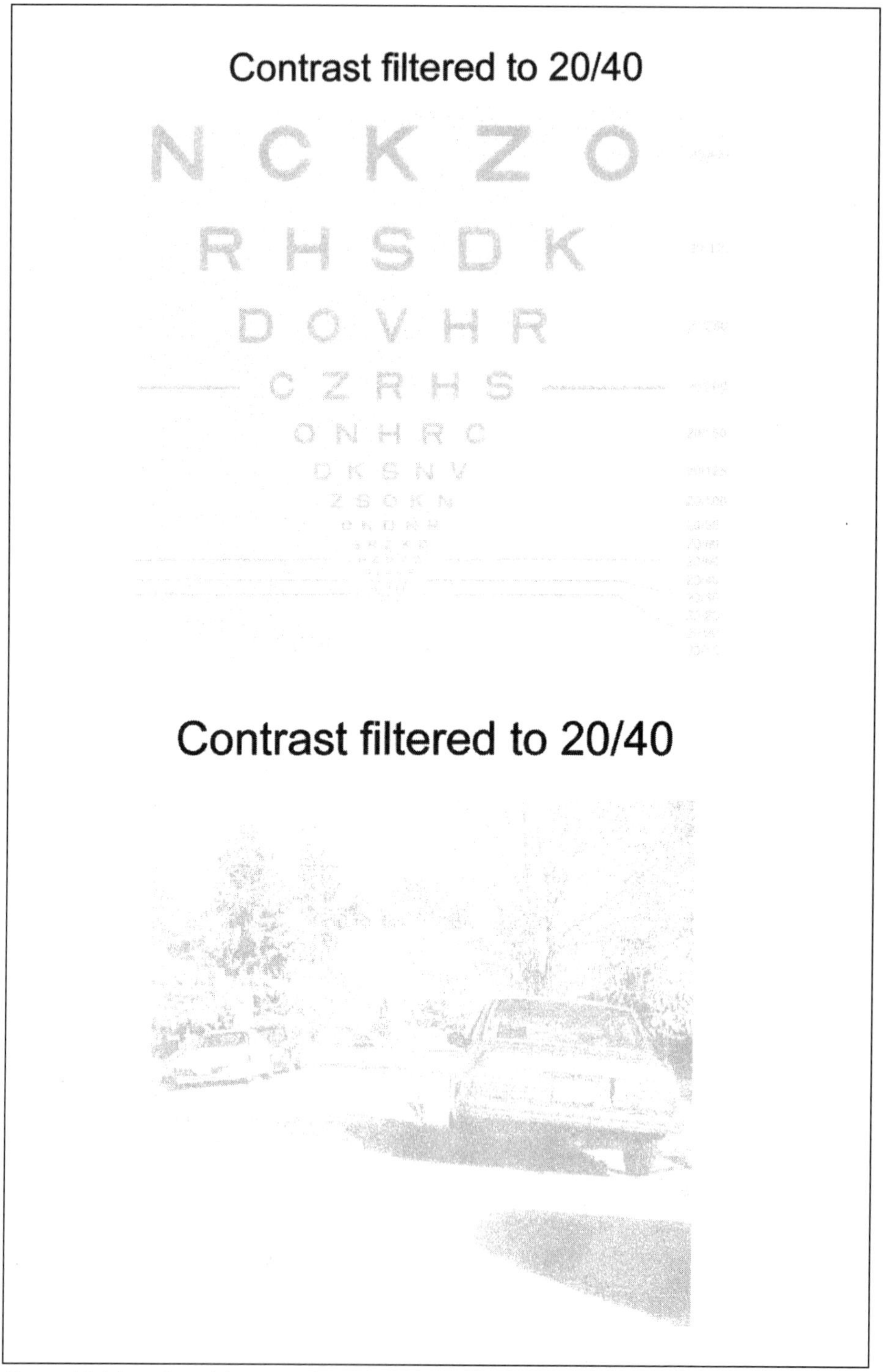

Figure 12.1 *(continued from previous pages)*

scene are blurred similarly to 20/40 acuity. The general features of the street scene are still easily visible. However, reducing the contrast of Snellen-type acuity charts can allow certain size letters to be read while the same amount of contrast loss on the real-world scene is visually debilitating. It is evident that the letters are less affected by the contrast loss than is the street scene. By the time loss of visual function reduces visual acuity to 20/40 due to reduced contrast (the general limit of most states for failure to visually qualify for a driver's license) the loss of functional vision may be a severe liability.

Nighttime brings a shift from primarily cone vision to rod vision, from the ability to see high contrast detail in color to that of low contrast form without color. Clearly, the standard acuity test taken under daytime luminance conditions has little relationship to what a person can see at night. The decreased contrast perception at night that shifts visual function primarily from one set of visual mechanisms to another is important to measure in order to understand why some people can see well during the day, but see poorly at night.

B. Visual channels

Another way to view visual function is in terms of visual cells (or channels) that filter a visual scene into functionally distinct or independent bits of information. For example, fine detail and color vision is mediated by cells most densely packed at the central retina, called cones. Coarse detail processed without color is mediated by cells most densely packed at the peripheral retina, called rods. Because rods, but not cones, are more light sensitive, general shapes (but not colors) are seen under low light levels at night.

Furthermore, the small central foveal area packed with cones provides the details of a scene. This is why we have eye and head movements to examine objects of interest due to their conspicuity. The much larger peripheral field surrounding the foveal area provides general shape and guidance information. Many drivers tend to speed in fog because although their foveal vision knows that the scene detail is limited by the fog, their peripheral vision is still stimulated in a manner similar to non-fog conditions by receiving gross low contrast stimulation while traveling down the road.

The purpose of accommodation is to create an "in focus" image onto the retina to ensure that the full range of size cells, from the largest to the smallest, which process contrast are used.

So far we have discussed static visual channels. Other channels include motion, color, depth, stereopsis and motion in depth. All of these channels operate in parallel and combine their information, resulting in the total perception of visual information in a scene.

The observer consciously and subconsciously selects and attends to information in a scene from these channels depending upon the perceived visual information associated with the task at hand.[4] The functional importance of each channel depends upon the scene information relevant to the particular visual tasks associated with accident. This is why each channel should be tested independently.

C. Contrast sensitivity testing

The limitations of Snellen acuity as a measure of functional vision and the channel nature of the visual system require a more comprehensive way to measure functional vision, to measure the breadth of channels a system using test targets of different sizes and shades of contrast which are detected at visual threshold. That measure is called contrast sensitivity. Contrast sensitivity measures the ability of the eye-brain system to visually separate an object from its background. There are a number of scientific and technological research results from others, such as human factors engineers, whose profession requires an understanding of the integration of visual capabilities into complex visual performance environments such as homes, roadways as well as in the air and space. These tasks require them to be intimately knowledgeable with analysis of functional vision. For example, the 1988 Engineering Data Compendium on Human Perception and Performance[5] had the following to say about visual acuity and contrast sensitivity:

> [T]he obtained acuity value . . . is a one-numbered characterization which says nothing about the ability to discern the basic shape or form of objects. However, the ability to discern low spatial frequencies which is not measured by letter tests, is vital for shape discrimination and sometimes has important clinical implications . . . . By measuring the contrast required for resolving the bars of a sine wave grating at each of several spatial frequencies, an observer's contrast sensitivity function is obtained. This function reveals far more about visual ability than a one-number limiting resolution value . . . . Since the spatial frequencies of other acuity targets can be analyzed, visual acuity can be predicted from contrast sensitivity.

Unlike visual acuity, contrast sensitivity does relate to complex visual performance in "real-world" situations. The scientific and engineering basis for using contrast sensitivity to assess functional vision is described elsewhere.[4] Considerable research linking contrast sensitivity to functional vision has been proven over the past twenty-five years. Sine-wave grating contrast sensitivity has been shown to be superior to Snellen acuity in measuring the functional vision performance of pilots for target detection in flight simulators and under field conditions.

These studies involve low contrast conditions of twilight, nighttime, fog, or rain; highway sign discrimination distance; identification of other complex targets such as faces, letters, and scenes; other complex military targets such as tanks and soldiers; and windscreen visibility analysis (see end notes 4 and 6 for review).

More recently a Pennsylvania Department of Transportation study involving 12,400 drivers demonstrated a correlation between older drivers and accident rate only when contrast sensitivity was added to the Snellen acuity and peripheral vision test scores.[7]

Furthermore, contrast sensitivity also overcomes many limitations of Snellen acuity in detecting and measuring visual loss of visual function due to contact lenses and refractive surgery[8] and a wide variety of visual disorders such as cataract.[9] In general, a 25 to 50 percent loss or gain in contrast sensitivity is functionally significant.[4, 8, 9] These results, coupled with the contrast sensitivity related to population norms, can help determine the functional significance of a particular contrast sensitivity function.

The most sensitive method of testing contrast sensitivity uses sine-wave gratings of different sizes and contrast levels as shown in Figure 12.2. The principal use sine-wave contrast sensitivity since the early 1960s has been to measure and describe the basic mechanisms of vision: channels. The visual channels of the retinal/brain system are discrete filters of size or spatial frequency which create

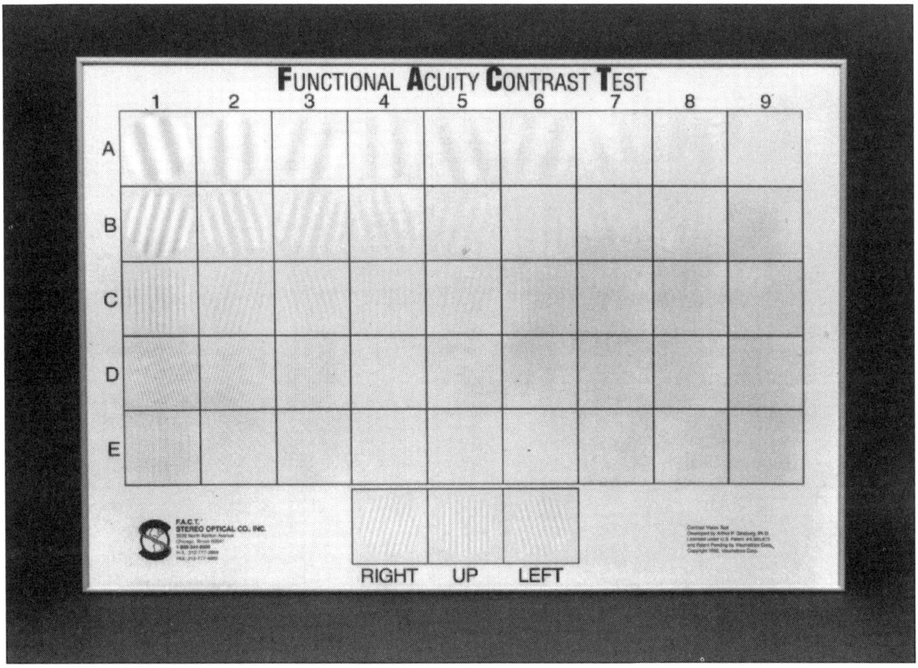

Figure 12.2

the fundamental building blocks of perception.[4] Sine wave gratings have been used not only to map out the perceptual properties of channels, but also to measure their sensitivity to contrast. It has been repeatedly demonstrated that only sine wave grating technology measures the elementary visual channels tuned to one spatial frequency at one orientation.

Therefore, in addition to measuring the optical quality of vision, like that of Snellen acuity, contrast sensitivity evaluates the quality of contrast perception at the next stages of visual processing, the retina-brain system. The retina-brain system, beginning with the rods and cones, converts the retinal image into neural codes for channel processing. The contrast channel information encodes the primarily shape, size and contrast of the image. Because visual objects come in a large range of shapes, size and levels of contrast, the sensitivity of the visual channels processing that information is important. Proper contrast sensitivity testing measures a relevant range of visual channels. The relationship between the contrast sensitivity function and channels is shown in Figure 12.3.

A contrast sensitivity evaluation curve or function is obtained by determin-

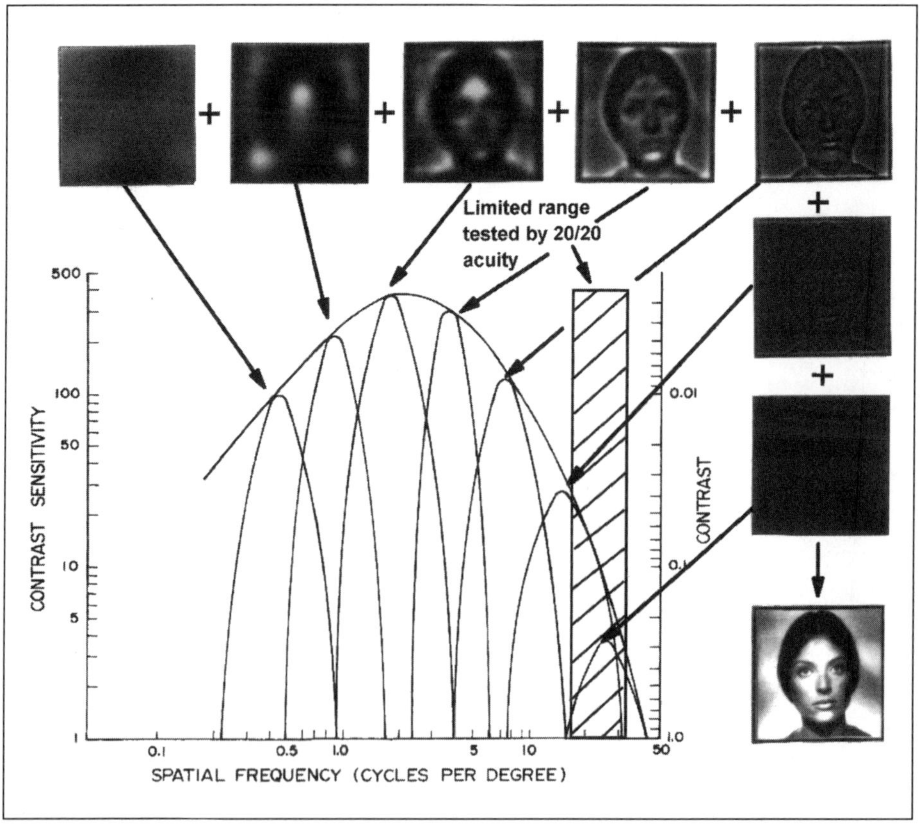

Figure 12.3

ing the minimum contrast to just see the sine wave grating as shown in Figure 12.4. The shaded area in Figure 12.4 represents the 5 to 95 percentile contrast sensitivity of the normal population.

The sine wave grating method of contrast sensitivity testing is very similar to audiometric testing. Just as an audiogram is created from using single fre-

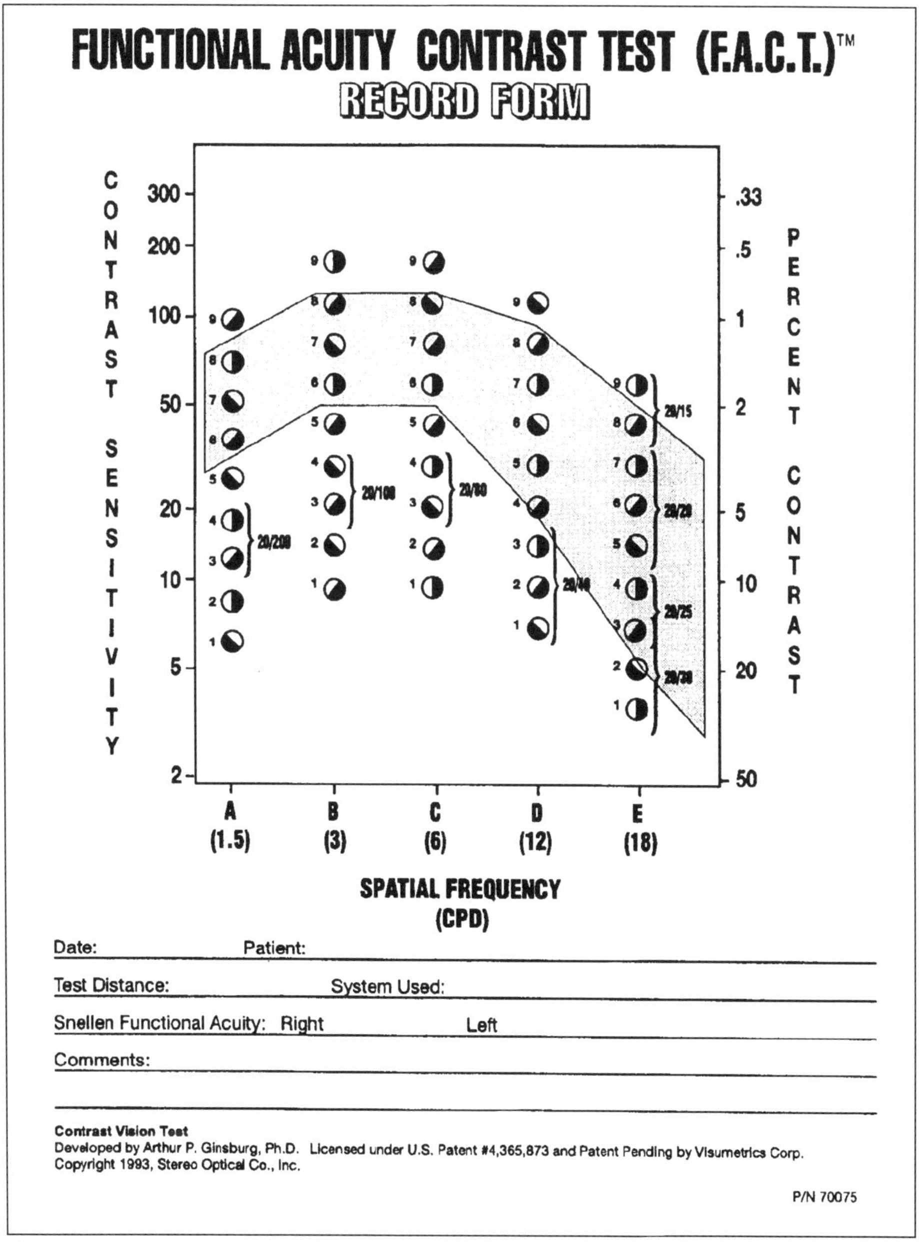

Figure 12.4

quency tones at different sound frequencies to measure hearing threshold, a contrast sensitivity curve is created by using pure space waves, sine wave gratings, at different spatial frequencies (sizes) to measure visual threshold. Therefore, just as sound frequency and loudness relate to hearing, spatial frequency and contrast relate to seeing. Similarly, just as an audiogram describes the capability of the auditory system, the contrast sensitivity function describes the capability of the visual system.

After thirty-two years of scientific, clinical and functional research, contrast sensitivity testing is standardizing vision testing just as pure tone audiometric testing standardized audiology in the 1940s.

Similar to visual acuity testing, there are neither "standards" nor a general

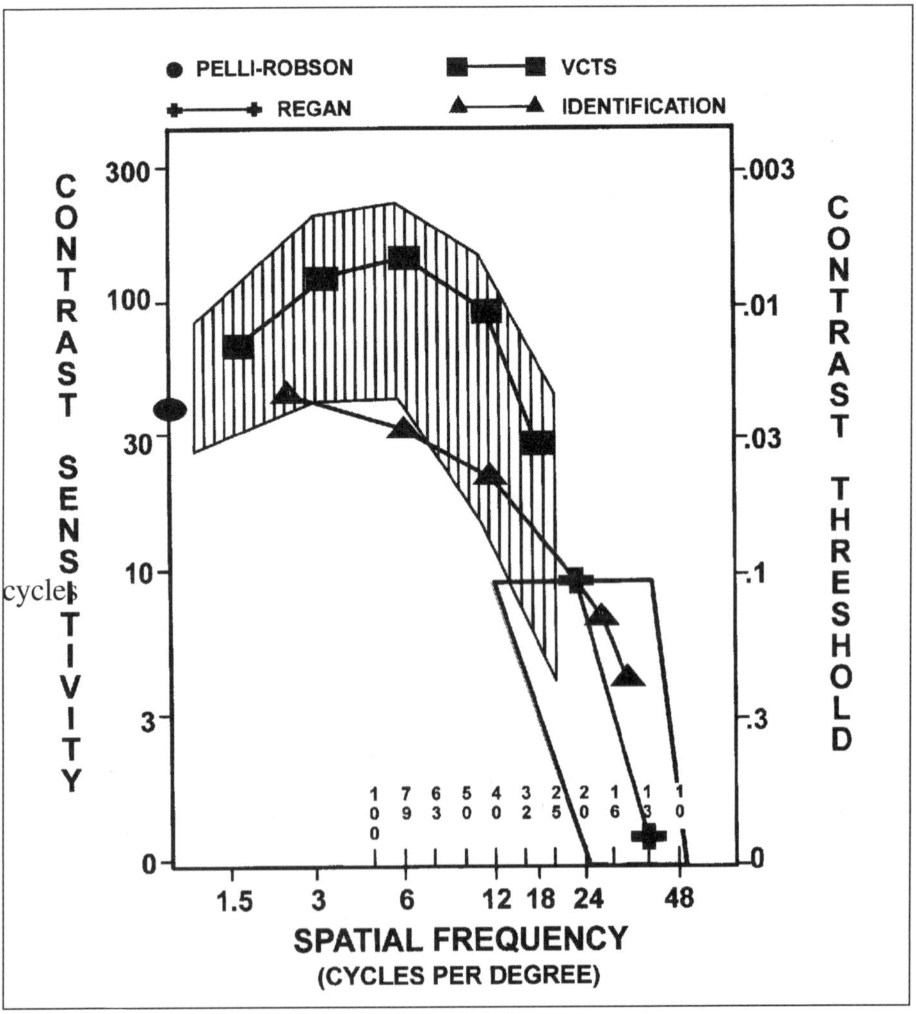

Figure 12.5

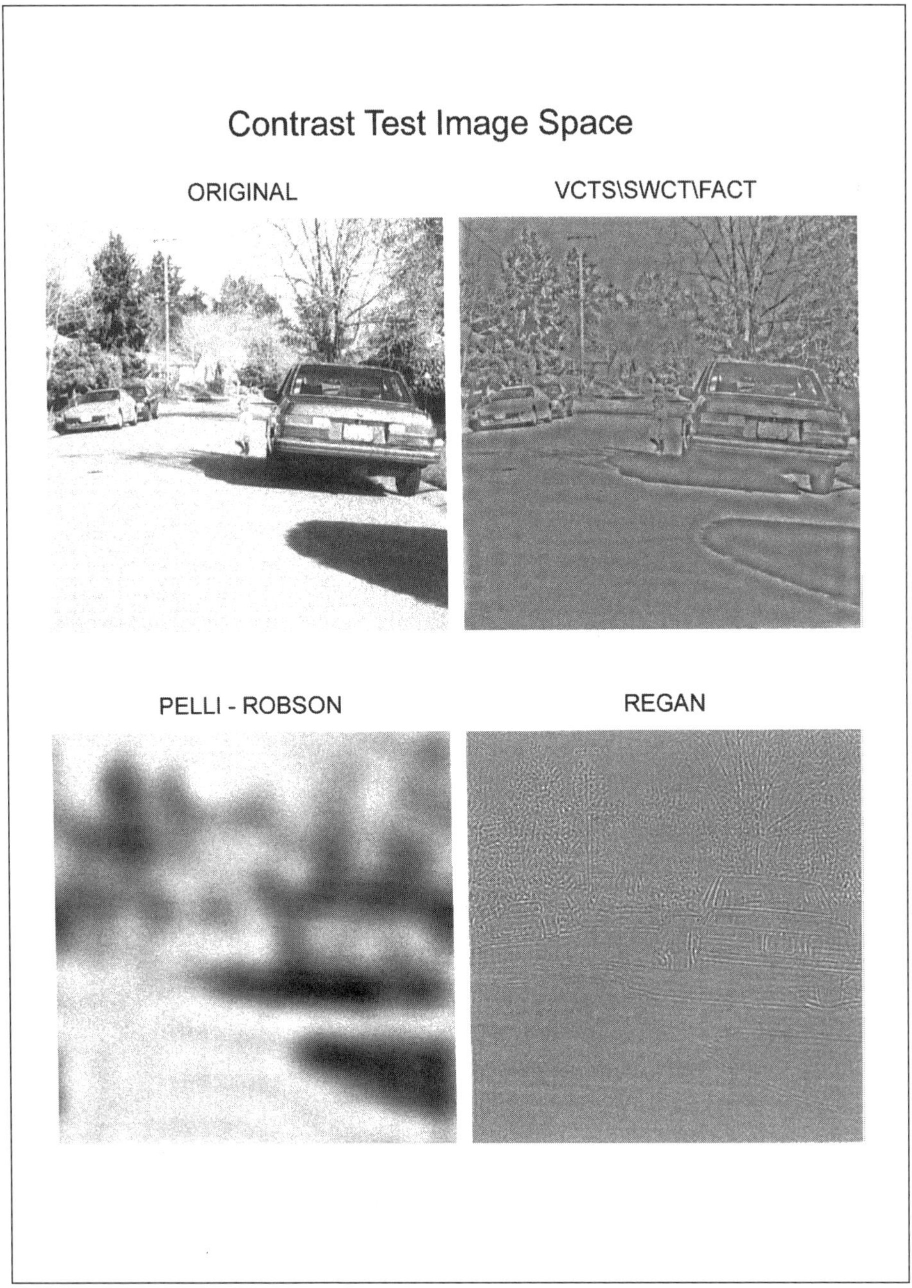

Figures 12.5a through 12.5d

consensus regarding contrast sensitivity testing. However, sine wave grating contrast sensitivity tests have long been considered the gold standard by many.

Other contrast tests have been developed. Although low contrast acuity tests have been used by some as contrast sensitivity tests, they do not provide a contrast sensitivity curve, comparable outcomes or function similar to that of sine-wave contrast sensitivity charts. Indeed, important differences between sine-wave grating and low contrast letter acuity charts have been discussed.[10, 11]

The functional size ranges of the sine wave grating and low contrast letter charts are shown in Figure 12.5. A street scene (Figure 12.5a) is spatially filtered using the spatial frequency test ranges of three contrast tests: sine wave gratings tests (VCTS, SWCT and FACT), single size letter charts (Pelli-Robson), and the multiple size letter charts (Regan). The filtering shows that the single size letter chart is testing a size too large to be relevant to the scene (Figure 12.5c). It may be useful for determining the contrast threshold of large trucks in fog, but not for determining the presence of smaller objects such as the little girl in the street. The multiple size letter charts test a larger range of size but the size range is for the sharper edges of the scene, not particularly relevant to image quality and the little girl (Figure 12.5d). The sine wave grating charts test a size range most relevant to the scene, especially the visibility of the little girl (Figure 12.5b).

Visual evoked potentials are one method for objectively determining visual function. Recently, the grating and Pelli-Robson charts were compared to visually evoked potential (VEP) measurements, a more objective measure of visual function.[12] It was found that grating chart measures were repeatable and, unlike the Pelli-Robson results, the grating chart measures of contrast correlated to that of the VEP.

D. Factors affecting contrast sensitivity functions

Contrast perception changes with luminance, age, normal individual variation, blur, media opacities and visual physiology (e.g., see end note 4).

Reducing light levels from day to night reduces contrast sensitivity first at the higher spatial frequencies (narrow gratings) and then at the middle and lower spatial frequencies (wider gratings), helping to explain why there is a loss of detail seen at night.

As with most other physiological functions, age takes its toll and vision is no exception. The visual capability of healthy 20-year-old is significantly reduced by age 60, due to the natural aging processes. The onset of a wide variety of age-related visual disorders such as cataract can reduce contrast perception dramatically without major losses in visual acuity as shall be shown later.

An important finding is that the considerable individual differences found in contrast sensitivity among normals are related to differences in functional vision.[4]

This means that what one person sees in any given scene does not necessarily mean that another person will see the same information. This has important implications for courtroom demonstrations when low contrast information is displayed, as will be discussed later.

In addition to improper refraction or eye disease, other factors which can affect vision include medication (prescription and nonprescription), alcohol, drugs and exposure to other toxic elements. Simple quinine found in tonic water can reduce vision, and many prescribed medications can also cause vision to degrade. Alcohol affects contrast vision differently for different individuals. Marijuana has been shown to reduce visual acuity. Exposure to toxic elements in the workplace can reduce contrast sensitivity. Microelectronics workers exposed to chemical cleaning agents (who reported a wide variety of symptoms) were found to have reduced contrast sensitivity—yet normal acuity. The reduced contrast sensitivity was found at middle spatial frequencies, indicating central nervous system effects.

E. Evaluation of contrast sensitivity test results

Certain patterns of contrast sensitivity loss can generally indicate specific visual problems. For example, neurological problems and glaucoma often cause midfrequency losses.[13] Small refractive errors typically cause high frequency losses. These may increase to middle and even low frequency losses with large refractive error.[8] Cataract can cause high as well as multiple frequency loss depending on the cataract type.[9, 13] High frequency loss is often attributed to narrow angle light scatter; low and high frequency loss is often attributed to wide angle light scatter.

F. Demonstrating the contrast sensitivity function: Functional vision analysis

Charting the sine-wave grating contrast sensitivity test results creates a contrast sensitivity curve, as shown in Figure 12.4. Although interpreting the different possible shapes that the contrast sensitivity function can obtain comes with experience, it can be difficult to translate those shapes into meaningful descriptions to others. A software product, EyeView™, was recently developed to illustrate contrast sensitivity test results.

EyeView is an image processing software program that creates newsprint and street scene pictures modified by either visual acuity or sine wave grating contrast sensitivity test result data. By comparing EyeView processed pictures to age-matched norms, acuity to contrast sensitivity or pre/post treatment, levels of visual disability are readily apparent.[9, 11] Other images relevant to the case at hand are used in place of the standard newsprint or street scene as needed for visual perceptual analysis and courtroom demonstrations. EyeView pictures allow one to begin to "see" the world through the eyes of the observer. The examination of images modified by vision test results is an important part of functional vision analysis.

12.3 Examples of Functional Vision Analysis

The following are examples of how functional vision analysis aids an understanding of visual loss in cases of medical malpractice and accident causation. In some cases, patient complaints require a functional visual analysis. Most common complaints occur due to untreated eye disease or malpractice. The key to the analysis is quantification and demonstration of visual function, in a manner easily understood by the jury.

A. Visual complaints after refractive surgery

The advent of refractive surgery offers distinct advantages to those encumbered by corrective lenses. However, most refractive surgery is generally irreversible and can leave some patients seriously functionally impaired. Using functional vision analysis, a quantitative determination of the patient's functional loss can be validated. The following is a recent case of refractive surgery malpractice that illustrates how functional vision analysis is used to understand patient complaints and loss of functional vision.

Functional vision analysis was conducted on a female patient who had undergone repeated radial keratotomy (RK) refractive surgery. The patient complained of poor near and distance fluctuating vision and would not drive at night. The following synopsis is from tests which were conducted to quantify her functional vision:

1. Visual acuity;
2. Near and far day and night sine wave contrast sensitivity with day and night glare;
3. Far sine wave contrast sensitivity with fog and glare;
4. Night driving simulation (using the VSRC Night Driving Simulator) which measured the visibility distances for the detection and identification of road warning signs, message signs and road hazards under various dynamic conditions; the simulated driving conditions are nighttime rural (with minimal lighting) and city (with street and store lights) under clear and inclement weather (fog) visibility conditions, and with and without glare; and
5. Visual function questionnaire.

1. Visual acuity measurements using near and distance charts.

a. Near visual acuity

Near without spectacles was:	OD: 20/125+1
	OS: 20/125
Near with her spectacles was:	OD: 20/80–1
	OS: 20/50

Although she is not functionally blind (her acuity is better than 20/200) her near vision, over twice as bad as 20/20, is poor.

b. Distance visual acuity

Test Condition	OD	OS	OU
daytime	20/80–	20/50–	20/50–
nighttime	20/100–	20/63–	20/63–
glare	20/100	20/80–	20/63–

Again the patient is not functionally blind, she has less than 20/40 visual acuity and therefore is not able to pass a driver's exam visual test.

2. Near and distance day and night sine wave contrast sensitivity with day and night glare.

The contrast sensitivity results are graphed and compared to 90 percent normal population limits (the grey area) in Figure 12.6. In general, she has significantly reduced contrast sensitivity below that of the normal population under all test conditions: day, day with peripheral glare, night and night vision with central glare, consistent with her low visual acuity. This patient would have difficulty seeing any size object, especially those at low contrast under reduced light levels such as dusk, dawn and nighttime.

3. Distance day and night sine wave contrast sensitivity with night fog and glare test conditions and simulated automobile mirror glare and fog (Figure 12.6).

The contrast sensitivity results are graphed and compared to 90 percent normal population limits (the grey area) for the day test condition and ± 2 standard deviations for the night clear, glare and fog test conditions. In general, the subject has significantly reduced contrast sensitivity below that of the normal population under all test conditions consistent with her low visual acuity.

4. Night driving simulation.

Night driving simulation measures the visibility distances for the detection and identification of road warning signs, message signs and road hazards under various conditions.

The simulated driving conditions are nighttime rural (with minimal lighting)

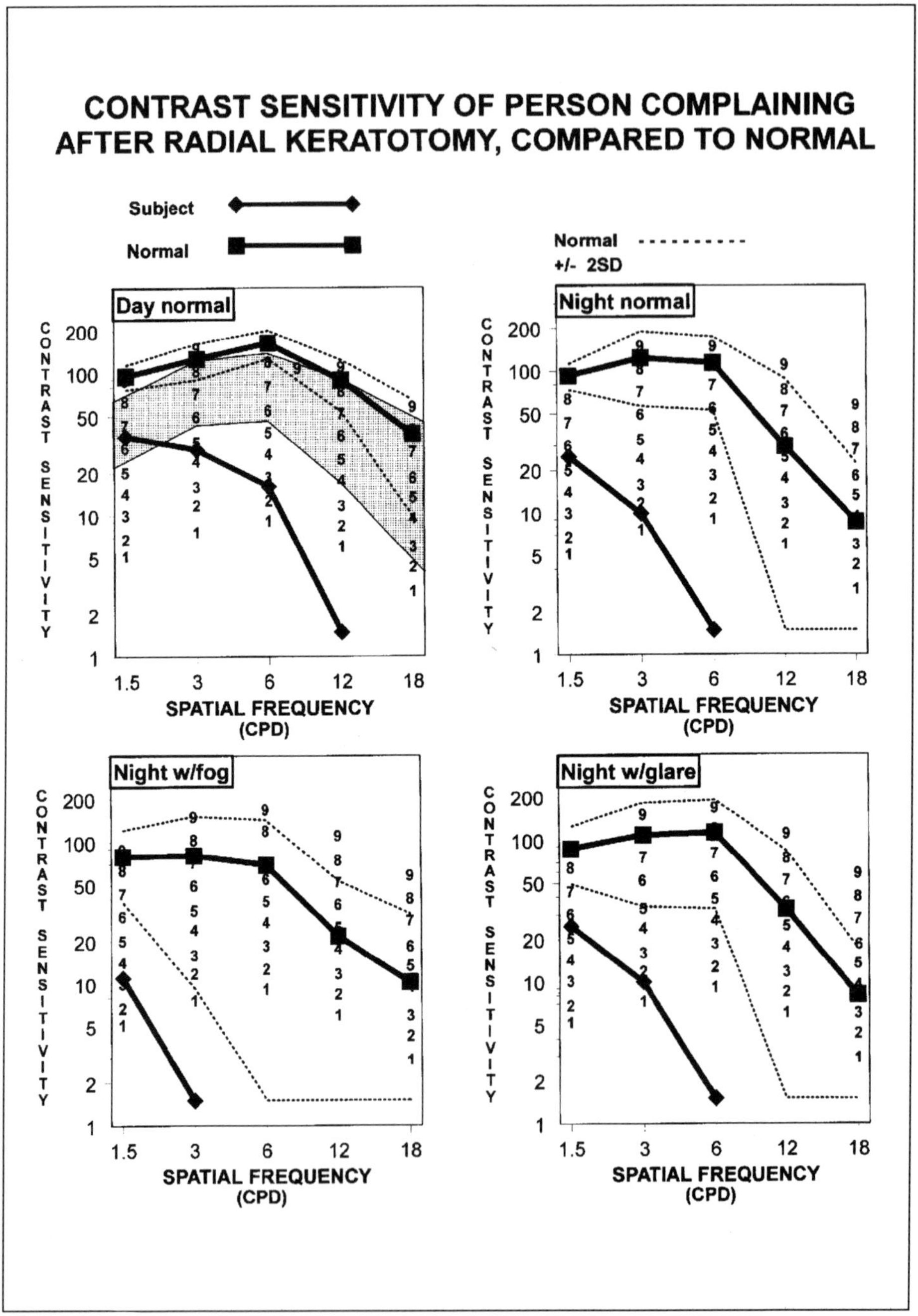
CONTRAST SENSITIVITY OF PERSON COMPLAINING AFTER RADIAL KERATOTOMY, COMPARED TO NORMAL
Subject
Normal
Normal +/- 2SD
Day normal
Night normal
Night w/fog
Night w/glare
CONTRAST SENSITIVITY
SPATIAL FREQUENCY (CPD)
1.5
3
6
12
18
200
100
50
20
10
5
2
1

Figure 12.6

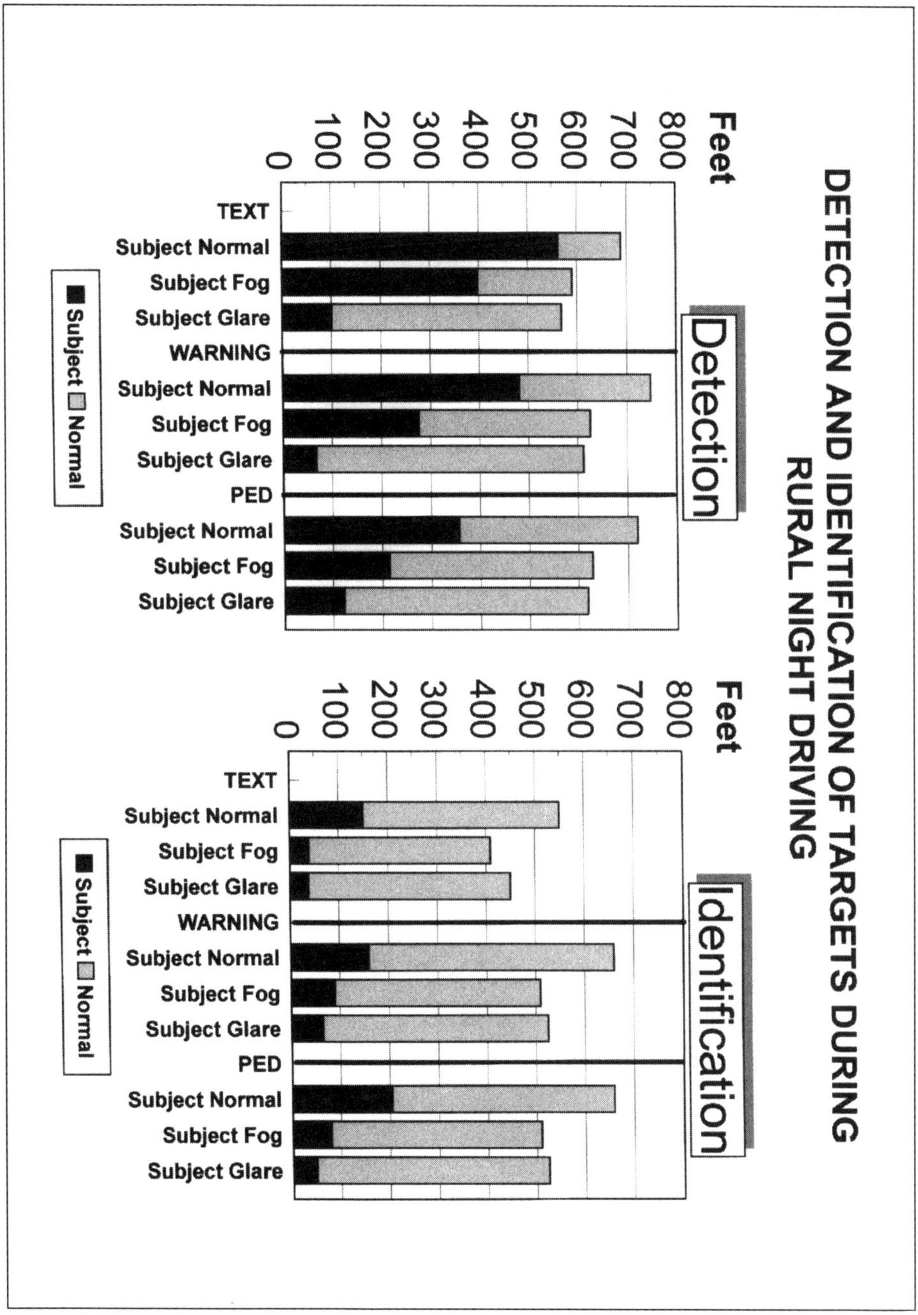

Figure 12.7 *(continued on next page)*

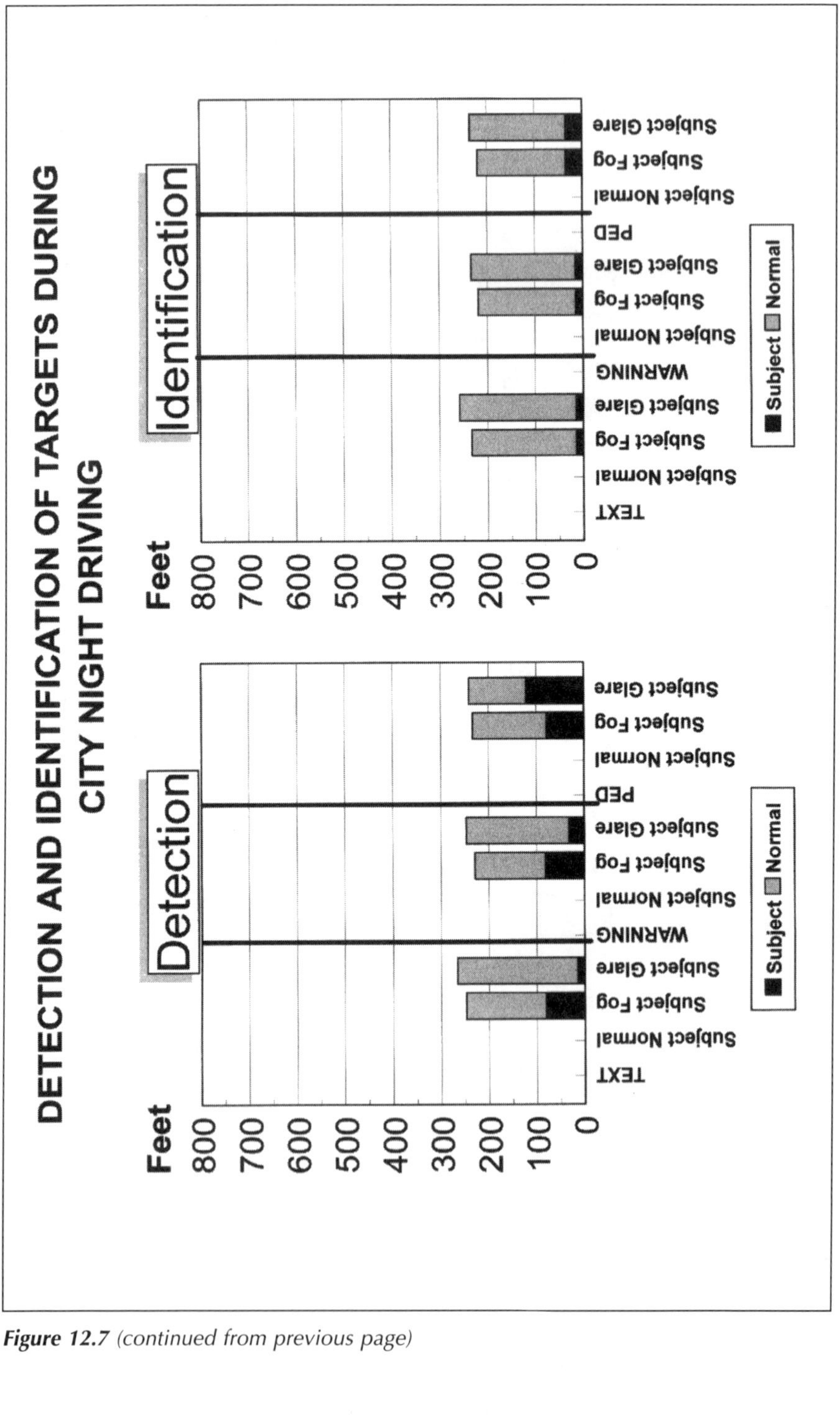

Figure 12.7 *(continued from previous page)*

and city (with street and store lights) under clear and inclement weather (fog) visibility conditions, and with and without glare.

The nighttime detection and identification distances for the rural driving conditions are graphed in Figure 12.7. The patient performs significantly less proficiently than normal under all conditions except for detecting message road signs. She has extreme difficulty reading the road message and warning signs and identifying the pedestrian hazard. While normal adults older (69.6 years) than she (60 years) could correctly identify the targets an average of 239.4 feet under all visibility conditions, this patient needed to be at an average distance of 77.8 feet, or 3.1 times closer, for correct target identification.

The nighttime driving detection distances for the city driving conditions are graphed in Figure 12.7. The data for the normal condition is missing due to an equipment malfunction. However, the fog and glare detection and identification distances in the city test condition are similar to that of the rural test condition: the patient performs significantly below that of the normal population.

In general, the driving simulation results confirm the serious functional vision loss as seen in the visual acuity and contrast sensitivity data.

5. The Activities of Daily Vision Scale

The Activities of Daily Vision Scale (ADVS) is one of several functional activity and personal perspective questionnaires providing some quantification of subjective quality of functional vision.[14] Although the ADVS was originally designed to evaluate visual function of persons with cataract, I have used it to provide a comparative baseline to evaluate the subjective functional vision due to other causes.

The ADVS uses visual activities such as seeing moving objects at night, reading typical newspaper print, climbing steps, and recognizing friends in bright sunlight. Those visual activities are categorized into five subscales (functional vision problem areas): (1) near vision activities; (2) distance vision activities that do not require driving; (3) glare disability; (4) night driving; and (5) daytime driving. Each subscale is scored between 100 (no difficulty) and 0 (cannot perform because of visual difficulty).

In a population of 223 presurgical cataract patients having an average age of 75 years (67 percent female), the scores (average ± standard deviation for in-person interview) and the refractive surgery subject are:

	Near	**Distance**	**Day Glare**	**Night Driving**	**Day Driving**
Patients	69 ± 25	66 ± 25	61 ± 31	69 ± 30	42 ± 32
Subject	30.3	16.4	0	0	0

The results of the ADVS show that this subject has significantly greater functional vision loss than that of an older presurgical cataract population. Although the use of these results by themselves may be questioned due to possible conscious and unconscious subject bias, when coupled with the more objective contrast sensitivity and driving simulator results they provide a well-rounded view of the subject's functional vision loss.

6. Visual acuity and contrast sensitivity processed pictures using EyeView.

The visual acuity and contrast sensitivity data were processed using the EyeView computer analysis program to create pictures depicting the functional vision loss of this patient.

The EyeView processed pictures of the street scene from the visual acuity data as compared to normal data are shown in Figure 12.8. The patient's significantly decreased visual resolution is very apparent in both pictures from the high degree of blur.

The below normal contrast sensitivity at all spatial frequencies, 1.5, 3, 6, 12 and 18 cycles per degree, will result in very poor contrast vision for most objects which are not high contrast black on white such as eye chart letters. The EyeView processed pictures of the newsprint and street scene from her contrast sensitivity

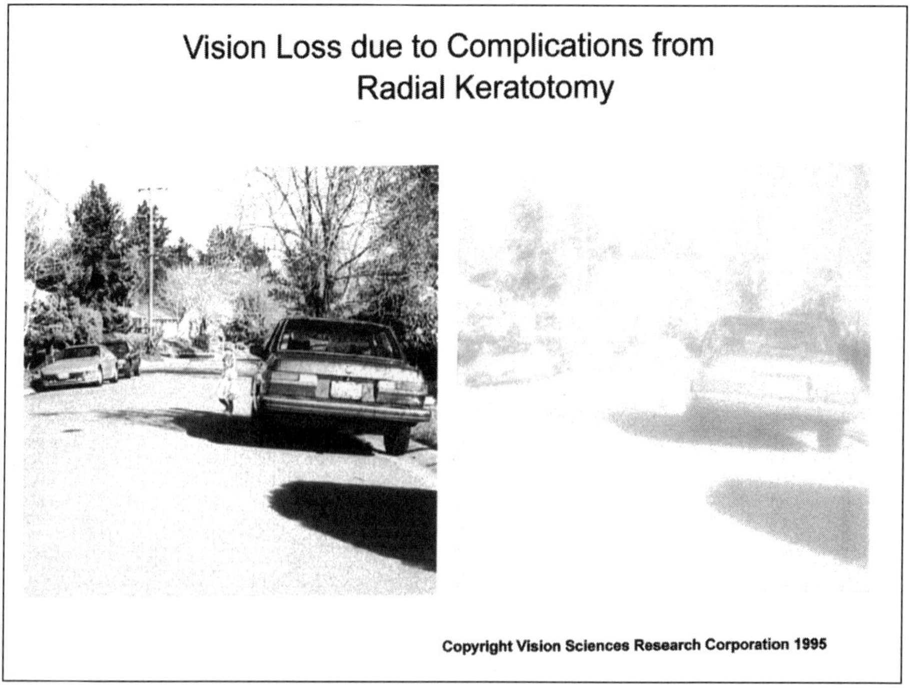

Figure 12.8

data shown in Figure 12.6 reveal very poor contrast perception as compared to normal data. The lack of detail in these pictures means that the patient will not see the same detail as that of a normal person when viewing the newsprint or street scene at the appropriate viewing distances. She will have to get considerably closer to the objects to see similar detail.

These computer processed pictures help to understand the patient's many visual complaints. She has considerable difficulty seeing low contrast objects during daytime, and much more difficulty at nighttime under reduced lighting conditions.

In summary, this patient has significant functional loss of vision that seriously impacts her daily activities and increases personal risk. A battery of functional vision tests was used to measure her visual capability. Visual acuity and contrast sensitivity, under daytime, nighttime, fog and glare conditions, all show large losses compared to normal population data.

Her severe functional vision loss due to poor visual acuity and contrast sensitivity is confirmed with poor performance on simulated nighttime driving tasks, an Activities of Daily Vision Scale and shown using EyeView processed pictures. The patient has significantly worse functional vision than that of typical older presurgical cataract patients.

Photorefractive keratectomy (PRK): The most recent refractive surgery technique is photorefractive keratectomy or PRK. PRK uses a laser to oblate the outer surface of the cornea, thereby changing its shape and, if all goes well, will eliminate refractive error. Although the FDA has recently approved PRK, prior European experience using PRK has shown that patients can suffer from hazy, poor night vision and glare for months after surgery. It is not surprising that some patients will have those vision problems considering that PRK creates a pitted corneal surface that scatters light. In addition, larger pupil sizes can reveal the edges of that pitted region to create glare conditions. Some researchers report that the vision loss is greatly diminished by one year and other laser surgery techniques claim to reduce those complaints.

Regardless of the laser surgery technique, proper functional vision analysis should be used to determine the functional vision capability of each patient. The visual complaints of these patients can be quantified by contrast sensitivity and glare testing, and using simulated driving conditions as needed, under day and nighttime light levels and ADVS-type questionnaires. These tests are similar to that used for patients suffering from cataract, because the causes of visual loss are similar: light scatter.

B. Functional vision loss due to cataract

We are entering an era of reduced medical care due to increased government Medicare costs and medical programs that in some cases reward doctors for *not* treating the patient. Many previously treated eye diseases and visual disorders will not be routinely treated in the future.

As the population ages, many age-related eye diseases not routinely treated will result in vision-impaired older individuals driving vehicles, putting themselves and others at serious risk. Cataract surgery reduction has been targeted by the government for cost-cutting measures through government guidelines. We can expect to see an increase in drivers with cataract causing accidents due to this new government policy. Therefore, individuals investigation accidents involving an elderly person should suspect eye disease such as cataract, even though the person may have 20/20 acuity. A simple review of medical records may reveal information about the cataract. However, other tests are needed to determine the affect of functional vision loss due to cataract. The main ideas outlined in a recent White Paper were accepted by the American Academy of Ophthalmology, who is attempting to restore scientific and clinical logic to those guidelines by supporting the need for contrast sensitivity and glare testing for the functional evaluation of cataract.[9, 15]

A cataract is an opacity of the lens which results in light being scattered or blocked at the retina. A cataract affects vision in several ways, primarily causing contrast losses, resulting in difficulty with object visibility (or target detection). Cataracts may also cause black spots, constant colored halos, monocular diplopia, desaturated color, discomfort and disability glare, lack of stereopsis and increased myopia and astigmatism.

Opacities may result in partial or total blockage of light to the retina. Patients experiencing partial light blockage may compensate by head or eye movement to locate the "clear" areas of sight.

Scattered light produces a veiling luminance which is superimposed on the retinal image. The scattered light reduces image and retinal contrast, resulting in overall hazy image quality across the complete visual field.

The degree of light scatter and/or blockage, hence the degree of loss of functional vision, is determined by the type and degree of opacities of the cataract as outlined in standard ophthalmic texts. Each type of cataract affects functional vision differently. Therefore, objective tests such as contrast sensitivity must be used to determine the degree of functional vision loss caused by cataract types.

Furthermore, a key problem of cataract is that contrast loss can be exacerbated by increased light in the form of glare, due to light sources such as the bright sun and oncoming headlights at night.

Although visual acuity may be spared, the effects of cataract on contrast are easily determined using contrast sensitivity and glare tests.[9, 13] Cataract reduces the quality of vision by light scatter from the opaque lens. Increased light results in increased light scatter. Therefore, an effective way to determine the functional loss of contrast due to cataract is to determine a contrast sensitivity function without, then with glare. An increased loss in contrast due to glare is an indication of increased light scatter due to the cataract.

Interpretation of the contrast sensitivity test may be accomplished by comparing the most recent evaluation to the patient's previous results, population "norms" and/or the fellow eye. For example, Figure 12.9, shows contrast sensitivity from 257 presurgical cataract patients divided into three regions: *Normal*, *Concern* and *Abnormal*.

These population data may be interpreted in the following manner; the minimum test result of any patient should be greater than the lower *Normal* population limit: the contrast sensitivity limit of a healthy 70-year-old. Of concern should be contrast sensitivity tests below the lower population limit and that of the least sensitive, healthy 70-year-old. This *Concern* range is where functionally significant contrast sensitivity loss occurs. Factoring these results with other objective measurements, the patients's lifestyle needs and surgical risks/expectations helps in evaluating the appropriateness of cataract surgery. The *Abnormal* range indicates serious functional vision loss and surgery is indicated unless other factors mitigate.

For example, a patient having a nuclear sclerotic cataract whose contrast sensitivity (shown in Figure 12.10) is tracked from initial measurement, three months pre-op, to two months post-op. Contrast sensitivity three months pre-op is in the *Concern* region. The pre-op contrast sensitivity degrades into the *Abnormal* region. The two months post-op contrast sensitivity recovers into the *Normal* region.

Unless one is familiar with the interpretation of these graphs, the degree of change in functional vision performance may not be readily apparent. However, the pictures processed from these contrast sensitivity data shown in Figure 12.10 illustrate the patient's functional vision loss from the initial visit through recovery that the patient.

The functional vision loss demonstrated by this patient over three months may be further examined by noting the quantitative differences in contrast sensitivity at the beginning and end of that time period. Functional relationships between target contrast and size and the contrast sensitivity function are straightforward.[4, 10, 11]

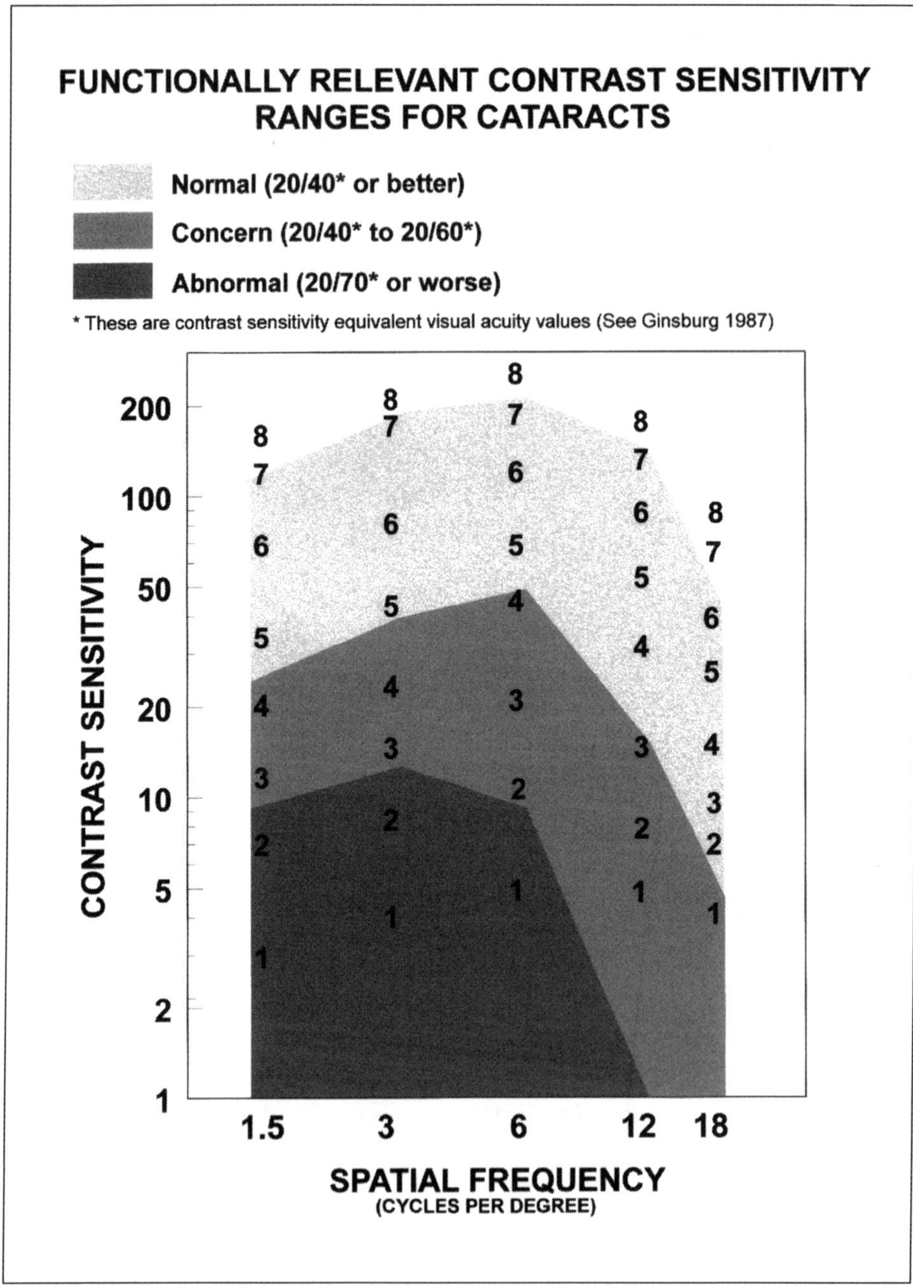
FUNCTIONALLY RELEVANT CONTRAST SENSITIVITY RANGES FOR CATARACTS
Normal (20/40* or better)
Concern (20/40* to 20/60*)
Abnormal (20/70* or worse)
* These are contrast sensitivity equivalent visual acuity values (See Ginsburg 1987)
CONTRAST SENSITIVITY
200
100
50
20
10
5
2
1
1.5
3
6
12
18
SPATIAL FREQUENCY
(CYCLES PER DEGREE)

Figure 12.9

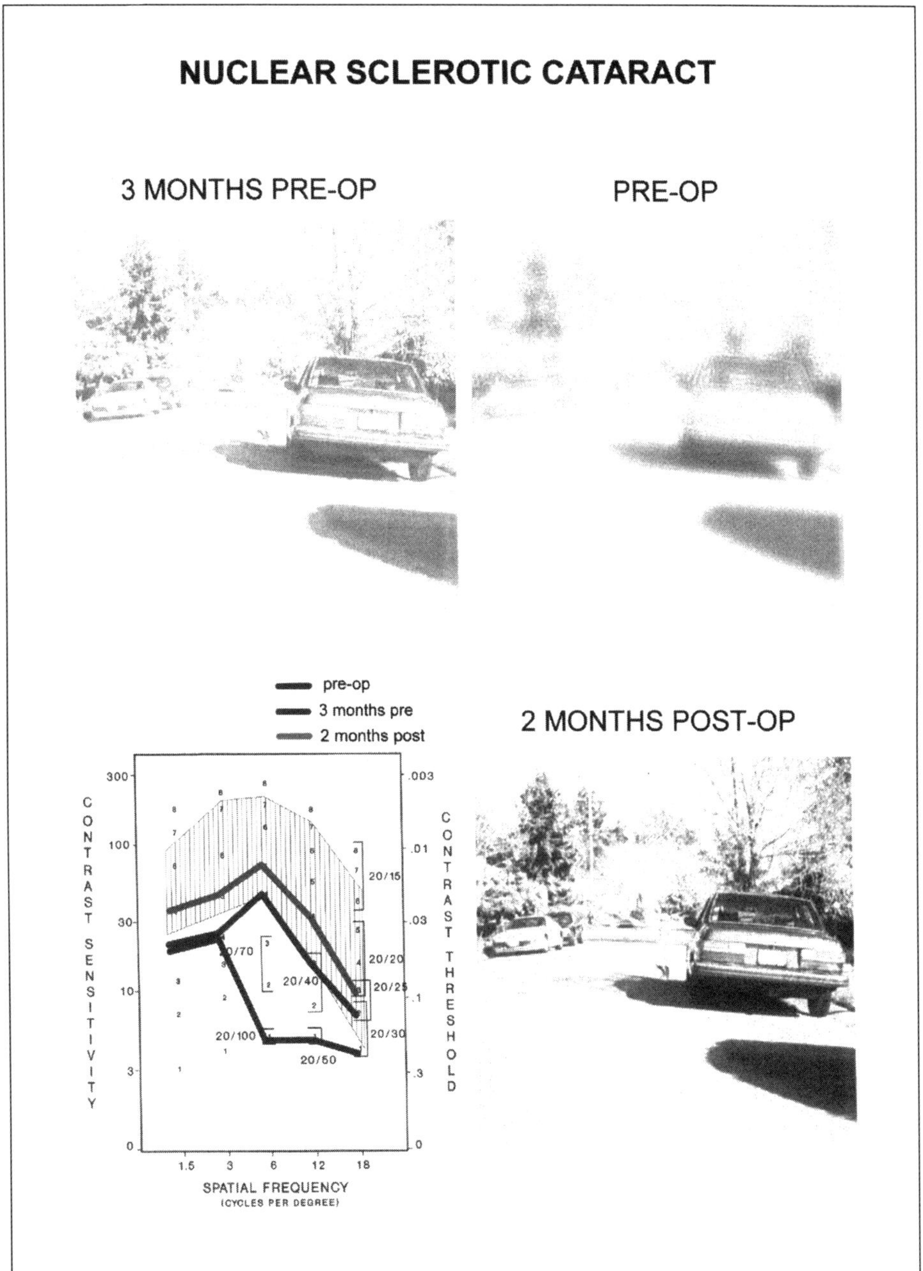
NUCLEAR SCLEROTIC CATARACT
3 MONTHS PRE-OP
PRE-OP
pre-op
3 months pre
2 months post
2 MONTHS POST-OP
CONTRAST SENSITIVITY
CONTRAST THRESHOLD
20/15
20/20
20/25
20/30
20/40
20/50
20/70
20/100
SPATIAL FREQUENCY
(CYCLES PER DEGREE)

Figure 12.10

For example, a 50 percent contrast target seen at 10 cycles per degree three months pre-op cannot be seen pre-op until it is 3.33 times closer at three cycles per degree. When viewed at 16 inches, the little girl in Figure 12.8 is the same size (visual angle) as when she is viewed by a driver at a distance of 88 feet. At that viewing distance, the size of critical features of the little girl, her face, dress and legs, are about 10 cycles per degree, and all but the legs are about 50 percent contrast. While travelling at 25 miles per hour, a driver has about 2.2 seconds to stop and avoid hitting the little girl on a dry road. In general, only 1.5 seconds perception/reaction time, or 81.1 feet, is needed and the three months pre-op driver has sufficient time to see the little girl and stop safely on a dry road.

However, three months later, the pre-op driver won't see the girl until one third the original 88 foot viewing distance, or 29 feet, which is too close to safely stop to avoid hitting her.

Thus, the contrast loss of this cataract patient and the intuitive effect of that loss of contrast as shown in these pictures has measurable adaptation for everyday functional vision performance such as driving.

Figure 12.11

C. Hitting an overturned trailer on a rainy night

Loss of contrast sensitivity is most debilitating under conditions of reduced contrast such as nighttime, rain, snow, glare, etc. Combining contrast reduced conditions such as nighttime rain can be particularly harmful to those who have reduced contrast perception. Some eye diseases can spare the central retina and leave visual acuity relatively unaffected. In such cases, good visual acuity masks the poor functional vision that may be the prime cause of the accident, as discussed in the following case.

A female having histoplasmosis (an eye disease caused by a protozoa which affects about 2 percent of people in the Midwest) drove into an overturned truck on a major highway on a rainy night. Although tested at 20/25 acuity, her contrast sensitivity was severely depressed. Compared to an age-matched normal shown in Figure 12.11, she has lost contrast sensitivity at the low and especially the middle spatial frequencies. However, high spatial frequencies were spared, allowing her to maintain good acuity.

The EyeView processed pictures show the severe functional consequences of the loss of contrast sensitivity. While the 20/25 acuity suggests good visual capability, the low contrast picture processed from the contrast sensitivity curve demonstrates otherwise. Note that the low contrast picture shows details just as sharp as that of the 20/25 picture. She has not lost the ability to see high contrast detail as evidenced by the 20/25 acuity. However, the loss of contrast of that detail as well as all the other scene information is the functional vision problem. While the contrast in the 20/25 picture could be greatly reduced before it would look similar to the low contrast picture, a similar reduction in contrast of the low contrast picture would render it virtually blank. Thus the 20/25 picture suggests that the person has a large contrast reserve that can tolerate contrast loss on a rainy night while in reality the low contrast sensitivity person has little. Although one can never prove that this degraded vision is the sole cause of the accident, clearly she would be visually handicapped under poor contrast conditions such as they were on a rural highway on a rainy night. The woman was not capable of seeing what an average person could see.

Most importantly, these EyeView pictures bring to the jury an understanding of the effects of vision loss from reduced contrast.

D. The unseen motorcycle: Foveal cone

In this case, a motorcyclist ran into the front side of a van that entered his path from a side street. Sight stopping distance analysis showed that the motorcyclist did not have sufficient time to see and avoid that accident. The van driver said he stopped at the stop sign and looked but didn't see the motorcycle, which would have been very easy to see had he looked. Why didn't the van driver see the motorcycle?

One possibility is that the van driver did look in the direction of the motorcycle but was visually attracted and paid attention to the cars travelling on the highway. The highway was on the far side of and parallel to the road on which the motorcycle travelled. By simulating the foveal cone view of the center of attention in this scene, the cars on the highway, as shown in Figure 12.12, the motorcyclist fades into the background with low conspicuity.

E. The invisible curb: Visual "illusion"

The cyclist's front wheel slips off the curb of a raised sidewalk, resulting in serious injury. The city had painted the curb white in an attempt to make the raised sidewalk stand out to cyclists. And, indeed, the white curb does stand out when viewed from the side. However, when viewed from a cyclist approaching the raised sidewalk from the front, the usual perspective, the white curb is perceived as just another lane marker, a flat white lane line, blending into the near and distance elements of the scene and becoming a visual trap (Figure 12.13). In this case it is the lack of visual cues required to perceive the white curb as part of a raised sidewalk that results in this accident. The solution to this visual hazard is to use different colored stripes for the curb along with warning signs, visual cues that would make the hazard conspicuous.

Figure 12.12

12.4 Visual Perceptual Analysis Methodologies

Documenting the information in a scene available to an observer becomes a crucial part of any accident analysis and is central to visual perceptual analysis.

This documentation is especially important to understand possible effects of abnormal vision as a possible cause of the accident. The use of contrast sensitivity and EyeView image processing as have been discussed here can, in certain cases, require the laying of a solid foundation for the scene information and personal visual performance levels. Typical documentation of scene content includes still photos and motion and video pictures. Each type of scene documentation has certain advantages and disadvantages in terms of being able to accurately depict scene information in perceptually valid ways.

A. Scene fidelity

The key to scene fidelity is to ensure that key scene elements are as similar to the accident scene as possible. If key scene elements have changed from original accident documentation, then they must be recreated for proper documentation. Attention is given to the background elements, for example, the roadway and its markings, buildings, vegetation such as trees and bushes, vehicles, pedestrians and at night, streetlights and other sources of light. The main visibility elements

Figure 12.13

such as a pedestrian or vehicles need to be essentially similar to that of the accident. Pedestrian size, race, gender and clothing color and style must be substantially similar. Vehicle make, model and color must be substantially similar. Eye height of the pedestrian and vehicle driver must be known and accounted for in certain exhibits.

B. Human factors issues

Many accidents typically involve perception/reaction time human factors issues. Analysis of perception/reaction time provides key locations based on speed and time from which to document the visibility of scene information. Other human factors issues involve the dynamic aspects of human vision such as dark and light adaptation, speed, distance and size judgments.

The time it takes the eye to dark adapt from entering a dark area after being in strong sunlight determines what can be seen immediately and how that changes over time. Conversely, leaving a dark room and entering the bright sunlight requires the eye to change adaptation state and results in time to adjust to normal performance levels. The amount of time to return to normal depends upon the initial and subsequent light levels and the age and visual health state of the person.

Speed, distance and size judgements made by principles and witnesses can be very misleading due to the simple fact that the visual system does not have mechanisms for absolute judgements along those dimensions. Rather, speed, distance and size judgements rely on relative evaluations based on personal experience and varying scene elements such as object overlap and texture, which can be misleading.

Therefore, visibility analysis based on speed, distance and size judgements from observers should be used with caution and verified by more objective analysis whenever possible.

The dynamic changes of the eye and limited precision of absolute judgements can play an important part in the visual perceptual analysis.

C. Documenting scene visibility

1. Controlling the process

Given that the exemplar accident scene integrates any pedestrians and vehicles with human factor considerations, such as critical sight stopping distances, the scene information available to the average observer is typically documented using still photos, film and video pictures.

The scientific validity of these photos and pictures depends upon the control with which they are obtained. Although the light levels, contrast and sizes of important features of objects in a scene can be measured and recorded, the visual system uses the interplay of such information in very complex ways. For example, visual mechanisms respond to emitted or reflected light of objects in a manner whereby the perceived brightness of objects depends upon the surrounding light, contrast, size and shape. Figure 12.14 shows how the same square is seen as dark or light depending upon the surround. (See end note 4 for other examples and how a channel filter model offers an explanation for how they are seen.) Therefore, it is the perceived brightness that determines the contrast of objects in a complex scene and consequently, how it is seen. By matching the visibility of an object in a scene to some recording medium, that record becomes the control for any other display medium.

Typically, Polaroid prints are used for recording visibility of scene information. By changing camera settings to provide a range of visible detail on the film and viewing the Polaroid print using similar scene information luminance, Polaroid prints provide rapid feedback as to the fidelity of scene information to the observer. This control technique, known as contrast matching,[4] compensates for the complex interrelationships of visual function relating to contrast, resolution, size, form and color into a single visibility judgement. Once obtained, that information can be used to develop larger format still photos, motion film, video or image processed pictures.

2. Creating scene documentation

The control print allows subsequent still photos, film, video and image processed pictures to accurately represent key scene information. However, each modality has certain advantages and disadvantages requiring careful attention, or certain biases can occur.

Large format still pictures (typically, 6×7 format cameras) provide large negatives producing good scene resolution of detail, especially important for creating enlargements for courtroom viewing. However, the still format can bias the information in a scene if perception/reaction time issues are important. The key scene information that may have been available for only a fraction of a second for the driver of a vehicle during the accident now is shown for unlimited time to the jury. Another drawback to still photography is that it cannot capture the dynamic range of brightness occurring over time in cases of sun or headlight glare.

Although still photographs can be very important, human factors issues must be considered when they are used as evidence The still photographs can demonstrate what information is available to be seen, but they need to be scientifically interpreted from a visual science and human factors perspective to understand what may have been seen.

Motion film has the advantage of providing the dynamic presentation of scene information over time. Motion film also has the advantage of being presented on large screens in front of the jury to create life-size simulations. However, motion film suffers from the same key limitation as still film: lack of dynamic range of brightness of different light sources in the same scene. Furthermore, careful control is required over nighttime variables such as film speed to ensure proper simulation of vehicle speed, flashing lights, etc. Uncontrolled vehicle lights will appear having motion too rapid under those conditions.

Video cameras offer the advantages of dynamic presentation but with the added advantage of a much larger dynamic range of brightness than that available from motion film. Since video presentation uses emitted light rather than reflected light of film media, video presentation appears more real and life-like, especially night scenes with different light sources at very different light levels. Another advantage is the possibility of real-time capture of scene information at night under conditions not realized using motion film. One disadvantage includes smaller display formats. However, proper sizing of the scene information with accurate viewing distance can also create life-size simulations. Arguments are often made that film captures more detail than does video at night. However, there needs to be objective tests to support that claim. Today's digital BetaCam rivals film resolution for night scenes.

Image processed pictures offer advantages over still pictures in allowing local changes to pictures, creating more accuracy to the control Polaroids than film developing techniques can provide. Furthermore, image processing can be used to bracket local information in a scene such as contrast and foveal viewing in ways unobtainable using photographic techniques.

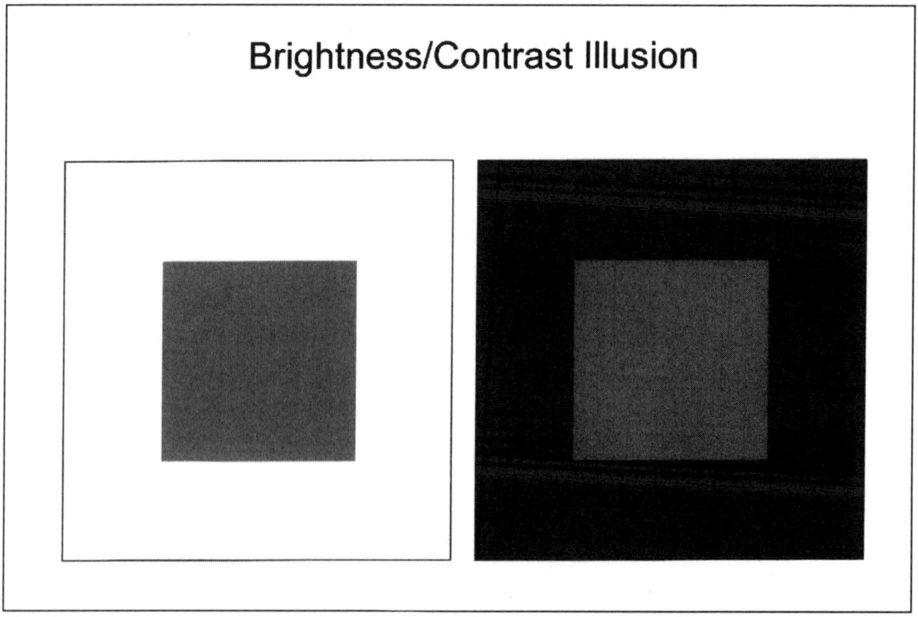

Figure 12.14

Latest animation tools coupled with video background are being used to create complex scene simulations under conditions that cannot be reconstructed with ease using other techniques. As advances are made with video camera resolution and light sensitivity, display size and resolution and animation, these digital tools will increasingly replace the analog photographic techniques providing far greater accuracy and flexibility of presentation of scene information.

3. Cautions relating to pictorial demonstrations

There can be many biases inherent in presenting pictorial demonstrations. For example, control techniques must be used with caution. First, only the scene information that is being matched by the observer is controlled on a control print. Because of the limited dynamic range and resolution of film, the control print cannot capture all the information in a scene with equal accuracy. Therefore, typically several control prints created with different exposures are needed to reliably capture the important features in a scene. Second, the control technique is only as good as the person making the scene feature match.

If that person does not have average contrast sensitivity, properly prescribed lenses or normal, healthy vision then the control print can be biased towards the observer's abnormality and affect subsequent documentation. This is also true for the person creating the demonstrative evidence from the control print. Third, in some cases, proper physiological controls must be used such as similar luminance for the contrast matching technique used at the scene to create the control Polaroid print and courtroom display to ensure similar adaptation state of the observers.

Along this line of thought, it is important to realize that judges, attorneys, jury members or other experts with dissimilar contrast sensitivity functions or visual disfunction may not see similar object detail in the demonstrative evidence and make evaluations accordingly. We have seen earlier that there are significant differences in contrast sensitivity due to normal individual variation and eye diseases that can affect target detection and visibility. Even with proper training and unlimited viewing distances and examination time, there is about a 25 percent error in reading low contrast x-rays, attesting to the fact of considerable individual differences in ability to see low contrast objects even among trained professionals. Although it is not currently being done, judges, attorneys, jury members and other experts should have certifiable normal contrast vision before being asked to evaluate any visual evidence requiring critical evaluation of scene content.

Presentation of pictorial evidence can be very biased without proper controls, especially due to the emotive content of certain scenes. Pictorial demonstrations typically show that key scene information such as a pedestrian in the street or overturned truck blocking the travel lane cannot be seen in time to stop safely. "Proof" of that fact is the jury's inability to "see" the information at a critical sight stopping distance or time in motion pictures. However, the accuracy of that judgement assumes similarity of events that may not have been established. For example, there may have been some flashing lights from traffic control signals or passing headlights that may have distracted the driver at a critical time which are not presented or presented accurately in the limited field of view of the display. There may have been changes in light and dark adaptation that change the ability to see key scene features such as the "slip and fall" pedestrian coming out of the dark mall into the bright sunlight or the vehicle driver entering the dark tunnel from the brightly lit roadway. Therefore, photographic skills alone are not always enough to ensure accurate observations and interpretation of pictorial demonstrative evidence. Vision test results of the person processing the pictures is also an important link to accuracy.

When these issues become important, one solution is to perform scientifically controlled experiments using matched observers to determine the statistical average and standard error of object visibility,[4] an example of which has been provided in this chapter. Only by determining the average sight distance seen in either a series of still photos or motion or video pictures can what the average reasonable person would have seen be scientifically determined, and establish the veracity of the pictorial demonstrative evidence. The courtroom display is only a display and cannot be used as the experiment in every case. The courtroom display should be supported by objective scientifically obtained sight distance and visibility data whenever possible.

A jury who is not age, sex and experience matched to the observer and has certifiable normal vision may be biased to see, or not see objects depending upon what information has preceded the pictorial demonstration. It is interesting to note that the term "substantially similar" that is used to allow pictorial evidence into court is not considered for the observers of that evidence in the courtroom. Given proper control of the pictorial evidence, it is a relatively simple step to use that evidence to conduct a proper study and obtain scientifically defensible information for presenting visibility analysis information in the courtroom.

End Notes

1. Henderson R.L., Burg A. (1974) *Vision and Audition in Driving*. Report TM(L)- 5297/000/00. System Development Corporation. Santa Monica, Calif.

2. Kinney J.A.S. (1968) Clinical measurements in night vision. In *Proc. Armed Forces NCR Committee on Vision*, National Academy of Sciences, Spring Meeting.

3 Shinar D. (1977) *Driver visual limitations, diagnosis and treatment.* Institute for Research and Public Safety, Indiana University School of Public and Environmental Affairs, Bloomington, Ind.

4. Ginsburg A.P. (1986) Spatial filtering and visual form perception. In *Handbook of Perception and Human Performance, II*, edited by Boff K., pp. 34–1, 34–41, John Wiley & Sons, New York.

5 *Engineering Data Compendium on Human Perception and Performance*, edited by Boff K., pp., John Wiley & Sons, New York.

6. Ginsburg A.P. (1987) Contrast sensitivity, drivers' visibility and vision standards. In *Visibility for Highway Guidance and Hazard Detection*, Transportation Research Record 1149, pp. 32–39. Transportation Research Board, National Research Council, Washington, D.C..

7. Decina L, Staplin L. (1993) "Retrospective evaluation of alternative vision screening criteria for older and younger drivers," *Accid Anl and Prev*, 25(3), pp. 267–275.

8. Ginsburg A, Waring G, Steinberg E. et al. (1990) "Contrast sensitivity under photopic conditions in the prospective evaluation of radial keratotomy (PERK) study." *Refract Corneal Surg*, 6, pp. 82–91.

9. Ginsburg A.P., Cheetham J.K., DeGryse, R.E. and Ableson, M. (1995) "The Effects of flurbiprofen and Indomethacin on Acute Cystoid Macular Edema: Functional Vision and Contrast Sensitivity," *J Cataract Refract Surg*, 21, pp. 82–92.

10. Ginsburg A.P. (1994) "Testing functional vision: important relationships between grating contrast sensitivity and low-contrast letter acuity tests." *Proc. Ophthalmic Lens Design and Fabrication II*, SPIE, pp. 36–43.

11. Ginsburg A.P. (1996) Next Generation Contrast Sensitivity Testing. In *Functional Assessment of Low Visio*n, edited by Rosenthal B. and Cole R., pp. 77–88, Mosby-Year Book Inc., St. Louis.

12. Ravelico G., Baccara F., Rinaldi G. (1993) "Contrast sensitivity in multifocal intraocular lenses." *J. Cataract Refract Surg*, pp. 22–25.

13. Ginsburg A.P. (1987) Clinical findings from a new contrast sensitivity test chart. In*Advances in Diagnostic Visual Optics*, edited by Fiorentini A., Guyton D.L. and Siegel I.M., pp. 132–140, Springer-Verlag, New York.

14. Mangione C.M. et al (1995) "Development of a questionnaire for the assessment of visual function." *Inv. Ophthal. Vis. Sci.*, abs., p.s428.

15. White Paper on Cataract Surgery. (1996) American Academy of Ophthalmology and American Society of Cataract and Refractive Surgeons, Ophthal, 103–7, pp. 1152–1156.

Chapter 13

Systemic Diseases and Highway Safety

Leslie Weintraub, O.D.

Synopsis

13.1 Metabolic Diseases

Metabolic disorders refer to dysfunctions of the endocrine glands. The endocrine glands work with the nervous system, to maintain homeostasis, or a balanced internal environment. Endocrine glands produce hormones, which regulate metabolic activities such as growth, utilization of nutrients by cells, salt and water balance, blood homeostasis and metabolic rate.

If the endocrine glands are not functioning properly, debilitating symptoms may occur. For example, a generalized lack of strength, muscle weakness, spasm or tetany, sudden episodes of vertigo, or unconsciousness. Motor vehicle operation should be restricted until the particular metabolic disease has been treated sufficiently to prevent these dangerous symptoms.

A. Diabetes mellitus

Diabetes, or the inability of the body to metabolize sugars, is very common. According to the 1988 National Health Survey, 26 out of every 1,000 people are

Table 13.1

Recent Studies Evaluating Accident or Violation Experience of Diabetic Drivers (Adapted from La Porte et al., 1991)

Study	N	Time	Type of Dbx	Accidents		Violations		Units	Comments
				Dbx	Ctl	Dbx	Ctl		
DeKlerk & Armstrong (1983)	8623	9 years	Both	72	73	-	-	hospital admissions for road trauma	Hospital-recorded accidents. Does not consider driving exposure. Diabetic males had more hospital admissions than expected.
Songer et al. (1988)	127	1 year	IDDM	14.2	7.1	-	-	per 100 drivers	Self-reported accidents. Small sample size for 1-year time.
	121	1 year	IDDM	10.4	3.9	-	-	per 100 drivers/per million miles	Adjusted for driving exposure.
Eadington & Frier (1989)	166	8 years	IDDM	5.4	10.0	-	-	per million miles	Self-reported accidents. Control was not age- or sex-matched.
Stevens et al. (1989)	354	5 years	ITDM	7.9	7.8	-	-	per 1.5 million kilometers	Self-reported accidents. Adjusted for driving exposure.
				7.1	7.1	-	-	per 100 drivers/year	
Chantelau et al. (1990)	241	2 years	ITDM	-	-	11%	16%	%	Comparison group not matched on age, sex or driving exposure.

N Sample size
Dbx Diabetics
Ctl Comparison group
IDDM Insulin-dependent diabetes mellitus
ITDM Insulin-treated diabetes mellitus
Both ITDM and non-insulin treated diabetics

res rpts/age related disability

diagnosed with diabetes mellitus (Hu et al. 1993). This survey also shows that the chances of developing diabetes increases with age. Non-insulin dependent, or NIDDM, is more common in the elderly than is insulin dependent, or IDDM. Reuben et al. found that 8.8 percent of individuals aged 65–74 have been diagnosed with NIDDM (Reuben et al., 1988).

Persons with NIDDM may experience hyperglycemia, or abnormally high levels of blood sugar. This will impair alertness, usually very gradually. Therefore, it does not inhibit one's safe driving ability, as long as they are properly counseled and monitored.

Persons with IDDM, and possibly those treated with oral hypoglycemic drugs such as diabeta, may experience hypoglycemia. Hypoglycemia, or abnormally low levels of blood sugar, can occur rapidly and without warning. Faintness or unconsciousness may result. For this reason, it is imperative for IDDM persons to self-monitor their blood-sugar levels. Only then can they ascertain their ability to drive safely. In fact, the U.S. Department of Transportation recommends a "restricted license" for persons subject to "stress hypoglycemia."

After reviewing several studies of driving records from the 1960s and 1970s, Janke, Peck, and Dreyer (1978), concluded that diabetes causes some increased driving risk. Both Janke et al., and Waller (1973), agree that the major cause of peril associated with diabetic drivers is most likely their susceptibility to hypoglycemic attacks. Table 13.1 shows a compilation of recent studies evaluating accidents or traffic violations of diabetic drivers (Janke, 1994). The results are mixed, but clearly show some increased risk associated with diabetes.

Diabetes may affect vision, and is one of the leading causes of blindness in our country. Eye disturbances associated with diabetic retinopathy, are discussed in the next chapter.

B. Thyroid disease

The thyroid gland, located in the neck, just anterior to the trachea, secretes two thyroid hormones. The two principal actions of the thyroid hormones, T3 and T4, are to stimulate metabolic rate and to promote growth.

Excessive amounts of thyroid hormone, or hyperthyroidism, causes an increase in metabolic rate, weight loss, and goiter. Symptoms of hyperthyroidism that may cause danger while driving include nervous excitability, tremors, breathlessness upon exertion, and a rapid heart rate.

Subnormal amounts of thyroid, or hypothyroidism, cause a decrease in metabolic rate, body temperature, pulse rate, respiration and mental capacity. Symptoms of hypothyroidism that may cause danger while driving, include physical and mental sluggishness, fatigue, and poor muscle tone.

Severe hyperthyroid or hypothyroid persons should not drive a motor vehicle at all. However, if well diagnosed and treated, persons affected with these disorders are able to safely drive motor vehicles.

C. Hyperparathyroidism and hypoparathyroidism

Disorders of the parathyroid glands, which surround the lateral lobes of the thyroid gland, may cause abnormally high, or abnormally low blood and bone calcium levels. Normal levels of calcium are essential for normal nerve and muscle function, bone metabolism, cell membrane permeability, and blood clotting.

If calcium levels in the blood are extremely low, as may occur with hypoparathyroidism, nerve fibers become more excitable. Twitching and muscle spasms may ensue. Neuromuscular excitability, cramps, spasms and tetany, are all contraindications for driving.

If calcium levels in the blood are extremely high, as may occur with hyperparathyroidism, muscular weakness and hypotonia may ensue. Since so much calcium is removed from the bones in this case, they are weakened and easily fractured. Muscular weakness, loss of muscle tone and brittle bones, may prevent safe driving. If calcium levels are stable, with or without treatment, persons affected with hyperparathyroidism or hypoparathyroidism should be able to drive safely.

D. Posterior pituitary insufficiency

The posterior lobe of the pituitary gland, releases oxytocin and antidiuretic hormones (ADH). ADH increases water reabsorption from the kidney, to conserve the body's water. Persons with insufficient pituitary function may experience enormous fluid loss. Hypoglycemic episodes, as do occur in hyperinsulin states, may ensue. This causes faintness and unconsciousness, which clearly make it unsafe to drive. Proper therapy, however, should prevent this from occurring.

E. Anterior pituitary insufficiency

The anterior lobe or the pituitary gland, releases six hormones, including the growth hormone, prolactin and several tropic hormones. Growth hormone has several actions that may directly or indirectly raise blood-sugar levels. Insufficiency may cause abnormally low carbohydrate levels and hypoglycemic events. This may impair alertness, making those persons unsafe drivers.

F. Pituitary tumor

Tumors of the pituitary gland may cause visual field loss. The pituitary gland sits at the base of the cerebellum, just under the intersection of the optic tracts. The classic visual field loss, in this case, is a bitemporal hemianopsia. This is the loss of both temporal fields of vision. Loss of peripheral vision can prove to be hazardous for a motor vehicle driver. Loss of peripheral vision results in a slower reaction time to objects appearing from the sides, which is the scenario for most motor vehicle accidents.

Visual fields may or may not return after treatment of a pituitary tumour. Visual field examinations are recommended every 6–12 months after treatment.

G. Adrenal cortical hypersecretion (Cushing's disease), and hyposecretion (Addison's disease)

The two adrenal glands, located on top of the kidneys, contain an inner medulla and an outer cortex. The adrenal cortex secretes corticosteroids. The corticosteroids help regulate water and electrolyte balance in body fluids, normal cell metabolism, blood glucose levels, and secondary male sex characteristics.

Hyperfunction of the adrenal cortex (Cushing's disease) causes excessive water and sodium retention, with consequential high blood pressure and potassium loss. When associated with muscular weakness and osteoporosis, it inhibits safe driving ability.

Hypofunction of the adrenal cortex (Addison's disease) causes excessive sodium and water loss. This is associated with muscle weakness, asthenia, low blood pressure, and possible hypoglycemia and syncope. These symptoms contraindicate driving.

H. Hyperfunction of the adrenal medulla

The adrenal medulla releases epinephrine and norepinephrine into the blood. This produces the "fight or flight" reaction during stressful situations. Epinephrine and norepinephrine increase heart rate, blood pressure, blood glucose, and blood oxygen. If hyperfunction of the adrenal medulla causes headaches, dizziness, weakness, blurred vision, a rapid pulse rate and increased blood pressure, driving a motor vehicle is clearly contraindicated.

13.2 Cardiovascular Disease

Symptoms of cardiovascular disease that would inhibit safe driving ability, are loss of consciousness, severe chest pain, and symptoms such as dizziness or blurred vision. Some heart conditions may also cause insufficient oxygenation of the brain. Lack of oxygen to the brain may impair mentation, or even cause sudden death behind the wheel. Cardiac deaths average about 4.6 per 1,000 man years, and 1.3 per 1,000 woman years in those aged 35–64 year of age (Shephard, 1987, cited in Janke, 1994). However, there is a 10 to 11 fold increase in the risk of cardiac deaths, in the age group of 60–64, as compared to the age group of 40–44.

A review of the more recent studies concerning the traffic accident risk of cardiovascular patients concluded that none of the well controlled studies have demonstrated a consistent increase in risk associated with cardiovascular disease (Potvin, Guibert, and Loiselle, 1993). Similarly, a review of studies done before 1978, concluded that the majority of cardiovascular patients pose no threat behind the wheel (Janke, Peck, and Dreyer, 1978). The researchers noted, however, that cardiovascular patients tend to reduce the amount of time they spend driving alone and driving in heavy traffic. This self restriction may account for the favorable results. Also, the researchers noted that the studies concerning cardiovascular patients and driving are full of methodological problems.

Although no definitive study has shown an increased private car crash risk associated with cardiovascular disease, persons afflicted with heart disease are usually restricted from obtaining a commercial drivers license. This is reasonable since commercial drivers, unlike private passenger car drivers, frequently need to drive long hours under adverse weather and lighting conditions. If a crash occurs, these large commercial vehicles can cause major damages and traffic congestion.

A. Congestive heart failure

If the heart fails to pump the blood throughout the body efficiently, blood backs up into the lungs, liver, and veins. The causes congestion of fluid in the lungs, legs, liver, and possibly other parts of the body. Persons affected with congestive heart failure will have difficulty breathing, and may be driving hazards. In 1993, Wielgosz and Asad found that the prevalence of congestive heart failure increases with age: 3 percent in those aged 45–64, 6 percent in those aged 65 and above, and 10 percent in those aged 75 and above (cited in Janke, 1994).

According to the American Medical Association (AMA), persons with congestive heart failure should not drive commercial or passenger transport vehicles, even if their condition is stable. Driving a private motor vehicle is considered safe, as long as their condition is stable.

B. Arrhythmias

Abnormal functioning of the ventricles, which pump blood out to the body, are very serious conditions that may cause sudden death. Rapid ventricular contractions tend to reduce cardiac output and may lead to heart failure. Therefore, any disorder of cardiac rhythm that causes very rapid ventricular contractions would contraindicate driving. For example, ventricular arrhythmias or atrioventricular blocks, associated with faintness or unconsciousness, contraindicate driving. The types of heart disease most frequently associated with ventricular tachycardia or ventricular fibrillation, are coronary artery disease (70 percent), dilated cardiomyopathy (7 percent), hypertensive heart disease (3 percent), and valvular disease (2 percent) (Larson, Stupey, et al., 1994).

Atrial rhythm disturbances, such as premature beats, or brief dysrhythmias, usually do not disturb safe driving ability. Atrial fibrillations or flutter, however, should be controlled by medication or a pacemaker, in order for the person to safely drive a private motor vehicle. The AMA advises that these persons should not drive a commercial or multi-passenger vehicle. Pacemakers usually alleviate disabling symptoms of cardiovascular disease, by maintaining proper cardiac rhythm. Thus, if a pacemaker has been implanted, the person should not be at risk to drive a private motor vehicle.

C. Angina pectoris (cardiac pain)

Persons with coronary artery disease, that experience angina at random times, are advised against driving, by doctors. This is because the resulting pain in the chest, arm or jaws can be so severe, it incapacitates the driver temporarily. Nitroglycerin dilates the coronary arteries, and usually alleviates cardiac pain.

Persons with coronary artery disease, whom experience angina only with moderate exertion, are advised by doctors against operating a commercial or multi-passenger vehicle. (No Class I or Class II licensing.)

D. Hypertension

Although hypertension normally does not preclude driving, some symptoms of hypertension may. Complications of hypertension that may contraindicate driving are: frequent and severe headaches, heart failure, weakness, mental disturbances, dizziness, retinal hemorrhages, and cerebral vascular hemorrhages. The potential for syncope caused by severe hypertension has also been mentioned as a great hazard to driving (Balkanyi, 1971).

Hypertension has been associated with an increased driving hazard. In a 1970 study, randomly selected groups of drivers with arteriosclerosis, hypertension, rheumatic heart disease, and other heart diseases, were compared to groups of drivers with the same age, sex, and city of residence, without medical conditions. The arteriosclerotic and hypertensive groups were found to have significantly higher accident rates than those of the comparison groups. The rates for the other cardiovascular disease groups, however, were not significantly different from those of the comparison groups. Violation rates for all groups were comparable (Crancer and O'Neal, 1970).

Hypertensive drugs may also cause side effects that contraindicate driving. These side effects include depressed reflexes, somnolence, syncope, and others. See Chapter 15 for more detail. Complications of hypertension, and antihypertensive drugs, should be evaluated in order to determine safe driving ability.

The AMA recommends that persons with:

Class I licenses have blood pressure < 180 / < 105.
Class II licenses have blood pressure < 200 / < 115.

E. Hypotension

Unless accompanied by syncope (faintness), hypotension does not preclude driving a motor vehicle.

13.3 Cerebrovascular Attacks (CVA)

Cerebrovascular accidents refer to those conditions where there is an interruption of blood supply to the brain. 80 percent of CVA's, or strokes, are ischemic, or due to lack of blood supply to the brain. They are caused by an embolus or thrombus. 20 percent of strokes are hemorrhagic, or due to leakage of blood out-

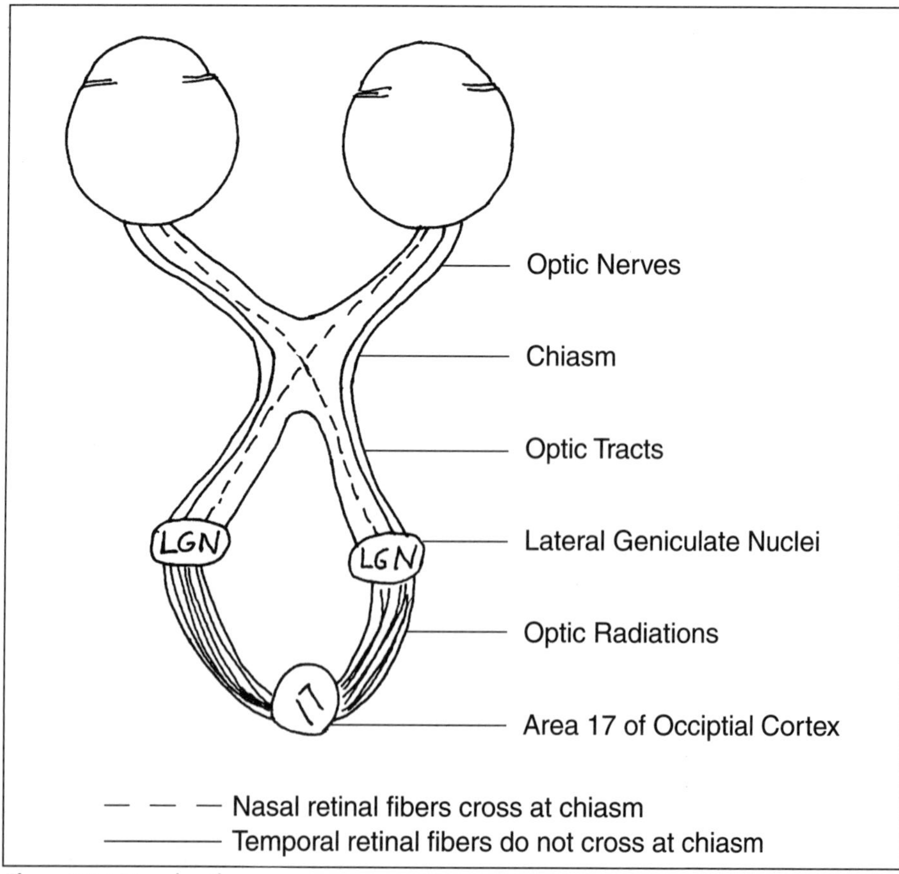

Figure 13.1 *Visual pathway.*

side the normal vessels. They can be caused by a ruptured aneurysm or hemorrhage from an arteriovenous malformation. It is estimated that each year 500,000 Americans have a stroke. Strokes are the third leading cause of death in the United States, and an estimated 2 million people are stroke survivors.

Brain tissue dies when it is deprived of adequate blood supply. Resulting disabilities that may increase crash risk include motor, sensory and behavioral changes, and visual and spatial deficits. Visual and spatial problems caused by stroke include visual neglect, and impairments in visual attention, oculomotor skills and visual fields. Up to 76 percent of stroke patients admitted to hospitals have visual and spatial deficits, which are a major cause of traffic accidents (Hills,

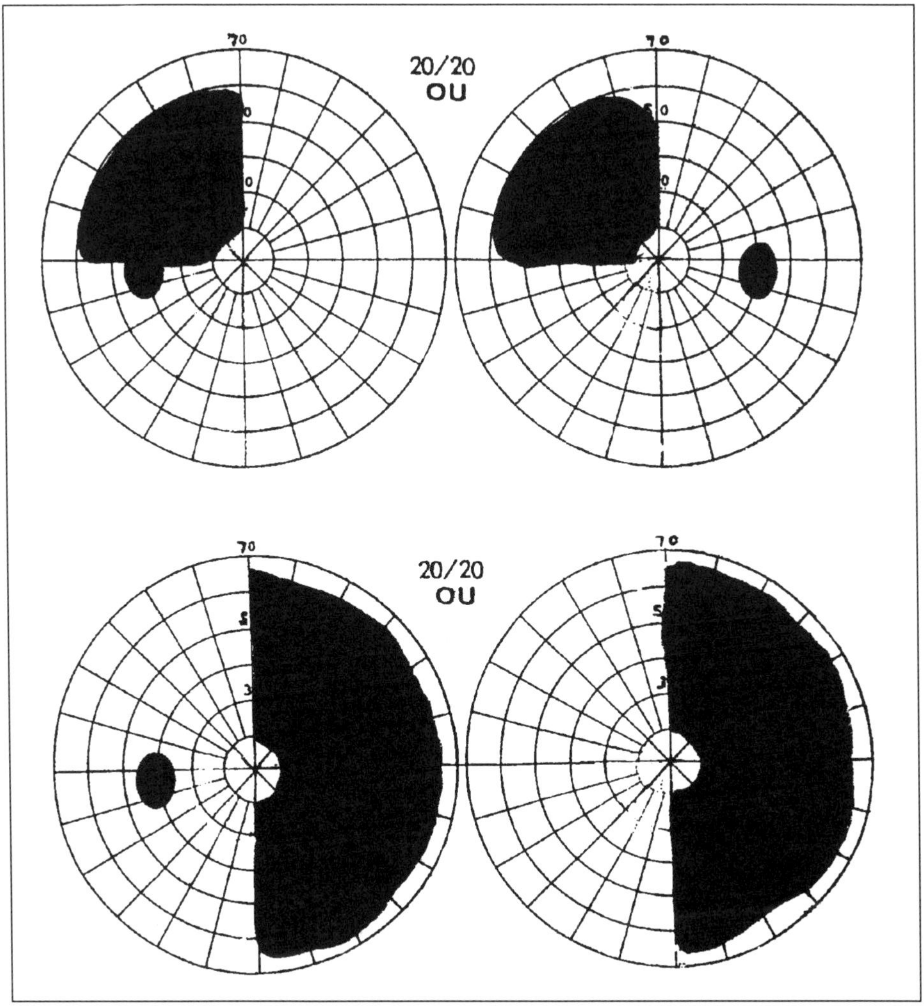

Figure 13.2 *Examples of post-CVA visual fields with resulting post-chiasmal lesions: left superior quadranopias (top), and right hemianopias (bottom). Both with 20/20 vision. Notice how they respect the mid-line.*

1980). In a 1983 study, stroke patients who had been cleared by hospitals to resume driving showed compromised driving skills and poor awareness of other vehicles. For example, these patients had difficulty entering and leaving the highway, driving in roundabouts, and performing two tasks at once in an emergency situation (Wilson and Smith, 1983).

Strokes may cause lesions of the nerves and pathways that control eye movements. Our extraocular muscles, which control eye movements, are innervated by cranial nerves (CN) located in the brain stem. They are the Oculomotor (CN III), Trochlear (CN IV), and Abducens (CN VI). Damage to them will most likely cause double vision, or oscillopsia (the sensation that objects are moving or oscillating).

Depending upon where the lesion is in the visual pathway, damage from stroke can affect one eye, or more commonly, one field of vision. Prechiasmal lesions will affect one eye, while postchiasmal lesions will cause hemianopias, or blindness in one-half of the visual field. In a study of over 100 hemianopias by Trobe et al., 89 percent were found to be caused by strokes (cited in *Clinical Ophthalmology*). Hemianopias or quadranopias may be extremely hazardous when driving. Objects or cars coming from the side can go completely unnoticed. See Figures 13.1 and 13.2.

Since the right cerebral hemisphere is dominant in visual and spatial abilities, while the left is dominant in language, we could assume that those persons suffering from right cerebral strokes would have more difficulty driving. In fact, this has been shown in a group of fifty post-CVA patients who underwent driver retraining: 74 percent of the patients with left CVA's passed the driving test, while 52 percent of the patients with right CVA's passed (Quigley and De Lisa, 1983).

If no new stroke occurs, deficits are stable within six to twelve months after the CVA. If antihypertensives are used to prevent future strokes, individuals can have visual impairments, drowsiness, light-headedness, and impaired attention in some (Toole, 1984). Stroke patients should be followed at least every six months with a visual field test, until stable, and counseled about their disabilities.

References

Balkanyi, A., "Various causes of disturbance in consciousness important for traffic medicine," *Praxis*, 60(17), 532-534, 1971.

Benzodiazepine/driving collaborative group, "Are benzodiazepines a risk factor for road accidents?", *Drug and Alcohol Dependence*, 33, 19-22, 1993.

Bell, Emslie-Smith, Paterson, *Textbook of Physiology*, Churchill Livingstone, London and New York, 10th Edition, 1980.

Crancer, A. and O'neall, P., "A record analysis of Washington drivers with license restrictions for heart disease", *Northwest Medicine*, 69, 409-416, 1970.

Doege and Engelberg, editors, *Medical conditions affecting drivers*, American Medical Association, Chicago, 1986.

Hedden and Raffle, *Medical aspect of fitness to drive: A guide for medical practitioners*, Medical Association of South Africa, 1990.

Hu, P.S., Young, J.R., and Lu, A., *Highway crash rates and age-related driver limitations: Literature review*, Oakridge National Laboratory, Oakridge, Tennessee, 1993.

Janke, Mary, "Age-related disabilities that may impair driving and their assessment," California Department of Motor Vehicles, 1994.

Janke, M., Peck, R.C., and Dreyer, D.R., "Medically impaired drivers: An evaluation of California policy", California Department of Motor Vehicles, Sacramento, 1978.

Larsen, G.C., Stupey, M.R., Walence, C.G., et al., "Recurrent cardiac events in survivors of ventricular fibrillation or tachycardia", *Journal of the American Medical Association*, 271, 1335-1339, 1994.

Physicians Guide for Determining Driver Limitation, American Medical Association, Chicago, 1968.

Potvin, L., Guibert, R., and Loiselle, J., "Cardiovascular disease and traffic accidents: Weighing the evidence", *Journal of Safety Research*, 24, 233-241, 1993.

Reuben, D.B., Silliman, R.A., and Traines, M., "The aging driver: Medicine, policy, and ethics", *Journal of the American Geriatric Society*, 36, 1135-1142, 1988.

Solomon and Davis, *Human Anatomy and Physiology*, Saunders College Publishing, Philadelphia, N.Y., 1983.

Stewart, Moore, Marks, et al., "Driving cessation and accidents in the elderly: An analysis of symptoms, diseases, cognitive dysfunction and medications," Dept. of Pharmacy Practice and Department of Statistics, University of Florida, Gainsville, Fla., 1993.

Waller, Julian, *Medical Impairment to Driving*, Thomas Pub., Springfield, Ill., 1973.

Chapter 14

Eye Disease and Highway Safety

Leslie Weintraub, O.D.

Synopsis

14.1 Introduction

Most eye diseases cause a reduction in contrast sensitivity, and an increased sensitivity to glare. Since visibility and conspicuity must always be evaluated when reconstructing motor vehicle accidents, contrast sensitivity and glare are major factors. Did the driver see the other motorist, pedestrian, road sign, etc., or not? Visual acuity measurements alone will not determine this. Contrast, glare and other factors need to be evaluated. If a person has decreased contrast sensitivity, decreased color vision and/or increased glare, it may be clearly determined that they could not see the obstruction in the road. This is especially significant in the presence of adverse weather conditions, such as rain, snow, or fog. Water on the pavement alone reduces its contrast by a factor of 5 to 10 times. A person with already reduced visual function may be "blinded" by this. Therefore, in order to evaluate one's ability to drive, ocular disease is a major concern.

14.2 Corneal Dystrophies/Degeneration/Scars

The cornea is the first surface through which light enters the eye. It is normally transparent, and regular, or undistorted in shape. The transparency and smooth curvature of the cornea allows the light rays to enter the eye, and bend clearly toward the retina. Any central corneal dystrophies, degenerations or scarring will blur vision by causing aberrations through the irregular or hazy surface. This will decrease visual acuity and increase glare.

14.3 Cataracts

Cataracts are any opacity in the lens of the eye. Most commonly, they are age related, but they can also result from trauma, long term oral steroid use, diabetes and other causes. Cataracts diffuse, scatter and back-reflect the light that enters the eye. This means that many aberrant light rays reach the retina, thereby increasing glare and causing a general decrease in visual acuity, contrast sensitivity, and possibly color vision.

A very common complaint of cataract patients is glare from light distortion and "halos" while driving at night. These people commonly suffer from posterior subcapsular type of cataracts, or opacities in the posterior subcapsular region of the lens, which is toward the back of the lens. These people will tend to see better under moderate to subdued lighting conditions, since reflex dilation of their pupils will allow more light to enter the eyes.

Visual acuity in persons with cataracts decreases significantly more than in those without cataracts, when exposed to glaring circumstances. For example, sun reflection, headlights from an oncoming car, and fog will decrease visual acuity and contrast sensitivity at all spatial frequencies even more in persons with cataracts than in persons without. In fact, of all ocular pathologies, cataracts and

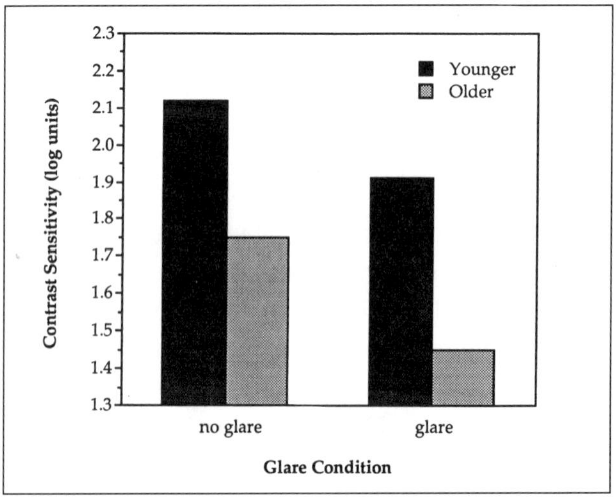

Figure 14.1 *Mean contrast sensitivity for younger men (mean age of 25.7 years) and older (mean age of 68.3 years) observers for the glare and non-glare conditions.*

glaucoma produce the most marked reductions in contrast sensitivity (National Research Council cited in Janke). A person with 20/20 visual acuity, and no cataracts, may "glare" to 20/40, while the person with 20/20 visual acuity and cataracts, may glare to 20/80. Since our contrast sensitivity normally drops off at low spatial frequencies, a low spatial frequency object, such as a truck, will be even more difficult to see through cataracts. This is why, in low contrast circumstances such as fog, an older person may not see a truck. Figure 14.1, adapted from "Dynamic Visual Contrast Sensitivity" (Liebowitz et al.), shows dramatic differences in contrast sensitivity between older and younger drivers, especially in glare conditions.

Cataracts significantly reduce night vision. Night driving and the ability to make out traffic signs becomes much more difficult. For example, an improperly placed traffic sign, or one with poor contrast, will be difficult to see. Low contrast objects will be difficult to view, and in combination with headlight glare, may become completely washed out.

Another possible symptom of cataracts is loss of color vision. "Yellowing" of objects is particularly common in those with nuclear sclerotic cataracts. Nuclear sclerosis, or a yellow to brunescent type discoloration the lens, causes the shorter blue and violet wavelengths to be absorbed, while the longer red and yellow wavelengths are transmitted. A brown or black lens can cause extensive color vision loss.

Patients with nuclear sclerosis also tend to become more nearsighted, and need frequent changes in their eyeglass prescriptions. Cortical opacities, on the other hand, may increase farsightedness. Also, different refractive indexes of the lens may even induce monocular diplopia, or two different images in one eye. This is due to a beam-splitting effect.

Cataracts can cause mild to severe impairments in visual-related driving skills. However, after successful cataract extraction with intraocular implants, these impairments are usually completely resolved.

14.4 Glaucoma

Glaucoma is a disease marked by increased intraocular pressure, optic nerve atrophy and visual field loss. This last characteristic, visual field loss, is the most detrimental to driving ability. Since objects of surprise, like a child running after his ball, usually appear from the sides, our peripheral vision is extremely important (see Figure 14.2).

The amount of peripheral vision loss in a glaucoma patient varies from none to an absolute loss. Generally, we see reductions of sensitivity in various areas of the visual field. This can translate into prolonged reaction times. Johnson and Keltner screened 10,000 volunteers with an automated visual field machine. They

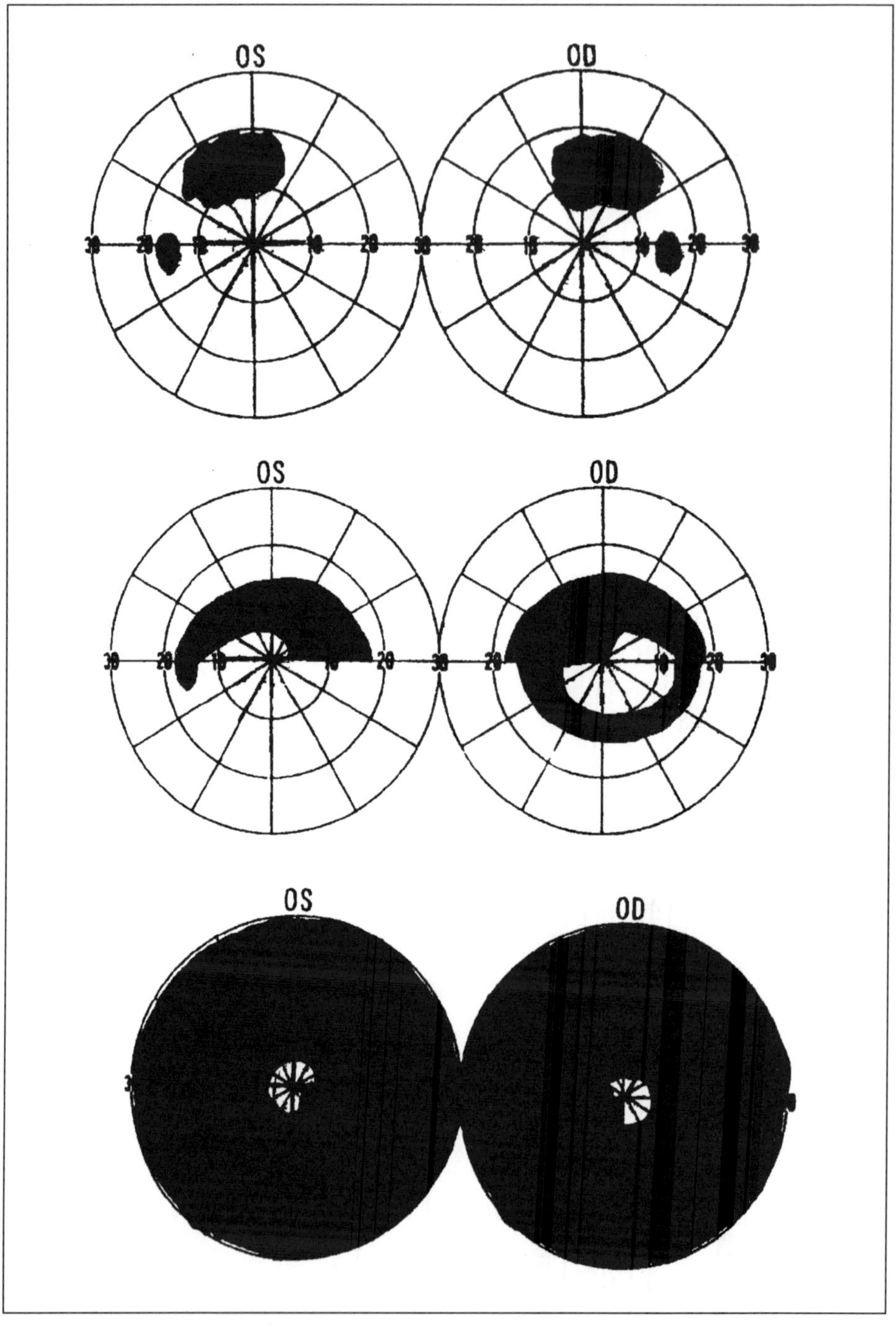

Figure 14.2 *Examples of glaucomatous visual fields: Paracentral scotmas (top), Bjerrum or arcuate type scotomas (middle), and advanced glaucomatous fields (bottom). All have 20/20 central vision. Notice how they do not respect the mid-line.*

found that approximately 13 percent of drivers above 65 years of age showed field loss, and 3.5 percent of them were severe. The most common cause of these visual field losses were glaucoma, retinal disorders and cataracts. They also found that drivers with binocular field loss have traffic accident and conviction rates twice as high as those with normal visual fields, over their three year test (Johnson and Keltner, 1983).

Persons with glaucomatous changes in their peripheral vision will have most difficulties driving at night. The rods, which are used for night vision, are the photoreceptors located in the peripheral retina that are most damaged by glaucoma. Also, contrast sensitivity is markedly reduced in persons with glaucoma (National Research Council, 1987).

14.5 Peripheral Visual Field Loss

Visual field tests are not routinely required in order to obtain a driver's license. States usually require a 100–140 degree field of vision with both eyes for a class III drivers license, but rarely test. Also, states do not specify how sensitive that visual field needs to be.

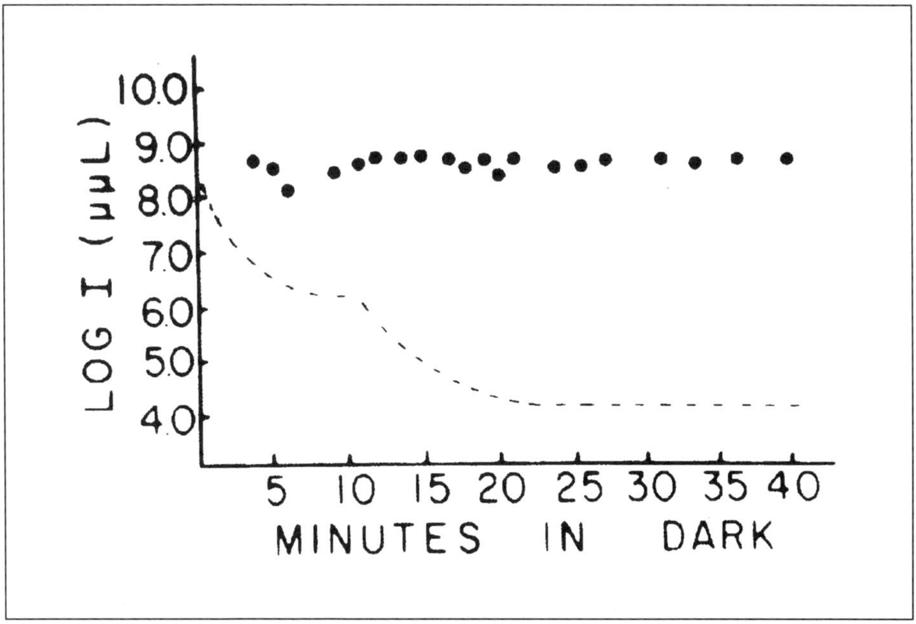

Figure 14.3 *Peripheral dark adaptometry. Dashes show a normal curve following a bleaching light. Dots represent a patient with retinitis pigmentosa, showing abnormalities of both cone and rod function (Duane & Jaeger,* Clinical Ophthalmology, *Vol. 3, Chap. 24, pg. 5, ©1988 Harper & Row).*

A 1991 study of peripheral vision loss and driving performance shows that real world accidents, as well as accidents on a driving simulator, increased for those with peripheral vision disabilities (Slyk, Severing, Fishman). They concluded that automobile accidents increased in frequency as the severity of the peripheral vision disabilities increased. Also, they showed that reaction time to peripheral stimuli was prolonged in those persons with peripheral vision loss as compared to people with normal peripheral fields of vision. (See Chapter 15 for more information.)

14.6 Macular Degeneration/Maculopathies

Age-related macular degeneration is the leading cause of blindness in the elderly population. However, maculopathies may occur at any age. They primarily involve the central retina. The cones, which are the photoreceptors located in the central retinal region, degenerate. This means they stop sending messages to the brain. This weakens visual acuity and color perception. Peripheral vision normally remains very good. Since static central visual acuity is most affected, persons with significant macular degeneration will probably not be able to pass a driving test.

14.7 Retinitis Pigmentosa

Retinitis pigmentosa, RP, are progressive, hereditary retinal diseases characterized by progressive photoreceptor and retinal pigment epithelium degeneration. Usually, rod degeneration is severe, causing drastic reductions in peripheral vision and night vision. The most common symptom is difficulty with dark adaptation, or night blindness. Dark adaptometry shows that in lower levels of illumination, people with RP can only see objects with extremely high luminosity (brightness). The rod and cone threshold are both highly abnormal. See Figure 14.3, adapted from *Clinical Ophthalmology*.

Less characteristic RP diseases involve the cone receptors more than the rods. Persons afflicted with this type of disease will have reduced central visual acuity, reduced color vision, or color blindness, and difficulty in bright lights.

RP has been associated with an increased motor vehicle accident rate. Subjects with RP reported significantly more accident involvement than visually normal control subjects, in a five year Illinois study. Total accidents, as well as accidents involving failure to detect peripheral information, was higher in the RP group than in the statistically equivalent in age, gender and years of driving experience group (Szlyk et al., 1991). Examples of binocular visual fields from that study are shown in Figure 14.4.

14.8 Diabetic Retinopathy

Diabetic retinopathy is one of the leading causes of blindness in the country, affecting approximately 50,000. It has many stages. Only persons with the initial stage, background diabetic retinopathy (BDR), may have visual driving abilities. Visual changes associated with pre-proliferative and proliferative diabetic retinopathy almost always preclude driving. However, Reuben et al. found 8 percent of diabetic drivers had proliferative diabetic retinopathy, 5 percent were blind in one eye, and 2.4 percent had severe decreases in visual acuity (Reuben et al., 1988).

BDR is usually associated with small intra-retinal hemorrhages. These hemorrhages block the transmission of light to the retina, and may cause small blind spots. The size of these resulting blind spots are proportional to the size of the retinal hemorrhages. Since the retina is unable to be stimulated through them, it follows that less information may reach the brain. Under circumstances with limited visual information, decreased retinal stimulation may result in slower reaction times.

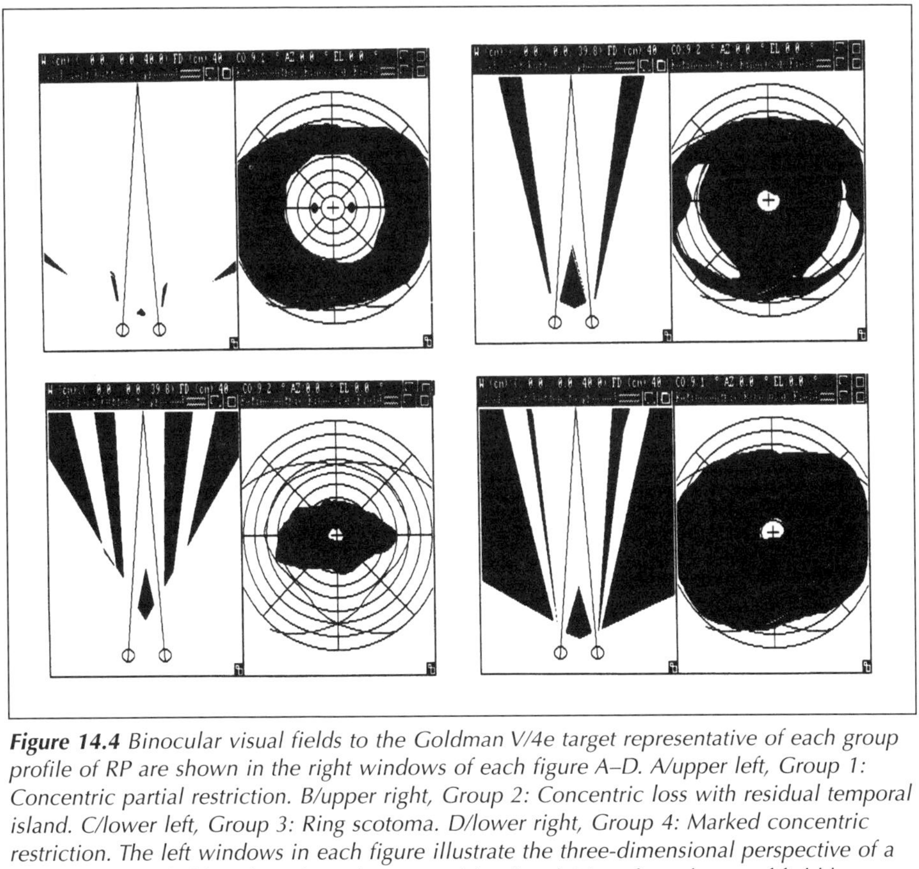

Figure 14.4 *Binocular visual fields to the Goldman V/4e target representative of each group profile of RP are shown in the right windows of each figure A–D. A/upper left, Group 1: Concentric partial restriction. B/upper right, Group 2: Concentric loss with residual temporal island. C/lower left, Group 3: Ring scotoma. D/lower right, Group 4: Marked concentric restriction. The left windows in each figure illustrate the three-dimensional perspective of a subject's visual field as the subject fixates straight ahead. Note the volumes of field loss shown in black in the peripheral field which are characteristic of RP.*

Another characteristic associated with BDR is macular edema. Persons with BDR may develop macular edema, or swelling of the central retina. This causes decreased visual acuity, decreased color vision, and slower dark adaptation. In fact, a common complaint among persons with macular edema is difficulty driving at night. In addition, accommodative ability is reduced in about 20 percent of diabetics.

Also common in diabetic persons is blurred vision caused by fluctuating blood-sugar levels. Patients with hyperglycemia have a tendency toward myopia, while those with hypoglycemia have a tendency toward hyperopia. Blurred vision in the absence of any retinal disease, is associated with changes in the hydration of the lens due to hyperglycemia. As blood-sugar levels fluctuate, visual acuity and refractive error can change, sometimes dramatically. Optimal eyeglass prescriptions may change frequently. This means that a person who has variable blood-sugar levels, whether or not they have been diagnosed with diabetes or not, may see perfectly well to drive safely one day, while on another day may not.

Surgeries, such as photocoagulation of the retina and vitrectomy, have been extremely successful in minimizing visual damages due to neovascularization and vitreal hemorrhages (proliferative diabetic retinopathy). However, regardless of how much vision is salvaged, it is rare that those surgically treated for proliferative diabetic retinopathy will be able to drive safely.

14.9 One-Eyed and Spectacle Corrected Aphakes

Persons with only one visually functional eye will have visual field limitations that may result in an increased risk of intersection crashes. Persons who have had their cataracts removed without intraocular lens implantation, who wear aphakic glasses, have visual field limitations as well. Certain aphakic eyeglasses cause ring scotomas, or a circular shaped blind spot in their mid-peripheral vision. Persons driving with this type of eyeglass correction also pose an increased risk for causing an intersection crash.

14.10 Postoperative Cataract and Refractive Surgery

Persons who have had their cataracts removed with intraocular lens implantation, as well as those who have had radial keratotomy (RK) or Lasik, experience increased glare. Discomfort and veiling glare may become significantly hazardous to these drivers. Headlight glare at night, is especially disturbing to many of these postoperative patients.

Complications from refractive surgery include irregular astigmatism and decreased contrast sensitivity. Irregular astigmatism will cause decreased visual acuity and may distort images. Decreased contrast sensitivity is a decrease in the ability to distinguish objects from their background. As discussed previously, contrast is a critical factor in determining whether an object is visible. Contrast sensitivity falls dramatically at night. In persons with lower than normal contrast sensitivity, signs or cars with low contrast may not be discernible.

Radial keratotomy weakens the cornea. A weakened cornea is much more susceptible than a normal non-operated cornea to severe corneal trauma, corneal abruptions, hyphemas and resultant cataracts. Automobile crashes and the force of air bags have been shown to more easily cause these types of traumas in post RK persons.

14.11 Ocular Muscle Imbalance

Ocular muscle imbalances, or heterophorias, are tendencies of the eyes to become misaligned. There may be an increased strain on these eyes to keep fused, or to maintain single binocular vision. Therefore, these conditions may indirectly cause fatigue. If sudden diplopia (double vision) occurs while driving, it may cause an automobile crash. Uncontrolled or intermittent diplopia represents a driving limitation.

14.12 Color Blindness

Most traffic lights have been standardized so that they can easily be distinguished by persons with red-green color deficiencies. Blue has been added to the green lights, and yellow has been added to the red lights, to increase their contrast. Color deficiencies are not considered hazardous for driving, except in severe cases of protanopia (red color blindness), completely color blind, or achromatic persons. Achromatic individuals have very poor vision, and should never drive.

14.13 Depth Perception

Stereopsis is the ability to use binocular cues to perceive depth. In other words, it is how well we use both eyes together to distinguish differences in nearness of objects. Stereopsis is significant only at near range, or within two meters. At far range we use mostly monocular cues to determine depth, not binocular cues. If depth perception is poor, it can affect near range driving tasks such as parking. Measurements of depth perception do not correspond with distance visual requirements, such as highway driving.

14.14 Age

Normal elderly people have been shown to have a reduction in contrast sensitivity and an increased sensitivity to glare. Whether this is a result of age, or age-related diseases is not definitively concluded. Either way, we all are at risk from their detrimental effects. Anything we can do to help increase visibility and conspicuity on the road would benefit us all.

References

Atlas of Clinical Ophthalmology, J.B. Lippincott Co., Philadelphia, 1988.

Doege and Engelberg, *Medical Conditions Affecting Drivers*, American Medical Association, Chicago, Ill, 1986.

Evans, D.W., and Ginsberg, A.P., "Contrast Sensitivity Predicts Age-Related Differences in Highway Sign Discriminability," *Human Factors*, 27, 637-642, 1985.

Johnson, C.A., Keltner, J.L., "Incidence of Visual Field Loss in 20,000 Eyes and Its Relationship to Driving Performance," *Archives of Ophthalmology*, 101, 371-375, 1983.

Kline, D., "Aging and the Visibility of Highway Signs: A New Look through Old Eyes," AAA Foundation for Traffic Safety, Washington, D.C., 1991.

Leibowitz, Tyrrell, et al., "Dynamic Visual Contrast Sensitivity," AAA Foundation for Traffic Safety, Washington, D.C., June 1993.

Owsley, C., Sekular, R., Seimsen, D., "Contrast Sensitivity throughout Adulthood," *Vision Research*, 23, 689-699, 1983.

Reuben, D.B., Silliman, R.A., Traines, M., "The Aging Driver: Medicine, Policy, and Ethics," *Journal of the American Geriatrics Society*, 36, 1135-1142, 1988.

Stewart, Moore, et al., "Driving Cessation and Accidents in the Elderly: An Analysis of Symptoms, Diseases, Cognitive Dysfunction and Medications," Dept. of Pharmacology and Dept. of Statistics, University of Florida, Gainsville, Fla., AAA Foundation for Traffic Safety, Washington, D.C., January 1993.

Szlyck, Severing and Fishman, "Peripheral Visual Field Loss and Driving Performance," The University of Illinois at Chicago, AAA Foundation for Traffic Safety, Washington, D.C., August 1991.

Chapter 15

Drugs and Alcohol Affecting Highway Safety

Leslie Weintraub, O.D.

Synopsis

15.1 Introduction

Prescription drugs, drugs of abuse, and alcohol may all affect highway safety. Sleepiness is the most common drug and alcohol reaction that causes dangerous driving. The National Highway Traffic Safety Administration (NHTSA) estimates that sleepy drivers cause 50,000 motor vehicle crashes each year. Also, according to The National Transportation Commission, sleepy drivers cause 57 percent of all fatal accidents. Adverse drug and alcohol reactions, overuse of medication, and polypharmacy (consuming many medications that could interact), must all be considered when evaluating one's ability to drive safely.

Medication use and polypharmacy increase with age. They become very common among senior citizens, 65 years and older. According to the 1988 National Disease and Therapeutic Index (NDTI), the 65 and older age group, which was 12 percent of the total population, received 29 percent of all the prescriptions. Medication use increases even more in those aged 75 and above. Three quarters of the population aged 75 and older use prescription medication. The average number of drugs taken daily by patients enrolled in Medicare is ten (Staplin et al., 1987). Elderly people not only take most of the medication, but they also experience three to seven times more adverse drug reactions than younger people do. This is due to a decrease in renal and hepatic functioning with age.

A. Narcotic analgesics (pain relievers)

Narcotic analgesics include codeine, hydrocodone/Hycodan, oxycodone/Percodan, propoxyphene/Darvon, meperidine/Demerol, hydromorphine/Dilaudid, morphine, opium, heroin, methadone and fentalyls. Heroin is the most commonly abused drug in this category. Methadone is a medication used to treat heroin addicts.

Narcotic analgesics inhibit pain neurons in the central nervous system (CNS) from releasing their neurotransmitters. This decreases the brain's perception of pain. These drugs induce drowsiness and impair driving ability. They also cause varying degrees of euphoria, inability to concentrate, dizziness, apathy, blurred vision and uncontrolled thought. Siegfried and O'Connolly (1986) have noted that opioid analgesics have adverse effects on driving, particularly in the older population. These drugs decrease blood pressure, decrease heart rate, decrease core body temperature, constrict pupils, and may cause eyelids to droop (ptosis). This category of drugs will not affect smooth pursuit eye movements, or nystagmus.

B. CNS depressants

Central nervous system depressants include: (1) non-barbiturates such as carisoprodol/Soma, cyclobenzaprine/Flexuril and methaqualone/Quaalude; (2) barbiturates such as phenobarbital, alurate and elixin; (3) antianxiety drugs, or the benzodiazepines, such as alprozolam/Xanax, triazolam/Halcion, diazepam/Valium, lorazepam/Ativan, flurazepam, oxazepam and chlordiazepoxide; (4) antidepressants such as amitriptyline/Elavil, imipramine/Tofranil, doxepin/Sinequan, fluoxetine/Prozac, nortriptyline and desipramine; (5)antipsychotics such as haloperidol/Haldol, chlorpromazine/Thorazine, fluphenazine, pericyazine and lithium; and (6) alcohol (ethyl alcohol).

CNS depressants inhibit neural transmission in the brain and spinal cord to varying degrees. Their effects can be additive. Smooth pursuit eye movements and saccades both have control centers at the cerebrum, cerebellum and brain stem. Therefore, these drugs can decrease smooth pursuit eye function, exaggerate normal endpoint nystagmus, and decrease angle of onset of nystagmus. Police officers may detect use of these drugs via horizontal gaze nystagmus (HGN) testing.

All CNS depressants increase the effects of alcohol, and can cause drowsiness, sleep, motor and sensory changes, and also a decrease in psychomotor skills. Small doses used to calm patients' nerves, usually have no affect on driving. However, if these drugs are abused, driving ability will be impaired. In a 1976 study of barbiturates and driving, these drugs were found to increase reaction times, impair motor control, reduce visual motor coordination and impair oculomotor function (Sharma et al., 1976). Also, ataxia, or poor balance and muscular incoordination, can occur with the benzodiazepines. Difficulties with pupillary function, accommodation, image fusion and dark adaptation, which may occur, will especially reduce night driving ability.

These drugs may be particularly dangerous in elderly drivers. Plasma concentrations of antianxiety drugs required for sedation dramatically falls between the ages of 20 and 80 years. Clinically significant drowsiness increases from 4 percent for those aged 40 or less, to 11 percent for those aged over 70 (Ray, Gurwitz, et al., 1992). Also, the benzodiazepines affect psychomotor function in the elderly more markedly than in younger people (Nolan, O'Malley, 1988). Side effects such as morning confusion, drowsiness, ataxia, and a decrease in psychomotor skills in persons taking benzodiazepines the prior evening, increases with age. As high as 39 percent of persons over 70 years old will have these significant side effects.

Many laboratory studies specifically show impaired driving-related skills as a side effect of antianxiety drugs. For example, Seppala, et al., showed increased critical flicker fusion threshold, increased choice reaction time, increased body sway, decreased hand-eye coordination and decreased divided attention, for both middle aged and younger subjects using these drugs. In a three-month study, 38 patients on chlordiazepoxide had ten times the normal amount of traffic accidents (Murray, 1960). Some estimate that accident risk doubles for people taking diazepam/Valium (Janke, 1994).

Table 15.1
Stages of Acute Alcohol Influence

BAC (g/100 ml)	Stage of Alcohol Influence	Impairment
below .05%	subclinical	possible
.05% – .08%	euphoria	judgement reaction time muscular coordination driving hazardous
.10% or more	excitement	emotional critical judgement visual acuity peripheral vision glare recovery

Antidepressants and antipsychotics sedate and impair psychomotor function more so in the elderly than in the young (Siegfried and O'Connolly). Antipsychotics, more so than antidepressants sedate their users. This type of sedation increases crash risk. If alcohol is used as well, motor skills become impaired (Scott and Mitchell, 1988). Also, phenothiazines may cause Parkinson-type reactions, such as muscle stiffness, slow reaction times and abnormal nystagmus.

Alcohol (ethyl alcohol)

As soon as you start to drink, your blood alcohol concentration (BAC) starts to rise. Driving impairment increases directly with BAC level. This is shown in Table 15.1, adopted from the *Blood Alcohol Concentration Calculator* and *Medicolegal Aspects of Alcohol* of Lawyers and Judges Publishing Company.

It is illegal to drive in all states with a presumptive BAC of .10% or above. In California, Florida, Kansas, Maine, Massachusetts, New Hampshire, New Mexico, North Carolina, Oregon, Utah, Vermont and Virginia, the illegal presumptive BAC is .08% and above.

Alcohol has been shown to impair vision. Static visual acuity decreased in 54 percent of subjects with BAC levels of .06–.10g/dL, and in 85 percent of subjects with BAC levels of .101–125g/dL (Newman and Fletcher, cited in Garriott, 1993). Other studies show a more significant reduction in dynamic visual acuity. In their 1975 study, Burns et al. showed that although low and high contrast static visual acuity was unaffected by alcohol, dynamic visual acuity was. In their 1993 study of dynamic visual contrast sensitivity, Leibowitz, et al. found that twice as much contrast was needed for detection after subjects imbibed an 8 ounce mixed drink containing 1.4 ml of 190 proof alcohol. This later study found that static visual acuity was also decreased, but to a much lower extent. Loss in both static and dynamic contrast sensitivity is a clear driving hazard.

Decreases in both light and dark adaptation, as well as resistance to glare and impaired color discrimination, have been observed in subjects with BAC levels of .09–.15g/dL (Wallgren and Barry, cited in Garriott). Adams, et al., in 1976 found a decrease in color discrimination in the blue and yellow zones. Also, alcohol may slow the response time to visual stimulation (Suzuki et al., 1957; Lewis et al., 1969; Idestrom et al., 1968).

Impairment of driving related visual skills may occur in persons with BAC as low .03%. Brecher demonstrated that in BAC levels as low as .03%, binocular coordination is reduced (cited in Garriott, 1993). Also, Moskowitz found decreased visual tracking performances at low BAC levels (Moskowitz, 1974).

Personality changes are associated with alcohol (Barnes, 1974). Alcohol may exaggerate one's mood, increasing depression or aggression. Aggression toward oneself may cause suicide, and aggression toward others may cause violent behavior. If driving, this may turn into suicide and/or homicide by an automobile accident.

Other detrimental effects of alcohol on driving ability include reduction in central processing of information and reductions in short term memory (Burns et al.). A decrease in risk judgement has also been observed (Dott, 1972). Furthermore, alcoholic hangovers have been shown to decrease reaction time, perception and motor performance.

C. Dissociative anesthetics (PCP and analogs)

This group of drugs includes phencyclidine/PCP, known as "angel dust," and ketamine/Ketalar, which is a veterinary anesthetic. They block pain information to the brain by dissociating the brain from pain information. These drugs stimulate the CNS, increase blood pressure, increase pulse rate, increase body temperature, cause hallucination and insensitivity to pain. These drugs also depress the CNS. They will decrease smooth pursuit ability, exaggerate endpoint nystagmus, and decrease the angle onset of lateral gaze nystagmus. Sometimes these drugs induce an upbeating vertical gaze nystagmus. There is no question that driving under the influence of these drug could be disastrous.

D. Cannabis (marijuana and hashish)

The active ingredient in cannabis is THC. Marinol and Nabilone are synthetic THC drugs prescribed for cancer and AIDS patients to increase appetite and reduce vomiting. This group of drugs acts within the CNS, but does not affect smooth pursuits or nystagmus. Visual disturbances associated with cannabis use include conjunctival injection (red eyes), a decrease in dynamic visual acuity (Brown et al.), and a decrease in color perception in the blue and red zones (Adams et al.).

Cannabis intoxication is clearly a driving danger. Cannabis reduces eye-hand and hand-hand coordination, increases reaction times and causes incorrect reactions (Kielholz et al., 1973). Cannabis intoxication can also cause incorrect estimates of time and distance, as well as increased brake time (Rafaelsen, et al, 1973).

The primary effects of marijuana are mood changes and disturbances in time perception (Barnes, 1974). It slows central thought processes and impairs short term memory (Burns et al.). Also, people often become oblivious and indifferent to their surroundings. Therefore, chronic marijuana users may have delayed thought processes and become dangerous drivers.

E. Hallucinogens (psychedelics)

This group includes mescaline, psilocybin (mushrooms), nutmeg, morning glory seeds, Jimson weed, bufotenene, lysergic acid/LSD, methylenedioxylamphetamine/ecstasy, and dimethoxylamphetamine/STP. These drugs act on the CNS to produce distorted information to the brain. Persons affected by these drugs become distracted, unable to concentrate, and unable to perform skilled tasks such as driving. These drugs will dilate pupils, but do not affect nystagmus or smooth pursuits.

F. Inhalants

This group includes acetone, toluene, benzene, gasoline, kerosene, hydrocarbons from aerosol containers, and anesthetic gases such as chloroform, nitrous oxide and amyl nitrate. These inhalants depress the central nervous system. Similar to other CNS depressants, using these drugs will show positive HGN test results: decreasing smooth pursuit eye movements, exaggerating endpoint nystagmus and decreasing the angle of onset of lateral gaze nystagmus. High doses may induce vertical nystagmus. These drugs distort the user's perception of time and space, which would be detrimental to driving ability.

G. CNS stimulants

This group of drugs includes cocaine, amphetamines, methylphenidate/Ritalin, pemoline/Cylert and phenmetrazine/Preludin. These drugs increase the amount of norepinephrine in the body by either inhibiting its uptake or increasing its release. They increase heart rate, increase blood pressure, increase respiration rate and body temperature. People who abuse these drugs will have dilated pupils that react slowly to light and normal HGN responses. Chronic use of amphetamines has been proven to be associated with crash risk (Waller, 1973).

H. Ophthalmic agents

Mydriatics and cycloplegics, such as phenylephrine, hydroxyamphetamine, tropicamide, cyclopentolate, scopolamine, homatropine, and atropine, are drugs that dilate the pupil. Except for phenylephrine and hydroxyamphetamine, they all cause cycloplegia, or inhibit accommodation, as well. They are used diagnostically for routine eye examinations, as well as therapeutically for treatment of certain ocular inflammations. A dilated pupil, and cycloplegia, will both blur vision and increase light sensitivity. Depending on the extent of the dilation and cycloplegia, caution while driving or no driving is recommended.

Glaucoma medication

1) *Adrenergics*, such as epinephrine and dipivefrin, cause mydriasis, or dilate the pupil. This may blur vision and cause increased light sensitivity.
2) *Miotics*, such as pilocarpine, carbachol, and echothiophate, and even more so, physostigmine, demarcarium, echothiophate and isofluro-phate, severely constrict pupil size. This decreases peripheral vision,

and in the presence of a cataract will also reduce central vision. Persons on topical cholinergic medication should never drive at night, and may not be able to safely drive during the daytime either.

15.2 HGN: Horizontal Gaze Nystagmus

The rate of major violations given for driving under the influence of drugs or alcohol is greatest for those aged under 25, and least for the elderly drivers (California Data). Crash risk is directly proportional to blood alcohol concentration, while the relationship between crash risk and drugs of abuse is unknown. However, the combination of even small amounts of alcohol and drugs increases the risk of automobile accidents for all age groups.

Police officers across the nation and in several foreign countries learn to evaluate whether suspected drivers are intoxicated or under the influence of drugs or alcohol (D.W.I. or D.U.I.). Major parts of these drug recognition evaluations are eye tests, or HGN tests. The HGN sequence tests for smooth pursuits, nystagmus at maximum deviation and angle onset of nystagmus. See Table 15.2.

Smooth pursuits are the slow, even eye movements used to track an object. We use them to keep low speed objects of interest on our central retinas. When the central nervous system is depressed, smooth pursuits become uneven or jerky.

Nystagmus is an involuntary movement of the eyes. Pendular nystagmus is an involuntary oscillation of the eyes with equal speed in both directions. Jerk nystagmus has a fast phase in one direction and a slow phase in the opposite

Table 15.2
Example of Score Card for HGN Sequence

Horizontal Gaze Nystagmus Sequence

Equal tracking?	Y	N
Equal pupil size?	Y	N

	Left Eye		Right Eye	
1) Smooth pursuits?	Y	N	Y	N
2) Normal endpoint nystagmus?	Y	N	Y	N
3) Nystagmus onset greater than 45 degrees?	Y	N	Y	N

4 or more "no" marks fails test

Last medications: ____________________

Comments: ____________________

____

direction. There are about 45 classifications of nystagmus, but only three types are considered normal. They are fatigue nystagmus, unsustained endpoint nystagmus and sustained endpoint nystagmus. Fatigue nystagmus occurs when eyes are maximally deviated for more than 30 seconds. Unsustained endpoint nystagmus is a few beats of nystagmus at gaze angles of 30 degrees or more. Sustained endpoint nystagmus is nystagmus at gaze deviations greater than 40 degrees. Normal, or physiological nystagmus in most of the population occurs with a very small amplitude of no more than three degrees. It is usually mild, difficult to see, or not visible at all. Whereas horizontal gaze nystagmus is exaggerated when the central nervous system is depressed, and clearly visible.

Before the HGN testing can commence, police officers need to have probable cause, or a reasonable suspicion that the driver is under the influence of drugs or alcohol. According to the NHTSA, the following constitutes reasonable cause:

Visual Cues	Probability (%) that driver is drunk
1. Turning with a wide radius	65%
2. Straddling center of lane marker	65
3. Appearing to be drunk	60
4. Almost striking object or vehicle	60
5. Weaving	60
6. Driving on other than designated roadway	55
7. Swerving	55
8. Speed more than 10 mph below the limit	50
9. Stopping without cause in traffic lane	50
10. Following too closely	50
11. Drifting	50
12. Tires on center or lane marker	45
13. Braking erratically	45
14. Driving into opposing or crossing traffic	45
15. Signaling inconsistently with driving actions	40
16. Slow response to traffic signals	40
17. Stopping inappropriately (other than in lane)	35
18. Turning abruptly or illegally	35
19. Accelerating or decelerating rapidly	30
20. Headlights off	30

After seeing one or more of the signs above, law enforcement officials may begin the HGN sequence. The police officers ask suspects to remove their eyeglasses and follow a slow-moving target, usually a penlight, horizontally at approximately 15 inches from their face. If the suspect tracks the penlight with both eyes moving equally in the same direction, the HGN results should be accurate. If suspects are unable to track objects with both eyes moving equally due to nerve or muscle disease, extreme refractive error, loss of one eye, stroke, medications, and so forth, then HGN testing will not be accurate.

The first part of the HGN sequence is testing smooth pursuits. This is to determine the ability to track a slow-moving object 120 degrees from left to right in four seconds. Smooth pursuits can be no faster than 30 degrees per second. Persons with good vision and binocularity can probably track an object smoothly. If the ocular system is depressed, tracking will be inaccurate, causing eyes to fall behind or jump ahead of their target. The eyes should be tested binocularly, without occluding one eye. The penlight should be held at 12–15 inches from the face, and slightly superior. The target moves from the midline of the face temporally to the maximum lateral deviation of one eye and then back to the midline again. Then, the target moves from the midline of the face temporally to maximum lateral deviation of the other eye and back to the midline. Each eye is graded separately for smooth pursuits.

The second part of the HGN sequence is testing nystagmus at maximum deviation, or sustained endpoint nystagmus. The penlight moves temporally from the midline of the face to maximum deviation and held there. A few beats of nystagmus are perfectly normal at lateral gaze deviation of 30 degrees or more. However, if nystagmus is markedly jerky for four seconds or more, this is considered outside normal limits. Neither eye should be covered, and each eye is tested and graded separately about whether endpoint nystagmus was exaggerated.

The third part of the HGN sequence is measuring the angle of onset of nystagmus, or unsustained endpoint nystagmus. The penlight is moved at a slower pace from the midline of the face temporally, and the angle of onset of nystagmus (AON) is recorded for each eye separately. According to precise laboratory testing, with the use of calibrated visual field devices and precise measuring:

51 degrees – 105 × BAC(%) =	**Angle Onset Nystagmus (AON)**
0.00%	51.00 degrees
0.05%	45.75 degrees
0.10%	40.50 degrees
0.15%	35.25 degrees

This shows that normal angle onset nystagmus (AON) occurs at 50 degrees or more. AON of 40–45 degrees indicates a BAC between 0.05–0.10, and AON of 0–30 degrees indicates significant intoxication. Police officers will fail a person with endpoint nystagmus of 45 degrees or less. A summary of occular responses to drugs is shown in Table 15.3.

A. HGN prosecution

The HGN sequence is the most accurate of all the psychophysical roadside sobriety tests for detecting 0.10 BAC. Government studies from 1977–1983 ("Psycho-physical Tests for D.W.I. Arrest," "Developmental and Field Test of Psychophysical Tests for D.W.I. Arrests" and "Field Evaluation of a Behavioral Test Battery for D.W.I.") show about an 80 percent accuracy level. More recently, the statistics show that nystagmus can be 96 percent accurate in detecting 0.10 BAC as the expertise of the police officer increases ("The Scientific Basis for Alcohol Gaze Nystagmus," 1987).

Most of the state courts recognize HGN as a scientific test. In other words, the majority of states accept that there is a scientific relationship between BAC and HGN. The American Optometric Association has passed a resolution endorsing the HGN test as an effective test for detecting alcohol impairment (see Figure 15.1). The scientific community accepts the test as reliable. Expert witnesses confirm to the jury that:

Table 15.3
Ocular Responses to Drugs

DRUG	HGN TEST	PUPILS	CONVERGENCE	PTOSIS (droopy eyelids)
Narcotic Analgesics	Pass	Constricted	Normal	Present
CNS Depressants	Fail	Slow reactions to light	Decreased	Present
Alcohol	Fail	Slow reactions to light	Decreased	Present
Dissociative Anesthetics	Fail	Normal	Decreased	No
Cannabis	Pass	May be dilated	Decreased	No
Hallucinogens	Pass	Slow reactions to light	Normal	No
Inhalants	Fail	Slow reactions to light	Decreased	No
CNS Stimulants	Pass	Dilated Slow reactions to light	Normal	None

1. There is a scientific relationship between BAC and HGN.
2. The HGN test is a reliable indicator of alcohol impairment.
3. A police officer can be trained to accurately administer the test and measure the results.
4. It is very unlikely to confuse alcohol gaze nystagmus with other forms of nystagmus.

B. HGN defense

Defense attorneys usually question the expertise of the police officer. After only one week of training, can they really be so exact in detecting angles of gaze without visual field gauges? Have they used half moon field devices or a 45-degree card to base their measurement on (see Figure 15.2)? How many intoxicated and sober people have they tested? Have they ever been trained at an eye doctor's office? How accurate are the guesstimates the law enforcement officers make as to the angle of onset of nystagmus?

The SFST (standard field sobriety test) manual instructs police officers how to perform the HGN sequence. Any variation from the manual may affect the validity of the test. Also, was the test area illuminated well enough for the officer to see the subject's eyes? How was the area illuminated? Was the subject facing passing cars, blinking lights or any other form of moving objects that can cause optokinetic nystagmus? Certain prescription drugs, such as antihistamines and anti-epilepsy drugs, can cause nystagmus. Some people normally exhibit AON of 20–40 degrees.

Defense attorneys should also question the vision of the arresting police of-

HORIZONTAL GAZE NYSTAGMUS AS A FIELD SOBRIETY TEST

WHEREAS drivers under the influence of alcohol pose a significant threat to the public health, safety, and welfare; and

WHEREAS optometric scientists and the National Highway and Traffic Safety Administration have shown the Horizontal Gaze Nystagmus (HGN) test to be a scientifically valid and reliable tool for trained police officers to use in field sobriety testing; now therefore be it

RESOLVED that the American Optometric Association acknowledges the scientific validity and reliability of the HGN test as a field sobriety test when administered by properly trained and certified police officers; and be it further

RESOLVED that the American Optometric Association urges doctors of optometry to become involved as professional consultants in the use of HGN field sobriety testing.

Adopted June 1993
House of Delegates

Figure 15.1 *American Optometric Association HGN resolution.*

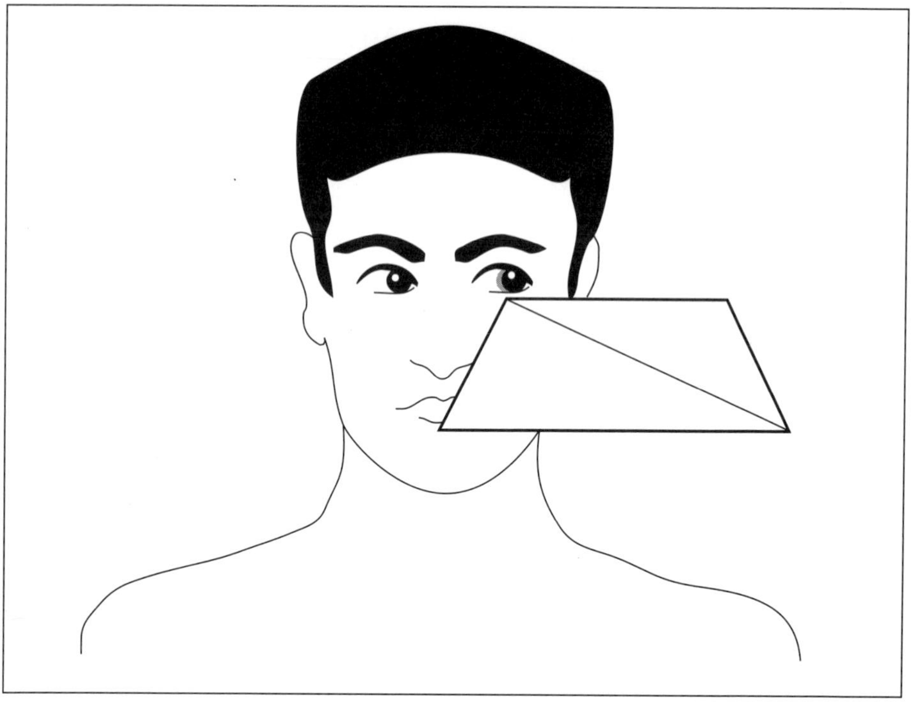

Figure 15.2 *45-degree card to score angle onset nystagmus (AON).*

ficer. HGN test results are based on visual observations of the officer. Not every police officer has 20/20 vision in each eye, normal binocular vision, normal color vision, or a high degree of depth perception. Also, if the police officer is close to forty years old or above, their focusing ability at near is almost always diminished (see Table 15.4). In other words they are not able to see as clearly up close any more due to a decrease in focusing, or accommodative ability. Accommodation decreases rapidly with age. By the mid-forties, most individuals can no

Table 15.4
Average Bifocal Power Needed Focus at 14–18 Inches Based on Age

Age	Average Bifocal Power
40	+1.00 D
45	+1.50 D
50	+2.00 D
55	+2.25 D
60	+2.50 D

longer see clearly at 24 or less inches away without eyeglasses and/or increased illumination. If HGN testing is done by a 45-year-old or older police officer, without his eyeglasses, at night, the results are suspect.

References

Abrams, Bernard, O.D., "HGN Police Testing and Other Fairy Tales," Feb. 1997, Las Vegas, Nevada.

Adams, Brown, Flom, Jones, and Jampolsky; "Alcohol and marihuana effects on static visual acuity" *American Journal of Optometry and Physiological Optics* 52 729–735, November 1975.

Adams, Brown, Haegerstrom-Portney, Flom, and Jones; "Evidence of the acute effects of alcohol and marihuana on color discrimination," *Perception and Psychophysics*, 20(2): 119–124, 1976.

Austin, Gregory, *Drug Users and Driving Behavior*, National Institute on Drug Abuse, Rockville, Md., 1977.

Barnes, T.H., *Drug Use and Driving*, Addiction Research Foundation, Toronto, 1974.

Bellak, L., and Karasu, T., *Geriatric Psychiatry: A handbook for psychiatrists and primary care*, Grune & Stratton, N.Y.

Blood Alcohol Concentration Calculator, Lawyers and Judges Pub. Co., Tucson, Ariz., 1993.

Brown, Adams, Haegerstrom-Portnoy, et al, "Effects of alcohol and marihuana on dynamic visual acuity," *Perception and Psychophysics*, 18(6): 441–446, 1975.

Burns, Marcelline, and Sharma, "Marihuana effects of driving: Performance and personality," *Proceedings of the 19th Conference of the American Association for Automotive Medicine,* San Diego, CA, Nov. 20-22, 1975, pp 274–284.

Castledon, C.M., George, C.F., Marcer, D., and Hallett, C., "Increased sensitivity to nitrazepam in old age," *British American Journal*, 274, 10–12.

Clayton, Betts, and Mackay, "A study of the effects of certain tranquilizers and small amounts of alcohol on driving performance," *European Journal of Toxicology*, 5(4): 254–256, 1972.

Council of Scientific Affairs, "Alcohol and the Driver," *Journal of the American Medical Association* (JAMA), January 24/31, 1986, vol 255.

Doege and Engelberg, *Medical Conditions Affecting Drivers*, American Medical Ass., Chicago, 1986.

Dott, A.B., *Effect of Marihuana on Risk Acceptance in a Simulated Passing Task*, Public Health Service Report, DHEW Pub. # HSM-72-10010, Washington, D.C., 197?.

Drugs of Abuse Calculator, Lawyers and Judges Publishing Co., Tucson, Ariz., 1993.

Duane and Yaeger, *Clinical Ophthalmology*, Vol 2, J.B. Lippincott Co., Philadelphia, Chapter 11, 1988.

Forkiotis, C.J., "Optometric Expertise: The Scientific Basis for Alcohol Gaze Nystagmus," vol. 59, Curriculum II, No. 7, April 1986.

Garriott, James, *Medicolegal Aspects of Alcohol Determination in Biological Specimens*, Lawyers and Judges Pub. Co., Tucson, Ariz., 1993.

Good, Gregory, and Augsburger, Arol, "Use of Horizontal Gaze Nystagmus as a Part of Roadside Sobriety Testing," *American Journal of Optometry and Physiological Optics*, vol. 63, 467, 1986.

Greenblatt, D.J., Allen, M.D., Shader, R.I., "Toxicity of high dose flurazepam in the elderly," *Clinical Pharmacology and Therapeutics*, 21, 355–361, 1977.

Halpern, Eric and Yolton, Robert, "Is the Driver Drunk? Oculomotor Sobriety Testing," *Journal of the American Optometric Association*, vol. 57, number 9, Sept. 1986.

"HGN test for D.U.I. Under Attack," *American Optometric Association News*, vol. 36, number 11, 12/8/97, pp. 1, 8.

Israelstrom and Lambert, *Alcohol, Drugs, and Traffic Safety*, Addiction Research Foundation, Toronto, 1975.

Kielholz, Hobi, Ladewig, et al, "An experimental investigation about the effect of cannabis on car driving behavior," *Pharmakopsychiatrie Neuro-Psychopharmakologie*, 6(2): 91-103, 1973.

Kosnoski, Yolton, Citek, Hayes, Evans, "The Drug Classification Program: Using ocular and other signs to detect drug intoxication," *Journal of the American Optometric Association*, vol. 69, Number 4, April 1998.

Moskowitz, H., Robinson, C.D., "Effects of low doses of alcohol on driving-related skills: A review of the evidence," U.S. Department of Commerce, National Technical Information Service, Springfield, Va., 1988.

National Highway Traffic Safety Administration, U.S. Dept. of Transportation, "Field Evaluation of a Behavioral Test Battery for D.W.I.," No. DOT-HS-475, Sept. 1983

National Highway Traffic Safety Administration, U.S. Dept. of Transportation, "Development and Field Test of Psychophysical Tests for D.W.I. Arrest," No.DOT-HS-805-864, March 1981.

National Highway Traffic Safety Administration, U.S. Dept. of Transportation, "Psychophysical Tests for D.W.I. Arrest," No. DOT-HS-802-424, June 1977.

National Traffic Law Center, *Horizontal Gaze Nystagmus: The Science and the Law*, July 1999, U.S. Department of Transportation.

Nolan, L., O'Malley, K., "Prescribing for the elderly," Part 1: Sensitivity of the elderly to adverse drug reactions, *Journal of the American Geriatrics Society*, 36, 142–149.

Owens, Alfred, "Differentiation of Visibility and Alcohol as Contributors to Twilight Road Fatalities," *Human Factors*, 38(4), 680-689, 1996.

Physicians Desk Reference, Medical Economics Data, 48th Edition, 1994.

Physicians Desk Reference Side Effects, Medical Economics Data.

Physicians Generix, Data Pharmaceutical, Inc., Smithtown, N.Y., 1992.

Rafaelson, Bech, and Rafaelson, "Simulated car driving influenced by cannabis and alcohol," *Pharmakopsychiatrie Neuro-Psychopharmakologie*, 6(2): 71–83, 1973.

Ray, W.A., Gurwitz, J., Decker, M.D., Kennedy, D.L., "Medication and the safety of the older driver": is there a basis for concern?" *Human Factors*, 34, 33–47, 1992.

Ray, W.A., Thapa, P.B., Shorr, R.I., "Medications and the older driver," *Clinics in Geriatric Medicine*, 9,413–438, 1993.

Scott, R.B., Mitchell, M.C., "Aging, alcohol, and the liver," *Journal of the American Geriatrics Society*, 36, 255–265, 1988.

Siegfried, K., O'Connolly, M., "Cognitive and psychomotor effects of different antidepressants in the treatment of old age depression," *Journal of Clinical Psychopharmacological Research*, 1, 231–243, 1986.

Sharma, and Satanand, "Barbiturates and driving," *Accident Analysis and Prevention*, 8:27–31, 1976.

Vaughn and Asbury, *General Ophthalmology*, Lange Medical Pub., Los Altos, Calif., chapter 17, 1983.

Willette, Robert, *Drugs and Driving*, Dept. of Health Education and Welfare, Public Health Service, Rockville, 1973.

Chapter 16

Introduction to Information in This Section and Why Visibility Is an Issue

Bernard S. Abrams, O.D.

Most frequently clients or attorneys need help in reconstructing a particular accident. Because most attorneys lack a knowledge of the basic principles of the visibility and human aspects of accident reconstruction, it is often difficult for them to know when to involve a visibility expert, reconstructionist, or both; what evidence is relevant; what questions to ask; and what types of accident reconstruction experts are needed. The point of this book is to familiarize the interested attorney with the various components of total accident reconstruction and to provide some guidance about how to use the various experts available.

At first glance it would seem hopeless to attempt to cover a field as vast as visibility aspects and accident reconstruction in one book. The variety of accidents with visibility factors[1] that occur is almost limitless, and each type of accident has its own literature. Fortunately, however, the majority of traffic accidents fall into a few fairly simple categories. For accidents in these categories, a person who has mastered the information in this book will be able to understand and reconstruct the visibility portion of what has occurred.

My chapters have been kept brief intentionally, and they have included both hypothetical and actual cases for two reasons. First, it can be read completely with a reasonable investment of time. Second, the method invites re-reading and some measure of mastery—thus giving the reader a fairly complete overview of traffic accident reconstruction.

This book is devoted to the basic concepts that underlie visibility aspects and accident reconstruction. Concepts such as visual acuity, lighting, contrast, color, perception reaction and disease have precise meanings which attorneys and experts frequently fail to explain to most juries. This leads to endless confusion. After completing the chapters, you will know what these terms mean. Be warned, however, that learning about basic visual concepts can be time consuming. Therefore, I suggest that you not attempt to master these concepts in a first reading. Simply get as much from each chapter as you can in reading, and then move ahead to the next chapter. Refer back to various chapters as needed—use the chapters as references.

Once you become familiar with the basic concepts established in the various chapters, you will be able to focus on how they can be used to analyze accidents. My section will be a series of real and constructed case studies. For the most part, the basic concepts developed in my chapters will not be sufficient to totally analyze the case studies; thus, it will be necessary to complete the entire book. Upon completion of the book and case studies, you should have a good idea of how visual reconstruction is done, what evidence is critical, and what questions are vital to ask.

The chapter on direct examination will look at how an attorney may make best use of a visibility reconstructionist. This will include suggestions about when to call the expert, what evidence will be needed, what kind of help can be expected, and how to structure testimony. This chapter will also include a survey of a brief review of evidence presentation that has proved useful in making testimony and forensic displays more understandable.

Several appendices have been included after each chapter that include references.

End Notes

1. See list of references in Appendix D.

Chapter 17

The Practice of Forensic Visibility

Bernard S. Abrams, O.D.

Synopsis

17.1 Introduction

The practice of forensic visibility by a vision specialist is, relatively speaking, in its infancy and growing with the general recognition that vision is of major importance, primarily in vehicular accidents. When litigation results from those accidents with a resultant question of fault, human visibility expertise is needed to understand what happened and why. Night visibility, in particular, has gained prominence due to the high injury and death rates related to vehicular accidents at night.

Forensic practice is distinguished from other areas of consultation largely by the system (legal) in which one works. Most practice is in the civil, as opposed to the criminal system (however, this author has worked in both areas), so most of what is important to the forensic consultant does not appear on *L.A. Law!* Most cases are settled before trial primarily as a result of the fact that both sides will know the theories, opinions, and basis for these opinions well in advance of trial through a "discovery" process.

For visibility experts the important parts of discovery are our depositions and/or written reports. A deposition is composed of questions asked of the vision specialist practitioner by the opposing attorney, answered under oath, and recorded for later typing by a court reporter. The practitioner's client (the attorney) will play a minor role here, possibly objecting (for the record and possible later ruling by the judge) to improper or confusing questions, or simply alerting the witness to a specific word in the question that might change its meaning. The expert witness might be asked his or her opinions, the analyses behind those opinions, his or her qualifications to render such opinions, and even questions concerning fees and other cases on which he or she has worked. Part of the deposition also examines a witness' communication style and evaluates how well the expert witness might impress a jury and stand up under cross-examination.

In the experience of this author, written reports are frequently called for; if they are, they are "discoverable" by the other side. Strong and well-presented reports and/or depositions may be used by one's own side to attempt a favorable settlement.

Trial testimony consists of direct examination by one's own attorney, followed by cross-examination by the opposing attorney (and occasionally redirect, recross, ad nauseam). "Direct" includes the expert witness' qualifications, work performed, and opinions formed. Because the witness can respond only to questions asked, it is important that direct be carefully worked out in advance with the attorney. One of the worst moments in court is when the employing attorney asks the expert witness a question to which the attorney really doesn't want the answer. Experienced, knowledgeable attorneys will need preparation, even if the expert's deposition or report and curriculum vitae (CV)[1] are fairly complete. This expert has found it useful to discuss a specifically exemplar case(s) with the retaining attorneys, outlining strengths and his experiences that might be related to the specifics of that case.

The visibility forensic practitioner has only one opportunity to communicate effectively to the judge and jury. A frustrating aspect of this occurs when objections are raised by the opposing attorney and ruled on by the judge. Although the jury will make the ultimate decision, the judge will make many decisions along the way in response to objections and motions. Sometimes the clear and complete analysis that had been prepared will not be allowed to reach the jury. If the jury doesn't understand what is said or doesn't believe it, then all of the expert witness' efforts may be for naught.

During cross-examination the visibility practitioner attempts to defend his or her credentials, opinions, analysis, and general credibility before the judge and jury. All manner of trick questions and emotional ploys might be used in an attempt to discredit the witness. He or she will be asked yes/no questions when either response would be misleading to the jury, and skill at squeezing in explanations around objections may be critical. The practitioner's decision to continue or no continue forensic practice will probably be made during cross-examination.

17.2 A Hypothetical Case

Consider an accident involving a small vehicle that during darkness went off a two-lane rural road onto the shoulder after swerving to avoid a nonlighted, stopped tractor/trailer. The vehicle then went out of control when its driver tried to re-enter the roadway. The tort liability against both the highway department and the tractor/trailer was based on improper road design and failure to place a retroreflective triangle, respectively. A civil engineer in road design presented analyses and opinions on these issues for the plaintiff.

The defense involved not only arguments about the roadway, but also the fact that the driver had sufficient time to avoid the crash based on .75 second alert reaction time. A visibility expert was retained by the plaintiff's attorney to assist in examining evidence, and analyzing the reaction times and visibility distances available to the driver.

The expert's testimony would be used chiefly in the direct testimony of the plaintiff's case, and/or in rebuttal of the defense's position, or not at all if analysis showed the driver had, in fact, had time to avoid the crash. (The various experts base their analyses on the accident site, the plaintiff's deposition, the police accident report, engineering reports, reaction time, light levels, and road drawings.)

The site in the hypothetical case was on a dark, nonlighted road which was curved and lined with trees and brush to create a "dark hole." Given this complexity of night visual observation of the scene and assuming the speed of the vehicles, the visibility expert should be able with headlight profiles to calculate a point of sighting, then explain to the jury when the cone of vision of the driver directly encompassed the other vehicle and the approximate time it appeared. Assuming this ideal, one estimates the distance of the first step of visibility between the vehicles and the perception/reaction time available for the vehicle to avoid the tractor/trailer. This perception/reaction distance at night in an unexpected situation would be, in this author's opinion, between 2.5 seconds to 3.5 seconds.

The four steps are detection, identification, perception, and reaction. Based on the plaintiff's testimony, the vision expert then divides this time (2.5 to 3.5 seconds) into four segments:

1. **Detection**: of the parked object and its position.
2. **Identification**: of the object as a parked tractor and the danger due to its inability to move.
3. **Decision**: that a danger or hazard condition existed due to the fact that movement of the object stopped, recognized that it is necessary to attempt an avoidance or evading maneuver.
4. **Reaction**: by sending a message to the muscular skeleton system to leave the road.

A chart was drawn for the jury showing these categories and the processes of visual and human factor detection, identification, decision making, and reaction with both estimated average and complex times and distances at the end of the four stages.

A critical question would be why the vehicle driver did not apply his brakes before going off the road. By entering this possible perception/reaction time into the analysis, the visibility expert was able to estimate that under the best reaction conditions, the distance between vehicles would have been only forty feet when the brakes could have been applied. The opinion of the reconstructionist was that had braking been selected, a head-on or out-of-control collision might have occurred. The visibility expert also gave opinions regarding factors that would increase processing time, such as non-expectancy or surprise.

Experience suggests that the jury's acceptance of opinions of vision experts is based on credibility in structuring four issues:

1. Estimates of the discernibility related to sight distance.
2. Explanation why 2.5 to 3.5 seconds for perception reaction was valid and .75 seconds was in error.
3. Explanation of what steps the driver had to accomplish within this critical period when 90 percent of the information necessary to guide a vehicle to a safe stop is processed.
4. The expert's credentials.

17.3 The Practitioner's Role

Accident causation and the surrounding technical and social systems and environment are often complex. Ideally, it might be desirable to have many experts. As in any field of practice, however, resources of both time and money are limited, so the attorney might employ, in addition to a night visibility specialist, a reconstructionist to cover all of the issues that the many experts might have addressed.

The practitioner must look at this from two opposing perspectives. The obvious primary perspective is one's ethical and professional responsibility not to offer opinions outside one's knowledge and experience. The other perspective is the difficult one. If the practitioner chooses not to express an opinion in some area, how will the judge and jury pursue questions related to that area? Either another, possibly less qualified expert fills in, or the judge and jury base their decisions on prior learning. Thus, the training, experience, education, background and research, if any, come into play.

Probably the clearest example is in the night vision area as related to visibility, discernibility, and reaction times, where so-called experts, lacking valid scientific training or experience, have been expressing opinions for many years. In today's world, these tests are the "Frye rule"[2] or the "Daubert rule."

Forensic visibility, in particular, is an important area for the professional who understands illumination, diseases, and vision. It has high visibility for both the practitioner and the profession. However, the forensic area is also fraught with difficulties and dangers ranging from procedural complexities and subtleties to ethical dilemmas. It is a challenge that can be worthwhile but should not be taken without forethought and preparation.

This introduction is a composite of the thoughts of many distinguished practitioners in the field of forensic human factors, visibility, and the jurisprudence system.

I am particularly indebted to the following individuals: Dr. Gordon H. Robinson, Dr. Merrill J. Allen, and Lyman Brownfield, Esq., from whose writings and thoughts I have borrowed liberally for this chapter.

End Notes

1. Note list of questions for basic qualification as visibility expert in Chapter 23.
2. Legal cases that have set scientific standards by which courts accept testimony of experts.

Chapter 18

Forensic Vision and Human Factors in the Courtroom

Bernard S. Abrams, O.D.

Synopsis

18.1 Section 1: Vision

A. Introduction

In this chapter the author presents a word pictorial of vision analysis and the part it may play in understanding and evaluating injuries and deaths on the highways during both daytime and nighttime.

Vision is primarily subjective in nature and, therefore, cannot be evaluated totally with any types of meters. However, this chapter presents certain scientific data and testing techniques that are available and permit the introduction of factual scientific information to aid the trier of facts to arrive at a decision as to the place of vision in the situation being evaluated. The theories, testing and evaluation of *quantitative* (Snellen acuity) and *qualitative* (contrast) are presented. Examples of how to mathematically evaluate the two theories and present them together in a courtroom are found in associated chapters and the Appendix E.

B. The role of vision

Vision and its place in forensic analysis of accidents involving vehicles, pedestrians, trains, airplanes, boats, motorcycles, bicycles, stairways, and farm equipment, to mention a few, has now become of prime concern in the court room.

Our research indicates it is only in recent years that serious attention has been given by the legal system to the quality and integrity of information presented in opinion reports, discovery depositions, trial testimony and forensic displays.

This author, as well as others, has reviewed documents purporting to be factual sworn data which, in my expert opinion, had deficiencies ranging from minor flawed facts to serious errors. A vast amount of this misinformation has been testified to, I believe, by individuals of all professions without any intention of misleading judges or juries. As a result, numerous cases may have been decided in error due to a lack of understanding of the visual system and how to properly present it to a jury.

This chapter will present information based on both the author's own and other visual scientists' research, training, education and experience; all of which may, in the future, be used as a factual basis to present more accurately both the visual and associated human factors in the area of forensic visibility analysis, and a review of literature.

C. Visual pathway

The eyes, essentially, are image catching devices, channels of vision that run to the brain. In the end, it is the brain that sees. The light entering the eye brings

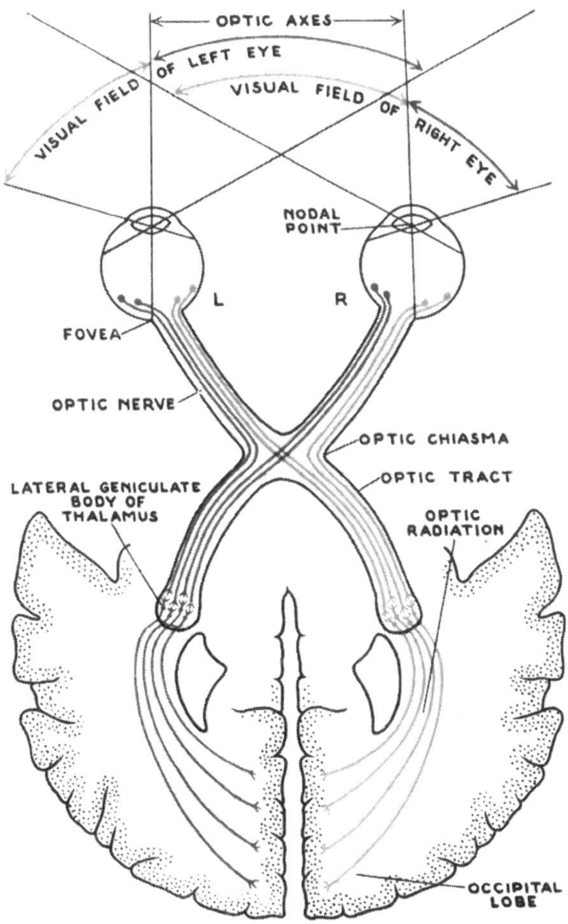

Plate IV.—Illustrating the neural connections between the retina and the occipital lobe.

Figure 18.1

with it crucial image information it has picked up by touching or passing through objects in the field of vision. Example: A newborn infant learns to identify and respond to its mother because the brain has been conditioned to understand that a certain pattern, shape and form striking the eye is a precursor to being fed or held or changed. The eye imprints the image on the brain, which sorts and reacts to information regarding that imprint (e.g., if the car is weaving or is in the wrong lane) (Figure 18.1).

In a pure mechanical sense, the eye (Figure 18.2) is an instrument that gathers light rays and focuses them into an image registered on its rear surface.

The light enters the eye through the cornea, a tough, transparent membrane at the front of the eye. Because the convex shape of the cornea is much like that of a camera lens, it tends to bend light rays together. The next tissue structure behind the cornea is the iris. The iris functions much like a diaphragm in a camera, a spillway in a dam. It regulates the amount of light permitted to enter the eye depending upon how much is needed for visual imprinting. The small circular hole in the middle of the iris is the pupil. Turn your eye toward the sun and the pupil will constrict to reduce the amount of light entering the eye. Walk from the bright outdoors into a darkened room and the pupil will dilate to gather as much light as possible.

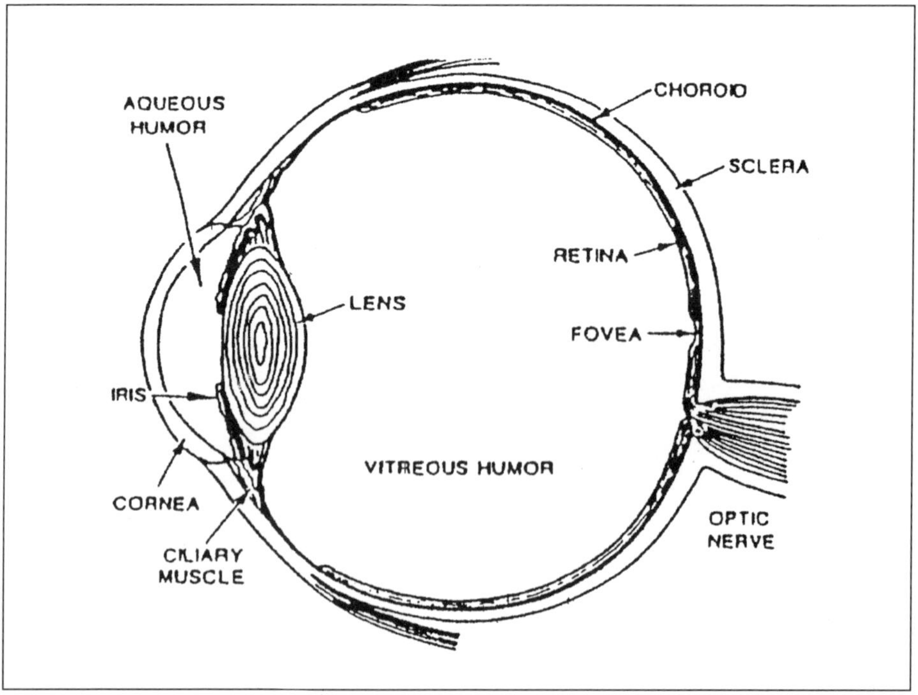

Figure 18.2

Light passes through the pupil and into the lens, the purpose of which is to make sure that the light focuses precisely on the retina. The retina is the anatomical equivalent of the film in a camera. It is a light sensitive layer located at the back of the eye. Its photosensitive cells translate light energy into images which then become signals carried to the brain by the optic nerve.

1. Structure and functions of the retina (Figure 18.3)

The human retina (the light-sensitive part of the eye) is tightly packed with two types of light receptors: cones and rods. The foveal region (cone of vision) of the retina (corresponding to the central 2–3 degrees of the visual field) contains exclusively cones; the periphery (corresponding to the remainder of the visual field) contains primarily rods (Osterberg, 1935).

As a consequence of these and other structural differences, the fovea and the periphery vary in their capabilities. In terms of detection, the differences between the fovea and periphery depend on light conditions. In photopic, or relatively

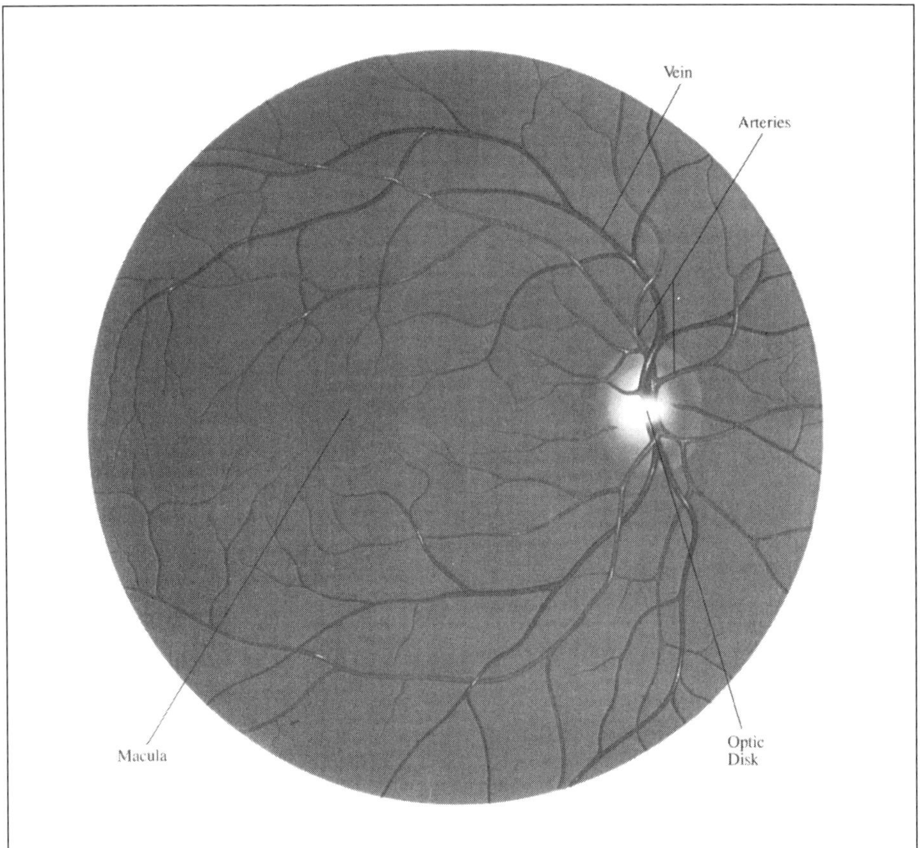

Figure 18.3

bright, conditions, the luminance threshold is highest at or near the fovea. In scotopic, or relatively dark, conditions, the threshold is lowest at 15–20 degrees in the periphery.

In terms of several processes needed for object identification, it is the fovea which excels. First, visual acuity (the ability to resolve small detail) is best in the fovea and worsens progressively with increasing peripheral eccentricity. This is true whether the target is moving or is stationary in relation to the observer. Second, motion perception is most efficient in the fovea. This implies that to detect movement of an object, the angular speed of the object must be greater if the image of the object falls in the retinal periphery rather than the fovea. Third, color discrimination is most accurate in the fovea and decreases with the increased eccentricity from the fovea.

The findings described above indicate that foveal identification (a function of visual acuity, motion perception, and color discrimination) is superior to peripheral identification. However, the fovea comprises less than 1 percent of the total active visual field. (As was noted earlier, the fovea includes the central 2–3 degrees, while the active visual field extends to about 175–180 degrees in the horizontal meridian and about 100 degrees in the vertical meridian.) (Figure 18.4) Therefore, the likelihood of an object's image falling on the periphery as opposed to the fovea is high. The inefficiency of the periphery in the identification

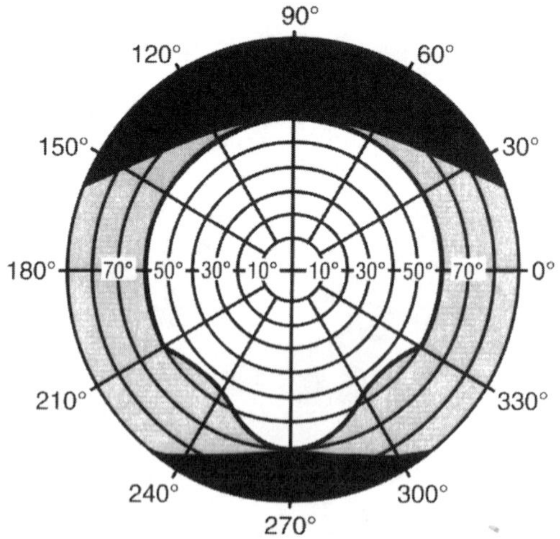

The normal field of view of a pair of human eyes. The white central portion represents the region seen by both eyes. The gray portions, right and left, represent the regions seen by the respective eyes alone. The cut-off by the eyebrows, cheeks and nose is shown by the dark areas.

Figure 18.4

process, however, implies that most of the objects are identified in the fovea (Waldram, 1960).

In general then, detection (monitoring) takes place in the periphery (due to the size of the periphery) while identification takes place in the fovea (due to the efficiency of the fovea). It follows the factors which will:

1. improve detection and/or
2. improve the likelihood of foveal fixation, will improve conspicuity, and will be beneficial for identification.

2. Dynamic visual acuity (motion)

The dynamic visual acuity studied in the California research is a complete skill involving the eye, the stato-kinetic vestibular mechanism and the muscles of the eye and neck. The test consisted of measuring the visual acuity with a target that moved from one side of the head around in front to the other side of the head at increasing velocities. The subject turned his head toward the anticipated appearance of the target and then followed it by turning his head and eyes in pursuit. The ability to maintain the eyes fixated upon the moving target at high velocities depends upon the degree of coordination between the neck and eye muscles that are controlled by both the retinal image and the vestibular apparatus. The fact that good, dynamic visual acuity performance correlates with good driving indicates that good coordination and freedom from confusion and dizziness in rapidly changing situations is important in driving. Impairments in the visual input or in oculomotor coordination, as by the need for a pair of glasses or for visual training, will reduce the performance on the dynamic visual acuity test. Other factors including interferences in the vestibular mechanism, as in Menier's disease, or limitations of head movement, as in arthritis, could also adversely affect the score.

3. Static visual acuity

Static visual acuity is usually tested with letters whose components give a measure of the ability of the eye to see, as well as separate, two objects that are very close together. It is usually conducted with chart luminances between 10 and 30 foot lamberts. Lower levels of illumination, less than 0.4 foot lamberts, as at night on the highway, will produce significantly reduced acuity performance, while the higher levels, up to 8,000 foot lamberts in the daytime, will give a higher visual acuity. A reduced visual acuity can also result from the need for a pair of glasses to correct a blurred retinal image condition or, more rarely, it can be the result of pathology.

Good central visual acuity and its associated clear retinal image is necessary for the early recognition and reading of road signs and the early detection of small but hazardous objects such as pedestrians, motorcycles, or other obstacles in the roadway. It is indispensable in determining such subtle information signs as the facial expressions and direction of attention of motorists and pedestrians when maneuvering in close quarters. Because good acuity allows the driver more time to make decisions about events, obstacles, or signs which are still at a great distance from him, it, in effect, slows down the action. On the other hand, poor acuity requires that the obstacle come closer to the driver before he can appreciate its significance. Thus, with poor acuity he has less time to act. He must be more alert, he will fatigue faster, and he will be more easily overloaded perceptually.

D. Night eye versus day eye

The questions facing most accidents investigators, reconstructionists, police officers, attorneys, and researchers are as follows:

Should it have been seen? If so, or not so: Why?

All visibility involves human subjective judgment. However, night vision (scotopic) is distinctly different from day vision (photopic). As previously stated, there are no devices which can measure visibility with sufficient reliability.

Perhaps of more importance is the fact that one of the most fundamental realties of visual anatomy is one that often goes unrecognized in court: the human

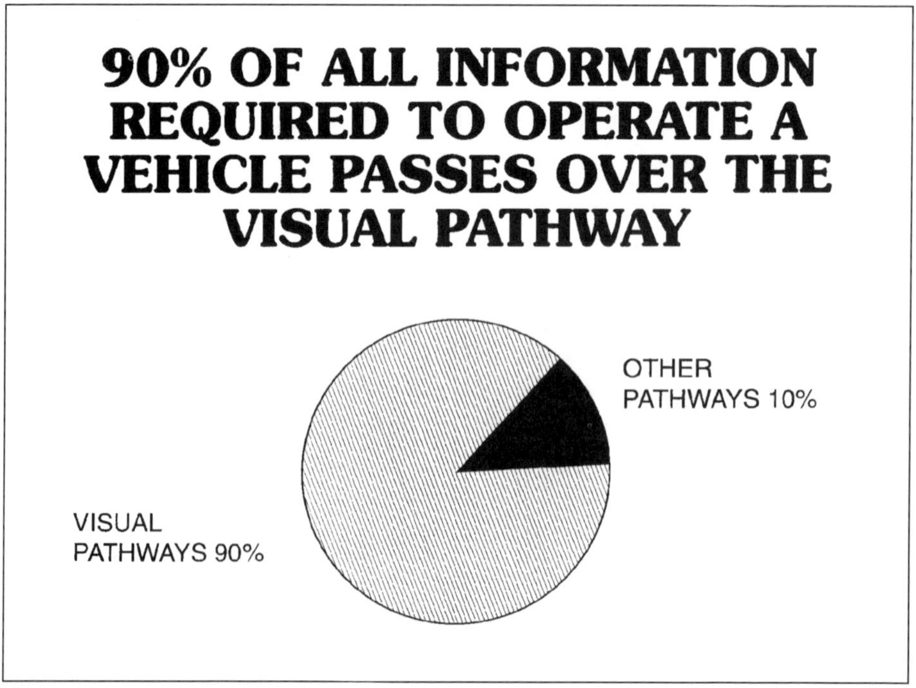

Figure 18.5

body has not one pair of eyes, but two. We have one pair of eyes for daytime vision and quite another for seeing at night. There exists a vast disparity in their Snellen acuity versus contrast sensitivity, and thus, their recognition skills. They each depend on different visual cues. In accidents in which a vehicle strikes and kills a pedestrian, only 11 percent of the daytime drivers indicated they did not see the victim in time. Yet 87 percent of the nighttime drivers claimed precisely that. For most of us, our assessment of that statistic would be both simplistic and superficial: people see better during the day. We ask nothing of the why, when and how that vision begins to change as the day moves from light to dusk to dark. To do this, one must understand the two accepted techniques of measuring human vision: Snellen acuity and contrast sensitivity.

It is no secret that a disproportionately greater number of U.S. traffic fatalities and injuries occur when we are using our "night eyes."

Transportation research scientists have long indicated that 90 percent (Figure 18.5) of all information necessary in operating a motor vehicle at night passes over the visual pathway system to the brain in order for detection, identification and decision to be made, and motor actions to occur.

This chapter focuses on how to arrive at essential scientifically accepted data required to evaluate the place of vision in vehicular accidents. Each and every case is different, and procedures discussed will help in an analysis related to visibility and discernibility. However, remember each situation requires its own analysis.

Important questions to be answered are as follows:

1. *What was observed, precisely, and when?*
2. *How certain is the witness, and why?*

OUR ABILITY TO SEE AN OBJECT
DEPENDS UPON HOW IT DIFFERS
FROM ITS SURROUNDING
IN TERMS OF:

SIZE
CONTRAST
MOTION
BRIGHTNESS
TIME
ILLUMINANCE

Figure 18.6

3. *Size, color, luminance and brightness of all factors existed?* (See Figure 18.6.)

In the give and take of the courtroom, the mind's camera and its acuity have been challenged to the point that it is not uncommonly the issue upon which the jury's decision turns. Yet too often we ask only what the plaintiff, defendant, or witness saw, without plumbing the subtleties that might well have impaired, impeded or colored what the mind registered through the eyes of the beholder.

This chapter is designed to be used as a guideline to permit the knowledgeable expert to make the following statement: *"It is my opinion within reasonable scientific and visual certainty based on my training, experience and research . . ."*

18.2 How We See (Figure18.7)

A. Day vision versus night vision

Vision begins with the energy of electromagnetic radiation—light that is either emitted or reflected from things—reaching the eye.

In the daytime the retina, often compared to a photographic plate, defines visual data primarily by means of a specialized set of about 5.5 million cells

HOW WE SEE

How well we see an object during the night or day is determined by the amount and color of the light it gives off compared to the amount of light given off by its surroundings. This light can be *emitted* by the object, or *reflected* from the object.

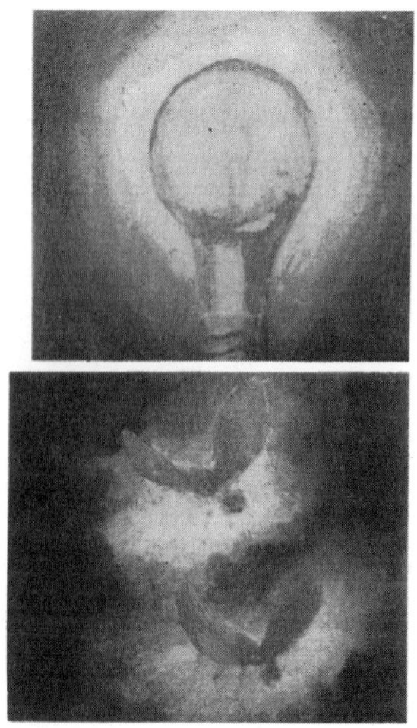

Figure 18.7

called cones that are wavelength color-sensitive and respond to bright light and color detail. This is known as *photopic* vision (3.4 cd/m^2).

There is a middle range of light levels in which both rods and cones function known as *mesopic* vision. Typically, night driving is done under mesopic conditions, depending upon the amount of light available; it may be compared to the end of Civil Twilight or beginning of Civil Dawn (.34 cd/m^2).

At nighttime, the eye relies chiefly on another more sensitive set of about 125 million cells called rods that are sensitive to small amounts of light. They are not, however, wavelength color sensitive; hence, a pure rod vision is in shades of gray to black. This is known as *scotopic* vision (.034 cd/m^2).

During the daytime the visual system is operating at the highest level of sensitivity—foveal vision which permits color discernment, depth perception, 20/20 vision—thus affording high contrast and the greatest capability for distinguishing differences between objects in the visual field.

Our vision is also shaped by our contrast sensitivity (Figure 18.8). How well do we see dark objects against a light background? How well do we see light objects against a dark background? As day becomes night, our contrast sensitivity diminishes accordingly. A vehicle or pedestrian framed against a daytime sky

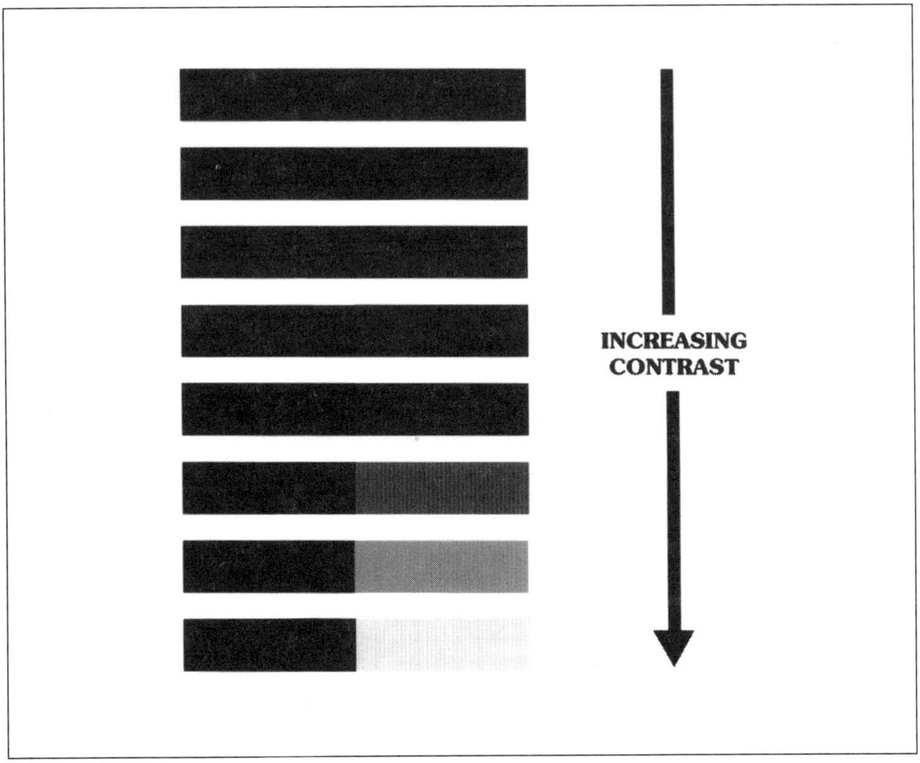

Figure 18.8 *The effect of contrast on visibility.*

may pose no problem for us. At night it is another matter altogether depending on size, luminance, color, and brightness.

What about external factors? Environmental factors? Physiological factors? We have discussed many of them here, yet there are many more. They affect our driving in subtle and profound ways, yet too often in the legal resolution of cases involving night driving, these factors and their intricacies go unproved, unexamined. In other areas, we rely on the best, most sophisticated evidence we can bring forward using everything from ballistics testing to genetic imprinting.

However, with vision we often ask only what the witness saw, without pondering the dozens of factors—some obvious, some obscure—that determine whether the answer we get is, in fact, reliable.

B. Daytime vision

Of all the elements of visual anatomy thus far discussed, the most crucial in terms of vision are the photosensitive cells at the back of the retina. These cells are of two types: rods and cones, named so because of their respective shapes. The cones require more light to stimulate them, whereas the rods are stimulated in very low intensity light. Cones are used for day or brightly illuminated conditions, and rods are used in lower light or night illuminations. Both contain chemicals which,

How The Eye Sees

Central visual acuity is measured by viewing targets (letters, numbers etc.) at a fixed distance of 20 feet (or 6 meters). Targets of progressively smaller size are viewed, each of which subtends a smaller and smaller angle on the retina. Larger targets, for example, subtend a large angle and correspond to a visual acuity of 20/400 (or less) while smaller targets which subtend a smaller angle correspond to a visual acuity of 20/20 (or better).

The best visual acuity is obtained in the central foveal area. If portions of the fovea or the macula are damaged, visual acuity will be reduced. Thus the visual acuity when viewing from the foveal area is 20/20. The falloff in vision is rapid, thus when viewing from 10° from the fovea visual acuity is 20/100 and falls off rapidly thereafter. The high density of cones in the fovea accounts for the high degree visual acuity discrimination in this area of the retina. It has been shown that the density of cones in the fovea is approximately 18 times greater than anywhere else in the retina where they reach a density of approximately 1900 cones/mm^2. Within 5° of the fovea there is a rapid falloff to about 200 cones/mm^2. Rods, which are absent from the fovea make their first appearance about 5° from the fovea and reach their maximum density approximately 20° from the fovea.

The cones which subserve the functions of sharp and color vision do not adapt to as low a light level as the rods. Indeed, the latter are a 1000 times more light-sensitive than the cones and during the course of dark adaptation the final lowest threshold for the eye takes about 25 minutes to achieve and is situated outside the fovea.

Figure 18.9

when excited or stimulated by light, become altered. The alteration of the chemicals marks the transition from light to electrical potentials which traverse the nerves to the brain.

We use the cones of the retina for daytime vision, and they are capable of producing the clearest signals to the brain. Not only is their signal the keenest, but the cones also possess light-sensitive pigments that make it possible for us to see things in color. By understanding the two types of receptors—rods and cones (Figure 18.9 and Figure 18.10)—and the difference in their ability to be stimulated by varying light intensities, it is easy to grasp the concept of "day eyes" and "night eyes."

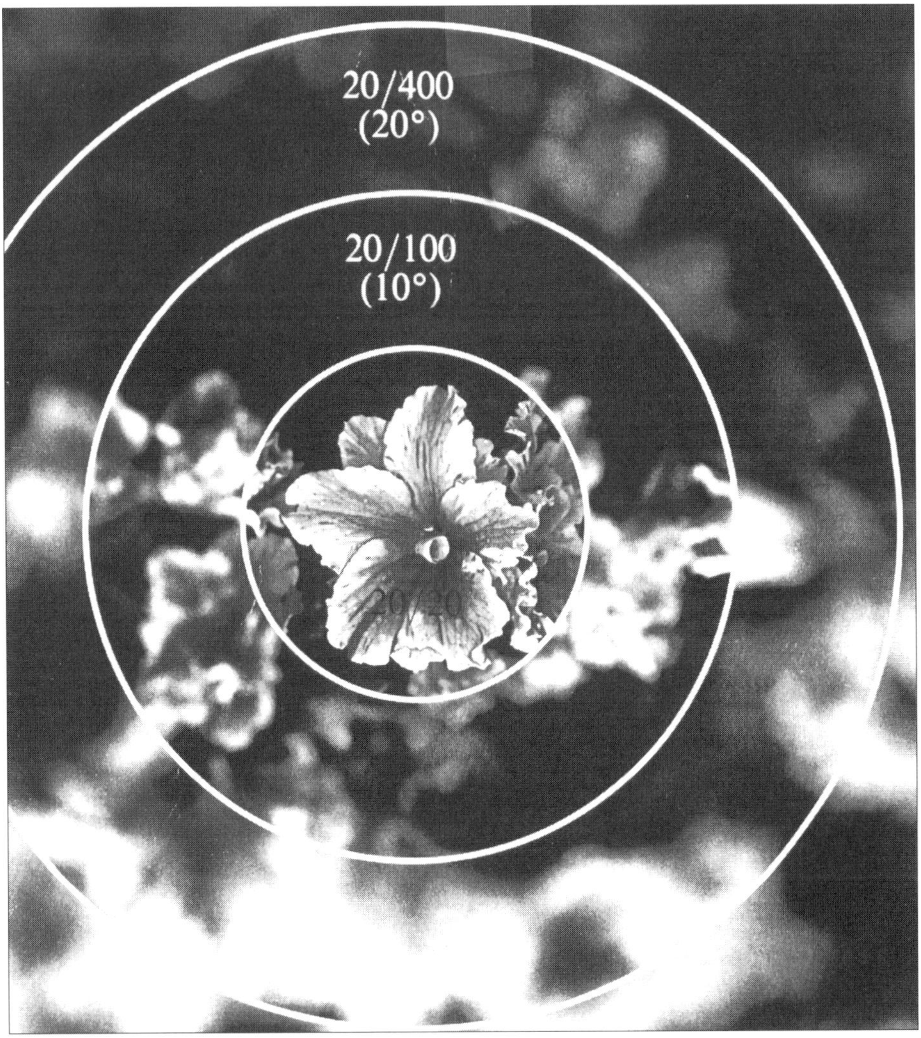

Figure 18.10

With our daytime vision we see best near the center of that photographic film we call the retina, but with our nighttime vision we see best at the periphery or near the edges of our film. Consequently, if we were standing watch on a ship at night, we could see the threatening periscope of the submarine in the distance better by not looking directly at it, rather training the eye a little above or below the horizon. To prove this, find a sharply visible star in the sky and look directly at it. You will find that if you shift your vision to either side of it, it will appear brighter.

We have talked about vision generally as a single sensory function. In fact, there are several components of vision that collectively form not only what we see, but how well we see it. Visual acuity is the most commonly discussed of these components. It is, quite simply, the clarity and sharpness with which we are able to imprint images on the retina. To use the camera analogy, good visual acuity is a well-focused lens on a very sensitive film. But even with the best of acuity, external factors can diminish the precision with which we see. A tinted or dirty windshield will dramatically reduce acuity, denying the eye the light it needs to clearly distinguish and interpret objects in the distance. Depth perception is another component. How accurately do we perceive the distance of objects before our visual field. Without strong depth perception, the eye sends faulty information to the brain, and the brain will respond accordingly, sometimes ignoring or misperceiving a true peril.

C. Darkness defined

Early astronomers identified three phases of twilight, separating daylight from full darkness, on the basis of functional changes in visual capability. Ambient illumination falls continuously during the three phases, which are referred to as (1) Civil Twilight, (2) Nautical Twilight, and (3) Astronomical Twilight. Each phase corresponds to a solar transit of six degrees below the horizon, and each lasts approximately 30 minutes in the middle latitudes of North America. Civil Twilight[1] occurs after sunset and before sunrise, when the upper limb of the sun is tangent with the horizon, and the moment when the center of the sun is six degrees below the horizon. This phase is of special interest for the present purpose because it was characterized as a period when "normal outdoor activities" could be conducted without supplementing ambient skylight. The middle phase, Nautical Twilight, occurs when the sun is between six and twelve degrees below the horizon. During this phase there is ample skylight to visualize the horizon for navigation at sea, but insufficient light for many other outdoor activities. The darkest phase, Astronomical Twilight, occurs when the sun is between twelve and eighteen degrees below the horizon. This phase approaches the darkness of full night when illumination from the sun is lower than that from the stars.

Civil Twilight is most interesting for our purposes because it includes a range of luminances over which there are dramatic changes in recognition vision. Assuming clear weather, natural ambient illumination at sunset—the beginning of evening Civil Twilight—is 30 foot candles (323 lux). By the end of Civil Twilight, ambient illumination has fallen two orders of magnitude to 0.3 foot candles (3.2 lux) (see Appendix C). Consistent with the astronomers' early observations, later research on visual processes showed that this range of illumination corresponds to the range of luminances over which photopic (cone) vision is degraded, approaching the level at which scotopic (rod) vision comes into use. As noted earlier, this is precisely the range over which we find great changes in basic visual functions, such as acuity and contrast sensitivity, which are critical for visual recognition. Recent research has also shown that visual accommodation and reaction time progressively deteriorate over luminances comparable to those that would be obtained during Civil Twilight.

In general, visual recognition functions depend on luminance, which is the product of illumination and the object's reflectance.

D. The visual system at night

At night there are only varying shades of gray and black and the resulting low contrast differences are generally the only method of distinguishing an object from its background. It is not visual acuity that guides our vehicles at night, but rather, contrast sensitivity. Thus, the visual system at night has a reduced capability for distinguishing differences between objects in the visual field. In order to be seen at night, objects must be conspicuous or, in other words, sufficiently brighter or darker than their backgrounds. It is the difference in viewing your flowers at high noon by sunlight versus viewing them at midnight by moonlight.

The information reaching a driver's eyes depends upon what quantity of illumination, was placed on various objects and, in turn, how much reflected visual energy (luminance) reached the driver's eyes from any objects, the roadway, the peripheral area (the berm), and the roadside lighting. At the simplest level, the average driver, depending on speed, needs to know what is ahead of him in approximately the next 200 to 250 feet in order to concentrate on it and to have his vehicle under control for any and all unexpected emergencies. At night, in the rain or darkness, the majority of the guidepath illumination is provided by luminaires, environment and the driver's headlights. It is essential that traffic and land uses near the roadway present important cues since this world does not reveal itself accurately at night, or even at all, without artificial visibility enhancement.

E. Nighttime detection/reaction

Nighttime detection of an object at distance cannot be determined by daytime visual scenes alone. Nighttime vision is far more complex, for basically, at night we use what is known as the "night portion" of the eye which is composed of nerve cells sensitive only to darkness. The portion of the eye that is stimulated at night is known as the peripheral retina and the cells involved are called the rods. It is important that these rods receive stimulus of sufficient intensity in order for an object to be detected. It is then necessary for the detected object to be identified in order for a driver to make a decision to activate orders at the motor center of the brain so the appropriate muscle group can initiate a proper response. Sufficient intensity is required in order to process this information at a higher brain center generally within a matter of 2.5 to 3.1 seconds. If the stimulus is not strong enough, the driver would either not respond or the response time would not be sufficient to avoid a collision. However, each situation is different and should be evaluated. Times vary with bits of data required to process.

F. Illuminance versus luminance

Illumination is the measure of the amount of light flux falling on a surface. Illumination is independent on the direction from which the light comes; the number of light sources, or their positions; the type of light source; and the type of surface on which it falls. A surface may be illuminated to a level of one foot candle by one concentrated source placed normal to the surface or by several less intense sources placed obliquely to the surface.

Luminance is a measure of the amount and concentration of light flux leaving a surface and is the light by which an object is seen. It is the luminance that controls the magnitude of the sensation of an object that the brain receives. The luminance of a surface depends on all of the quantities of which illumination is independent, such as the direction from which the light reaches the surface, the direction from which it is viewed, and the reflective properties of the surface itself. The amount of light falling on a small area of a surface is measured as the illumination on that area. This incident light is generally reflected in all directions by the surface, and its directional distribution is determined by the properties of the surface and the manner in which the light strikes the surface. The apparent luminance of the area on the surface is determined by the amount of light reflected toward the observer's eye.

1. Illumination cues

Brightness, especially at night, is a major clue to distance, partly because there are few others. When an object is far enough away that it subtends about one minute of arc (3.5 inches at 1,000 feet), further increase in its distance causes no change in point image size, but rather causes a loss in retinal image illumination per unit area in compliance with the inverse square law; that is, twice the distance reduces the light on the retina to one-fourth. For people with 20/40 acuity, the critical size is 2 minutes or 3.5 inches at 500 feet. Thus, past experience leads us to believe that dim points of light are farther away than bright ones, though they are at exactly the same distance. Errors in judgment are regularly made when judging small lights at a distance; for example, in one test red tail-lights at 270 feet were judged to be much farther away than white lights at 750 feet.

Larger sources such as automobile surfaces or signs do not lose brightness with ordinary driving distances, except for atmospheric losses. They must be very far away to subtend one minute of angle or less at the observer's eye.

2. Illumination[2] and luminance.[3]

Illumination is an effective tool which can be used to improve traffic operations on rural and urban streets and highways. Studies indicate that the traffic incident rate is two or three times greater at night than in daytime. Despite lower traffic volumes, the night rate is principally so high because of reduced visibility.

Visibility is defined as the distance at which the driver with normal vision will detect road details, objects and potential hazards. Visibility is considered adequate if this detection is at a sufficient distance to allow the motorist to react appropriately. This distance normally increases with the speed of travel. Similarly, the distance at which the driver can see an object varies with the amount and distribution of light on the object on the roadway. During the daytime, adequate illumination is usually provided by sunlight; however, at night the driver must rely essentially on the illumination provided by the vehicle's headlights and other light sources including roadway lighting systems (i.e., lighting, sign lighting or combinations thereof).

3. Colored light signals

The threshold for the identification of the color of a light signal is about the same as the cone-threshold for detection of that light. At the spectral extremes these threshold values are nearly identical, but at the center of the visible spectrum the cone-threshold for detection may be as much as a half a log unit lower. In the luminance range between absolute rod-threshold and the cone-threshold for identification of color (about three log units), no perception of hue can be made. This luminance range is known as the photochromatic interval. Thus, color discrimination should not be required when signal light luminances are in this interval.

As noted before, color perception of very small lights may not be good due to small field tritanopia. For this reason, color identification is rarely required for signal lights that have to be seen at great distances. Lights of larger areal extent should be used when color discrimination is necessary. Traffic lights, for example, are usually of sufficient areal extent when color judgments are required (i.e., near a road intersection). Similarly, atmospheric pollutants may selectively attenuate certain regions of the spectrum. In such circumstances the apparent hue of the signal light may change, and color discrimination may be impaired.

4. Glare

Two kinds of glare have a critical influence on driver visual performance:

1. Discomfort glare (psychological glare): ocular discomfort from a bright light source.
2. Disability glare (physiological glare): stray light that reduces contrast sensitivity and, thus, produces a loss of visual efficiency.

Glare is an especially disturbing influence when one is viewing a difficult visual task under low brightness conditions.

a. Discomfort glare. Discomfort glare effects can be diminished by reducing luminaire brightness, by increasing mounting height, and by increasing the background brightness in the observer's field of view. Luminaire brightness may be reduced by increasing the effective luminaire area and by decreasing the intensity of light at angles higher than that required for optimum pavement brightness (luminance). The background brightness is increased by raising the general level of illumination.

b. Disability glare. Glare that directly interferes with visibility and ultimately with visual performance is of prime concern and is considered to be disability glare. Trotter (1982) distinguishes two causes of disability glare: intraocular veiling luminances and transient adaptation. Light that enters the eye is scattered within the eyeball by irregularities in the lens and the fluid that fills the eyeball. This scattered light creates a "veiling luminance" on the retina and reduces the contrast of the target being viewed; in effect, it "washes" out the image. Any source of light, direct or reflected, in the field of view causes some veiling luminances on the retina. The effect on foveal vision is a function of the intensity of the glare source and the angle of the source to the line of sight. The smaller the angle, the greater the effect on visibility.

There is a tendency for the eyes to turn toward a bright light (such as an oncoming automobile headlight); this phenomenon is called phototropism. Store owners and department store window designers take advantage of this human tendency when they direct bright light towards a particular part of the store (perhaps where the high-profit items are) or at a particular item in the window. This is but one example of the artistic aspects of illumination.

As a result of phototropism, the eyes are drawn to a bright glare source and become adapted to the higher luminance level. This is called transient adaptation. This, in turn, reduces the eyes' sensitivity to light. When the person looks back to the task, the eyes are less sensitive and visibility is reduced. It is like going into a dark movie theater on a bright sunny day, only the effect is not so pronounced. Windows are an especially good source of disability glare and transient adaption because the illumination levels can be 1,000 times more intense than normal indoor light levels.

The effects of phototropis are reduced by the use of fixed roadway lighting as the eye is more adapted to oncoming headlights. Disability glare can be reduced by increasing mounting height, moving the luminaire from the line of sight, and increasing background brightness.

Current practices in light design, such as high mounting heights, increased lateral set-back of supports, and restriction of light from the luminaire at vertical and horizontal angles where interference with driver visibility is most significant are effective in controlling discomfort and disability glare.

5. Process of seeing (Figure 18.11)

The purpose of this figure is to give an overall picture of the activities involved in seeing and its improvement. You will find that the text will cover the same visual processes and their improvements, but in much greater detail. It will thus be of considerable value if you will consistently bear in mind this overall picture, so that you will see each particular topic which follows in its larger context, and will, so to speak, not lose the woods from the trees.

Figure 18.11 presents the total process of seeing and the three parts of the

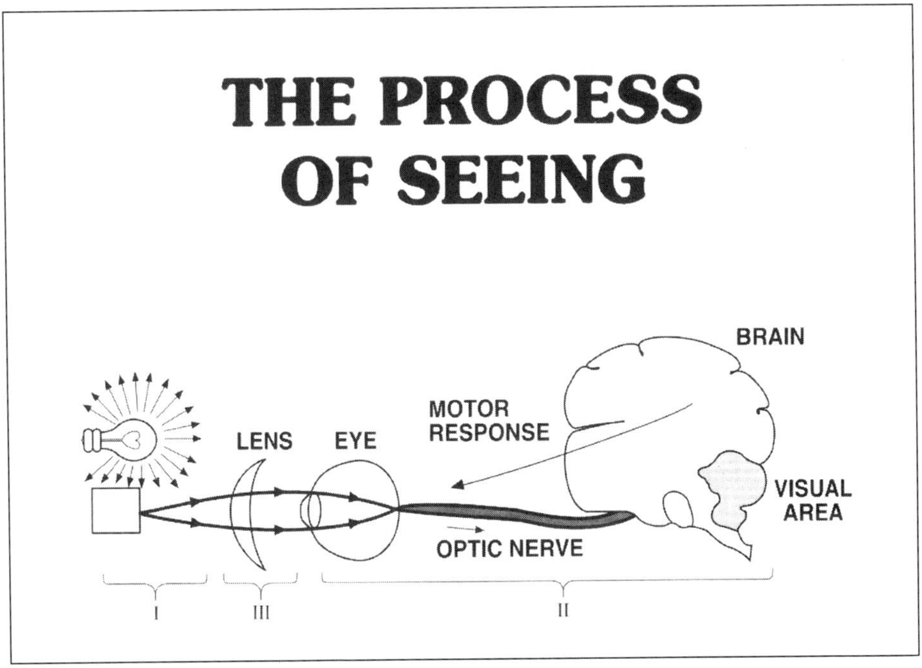

Figure 18.11

present text. Part I pertains to the light source and the objects reflecting light into the eye. Part II deals with the eye, the sensory nerve impulses passing to the visual area of the brain, and the motor impulses which pass from the brain back to the eye. Part III concerns the lens placed in front of the eye.

6. Effects of the atmosphere[4]

The atmosphere is never perfectly transparent. Hence, unless the viewing distance is short, atmospheric losses may have a significant effect upon the illuminance at the observer's eye. In fog the law of diminishing returns takes effect at relatively short distances. For example, if the transmissivity is 0.01 per mile (light fog), a light with an intensity of 100 candelas will produce an illuminance of one mile candle at a distance of one mile; an intensity of 40,000 candelas is required to produce that illuminance at two miles; and 9,000,000 candelas is required at three miles.

The clarity of the atmosphere may be conveniently expressed by a distance defined as the meteorological optical range, the distance at which the transmittance of the light path for light of color temperature of 2700 degrees K is equal to 0.05. This distance corresponds closely with the maximum distance at which dark objects may be observed through such an atmosphere in the daytime.

7. Photochemical reaction/sun glare

The eyes ability to see are a result of a photochemical reaction that takes place. There is a chemical called visual pigment present within the cells of the retina. When light is exposed to the visual pigments of the rods and cones, the visual pigments undergo a chemical change and elicit an electrical response. As the chemicals are used up, the retina becomes "bleached" of its visual pigments, and become less sensitive to lower light stimulation. When the light stimulation is removed, the process of pigment regeneration takes place to re-sensitize the retina to light (see Figures 18.7–18.9). Differences in size, spectral composition and duration of the stimulation of light levels. Thus, a strong pre-adaptation light will prolong the course of dark adaptation, and the effects of very bright sun light may last 24 hours or longer.

In order to detect an object, there must be a contrast difference between the object and its background. If L is the background luminance, ΔL would be change in luminance required to just recognize the object. This amount of change is called the threshold. The ratio of $\Delta L/L$ is found to be approximately constant for a range of average luminances. This is known as Webber's Law. The L that is just detectable is the threshold. (See Figures 18.7–18.9.)

When the eye is exposed to a bright stimulus source, the external stimulus induced a state of local adaptation which produces an apparent negative image of the original stimulus called a negative after-image. The after-image may be due to the regeneration of the visual pigments or a continuation of stimulation. The darkened after-image will temporarily reduce the retinal sensitivity in that particular area of the retina. Since sensitivity is reduced, it will reduce contrast and therefore, a higher I threshold is required under these conditions. The after-image leaves a veil over the object of regard making it more difficult to distinguish it from its background. A negative after-image is the most likely to show a latency of a second or so and a duration of a half a minute or so. (See Figures 18.7–18.9.)

Through personal research and the literature I was able to review, it is my opinion that if someone were exposed to bright headlight, the resulting veiling effect of the after-image would result in decreased sensitivity, contrast and visibility of the object of regard immediately following the exposure to a bright headlight.

G. Geometric optics—Visual acuity

While contrast detection may be considered the simplest visual function, visual acuity is somewhat more complex. The word "acuity" is often used to describe the visibility of fine details involved in various kinds of displays. Several different kinds of acuity are recognized.

1. Resolution acuity

Resolution acuity is the ability to detect that there are two stimuli, rather than one, in the visual field. It is measured in terms of the smallest angular separation, measured at the eye, between the two stimuli that can be present and still have the targets seen as separate.

2. Recognition acuity

Recognition acuity is the ability to correctly identify a visual target, such as differentiating between a "G" and a "C." Usually, but not always, it is measured in terms of the smallest size target, in angular measure, that can be discriminated. Visual acuity testing performed using letters, such as done clinically, is a form of recognition acuity.

Recognition acuity can involve very complex perceptual processing and often cannot be simply related to resolution acuity. Although detecting the difference between an "O" and a "C" may be identical to resolution acuity, differentiating between a circle and an octagon is a more complex task.

The chapter on geometric optics describes and illustrates how a visual angle is determined: the "E" could be measured in terms of either its critical detail (as shown) or in terms of its overall angular size.

Visual acuity, like detection, varies with exposure duration and luminance (retinal illuminance).

18.3 Measurement of Visibility

Visibility is a complex function of physical stimulus variables, physiological processes, and psychological predispositions and attitudes, all of which interact to determine the appearance of each display. Over the years, there have been many definitions of visibility, but most have recognized that visibility indicates something about how easy or difficult a target is to see. Accordingly, attempts have been made to measure target difficulty in terms that would be meaningful to lighting designers.

A. Snellen acuity

1. Measurement of visual performance—visual acuity by Snellen fractions and contrast sensitivity (quantitative)

The measure of visual performance with which most people are familiar is static acuity. Static acuity is a measure of the ability to distinguish fine detail in a stationary target with high luminance contrast.

Acuity is generally expressed by the Snellen fraction, such as 20/15, 20/20, 20/30, and so on. The numerator of the fraction tells how far the individual was from the letters which he was able to read. In most examinations, the individual is 20 feet from the letters. Thus, the numerator of the Snellen fraction is usually 20. The denominator tells the distance which the letter must be from the eye in order to produce a visual angle of five minutes. If the letter produces a visual angle of five minutes when it is twice as large, then it must be 40 feet from the eye to produce the same size visual angle. A visual acuity of 20/40, therefore, means that while the person was 20 feet from the letter, the letter could produce a visual angle of five minutes when it was 40 feet distant. Thus, the visual acuity of 20/40 is approximately half the normal amount.

The usual chart which is used for measuring the visual acuity is called the Snellen chart. This chart consists of a series of letters, each of which is a different size. It has been found that the average individual can make out the details of a letter sufficiently to detect what the letter is when the visual angle produced by the letter is approximately five minutes. Various size letters or objects can be placed at various distances, each of which will produce the same visual angle and the same size retinal image. The individual who can distinguish the details for the smallest size retinal image has the best acuity. Thus, visual acuity is the inverse of the visual angle size, and if a person needs a visual angle of ten minutes instead of five, his acuity is only half of normal.

A score of 20/20 does not mean "perfect vision," as people sometimes claim. A score of 20/40, which is sometimes set as the lower limit of acuity for a driver's license, means the person being tested can only resolve fine detail as well at 20 feet as can the standard observer at 40 feet. A person with an acuity of 20/40 can read a highway sign at only half the distance of someone with an acuity of 20/20.

2. The current vision standard—visual acuity

The Snellen Visual Acuity Test, the current measure to evaluate vision by use of the standard, well known eye charts, is designed to evaluate an individual's ability to see black letters on a white chart background. Because it tests the resolution ability of the eye, or how well the eye can focus an image, Snellen acuity corresponds to the static *quantity* rather than the quality of vision.

This type of test indicates the state of a person's vision in an ideal high-contrast situation such as reading well-lit black letters on a white background. Real-life objects have different sizes, shapes, and contrasts, and are viewed under such diverse conditions as dusk and twilight, rain, snow, fog, or smoke, all of which are low-contrast environments. There is a direct relationship which must be adjusted for the prior factor.

3. 20/20 Snellen quantitative vision

However, 20/20 (5' of arc) represents detection of an area (or object), not always positive identification as E. Identification through evaluation (discernment) requires ability to distinguish an arc of one minute of angle.

In 20/20 this means:

$$5' = .348'' \text{ (object) at 20 feet}$$

$$1' = \frac{.348''}{5} \text{ or } .0696'' \text{ (object) at 20 feet}$$

4. Summary: 20/20 vision*

Thus, to have true 20/20 vision one must be able to *discern* a 20/20 object in detail which requires the ability to differentiate spokes on a .348" E at 20 feet. This requires the ability to distinguish object separation of .069" at 20 feet in a doctor's office with the following contrast relation between bright screen and black letter:

Screen brightness = 10 to 40 fl (foot lamberts)

Letters = approximate reflectance 3 fl

**This is not qualitative vision (contrast sensitivity).*

5. 20/40 Snellen acuity

The designation 20/40 is also Snellen acuity terminology and in most states is minimum uncorrected vision to obtain a drivers license. Basically it states *what* a person *with* 20/20 vision can see at 40 feet that the subject with 20/40 must have at least 20 feet to resolve.

To compute the angle for 20/40, the following is an example:

Example: (Review Chapter 22)

Fact: 20/20 = tan 5' min of arc

20/40 = tan 10 min of arc at 20 feet (240")

tan 1' min of arc = .00029091

$$10' = 10 \times .000292 = \frac{x''}{240''}$$

x'' (object) = .6982026 inches in height (240 × .0029)

B. Snellen acuity versus contrast sensitivity

Following is a discussion of the original vision standard of Snellen acuity (quantitative) or standard eye chart and an emerging new contrast sensitivity testing technology (qualitative) for evaluating the health and performance of vision, low light level. A number of eye diseases, including cataracts, represent a major safety problem for drivers, especially considering the fact that they are not being properly detected by Snellen visual acuity testing. In recent years approximately 7000 eye doctors have added contrast sensitivity to their battery of tests to give a more comprehensive evaluation of a person's visual function for lowered light levels.

1. Contrast sensitivity[5]

Emerging as a more comprehensive way to measure vision, contrast sensitivity evaluates the ability of the eye-brain system to distinguish between an object and its background. Previous research has shown that, unlike visual acuity, contrast sensitivity does relate to visual performance in real-world situations. In visual processing, the retinal image is converted into a visual code by the retina-brain system. Contrast sensitivity tests this part of vision, which processes an object's size, shape and contrast.

Indeed contrast sensitivity testing is standardizing vision testing as pure tone audiological testing standardized audiology in the 1940s. After twenty years of scientific and clinical testing, contrast sensitivity, the ability to discern subtle changes in shades of gray, is emerging as a more comprehensive way to describe vision than Snellen acuity. In addition to measuring the optical quality of contrast, sensitivity evaluates the quality of contrast perception at the next stage of visual processing—the retina-brain system.

Contrast sensitivity refers to characteristics of an object that cause it to appear different or separate from something else. The eye responds to contrast. Under daylight levels of illumination, there are a variety of forms of contrast available (for example, color, texture, brightness). In addition, during daylight, the visual system is operating at the highest level of sensitivity and has the greatest capability of distinguishing differences between objects in the visual field. However, at night, *brightness contrast* is generally the only form of contrast of any consequence, and the visual system has a reduced capability to distinguish differences between objects in the visual field. Thus, in order to be seen at night, objects must be sufficiently brighter or darker than their background.

2. Luminance contrast[6]

Luminance contrast is defined in several ways:

1. $$C = \frac{L_d - L_b}{L_b}$$

Where:

L_d = luminance of detail (object)
L_b = luminance of background

2. $$C = \frac{L_g - L_l}{L_g}$$

Where:

L_g = greater luminance
L_l = lesser luminance

3. $$C = \frac{L_g - L_l}{L_l}$$

Where:

L_g = greater luminance
L_l = lesser luminance

4. $$M = \frac{L_{max} - L_{min}}{L_{max} - L_{min}}$$

Where:

L_{max} = maximum luminance
L_{min} = minimum luminance

Equation number one will result in contrasts that range between 0 and 1 for objects that are darker than their backgrounds and 0 and –1 for objects that are brighter than their backgrounds. This equation is recommended by some because the contrasts so determined represent relative visibilities.

Equation number two results in contrasts between 0 and 1 for all objects whether brighter or darker than their backgrounds. It is especially applicable in a situation like a bipartite pattern in which neither of the areas on the two sides of the border can be identified as object or background. It also applies to square wave gratings where neither the dark nor the bright bars can be designated as objects as opposed to backgrounds.

Equation number three is an alternative to equation number two which is commonly used when the object is brighter than the background.

The quantity defined by equation number four is often called contrast but is usually, and more properly, called modulation. It applies to periodic patterns such as gratings, which have one maximum and one minimum in each cycle.

When the contrast of an object is specified, one must know which definition is being used.

When an object and its background are illuminated by a single source and the luminances are dependent on their reflectances, the contrast is not affected by changing the intensity of the source. A target that consists of a disk (50 percent reflectance on a background of 90 percent reflectance) will have a contrast (equation number one) of 0.44 regardless of the illuminance on the scene. The contrast is determined by the reflectances.

It should be noted that because reflectances are rarely uniform in all directions, the contrast may be changed by varying the position of the observer or that of the source. This situation is described by saying that changing the position of the observer or of the source affects the *contrast rendition.*

3. Chromatic contrast

Visual targets that have the same luminance as the background may still be discerned by color information. These equal luminance chromatic contrasts are generally less distinct than achromatic contrasts, but under some conditions they can be quite visible. This is especially true if there is a sharp, spatial discontinuity between the two colors. The distinctness of such a chromatic border can be estimated by matching it to the contrast or an achromatic border, compared in this way, a chromatic threshold to about 0.30. A model for chromatic contrast has been developed using the responses of the long and middle wavelength-sensitive cones.

Because color contributes to the perceptions of scenes, predictions of visibility based only upon achromatic luminances can be wrong. These errors can arise not only because of chromatic contrast, but also because perceived brightness is modified by color information. Brightness is not based only upon achromatic luminance. The input from the color channels can also modulate luminance information to make borders more or less distinct. Roughly, the larger the difference in saturation between the target and the background, the larger the discrepancy between the perceived contrast and the estimated contrast based only on achromatic luminance.

4. Contrast detection

Contrast detection is the basic task from which all other visual behaviors are derived. The visual system gives virtually no useful information when the retina is uniformly illuminated, but it is highly specialized to inform about luminous discontinuities and gradients in the visual field.

The simplest visual function is one in which a small change in luminance must be detected in an otherwise uniform surrounding. This function has been studied in great detail and has related the probability of detecting a small round test object on a uniform background to the contrast and the luminance of the background.

As the contrast is raised, the probability of seeing a test object increases until, at a certain contrast, the object can be detected 100 percent of the time. The contrast at which the object can be detected 50 percent of the time is called *threshold contrast* and will vary among individuals, with the duration of exposure to the object, with the size of the object, and with the luminance of the background.

The change in threshold contrast as a function of background luminance represents a specific group of observers and a particular test object on a uniform background. This curve has been used by the Illuminating Engineering Society (IES) to illustrate a fundamental relationship between object detection and the luminance of the background. It is called the *visibility reference function.*

C. Quantitative versus qualitative

Commentary: The distinction between the two is best explained in the following example by use of the following two distinct approaches.

Problem: If we have a five-foot tall human at a distance of 400 feet, how does one determine if that person is both visible to the human eye and cognitively discernible[7] to the human mind? During daylight (photopic) and end of twilight—photopic, mesopic and scotopic times.

1. Snellen visual acuity approach (quantitative)

(Review Chapter 22)

Given: 5' (minutes) of arc at 20 feet = 20/20

Math: Tangent of side opposite over side adjacent = .348

20/20: tan 5' = .348"

$$\frac{400}{20} = 20$$

20/20 at 400 = 20 × .348 = 6.960" or 7 inches.

$$60'' = 5\text{ ft object} = \frac{60}{7} = 8.5 \times 20 = 170 \text{ or } 20/170 \text{ visual acuity}$$

Summary: A 5-foot object requires 20/170 visual acuity. It is quantitatively visible to a person with 20/20 visual acuity.

Problem: Under what lighting conditions (quality)?

To answer this problem one must understand contrast sensitivity or the ability to tell an object from its background.

2. Contrast sensitivity approach (qualitative)

Given: The brain has five channels that are sensitive to various light levels and object size.

Example: In our example we must determine the light level and the amount of reflected light from the object and its background.

Daylight: Facts: Available light (1) is 500 foot candles, (5380 lux), the (photopic)[8] object (2) is off-white or 60 percent reflectivity (300 foot lamberts =1038 cd/m²),[9] the background (3) is a dark blue wall of 5% reflectivity 25 (86.5 cd/m²).

Formula: $$\text{The contrast} = \frac{\text{object} - \text{background}}{\text{background}} = 11$$

11 is a positive image that is discernible to the mind.

Summary: In this simplistic example during daylight (photopic), a 5-foot object dressed in white with a dark background has a visual acuity requirement of 20/170 and a contrast ratio of 11:1, both satisfy the discernibility requirement of quantity and quality.

Civil Twilight:

By definition, p.m. Civil Twilight is between 30 foot candles and .3 (mesopic) foot candles (or civil darkness) which we shall use in this example. Sun center is 6 degrees below horizon.

3. The end of Civil Twilight

The prior number of 20/170 *Snellen acuity* still exists and the object will still be quantitatively visible to the eye; however, in order to understand if it is discernible to the cognitive center of the brain, we must turn to *contrast.*

Qualitative approach:

Facts: Available light is .3 foot candle.

Twilight: Assuming the previous data, white object 60 percent reflectivity; with a .3 (mesopic)[10] foot candle illumination, we now have .18 foot lamberts (.62 cd/m^2).

Dark background of 5% reflectivity with a .3 foot candle illumination, we now have .015 foot lamberts (.052 cd/m^2).

Formula: $$\text{contrast/sensitivity} = \frac{\text{object} - \text{background}}{\text{background}}$$

$$= \frac{.18\ \text{fl} - .015\ \text{fl}}{.015\ \text{fl}} = 11 = \frac{.62\ \text{cd/m}^2 - .052\ \text{cd/m}^2}{.052\ \text{cd/m}^2} = 11$$

= ratio 11:1

Answer: The eye would perceive a visible object but the mind would normally *not* discern what the object is due to low light level. Even though the acuity and contrast ratio are the same as the previous example, we are required to use the lower end *mesopic* vision (.34 cd/m^2) or rod/cone retinal cell usage, with a discernibility bordering scotopic vision (which has a sensitivity of .034 cd/m^2 and of rod retinal cells). However, they would identify an object's existence.[11]

Astronomical Twilight:

By definition, Astronomical Twilight is when the center of the sun is 18° below the horizon or commonly the darkest part of the night, or .01 foot candles or .1076 lux (scotopic).

Assuming the previous facts of object 60 percent reflectivity; we now have .006 foot lamberts (.02 cd/m^2); background is 5 percent reflectivity .0005 foot lamberts (.0017 cd/m^2).

Contrast ratio: $$\frac{\text{object} - \text{background}}{\text{background}}$$

$$= \frac{.006\ \text{fl} - .0005\ \text{fl}}{.0015\ \text{fl}} = 11 = \frac{.02\ \text{cd/m}^2 - .0017\ \text{cd/m}^2}{.0017\ \text{cd/m}^2} = 11$$

= ratio 11:1 visual acuity 20/170

Summary: The object is now neither visible or discernible.[12] It is well below the contrast detection and acuity detection at this light level for a static reflective white object.

Note: The lesson to be derived is that size, contrast, illumination, luminance, and color are necessary to determine object discernibility. The author wishes to note this hypothetical example is a simplistic static situation, and each situation must be evaluated on its own merits by a competent expert.

18.4 Section II: Human Factors

The Human Factors Society is an interdisciplinary organization of professional workers with the role of humans in complex systems, the design of equipment and facilities for human use, and the development of environments for comfort and safety. The membership is composed of psychologists, engineers, physiologists, and other scientists from the United States and around the world. The Human Factors Society promotes research and application of human factors in the design, development, use, and evaluation of machines, systems, environments, and devices.

A. What exactly is human factors?

Let me start with something very basic. Exactly what do we do? Human factors has been defined in several ways. My definition is that:

Human factors is a body of knowledge about human abilities, human limitations, and other human characteristics that are relevant to design.

In forensic aspects of highway safety, we are primarily interested in three aspects:

1. perception/reaction for highway design;
2. expectancy; and
3. detection/response time.

B. Perception/reaction time

Stopping sight distance is calculated as the sum of two distances: the distance traversed between the time an object is detected and the brakes are applied, and the distance required to bring a vehicle to a full stop. In highway design the perception-reaction time of 2.5 seconds is assumed for determining the four steps of the behavioral component of stopping sight distance with an additional 1.5 seconds allowed for braking. When adopted by the American Association of State Highway and Transportation officials, the 2.5 second assumption was considered long enough to cover nearly all drivers under most driving conditions. However, with an unexpected event, a new assumption of 3.5 seconds is recommended for the perception/reaction time formula.

C. Expectancy

Expectancy relates to a driver's readiness to respond to situations, events, and information in predictable and successful ways. As such, it is a key factor in driving task performance since it affects the speed and accuracy of a driver's response. Prevalent expectancies that are reinforced aid drivers, while expectancies that are violated increase reaction time and driver error.

Expectancy and expectancy violations operate at all levels of the driving task, from vehicle control through guidance in the traffic stream to navigation of the road network. They include a priori (brought by the driver as a result of culture and experience) and ad hoc (caused by exposure to a set of site specific practices and conditions) aspects. They encompass all phases of geometric design and traffic control.

Because of these considerations, engineers and designers need to maintain an appreciation of the expectancy concept and the adverse effects of expectancy violations. They should assure that their designs, traffic operations, and traffic control devices do not violate expectancies by surprising drivers. Finally, they should rectify expectancy violations through information system improvements based on the principles of Positive Guidance. To emphasize the point, when drivers get the information they expect from the highway and its traffic control devices, performance tends to be timely and error free. When they do not get what they expect or get what they do not expect, response delays, errors, and system failures are the usual result.

"Expectancy" is a predisposition of drivers to believe that things will happen or be configured in certain ways. All drivers have expectancies that are based on exposure to general practices in civil and traffic engineering, as well as the behavior of other drivers. Recognizing that drivers develop expectations, there has been a strong trend toward making road design, signing, and signalling practices as uniform as possible. When expectancies are violated, a more potent stimulus and/or more information is required to reliably capture the driver's attention and communicate the essential data than would otherwise be the case. The result is that perception-response time may be increased, primarily because the detection and/or identification intervals are lengthened.

D. Detection/response

A driver's reaction to any stimulus of a traffic situation or hazard is a four-step process—a process that takes time. (That time is now accepted in road sight design as 2.5 seconds.) The time required for a response equals the time it takes for the driver to recognize the situation, understand the situation, decide to take action, and take action. Or, put more simply, *detection*, *identification*, *decision*, and *reaction*. However, the time is "elastic," and each situation must be evaluated.

More specifically defined, those four processes are:

1. *Detection* or information, which is based on "visibility," is the visual awareness that an object is present in the roadway. At night it depends entirely on contrast sensitivity.
2. *Identification* is the process of gathering information about the object until enough information is gathered for the driver to make an appropriate decision as to what it is, whether it poses a threat, and whether its existence calls for some responsive action.
3. *Decision* is the next step; it involves the driver making a choice as to the appropriate action to take to avoid the object or condition.
4. *Reaction* occurs when orders are issued by the driver's brain to the appropriate muscle groups in order to initiate the responsive action decided upon.

A key point is that detection, identification, evaluation, and reaction are four different processes. It does not always guarantee that correct identification or discernment will automatically follow detection, and failure in either one can result in tragedy.

Existing tables and charts of reaction times based on alerted studies are relevant only as generalities. The brain can be fooled by optical illusions, misinterpretations, and errors in visual performance in non-alerted situations. *Every situation must be evaluated on its own characteristics.*

The following ten figures show comparisons of various situations. Work

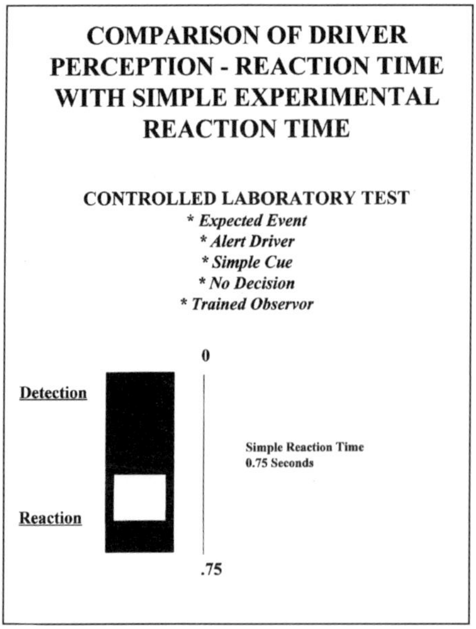

Figure 18.12

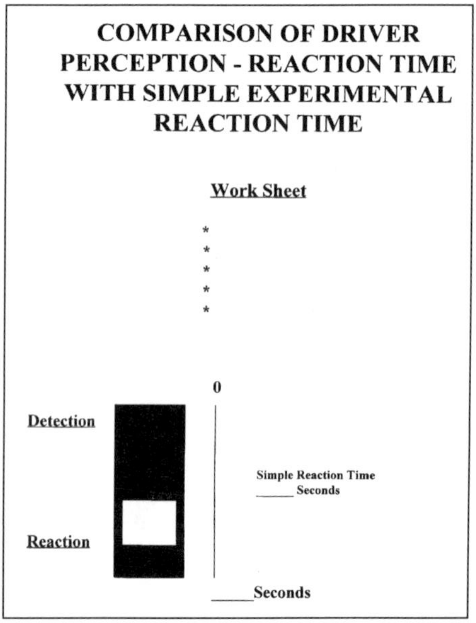

Figure 18.13

sheets are provided for the reader's use (Figures 18.12 through 18.21).

E. Human factors considerations related to perception/reaction

Available perception-reaction time can have a direct impact on a driver's ability to respond in such fashion to avoid having an accident. Many lay persons believe that the perception-reaction times for drivers are short and that a driver can and should respond very quickly to any condition encountered on the roadway. However, this is not a correct assumption to make for a driver. Perception-reaction time can vary significantly depending upon a given situation and can be quite long under certain conditions. AASHTO addresses the perception-reaction time issue as it relates to the design and operation of highway facilities:

> Information takes time to process. Drivers' reaction times increase as a function of increased decision complexity and information content. The longer the reaction time, the greater the chance for error. Johannson and Rumar [14] measured brake reaction time for expected and unexpected signals. Their results show that when the signal is expected, reaction time averages about .66 second, with a few drivers taking as long as 2 seconds. With unexpected signals, reaction times increased by 35 percent. Thus, for a simple, unexpected decision and action, some drivers may take as long as

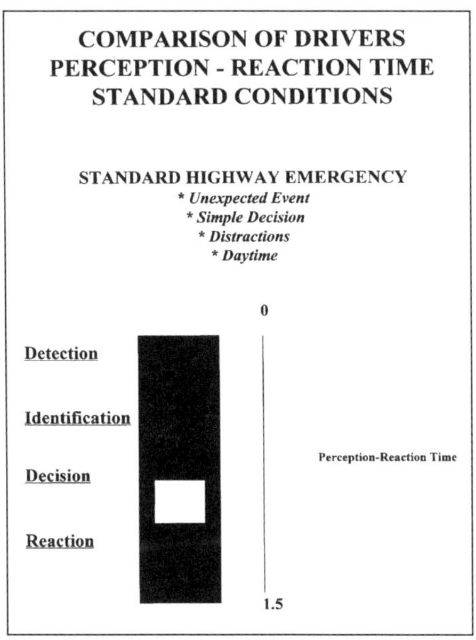

Figure 18.14

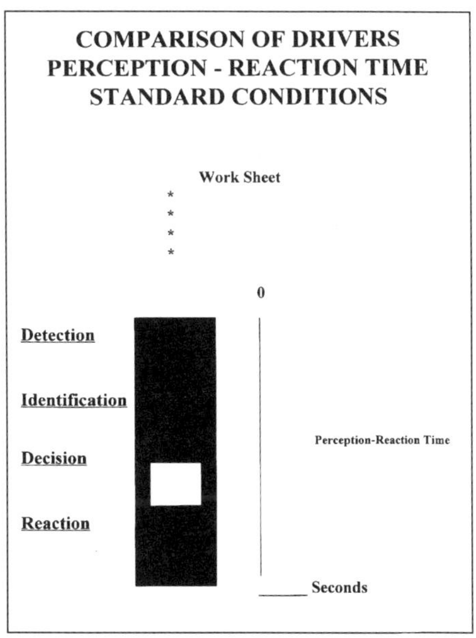

Figure 18.15

> 2.7 seconds to respond. A complex decision with several alternatives may take several seconds longer than a simple decision [13].
>
> Designs should take reaction times into account. It should be recognized that drivers vary in their response and take longer to respond when decisions are complex or features are unexpected [13]. Clear sightlines and adequate decision sight distances provide margins for error [13].
>
> A reaction time of 2.5 seconds is considered adequate for more complex conditions than those of the various studies, but it is not adequate for consideration of the most complex conditions encountered by the driver [13].

One can see that perception-reaction times can vary substantially from driver to driver and from driving situation to driving situation. The more complex the driving situation is and the more unfamiliar the driving situation is, the longer the perception-reaction time will be. Inadequate perception-reaction times simply lace the driver in a position that will lead to wrong decisions and/or responses that are too late, thus resulting in an accident.

There are some who believe that the 2.5 seconds used by AASHTO for perception-reaction time may not be long enough and that the time should be increased if an adequate level of safety is to be provided to all of the traveling

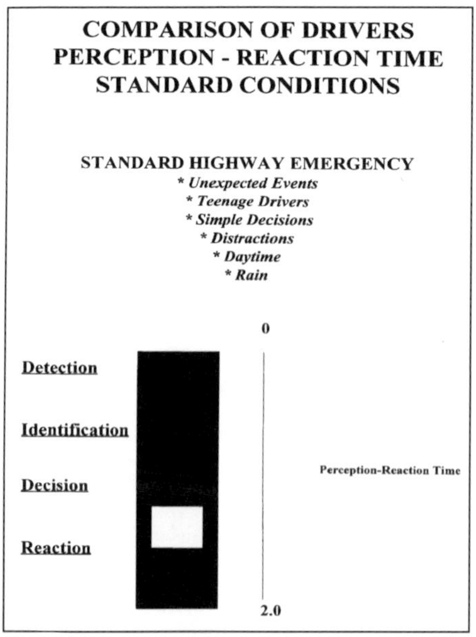

Figure 18.16

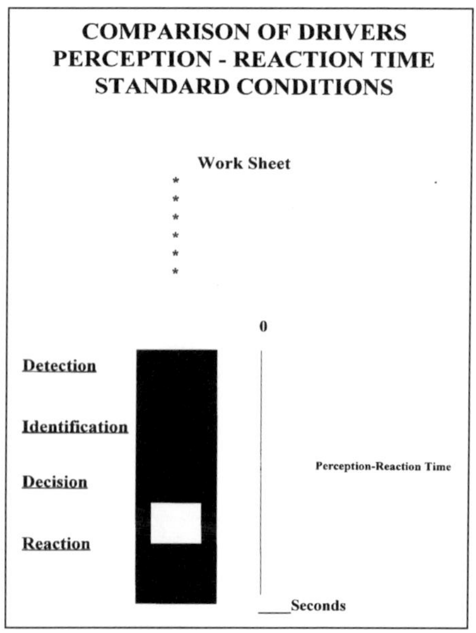

Figure 18.17

public. Specifically, the Institute of Transportation Engineers (ITE) addresses this issue in their handbook for traffic engineers:

> A significant component in the successful processing and use of information is the speed with which this processing is done. One of the human factors often cited by traffic engineers concerned with safety is perception-reaction time (PRT), or how quickly a driver can respond to an emergency situation. A good deal of research has been done on this topic, but there is still not complete agreement on what PRT is appropriate for use in the design of roadways and traffic control devices. The concept of decision sight distance is an important part of roadway engineering, as it relates to stopping, steering, and overtaking. Adequate sight distance depends, of course, on vehicle speed and size as well as driver PRT. It plays a role in many traffic accident litigation cases where a central issue is how much time or distance was available for the driver to respond to a hazard [15].
>
> The PRT used for design standards by the American Association of State Highway and Transportation Officials (AASHTO) was derived from research done some time ago and includes 1.5 seconds for perception and decision and 1.0 second for making the response, for a total of 2.5 seconds [15].

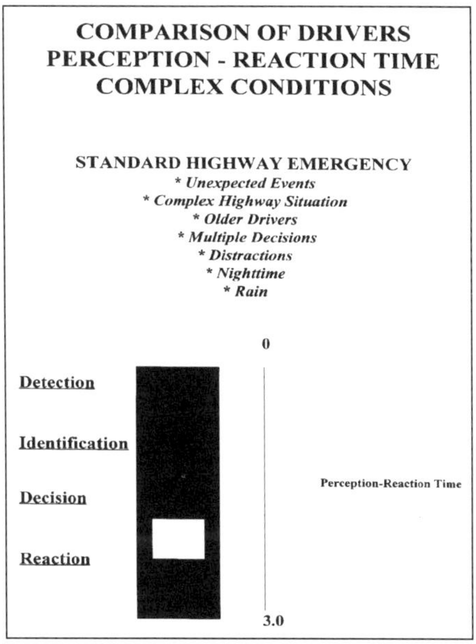

Figure 18.18

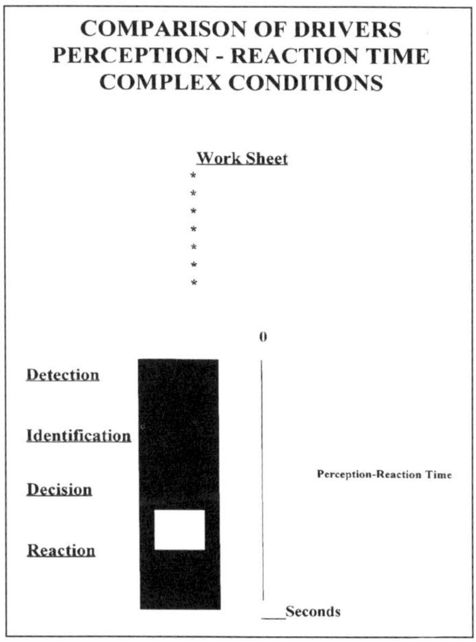

Figure 18.19

The complexities of driver PRT are often not appreciated by those who use the concept. The total time to complete an appropriate response involves the following elements: detection (is something there?), identification (what is it?), decision (what should I do?), response execution (including movement time—e.g., getting the foot from accelerator to brake, and completing the response of pressing the brake), and time for the vehicle to respond (come to a stop or move laterally to avoid an obstacle). The last element is not a component of PRT, but is part of the total time required for the vehicle to come to a stop or move laterally to avoid a collision. All of this takes considerable time. This time is increased under conditions where the hazard is unexpected (which is most of the time in emergency situations), the driving scene is visually complex or dark, and when the driver is impaired, distracted by other components of the driving task, not paying attention, fatigued, or elderly. Hence the need to take into account not the "average" driver, but the one whose performance is much below that of most others on the road [15].

The complexities of driver reaction time have been described in detail by Triggs, who points out that a PRT in excess of 2.5 seconds should be the standard in design of roads, traffic control devices, etc. He examined PRT in a variety of driving situations ranging from

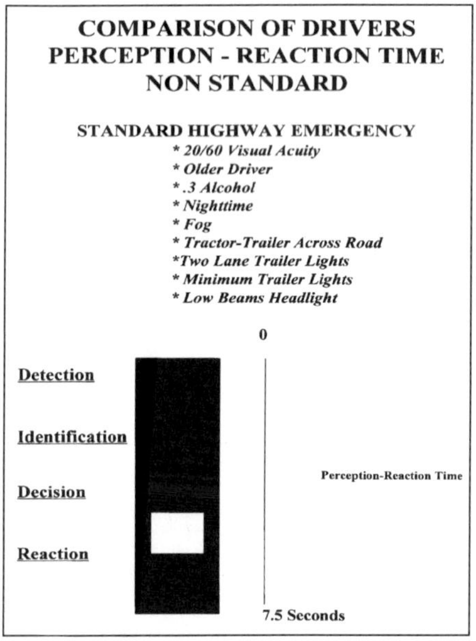

Figure 18.20

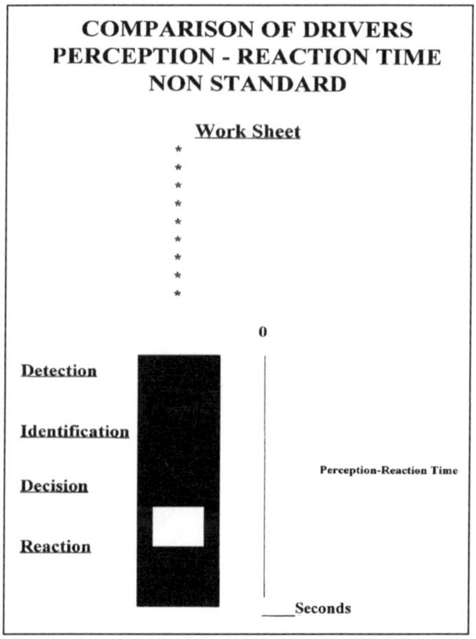

Figure 18.21

braking to traffic signs and the presence of police to emergency situation (e.g., braking by a lead vehicle). The 85th percentile reaction times to brake ranged from 1.26 seconds to over 3 seconds, and 7 of the 12 situations tested produced times greater than 2.5 seconds, suggesting that the standard of 2.5 seconds is too low [15].

An examination of the current standards for PRT was carried out by Hooper and McGee. On the basis of available literature on the topic they determined that the current time of 2.5 seconds was too short, in view of the complexities of the driving task. They suggest 3.2 seconds as a more reasonable figure [15].

Olson has also summarized some of the literature on PRT and drawn similar conclusions. The element of surprise increases PRT by about one-third to one-half, emphasizing the need to be cautious in the interpretation of much of both the laboratory and the roadway research on this topic. Surprise is a typical component of the emergencies that arise in a driving task [15].

Taoka has also challenged the 2.5 second PRT used by AASHTO in design considerations following a review of recent work on this topic. He points out that the research on which the 2.5 second figure was based has definite limitations. Specifically, subjects were alert (expecting to have to make a braking response), young (usually under 30), and driving in an uncluttered environment during daylight and in good weather. Such conditions are not representative of those found in typical driving. On the basis of his analysis of these problems and the existing research, Taoka concludes that a PRT of 3.5 seconds would be more appropriate to take into account the 85th percentile driver. Even using the 85th percentile as the design standard, there will still be 15 percent of drivers who will be unable to respond within this time frame [15].

Discussions of PRT assume the process begins when the driver first detects the object of concern. However, active search often precedes the beginning of the detection/perception phase of information processing. Alexander points out the need to take this factor into account, challenging the idea that the process of responding to a hazard begins with detection. A certain amount of time is required for head and eye movement, as the driver scans the roadway environment for information. In some cases it takes on the order of seconds (not fractions of a second) for a successful search, even when the hazard, traffic sign, or whatever is readily visible. This

> is especially the case with older drivers and in complex environments [15].
>
> On the basis of the work on PRT and its recent reevaluation and criticism, it is clear that caution must be exercised in applying this concept to the design of roadways and traffic control devices. More time than is typically allowed for emergency responses will be required by a sizable proportion of drivers. The implications for design and placement of traffic control devices, intersections, and curves are clear [15].

One can see that ITE feels that a perception-reaction time of 2.5 seconds is a minimum value in which a sizable proportion of drivers may not be able to accommodate their needs. Thus, the distances shown for minimum stopping may not be adequate for a reasonable number of drivers for a reasonable number of situations due to a longer perception-reaction time being required.

End Notes

1. See Appendix C for Civil Twilight example.
2. *Illumination* is the measure of the amount of light flux falling on a surface. Illumination is independent of the direction from which the light comes; the number of light sources, or their positions; the type of light source; and the type of surface on which it falls.
3. *Luminance* is a measure of the amount and concentration of light flux leaving a surface and is the light by which an object is seen. It is the luminance that controls the magnitude of the sensation that the brain receives of an object. The luminance of a surface depends on all of the quantities of which illumination is independent, such as the direction from which the light reaches the surface, the direction from which it is viewed, and the reflective properties of the surface itself. The amount of light falling on a small area of a surface is measured as the illumination on that area. This incident light is generally reflected in all directions by the surface, and its directional distribution is determined by the properties of the surface and the manner in which the light strikes the surface. The apparent luminance of the area on the surface is determined by the amount of light reflected toward the observer's eye.
4. *Illuminating Engineering Society Handbook*, 1987.
5. Review chapter by Dr. Arthur Ginsburg.
6. See *Illuminating Engineering Society Handbook*, 1987.
7. Cognitive to senses (vision).
8. Photopic vision = 3.426 cd/m^2 (candelas per square meter) or more.
9. 3.426 x foot lamberts = cd/m^2.
10. Mesopic vision = .34 cd/m^2.
11. Review human factors section.

12. Scotopic Sensitivity is .034 cd/m^2.

13. *A Policy on Geometric Design of Highways and Streets*. Federal Highway Administration, U.S. Department of Transportation, 1984.

14. *A Policy on Geometric Design of Highways and Streets*. Federal Highway Administration, U.S. Department of Transportation, 1990.

15. *Traffic Engineering Handbook*, (4th edition), Institute of Transportation Engineers, Prentice Hall, Inc., 1992.

References

Manual on Uniform Traffic Control Devices. Federal Highway Administration, U.S. Department of Transportation, 1988.

A Policy on Geometric Design of Highways and Streets, American Association of State Highway and Transportation Officials, Washington, D.C., 1990.

Positive Guidance in Traffic Control, G.J. Alexander and H. Lunenfeld, Federal Highway Administration, U.S. Department of Transportation, Washington, D.C., 1975.

An Examination of Driver Reaction Times, Albert T. Baxter.

Human Factors in Engineering and Design, Mark S. Sanders and Ernest J. McCormick.

Real Time, Accurate Recall, and Other Myths, Malcolm Stewart-Morris, M.D.

Chapter 19

Assured Clear Distance Discussion

Bernard S. Abrams, O.D.

Synopsis

19.1 Memorandum for Plaintiff

This motion is made on the ground that there is genuine issue as to material fact and that Plaintiff is entitled to a jury trial as a matter of law.

A. Hypothetical facts

The hypothetical accident which forms the basis for the lawsuit in this matter occurred on February 1, 1993, on State Route 48, a two-lane asphalt road in Miami County, Ohio, between 5:30 a.m. and 6:00 a.m. The roadway was dry without luminaries and the light conditions are in dispute. The Plaintiff says that it was "pitch dark" at the time of the accident. The Defendant says that the accident happened when it was starting to get light, just as dawn was breaking.

A car driven by Defendant ran off State Route 48 into the ditch, then returned to the roadway and sat across the southbound lane and a portion of the northbound lane of State Route 48. Plaintiff came upon the defendant's stalled vehicle which was without lights at a time when the vehicle was sitting perpendicular on the road. Plaintiff saw something and was not certain if it was a shadow, but then determined that it was a car sitting across the roadway. When Plaintiff finally recognized that what he was viewing was a vehicle, rather than a shadow, he put on his brakes and his vehicle struck the defendant. The distance and time frame required to avoid this accident would have been 345.76 feet or 6.07 seconds (Table 19.1). The beginning of isocandela distance available on low beam headlights under currently required vehicle conditions would have been approximately 175–200 feet. This early detection distance would have been insufficient to avoid or evade an incident.

Plaintiff cannot estimate how far he was from the defendant vehicle when he first saw it, and states he only had the opportunity to put on his brakes and lock up his tires. His vehicle continued straight and the front of his vehicle hit the defendant vehicle. This, when analyzed by a visibility expert, indicates a correlating distance to current low beam headlights. The element of discernibility and when it occurred is stated to be a jury question. However, the understanding of scientific and technical knowledge related to visibility and human factors will assist the jury in understanding the evidence. To accomplish this, an expert in the area of visibility, human factors, and traffic engineering is recommended.

B. Rules of evidence

Rule 702. Testimony of experts. If scientific, technical, or other specialized knowledge will assist the trier of fact to understand the evidence or to determine a fact in issue, a witness qualified as an expert by knowledge, skill, experience, training, or education may testify thereto in the form of an opinion or otherwise.

C. Law and argument

A violation of Ohio Revised Code 4511.21, dealing with the assured clear distance ahead statute, is negligence per se. The criteria needed to show a violation, and negligence per se, have been set forth in the case *Blair v. Goff-Kirby Company*, 48 Ohio St. 2d 5, 358 N.E. 2d 634 (1976). There, the Supreme Court wrote:

> Violation of the statute and a finding of negligence per se depends on whether there is evidence that the driver collided with an object which (1) was ahead of him in his path of travel, (2) was stationary or moving in the same direction as the driver, (3) did not suddenly appear in the driver's path, and (4) was reasonably discernible.

Since there is no question about the first three elements required under *Blair*, the only issue usually left is whether the forward object or vehicle was reasonably discernible in sufficient time to avoid impact. The doctrine of *Sharp v. Norfolk & Western Ry. Co.*, 36 Ohio St. 3d 172 (1988), says that whether an object is reasonably discernible on a highway during the nighttime is usually a question of fact for a jury, if there is conflicting evidence. However, there is conflicting evidence in most cases. It is generally presented through different perspectives, but the facts are that the discernibility of a vehicle or object on the highway is a matter that is best explained by a nighttime visibility human factors expert with the aid of a reconstructionist.

A common misconception is that visibility means discernibility, which is just as incorrect as the assertion that a collision equals a violation of the assured clear distance ahead statute. The fact is that discernibility will depend upon several factors such as lighting, visual contrast, distance, and so forth. Discernibility results when it is perceived at a higher brain level that there is something on the highway that requires action by a driver to avoid a collision. The concept can be found in the case of *McFadden v. Elmer C. Breuer Transp. Co.,* 156 Ohio St. 430, 103 N.E. 2d 385 (1952), where the Ohio Supreme Court cited the Pennsylvania Supreme Court, which had decided a case under Ohio law. There, it wrote:

> The Court stated that none of the cases revealed an intention to "ascribe to the word 'discernible' a fixed and rigid meaning applicable to every possible situation. The word 'discernible' ordinarily implies something more than 'visible.' 'Visible' means perceivable by the *eye* whereas 'discernible' means *mentally* perceptible or distinguishable—capable of being discerned by the *understanding* and not merely by the senses."

Whether it was an automobile on the highway, a motorcycle, or a person, the approaching vehicle operator can only discern that there is something (an object) on the highway which required his or her attention when certain visual and human factor criteria are satisfied by the stimulus given off by that object. Thus, it is the opinion of this author, based on physics, human factors and visual research, that under *McFadden* the mental perception of a potential problem requires (1) detection, (2) identification, (3) recognition (before it can or cannot be perceived as a danger), and (4) reaction (i.e., message sent to the muscular skeleton system before a maneuver can occur). These four steps lead from visibility on the photographic plate of the eye to discernibility at the mentally perceptible brain level, all of which takes time. It is only after these steps that a maneuver such as braking can, in fact, occur.

The second issue for consideration by a court may be the effect of the violation of the assured clear distance rule by an "intervening agency." This discussion can be found in the case of *Hurt v. Charles J. Rogers Transp. Co.*, 164 Ohio St. 323, 130 N.E. 2d 824 (1955). There, the Supreme Court wrote:

> Where there intervenes between an agency creating a hazard and an injury resulting from such hazard another conscious and responsible agency which could or should have eliminated the hazard, the original agency is relieved from liability. A break in the chain of causation thereby takes place which operates to absolve the original agency.

As there were no intervening factors, this area is not applicable in this case.

D. Conclusion

Failure to discern evidence of an object in darkness in the path of one's vehicle, regardless of the nature of that object, will, in all probability, occur if there is insufficient time, lighting, contrast, or a combination of the three factors.

As clearly noted, the facts in this hypothetical case, when evaluated as in Chart II, indicate adequate stimulus required at a minimum of 346 feet. Low beam headlights have a twilight envelope at their peak of .3 foot candles at approximately 175 to 200 feet. There would, in all probability, have been insufficient distance for an approaching driver to accomplish the necessary steps, including maneuver, to evade or avoid this incident.

E. Summary

It is the opinion of Dr. Abrams, within a reasonable degree of scientific and visual certainty, that the responsibility for this accident belonged to the defendant.

Table 19.1
Brake and Stop Distance

Enter the speed of the vehicle (m.p.h.)

Iterate	Value
N	55

Enter coefficient of friction

Iterate	Min. Value	Max. Value
Y	.4	.7

Enter reaction time of driver (sec.)

Iterate	Value
N	2.5

Friction	Stop Time	Brake Dist	Total Time	Total Dist	Reaction Dist
.40	6.25	252.08	8.75	453.80	201.71
.43	5.88	237.25	8.38	438.97	201.71
.45	5.56	224.07	8.06	425.79	201.71
.48	5.26	212.28	7.76	413.99	201.71
.50	5.00	201.67	7.50	403.38	201.71
.53	4.76	192.06	7.26	393.78	201.71
.55	4.55	183.33	7.05	385.05	201.71
.57	4.35	175.36	6.85	377.07	201.71
.60	4.17	168.06	6.67	369.77	201.71
.62	4.00	161.33	6.50	363.05	201.71
.65	3.85	155.13	6.35	356.84	201.71
.67	3.70	149.38	6.20	351.10	201.71
.70	3.57	144.05	6.07	345.76	201.71

The above is an actual case from the files of The Institute of Vehicular Safety with names and locations changed.

19.2 Definitions

Assured clear distance: A driver must not operate a vehicle at a greater speed than will permit him to bring it to a stop within the assured clear distance ahead. Assured clear distance ahead is the distance between the vehicle he is operating and a reasonably visible object in his path of travel. It constantly changes and is measured at any moment by the distance between the driver and any reasonably visible object ahead of him or in his path of travel.

Legal excuse: Without fault on his part and because of circumstances over which he had no control, the driver was confronted by a sudden and unforeseeable emergency which made compliance with the assured clear distance statute impossible.

Table 19.1
Data & Information

Data Required:	Facts:
Lighting Conditions	Dark No Light
Coefficient Friction	.7
Color Road	Asphalt
Color Defendant Car	Dark Blue
Ambient Light	None
Weather Conditions	Clear
Road Contour	Straight and Level
Plaintiff Headlights	Low Beams
Detection Reaction Time	2.5 Seconds
Speed	55 MPH
Sunrise	6:30 A.M.
Time of Collision	5:30-6:00 A.M. (Darkness)
Legal Speed	55 MPH
Braking Time (stop)	3.57 seconds

Problems to Solve and Methods Used:	
Distance Required?	TAAR, Model B-1
Time Required?	TAAR, Model B-2

Enclosures:
Enclosed are 3 TAAR computer charts relating to various speeds, perception-reaction times and coefficient of road friction.

Reasonable or proper speed: That which has due regard to traffic, surface and width of the street or highway and to any other condition. This includes consideration of permanent physical features at the scene, hour of day or night, extent of other traffic, width and nature of the roadway, and any other circumstances.

Discernible object: The element of discernibility is at issue. *Discernible* implies something more than *visible*. *Visible* means perceivable by the eye, whereas *discernible* means mentally perceptible, distinguishable, capable of being discerned by the understanding, not merely by the senses.

Reasonably modified, "discernible" in this statute means an object which the driver should or could have seen if he was operating his vehicle at a speed which would have permitted him to bring the vehicle to a stop within an assured clear distance.

Chapter 20

The Eye Is Not a Camera, the Camera Is Not an Eye

Bernard S. Abrams, O.D.

Synopsis

20.1 Foreword

Ansel Adams in his photography series book, *The Camera,* states in Chapter 1, *Visualization*:

> Photography involves a series of related mechanical, optical, and chemical processes which is between the subject and the photograph of it. Each separate step of the process takes us one stage further away from the subject and closer to the photographic print. Even the most realistic photograph is not the same as the subject, but separated from it by the various influences of the photographic system. The photographer may choose to emphasize or minimize the "departures from reality," but he cannot eliminate them.
>
> The process begins with the camera/lens/shutter system which "sees" in a way analogous, but not identical, to that of the human eye. The camera, for example, does not concentrate on the center of its field of view as the eye does, but sees everything within its field with about equal clarity. The eye scans the subject to take it all in, while the camera (usually) records it whole and fixed. Then there is the film, which has a range of sensitivity that is only a fraction of the eyes'. Later steps, development,

> printing, etc., contribute their own specific characteristics to the final photographic image.

He further clarifies the difference in Chapter 7, *Basic Image Management*:

> [W]e must understand the differences between the image seen by the human eye and the one seen by the camera. The photographic image, for example, is flat and two-dimensional. It has borders that define what is included and what is not; its focus, content, and point of view are fixed at the moment of exposure. These characteristics are very different from what we are accustomed to, and take for granted, in our visual contact with the world. Whether we realize it or not, we observe the world from many points of view, not just one, by means of our binocular vision (using our two eyes), and through continuous movements of the eyes, head, and body. The brain synthesizes this continuous exploration into a unified experience.

Louis Erhardt, in *Views on the Visual Environment* under the subheading of *Light as a Stimulus for Vision,* states:

> Edward T. Hall clarifies, "Quite simply, man does not see the way he thinks he sees. Instead of a passive-receptive act in which scenes in the outside world are simply recorded like a camera with film in it the act of perceiving visually is one in which man is totally involved and in which he participates actively, screening and structuring very much in the same way that one selects and constructs when talking or writing. The visual process is therefore active and creative."

20.2 The Eye versus the Camera

A. The eye: A living camera?

Light reflects from an object in space and comes to the eye. This is the first step of the visual process which leads over a visual pathway to the brain and, eventually, to a decision or an opinion. After the light enters the eye and passes through the cornea, the black shutter known as the pupil shrinks or expands. The light passes through this opening and is focused by a lens system which forms images on a photographic plate called the retina. It might be noted here that a man-made camera can only take a single exposure on a single photographic plate—not so with the eye. When you take a picture with a camera, you have to take special pains to hold the camera still—not so with the eye. With the eye we are able to observe a constant succession of changing scenes. A very remarkable moving picture goes on before us.

B. The brain: A picture developing room

The scene before our eyes has been photographed. The light entering the eyes has played its major role. The light can go no farther than the photographic plate, the retina. A new form of energy relays the image-message to the brain before seeing is possible. This form of energy is called the nerve impulse. Here in the dark confines of the skull where light never enters, vision is created. The brain is a dark room where the pictures, taken by the eyes, are developed.

Not only is visual consciousness created in the brain but also hearing, tasting, smelling, feeling, and the still more complex forms of consciousness, our memories, our thoughts, our loves, our hopes and our fears.

It is evident from the previous two brief paragraphs that visual perception is the final outcome of a long chain of complex events. It is dependent upon the light rays which come into the eyes and form the retinal images. It is further dependent upon the complex physiological process that takes place from the retina to the occipital lobe in the brain. Finally, it is directly dependent upon the brain activity itself. The termination of the impulse from the eye is in the occipital lobe of the brain along what is known as the optical pathway. This traveling of impulse can be measured by noninvasive technology and renders great information about not only what one is seeing, but how one is thinking. Thus, it is very logical to understand and believe that visual perception is not the only end product of a chain of events starting with reflective light, but it is also within a great interwoven field of activity—the cerebral cortex—which is responsible for all forms of human consciousness. It is for this reason that physicists, physiologists, and anatomists have dealt with the sequence of events leading to visual perception. In addition, psychologists and physicians have dealt with the various interrelationships between visual perception and various other nonperceptual mental processes.

In summary, visual perception involves the interrelationships between visual perception and such processes as learning, memory, emotion, thinking, attitude, and decision making.

C. Camouflage/optical illusion

The eye is normally an accurate and sensitive receiver.[1] It is the conduit or connecting link between what is really there and what we perceive to be there. When we see an object, our eye gives us immediate information. A picture is seen in the third dimension and is easily evaluated by the brain.

The eye can, however, be deceived. Camouflage is, after all, another word for an illusion.[2] It is possible for the eye to perceive objects differently than they really are. Confusing the eye results from the lack of certain factors of recognition which help the eye and brain identify the object. Although psychologists, military tacticians, scientists and ophthalmologists all have different names for these factors of recognition, they are in agreement that there are six factors generally present. If any one of these factors is absent, an illusion in the process of vision may result. These six factors are as follows:

1. Color

Color is an aid to the observer when there is a contrast between the color of an object and its background. The greater the contrast in color, the more visible the object appears. While color alone will usually not identify an object, it is often an aid in locating the object or confirming a tentative identification. A secondary consideration is a tone of a color. The tone of color is a modification of color in varying shades. Usually darker shades of a given color will be less likely to attract an observer's attention than lighter, more brilliant shades. Use of colors that blend in with the surroundings is probably the most basic of the fundamentals of camouflage.

2. Shape

Experience teaches people to associate an object with its shape or outline. Because shapes have become familiar through experience, the object can be identified long before all its details are identified. When the shapes of solid forms or outlines are not easily identifiable based on past experience, however, the perception, based upon experience and association with objects, is more likely to be in error. The lack of shape identification often gives rise to false assumptions and incorrect associations.

3. Texture

Texture is the relative smoothness or roughness of a surface. It affects how much light an object reflects or absorbs and whether it appears light or dark.[3] Lack of texture causes shine which is extremely revealing. A rough surface reflects little light and casts many shadows on itself. Consequently, it appears very dark to the eye. A smooth surface reflects more light. This alone can attract attention to a location or to an object. Shine is generally associated with the reflection of sunlight from windshields, windows and other such almost textureless surfaces. When an object has a rough surface, the visual sense or intellect may not alert itself to the existence of the object.

4. Movement

This factor seldom reveals the identity of an object by itself, but it does have importance in revealing the existence of the object. If an object moves, obviously it will attract the attention of the observer just as a shiny object, which lacks texture, will cause attention. If the object is not capable of movement, the attention of the observer to the object must come by other means.

5. Position

An object is often identified by its position with relation to its surroundings. Position is nothing more than the relative space relationship of one object to another object or objects. A long object on a railroad track, for instance, is often assumed to be a train. Similar objects on a river and parallel to its banks are assumed to be boats or barges. If an object is expected to be present in relation to its surroundings, the observer will be or should be aware that its existence may be imminent.

6. Shadow

Shadow is principally a projection of shape. It is primarily even more revealing than the object itself. However, if there is no shadow, then the attention of the observer, if drawn at all, must be drawn by another factor of recognition.

Applying the factors of recognition to the law of camouflage, a person who claims to have exercised ordinary care in maintaining a lookout, but nevertheless failed to see an object in plain sight, is not negligent because of failure to see an object in plain sight if the object is not seen because at least one of the factors of recognition was not present thereby causing the object to blend with its background, obscuring its presence and diminishing the reasonable prospect of its perception.

Obviously, the nighttime will present the most usual case for camouflage since factors of recognition are more apt to be absent than during the daytime. One cannot, however, restrict the camouflage instruction to the nighttime since one factor of recognition could be missing during a daytime observation, thereby causing a camouflage effect.

20.3 Author's Commentary

The author, as an expert on forensic night/day visibility, has frequently been called upon to make evaluation of the reliability of photographs and videos compared to the eye.

All too often in the courtroom, to simplify science, functional aspects of the eye are compared to those of a camera. The facts are that the eye is not like a camera, and the camera is not like an eye.

This author has pieced together the following series of random facts from the world of mechanical optics, psychology, physiological optics and common sense to validate his viewpoint.

1. I have experience in and have undertaken research relative to the issue of whether a photograph accurately reflects what is perceived by the human eye.

2. Humans do not see the way they think they see. Instead of a passive-receptive act in which scenes in the outside world are simply recorded like a camera with film in it, the act of perceiving visually is one in which the person is totally involved and in which he/she participates actively, screening and structuring very much in the same way that one selects and constructs when talking or writing.
3. The human process of seeing involves all of the functions of the eye and vision adaptation, accommodation and sensitivity to size, color, brightness, contrast and motion.
4. The eye's response to brightness or luminance is logarithmic.
5. The human eye is not like a camera.
6. While a photograph is usually sharp and in focus over its entire surface and the edges are clear, that is not the way the human eye sees things.
7. A driver looking straight ahead cannot read road signs or directional signs on the side of the road because the "visual field"[4] of the eye is not covered by a clear image as is the visual field of a camera.
8. When a human being looks straight ahead, light rays from this direction strike the fovea, an area of two-degree size, where vision is sharpest. Only five-degrees to the left or right of the fovea, visual acuity drops to half as much as foveal acuity.
9. In the eye, there is a "blind spot" which consists of an area where the optic nerve and blood vessels connect the eye, the brain and the heart. Absolutely no image is recorded in that part of the eye.
10. In a human-made camera, the designer and manufacturer use rigid materials.
11. This combination of rigid materials and geometrically exact box-like construction is not available in the eye. The human eye is made of soft tissue, liquid, and gel. The liquid is the aqueous humor, which is continually produced in the eye and continually drained away maintaining an intraocular pressure that is relatively stable. The gel is the vitreous humor and is the largest component of the eye.
12. The most important difference between the human eye and a camera is that the human eye sees selectively and the camera sees indiscriminately.
13. Human beings tend to observe only those details that are important to them. The human mind filters out all details except those to which it is paying attention.

14. Those who have taken photographs have the experience of finding in a finished print a strange object which they did not notice when they snapped the photograph because, as photographers, they had been concentrating on the subject of the photograph.
15. The camera sees objects differently from the human eye because human beings mentally correct distortions while the camera does not.
16. The lens of a camera does not correct distortions, and what it does record on film is often not what the human being sees or what the human being thinks he sees.
17. An important characteristic of the lens in the human eye is that, unlike its glass counterpart in a camera, it is, in fact, highly pliable. This difference is fundamental.
18. The focus mechanism in the eye is different from the focus mechanism in a camera. When the human eye looks around at things across the room or across the street, the lens in the human eye makes fine focus adjustments from near to middle to far distances with such rapidity that the human being is unaware that his/her mind is directing a change of focus. Not even the most skilled photographer with the finest equipment can shift a camera's focus with anything like the speed of the human eye.
19. The retina of the human eye is not completely analogous to the film in the camera although both the retina and the film are receptors of visual images. The human retina uses one system to perceive objects in daylight and another system to perceive objects in darkness. The system used in darkness produces a different and less distinct image on the retina from that produced under daylight conditions. The camera uses a single system, and the images recorded in darkness are no different in quality from the images recorded in daylight. In the human eye the image quality in darkness is far inferior to the image quality of a daytime perception.
20. Hermann von Helmholtz, the nineteenth century's greatest authority on the nature of vision, wrote the following concerning the human eye: "If an optician wanted to sell me an instrument which had all these defects, I should think myself quite justified in blaming his carelessness in the strongest terms."
21. Compared with a modern camera or telescope, the eye suffers from optical limitations. Though its overall visual horizon is broad, the eye sees sharply only in good light and then only in a small central area. In dim light, the human eye sees poorly and loses all color perception,

unlike a camera. Each human eye, also unlike a camera, has a built-in blind spot, a hole in its field of vision where no image registers. In addition, all sorts of ailments affect the eye's function which could have no such effect on a camera.

22. Myopia, glare, blur, and under-illumination are visual degradations common to human vision but not to photographs.
23. Minimum Angle Resolution (M.A.R.) and Modulation Transfer Function (M.T.F.):
    (a) *Minimum Angle Resolution (M.A.R.)*: Visual acuity is traditionally measured by means of the Snellen eye chart which tells how well an individual sees small black letters on a white background. These types of legally accepted visual acuity measurements are done for every patient who receives a vision examination (Snellen acuity is accomplished with high contrast to determine under optimum seeing conditions if the patient can determine the smallest letters on the chart). This is equivalent to Minimum Angle of Resolution (M.A.R.).
    (b) *Modulation Transfer Function (M.T.F.)*: Contrast sensitivity is the only way of evaluating the patient's true overall vision under everyday conditions in which things do not consist of small black letters on a bright background, but rather, objects of every different size and every different contrast level. Contrast sensitivity thus evaluates the entire visual pathway from cornea, crystalline lens, retina, optic nerve, optic chiasm, optic radiations, and cerebral cortex—the occipital region. This is done by using fuzzy lines (technically, sine wave grating patterns) and reducing the contrast until the patient no longer can see the lines. This is equivalent to the term Modulation Transfer Function (M.T.F.)

Commentary: *It is interesting that vision specialists and photo specialists are very aware of how modulation transfer function (M.T.F.) affects the photographic system in its relationship to human M.A.R.; however, few photo/video specialists understand the fact that the modulation transfer function of an individual is fairly easily determined by contrast sensitivity measurements which are routine in an eye doctor's office, both in a screening mode which takes less than five minutes and in a comprehensive mode which requires about thirty to forty-five minutes of testing using computers and sine wave grating patterns electronically introduced on a television monitor.*

20.4 Photorealistic Simulation

The images produced by the Institute of Vehicular Safety are photorealistic simulations of accident environments created by adjusting and compositing still photographs using Adobe Photoshop. These images are not illustrations or drawings hand produced by an artist nor are they artificial images generated by a computer program.

The term, *photorealism*, does not have a single, unequivocal definition. It has evolved and broadened from its pre-computer era artistic meaning of "a painting that looks like a photograph." In this age of virtual reality 'photorealism' has acquired a range of meanings which may generally be described as "a reasonable believable recreation of a physical scene." Because the cognitive processes in the human brain cause the eye to process images differently than a still camera, this discussion defines its own variation of "photorealism" as "an image that closely represents the view seen by human eyes."

Adobe Photoshop is a standard product used in the advertising and publishing industry to produce images for print, multimedia, and Internet applications. In fact, it is generally considered the best and most widely-used product of its type and is the "flagship" product of Adobe Systems, Incorporated. A large number of books and magazine publications are devoted to this product, as well as a variety of Internet sites.

Note that whenever a reference is made in this discussion to the source of an image being a "photograph," it may refer to any photographic product, including, but not limited to slides, negatives, or photostatic copies or an original. When a source is truly a photograph, it may range in quality from Polaroid to professional 35mm. enlargements, but is most commonly a standard 3x5 or 4x6 snapshot.

Unfortunately, a sharp, enlargeable photograph of a scene just prior to an accident almost never exists. Occasionally a photograph exists from a different perspective or for different lighting conditions and these may be incorporated as a component of the final product. Other potential components that may be included in composites include studio photographs of safety objects such as orange barrels or cones, current photographs of the accident scene, and photographs of other similar scenes or objects.

Creating a finished product representing a simulated accident scene is a multistage process. In the first stage, the available components are scanned and then combined, using Adobe Photoshop, to produce an image that closely resembles the accident location, even though it may not, in this initial stage, reflect the desired lighting or perspective. The compositing technique involves selecting areas from various photographs, normalizing their colorization and brightness, then seamlessly blending their edges. Gaps are filled in by "cloning" or copying similar areas from one of the sources.

In the second stage, any minor changes in perspective, area enlargements, or cropping are performed. Significant changes in perspective are not feasible using the techniques described herein and are not attempted.

The third stage involves making any changes required to realistically simulate variations on the original. For example, changes in ambient lighting, addition of flares, or alteration of sun or moon position may be made. Also, if necessary, extra safety devices may be added or alternate versions may be composited to replace obsolete versions. Examples would include addition of orange barrels, yellow lines, or changing the version of railroad crossbucks.

In the fourth and final stage any noticeable defects are removed, a textual title is added and a small border. Defects, sometimes called artifacts, are defined as irregularities in the image which are not part of the actual scene. These may arise from the photographic process itself, scanning, or the earlier compositing stages. Examples would include lint on a camera lens, scratches on a negative, or irregular edges causes by enlarging sections of a photograph. Defects are not always correctable if the original photographs are of poor quality.

The images are printed using inkjet printers and papers that are readily available in any large computer store.

20.5 Qualification Questions You May Be Asked About Photographs

1. What are some primary issues of whether a photograph accurately reflects what is perceived by the human eye? Day? Night?
2. What is the difference between dynamic and static photographs as to accurately reflect what is perceived by the human eye?
3. How would you describe the way a human eye sees?
4. What is meant by passive-receptive act.
5. How would you describe the act of the mechanical camera? of video (VHS)? of 16 mm?
6. Is human sight participatory or non-participatory?
7. What is meant by participatory?
8. Describe a photograph or video in terms of sharpness of focus at various distances.
9. How is the edge of a photograph different from the edge of what appears to the human eye?
10. Describe visual field of camera; of video.
11. Describe visual field of the human eye.

12. Where is vision sharpest in the human eye?
13. How big is this fovea?
14. What is visual acuity?
15. How does the visual acuity change five degrees to the left or right of the fovea?
16. What is the blind spot in a human eye?
17. How much vision takes place in that spot?
18. Where are blind spots to be found in the camera?
19. How is sight different in different parts of the human eye?
20. What are the differences in materials that make up the camera and the human eye?
21. What are the greatest differences between the way the human eye sees and the way the camera sees?
22. What does the human brain do to images that the brain does not consider important?
23. What is a common experience encountered after a photograph is taken?
24. What does the human eye do to visual distortions?
25. What does the camera do to visual distortions?
26. What is the difference between a lens in a camera and the lens in the human eye?
27. How is the focus mechanism in the eye different from the focus mechanism in the camera?
28. What is the difference in the speed of focusing between a camera and the human eye?
29. How is the retina of the human eye like the film in a camera?
30. How are they different?
31. How many systems does the human eye use for daylight vision; for nighttime vision?
32. How many systems does the camera use in daylight photography; in nighttime photography?
33. In the human eye, which perception is better, daytime or nighttime?
34. What optical limitations does the eye have in relation to the modern camera?
35. Under what conditions does the eye see sharply? Photopic? Mesopic? Scotopic?
36. What happens to the eye's perception at night?
37. What visual degradations are common to human vision?
38. What is meant by "visual degradation"?

39. What is parallax effect?
40. Is that found in human vision?
41. Is it found in the camera?
42. What visual distortions are created by the camera?
43. What effect does the flatness of the photographic image have?
44. What distortion is created by a telephoto lens?
45. What distortion is created by a wide angle lens?
46. How many photos are taken by the human eye?
47. Describe minimum angle resolution (M.A.R.).
48. Describe modulation transfer function (M.T.F.).

End Notes

1. Department of the Army, Department of the Army Field Manual FM 5-20, *Camouflage 4* (May, 1968).
2. See Appendix E, "Cone of Vision," and Chapter 22, "Geometric Optics."
3. M. Lacklesh, *Visual Illusion* 210 (1965).
4. United States Army, Training and Doctrine Command, Tradoc Bulletin 6, at 6 (Jan. 30, 1976).

Chapter 21

Measurement and Evaluation of Motor Vehicle Lighting: A Systematic Approach

Developed by Bernard S. Abrams, O.D.
Measurement and Case Example by Sgt. Gregory Vandenberg
Graphics Designed for: The Institute of Vehicular Safety
by Charles H. Matthews, Evidence Research Services

Synopsis

21.1 Preface

The objective of this block of instruction is to familiarize the reader with a methodology whereby vehicle lighting systems may be tested accurately, and useful application may be made of the data collected. We have designed a testing platform, together with programmed data collection and presentation formats, which provide a consistent approach throughout the process, from the establishment of a testing range, through the final courtroom presentation. It is assumed that the reader is already proficient in certain skills necessary in the technical evaluation and reconstruction of traffic crashes, particularly with regard to the taking of routine field measurements, the subjective evaluation of road surface characteristics, and, most especially, proper mechanical drawing or engineering graphics techniques.

While not discussed in the main text, we would add that conditions of adverse weather (rain, snow, fog) should be avoided in the testing of lighting profiles. Equally, the testing would ideally be conducted during a no-moon period (this does not necessarily mean a *new* moon; rather, a period during which moonrise allows for sufficient dark periods, or there is sufficient heavy overcast to obscure the moon). We assume that you are all innovators, or you would not be reading this book.

As a final word, we would note that while we have made every effort to simplify this process, the underlying precepts have a certain degree of complexity. These can best be overcome through patience and scrupulous attention to detail, both cornerstones on which good science is founded.

21.2 Establishing the Test Range

A. Desirable qualities of the test range

Before establishing a range for the testing and measurement of vehicle lighting systems, a suitable site must be chosen. If the basic qualities presented below are met at the test site, the chances of consistent, accurate test results are greatly improved.

The *surface material* on the test range should closely duplicate that found in the vehicle's usual highway environment. In most instances, this means an asphalt concrete material. Probably the best surface selection is what is commonly termed a "travelled" surface (i.e., one on which the sharp edges of the stone have been degraded somewhat, and the surface color appears generally as a dull gray-brown), as this is the most likely surface to be encountered in the field. Newly-applied asphalt has an excessively high surface content of tar, and thus reduced reflectivity, while a badly worn ("traffic polished") surface develops a sheen, thus increasing reflectivity.

The *surface contour* should be as flat as possible. If it is necessary to conduct testing on a grade, the grade must be maintained throughout the length of the test range. Any drainage crowns or slopes should be minimal or absent.

It is helpful to imagine a plane projected horizontally through the centers of the beams of a vehicle's headlamps. On the ideal test range, this plane would be parallel to the ground with the vertical height between the ground and the imaginary plane being equal at all points of measurement. The ideal facility to meet this requirement may be a drag strip or unused runway.

The *ambient lighting* (i.e., light from sources other than the source being measured) must be kept at a minimum. Any adjacent light sources must be sufficiently distant, or of sufficiently low intensity, to prevent skewing of the test measurements. The headlamps of passing vehicles may severely skew the test results; thus, the site should be selected with a view to minimize or eliminate the effect of such traffic.

The *access* to the test range should allow for the greatest flexibility, as testing dates must be adjusted to accommodate the vagaries of weather, priority demands, and so forth. Ideally, we would have exclusive access and control over the test facility, thus enabling us to make adjustments to the surface conditions, range dimensions, and so on, as may be required by individual circumstances.

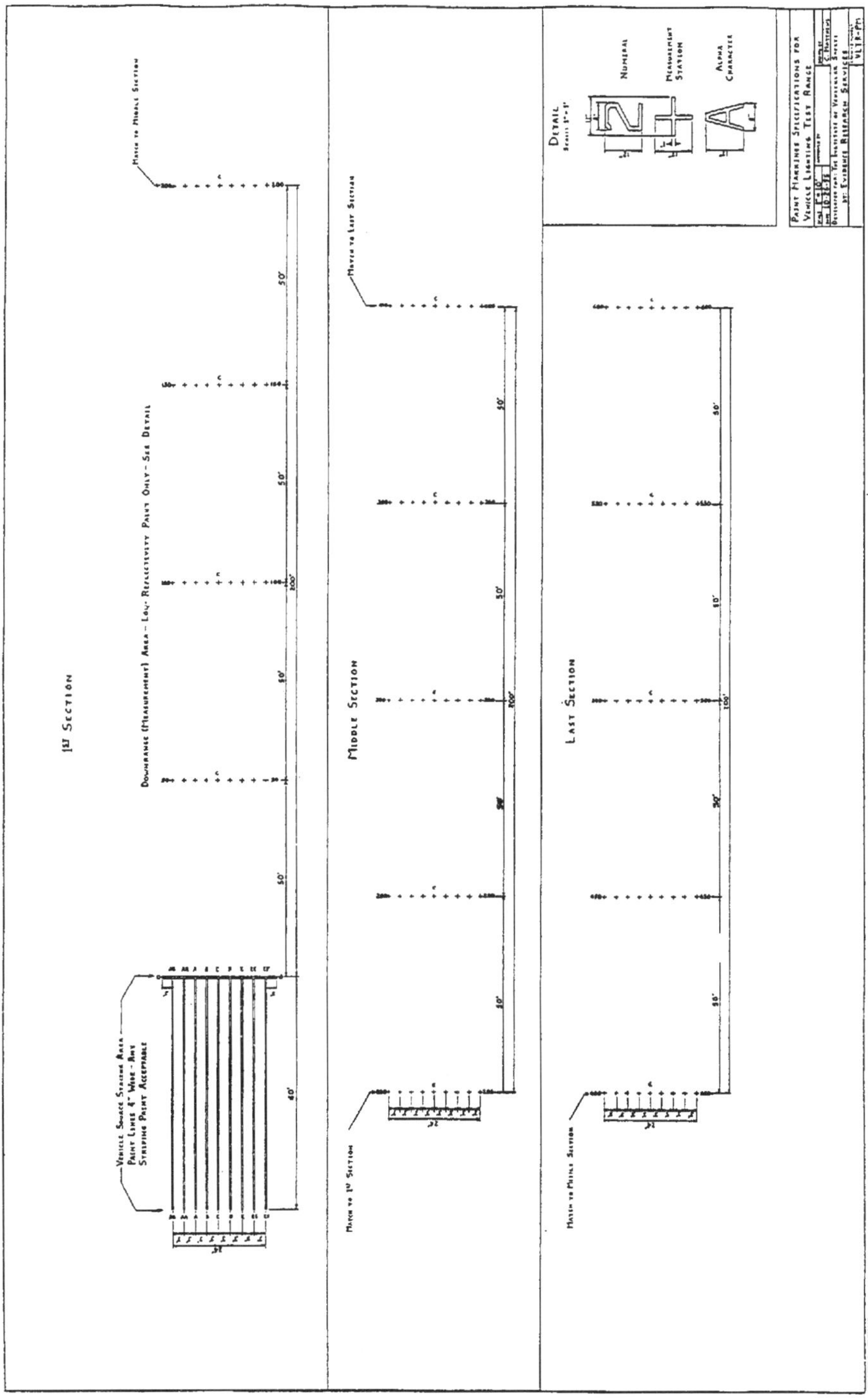

Figure 21.1 *Instruction Packet Drawing 1.*

B. Construction of the test range

Having located a suitable site for out test range, the next step is to construct the facility. You should refer to **Instruction Packet Drawing 1** (Figure 21.1), which provides the layout and dimensions of the surface markings which constitute the test range. In addition, we have enclosed an actual case example.

This design contemplates the construction of a permanent facility, with a 600-foot length and a 24-foot breadth, providing for a variety of potential testing requirements.

The *vehicle staging area* is intended to aid in the proper alignment of motor vehicles to the measurement area and should be of sufficient depth to accommodate even large, commercial vehicles. As noted, this area may be marked with any suitable highway-striping paint, as surface reflectivity is not critical here.

The *downrange*, or measurement area, must be given different treatment. Obviously, highly reflective paints would not be suitable here. In the case of a permanent test range, we would suggest the use of a flat, "red oxide" type primer for markings in this area. This has reasonable durability and low reflectivity, yet it provides reasonable contrast to the surface to allow the testing personnel to locate the measurement station with the aid of a flashlight.

When a field-expedient test range is used, chalk, crayon, or similar temporary markings may be used.

Ultimately, the objective is to position a uniform set of measurement stations at known distances from the light source, thus providing for a consistent method of taking the required measurements on every occasion.

In the case of a *permanent test range*, we would recommend that the layout be done with the aid of a transit level. This will not only ensure that the various lanes are established parallel to one another, but allow for the discovery of substantial departures from level for the various stations. If such a departure is found, the difference should be noted for later use in the actual conduct of the light measurements.

Fully recognizing that the ideal, permanent facility may not be such an easy matter to establish, we will also offer some guidance for the construction of a *field-expedient test range*. The layout is best done in daylight.

A *field-expedient* test range requires the same basic characteristics as the permanent facility in the way of surface material, ambient light, and surface contour, but it may be used anywhere these conditions are found.

In this case, the vehicle staging area is omitted. The downrange area is established to permit the testing required for the particular circumstance.

This range is constructed around the test source; the first step being to position the test source (usually a vehicle) at one end of the contemplated range.

The next step is to define a centerline extending through the centerline of the source. This can easily be done with the aid of an assistant sighting along the centerline of the vehicle, and directing you right or left, as may be necessary, as you move downrange.

Along this centerline, mark small crosses every 50 feet (the front of the vehicle is considered to be "0" feet), and label each with a letter "C." Continue this to the desired length of the range.

Having done this, measure distances in increments of three feet to either side of the crosses mentioned above, taking care that these lie along lines that are perpendicular to the established centerline. At each of these incremental distances, also make a small cross, but do not label these.

Once you have measured to the desired distance on both sides of the centerline, move up the extreme edge of the range on each side, and label the edge crosses with the appropriate depth (50', 100', etc.) and with the lane designator as taken from Instruction Packet Drawing 1.

As an example, let us assume that we are using a conventional automobile as a source and wish to establish a field-expedient test range that is 250 feet long and 12 feet wide; we will be testing the headlamp pattern.

We park the vehicle at one end of the selected surface with the front of the vehicle facing downrange, assuring that we have at least 250 feet of surface ahead of the vehicle and six feet of surface to either side of its centerline.

We position an assistant behind the vehicle; he looks through the car and establishes a line-of-sight using the "third" brake light and the mounting post of the rear-view mirror.

Starting at the front of the vehicle, using either a conventional tape measure or wheel measure, we measure a distance of 250 feet and stop here. Our assistant directs us to the right or left, as necessary, until we are standing on the centerline projected through the vehicle.

At our feet, we make a cross, labelled with a "C"; we then measure back toward the vehicle, stopping every 50 feet, and mark identical crosses, taking direction from the assistant to assure that we remain on the centerline. Note that it is helpful to orient the crosses such that one bar lies directly on the centerline and the other perpendicular to the centerline.

We then measure distance of three feet and six feet, respectively, to either side of the centerline, taking care to move at a perpendicular to the centerline, and mark a cross at each of these locations; this is repeated at each of the centerline crosses.

Standing at the front of the vehicle and facing downrange, we now move to the far left-hand cross at 50 feet downrange. This is labelled "A 50." The far right-hand cross at 50 feet is labelled “E 50.” You will note that this corresponds to the lane designators on the referenced drawing.

Moving downrange, the farthest outside crosses are similarly labelled, with the numeric figure corresponding to the downrange distance in feet.

The example cited above is typical of a field-expedient test range established to measure the headlamps of a car in the confines of an ordinary traffic lane.

If the circumstances require a “bias” to one side of a traffic lane (e.g., in a circumstance involving a pedestrian or animal outside of the travel lane), it will be necessary to add measurement lanes to the appropriate side of the test source. This is accomplished by either adding a lane farther away from “C,” as specified on the drawing, or by establishing the centerline of the vehicle on an alternate measurement lane to one side or another of “C.”

Please note that, whatever type of test range is established, it is necessary to use the lane designators indicated to successfully utilize the measurement system presented here.

21.3 Taking Measurements

Having previously established our test range, we will now proceed to take measurements of the light produced by our test source.

We will continue with the example set forth in the previous section, “Establishing the Test Range.” For the purposes of this discussion, we will assume that we are using a 1991 Cadillac Brougham, around which we constructed the field-expedient test range previously discussed. During this discussion, you should refer to the completed sample of Form VLP-FM, which is part of the instruction packet (Figure 21.2).

To take and record measurements, we will require a copy of **Form VLP-FM**, a clipboard, a small flashlight, a tape measure or folding rule (the latter gives better service), a pencil, a wheel measure, and, naturally, a reliable light meter. The light meter is to be calibrated in accordance with the instructions you have received previously.

It is very helpful to have an assistant or two to aid in taking the measurements and recording the results. We highly recommend that whoever records the results be chosen with a consideration of good penmanship.

You will note that the form VLP-FM consists primarily of a matrix upon which the test results are recorded; along the margins are areas where additional data is requested. At this point, our primary concern is with the sections marked “**Vertical Stations**” and “**Target Value =**.”

DATE: 10-25-93 TIME: 1745 PAGE 01 OF 01 PAGES

VEHICLE LIGHTING FIELD MEASUREMENTS

		0'	50'	100'	150'	200'	250'	300'	TARGET (o) AT:
AB	5								
	4								
	3								
	2								
GROUND	1								
AA	5								
	4								
	3								
	2								
GROUND	1								
A	5								
	4								
	3		.295	.094	.050	.035	.021		50'
	2		.684	.143	.060	.041	.025		71'
GROUND	1		3.78	.563	.107	.057	.037		116'
B	5								
	4								
	3		.291	.190	.052	.034	.029		50'
	2		.912	.145	.067	.042	.029		75'
	1		4.55	.611	.116	.058	.038		114'
C	5								
	4								
	3		.315	.112	.131	.034	.023		50'
	2		1.52	.192	.072	.042	.024		80'
GROUND	1		5.34	.920	.054	.055	.039		125'
D	5								
	4								
	3		.338	.126	.056	.032	.021		56'
	2		3.23	.278	.088	.039	.028		87'
GROUND	1		4.61	1.60	.201	.078	.036		130'
E	5								
	4								
	3		.305	.132	.071	.041	.036		59'
	2		1.43	.409	.103	.058	.036		106'
GROUND	1		4.95	.219	.368	.087	.028		150'
EE	5								
	4								
	3								
	2								
GROUND	1								
EF	5								
	4								
	3								
	2								
GROUND	1								

COMPLETED SAMPLE

RANGE TYPE / LOCATION: FIELD EXPEDIENT / ADAMS CO. AIRPORT

PERSONNEL: TPR. B. JONES, SGT. R. ROE

SOURCE: 1991 CADILLAC BROUGHAM 4-DR. (EXEMPLAR)

VIN: 1G6DW53A6MB700001

CASE TITLE / NUMBER: STATE VS DOE / 01-2345

VERTICAL STATIONS:
5 = N/A
4 = N/A
3 = DRIVER HEIGHT-OF-EYE - 46"
2 = CTR. OF HEADLAMP BEAM - 26"

TARGET VALUE = .3 Fc ± 5% (.285 - .315 Fc)
NOTES: CTR.-TO-CTR. DISTANCE BETWEEN HEADLAMPS 53"
LOW BEAM LAMPS TESTED

***Figure 21.2** Completed sample of form VLP-FM.*

The Vertical Stations are designated numerically and, in the case of stations 2 through 5, arbitrarily. Station 1 will always be *ground level* as it forms the foundation line for other vertical measurements.

Stations 2 through 5 may be any height above ground level which the particular testing program may require. In our example, Station 2 is the vertical height of the center of the headlamp beams (assumed to be symmetrical—if actual measurement of a vehicle reveals minor differences in the dimension, an average of the two will probably suffice), and Station 3 is the height of the driver's eye (measured on-site). In our example, Station 2 is 26 inches above ground level, and Station 3 is 46 inches above ground level. Stations 4 and 5 are not used in this instance, and are lined through.

The Target Value is determined to be 0.2 foot candle, plus or minus 5 percent. The range is, therefore, from .285 to .315 foot candle. *Note that whatever target value is selected, it is best to hold the error tolerance to as small a value as possible. For reasons which will become apparent in a later section, even the 5 percent tolerance we have used in this example is too great.*

Recorded in the "Notes" section is the horizontal, center-to-center distance between the headlamps, in this case 53 inches; it is also noted that this is a test of the *low beam* lamps. Other marginal data blocks are relatively self-explanatory.

The main data area consists of a matrix on which the measured values are recorded. There are nine primary horizontal rows, lettered from "AB" through "EF"; you will note that these designators correspond to the lane designators specified in Instruction Packet Drawing 1.

Lanes AB, AA, EE, and EF are not used in this example; therefore, they are lined through.

Each of the primary horizontal rows is subdivided into five individual rows, each labelled "1" through "5." These correspond to the "Vertical Stations"; again 4 and 5 are not used in this example and are lined through.

The matrix uses eight vertical columns. The first seven columns are designated, in increasing order, with the downrange distance of the measurement stations in fifty-foot increments. In this instance, we have not taken measurements at either 0 feet or 300 feet, and these columns are lined through.

The eighth column is for recording target value and will be discussed in a later paragraph.

In our example, we will begin at 50 feet along lane "A" and commence to take and record measurements. A measurement is taken at the ground at this point and recorded in Row A, subdivision 1, in the 50 foot column. Using the tape measure or folding rule, we take a second measurement 26 inches above the ground, and record this in the space immediately above the last value (i.e., row

A, subdivision 2, 50 foot column). We next measure to 46 inches above ground and repeat the procedure, with the value being recorded above the last.

When an assistant is recording the measurements for you, we recommend that the assistant read back each value as it is recorded, to assure that it is correct.

If you have followed this example, you should find values at Vertical Stations 1, 2 and 3 of .295, .684, and 3.78 respectively, in Row A of the 50 foot column.

Having recorded these measurements, we move to Lane B on the test range (still at 50 feet downrange), and repeat the process; we continue this until all values are obtained.

Once we have obtained measured values for each of the pre-established measurement stations, we must seek the target values.

It can be easily seen that we found values meeting the target parameters at Vertical Station 3, 50 feet downrange, along Lanes A, B, and C. Equally, we found a target value at ground level (Vertical Station 1) along Lane E at 150 feet downrange.

In our example, we can observe that for Vertical Station 3, along Lanes D and E, we would expect to find a .3 foot candle value between 50 and 100 feet downrange. Moving along the lanes and taking measurements every foot or so, we find that this is indeed true; we find our target value at 56 feet on Lane D, and at 59 feet along Lane E.

Moving to the "**Target Value**" column on the work form, we record the downrange distance at which we found the target values at Vertical Station 3. Again, if you have followed along with the example, you will note that for Vertical Station 3, we recorded target values at 50 feet for each of Rows A, B and C and at 56 feet and 59 feet, respectively, for Rows D and E.

The same procedure is followed for the remaining vertical stations on each lane, and the figures are recorded in the appropriate columns.

It should be noted that assistants must not be between the light source and the measuring instrument. Equally, while it will be necessary to use a light to read the instrument and record data, all lights should be extinguished while the instrument is actually directed at the source.

In the case of field-expedient ranges, a lookout must be kept for passing vehicles, as lights from which may skew the test results.

As a final note, all personnel should clearly hear the measured values and take note of them in relation to previously-obtained values. Any station at which a suspect value is obtained should have sufficient repeated tests to assure that the value obtained is accurate. (For example, if we find a reading of .9 foot candle in a field of .2 or lower values, we would tend to suspect that this was inaccurate and probably the result of an unnoticed, passing vehicle. Certainly, this must be retested.)

21.4 Final Presentation of Data-Profile Plots

Now that we have collected the measurements of the light produced by our source, we must present the data in a useful form. Here again, we will continue with the example we have begun in previous sections. In this section we will make use of **Form VLP-1**; a blank version of this form is included as **Instruction Packet Drawing 2** (Figure 21.3), and a sample completed version, in accordance with our example, is included as **Instruction Packet Drawing 3** (Figure 21.4).

This form is a representation of 300 feet of the downrange portion of the test range; the original scale is 1 inch =10 feet, which we find to be a very convenient scale in which to work for crash reconstruction purposes. You will note that we use a graphic scale; we do this against the possibility that we may later wish to enlarge or reduce the drawing, in which case the graphic scale allows for accurate measurements without the need of developing "odd" scale.

The **Plan View** section of the drawing represents the horizontal plane of measurement. All of the measurement lanes are represented here; downrange distances have been left blank, as it may be necessary to use two forms if more than 300 feet of downrange distance is used for testing.

In the **Side Views** section, we have divided the range into nine vertical planes, each corresponding to one of the test lanes. Allowance is made for vertical stations to a maximum of 10 feet above ground; you will note that the ground level foundation line is pre-established.

The **Data & Notes** section contains a reproduction of the data area of **Form VLP-FM** (Figure 21.2), as well as pre-established lines for the recording of Vertical Station and Target Value information. Ample space is provided for additional notes which may be required. The form is to be set up on a drawing board, and brought into square with either a T-square or drafting machine.

To complete the form, we begin by carefully recording the data we obtained in our measurements. These are simply copied into the appropriate locations in the data area.

We will next carefully record the approximate downrange distance figures in their respective locations. In the case of our example, these range from 0 feet through 300 feet.

The next step is to define the boundaries of the test range on the drawing. This is done with the use of long-dashed lines drawn *just outside* the area in

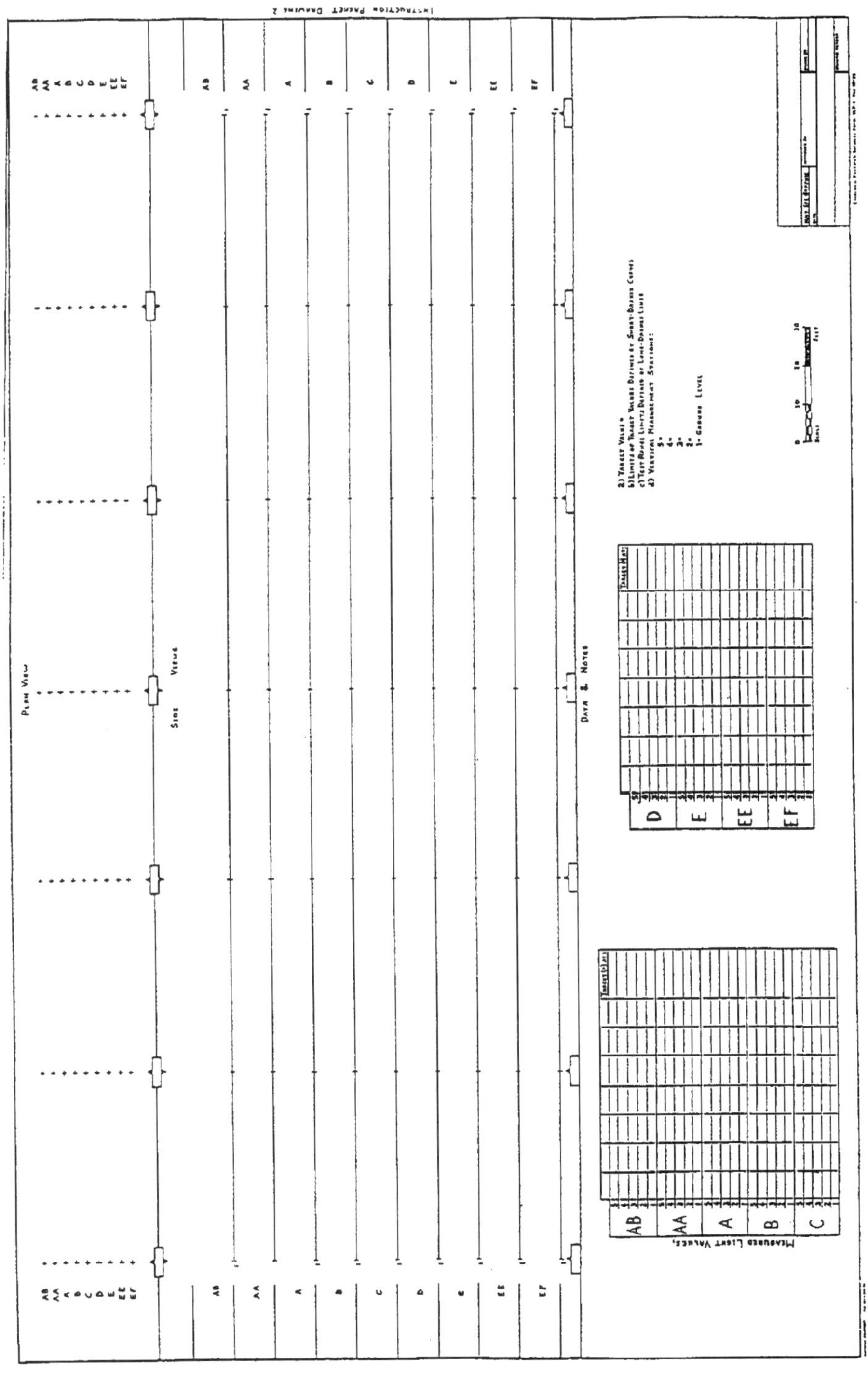

Figure 21.3 *Instruction Packet Drawing 2.*

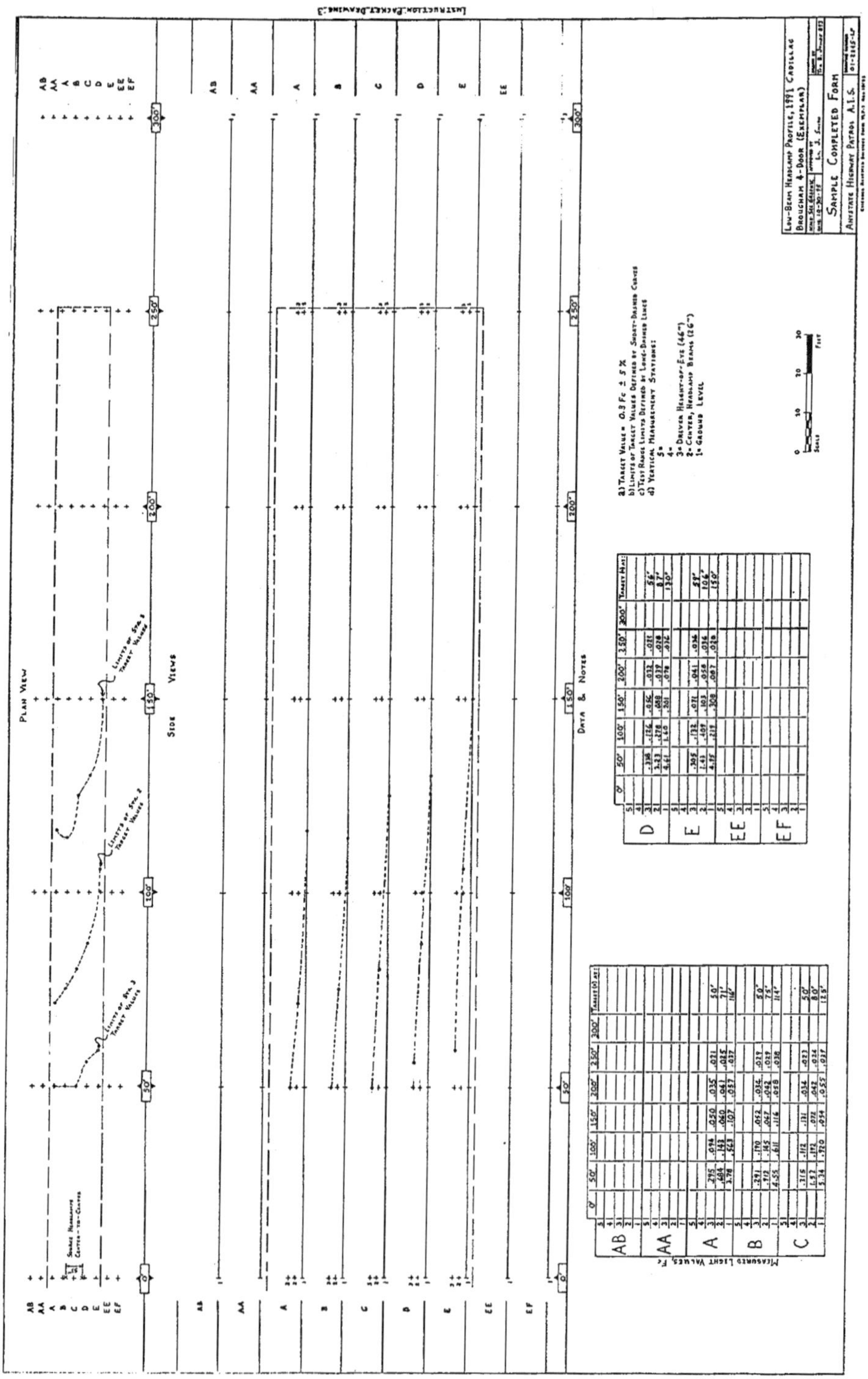

Figure 21.4 Instruction Packet Drawing 3.

which measurements were made. This is done on both the Plan and Side views, with ample space being allowed on the latter for the plotting of Vertical Stations.

The source lamps are then represented to scale on the Plan View; we have used a small letter "x" to represent each of these. As the headlamps in the example are located at Vertical Station 2, 0 feet, their location is assumed in the Side Views.

We now plot, again to scale, the vertical stations on each of the Side Views, in this case on Views A through E. Each pre-established vertical station is represented by a small cross, as was the case with the horizontal stations. There will be a vertical station at each 50-foot downrange increment, on each Side View, for every vertical station used. These stations are pre-plotted for Station 1, Ground, but must be individually plotted for Stations 2 and 3.

Next, we establish construction lines between the downrange increments where we will have Target Values on both the Plan and Side Views. (Note that these should be very light, erasable lines.)

We measure along these lines in the Plan View to the appropriate location at which we found target values for each lane and for each Vertical Station. At these locations, a small circle is plotted. It is helpful to place a small number adjacent to these circles to identify the respective vertical station of each. This may be erasable.

The target value locations thus established on the Plan View are simply projected down to their respective locations on the appropriate Side View.

This done, our next task is to illustrate the approximate limits of the target values in each view. This is done by drawing the best smooth curve through the target values within the same measurement plane.

In the case of the Plan View, a curve is drawn through all target value circles designated Station 1, then another through Station 2 circles, and, finally, through Station 3 circles.

It is here that we will further address the subject of the selection of target values. In our example, you will recall, we selected a target value of 0.3 foot candle, with an error tolerance of plus or minus 5 percent, which yielded a range of from .285 to .315 foot candle. You will also recall that we found values within these tolerances at 50 feet downrange, along Lanes A, B, and C, at Vertical Station 3 for each lane.

Look closely at the plot example in the Plan View on Instruction Packet Drawing 3, where the Vertical Station 3 plot is indicated.

The "best smooth curve" through the values specified for Lanes A, B, and C is a straight line! If we had accepted the default value for this station in Lane E (you will see that we found a .305 foot candle value at 50 feet here), all of our plot points but one would have been in a line. The resulting "best smooth curve" would have appeared as essentially a straight line across the 50-foot marker, punctuated by a sort of "spike" extending to 56 feet downrange and lying between Lanes C and E; hardly an accurate representation of the true limits of the target value area!

With this in mind, we will reiterate the importance of selecting the narrowest error tolerance possible for the target value, particularly when dealing with very small values in the first instance. In this example, the difference between the default value of .305 foot candle and the true target of .3 foot candle is only about 1.64 percent, but we found the true value nine feet downrange from the default value location, which made a considerable difference in our resultant plot.

The search for precise values entails considerable effort, patience, and attention to detail, but is necessary.

To return to the completion of the plots, we next direct our attention to the Side Views. Here again, we simply draw the best smooth curve through the target value locations in each measurement plane. These curves are readily observable on the example.

Once this is done, the construction lines are erased, the title block completed, and the drawing is complete. The curves we have plotted can now be used as the basis for evaluation of visibility in crash reconstructions and for the construction of models to illustrate the dynamics of visibility issues in court.

With the availability of low cost Computer Aided Drawing (CAD) software programs, isocandella maps of headlamp patterns can be quickly and easily constructed as an alternative to the hand drafting method described.

By plotting the target values and drawing a curved line through the target value control points, an acceptable scale representation of the pattern can be constructed. This headlamp pattern, attached to a vehicle symbol, can in turn be placed in a CAD site diagram to provide a graphic representation of the vehicle's

0.3 Foot Candle Isocandella Map of 1988 Chevrolet Cavalier Low Beam Headlamps

	10 ft Left	6 ft Left	3 ft Left	Center	3 ft Right	6 ft Right	11 ft Right
@ Ground	$91^{\underline{10}}$	$110^{\underline{7}}$	$127^{\underline{0}}$	$157^{\underline{3}}$	$191^{\underline{1}}$	$213^{\underline{11}}$	$228^{\underline{10}}$
@ 25 in.	$66^{\underline{0}}$	$66^{\underline{10}}$	$73^{\underline{6}}$	$127^{\underline{5}}$	$170^{\underline{0}}$	$191^{\underline{6}}$	$203^{\underline{11}}$
@ 43 in.	$36^{\underline{10}}$	$50^{\underline{8}}$	$59^{\underline{7}}$	$71^{\underline{10}}$	$107^{\underline{10}}$	$138^{\underline{2}}$	$58^{\underline{2}}$

Measurements taken at ground level, center of headlamp (25 inches), and driver's eye level (43 inches).

All measurements listed in feet and inches.

Figure 21.5

headlight pattern for evaluation purposes.

Following are two examples of field-expedient headlamp profiles where only the target value foot candle readings (.3 foot candle) are recorded (Figures 21.5 and 21.6) and plotted (Figures 21.7 and 21.8). These examples were created using a CAD program. Although both examples document low beam headlamps, note the differences in the patterns due to headlight condition, age, and aim.

Isocandella Map for Pontiac 6000					
Distance from Vehicle	6ft Left	3 ft Left	C/L of Vehicle	3 ft Right	6 ft Right
50 @ Ground	.635	1.53	3.70	2.18	2.75
@ Headlamp	.265	.300	.410	.40	.308
@ Eye Level	.200	.215	.236	.224	.206
100 @ Ground	.115	.160	.230	.271	.276
@ Headlamp	.083	.097	1.01	1.16	.095
@ Eye Level	.065	.072	.078	.071	.070
150 @ Ground	.052	.061	.065	.078	.094
@ Headlamp	.042	.048	.054	.055	.056
@ Eye Level	.036	.040	.041	.044	.041
200 @ Ground	.030	.050	.051	.057	.042
@ Headlamp	.026	.029	.031	.031	.031
@ Eye Level	.025	.025	.026	.027	.028
250 @ Ground	.021	.021	.024	.025	.026
@ Headlamp	.019	.020	.021	.022	.023
@ Eye Level	.017	.018	.019	.019	.022
.3 fc @ Ground	62 ft	71 ft	87.5 ft	92.5 ft	64 ft
.3 fc @ Headlamp	41 ft	50 ft	55.5 ft	57.5 ft	51.5 ft
.3 fc @ Eye Level	10 ft	38 ft	40 ft	38 ft	22.5 ft

All values are given in foot candles.

Figure 21.6

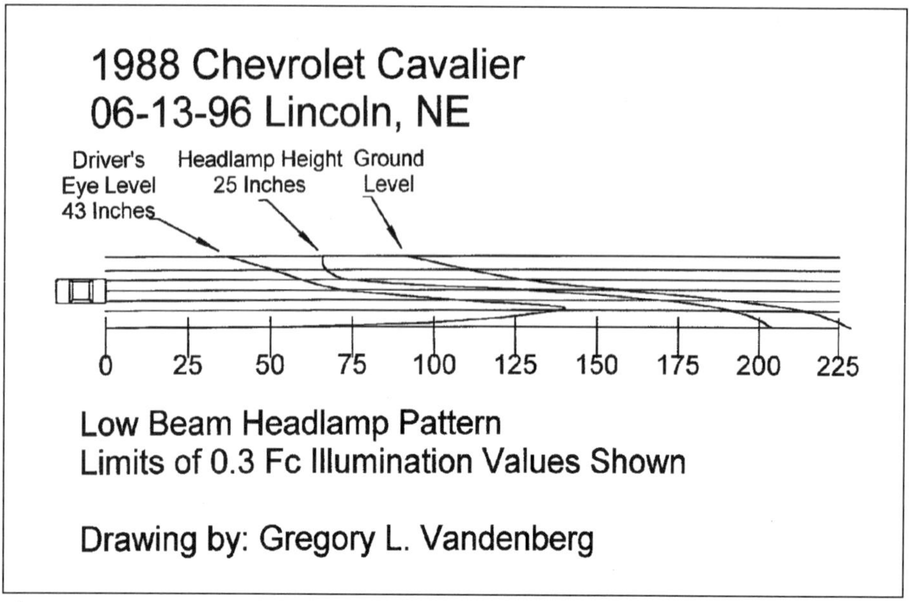

Figure 21.7

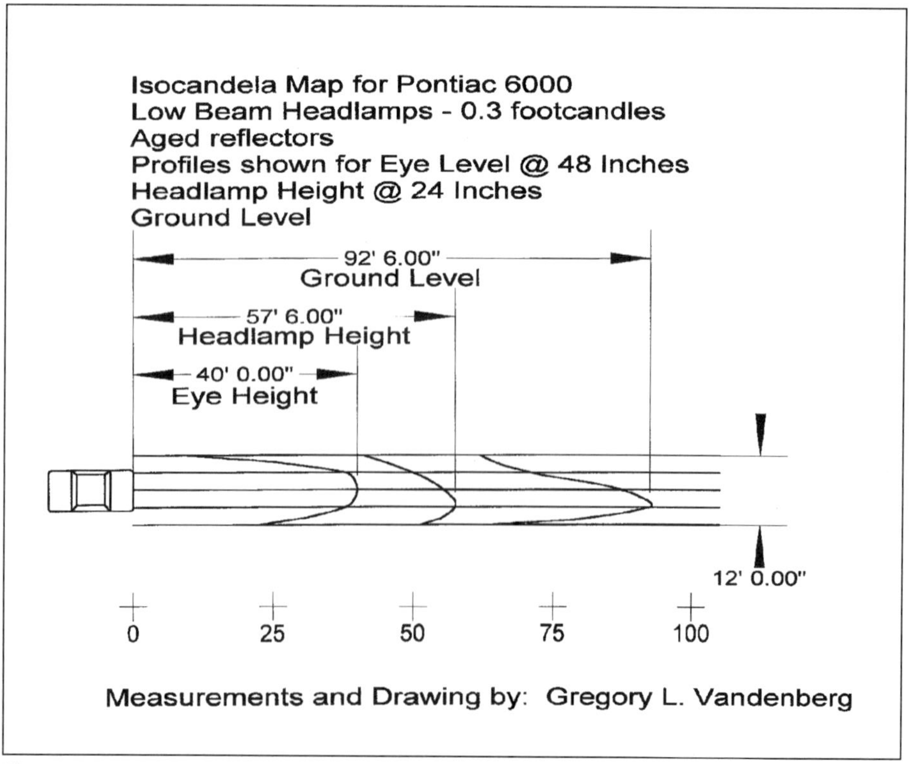

Figure 21.8

Chapter 22

Geometric Optics

Bernard S. Abrams, O.D.

Synopsis

22.1 Master Formulas
- A. Tangent function
- B. Area of a circle
- C. Cosine function
- D. Light transmission
- E. Contrast

22. Sample Work Problems
- A. Retinal cells
- B. Time and distance required with 20/20 acuity
- C. Read signs with reduced acuity
- D. Read signs with minimum driver visual acuity of 20/40
- E. Angular separation headlights
- F. Visual acuity required to detect 5-foot object
- G. Visual acuity required to see a bicycle rider
- H. Telephone poles' size at various distances

22.1 Master Formulas

A. Tangent function

A *tangent* is defined as an angle created by: $\frac{\text{side opposite}}{\text{side adjacent}}$

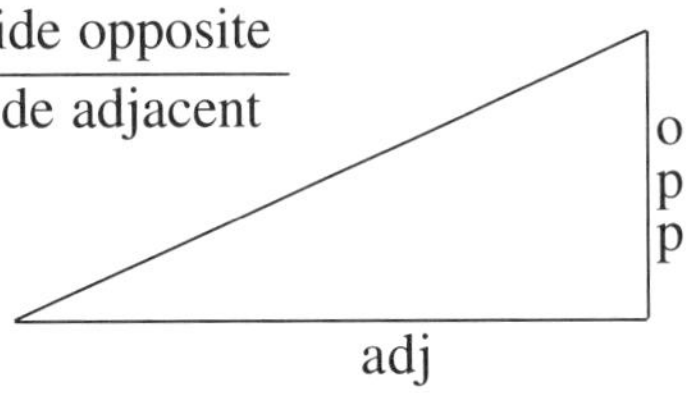

$$\tan = \frac{\text{opp}}{\text{adj}}$$

Example: tangent relation to 20/20

20/20 visual acuity, commonly referred to as Snellen acuity, has been established as follows:

$$\tan 5 \text{ minutes of arc} = \frac{\text{opp}}{\text{adj}}$$

The side opposite is .349"
The side adjacent is 20 feet (240").

Proof: tan 1 degree = .017455

tan 1 minute or $^1/_{60}$ of 1 degree = $\frac{.017455}{60}$ = .000291

tan 5 minutes = 5 × .000291 = .0014545

.0014545 = $\frac{X}{240}$ [all measurements in same unit]

240 × .0014545 = .349"

How used: To determine visual acuity required to see object when size and distance is known.

B. Area of a circle

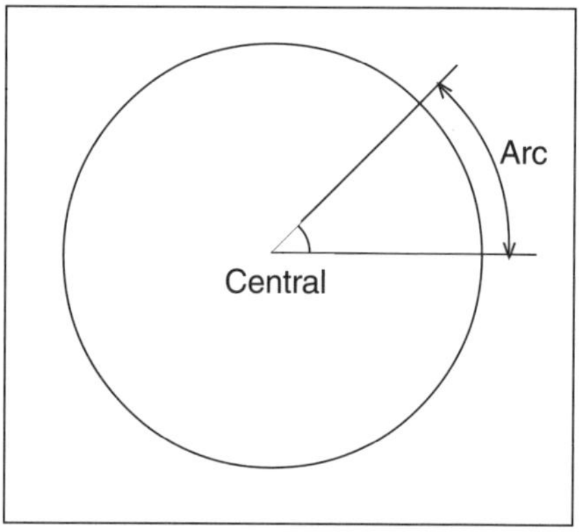

Defined as:

Each circle has 360 degrees (°).
Each degree has 60 minutes (').
Each minute may be separated into 60 seconds or 100 parts.

(However, for geometric optics we generally use 100 parts of a second if that fine a detail is required.)

Area = πr^2
π = 3.14
r = radius

Examples:

A: What is area of pupil (circle) with 2 mm diameter?

Pupil = 2 mm
r = 1 mm
Area = $\pi r^2 = 3.14 \times 1^2 = 3.14$ mm of area

B: What is area of pupil with 8 mm diameter?

Pupil = 8 mm
r = 4 mm
Area = $3.14 \times 4^2 = 50.24$ mm

C: What is ratio of older person with 2 mm pupil and a youth with 8 mm pupil?

$\frac{50.24}{3.14}$ = 16:1

How used: Older individuals from above derivation require more light at night due to pupil size reduction.

C. Cosine function

A *cosine* is defined as an angle created by: $\frac{\text{side adjacent}}{\text{hypotenuse}}$

$$\cos = \frac{\text{adj}}{\text{hyp}}$$

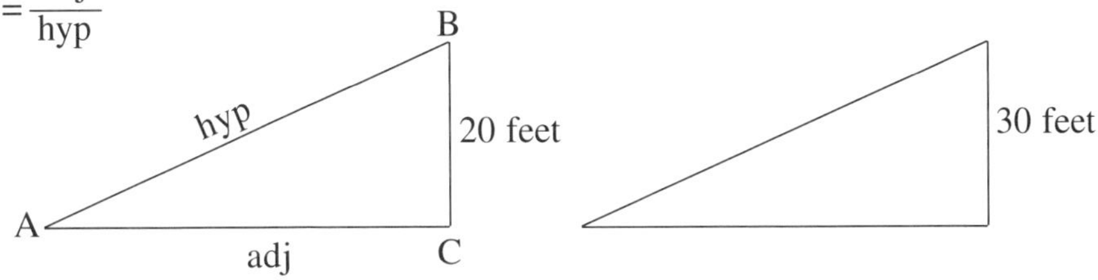

Example: How is cosine used in a problem if a 15 fc light is moved from point C to point B, 20 feet to 30 feet directly vertical from a point 50 feet from point A or < a?

What is its effect in candle power to a person at point A (A to C = 50 feet)?

Solve for < a:

$$\tan X = \frac{30}{50} = .6$$

$$\tan 1^\circ = .017455$$

$$\tan .6 = \frac{.6}{.017455} = 34 \text{ degrees}$$

cos 34 degrees = .829 or 83% of 15 fc

D. Light transmission

Light emitted X = 12.4 fc

Proof: What is distance from A to B?

A to B = $34 = \frac{X}{50}$ or $.83 = \frac{X}{50} = 41.45$

How used: To determine light intensity when source is no longer perpendicular to original location.

Transmission of light is generally defined as the amount of light passing through a transparent material.

The amount of light transmitted [T_1] is determined primarily by four factors:

1. Surface curvature front [S_1] and back [S_2]
2. Index of material or transmissivity [m]
3. Color (tint) absorptive value
4. Thickness of material [t]

Each of the four factors detracts or reduces the amount of light passing from point A to point B through a transparent material.

$$T_1 = (S_1 + S_2)(t/m)$$

Example: If 100 fc is falling on a pane of windshield with 25% tint, what quantity of light is transmitted?

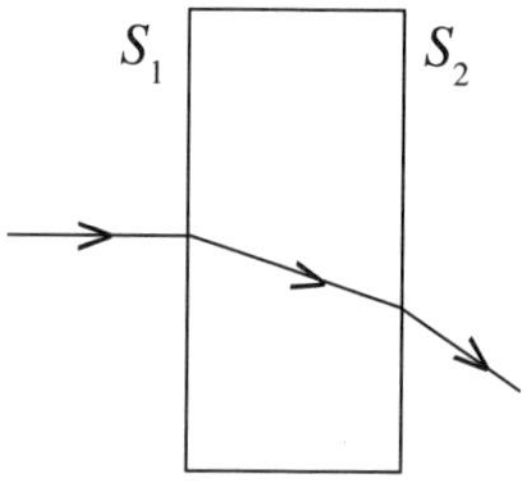

Answer: A clear windshield has parallel surfaces. 4% is reflected at each surface.

[S_1 reflected 4% + S_2 reflected 4%] = 92%

92% × 100 fc = 92 fc transmitted (if clear)

S_1 absorption 4% + S_2 absorption + actual tint 25%

25% × 100 fc = 75 fc transmitted (if classified 25% tint)

Further discussion:

Angle of window, thickness, and color are factors which should be considered.

How used: To determine loss of transmission through a transparent surface that has absorptive properties such as a tinted windshield.

E. Contrast

Contrast is defined as the reflectance (luminance) difference between an object and its background. It is generally stated as a ratio of the percent of reflectivity or as a positive or negative image.

Example: A person is wearing dark blue denim of a 3% reflectivity. The person is standing in front of a diffuse reflective wall of light sandy color with a reflectivity of 40%. The incident light falling on both object and background is 100 fc.

Question: What is quantity of reflected light?

formulate $C = \dfrac{L\ \text{Object} - L\ \text{Background}}{L\ \text{Background}}$

% × illumination = reflected light

Object: blue jeans = 3% × 100 fc = 3 fl

Background: sandy wall = 40% × 100 fc = 40 fl

Question: What is ratio of contrast?

$$C = \frac{L_O - L_B}{L_B} = \frac{3 - 40}{40} = -\frac{37}{40} = -.925 \text{ (negative object)}$$

C = Object is detectable negative image

Contrast ratio $\dfrac{40}{3} = 13.3{:}1$

How used: Please read the chapter by Dr. A. Ginsburg for a detailed explanation. In addition, the 8th edition of the *Illuminating Engineering Society Handbook* has additional data. The visibility expert will use this formula as a guide in arriving at discernibility conclusions.

22.2 Sample Work Problems

A. Retinal cells

Problem: Which retinal cells are activated?

Illumination: 5000 fc
Object reflectivity: 50%
Background reflectivity: 3%

.50 × 5000 = 2500 fl
2500 × 3.4 = 8500 cd/m^2

Answer: Photopic vision (3.4 cd/m^2) with pure cone cell = equal to normal day.

Problem: Which cells are activated?

Illumination: 1.5 fc
Object reflectance: 50%
Background reflectivity: 3%

.50 × 1.5 = .75 fl
.75 Fl × 3.4 = 2.5 cd/m^2

Answer: Mesopic vision (.34 cd/m^2) = dusk driving with combination of cone and rod cells.

Problem: Which cells are activated?

Illumination: .1 fc
Object reflectance: 50%
Background reflectivity: 3%

$.50 \times .1 = .05$ fl
$.05 \times 3.4 = .017$ cd/m^2

Answer: Scotopic vision (.034 cd/m^2) = night; rod cells.

B. Time and distance required with 20/20 acuity

Problem: Time and distance required for driver with 20/20 acuity to read signs on highway.

Sign letters:	6"
Speed:	60 mph
Driver visual acuity:	20/20

20/20 =	5' of arc
tan =	side opposite/over side adjacent
1 degree =	60 minutes
tan 1 degree =	.017455
1 minute =	$\frac{.017455}{60} = .0002909$

$5' = 5 \times .0002909 = .0014545$

Distance

$$\tan 5' = .00145 = \frac{6\text{" (letters)}}{X\text{" (distance)}}$$

$$.00145X = \frac{6\text{"}}{.00145X}$$

Distance required = $4137\text{"} = \frac{4137}{12} = 344.75$ feet

Time
feet per second:
1 hour = 60 minutes
1 minute = 60 seconds

1 hour = 3600 seconds
1 mile = 5280 feet

$\frac{5280}{3600}$ = 1.466 feet per second × mph = feet per second traveled

1.47 × speed = distance traveled at known speed

60 mph = 1.47 × 60 = miles per second = 88.2 feet per second

$\frac{344.75}{88.2}$ = 3.9 seconds

Time required = 3.9 seconds

A driver with 20/20 visual acuity will have 3.9 seconds available to read the sign at 60 mph or 88 feet per second.

Commentary: Ample time for decision making.

C. Read signs with reduced acuity

Problem: Read signs/time/speed with reduced acuity.

Facts:	Acuity:	20/100
	Letter/signs:	6" (inches)
	Vehicle speed:	60 mph
	Design used for 20/20 visual acuity (344 feet)	

Each 5' arc= 20/20

20/20 = tan 5' arc= .0014545 *(See Section B.)*
20/100 = tan 25' arc= .0072729 *(Calculated similarly to Section B.)*

Distance calculation 20/100 acuity to read sign

Tangent = $\frac{\text{side opposite}}{\text{side adjacent}}$

$$.0072729 = \frac{6''}{X''}$$

.0072729 X" = 6"

Distance
X" = 825" (inches) 825 ÷ 12 = 68.7 feet
X" = 68.7 (feet)

68 feet = .78 seconds time available to read a 6" letter/sign at 60 mph or 88 feet per second for driver with 20/100 visual acuity

A driver with 20/100 visual acuity will have only 0.78 seconds available to read the sign at 60 mph or 88 feet per second.

Comparison 20/20

$$20/20 \text{ visual acuity time} = \frac{344}{88} = 3.9 \text{ seconds}$$

Time reduced 3.9 – .78 = 3.12 seconds shortage for 20/100 acuity

Commentary: Foreseeable driving errors.

D. Read signs with minimum driver vision acuity of 20/40

Problem: Read signs/time/acuity/speed with minimum driver visual acuity of 20/40.

Facts:	Acuity:	20/40
	Sign/letters:	6" (inches)
	Speed:	60 mph
	Design time:	6" letter for 20/20 requires 3.95 seconds

Distance

20/40 = 10' arc (tangent)

tan 10' = $10 \times .0002909 = .002909$

$$.002909 = \frac{6''}{X''}$$

$$.002909X'' = 6''$$

$$X = \frac{6}{.002909}$$

$$X = 2062''$$

$$X \text{ ft} = \frac{2062''}{12} = 171.8 \text{ ft}$$

X = 171.8 feet required for 20/40 acuity to read 6" sign

Time

60 mph = $1.47 \times 60 = 88.2$ feet/second

$$\frac{171.8}{88.2} = 1.94 \text{ seconds}$$

Available time = 1.94 seconds for 20/40 visual acuity.

Answer: 20/40 vision permits only 1.94 seconds to read a sign with 6" letters or 171.8 feet from sign at 60 mph.

Commentary: Signs of 6" are designed for 20/20 visual acuity and a time of 3.9 seconds. With 20/40 visual acuity there is still a time shortage of 1.95 seconds when compared to an individual with 20/20 acuity. Obviously, signs need to be larger for a licensed portion of driving population.

E. Angular separation headlights

Problem: Angular separation headlights (Figure 22.1),

Solve for: Time it takes for headlights to double and be resolvable for driver with acuity of 20/20 visual acuity.

Headlight separation = 5 feet
Dist: A) 1 mile = 5280 feet
B) .5 mile = 2640 feet

Vehicle speed = 60 mph

Acuity

A) Solve for angular separation and acuity at 1 mile.

$$\tan a = \frac{5 \text{ (headlight)}}{5280 \text{ (1 mile)}} = \text{angular separation}$$

$$\tan a = .000946$$

$$\tan 1' = .00029$$

$$\tan a = \frac{.000946}{.00029} = 3.2 \text{ minutes of 1 degree (angular separation)}$$

$$\frac{20}{X} = \frac{5}{3.2}$$

Acuity required: $X = 12$ (20/12 visual acuity)

3.2' of arc = requires 20/12 visual acuity

Distance

Distance = 5280 feet

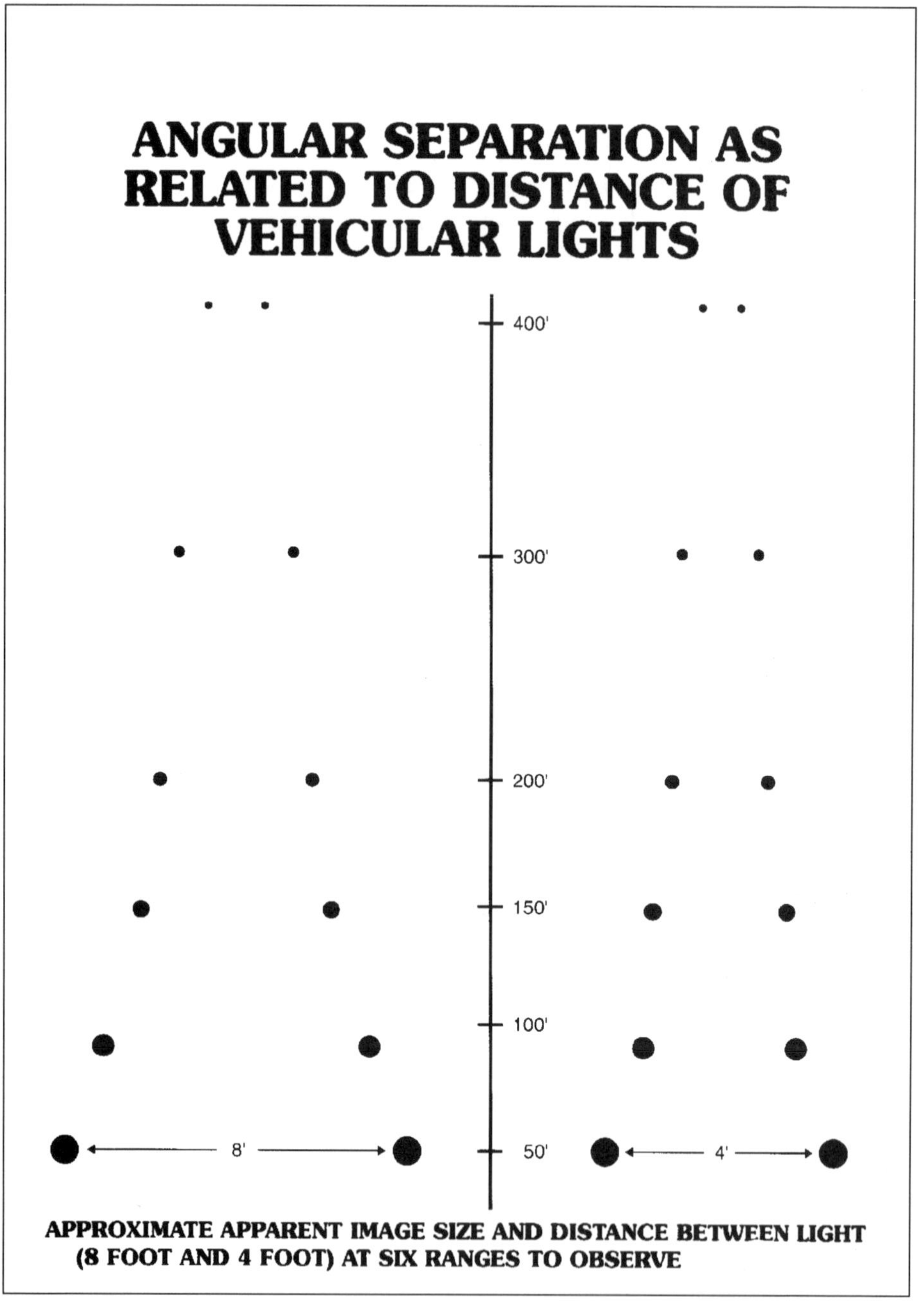
ANGULAR SEPARATION AS RELATED TO DISTANCE OF VEHICULAR LIGHTS
400'
300'
200'
150'
100'
50'
8'
4'
APPROXIMATE APPARENT IMAGE SIZE AND DISTANCE BETWEEN LIGHT (8 FOOT AND 4 FOOT) AT SIX RANGES TO OBSERVE

Figure 22.1

60 mph time = 88 feet per second

$$\frac{5280}{88} = 60 \text{ seconds}$$

Commentary: Nonresolvable separation for most individuals with 20/20 visual acuity at 5280 feet or 60 seconds away. Pair of headlights appear as a single point source of light.

B) Solve for angular separation and acuity at .5 mile (2640 feet).

$$\tan b = \frac{5}{2640} = .0018939$$

$$\tan 1' = .00029 \qquad \frac{.00189}{.00029} = 6.5$$

tan b = 6.5' minutes

20/20 = 5' minutes

Visual acuity required = $\frac{6.5}{X}$ = 1.3 × 20 = 26 or 20/26 visual acuity at 2640 feet (.5 mile)

Time 60 mph = 1.47 × 60 = 88 feet per second

Distance traveled = $\frac{2640}{88}$ $\frac{\text{(.5 mile)}}{\text{feet per second}}$ = 30 seconds

Time = 30 seconds required to double angular separation of 5-foot headlight separation from 1 mile to .5 mile for person with 20/20 visual acuity

Commentary:

1. A 5–foot separation of headlights when dividing distance traveled by half doubles its angular separation.
2. As distance shortens, the brightness of each headlight increases.
3. As distance shortens, the visual stimulus requires less acuity to judge separation and indicates increasing closeness.

F. Visual acuity required to detect 5-foot object

Problem: What visual acuity is required to detect a 5-foot object at 500 feet [or tan *X*]?

Facts: 20/20 = tan 5' arc

circle = 360 degrees
1 degree = 60'

$$\tan 1' = .017455$$

$$\tan 1' = \frac{.017455}{60} = .00029$$

$$\tan 5' = 5 \times .00029 = .0014545$$

Solve: $\tan X = \dfrac{5 \text{ ft}}{500 \text{ ft}} = .01$

$$\tan 1' = .01745$$

$$\tan 1' = \frac{.01745}{60} = .00029$$

$$\tan X' = \frac{.01}{.00029} = 34.4'$$

$$5' = 20/20$$

$$X = \frac{34.4}{5'} = 7$$

Acuity required

Answer: Visual acuity = 7 × 20 = 20/140 visual acuity.

Proof: 20/140 = tan 34.4 minutes of arc

$$\tan 1' = .00029$$

$$\tan 35' = .01$$

$$.01 = \frac{5 \text{ ft}}{500 \text{ ft}} = \frac{\text{object}}{\text{distance}}$$

Commentary: By use of tangent formula, one can compute the Snellen visual acuity required to see an object of known size at a known distance.

G. Visual acuity required to see a bicycle rider

Problem: What acuity is required to see a bicycle rider when the total object size is 6 feet high at 100 fc?

Facts: 1 mile = 5280 feet

bicycle and rider: 6 feet high
lighting: 100 fc [approaching sunset]

Acuity calculation:

1 mile

$$\tan X = \frac{6 \text{ ft}}{5280 \text{ ft}} = .0011$$

tan 5' = .00145 = 20/20

$$\text{Visual acuity} = \frac{.0011}{.00145} = .78$$

Visual acuity = .783 $.78 \times 20/20 = 20/16$ visual acuity

X = 20/16 visual acuity required

Commentary: Border line to distinguish object at 100 fc level due to size and amount of light.

H. Telephone poles' size at various distances

Problem: Why do telephone poles of equal size appear smaller at various distances?

Facts: Each telephone pole is 40 feet high.

Distances: (a) 2 miles, (b) 1 mile, (c) .5 mile, (d) .25 mile

(a) 2 miles (10,560 feet):

$$\tan X = \frac{40 \text{ ft}}{10{,}560 \text{ ft}} = .003788$$

tan 1' = .00029

$$\text{Visual acuity } \tan X = \frac{.003788}{.00029} = 13 \text{ minutes of arc}$$

$$20/20 \text{ visual acuity} = 5' \qquad \frac{13}{5} = 2.6 \times 20 = 52$$

20/52 visual acuity required

(b) 1 mile (5280 feet):

$$\tan X = \frac{40 \text{ ft}}{5280 \text{ ft (1 mile)}}$$

$\tan X = .00757$

$\tan 1' = .00029$

Visual acuity $\tan X = \frac{.00757}{.00029} = 26$ minutes of arc

20/20 visual acuity = 5' $X = \frac{26}{5} = 5.2 \times 20 = 104 = 20/104$

20/104 visual acuity required

(c) .5 mile

$\tan X = \frac{40 \text{ ft}}{2640 \text{ ft } (.5 \text{ mile})}$

$\tan X = .01515$

$\tan 1' = .00029$

Visual acuity $\tan X = \frac{.01515}{.00029} = 52.2$ minutes of arc

20/20 visual acuity = 5' $X = \frac{52.2}{5} = 10.45 \times 20 = 208 = 20/208$

20/208 visual acuity required

(d) .25 mile

$\tan X = \frac{40 \text{ ft}}{1320 \text{ ft } (.25 \text{ mile})}$

$\tan X = .03030$

$\tan 1' = .00029$

Visual acuity $\tan X = \frac{.02985}{.03030} = 104.4$ minutes of arc

20/20 visual acuity = 5' $X = \frac{104.4}{5} = 20.9 \times 20 = 417 = 20/417$

20/417 visual acuity required

Commentary: The angle subtended diminishes with distance. The pole at a distance of 1320 feet is equivalent 20/417. At a distance of 10,560 feet, the visual acuity is equivalent 20/52 or an 8:1 ratio.

End Notes

1. Fact. Miles per hour × 1.47 = feet per second
   60 miles per hour × 1.47 = 88 feet per second

Chapter 23

Questions

Bernard S. Abrams, O.D.

Synopsis

23.1 Work/Note Questions You May Be Asked to Answer in Order to Qualify As a Nighttime Visibility Expert

1. Any formal training in the visual function of the human eye?
2. Any formal courses or degrees in physiological optics? Please describe your understanding of physiological optics.
3. Are you a member of the Illuminating Engineering Society of North America?
4. Are you a member of the Human Factors Society?
5. Are you a member of the National Safety Council?
6. Are you a member of the International Traffic Engineers Society?
7. Are you a member of the Forensic Engineers Society?
8. Are you a member of the American Institute of Physics?
9. Are you a member of the Optical Society of America?
10. Have you ever been qualified as an optical or visibility consultant? Do you consider yourself an expert in visibility?
11. Have you ever been certified as an accident reconstructionist?
12. Have you ever been qualified as an accident reconstructionist?
13. Have you ever read the nighttime concepts of traffic reconstruction issued by the University of Michigan Transportation Institute?
14. Is it your testimony that you performed a nighttime accident reconstruction of this accident including a nighttime visibility reconstruction?
15. Isn't nighttime visibility reconstruction more effective when accomplished by one trained in physiological optics?

16. Have you ever written any books, articles, or papers on nighttime visibility? Discernibility? If not, what learned treatises have you read?
17. What is the difference between visibility and discernibility?
18. Have you ever heard of Dr. Merrill Allen?
19. Have you read his book? Papers? If so, which?
20. Have you ever heard of Dr. Herschel W. Liebowitz? In what respect?
21. Have you ever taught courses related to accidents? What subjects? Any visibility? Any visibility human factors? Have you attended such courses? Full-time or single lectures? Name instructors.
22. Define human factors.
23. Are you familiar with the terminology "perception/reaction"? Explain.
24. What steps are involved in perception/reaction?
25. Can you explain the visual pathway components from visual stimulus to discernment?
26. Do you have formal training in human factors?
27. Do you know of Dr. Paul Olson?
28. Have you read any of his treatises? Do you agree with them?
29. Is he an expert in perception/reaction? Was his training as a visibility professional?
30. Are you familiar with the theory of veiling glare? Disability glare? Discomfort glare? If so, describe.
31. Do you know the definition of low luminance acuity?
32. Do you know the definition of low contrast acuity?
33. Do you know the definition of glare susceptibility?
34. Do you know the definition of glare recovery?
35. Do you know the definition of low contrast target detection threshold?
36. Do you know the definition of photopic vision? If so, describe.
37. Do you know the definition of scotopic vision? If so, describe.
38. Do you know the definition of mesopic vision? If so, describe.
39. What cellular tissue of the eye is used in each (Nos. 36, 37 and 38 above)?
40. Do you know what the fovea is? Describe.
41. What is foveal cone of vision? Can you calculate foveal cone at 200 feet?
42. Do you know what rods and cones are? Define the function.
43. Define illuminance. How is it measured?
44. Do you know the patterns or isocandela of headlights? Low beam? High beam? What are SAE recommendations?

45. Do you have any idea whether visual function declines as illumination declines? At what light levels does function change?
46. Have you done research work in reaction time? In automobile accidents?
47. Can expectancy affect reaction time?
48. What is positive guidance?
49. Who is Hal Lunenfield?
50. Have you done any studies dealing with how driving at night differs from driving in the day time? Research? Do you research?
51. In reaching your conclusions, did you take into account any optical factors?
52. In reaching your conclusions, did you take into account any vision factors?
53. What is a vision time line?
54. Do you consider yourself an expert in the field of driver response time? Visual pathway? Nighttime visibility?
55. In your calculations did you use perception and reaction times? Before or after motor reaction?
56. Isn't the standard perception/reaction time used in highway design 2.5 seconds (AASHTO)?
57. If it takes a driver longer to perceive and react, is it going to take him longer to stop his car?
58. Does expectancy enter into your calculations?
59. Have you ever done any research yourself into perception/reaction time as applied to automobiles?
60. Are you familiar with the term "surprise intrusion"?
61. Are you qualified to formulate opinions about properties and characteristics of light?
62. Do you have sufficient training expertise to give opinions about light properties? If so, explain.
63. Do you know the meaning of scientific terms related to light? Lux?
64. Are you or have you been licensed in this or any other state as an eye doctor? Optometrist? Ophthalmologist?
65. What degree do you have?
66. Do you consider your visual background to qualify you in the same manner as a trained eye doctor?
67. Can you define Snellen acuity? (quantity)
68. What is the formula?
69. If an object is 40 feet by 5 feet, what acuity is required at 1000 feet?

70. What is static acuity? How is it measured? What is 20/20?
71. What is dynamic acuity? What happens at night when it is used?
72. What is contrast sensitivity?
73. What articles have you reviewed on contrast? Have you ever been tested for contrast sensitivity?
74. What is the formula for contrast?
75. What was contrast at the scene? How did you measure it?
76. Have you taken courses relating to human factors? Vision?
77. When? Where?
78. Who were the instructors?
79. Have you heard of Dr. Bernard Abrams?
80. Have you read any of his articles? Attended his courses?
81. Do you recognize him as a visibility consultant?

23.2 Questions You May Be Asked Relating to Nighttime Accidents on Cross-Examination

1. Please give a brief description of your former subspecialty in nighttime visibility as related to vehicular accidents.
2. What training and studies have you had in the area of nighttime vision?
3. Have you been qualified as an expert in other cases? If so, what percentage for plaintiffs and what percentage for defendants?
4. Are you being compensated for your time here today based on your knowledge of the human eye?
5. Can you describe briefly for us how it is that we see? Do you wish to use diagrams or exhibits?
6. What is it that enables us to see and recognize objects at night?
7. How does the eye work?
8. Function of cones.
    a. Day or bright conditions
    b. Produce clearest image
    c. Able to perceive color
    d. Area of foveal cone
9. How do the following aspects of vision form what we see and how well we see?
    a. Visual acuity—clarity and sharpness
    b. Depth perception

10. How many vision systems does a human have?
11. What are these systems?
12. How do they differ?
13. According to your research, the use of which vision system is found in most accidents during scotopic, mesopic, and photopic conditions?
14. What is required for an object to be discernible at night?
15. What visual conditions are important to the nighttime driver?
16. Can you explain to the jury what is meant by the term "human factors"?
17. Can you explain some of the human factor considerations applicable to motor vehicle collisions and nighttime driving?
18. What four steps of driver information processing are important to you in evaluating a case?
19. Is driver response time different in daylight hours as opposed to when it is dark? If so, why?
20. Can you explain to the jury the meaning of the following terms?
    a. Illumination
    b. Luminance
    c. Reflectivity
21. Can you explain what the term "visibility" means?
22. Can you explain what the term "cognitive discernibility" means?
23. Can you describe nighttime visibility with headlight illumination?
24. What is it that enables us to see and recognize objects at night?
25. At the scene, did you conduct any of the following testing?
    a. What sources of light are available at this nighttime scene? Did you take into account the following:
        1) Environment?
        2) Luminaires?
        3) Headlights?
        4) Signs?
    b. What about the moon?
        1) What effect did it have on your analysis? How did you arrive at your conclusions?
    c. What is "valley of darkness" or "black hole"?
        1) Where can you find "black hole" literature?
    d. What readings were taken?
        1) Ambient light?

   2) Reflectivity?

26. What steps in your analysis have you done as it relates to vision?
    a. Review data.
       1) Transcripts of depositions?
       2) Summaries of depositions?
       3) Discuss case with counsel?
       4) View state highway patrol photographs and reports?
       5) Review learned treatises?
       6) Site visit?
    b. When did you visit the accident scene?
       1) Dates: day/night?
       2) What did you do at accident scene?
       3) Take any measurements?
       4) Consult photographs/deposition transcript?
       5) Describe the road at the scene of the accident?
    c. Have you had an illumination map prepared to show lighting conditions at night on the scene?
    d. Third step in your analysis—weather report.
       1) Why is it important?
       2) How do you check the weather?
       3) What assumptions were made about weather at the time of the accident?
27. Will your testimony help the jury in understanding how this incident took place?
28. Unless otherwise indicated, will you state all of your opinions today with a reasonable degree of professional and scientific probability based on your experience, training, background, and research?
29. What makes your knowledge and expertise different from:
    a. an accident reconstructionist?
    b. a mechanical engineer?
    c. a photographer?
    d. a state trooper?
    e. a visibility expert?
    f. a human factors expert?

Chapter 24

Nighttime Visibility Expert on Direct Examination

Bernard S. Abrams, O.D.

Synopsis

24.1 Hypothetical Case Review and Decision

IN THE COURT OF APPEALS, COUNTY OF UNKNOWN

George H. Ogle, et al.
Plaintiff: No. 33XY-196-53

v.

Arthur Greene
Defendant
Jonathan Edwards, L.P.A., for the Plaintiff
Smith, Smith & Smith, for the Defendant

Plaintiff George Ogle, on August 13, 1983, at approximately 10:30 p.m., was walking along the right edge of State Route 631. His car had broken down and he was walking to the nearest town or village to seek assistance. As he was walking along the roadway, he was struck from behind by a vehicle driven by Arthur Greene, the defendant, who was traveling southbound on State Route 631, an unlit, rural, two-lane highway with rolling hills. It was a clear night.

Ogle alleges that defendant Greene negligently operated the motor vehicle he was driving by failing to maintain assured clear distance ahead.

The plaintiff, Ogle, a dentist, age 40, said the personal injuries he sustained had required multiple surgeries and lengthy therapy and that said injuries and resultant handicap made it impossible for him to return to work for his lifetime.

The plaintiff seeks compensation for personal injury, pain, and suffering in the amount of $4 million. Additionally, he seeks compensation for hospital, medical, and therapy expenses incurred during his recovery from said injuries in the amount of $178,365.33. The plaintiff also seeks compensation for loss of wages, both past and future, in the amount of $2,500,000.00 (25 years × $100,000.00).

Additionally, the plaintiff's spouse, Mary Ogle, joins in the suit, seeking compensatory damages for mental anguish plus loss of services and, on behalf of the plaintiff's children, seeking compensatory damages for mental anguish and loss of society with the plaintiff in the amount of $2 million.

The defendant Greene was driving at approximately the posted speed limit of 35 miles per hour with his headlights on low beam. Greene said that as his vehicle approached a small crest in the road, he saw Ogle just before he struck him with the right front fender of his vehicle, knocking him to the pavement.

Green stopped his vehicle immediately and went back to assist Ogle who was unconscious and appeared to be severely injured. After putting a blanket over the injured man, Greene called for assistance on his cell phone.

The defendant, Greene, claimed that he saw Ogle just before impact and did not have enough time to stop or swerve out of the way. Greene claimed that he had no control over the circumstances as he was confronted by a sudden and unforeseeable emergency which made compliance with statute impossible.

Greene stated that the plaintiff was dressed in dark clothing and was walking on the right side of the road with his back to traffic, which is contrary to the State Revised Code. This requires that a pedestrian on a highway, where neither sidewalk nor a shoulder is available for use, must walk as near as he can to the outside edge of the roadway and on the left side of the roadway, facing oncoming traffic.

Defendant further claimed that the plaintiff was wearing dark clothing which made him difficult to discern. Under State Revised Codes, a "discernible object is a reasonably visible object. An object is discernible when it is visible or can be detected or perceived." Ogle contended that the plaintiff was nondiscernible until just before the impact, and therefore, the plaintiff committed an act or acts of negligence which directly and proximately caused his injury.

The plaintiff, Ogle, called Paul Jones, an expert in accident reconstruction, to discuss the issue of driver sight distance and reaction time. Quoting from a manual for drivers, Jones stated that visibility distance with low beams is 350 feet. Mr. Jones points out that on that basis, in his opinion, the driver should have had plenty of time to detect the plaintiff and avoid the impact. He further quoted numerous articles that stated perception reaction time was 1.5 seconds. Therefore, at 35 miles per hour (1.46×35) Green would need only to travel approximately 80 feet in 1.5 seconds and, with 350 feet sight distance, should have been able to view the plaintiff in time to avoid a collision.

Counsel for the plaintiff cited the statute relating to assured clear distance where there is a curve, hill, or an obstruction of view in the highway, the assured clear distance is that distance between the driver of a vehicle and the point where his vision ends or is cut off. The driver must drive at such a speed that he can stop within the distance between him and the point where his vision ends. The plaintiff alleged that the defendant was negligent in not maintaining assured clear distance ahead as defined by the State Revised Code.

The plaintiff's counsel also cited the State Revised Code referring to light. "Distribution of lights must be high enough to reveal persons, vehicles and substantial objects on the highway at a safe distance in advance of his moving vehicle." Plaintiff alleges that the defendant is negligent for not providing adequate illumination for the section of highway he was traveling.

In charging the jury, the judge explained to the jurors that the element of discernibility is at issue in the case and that in the statute, "discernible" implies something more than "visible." "Visible" means perceivable by the eye, whereas "discernible" means mentally perceptible or distinguishable; capable of being discerned by the understanding, not merely by the senses. Reasonably modified, "discernible" in this statute means an object which the driver should or could have seen if he was operating his vehicle at a speed which would have permitted him to bring the vehicle to a stop within an assured clear distance.

The judge further explained that the fact that some other cause concurred with negligence of the defendant in the production of an injury does not relieve him from liability, unless it is shown such other causes would have produced the injury independently.

The judge charged the jury to determine if the car driven by the defendant did strike an object—to wit, the plaintiff—that the object was ahead of the driver in his path of travel, that the object was stationary or moving in the same direction as the driver, that the object did not suddenly appear in the driver's path, and that the object was easily discernible.

Comparative negligence also was explained to the jurors. They were told that if comparative negligence was found to be involved, they would have to determine to what degree each party was at fault.

The jury rendered a verdict in favor of the plaintiff, against Greene. The jury found the defendant, Greene, 51 percent negligent and the plaintiff 49 percent negligent.

The *Ogle v. Greene* case is hypothetical and is an atypical conclusion to the vast number of night pedestrian traffic accident cases argued before juries all over the country. Most cases of "assured clear distance" and/or discernibility are found for the defendant.

The cases always involve questions of driver visibility and discernibility or when a driver could have or should have seen, or at what distance the driver should have discerned something, and what reaction time is involved.

Prior to the introduction of visibility experts, a common practice is for an accident investigator, usually a former police officer or possibly an engineer, to prepare a reconstruction of the event in an effort to determine answers to the questions. In the past, reconstructionists of night accidents, however, had some distinct limitations. They were not trained in accident reconstruction to understand how human factors and the visual information gathering system interact under nighttime conditions.

A paper by Olson (SAE 870600)[1] titled "Visibility Problems in Nighttime Driving" states that:

> Estimating something like nighttime detection distance for an object by measuring the distance at which one or even several persons can see it in a daylight reconstruction is like trying to estimate the stopping distance of a large truck by using a sports car. No judge would allow the latter type of evidence to be introduced. No judge should allow the former evidence to be introduced either.

There are visibility experts with backgrounds in vision, human factors, and a vast body of literature. In addition, Abrams[2] is conducting classes across the land for reconstructionists, engineers, and other interested parties.

This chapter is intended to summarize information on the question of driver visibility and discernibility under nighttime operating conditions and not to state a case for the defendant or plaintiff. The hope is that it will aid individuals involved in accident cases to better understand the information-gathering process. Then, with this knowledge each case can be judged on its own merits and an equitable decision can be rendered after a full disclosure of all of the facts to the jury.

It is absolutely essential for those who are involved in accident analysis to understand that 90 percent of all information-gathering is over the visual pathway and to be able to qualify as an expert who can assist the jury in understanding how the collision occurred.

Vital to that understanding are the steps in driver information processing. This is a four-step process that takes time, and that time varies from person to person. The four-step process involves detection, identification, decision, and response.

This multistep process is a general rule that applies to every driver. It means that before a driver can be expected to make an appropriate response to any roadway situation, four things have to happen: detection, identification, decision, and response. Detection is the conscious awareness that something is present in the roadway. Identification is the process of gathering information about the object in the road until enough information is gathered that the driver can make an appropriate decision as to what it is, whether it poses a threat, and whether its existence calls for some responsive action. The next step is decision, and this is the process of the driver's deciding on a response to the condition which has been identified. Then, finally, we have response. This occurs when orders are issued by the driver's brain to the appropriate muscle groups in order to initiate the responsive action decided upon.

24.2 Use of Qualified Expert Witness with a Visibility Background

The previously discussed hypothetical case was a close decision for the plaintiff; however, let us now inject an expert on vision and associated human factors.

Let's presume in the testimony of the Ogle v. Greene case that the defendant, Greene, calls in visibility expert Tom Jackson who on direct examination can discuss such concepts as how we see and the average driver's night visual capabilities. He also defines what are reasonable response times to either an expected or unexpected object in the roadway ahead:

Tom Jackson—Direct Examination

Section II
(After qualifying as an expert)

Mr. Jackson, will your testimony and your opinions assist the ladies and gentlemen of the jury in understanding how this collision occurred? And why?

Jackson: It is a well-known fact that a disproportionately greater number of U.S. traffic fatalities and injuries occur at night. He points out that night vision is distinctly different from day vision (photopic) and that these different factors involved in night (scotopic) visibility need to be given consideration by the court as do the questions of what are reasonable responses. Understanding how humans function visually at night is a missing piece in case law and in sections of various State Revised Codes.

Can you describe for us how it is that we see?

Jackson proceeds to present basic information concerning visual perception to provide the jury with a foundation for understanding how the visual system works under nighttime driving conditions.

Jackson: Vision begins with the energy of electromagnetic radiation reaching the eye—that is, light that is either emitted or reflected from things.

Before seeing is possible, however, a new form of energy called a nerve impulse must relay the image message to the brain. It is within the dark confines of the skull where vision is created. Thus, it becomes evident that visual perception is the final outcome of a long chain of complex events.

It is dependent upon light rays that come into the eyes and form retinal images. It is further dependent upon the complex physiological process that takes place from the retina to the occipital lobe in the brain. Finally, it is directly dependent upon the brain activity itself. The termination of the impulse from the eye is in the occipital lobe of the brain along what is known as the optical pathway. This traveling of impulse can be measured by noninvasive technology and renders great information about what one is seeing, plus how one is thinking.

The cornea is the transparent front surface of the eye through which light enters. This lens helps bring light to focus on the retina while the iris controls the size of the opening in front of the lens (the pupil).

The retina is the light-sensitive layer of the eye which covers about two-thirds of the interior of the eye. The central portion of the retina is the fovea which plays a central role in visual acuity. The fovea is an area about two degrees in size where vision is the sharpest. Only five degrees to the left or right of the fovea, visual acuity is only half as much.

The retina contains two different types of cells—the rods and the cones. These cells differ functionally as well as in their distribution throughout the retina.

The cones function at higher (daytime) light levels, providing what is call *photopic* vision. They are wavelength sensitive, producing the sensation of color. Cones have far fewer neural interconnections and are hence capable of finer discriminations. Cones are found exclusively in the fovea and in rapidly diminishing numbers as one moves away from the fovea.

At low light levels (darkness or nighttime) the eye relies chiefly on a set of about 125 million cells called rods that are sensitive to small amounts of light and provide what is called *scotopic* vision. Rods are found throughout the retina with the exception of the fovea. They are not wavelength sensitive. Hence, a pure rod vision is in shades of gray.

There is a middle range of light levels in which both rods and cones function. This is called *mesopic* vision. Typically, night driving is done under mesopic conditions, depending on the amount of light available.

How is nighttime defined?

Jackson: Here is the definition of nighttime illumination as stated in the *Illuminating Engineering Society Lighting Handbook*, 1987 Reference Volume:

Nighttime: those hours between the end of evening civil twilight and the beginning of morning civil twilight when auxiliary illumination is needed to perform a task, such as driving.

Note: Civil twilight ends in the evening when the center of the sun's disk is six degrees below the horizon and begins in the morning when the center of the sun's disk is six degrees below the horizon.

Can you explain why and how low-beam headlights are used?

Jackson: Because of the limitations imposed by traffic flow and highway design, we primarily must use low beams to guide vehicles at night even though all vehicle headlamps offer two beams: a low-beam and a high-beam. However, drivers must use the low-beam headlight the vast majority of the time. The object of a low-beam headlight design is to get as much of the illumination below the horizontal axis (that is, approximately thirty-six inches above the ground) to reasonable levels, because it causes glare for other drivers. Typically, low-beam headlamps in automobiles produced for use in America illuminate an area between 150 and 175 feet in front of the automobile. They attenuate rapidly as they leave the headlamp, and at 175 feet the light drop off is approximately .3 foot candles or darkness by definition.

Can you explain to me the meaning of the terms: illumination, luminance and reflectivity?

Jackson: Illumination is the measure of the amount of light falling on a surface without respect to the direction from which the light comes, the type of light source, or the type of surface upon which it falls. The illumination will be the same whether the surface is a polished steel plate or a piece of black felt cloth. Luminance, on the other hand, is the measure of the amount and concentration of light *leaving* a surface. It is luminance that controls the magnitude of the sensation that the brain receives off an object. In other words, luminance is the amount of light reflected or "thrown off" by the object and is a key factor in how well we can see the object. The luminance of a surface depends upon the direction from which it is viewed and the reflective properties of the surface itself.

What is it that enables us to see and recognize objects at night?

Jackson: There are a number of factors that determine whether we will be able to observe and recognize an object at night. One of these is "conspicuity." Conspicuity (stemming from the word "conspicuous") is the sum of the characteristics of an object that determines the likelihood that the object will come to the attention of the observer. The fact that something may be present in the visual field does not necessarily mean that it will be detected because it may have less conspicuity than other visible features. Another important concept is that of "visibility." Visibility refers to how well something can be seen by the human eye. Visibility, therefore, involves human judgment. There is no device that can measure visibility directly. However, one key factor influencing visibility of an object is "contrast." Contrast refers to characteristics of an object that cause it to appear different or separate from something else. The eye responds to contrast. Under daylight levels of illumination, there are a variety of forms of contrast available—for example, color, texture, brightness. In addition, during daylight the visual system is operating at the highest level of sensitivity and has the greatest capability of distinguishing differences between objects in the visual field. However, at night, *brightness contrast* is generally the only form of contrast of any consequence and the visual system has a reduced capability for distinguishing differences between objects in the visual field. Thus, in order to be seen at night, objects must be sufficiently brighter or darker than their backgrounds. Specifically, in nighttime driving conditions, an object will be discernible in the forward visual field if it is illuminated by the headlights of an approaching vehicle until it is sufficiently brighter than the background to be seen. White or reflectorized objects are discernible at approximately twice the distance as dark objects.

Why is it that sometimes we humans do not see an object?

Jackson: Because the foveal area or cone of vision of the retina is so small relative to the entire visual field, detection typically occurs in the periphery. It may take several "glimpses"—combinations of eye movements and fixations—before an object, depending on reflectivity, in the peripheral visual field can be recognized. However, in order to be detected, an object in the periphery must be much more conspicuous than if its image had fallen on the fovea.

This multiple-glimpse requirement for recognition is one reason why accepting a "standard human reaction time" of 0.75 seconds for response often is not applicable in non-laboratory settings and tasks.

This presents a simple scientific fact: The variation of object reflectivity accounts for why people, even careful observers, sometimes don't see what is there to be seen.

Responding to what is seen takes time. The time for a driver to respond to the stimulus of a traffic situation or hazard equals the time it takes for the driver to recognize the situation, understand the situation, decide to take action, and take that action. In brief, that four-step process, as mentioned above, is detection, identification, decision-making, and reaction.

Why are the four steps of driver information processing important to us in this case? And why is expectancy a factor?

Jackson: They are important to us, quite simply, because taken together, they constitute "driver perception/reaction time." These four steps, which will always occur in sequence, require time to accomplish. How much time varies, depending upon the circumstances, and that is very important to our understanding of the collision we are concerned with here. In order to fully appreciate the concept of driver response time, it is necessary that we consider one other fact, and that is driver *expectancy*.

Based upon their driving experience, people develop expectations about matters such as traffic control devices, roadway design, and driver behavior. This is true for both night and day driving although it becomes more important at night because so much of the information available during the day is lost when it becomes dark. Accordingly, a driver's response time will be affected by his expectations of the environment. For example, in a school zone, one is cautioned to expect children. Most drivers know that children are sometimes unpredictable. Hence, a driver will be alert to a child's darting out into the street after a ball or otherwise in the furtherance of some childhood endeavor. Because the driver has been alerted to expect such an occurrence, his or her response time will be less. Likewise, if a driver is cautioned to be alert to falling rock and the driver rounds a curve to find a boulder in the roadway, his or her response time will be less than if he or she had not been warned of the possibility of such an occurrence. The important points to be made are that all drivers have expectations, and these expectations are based on general experience. When these expectations must be violated, great care should be taken to alert approaching drivers to the condition in sufficient time so that they can make the necessary adjustments. It is very important to understand that this is not a question of whether a driver is *paying attention* or not. It is a question, rather, of how long it takes the driver to process information that comes to his attention in order to create object discernibility.

At any given point in time there may be a great deal of information imaged on the retina. However, while the brain handles information very rapidly, it also handles it serially. At night new information is most likely to appear on the retinal periphery where it is less well seen, and it must be strong enough to capture the attention of the observer. In motor vehicle operation, the time available for this to happen is typically fairly short.

In recent years, it is generally accepted in the field that driver response time is "elastic," and during non-daylight hours the time is between 2.5 and 3 seconds. It is important to understand, however, that perception reaction time begins when the driver becomes aware of an object in his field of vision.

What does the term peripheral filter mean to us? And how does it affect conspicuity?

Jackson: The peripheral filter is a mechanism which determines what will come to the attention of the observer. While the way the filter works is not yet understood, the types of stimuli that are likely to create a foveal fixation or saccade are known. In general, they are objects that differ greatly from their backgrounds in terms of brightness, texture, and color; objects that are flickering or flashing; objects of large size; and object that are moving.

The fact that something may be present in the visual field does not necessarily mean that it will be detected because it may have less conspicuity than other visible features.

What is visual acuity?

Jackson: The measure of visual performance at a doctor's office which most people are familiar with is called static acuity, or a measure of the ability to distinguish fine detail in a high contrast stationary target and generally represented as a comparative figure—for example, 20/20. This is the standard test used for obtaining a driver's license. A number of other measures of visual acuity are more meaningful in the night driving such as low-luminance acuity, low-contrast acuity, glare susceptibility, glare recovery time, and low-contrast target detection threshold.

Why is driver response different during nighttime as opposed to when it is daylight in this case?

Jackson: Things become even more complicated with night driving because of low light and low contrast. They are important elements in being able to discern various objects, including pedestrians from their background.

"Contrast" is defined as those characteristics that cause something to appear different or separate from something else. The eye responds to contrast. Contrast is far more important in determining whether something will be visible and depends primarily on illumination—incident lighting on an object—and the luminance—reflected light of an object.

For example, a person with a white shirt has a reflectance factor of 80 percent and will stand out from a darker night surrounding while a person wearing blue jeans has a reflectivity of 6 percent and will be difficult to distinguish at nighttime.

During daytime levels of illumination, due to the photopic eye functioning, there are a variety of forms of contrast available—color, texture, brightness. In addition, the visual system is operating at its highest level of foveal sensitivity and has its greatest capability of distinguishing differences and finite details.

However, under nighttime driving conditions, when this accident occurred, due to the scotopic eye function, the visual system has a significantly reduced capability of distinguishing differences. Brightness contrast is generally the only form of contrast of any consequence. The job of the headlights is to provide the necessary illumination to create object brightness contrast from its background.

Why is your opinion different than Mr. Jones'? (Plaintiff's expert)

Jackson: The setting in which the accident involving Ogle and Greene took place was a rural area with many trees at both sides of the roadway creating a black tunnel effect. There were no streetlights and no ambient lighting. The plaintiff was wearing low reflective (6 percent) dark denim clothing which, due to its low contrast, blended into the background making him difficult to discern.

Why do you feel Mr. Jones' opinion of low beams 350 feet sight distance at night is in error?

Jackson first points out 350 is an error and is used for high beams which, due to opposing traffic, were not permitted. In addition, this State Code requires object visibility at 175 feet but does not specify object color.

Jackson then proceeds to introduce results of a field test of different head-lighting systems and four possible pedestrian targets wearing various types of clothing—three clad in various denim and one in a white vest.

Jackson: The analyses suggest that when confronted with a low-contrast object, such as an unexpected pedestrian wearing dark clothing in a rural setting, low-beam headlights will not provide adequate detection-identification distance at speeds in excess of 35 mph. If the pedestrian is approaching from the left side of the vehicle, with most of the energy from headlights focused on the right, the detection-identification problem became more pronounced.

The data indicated that pedestrians who must venture forth at night can make themselves much more likely to be seen by wearing light-colored garments and/or reflective tapes; otherwise, they are laying a trap for approaching drivers.

Additionally, there is evidence (Allen, Hazlett, 1970) that indicates that individuals who walk in traffic at night overestimate by a factor of two the driver visibility distance provided by the oncoming vehicle's lighting system.

Assuming all of the facts you have stated to be true, and based upon your education, training and experience, as well as your investigation of this occurrence, do you have an opinion, which you can state with a reasonable degree of professional and scientific probability as to the visibility of Mr. Ogle on the roadway at the scene of this occurrence?

Jackson: Yes.

In your opinion, was Mr. Ogle discernible to Mr. Greene in time for him to avoid or evade this incident? And what facts do you base your answer on?

Jackson: Based on the facts presented in this case, in my opinion, the plaintiff, Ogle, was non-discernible to the defendant, Greene, in sufficient time to avoid or evade a collision. I base my opinion on the following facts:

1. Low contrast factors of pedestrian and background
2. Headlight profile
3. Perception/reaction times
4. Distances at which the prior three items occur
5. Time required to avoid prior to maneuver

. . . *Now, with this new information, you be the judge and jury and decide if the original decision was correct or in error in this case.*

End Notes

1. Dr. Paul Olson, U.M.T.R.I.
2. Dr. Bernard Abrams, Institute of Vehicular Safety.

Chapter 25

Suggested List of Documentation Which May Be Needed for Visibility and Human Factors Evaluation

Bernard S. Abrams, O.D.

All accidents require pre- and post-impact data. The sensory mechanism most basically involved is vision. It is essential to comprehend the physiological visual functions in order to assess the human factors that guide a driver's response.

From the case studies, it is relatively easy to infer the kind of evidence that will be needed in a given type of accident. For example, in a simple skid to a stop with no collision, the key elements are length of skid, slope of roadway, type of road surface, and condition of road surface. The vehicle weight is irrelevant in this case.

For collisions, in addition to the evidence cited above, vehicle weights become important. In addition, it is important to determine exactly where the collision took place—the point of impact. Photographs or diagrams should document the precise angles that any skid marks have relative to each other and to clearly defined road directions such as center lines. Furthermore, any collateral damage to obstacles such as trees, fire hydrants, buildings, and the like should be documented as completely as possible. Photographs should be taken of each vehicle from angles such that the depth of crush can be estimated fairly accurately.

For accidents involving loss of control due to travelling around a curve, the exact shape of the yaw mark (assuming there is one) should be documented. The critical measurement is the radius of curvature of this mark and any bank angle of the roadway.

For accidents involving visibility/discernibility problems, it is important to determine the sight distance, lighting, and weather conditions at the time to name a few. If the accident occurred at night, then it is critical to determine the position of any lights that may have distracted or blinded a driver involved in the incident. If the accident occurred at dawn or dusk, then it is important to determine the exact time of the accident and the sky conditions that existed at that time—an overcast sky will greatly reduce light, while a sunset will greatly increase it.

For accidents involving an airborne object, it is important, if possible, to determine the point from which the object left the ground, the point at which it returned to the ground, and the point where it finally came to rest. Often the mistaken assumption is made that where the object finally came to rest is where it first hit the ground. This is not usually the case. However, it will require a careful examination of the ground to find where the object first struck.

The following pages list suggested information which you may need to document the forensic visibility aspects of this incident. The information obtained should be divided into two sections: (1) pre-impact and (2) post-impact.

Vehicle at Scene Documentation
Visibility Aspects
Pre-Impact

A. Minimum View 1000 Feet Prior to Impact
   1. Written Description

B. Obtain Light Level
   1. Time:________________ Environmental:_________
      Luminaire:____________ Other: _________________
   2. Sun Rise _______ Sun Set _______ Both ________

C. Obtain Vehicle Windshield Data
   1. Windshields: Clear _____ Tint _____ Color _____
      Dirty _____ Scratched _____ Sloped _____
      Other _______ Photo _____

D. Color of Car __________ Pantone ________ Y _____ X ______
   1. Sample Paint
   2. Percent Reflectance

E. Inspect Lighting System
   1. Headlight
      a. Lens: Dirty _____ Scratched _______
      b. Filament _________
      c. Low/High: ________
      d. Ground to Bulb: _________ to Center: _________
      e. Separation: __________
      f. Type: _______________
   2. Taillight
      a. Dirty _____ Pitted _____ Scratch _______

SAE #________ Lens Color _________
Stop _________ Turn _______ Regular __________
Transmission % _____ Y _______ X ________ Each ________
Other __________

F. Sight Distance/Site Distance
   1. Day
   2. Night
   3. Obstruction—Describe

G. Road: Asphalt _____________ % Ref.
   Concrete ____________ % Ref.

H. Background: Visual Clutter: _______ Clear _______
   Luminance: Absolute ________ % _________
   Other: _________________________________

I. Driver V-1
   a. Wear Glasses _______ Tint
   b. Age ______
   c. Size ______

   Driver V-2
   a. Wear Glasses _______ Tint
   b. Age ______
   c. Size ______

J. Other Involved
   a. Pedestrian
      Clothes Color: ________ Pants ________ Shirt ________
      Size ________ Shoes ________ Other ________
   b. Locomotive (See Railroad Work Up)
   c. Bicycle
      Color ______ Headlamp _________
      Reflector _________ % _______ Size _________
      Location: _________________

K. Weather/Climatology
   Rain _______ Estimate Light, Medium, Heavy

Fog ________ Estimate Light, Medium, Heavy

Snow _______ Estimate Light, Medium, Heavy

Mist _______ Estimate Light, Medium, Heavy

Condition: Wet ___ Dry ____ Snow _____ Ice _____

L. Road Design: 1000 Feet Prior to Scene

Draw Map

Items: Signs, Houses, Driveways, Contour, etc.

2 Lane ______ 4 Lane _______ Other _________

M. Visual Clutter—Describe

N. Traffic Controls/Location

1000 Feet Prior Signs ______ Road _______ Berm _______

Signals _______ Other _______

O. Special Conditions

a. Construction

Describe Controls ___________________________

b. School

c. Hospital

d. Urban _____ City ________ Township _________

e. Other/Describe

Post-Impact Documentation
Visibility Aspects
Scene Data Required

1. Moon Evaluation as to Light Quantity, Azimuth, Bearing.
2. Sun Evaluation as to Azimuth and Location.
3. Percent Transmission of Windshield
4. Taillight/Headlight SAE Number: _________

   Height/Ground Center Bulb _____________

   Angular Separation: Center to Center___________
5. Retro-Reflection Signs

   a. Age

   b. Type
   c. Condition
6. Truck Light/Lens Inspection
   a. Age
   b. Condition
   c. Emission
   d. Lens
7. Retro-Reflection Tapes
   a. Location
   b. Condition
   c. Type
8. Photographs
9. Dynamic Photo Documentation

Appendices

Appendix A

Color References

Merrill J. Allen, O.D., Ph.D.

Figure A.1 *(referenced in Chapter 3, page 20) Shape coding of signal lights.*

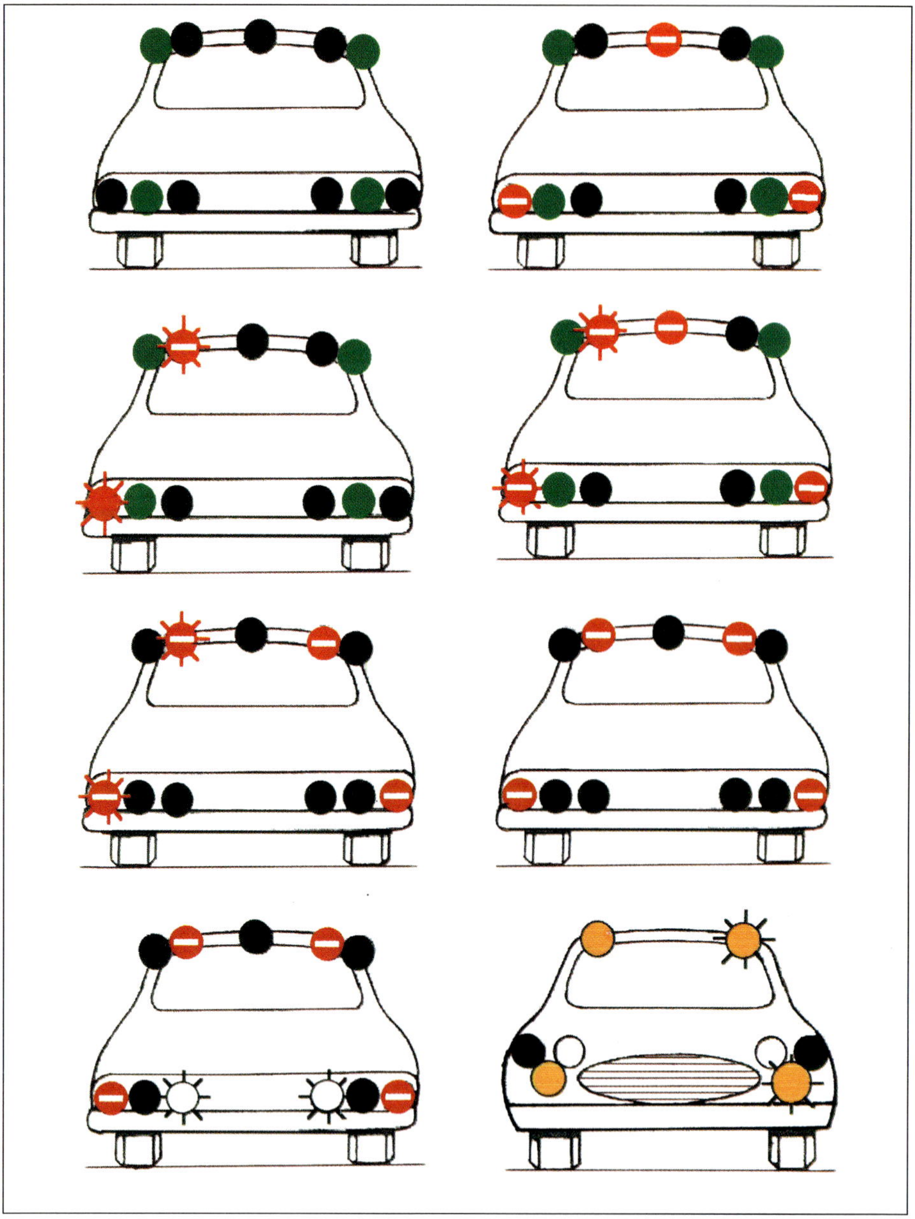

Figure A.2 *(referenced in Chapter 8, page 141) An improved motor vehicle signal light system. As seen from the rear, the "follow me" color would be green. Red would be the color for braking, stopping, or turning. To guarantee that colorblind drivers can see the red color, the stop and turn signals are shape coded by adding a white horizontal bar. In the front view of the vehicle, the amber would be the "engine running" and the "turn signal" color. Note that both the front and the rear lights have low and high locations. This is extremely important in judging the distance and speed of the vehicle at night. A roof mounted add on light system called the Life Lite was tested in Iowa. A preliminary report indicated a 69 percent accident reduction (Brown, G., 1969; Moran, M., 1976; Allen, M.,* Running Lights, *1979).*

Figure A.3a *(referenced in Chapter 10, page 191) Principal signs used on streets and highways in the USA. Relative sizes are of no importance. Local conditions, traffic speed and legislative requirements determine the sizes in actual use.*

Figure A.3b *(referenced in Chapter 10, page 191) Principal signs and signals used in the USA. At the top are three old style signs. They are superior to the new signs replacing them.* Information signs *are rectangular. Of the* prohibitory signs, *the Do Not Enter sign shows us how to shape code our red signal lights so that color blind drivers can recognize the red. In* signal lights *at the bottom, note that red is at the top in vertical signals and on the left in horizontal signals.*

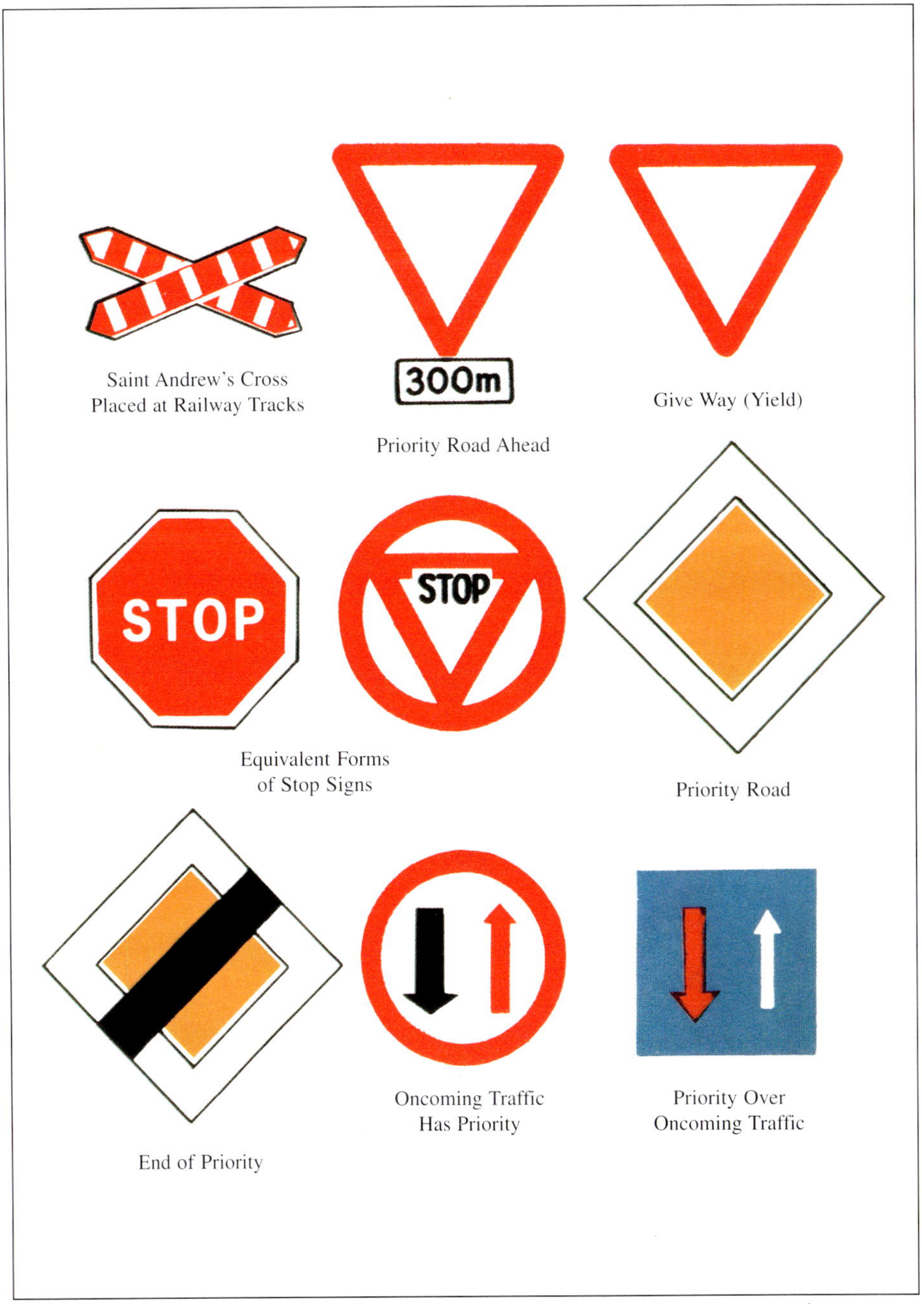

Figure A. 4 *(referenced in Chapter 10, page 192) United Nations motorway mandatory signs.*

Figure A.5 *(referenced in Chapter 10, page 192) United Nations motorway prohibitory signs. The red circle signifies negative action; the black figure signifies the act or vehicle that is negated.*

Figure A.6 *(referenced in Chapter 10, page 192) United Nations motorway warning signs. The red triangle, apex up, is interchangeable with the diamond for all warning signs.*

Appendix B

Definitions

Bernard S. Abrams, O.D.

Absorptive lenses: Frequently called tinted lenses because the material is not as clear as ordinary material. The tint is not a major factor, but merely a result of the chemicals used to increase the absorption of the material. The major factor is the absorption curve of the lens.

Accommodation: The process by which the eye changes focus from an object at one distance to an object at another distance.

AMP: A generic term for a man-made source of light.

(Author's note: Sometimes used to describe a lighting fixture or luminaire, this term is commonly referred to as a "bulb.")

Attenuation: (A) is the amount of light, usually expressed in percent, that does not pass through the lens. Attenuation includes the light lost by reflection, scattering, and absorption. T(%) = 100 – A(%).

Blind spot: The area of the retina at which the fibers of the optic nerve leave the eye. It contains no light receptors and therefore does not mediate visual experiences. The nerve fibers themselves are insensitive to light.

Blindness: Generally legally defined in the United States as visual acuity for distance, vision of 20/200 or less in the better eye, with best correction or visual acuity of better than 20/200 if the widest diameter of field of vision subtends an angle no greater than 20 degrees. (Some states include up to 30 degrees.) (A measure of 20/200 visual acuity means that a person can see a distance no greater than 20 feet [6.5 meters] what one with normal sight can see at 200 feet [65 meters].)

Candela: The unit of luminous intensity. One candela (cd) is defined as the luminous intensity of 1/60th of 1 cm^2 of projected area of a black-body radiator operating at the temperature of solidification of platinum (2046° K).

Candlepower: It is defined as 1/60th of the intensity of 1 cm^2 of a blackbody radiator at the temperature of solidification of platinum (2046° K). Luminous intensity expressed in candelas.

Central vision: The seeing of objects in the central part of the visual field, approximately 3 degrees in diameter. (Also called foveal vision.)

Civil Twilight: Averages 30 minutes as the light level goes from 30 foot candles to .3 foot candle and color to non-color (may be 28 to 32 minutes).

Contrast: The subjective assessment of the difference in two parts of a field of view seen simultaneously or successively. (Hence, luminosity contrast, lightness contrast, color contrast, simultaneous contrast, successive contrast.) Amount of light reflected from an object compared with the amount of light reflected from its background.

Darkness: Less than .3 foot candle.

Deuteranopia: The more common form of red-green blindness, in which the visible spectrum is not shortened at the red end.

Foot candles: Measurement of light falling on an object. 1 foot candle (fc) = 10/76 lux or 1 lumen per square foot.

Foot lamberts: The amount of light reflecting off of an object.

Hyperopia: A refractive error in which, with the lens inside the eye in the resting state (least convex), parallel rays of light are focused behind the retina.

Illuminance: The density of the luminous flux incident on a surface; it is the quotient of the luminous flux divided by its uniformly illuminated area. Units: footcandle (lumens/square foot or lux (lumens/square meter).

(Author's note: This is simply the light incident on a surface divided by its area; i.e., the density of light falling on a surface. Most lighting level recommendations are given in foot candles in the U.S.)

Illumination: The act of illuminating or state of being illuminated. Units in foot candles or lux (10.76 lux = 1 fc).

Inverse square law: The illumination (E), at a point in a plane perpendicular to the line joining the point and the source, is directly proportional to the luminous intensity (I) of the source in the direction of the point, and inversely proportional to the square of the distance (D) from the point to the source. For a point source: $E = I/D^2$.

Lighting fixture (luminaire): A complete lighting unit consisting of a lamp or lamps together with the parts designed to distribute the light, to position and protect the lamps, and to connect the lamps to the power supply.

Lumen: The luminous flux through a unit solid angle of 1 sr from a uniform point source of 1 cd. 1 lumen per square foot = 1 foot candle.

Luminance: The intensity of light leaving a surface in a given direction (author's simplified definition). Units: candelas per square meter or sometimes foot lamberts (used to be deprecated). Units in foot lamberts or cd/m^2 ($3.426 \times \text{fl} = \text{cd/m}^2$).

Lux: 1 lumen per square meter or 1 lux = .1 foot candle.

Mesopic: Or dusk vision: is generally associated with adaptation to luminance between 3.4 candelas and .34 candelas per square meter—combination cone and rod vision.

Myopia: Refractive defect of certain eyes so that, with accommodation of the lens for infinity, parallel rays of light are brought to a focus before they reach the retina.

Perception/reaction: A driver's reaction to any stimulus of a traffic situation or hazard is a four-step process—a process that takes time. That time is now accepted in road sight design as 2.5 seconds. The time required for a response equals the time it takes for the driver to recognize the situation, understand the situation, decide to take action, and take action. Or, put more simply, *detection*, *identification*, *decision*, and *reaction.*

More specifically designed, those four processes are:

1. **Detection** of information, which is based on "visibility," is the visual awareness that an object is present in the roadway. At night it depends entirely on contrast sensitivity.
2. **Identification** is the process of gathering information about the object until enough information is gathered for the driver to make an appropriate decision as to what it is, whether it poses a threat, and whether its existence calls for some responsive action.
3. **Decision**, the next step, involves the driver making a choice as to the appropriate action to take to avoid the object or condition.
4. Finally, we have **reaction**. This occurs when orders are issued by the driver's brain to the appropriate muscle groups in order to initiate the responsive action decided upon.

Photopic: Or day vision: is generally associated with adaptation to luminance at least 3.4 candelas per square meter—essentially cone vision.

Protanopia: Form of dichromatism (colorblindness) in which red and bluish-green are confused, and relative luminosity of red is much lower than for normal observer.

Reflectance: The ratio of the reflected flux to the incident flux. Units: none; expressed as a percentage.

(Author's note: Simply a property of different materials, reflectance refers to the ratio of the amount of light reflected from a material to the amount of light incident on that material.)

Retina: An outgrowth of the brain forming a thin lining at the back of the eyeball containing the light-sensitive rods and cones which are the peripheral end organs of the optic nerve.

Saccadic movements: The sudden movement of the eyes from one fixation point to another.

Scotopic: Or night vision: is generally associated with adaptation to a luminance below 0.034 candelas per square meter—essentially rod vision.

Specular reflection: Reflection in accordance with the laws of optical reflection, as in a mirror.

Transmission: (*T*) is the amount of light, usually expressed in percent, that passes through the lens compared to the light incident upon it.

Transmissivity: (*t*) is the transmission for a unit of thickness of the material. In ophthalmic work the standard thickness is usually 2.0 millimeters, although occasionally a 1.0-millimeter standard thickness is employed.

Appendix C

Example: Civil Twilight Time Line

Gregory L. Vandenberg, Sergeant
Nebraska State Patrol

As part of a class of instruction on night visibility in Lincoln, Nebraska, (40 degrees 48 minutes latitude, 96 degrees 39 minutes longitude) ambient light levels were measured using a Minolta T-1 illuminance meter. Measurements began approximately 7 minutes before sunset, or the beginning of Civil Twilight, and continued until a level of .30 foot candles was achieved—approximately 2 minutes before the end of Civil Twilight (21:32).

Sunset and Civil Twilight times were determined using Zephyr Services SunTimes Plus software. A plot of the sun's position for the day, June 12, 1996, is included (Figure C.1). Sunrise occurred at 05:55 with the sun at an azimuth of 57 degrees 49 minutes (north of east). It set at 20:59, after 15 hours and 4 minutes of daylight, at an azimuth of 302 degrees 13 minutes (north of west). Civil Twilight ended at 21:32, 33 minutes after sunset.

The Civil Twilight Time Line which follows clearly shows how the ambient light from the sun, before, during, and after sunset, falls in a logarithmic fashion from a photopic level of 31.4 foot candles to a mesopic level of .30 foot candles during this time period.

Military Time:	foot candles:
20:52	31.4
20:54	31.0
20:56	30.1
20:58	29.8
21:00	26.4
21:02	22.4
21:04	19.8
21:06	16.7
21:08	15.1
21:10	13.2
21:12	10.5
21:14	8.7
21:16	6.6
21:18	4.5

(continued on next page)

(continued from previous page)

Military Time:	foot candles:
21:20	3.1
21:22	2.1
21:24	1.0
21:26	.62
21:28	.41
21:30	.30

Facts:
Civil Twilight
Lat: 40° 48'
Long: 96° 39'
Lincoln, Nebraska
June 17, 1996

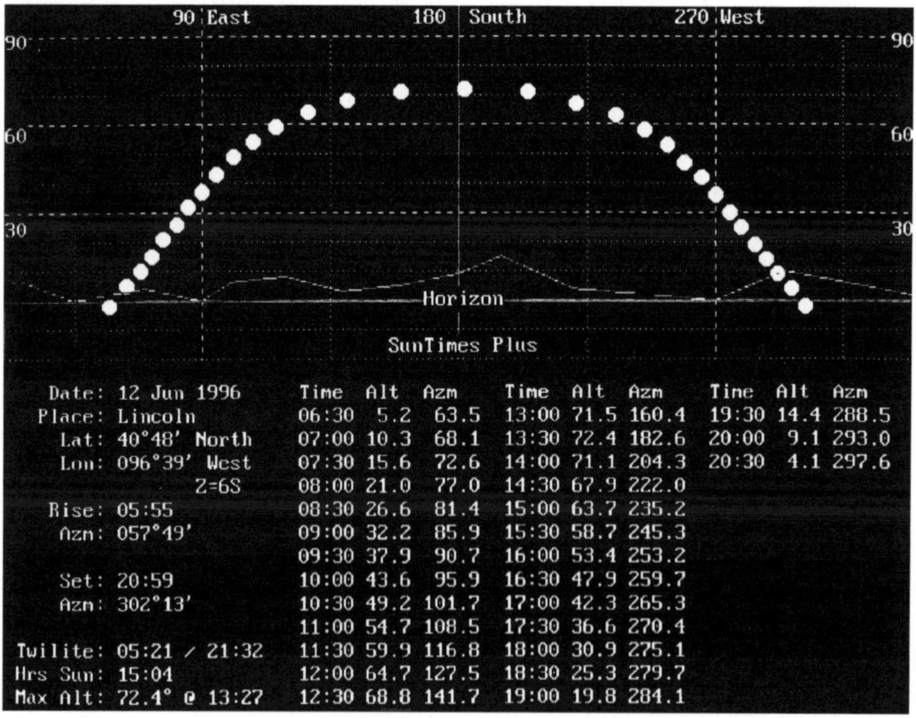

Figure C.1

Appendix D

Recommended Sources

Bernard S. Abrams, O.D.

---

1. *Adler's Physiology of the Eye,* Clinical Application, Seventh Edition, Edited by Moses.
2. *Auto Accident Checklist*, 1995, Jon Abele, Esq, Lawyers and Judges Publishing.
3. *Basic Collision Analysis and Scene Documentation*, 2000, Second Edition, David A. Casteel and Steven D. Moss, Lawyers and Judges Publishing.
4. *Bus and Recreational Vehicle Accident Reconstruction and Litigation*, 2000, Dr. Roy Scitt Hickman and Paul F. Hill, Esq., Lawyers and Judges Publishing.
5. *Defensive Driving Course*, Professional Truck Driver, Driver's Notebook, National Safety Council.
6. *Federal Motor Carrier Safety Regulations*, July, 1990, U.S. Department of Transportation, Federal Highway Administration, American Trucking Association.
7. *Forensic Aspects of Driver Perception and Response*, 1996, Paul Olson, Lawyers and Judges Publishing.
8. *Handbook of Human Factors*, Gavriel Salvendy.
9. *The Human Element—Proceedings,* Volume II, 1990 International Motorcycle Safety Conference.
10. *Human Factors in Engineering and Design*, 6th Edition, Mark S. Sanders, Ernest J. McCormick.
11. *Human Factors in Highway Traffic Safety Research*, Edited by T.W. Forbes, Michigan State University, East Lansing.
12. *IES Lighting Handbook*, 1984 Reference Volume, Illuminating Engineering Society of North America.
13. *IES Lighting Handbook*, 1987 Application Volume, Illuminating Engineering Society of North America.

14. *Low Speed Automobile Accidents: Accident Reconstruction and Occupant Kinematics, Dynamics and Biomechanics*, 1999, Second Edition, Alan J. Watts, Dale R. Atkinson and Corey J. Hennessy, Lawyers and Judges Publishing.

15. *Manual on Uniform Traffic Control Devices*, 1988 Edition for Streets and Highways, U.S. Department of Transportation. Available from Lawyers and Judges Publishing.

16. *Motorcycle Accident Reconstruction and Litigation*, 1997, Second Edition, Kenneth Obenski, P.E., and Paul F. Hill, Esq. Lawyers and Judges Publishing.

17. *The Old Farmer's Almanac*, Annually.

18. *A Policy on Geometric Design of Highway and Streets*, 1990, American Association of State Highway and Transportation Officials.

19. *Pedestrian Accident Reconstruction and Litigation*, 1999, Second Edition, Jerry Eubanks and Paul F. Hill, Esq., Lawyers and Judges Publishing.

20. *Roadway Defects and Tort Liability*, 1996, John C. Glennon, D. Engr., P.E., Lawyers and Judges Publishing.

21. *Roadway Through the MUTCD: Vision and Other Human Factors in the Manual on Uniform Traffic Control Device*s, 1998, Archie C. Burnham, Jr., and Bernard S. Abrams, Lawyers and Judges Publishing.

22. *1996 SAE Ground Vehicle Lighting Manual.*

23. *SAE, CD ROM, Database–2000.*

24. *Taar Safety Engineering*, Accident Investigation Software.

25. *Tractor-Trailer Driver Manual,* A Guide for Professional Drivers, Professional Truck Driver Institute of America, American Trucking Association.

26. *Traffic Accident Investigation and Physical Evidence,* D.R. McGrew, Certified Legal Investigator, National Director, National Association of Legal Investigators.

27. *Traffic Engineering Handbook*, Fourth Edition, Institute of Transportation Engineers.

28. *Train Accident Reconstruction and FELA & Railroad Litigation*, 1998, Third Edition, James Loumiet and William Jungbauer, Lawyers and Judges Publishing.

29. *Transportation in an Aging Society*, Improving Mobility and Safety for Older Persons, Special Report 218, Volume 2, Transportation Research Board, National Research Council.

Appendix E

Cone of Vision

Bernard S. Abrams, O.D.

Area the Eye Sees at Various Distances from the Fovea

Central visual acuity is measured by viewing targets (letters, numbers, etc.) at a fixed distance of 20 feet (or 6 meters). Targets of progressively smaller size are viewed, each of which subtends a smaller and smaller angle on the retina. Larger targets, for example, subtend a large angle and correspond to a visual acuity of 20/400 (or less) while smaller targets which subtend a smaller angle correspond to a visual acuity of 20/20 (or better).

The best visual acuity is obtained in the central fovea area.[1] If portions of the fovea or the macula are damaged, visual acuity will be reduced. Thus the visual acuity when viewing from the foveal area is 20/20. The fall-off in vision is rapid, thus when viewing from 10° from the fovea, visual acuity is 20/100 and falls off rapidly thereafter (refer to Figures 18.9 and 18.10 in Chapter 18). The high density of cones in the fovea accounts for the high degree visual acuity discrimination in this area of the retina. It has been shown that the density of cones in the fovea is approximately 18 times greater than anywhere else in the retina where they reach a density of approximately 1900 cones/mm^2. Within 5 degrees of the fovea there is a rapid fall-off to about 200 cones/mm^2. Rods, which are absent from the fovea, make their first appearance about 5 degrees from the fovea and reach their maximum density approximately 20 degrees from the fovea.

The cones which subserve the functions of sharp and color vision do not adapt to the low light levels of the rods. Indeed, the latter are a 1000 times more light-sensitive than the cones, and during the course of dark adaptation, the final lowest threshold for the eye takes about 25 minutes to achieve and is situated outside the fovea.

Example

Problem: Acute cone of vision at 150 feet

Facts: Foveal acute cone = 3 degrees
Distance = 150 feet
Visual acuity = 20/20
Solve for: area X

Distance:

tan 1° = .01745

tan 3° = 3 × .01745 = .05236

$$\tan = \frac{\text{side opposite}}{\text{side adjacent}}$$

tan 3° = .05236

$$.05326 = \frac{X}{150 \text{ feet}}$$

X = 7.85 feet

Commentary

This is the area that is considered the cone of vision and has the most acute vision.

If an individual has Snellen visual acuity of 20/20, said vision will cover a width of 7.85 feet at a distance of 150 feet.

Example

Problem: Sub-acute cone of vision at 150 feet

Facts: Sub-acute foveal cone of vision = 10°

Distance =	150 feet
Visual acuity at 10° =	20/100
Solve for:	area X

Distance:

tan 1° = .01745
tan 10° = 10 × .01745 = .1745

$$\tan = \frac{\text{side opposite}}{\text{side adjacent}}$$

tan 10° = .1745

$$.1745 = \frac{X}{150 \text{ feet}}$$

X = 26.18 feet

Commentary

When viewing in the sub-acute retinal area or 10 degrees from the fovea, the area is 26.18 feet in width. At the periphery the vision is 20/100. An object to be seen would need to be 5 times larger to be equivalent to that in the cone of vision. The area between 3 degrees to 10 degrees has a visual transformation from 20/20 to 20/100.

End Notes

1. The area varies with researchers; however, the standard conservative is 3 degrees in width.

Appendix F

Dynamic Visual Forensic Displays

Bernard S. Abrams, O.D.

The Art of Presenting Evidence Based on Physiological Optics, Newtonian Physics, and Human Factors

In the presentation of evidence, the usual method is verbal testimony aided by simple diagrams. A useful improvement over the simple diagram is to show the evolving positions of vehicles at short intervals of time throughout the time preceding the accident. This permits a somewhat dynamic visualization of how the accident evolved. In addition to diagrams, photographs are used as well, provided they are taken at the approximate time and conditions of the accident. Starting in the early 1990s, a number of new techniques started to make their appearance. Among them are video tapes and animations. Today, cinema photography has proceeded to a new level of dynamic visual forensic documentation based on real scenes and digitized simulation of objects with audio explanations using 16mm film.

Although video tapes and animation are well known, simulation on 16mm film requires some comment. The idea behind animation is to construct a "moving picture" of a theory of the accident, usually done with the aid of a computer. However, an animation does not necessarily conform to the laws of physics or vision nor does the subject observation seem to be, for lack of better words, "real life." Like the Saturday morning cartoons, an animation can be made to behave in any way that can be imagined regardless of whether the behavior is physically possible. Because the objects in an animation can be made to move in physically impossible ways, the unrestricted use of animation should be avoided in legal proceeding. However, if the documentation is based on real scenes concurrent with actual underlying simulation, then it becomes a useful and justifiable dynamic visual forensic display for courtroom use. Basically, this newer technique using simulation is the outcome of a series of mathematical computations based on the laws of physics, visual science, and human factors. That is, all the known parameters of the accident are used, together with the laws of visual physiology and physics, to contrast in real time—second by second—how the accident evolved. The result of this computation is a series of numbers, but these numbers can be made more visually meaningful by using them as the basis of simulation by digital input. In this type of rendition, the motion of objects conforms rigorously to the laws of geometric optics, Newtonian physics, and science of human factors to show exactly how the accident evolved in real time based on the assumed initial pre-impact conditions of the involved vehicles, objects, humans, and so on.

The idea of using 16mm scenes in combination with simulations is to test different theories of the accident by making each theory the basis for a real time production. Thus, one recreation theory might assume that if certain human factors were true, then each vehicle had a certain velocity and position at some point prior to the accident and that each driver had certain visual and human factor capabilities. By using these assumed velocities and positions, together with the laws of physics, geometric optics and visual physiology, a 16mm combination/simulation would show each vehicle movement, object locations, and visual and human factors. The visual and scientific creation would show, based on the theory being tested, (1) the pre-impact, (2) just where the collision would take place, and (3) where the vehicles would come to rest. These results can then be compared to the actual results of the accident. If there is agreement, then the theory being proposed is supported. Disagreement obviously disqualifies the theory. The strength of this technique, made by a faithful adherence to science, is that it shows *one* physically possible theory of the accident and makes that theory visually apparent. It should be noted that there may be more than one theory of the accident that conforms to the facts. This can occur usually because the physical evidence is incomplete. It should also be noted that not all courts will permit motion forensic displays based on use of this newly evolving technique. Therefore, strict attention to known visual and scientific certainty must be adhered.

With the advent of digital video camcorders, comes the prospect of higher resolution, low light video which may prove to be a cost effective method of producing dynamic visual displays.

Appendix G

Relationship of Visual Angles/Visual Acuity

Bernard S. Abrams, O.D.

Visual Angles/Visual Acuity

An object subtends different visual angles at various distances. This visual angle may then be corrected to an approximate visual acuity level.

The standard equation used in these calculations is:

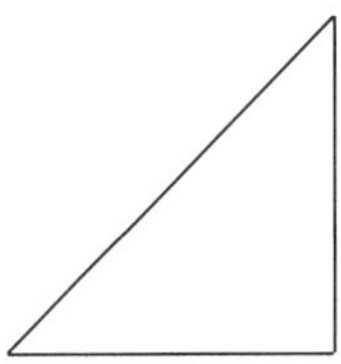

$\tan \theta$ = opposite/adjacent

θ will be in degrees

We change the value in degrees to minutes.

Visual Acuity	Visual Angle (mins of arc) at 20 feet
20/20	5
20/25	6.25
20/30	7.5
20/40	10
20/50	12.5
20/60	15
20/70	17.5
20/80	20
20/100	25
20/150	37.5
20/200	50
20/300	75
20/400	100

(a) The Snellen fraction is:

$$\text{Visual acuity} = \frac{\text{distance at which test is made}}{\text{distance at which the smallest letter read subtends an angle of } 5'}$$

If at 20 feet patient can read a letter "E" of a size .349" (inches), the fraction is recorded as 20/20.*

If at 20 feet patient can read a letter "E" of a size 1.392" (inches), the fraction is recorded as 20/80.**

* "E" subtends 5 minutes of arc at 20 feet.

** "E" subtends 5 minutes of arc at 80 feet (4 times taller letter/4 times the distance).

(See Figure G.1.)

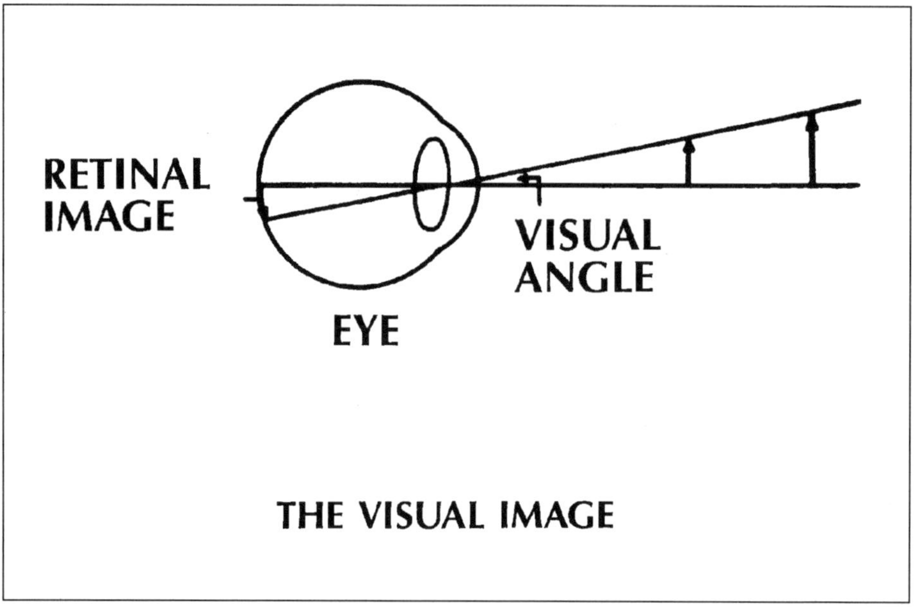

Figure G.1

Bibliography

Merrill J. Allen, O.D., Ph.D.

Abbott Laboratories. "Glaucoma," *What's New* (North Chicago, Ill.), 1962.

Abelson, Philip H. "A Damaging Source of Air Pollution," *Science,* Vol. 158, No. 3808, Dec. 22, 1967.

Abernethy, Roy. "We Care Very Much," *Highway User,* Vol. 30, No. 5, May 1965, 16–17.

"Accident Prevention Spotlighted at Annual SAE Meeting," *Traffic Safety,* March 1968, 16–18ff.

Adams, Anthony J., and John R. Levene. "Stereoscopic Depth Associated with Cyclotorsional Eye Movements," *British Journal of Physiological Optics,* Vol. 24, No. 3, 1967, 217–220.

Adams, James R., and E. Belvin Williams. "Association Between Smoking and Accidents; Overdependency As an Influencing Variable," *Traffic Quarterly,* Vol. 20, No. 4, Oct. 1966, 583–588.

Adams, Leon D. "Stupid Highway Signs Can Kill," *Popular Science,* Vol. 186, No. 5, May 1965, 104–108ff.

Adler, F. H. *Physiology of the Eye,* C. V. Mosby Co., St. Louis, Mo., 1965.

Adrian, Werner. "Principles of Disability and Discomfort Glare," *Proceedings, Symposium on Visibility in the Driving Task*, sponsored by Highway Research Board, Illuminating Engineering Research Institute, and Texas A & M University, May 13–15, 1968, 75–95.

Ady, R. W. "Investigation of the Relationship between Illuminated Advertising Signs and Expressway Accidents," *Traffic Safety Research Review*, Vol. 11, No. 1, 1967, 9–11.

Aerospace Systems Safety Society. *Hazard Prevention*, Vol. 3, No. 3, Dec. 1965.

"Alcohol and Vision Experiment," *Accident Facts,* 1967 (New York State Department of Motor Vehicles), 15.

"Alcohol in Perspective," *Consumer Reports*, Vol. 31, No. 2, Feb. 1967, 97–99.

"Alcohol or CO Found in Half the Driver Dead," *Highway Research Abstracts*, Vol. 36, No. 6, June 1966, 3.

Allen, Merrill J. "Influence of Age on the Speed of Accommodation," *American Journal of Optometry and Archives of American Academy of Optometry,* Vol. 33, 199, 1956.

______. *Study of Visual Performance Using Ophthalmic Filters,* A.S.D. Technical Report 61–576, Wright Patterson Air Force Base, Ohio, Oct. 1961, 29 pp.

______. "How Do You Fit Spectacles?" *Indiana Journal of Optometry*, Vol. 32, No. 2, April 1962, 5–7.

______. "Effective Means of Increasing Highway Illumination and Reducing the Headlight Glare," *Journal of the American Optometric Association*, Vol. 34, No. 3, Oct. 1962, 225–226.

______. "Indiana State Fair Vision Screening Booth," *Indiana Journal of Optometry,* Vol. 32, No. 4, Oct. 1962, 10–11.

______. Certain Visual Aspects of the Average Modern American Automobile," *Journal of the American Optometric Association,* Vol. 34, No, 5, Dec. 1962, 380–383.

______. "On Automobile Auxiliary Side Lights," *Science News Letter*, Jan. 26, 1963.

______. "Daytime Automobile Windshield and Dash Panel Characteristics," *American Journal of Optometry and Archives of American Academy of Optometry,* Vol. 40, No. 2, Feb. 1963, 61–72.

______. "Special Motor Vehicle Auxiliary Lights Designed to Reduce the Effects of Glare and Aid Highway Visibility," *Highway Research News,* No. 5, May 1963, 24.

______. "Darkness at Noon Covering Daytime Automobile Windshield and Dash Panel Characteristics," Human Engineering news item, *Product Engineering*, Vol. 34, No. 16, Aug. 1963.

______. "Glasses for Automobile Driving?" *Optometric Weekly,* Vol. 54, No. 48, Nov. 28, 1963, 2238–2239.

______. "Volkswagen's 'Outlook'," *Small World* (VW of America, Englewood Cliffs, N. J. Vol. 2., No. 4, Fall 1963.

______, and William M. Lyle. "Relationship Between Night Driving Ability and the Amount of Light Needed for a Specific Performance on a Low Contrast Target," *Journal of the American Optometric Association,* Vol. 34, No. 16, Nov. 1963, 1301–1303.

______, and John H. Carter. "Visual Problems Associated with Motor Vehicle Driving at Dusk," *Journal of the American Optometric Association,* Vol. 35, No. 1, Jan. 1964.

______, and John K. Crosley. "Automobile Liquid Glass Tint, A Research Report," *American Journal of Optometry and Archives of American Academy of Optometry,* Vol. 42, No. 6, June 1965, 344–350.

______, and ______. "Automobile Liquid Glass Tint," *Highway Research Abstracts*, Vol. 36, No. 3, March 1966, 6.

______, and ______. "Auxiliary Lighting to Improve Rear Visibility of Trucks and Buses," *American Journal of Optometry and Archives of American Academy of Optometry,* Vol. 44, No. 5, May 1967.

______, and G.R. Courtney. "Photomyoclonic and Photoconvulsive Responses to Flickering Light," *Journal of the American Optometric Association,* Vol. 38, No. 2, Feb. 1967, 111–112.

______, Jerald Strickland, and Anthony J. Adams. "Visibility of Red, Green, Amber, and White Signal Lights in a Highway Scene," *American Journal of Optometry and Archives American Academy of Optometry,* Vol. 44, No. 2, Feb. 1967, 105–109.

______, and Johannes J. Vos. "Ocular Scattered Light and Visual Performance As a Function of Age," *American Journal of Optometry and Archives of American Academy of Optometry,* Vol. 44, No. 11, Nov. 1967, 717–727.

______. "Automobile Running Lights, A Research Report," *American Journal of Optometry and Archives of American Academy of Optometry,* Vol. 41, No. 5, May 1964, 293–315.

______. "Eye Injuries in Automobile Accidents," *Journal of the American Optometric Association,* Vol. 35, No. 7, July 1964, 623.

______. "Automobiles and Yellow Lights," *Journal of the American Optometric Association,* Vol. 35, No. 7, July 1964, 607.

______. "Painted Bulbs in Turn Signals Dangerous," *Journal of the American Optometric Association,* Vol. 35, No. 6, Aug. 1964, 662.

______. "Automobiles and Yellow Lights, Part II," *Journal of the American Optometric Association,* Vol. 35, No. 10, Oct. 1964, 871–872.

______. "Automobile Dash Panel Visibility Impairment Due to Wearing Fit-Over Sunglasses"' *American Journal of Optometry, and Archives of American Academy of Optometry,* Vol. 41, No. 10, Oct. 1964, 595–598.

______. "Vision Screening at Indiana State Fair," *Journal of the American Optometric Association,* Vol. 35. No. 11, Nov. 1964, 974–977.

______. "Misuse of Red Light on Automobiles," *American Journal of Optometry and Archives of American Academy of Optometry* Vol. 41, No 12, Dec. 1964, 695–699.

______. "Running Light Questionnaire," *American Journal of Optometry and Archives of American Academy of Optometry,* Vol. 42, No. 3, March 1965, 164–167.

______. "Visibility Problems Cause Automobile Accidents," *Indiana University Review,* Vol. 7, No. 3, May 1, 1965, 1–6.

______. "Tinted Windshields are a Hazard," *Optometric Weekly*, May 6, 1965, 76–77.

______. "Automobile Visibility Problems," *Journal of the American Optometric Association,* Vol. 36, No. 9, Sept. 1965, 807–810.

______. "Eye Position on the Highway," *Journal of the American Optometric Association,* Vol. 37, No. 5, May 1966, 460.

______. "Automobile Windshields, A New Car Study, 1966 Models," *Optometric Weekly,* Vol, 57, No. 28, July 14, 1966, 14–17.

______. "Vision, Vehicles, and Highway Safety," *Highway Research News,* No. 25, Autumn 1966, 57–62.

______. "How to Avoid Dying with Your Boots On," *Bulletin of the Woman's Auxiliary to the American Optometric Association,* Vol. 21, No. 2, Nov. 1966, 6.

______. "Chromium Headlight Covers, A Possible Hazard," *American Journal of Optometry and Archives of American Academy of Optometry,* Vol. 44, No. 1, Jan. 1967, 34–41.

______. "Visual Environment in the Modern Automobile," Prevention of Highway Injury Symposium, University of Michigan Highway Safety Research Institute, April 1967, 118–121.

______. "Tips for the Older Driver," *Optometric Weekly,* Vol. 58, No. 23, June 8, 1967, 31–32.

______. "Headlight Ring Retroreflectors," *American Journal of Optometry and Archives of American Academy of Optometry,* Vol. 44, No. 12, Dec. 1967, 765–768.

______. "Report on Windshield Tint and Angles," *Physicians for Automobile Safety News Letter* (537 Morris Ave., Springfield, N.J.), April, 1968.

______, Richard, D. Hazlett, "The Ability to See a Pedestrian at Night, the Effects of Clothing, Reflectorization and Driver Intoxication," *American Journal of Optometry and Archives of the American Academy of Optometry*, Vol. 45, No. 4, April 1968, 246–258.

______. Glare and Driver Vision Report," Contract FH–11–6550, *National Highway Safety Bureau,* submitted Spring 1968.

______, "White Tire Treads and Truck Visibility," *Journal of the American Optometric Association*, Vol. 39, No. 9, Sept. 1968, 827.

______, Strickland, J. and Seigel, A., "Daytime Headlights and Position on the Highway," *American Journal of Optometry and the Archives of the American Academy of Optometry*, Vol. 46, No. 1, Jan. 1969, 33–36.

______. "Vision and the Driving Task," *The Canadian Journal of Optometry*, June 1969, Vol. 31, No. 1, 41–50.

______. "Automobile Windshields Surface Deterioration," *American Journal of Optometry and Archives of the American Academy of Optometry*, Vol. 46, 1969, 594–598.

______. "Vision and Driving." *Traffic Safety*, Vol. 69, No. 9,1969, 8–12.

______. "Chrysler Corporation's Super Lite, An Evaluation," *American Journal of Optometry and Archives of American Academy of Optometry*, Nov. 1969.

______. "Disappearing Headlights," *Journal of the American Optometric Association,* Vol. 40, No. 6, June 1969, 601–602.

______. "Automobile Windshields Surface Deterioration," *American Journal of Optometry and Archives of American Academy of Optometry,* Aug. 1969, 594–958.

______, Hazlett, Richard D., Courtney, George R., Stockley, L. A. F., "Motorcycle Helmet Visibility and Retroreflectorization," *American Journal of Optometry and Archives of the American Academy of Optometry*, Vol. 46, No. 9, Sept. 1969, 666–675.

______. "Vision and Driving." *Traffic Safety*, Vol. 69, No. 9 1969, 8–12.

______. "Chrysler Corporation's Super Lite, An Evaluation," *American Journal of Optometry and Archives of American Academy of Optometry*, Nov. 1969.

______, et al. "Visibility Distances of a Pedestrian, With and Without Glare, and the Pedestrian's Estimation of His Own Visibility," *American Journal of Optometry and Archives of American Academy of Optometry,* Dec. 1969.

______. "Automobile Windshield, Surface Deterioration," Society of Automotive Engineers, Mid Year Meeting, Detroit, May 18–22, 1970.

______. *Vision and Highway Safety*, Philadelphia, Chilton Book Co. 1970 (out of print).

______. "Seeing and Safety," *Analogy No. 9*, Published by all State Insurance Co., All State Plaza, Northbrook, Illinois, 60062, 13–17.

______. "Some Popular Misconceptions about Vision and Driving," *Traffic Safety*, Feb. 1972, pp8ff.

______, Miller, Stanley D. and Short, James., "The Effect of Flares and Triangular Distress Signals on Highway Traffic," *American Journal of Optometry and Archives of the American Academy of Optometry*, Vol. 50. No. 4, April, 1973, 305–315.

______. "Windscreen and Dirt Surface Damage Effects," *Australian Research*, Vol. 5, No. 6, Dec. 1974, 7–19.

______. "How to See Better at Night," *Family Safety*, Winter 1976–77. (This article was converted to an interview format by an anonymous author.) National Safety Council.

______. "The Current Status of Automobile Running Lights," *Journal of the American Optometric Association*, Vol. 50, No. 2, Feb. 1979, 179–180.

______. "The current Status of Automobile Running Lights," *Journal of the American Optometric Association*, Vol. 50, No. 9, Sept. 1979, 1023–1027.

______. *Vision of the Older Driver: Implications for Vehicle and Highway Design and for Driver Testing*. Proceedings of the Older Driver Colloquium, Feb. 1985, Edited by James L Malfetti, sponsored by AAA Foundation for Traffic Safety, 1730 M Street, N. W., Suite 401, Washington, D.C. 20036.

______, Whillans, M. G. "Color Defective Drivers and Safety," *Optometry and Vision Science*, Vol. 69, No. 6, June 1992, 463–466.

Allen, Merrill J. & R.W. Lowry, OD, "Successful Reversal of Retinitis Pigmentosa," *The Journal of Orthomolecular Medicine,* Vol. 13, No. 1 First Quarter 1998, 41–44.

Allen, Merrill J., John Jarding, OD, Ralph Zehner, OD., "Macular Degeneration Treatment with Nutrients and Micro Current Electricity." *The Journal of Orthomolecular Medicine, #4,* Fourth Quarter 1998, 211–214.

Allen, T. M. "Visibility of Signs," *Proceedings, Symposium on Visibility in the Driving Task,* sponsored by Highway Research Board, Illuminating Engineering Research Institute, and Texas A & M University, May 13–15, 1968, paper not avail.

______, and A. L. Straub. "Sign Brightness and Legibility," *Highway Research Board Bulletin 127,* 1955, 1–14.

Allgaier, E. "Better Visibility for Civilian Night Driving," *Optometric Weekly*, Vol. 5, 1960, 2570–2573.

______. "Better Vision Makes Better Drivers," *Journal of the American Optometric Association,* Vol. 32, 1960, 217–219.

Alpern, S. E. "Contact Lenses and Automobile Driving," *Journal of the American Optometric Association,* Vol. 32, 1960, 221–223.

American Association for Automotive Medicine. *Pre–Crash Factors in Traffic Safety,* 12th Annual Symposium, Sacramento, Calif., 1968.

American Automobile Association. *Seat Belts for Passenger Cars* (1712 G Street NW, Washington, D.C.), 1963.

______. *Foundation for Traffic Safety, Manual on Pedestrian Safety* (Washington, D.C.), 1964.

______. *Driver Education Equipment* (Washington, D.C.), 1965.

"American Massacre," *American Trial Lawyers,* I, No. 1, Dec. 1964.

American Optometric Association. *Manual on Drivers' Vision Test,* St. Louis, Mo., 1949.

American Trial Lawyers Association. *Stop Murder by Motor,* New York, 1966.

Andreotti, Francesco, "Universal Type of Metal Number Plate in All Countries of the World," *International Police Chronicle,* No. 70, Jan–Feb. 1965, 45–51.

"Antiskid Road Works," *Science News,* Vol. 95, Jan. 4, 1969, 14.

"Are You a Defensive Driver?" *U.S. Navy Medical News Letter,* Vol. 48, No. 7, Oct. 1966, 22.

Armand, Harry "Make the Automobile Safer," *Safety Engineering,* parts 1–15, Jan. 1937 to March 1938.

______. "Criticism and Safer Automobiles," *Safety Engineering,* Feb. 1938.

______. "This Year It's Hudson," *Safety Engineering,* Nov. 1940, 14–16, 34.

Armistead W H. and S. D. Stookey. "Photochromic Silicate Glasses Sensitized by Silver Halides," *Science,* Vol. 144, April 1964, 150–154.

Atkin, Dorothy. "Safety Forum: Running Lights in Daytime?" *Fleet Owner,* Jan. 1965, 138–139.

"Atmospheric Opacity, a Study of Visibility Observations in the British Isles," *Quarterly Journal of Royal Meteorological Society,* Vol. 65, 411–442, 1939.

Automotive Safety Foundation. "Railroad Grade Crossings," *Traffic Control Elements: Their Relationship to Highway Safety/Revised,* Chapter I, Washington, D.C., 1968.

______. "Traffic Volume," *Traffic Control Elements: Their Relationship to Highway Safety/ Revised,* Chapter II, Washington, D.C., 1969.

______. "Illumination," *Traffic Control and Roadway Elements: Their Relationship to Highway Safety/ Revised,* Chapter III, Washington, D.C., 1969.

Aulhorn, E. "Die Blendung aus der Sicht des Ophthalmologen," *Berichte dei Deutschen Ophthalmologischen Gesellschaftin Heidelberg,* Vol. 65, 1963, 454.

______. "Uber die Beziehung zwischen Lichtsinn und Sehscharfe," *Albrecht von Graefe's Archiv fur Ophthalmologie,* Vol. 4, 1964, 167.

______, and H. Harms. "Untersuchungen uber das Wesen des Grenzkontrastes," *Berichte der Deutschen Ophthalmologischen Gesellschaft in Heidelberg,* Vol. 60, 1956, 7.

Automobile Manufacturers Association. *The State of the Art of Traffic Safety,* Part 1, Arthur D. Little, Cambridge, Mass., 1966, 16–31.

______. *1968/ Automobile Facts / Figures,* Detroit, Mich., 1968.

Automotive Medicine Association. "Effect of Drugs on Drivers' Vision Stressed," *Medical Tribune and Medical News,* Vol. 8, No. 119, Dec. 11, 1967, 24.

"Automotive Safety and Engineering Responsibility," *American Engineer,* Oct. 1965, 31–36.

Automotive Safety Research Office. *Data on the Motor Vehicle Transportation System in the United States, A Delineation of the Motor Vehicle Accident Problem,* Engineering Staff, Ford Motor Company (Dearborn, Mich., 48121), Nov. 1968.

"Auxiliary Lights Urged," *Automotive Industries*, Feb. 1, 1963, 26.

Baglien, J. W. "Driving Vision," *Optometric Weekly*, Vol. 51, 1960, 1811–1814.

Bailey, Neal J., and Henry W. Hofstetter. "Effect of Ophthalmic Lens Fluorescence on Visual Acuity," *American Journal of Optometry and Archives of American Academy of Optometry,* Vol. 36, 1959, 634.

Baker, C. A., and W. C. Steedman, "Perceived Movement in Depth As a Function of Luminance and Velocity," *Human Factors,* Vol. 3, No. 3, 1961, 166.

Ball, R. J., and S. Howard Bartley. "Induction and Reduction of Color Deficiency by Manipulation of Temporal Aspects of Photic Input," *American Journal of Optometry and Archives of American Academy of Optometry,* Vol. 44, No. 7, July 1967, 411–418.

Baluyut, Lolita C., and Henry W. Hofstetter, "Statistical Review of 1,000 Vision Certificates," *Journal of the American Optometric Association,* Vol. 35, No, 8, August 1964, 664–668.

Banks, Anderson. "Retinal Responses to Ischemia and Hyperoxia," *North Carolina Medical Journal,* Vol. 26, Oct. 1965, 446–449.

Barach, A. L., Ross A. McFarland, and C. P. Seitz. "Effects of Oxygen Deprivation on Complex Medical Functions," *Journal of Aviation Medicine,* Vol. 8, No. 4, 1937, 197–207.

Barbarik, Paul. "Auto Accidents and Driver Reaction Patterns," *Journal of Applied Psychology,* Vol. 52, No. 1, 1968, 49–54.

Barmack, J. E., et al. "Field Evaluation of the Smith–Cummings–Sherman Driver Performance Rating Scale," *Traffic Safety Research Review,* Vol. 6, No. 2, 1962, 25–30.

______, and D. E. Payne. "Injury–producing Private Motor Vehicle Accidents Among Airmen: Psychological Models of Accident Generating Process," *Traffic Safety Research Review,* Vol. 6, No. 3, 1962, 24–32.

Bartlett, N. R., and S. MacLeod. "Effect of Flash and Field Luminance Upon Human Reaction Time," *Journal of the Optical Society of America,* Vol. 44, No. 4, 1954, 306–311.

Bartley, S. Howard. "What Optometrists Should Know About Fatigue," *Michigan Optometrist,* March 1952.

______, G. Paczewitz, and E. Valsi. "Brightness Enhancement and the Stimulus Cycle," *Journal of Psychology,* Vol. 43, 1957, 187.

Belzer, E. G., and W. J. Huffman. "Quickness of Selected Right–foot and Left–foot Braking Techniques," *Traffic Safety Research Review,* Vol. 10, No. 3, 1966, 72–77.

Berger, C. et al. "Effect of Anoxia on Visual Resolving Power," *American Journal of Psychology,* Vol. 56, July 1943, 395–407.

Bergevin, J., and Michael Millodot. "Glare with Ophthalmic and Corneal Lenses," *American Journal of Optometry and Archives of American Academy of Optometry,* Vol. 44, April 1967, 213–221.

Bewley, Lawrence A. "Spectacle Frames Reduce the Field of Vision: A Driving Hazard," *Journal of the American Optometric Association,* Vol. 40, No, 1, Jan. 1969, 64–69.

Bhatia, B. "Some Factors Determining the Maximum Angular Velocity of Pursuit Ocular Movements," *Journal of the Optical Society of America,* Vol. 50, 1960, 149–150.

Bickford, R. G. "Thresholds for Production of Seizures by Photic Stimulation in Man," *American Journal of Physiology,* Vol. 155, 1948, 427 (abstract).

Birkhoff, A. J., and H. R. Blackwell. "A Visual Evaluation of Illumination in the Roadway

Environment," Proj. HR63–5–2 *National Cooperative Highway Research Program, Institute for Research in Vision and Transport,* Sept. 1966, 1–42.

Birren, Faber. "Safety on the Highway: A Problem of Vision, Visibility, and Color," *American Journal of Ophthalmology,* Vol. 43, No. 2, 1957, 265–270.

Blackwell, H. R. "Effect of Tinted Optical Media upon Visual Efficiency at Low Luminance, *Journal of the Optical Society of America,* Vol. 43, 1953, 815.

______. "Visual Detection at Low Luminance through Optical Filters," *Highway Research Board Bulletin 89*, 1954, 43.

______. "Use of Visual Brightness Discrimination Data in Illuminating Engineering," Commission Internationale de l'Eclairage, 13th Session, Zurich, 1955.

______. "'Visual Capabilities of the Automobile Driver,' Report of the Armed Forces National Research Council Committee on Vision Symposium on the Visual Factors in Automobile Driving," *National Academy of Sciences—National Research Council Publication 574,* Washington, D.C., 1958, 8–9.

______. "Discussion of Paper Entitled 'Practical Application of Polarization and Light Control for Reduction of Reflected Glare,'" by C. L. Crouch and J. E. Kaufman, *Illuminating Engineering,* Vol. 58, 1963, 283–290.

______. "Visibility of Signals," *Proceedings, Symposium on Visibility in the Driving Task,* sponsored by Highway Research Board, Illuminating Engineering Research Institute, and Texas A & M University, May 13–15, 1968, 146–154.

______, and O. M. Blackwell. "Visibility of Objects on Highways," *Proceedings, Symposium on Visibility in the Driving Task,* sponsored by Highway Research Board, Illuminating Engineering Research Institute, and Texas A & M University, May 13–15, 1968, 106–123.

______, and B. S. Pritchard. "New instruments for Field Measurements of Illumination Requirements and Disability Glare," *Proceedings, 3rd Research Symposium of the Illuminating Engineering Research Institute*, New York, 1961, 10.

______, and ______. "Sight Through Fog," *Proceedings, 3rd Research Symposium of the Illuminating Engineering Research Institute,* New York, 1961, 10.

______, ______, and R. N. Schwab. "Illumination Requirements for Roadway Visual Tasks," *Highway Research Board Bulletin 255*, 1960, 117–127.

______, ______, and ______. "Light for Safety on Streets and Roadways," *Proceedings, 3rd Research Symposium of the Illuminating Engineering Research Institute*, New York, 1961, 16.

______, ______, and ______. *Test Data on Visibility and Illumination Variables in Roadway Visual Tasks,* Ohio State University, Institute for Research in Vision and Engineering Experiment Station, Report on Project 47, *Illuminating Engineering Research Institute,* 1963, 50.

______, ______, and ______. "Visibilily and Illumination Variables in Roadway Visual Tasks," *Illuminating Engineering,* Vol. 59, No. 5, Sec. I, May 1964, 277.

______, ______, and ______. "Illumination Variables in Visual Tasks of Drivers," *Public Roads,* Vol. 33, No. 11, 1965, 237–248.

Blanche, Ernest E. "Roadside Distraction," *Traffic Safety*, Vol. 65, No. 11, Nov. 1965, 24–25, 36–37.

Blikra, Georg, and Rolf Ringkjob. "Personskader Ved Trafikkulykker, Behandlet I Ullerval Sykehus 1966" (Personal Injuries Caused by Traffic Accidents, Treated at Ulleval Hospital, 1966), *Report No. 2, UTVALG for Trafikksikker–Netsforskning*, Statsjousveien 4, Oslo, Sentralboro 608280, Slemdal, Aug. 1968.

Boelter and Ryder. "Notes on the Behavior of a Beam of Light in Fog," *Illuminating Engineering,* Vol. 35, 1940.

Boettner, A. E., and J. R. Wolter. *Transmission of the Ocular Media,* Technical Documentary Report No. MRL–TDR–62–34, Wright–Patterson Air Force Base, Ohio May 1962. Also in *Investigative Ophthalmology,* Vol. 1, No. 6, Dec. 1962, 776–783.

Box, Paul C. "Driver Age As Related to Freeway Accidents," *Proceedings, Symposium on Visibility in the Driving Task,* sponsored by Highway Research Board, Illuminating Engineering Research Institute, and Texas A & M University, May 13–15, 1968, 44–55.

Boynton, Robert M., and Frank J. Clarke. "Sources of Entoptic Scatter in the Human Eye," *Journal of the Optical Society of America,* Vol. 54, No. 1, Jan. 1964, 110–119.

Brecher, Gerhard A., A. P. Hartman, and D. D. Leonard. "Effect of Alcohol on Binocular Vision," *American Journal of Ophthalmology,* Vol. 39, No. 2, pt. 2, 1955, 44–52.

Breckenridge, F. C. "United States Standard for the Colors of Signal Lights," *U.S. Department of Commerce,* Washington, D. C., 1964.

Brody, L. "Role of Vision in Motor Vehicle Operation," *International Record of Medicine,* Vol. 167, June 1954, 365–377.

Bombrach, T. A. "Contact Lenses and Visual Fields," *Contacto,* Aug. 1961, 265–277.

Broschmann, D. "To the Question of Driving Ability in Uniocular Mydriasis," *Klinische Monatsblãtter fiir Augenheilkunde,* 1967, 151, 116–119.

Brown, Edward G. *Report of Reflectorization of License Plates,* Joint Committee on Highways, Washington State Legislature, 1964, 1–3.

Brown, R. H. "Analysis of Visual Sensitivity to Differences in Velocity," *U.S. Naval Research Laboratory Report 5478,* 1960, 16 pp.

______. "Weber Ratio for Visual Discrimination of Velocity," *Science,* Vol. 131, 1960, 1809–1810.

Bryan, W. E. "Research in Vision and Traffic Safety," *Journal of the Optometric Association,* Vol. 29, No. 3, Oct. 1957, 169–172.

______. "Lenses for Night Driving," *Highway Research Board Bulletin 336,* Jan. 1962, 104.

______, and Henry W. Hofstetter. "Statistical Summary and Evaluation of the Vision of Automobile Drivers," Journal of the American Optometric Association, Vol. 29, 1958, 513.

Bugelski, B. R. "Traffic Signals and Depth Perception," *Science,* Vol. 157, 1967, 1464.

Bureau of Public Roads. *Federal Role in Highway Safety* (A Report to Congress), 1959.

Burg, Albert. "Visual Acuity As Measured by Dynamic and Static Tests: A Comparative Evaluation," *Journal of Applied Psychology,* Vol. 50, No. 6, 1966, 460–466.

______. "Relationship Between Vision Test Scores and Driving Record: General Findings," University of California Department of Engineering, 1967.

______. "Horizontal Phoria As Related to Age and Sex," *American Journal of Optometry and Archives of American Academy of Optometry,* Vol. 45, No. 6, June 1968, 345–350.

______. "Relation Between Vision Quality and Driving Record," *Proceedings, Symposium on Visibility in the Driving Task,* sponsored by Highway Research Board, Illuminating Engineering Research Institute, and Texas A & M University, May 13–15, 1968, 5–16.

______. *Vision Test Scores and Driving Record: Additional Findings,* Institute of Transportation and Traffic Engineering, California Department of Motor Vehicles, Dec. 1968.

______, and S. F. Hulbert. "Dynamic Visual Acuity and Other Measures of Vision," *Perception and Motor Skills,* Vol. 9, 1959, 334.

______, and ______. "Dynamic Visual Acuity As Related to Age, Sex, and Static Acuity,"

Journal of Applied Psychology, Vol. 45, No. 2, 1961, 111–116.

Byrnes, Vistor A. "Visual Factors in Automobile Driving," *Transactions of the American Ophthalmological Society,* Vol. 60, 1962, 60–79.

______. "Vision and Its Importance in Driving," *Sight–Saving Review*, Vol. 37, No, 2, Summer 1967, 87–90.

Cadle, R. D. *Particle Size Determination*, Interscience Publishers, New York, 1955.

California Department of Motor Vehicles. *Vision Research Project Progress Report*, Research Report No. 2, Oct. 1, 1959.

California Highway Patrol. *Motorcycle Accident Study* (P. O. Box 898, Sacramento, California 95804), Jan. 1968.

Campbell, B. J., and W. S. Rouse. "Reflectorized License Plates and Rear End Collisions at Night," *Traffic Safety Research Review*, Vol. 12, No. 2, June 1968, 40–45.

Campbell, H. E. "Carbon Monoxide, Smoking in Automobiles and Haylofts," *Journal of the American Medical Association,* Vol. 207, No. 5, Feb. 3, 1969, 951.

"Canada Instituting Uniform Traffic Sign, Signal and Marking Program," *Highway Research News,* 42–43.

Chalfont, M. W. "Who the Problem Drivers Are," *Optometric Weekly*, Vol. 52, 1961, 2311–2312.

Chapman, B. G. "Techniques and Variables Related to Driving, Part 1," *Rehab Optometry,* 2(2) 1984, 18–20.

______, B. G. "Techniques and Variables Related to Driving, Part 2," *Rehab Optometry*, 2(3), 1984, 12–18

Chapman, Albert L "Accident Prevention," *Pennsylvania Medical Journal,* Vol. 61, Sept. 1958, 1201–1203.

Chesebrough, Harry E. "Cars in the Future—An Engineer Dreams Ahead." *Highway Research Abstracts,* Vol. 36, No. 6, June 1966, 15.

Chessman, Max R., and William T. Voss. *Motor Vehicle Headlight Beam Usage Study on a Section of Interstate Highway 90 in South Dakota,* South Dakota Department of Highway Research and Planning Division, 1964.

Christie, A. W. "Night Accident Problem and the Effect of Public Lighting," Reprinted from the *Journal of the Association of Public Lighting Engineers, Public Lighting*, Vol. 33, No. 141, June 1968, 98–101.

______, and A. J. Fisher. "Effect of Glare from Street Lighting Lanterns on the Visibility of Objects for Drivers of Different Ages," *Proceedings of the Third Conference of the Australian Road Research Board,* Vol. 3, Part 1, 1966, 570–588.

Cibis, Paul A., and Fritz Haber. *Studies on Effects of Windshields and/or Air of Different Densities on Stereoscopic Vision,* Mathematical Principles concerning Displacement Effects on Bi–dimensional Perception of Direction, Size, and Distance, and Tri–dimensional Perception of Depth, Unnumbered project report No. 1, Department of Ophthalmology, USAF School of Aviation Medicine (Randolph Field), Texas, Nov. 1950.

______, and Max Halperin. *Faulty Depth Perception Caused by Cyclotorsion of the Eyes,* USAF School of Aviation Medicine Project Report, Texas, 1951.

Cobb, Percy W., and Frank K. Moss. "Four Variables of the Visual Threshold," *Journal of the Franklin Institute,* Vol. 205, No. 6, June 1928, 831–847.

______, and ______. "Effect of Dark Surroundings upon Vision," *Journal of the Franklin Institute,* Vol. 206, No. 6, Dec. 1928, 827–840.

Cocke et al. "Chloramphenicol Optic Toxicity," *Journal of Pediatrics*, Vol. 68, Jan. 1966, 27.

Coldwell, B. B. "Highway Investigations (Effects of Alcohol)," *R.C.M.P. Quarterly* (Royal Canadian Mounted Police, Ottawa, Canada), Vol. 31, No. 2, Oct. 1965, 17–24.

Cole, Ben. "Blinking Devices May Cut Traffic Toll," *Indianapolis Star*, Sept. 19, 1965, 1.

Cole, B. L. "Distribution of Intensity for Road Traffic Light Signals," *Australian Road Research,* Vol. 2, 1966, 13–20.

______, Nathan, J. Henry, G. H. and Cole, B. L. "Recognition of Colour and Road Traffic Light Signals by Normal and Colour Defective Observers," *Journal of Optometric Society of America* 54, 1964, 1041–1045 and Preliminary Report in *Australian Road Research,* Vol. 1, 30, 1963.

______, et al. "Transport Lighting," *Australian Road Research,* Vol. 2, No. 6, Dec. 1965, 51–57.

______, and B. Brown. "Intensity of In Service Road Traffic Signal Lights," *Australian Road Research,* Vol. 2, No. 6, Dec. 1965, 58–69.

______, and ______. "Note on the Effectiveness of Surround Screens for Road Traffic Lights," *Australian Road Research*, Vol. 2, 1966, 21–23.

______, and ______. "Preliminary Examination of the Optical Performance of Road Traffic Signal Lights," *Australian Road Research*, Vol. 2, 1966, 24–32.

______, and ______. "Optimum Intensity of Red Road Traffic Signal Lights for Normal and Protanopic Observers," *Journal of the Optical Society of America*, Vol. 56, 1966, 516–522.

______, and ______. "Specification of Road Traffic Signal Light Intensity," *Human Factors,* Vol. 10, 1968, 245–254.

______, and Brown B. "An Analysis of Sun Phantom in Road Traffic Signal Lights," *Australian Road Research*, 3, 1969, 35–49.

______, and Brown B. "Effect of Visual Noise on the Visibility of Road Traffic Signal Lights," *Australian Road Research*, 4, 1969, 35–49.

______. "The Colour Blind Driver," *Australian Journal of Optometry*, 53, 1970, 261–269.

______. Visual Standards for Drivers of Motor Vehicles," *Australian Journal of Optometry*, 55, 1972, 135–142.

______. "Visual Aspects of Road Engineering," *Proceedings of 6th Conference of Australian Road Research Board* 6(1), 1972, 10148.

______, Fisher, A. J. "Photometric Requirements of Traffic Signal Lanterns," *Proceedings of 7th Conference of Australian Research Board* 7(5), 1974, 246–265.

______, Anderton, P. J., Johnson A. W. "The Effect of Letter Spacing on The Legibility of Direction and Information Signs," *Australian Road Research*, 5, 1974, 100–102.

______, Jacobs, R. J., Johnston, A. W. "The Visibility of Alphabetic and Symbolic Traffic Signs," *Australian Road Research*, 1975, 68–86.

______, Johnson, A. W. "The Effect of Blurred Vision on the Contrast Sensitivity Function," P–75–31, Compte Rendu Commission Internationale de l'Echanage 18th Session, London CIE Publication No. 36, Paris.

______, Johnson, A. W. "Investigation of Distraction by Irrelevant Information," *Australian Road Research*, 6, 3–23.

______, Jacobs, R. J. "A Comparison of Alternative Symbolic Warning Signs for Railway Level Crossings," *Australian Road Research*, 11, 1981, 37–45.

______, Jacobs, R. J. "A Resolution Limited Model for the Prediction of Information Retrieval from Extended Alphanumeric Messages," Proceedings 9th Conference of the Australian Road Research Board 9(5), 1978, 383–389.

______, Jacobs, R. J. "Acquisition of Information from Alphanumeric Road Signs," Proceedings of the 9th Conference of the Australian Road Research Board 9(5), 390–395.

______, Jacobs, R. J. "Searching Vertical Stack Direction Signs," Proceedings of the 9th Conference of the Australian Road Research Board, 9(5), 1978, 396–400.

______, Jenkins, S. E. "Conspicuity of Traffic Control Devices," *Australian Road Research*, 12, 1982, 223–238.

______, Jenkins, S. E. "The Nature and Measurement of Conspicuity," Proceedings of the Conference of the Australian Road Research Board 10(4), 1980, 99–107.

______, Jacobs, R. A. "A Comparison of Alternative Symbolic Warning Signs for Railway Level Crossings," Australian Road Research Board, 1981 11, 37–45.

______, Jenkins, S. E. "The Effect of the Density of Background Elements on the Conspicuity of Objects," *Vision Research*, 22, 1241–1252.

______,Vingrys, A. J. "A Survey and Evaluation of Lantern Tests of Color Vision," *American Journal of Optometry and Psychological Optics*, 59, 1982, 346–374.

______, Anderton, P. J. "Contour Separation and Sign Legibility," *Australian Road Research*, 12, 1982, 103–109.

______, Vingrys, A. J. "Validation of the Holmes Wright Lantern," *Ophthalmologist Physical Optics*, 3, 1982, 137–152.

______, Steward, J. M. and Pettet, J. L. "Visual Difficulty driving at Night," *Australian Journal of Optometry*, 66, 1983, 20–24.

______, Vingrys, A. J. "Who Fails Lantern Tests," *Documentary Ophthalmology*, 55,1983, 157–173.

______, Vingrys, A. J. "Do Protonormals Have Difficulty Seeing Red Lights" Compte Rendu Commision Internationale de l'Eclairage 20th Session, Paris, CIE Publication No. E04, 1983, 1–3.

______, Hughes, P. K. "Search and Attention Conspicuity of Road Traffic Control Devices." *Australian Road Research*, 14, 1984, 1–9.

______, Jenkins, S. E. "The Effect of Variability of Bad Background Elements on the Conspicuity of Objects," *Vision Research*, 24, 1984, 262–270.

______, Jenkins, S. E. "Daytime Conspicuity of Road Traffic Control Devices," *Transportation Research Record*, 1093, 74–80.

______, Hughes, P. K. "A Field Trial of Attention and Search Conspicuity." *Human Factors,* 1984 26(3), 299–313.

______, Hughes, P. K. "What Attracts Attention When Driving," *Ergonomics*, 29, 1986, 377–391.

______, Hughes, P. K. "Can the Conspicuity of Objects be Predicted from Laboratory Experiments?" *Ergonomics*, 29, 1986, 1097–1111.

______, Vingrys, A. J. "Origins of Colour Vision Standards Within the Transport Industry," *Ophthalmological Physical Optics*, 6, 1986,369–374.

______, Vingrys, A. J. "Are Colour Vision Standards Justified for the Transport Industry?" *Ophthalmological Physical Optics*, 8, 257–274.

______, Hughes, P. K. "The Effect of Additional Demand on Eye Movement Behavior When Driving," In: Gale, A. G. , Freeman, M. H., Haselgrave, C. M., Smith, P and Taylor, S. P. (eds.), *Vision in Vehicles II, Proceedings of 2nd International Conference on Vision in Vehicles*, Elsevier Publishers, Amsterdam 221–230.

______, Steward, S. M. "What Do Colour Vision Detectives Say About Everyday Tasks?" *Optometry and Vision Science*, 66, 1989, 288–295.

______, Hughes, P. K. "Drivers Don't Search; They Just Notice," Brogan, 'DVisual Search Proceedings 1st international Conference on Visual Search University of Durham, September 1988, Taylor and Francis, London, 407–417.

______. "Does Defective Colour Vision Really Matter?" In: Drum, B. (ed). *Colour Vision Deficiencies*, XI, Kluwer, Dordrecht, 1992, 67–86.

______, Vingrys, A. J. "The Ability of Colour Vision Detective Observers to Recognize an Optimized Set of Red, Green, and White Signal Lights," In: Drum, B. (ed). *Colour Vision Deficiencies*, XI Kluwer, Dordrecht, 1992. 87–95.

______, Steward, J. M. "Some (But Only a Few) Colour Vision Defectives Have No Difficulty with Colour," In Dickinson, C. M., Murray, I. J. and Carden, D. (eds.) *John Dalton's Color Vision Legacy*, 1996. Taylor and Francis, London (in Press).

______, Maddocks, J. D., "Revision of the CIE Recommendations for the Colours of Signal Lights," In Dickinson, C. M., Murray, I. J., and Carden, D. (eds.) *John Dalton's Color Vision Legacy*, Taylor and Francis, Lond (in Press).

______, Maddocks, J. D. "Defective Colour Vision Is a Risk Factor In Driving," In Cavonius, C. R. (ED) *Colour Vision Deficiencies*, XIII (submitted).

Collins, William E. "Vestibular Responses from Figure Skaters," *Aerospace Medicine,* Office of Aviation Medicine, Civil Aeromedical Institute, Federal Aviation Agency (Oklahoma City, Okla. 73101), Nov. 1966, 1098–1104.

Colorado State Department of Highways. "Colorado's Reflective Bead Study," Planning and Research Division (4201 Arkansas Ave., Denver, Col. 80222), Nov. 1968.

"Colored Pavements," *Traffic Safety*, March 1968, 26.

Colson, W. "Effect of Alcohol on Vision," *Journal of the American Medical Association,* Vol. 115, Nov. 2, 1940, 1525–1526.

Conners, M. M., and J. A. S. Kinney. "Relative Red–Green Sensitivity As a Function of Retinal Position," *Journal of the Optical Society of America,* Vol. 52, 1962, 81–84.

Connolly, Paul L. "Vision and Headlight Glare," *Michigan Optometrist,* Vol. 16, No. 5, May 1947.

______. "Recent Developments in Automotive Lighting," Monograph 305, *American Journal of Optometry and Archives of American Academy of Optometry, Aug. 1962, 415.*

______. "In the Vehicle and on the Road," Society of Automotive Engineers publication SP 253, March 1964.

______. "About Cars and Vision," *Industrial Design*, Part 1, Vol. 11, No. 1, Jan. 1964, 38; Part II, Vol. 12, No. 5, May 1965, 66.

______. "Automobiles, Vision and Driving," *Optometric Weekly*, Vol. 56, No. 48, Dec. 1965, 26–28; Vol. 57, No. 2, Jan. 1966, 36–38.

______. "Visual Considerations: Man, the Vehicle, and the Highway," *Police,* July–August, 1966.

______. "An Optometrist Analyzes Safe Driver Vision," *Autoproducts* (Cummins Publishing Co., Oak Park, Mich.), Vol. 4, No. 8, Aug. 1966.

______. "Vision, Man, Vehicle and Highway," reprinted from *Prevention of Highway Injury,* Proceedings from Symposium, University of Michigan Highway Safety Research Institute, 1967.

______. "Human and Visual Factors Considerations for the Design of Automotive Peroscopic Systems," Society of Automotive Engineers Mid Year Meeting, Detroit, May 20–24, 1968.

______, and Ingeborg Schmidt. *Visual Considerations of Man,* the Vehicle and the Highway, SP–279, 1966.

______, W. A. Devlin, Jr., and Konrad H. Marcus. "Design Aspects for Rear Vision in Motor Vehicles," SP–253 presented at SAE Automobile Meeting, Detroit, March 1964.

______, ______, and ______. "A Look to the Rear with an Eye to Safety, *SAE Journal*, Vol. 73, No. 7, July 1965, 30–41.

Coppin, R. S., et al. "Effectiveness of Short Individual Driver Improvement Sessions, *Highway Research Abstracts,* Vol. 36, No. 6, June 1966, 3.

Cornell Aeronautical laboratory. "ACIR Evaluates Safety of New Windshield," *Transportation Research Review* (Buffalo, N.Y.), Third/Fourth Quarter 1968.

"Countdown Traffic Light Ticks off Seconds," *Popular Science,* June 1966, 131.

"Country Driving Dangers Outlined," *AMA News,* March 21, 1966, 3.

Crancer, A., et al. "Comparison of the Effects of Marihuana and Alcohol on Simulated Driving Performance,"' *Science,* Vol. 164, No. 3881, May 16, 1969, 851–854.

Crandell, Frank J. Packaging the Passenger, Liberty Mutual Insurance Company (Boston, Mass.).

Crawford, W. A., "Perception of Moving Objects: II. Eye Movements," RAF Flying Personnel Research Commission, Farnborough, England. Memo 150b, July, 1960.

Cresswell, W. L., and P. Froggatt. "Causation of Bus Driver Accidents," published by Oxford University Press for Nuffield Provincial Hospitals Trust, London, 1963, 101–102.

Crinigan, R. P. "Survey of Motorists' Vision Requirements," *Traffic Safety Research Review,* Vol. 4, No. 3, 1960, 29–32, and *Journal of the American Optometric Association,* Vol. 32. 1960, 209–210.

Crosley, John, and Merrill J. Allen. "Automobile Brake Light Effectiveness: An Evaluation of High Placement and Accelerator Switching," *American Journal of Optometry and the Archives of the American Academy of Optometry,* Vol. 43, No. 5, May 1966, 299–304.

Cross, Millar, and Simpson. "Vital Importance of Fixed Lighting on Public Roads," *Illuminating Engineering,* Vol. 41, 1946.

Cumming, R. W. "Analysis of Skills in Driving," *Australian Road Research,* Vol. 1, No. 9, March 1964, 4–14.

Damon, A., and Ross A. MacFarland. "Physique of Bus and Truck Drivers: With a Review of Occupational Anthropology," *American Journal of Physical Anthropology,* Vol. 13, No. 4, Dec. 1955, 711–742.

Danielson, R. W. "Relationship of Fields of Vision to Safety in Driving," *American Journal of Ophthalmology,* Vol. 44, No. 5, Part I, Nov. 1957, 657–680.

Darrell, J. E. P., and M. D. Bunnette. "Driver Performance Related to Interchange Marking and Nighttime Visibility Conditions," *Highway Research Board Bulletin* 137, 1960, 128–137.

Davey, J. B. "Road Safety: Some Visual Aspects," *Optician*, Vol. 139, 1960, 436–438.

______.Vision and Eye Movements of Auto Drivers," *Optician*, Vol. 140, 1961, 676.

______. Visual Task of Road Users, *Optician*, Vol. 141, 1962, 669–673.

______."Reflections at the Motor Show," *Ophthalmic Optician*, Nov. 28, 1964, 1205–1214.

______."Incidence and Causes of Blindness in England and Wales, 1948–1962," *Ophthalmic Optician*, April 2, 1966, 325–327.

______."Night Driving, Two Important Papers," *Ophthalmic Optician,* Vol. 7, No. 2, Jan. 1967, 73–79.

David, J. H., and Larry Lett. "Study of the Effect of Using Colored Guide Posts in Interstate Highways to Reduce Accidental Damage," *Alabama State Highway Department* (Montgomery, Ala. 36104), HPR Report No. 33, Aug. 1968, 22 pp.

Davis, Adelle. *Let's Get Well,* Harcourt, Brace, & World, New York, 1965.

Dawson. Report of Department of Transportation Act: H.R. 1701, Washington, D. C., House of Representatives of Eighty Ninth Congress, Second Session, 1966.

Dawson, Noel K. "Too Dangerous to Drive," *Popular Mechanics,* Vol. 127, No. 1, Jan. 1967, 99–101, 212.

DeMott, D. W., and R. M. Boynton. "Retinal Distribution of Entoptic Stray Light," *Journal of the Optical Society of America,* Vol. 48, 1958, 13.

Department of Scientific and Industrial Research. *Research on Road Safety,* Her Majesty's Stationery Office, London, 1963.

______. *Dipped Headlights Campaigns in 1963–64,* Road Research Technical Paper No. 73, Her Majesty's Stationery Office, London, 1964.

______. *Use of Headlamps*, Working Party on the Lighting of Motor Vehicles, Report to the Minister of Transport, Her Majesty's Stationery Office, London, 1967.

"Designing the 100 MPH Expressway," *Highway Research News,* No. 34, Winter 1969, 48–52.

"Doctors Prescribe for Highway Safety," *Traffic Safety*, Vol. 65, No. 11, Nov. 1965, 16.

Domey, Richard G. "Flicker Fusion, Dark Adaptation and Age As Predictors of Night Vision," *Highway Research Board Bulletin 336*, Jan. 1962, 22–25.

______."Predictors of Night Vision," *Proceedings, Symposium on Visibility in the Driving Task,* sponsored by Highway Research Board, Illuminating Engineering Research Institute, and Texas A & M University, May 13–15, 1968, 69–74.

______, and Ross A. McFarland. "Dark Adaptation As a Function of Age: Individual Prediction," *American Journal of Ophthalmology,* Vol. 51, No. 6, 1961, 1262–1268.

______, and ______. "Operator and Vehicle Design," *Human Factors in Technology,* E. M. Bennett, J. Degan, and J. Spiegel (eds.), McGraw Hill, New York, 1963.

______, ______, and Ernest Chadwick. "Threshold and Rate of Dark Adaptation As Functions of Age and Time," *Human Factors,* Vol. 2, No. 3, 1960, 109–119.

______, ______, and ______. "Dark Adaptation As a Function of Age, II," *Journal of Gerontology,* Vol. 15, No. 3, July 1960, 267–279.

Drinking Drivers at Fault in One Half of Auto Deaths, *Highway Research Abstracts,* Vol. 36, No. 11, Nov. 1966, 14.

"Driver Behavior," *Proceedings of the Second Annual Traffic Safety Research Symposium of the Automobile Insurance Industry,* Insurance Institute for Highway Safety (Suite 711, Watergate Office Bldg., 2600 Virginia Ave. NW, Washington, D.C., 20037).

"Drivers' Medical Screening Urged," *AMA News,* March 21, 1966, 1.

"Drivers' Vision and Car Design," Optician, May 3, 1963, 445.

Dureman, Ingmar, et al. "A Dose Response Study of Diazepam (Valium) and 4306 CB (Tranxilen) During Prolonged Simulated Car Driving," Department of Psychology, University of Uppsala, Sweden, Report 54, Sept. 1968.

Eastman, A. A., S. K. Guth, and G. A. Brecher. "Instrument with Variable Beam Splitter for Measuring Contrast Sensitivity," *Investigative Ophthalmology*, Vol. 2, Feb. 1963, 37–46.

"Effect of Glare on Drivers' Vision," *Ophthalmic Optician,* April 2, 1966, 363.

Elliott, F. R., and C. M. Louttit. "Auto Braking Reaction Time to Visual vs. Auditory Warning Signals," *Proceedings of the Indiana Academy of Sciences,* Vol. 47, 1937, 220–225.

Elstad, J. O., J. T. Fitzpatrick, and H. L. Woltman. "Requisite Luminance Characteristics for Reflective Signs," *Highway Research Board Bulletin 336*, Jan. 1962, 51–60.

Eneke, Kurt, "Possibilities for Improving Safety within the Driver, Vehicle, Environment Control Loop," Seventh International Technical Conference on Experimental Safety Vehicles, Paris,

France, NHTSA, U.S. Department of Transportation, June, 1979.

Engelking, E. "Die Tritanomalie, ein bisher unbekannter Typus Anomaler Trichromasie," *Albrecht von Graefe's Archiv für Ophthalmologie,* Vol. 116, 1925, 196.

"Environment: Visual Effects of the Atmosphere," *Visual Factors in Automobile Driving,* Stanley S. Ballard, and Henry A. Knoll (eds.), Highway Research Board of the National Academy of Sciences–National Academy of Engineering, Washington, D.C., 1958, 6.

Ercoles, A. M. "On the Recovery of Sensitivity Subsequent to Either White or Yellow Glare," *Atti Fond Ronchi,* Vol. 15, 1960, 164–271.

Evans, J. N., and Ross A. McFarland. "Effects of Oxygen Deprivation on the Central Visual Field," *American Journal of Ophthalmology,* Vol. 21, No. 9, 1938, 968–980.

Ezell, Walter K., Court Case Reveals Lighting Problem (A report of bicycle accident lawsuit with Merrill J. Allen appearing As an expert witness) American Wheelman, Vol. 15, No. 12, Dec. 1979, 8–9.

Factors Influencing Safety at Highway Rail Grade Crossings, National Cooperative Highway Research Program Report 50, National Research Council, National Academy of Sciences, National Academy of Engineering, Alan M. Voorhees & Associates, McLean, Va., 1968.

Faulkner, C. R., and S. J. Older. "Effects of Different Systems of Vehicle Lighting on a Driver's Ability to See Dark Objects in Well Lit Streets," *Road Research Laboratory, Ministry of Transport* Report LR113, Crowthorne, 1967.

Federal Government of Canada, Brief on Traffic Accident Deaths and Injuries in Canada, Ottawa, 1965.

"Federal Specifications and Standards: Standard Safety Devices for Automotive Vehicles," *Federal Register,* Vol. 30, No. 125, June 1965, 8319.

Feinbloom, W. "Recent Developments in Bioptic Aids for Driving," in Proceedings of the National Conference on Telescopic Devices and Driving, June 1976, 11–12 Arlington Heights, Ill., American Association for Automotive Medicine, Feinbloom, W. Driving with Bioptic Telescopic Spectacles, *American Journal of Optometric Physiological Optics* 54(1), 1977, 348–349.

Feldhaus, J. L., Jr. "Dynamic Visual Acuity Effect on Night Driving and Highway Accidents," *Highway Research Board Bulletin 298*, Washington, D.C., 1961.

Feinbloom, W. Recent "Developments in Bioptic Aids for Driving," *Proceedings of the National Conference on Telescopic Devices and Driving* 1976, June 11–12, Arlington Heights, Illinois, American Association for Automotive Medicine.

_____, "Driving with Bioptic Telescopic Spectacles," *American Journal of Optometric Physiological Optics* 54(1)1977, 35–42.

Ferguson, H. H. "Road Accidents: Pedestrians' Beliefs Regarding Visibility at Night," *Journal of Applied Psychology*, Vol. 28, 1944, 109–116.

______, and W. R. Geddes. "A Dangerous Pedestrian Belief," *Road Accidents,* Psychological Laboratory, University of Otago, New Zealand (the experiment described was carried out in July 1939), 199–205.

Filderman, Irving P. "Clinical Procedure for Adapting the Telecon Lens," *Journal of the American Optometric Association,* Vol. 30, No. 8, March 1959, 561–562.

Finch, D. M., "Factors Influencing Night Visibility of Roadway Obstacles," *Illuminating Engineering,* Vol. 51, 1956.

______. "Roadway Delineation with Curb Marker Lights," *Highway Research Board Bulletin 336,* 1962, 105–109.

Fine, Jerome L. "Development of a Criterion for Driver Behavior," *Highway Research Abstracts,* Vol. 36, No. 6, June 1966, 4.

Fisher, A. J. "Photometric Specification for Vehicular Traffic Signal Lanterns, Part I," Institute of Highway and Traffic Research, University of New South Wales, Kensington, Australia, Feb, 1969.

______, and Christie, A. W. "Note on Disability Glare," *Vision Research,* Vol. 5, 1965, 565–571.

______, and A. B. Crouch. "Measurement of Coloured Lights of High Luminance Using a Spectra Pritchard Photometer," *Australian Road Research,* Vol. 3, No. 7, 1968, 21–24.

Fisher, R. L., "Accident and Operating Experience at Interchanges," *Highway Research Bulletin 291,* 126.

"Fitness to Drive Motor Vehicles," *Optician,* Vol. 136, 1960, 666–668.

Fitzpatrick, J. T. "Uniform Reflective Sign, Pavement and Delineation Treatments for Night Traffic Guidance," *Highway Research Board Bulletin 255*, 1960, 138–145.

Flom, Merton C. "Prognosis in Strabismus," *American Journal of Optometry and Archives of the American Academy of Optometry,* Vol. 35, No. 10, 1958, 509–514.

Fonda, G., A "Bioptic Telescopic Spectacle: Advantages and Limitations." *Sight Saving Review* 48(3) 1978, 125–128.

_____, G., "Bioptic Telescopic Spectacle is a Hazard for Operating a Motor Vehicle," *Archives of Ophthalmology* 101, 1983, 1907–1908.

_____, G. "Legal Blindness Can be Compatible with Safe Driving," *Ophthalmology* 96(10) 1989, 1457–1459.

"Fog Surrounding the Fog Problem Being Swept Away by N.J.'s Unique Nylon Broom," *Highway Research News,* 5.

Foldvary, L. A. "Effect of Compulsory Safety Helmets on Motorcycle Accident Fatalities," *Australian Road Research,* Vol. 2, Sept. 1964, 9.

______. "Analysis of Age and Experience of Responsible and Non Responsible Drivers Involved in Motorcycle vs. Other Motor Vehicle Collisions in Victoria, 1961 and 1962," *Australian Road Research,* Vol. 2, No. 3, March 1965, 48.

Forbes, T. W. "Psychological Applications to the New Field of Traffic Engineering," *Journal of Applied Psychology*, Vol. 25, No. 1, Feb. 1941, 52–58.

______."Driver Characteristics and Highway Operation," *Traffic Engineering*, Nov. 1953.

______."Some Factors Affecting Driver Efficiency at Night," *Highway Research Board Bulletin 255*, 1960, 66.

______. "Driver Behavior Requirements and Discovering Deficiencies," *Optometric Weekly*, Vol. 51, 1960, 2556–2558.

______."Human Factors in Highway Design, Operation and Safety Problems," *Human Factors,* Vol. 2, Feb., 1960, 1–3.

______. "Study of Accident Hazard in Relation to Fenders and Mudguards for Motor Vehicles," *Traffic Safety Research Review*, Vol. 6, No. 1, 1962, 16–19.

______. "Predicting Attention–Gaining Characteristics of Highway Traffic Signs: Measurement Technique," *Human Factors,* Aug. 1964, 371–374.

______."Traffic Engineers and Driver Behavior," *Traffic Safety Research Review*, Vol. 9, No. 3, Sept. 1965, 87–89.

______, K. Moscowitz, and G. Morgan. "A Comparison of Lower Case and Capital Letters for Highway Signs," *Proceedings of the Thirteenth Annual Meeting of the Highway Research*

Board, 1950, 355–377.

______, and M. S. Katz. "Summary of Hunian Engineering Research Data and Principles Related to Highway Design and Traffic Engineering Problems," *American Institute for Research,* Pittsburgh, April 1957.

______, et al. "Measurement of Driver Reactions to Tunnel Condition," *Highway Research Board Proceedings,* Vol. 37, 1958, 345–357.

______, E. Gervais, and T. Allen. "Effectiveness of Symbols for Lane Control Signals," Michigan State University, Highway Traffic Safety Center and Michigan State Highway Department, East Lansing, Dec. 1958.

______, T. E. Snyder, and R. F. Pain. *A Study of Traffic Sign Requirements—An Annotated Bibliography,* East Lansing, Mich., 1964.

______, ______, and ______. "Traffic Sign Requirements," *Highway Research Board Bulletin 70,* 1963 and 1964, ten reports.

______, et al. "Low Contrast and Standard Visual Acuity under Mesopic and Photopic Illumination," Highway Traffic Safety Center and Department of Psychology, Michigan State University (East Lansing), Dec. 1967.

______, et al. "Letter and Sign Contrast, Brightness, and Size Effects on Visibility," *Highway Research Board Bulletin 216*, 1968, 48–54.

______, et al. "Color and Brightness Factors in Simulated and Full Scale Traffic Sign Visibility," *Highway Research Board Bulletin* 2J6, 1968, 55–65.

Ford, Richard, and Alfred L. Mosley. "Motor Vehicle Suicides," *Highway Research Abstracts,* Vol. 33, No. 6, June 1963, 14.

Ford, Henry, II. "Henry Ford II Talks About Car Safety," *Popular Science*, Vol. 187, No. 6, Dec. 1965, 62–65.

Forney, Robert B. "Combined Effect of Ethanol and Other Drugs," *Prevention of Highway Injury,* Selzer, Gikas, and Huelke (eds.), Highway Safety Research Institute, University of Michigan (Ann Arbor), 1967, 70.

Fortuin, G. J. *Visual Power and Visibility* (Rijks–Universteit of Groningen, The Netherlands, Doctoral Dissertation, 1951.

Fosberry, R. A. C., and R. L. Moore. "Vision From the Driver's Seat," reprint of paper to JIDITVA Conference on Technical Inspection of Motor Vehicles, Brussels, by Motor Industry Research Association, England, 1963.

Fox, Phyllis, and Frederick Lehman. *Computer Simulation of Single Lane Automobile Traffic,* Newark, 1965.

Fry, Glenn A. "Reevaluation of the Scattering Theory of Glare," *Illuminating Engineering,* Vol. 49, 1954, 98.

______. "Relation of the Configuration of a Brightness Contrast Border to Its Visibility," *Journal of the Optical Society of America,* Vol. 37, 1947, 166.

______. "Assessment of Visual Performances," *Illuminating Engineering*, Vol. 57, No. 6, 1962.

______. "Transient Adaptation of the Eyes of a Motorist," *Highway Research Board Bulletin 366,* 1962, 110.

______. "Visual Performance Under Varying States of Adaptation," *Proceedings, Symposium on Visibility in the Driving Task,* sponsored by Highway Research Board, Illuminating Engineering Research Institute, and Texas A & M University, May 13–15, 1968, 96–105.

______, and P. W. Cobb. "Visual Discrimination of Two Parallel Bright Bars in a Dark Field," *American Journal of Psychology,* Vol. 49, 1937, 265.

______, B. S. Pritchard, and H. R. Blackwell. "Design and Calibration of a Disability Glare Lens," *Illuminating Engineering,* Vol. 58, 120–123, 1963.

Gallaway, Bob M. "Skid Resistance and Polishing Type Aggregates," *Texas Transportation Researcher,* Vol. 5, No. 1, Jan. 1969, 3–7.

Garrett, John W. *Ocular Orbital Injuries in Automobile Crashes,* Bulletin No. 4, Automobile Crash Injury Research, Cornell Aeronautical Laboratory, March 1963.

Gasson, A. P., and G. S. Peters. "Effect of Concentration Upon the Apparent Size of the Visual Field in Binocular Vision" (student research project under direction of Prof. J. B. Davey, London), *Optician,* Jan. 1, and 8, 1965.

Gerathewohl, S. J. "Conspicuity of Steady and Flashing Light Signals: Variation of Contrast," *Journal of the Optical Society of America,* Vol. 43, No. 7, July 1953, 567–571.

Gibson, J. J. "Motion Picture Testing and Research," U.S. Army Air Force Aviation Psychology Program, Research Report No. 7, 1946, 62.

Gibson, Jack R. "Visibility: A Bibliography" (2,100 references), Library of Congress Technical Information Division, Washington, D.C., 1952.

Gioia, Anthony J., and Clarence Morphew. "Evaluation of Driver Vision," Proceedings of General Motors Corp. Automotive Safety Seminar, July 11–12, 1968, Paper No. 10. General Motors Proving Ground (Milford, Mich. 48042), 14 pp.

"Glass in New Car Reacts to Light," *New York Times,* Nov. 28, 1965.

"GM Experiments with New Road Vehicle Communications System Dubbed 'Dair'," *Highway Research News,* No. 24, Summer 1966, 33–35.

Goldberg, L. "Quantitative Studies on Alcohol Tolerance in Man," *Acta Physiologica Scandinavica,* Vol. 5, 1943.

______."Alcohol Induced Nystagmus," *Alcohol and Road Traffic*, Proceedings of 3rd International Conference, B.M.A. House, London, 1963.

Goldsmith, John R., and Stephen A. Landaw. "Carbon Monoxide and Human Health," *Science*, Vol. 162, No. 3860, Dec. 20, 1968, 1352–1359.

Goldstein, A. G. "Linear Acceleration and Apparent Distance," *Perceptual and Motor Skills,* Vol. 9, 1959, 267–269.

Goldstein, Leon G. *Research on Human Variables in Safe Motor Vehicle Operation: A Correlational Summary of Predictor Variables and Criterion Measures,* George Washington University, Washington, D.C., 1961.

______. *Human Variables in Traffic Accidents,* National Academy of Sciences, National Research Council, Washington, D.C., 1962.

Gonseth, A. T. "Effectiveness of Holland Tunnel Transitional Lighting During the Winter Months," *Highway Research Board Bulletin 255*, 1960, 79–91.

Goodwin, H., et al. "Investigation of the Effects of Ethyl Alcohol on Visual Functions," paper presented before the American Academy of Optometry, Denver, Dec. 1966.

Gordon, Donald A. *Experimental Isolation of the Driver's Visual Input,* U.S. Department of Commerce, Bureau of Public Roads, Washington, D.C.

______. "Static and Dynamic Visual Fields in Human Space Perception," *Journal of the Optical Society of America*, Vol. 55, No. 10, Oct. 1965.

Gramberg, Danielson B. "Ursachen des Pulfrich Phenomenon and seine Bedeutung im Strassenverkehr," *Klinische Monatsblätter für Augenheilkunde,* Vol. 142, 1963, 738.

______, "Das Sehen im Strassenverkehr," *Klinisch Monatsblätter für Augenheilkunde,* Vol. 143, 1964.

Greenshields, B. D. and F. N. Platt. "Driver Behavior Study," Aug. 1961, quoting *Traffic Engineering* by Matson, Smith, and Hurd, McGraw Hill, 1955.

______, and ______. "Driver Behavior Study," University of Michigan Transportation Institute, Aug. 1961.

______, and ______. "Objective Measurements of Driver Behavior," Paper 809A presented at SAE Automotive Engineering Congress, Detroit, Jan. 1964.

Grey, Michel. "Road User and the Improvement of Vehicle Registration Plates, *International Police Chronicle,* No. 70, Jan.–Feb. 1965, 8–20.

Grime, G. Crompton Lanchester Lecture: *Automobile Lighting and Visibility, Institution of Mechanical Engineers,* England, 1960.

______. "Car Design and Operation in Relation to Road Safety," *Practitioner*, Vol. 188, April 1962, 447–456.

______, and R. D. Lister. *Inspection of Vehicles for Road Worthiness with Special Reference to Methods and Equipment,* Road Research Laboratory, Harmondsworth, Middlesex, Eng., 1957.

Grindley, G. C. "Notes on the Perception of Movement in Relation to the Problem of Landing an Aeroplane," WAM–100–15, FPRC 426, March 1942.

Guerry, Du Pont. "Ophthalmological Aspects of Driver Licensing and Repeat Offenses," *Journal of the American Medical Association,* Jan. 26, 1957, 227–228.

Guth, Sherman L. "The Effect of Wavelength on Visual Perception Latency," *Vision Research,* Vol. 4, Dec. 1964, 567–578.

Guth, Sylvester K. "Effects of Age on Visibility," *American Journal of Optometry and Archives of American Academy of Optometry,* Vol. 34, No. 9, 1957, 463–477.

______. "Method for the Evaluation of Discomfort Glare," *Illumination Engineering,* Vol. 58, No. 5, May 1963, 351–364.

______, and Arthur A. Eastman. "Brightness Difference in Seeing," *American Journal of Optometry and Archives of American Academy of Optometry,* Monograph No. 169, Nov. 1954.

Haber, Heinz. "Safety Hazard of Tinted Automobile Windshields at Night," *Journal of the Optical Society of America,* Vol. 45, No. 6, June 1955, 413–419.

Haddon, William Jr. "Changing Approach to the Epidemiology, Prevention, and Amelioration of Trauma: The Transition to Approaches Etiologically Rather Than Descriptively Based," Presented at the 95th Annual Meeting of the American Public Health Association, program on Epidemiology of Traffic Accidents, Miami Beach, Fla., Oct. 26, 1967.

______, Edward A. Suchman, and David Klien *Accident Research,* Harper and Row, New York, 1964.

______, et al. "Controlled Investigation of the Characteristics of Adult Pedestrians Fatally Injured by Motor Vehicles in Manhattan," *Journal of Chronic Diseases,* Vol. 14, 1961, 655–678.

Haight, Frank A. "Traffic Death and Suicide: A Statistical Study," Institute of Transportation and Traffic Engineering, University of California (Berkeley), Special Report, 1965, 38 pp.

Halperin, Meyer H., et al. "Time Course of the Effects of Carbon Monoxide on Visual Thresholds," *Journal of Physiology,* Vol. 146, No. 3, 1959, 583–593.

Hare, Charles T., and Robert H. Hemion. *Headlight Beam Usage on U.S. Highways,* Project No. 11–1908, Final Report on Phase III of a Study for the Bureau of Public Roads, Federal Highway Administration, U.S. Department of Transportation under U.S. Contract No. 11–4126, Southwest Research Institute, San Antonio, Tex., Dec. 2, 1968.

Harrington, T. L., and K. Johnson McRae. "Improved Instrument for Measurement of Pavement Marking Reflective Performance," *Highway Research Board Bulletin 336,* 1962, 111–113.

Harris, A. J. *Vehicle Headlighting: Visibility and Glare,* Department of Scientific and Industrial Research, London, 1954.

Hartmann, E. "Disability Glare and Discomfort Glare," in Eric Ingelstam, ed., *Lighting Problems in Highway Traffic,* Macmillan Co., New York, 1963, 95–109.

______. "Die Blendung aus der Sicht des Physikers," *Berichte der Deutschen Ophthalmologischen Gesellschaft in Heidelberg,* Vol. 65, 1963, 446.

______. "Threshold of Disability Glare," *Highway Research Abstracts,* Vol. 34, No. 7, July 1964, 12.

Harvard School of Public Health. "Human Factors in Highway Transport Safety" (description of research reports), 1955 (4).

Havens, James H. and Allie C. Peed, Jr. "Spherical Lens Optics Applied to Retrodirective Reflection," *Highway Research Board Bulletin 56,* 1952, 66–77.

Head, J., *et al. Pedestrian Traffic Accidents Involving Children in the City of Vancouver, Canada,* University of British Columbia, Vancouver, 1963.

Heath, Gordon G. "Luminosity Curves of Normal and Dichromatic Observers," Science, Vol. 128, 1958, 775.

______, and Ingeborg Schmidt. "Signal Color Recognition by Color Defective Observers," *American Journal of Optometry and Archives of American Academy of Optometry,* Vol. 36, No. 8, Aug. 1959, 421–437.

Heath, Warren M., and Dan M. Fitch. "Determination of Windshield Levels Requisite for Driving Visibility," *Highway Research Board Bulletin 56,* 1952, 1–16.

Hecht, S., and C. G. Muller. "Visibility of Lines and Squares at High Brightness," *Journal of the Optical Society of America,* Vol. 37, 1947, 500.

Hecht, S., and E. U. Mintz. "Visibility of Single Lines at Various Illuminations and the Retinal Basis of Visual Resolution," *Journal of General Physiology,* Vol. 22, 1939, 593.

Heinsen, Arthur C., Jr. *Reflectorized License Plates: Their Advantages,* San Jose, Calif., 1965.

Hemion, Roger H. "Glare Factor on Two Lane Highways," *Proceedings, Symposium on Visibility in the Driving Task,* Sponsored by Highway Research Board, Illuminating Engineering Research Institute, and Texas A & M University, May 13–15, 1968, 145–146.

______."Effect of Headlight Glare on Vehicle Control and Detection of Highway Vision Targets," Project No. 11–1908, Southwest Research Institute, San Antonio, Tex.

Henderson, Harold L. and Angelo Dispenzieri. *Automobility: Adding a New Dimension Total Physical Rehabilitation,* Drivers Safety Service, New York, N.Y., 1964.

Herbert, Evan. "Traffic Safety," *International Science and Technology* (205 E. 42nd St., New York, N.Y.), Sept. 1966.

Herman, R., et al. "Traffic Dynamics: Analysis of Stability in Car Following," *Operations Research,* Vol. 6, No. 2, March, April 1958, Vol. 7, No. 1, Jan., Feb. 1959.

______, and K. Gardels. "Vehicular Traffic Flow," *Scientific American,* Vol. 209, No. 6, Dec. 1963.

Herrington, C. G. "Design of Reflectorized Motor Vehicle License Plates," *Highway Research Board Proceedings,* Vol. 39, 1960, 441–466.

Hess, E. H., and J. M. Polt. "Pupil Size As Related to Interest Value of Visual Stimuli," *Science,* Vol. 132, 1960, 349–350.

Hicks, Clifford B. and Merrill J. Allen. "Are You an Invisible Driver?" *Popular Mechanics,* Vol.

122, No. 5, Nov. 1964, 114–117.

Highway Research Board. *Bibliography Night Visibility, Selected References,* National Academy of Sciences, National Academy of Engineering, No. 45, 1967.

______. *Proceedings, Symposium on Visibility in the Driving Task,* sponsored by Highway Research Board, Illuminating Engineering Research Institute, and Texas A and M University, May 13–15, 1968.

______. *Highway Research Record No. 216, Lighting, Visibility, and Driving, 6 Reports,* National Academy of Sciences, National Academy of Engineering, 1968.

Highway Safety, Design and Operations: Roadside Hazards, Hearings before the Special Subcommittee on the Federal Aid Highway Program of the Committee on Public Works, House of Representatives, Ninetieth Congress, U.S. Government Printing Office, Washington, 1968.

Hildebrand, G. and H. Wakeland. *Feasibility Study,* N*ew York State Safety Car Program Final Report,* Fairchild Hiller, Republic Aviation Division, Farmingdale, L.I., N.Y., 1966.

Hill, N. E. G. "Recognition of Colored Light Signals Which Are Near the Limit of Visibility," *Proceedings, Physical Society* (London), Vol. 59, 1947, 560–574.

Hirsch, Monroe, and Ralph E. Wick. *Vision of the Aging Patient,* Chilton Co., Philadelphia, 1960, xviii and 328.

Hockenbeamer, E. F. "Side Vision Versus Speed," Claims and Safety Department, Pacific Gas and Electric Co., San Francisco, Calif., 1952.

Hofer, Rudolph, Jr. "Glare Screen for Divided Highways," *Highway Research Board Bulletin 336,* Jan. 1962, 95–101.

Hoffman, Errol R., and Peter N. Joubert. "Effect of Changes in Some Vehicle Handling Variables on Driver Steering Performance," *Human Factors*, Vol. 8, No. 3, June 1966, 245–263.

Hofstetter, Henry W. "Illumination for Sight Testing," *Illuminating Engineering,* Vol. 46, No. 3, March 1951, 116–118.

______. *Industrial Vision,* Chilton Co., Philadelphia, 1956.

______. "Visual Performance Following Optometric Correction," *Optica International,* Vol. 3, No. 2, June 1966, 46–51.

______. "Computed Distances of Legibility of Standard Traffic Control Signs," *Journal of the American Optometric Association,* Vol. 38, No. 5, May 1967, 381–385.

______. "Alpascope, An Instrument Review," *Journal of the American Optometric Association,* Vol. 39, No. 1, Jan. 1968.

______, and Lowell B. Zerbe. "Prevalence of 20/20 with Best, Previous, and No Lens Correction," *Journal of the American Optometric Association,* Vol. 29, No. 12, July 1958, 772–774.

______, and W. M. Lyle. "Modification of the Bio Photometer for Alterocular Fixation Control," *Highway Research Board Bulletin 336, Night Visibility,* 1962, National Academy of Sciences, National Research Council publication 1018; also in *American Journal of Optometry and Archives of American Academy of Optometry,* Vol. 40, No. 1, Jan. 1963, 35–40.

______, and R. Reading. "Extra Horopteral Steropsis in Vehicle Operator Orientation," *Highway Research News,* No. 17, Feb. 1965, 84–90.

Holladay, L. L. "Fundamentals of Glare and Visibility," *Journal of the Optical Society of America,* Vol. 12, 1926, 271.

Hon, Conrad C., Jr. "Headlight Glare Solved by Rearward Directed Fender Mounted Side Light," personal correspondence to Senator Abraham A. Ribicoff from 521 Old Bridge Road, Northport, L.I., N.Y., Nov. 1955.

Honegger, Von H. and W. D. Schafer. "Sehscharfe für bewegte Objekte Einige Gesichtspunkte für die Verkehrmedizin, *Zentralblatt," für Verkehrs–Medizin, Verkehrs Psychologie, Luft– und Raumfahrt–Medizin,* Vol. 14, No. 1968, 160–167.

Hopkin, V. D. "A Selective Review of Peripheral Vision," *Great Britain Flying Personnel Research Commission,* Vol. 1128, 1959.

Hopkinson, R. G., and R. C. Bradley. "Study of Glare from Very Large Sources," *Illuminating Engineering,* Vol. 55, 1960, 288–294.

Hoppe, Donald A., and A. R. Lauer. "Factors Affecting the Perception of Relative Motion and Distance Between Vehicles at Night," *Studies in Night Visibility,* Highway Research Board, Washington, D.C., 1951, 11–16.

Houghton, H. G. "On the Relation Between Visibility and the Constitution of Clouds and Fog," *Journal of Aeronautical Sciences*, Vol. 6, 1939, 408–411.

______, and W. H. Radford. On the Measurement of Drop size and Liquid Water Content in Fogs and Clouds," *Papers in Physiological Oceanography and Meteorology* (Cambridge, Mass.), Vol. 6, No. 4, 1938.

______, and W. R. Chalker. "Scattering Cross Section of Water Drops in Air for Visible Light," *Journal of the Optical Society of America,* Vol. 39, No. II, Nov. 1949, 955–957.

Howard, J. and D. M. Finch. "Visual Characteristics of Flashing Roadway Hazard Warning Devices," *Highway Research Board Bulletin 255,* 1960, 146–157.

Howell, W. C., and G. E. Briggs. "Effects of Visual Noise and Locus of Perturbation on Tracking Performance," *Journal of Experimental Psychology,* Vol. 58, 1959, 166–173, from *Aerospace Medicine*, Vol. 331, 1960, A8.

Huber, Mattew J. "Traffic Operations and Driver Performance As Related to Various Conditions of Nighttime Visibility," *Highway Research Board Bulletin 336*, 1962, 37–50.

Hulbert, Slade F. "Signing a Freeway to Freeway Interchange (Guide Signs)," Institute of Transportation and Traffic Engineering, University of California (Los Angeles), Sept. 1965, 1–19.

______, *et al.* "Preliminary Study of Dynamic Visual Acuity and its Effect in Motorists' Vision," *Journal of the American Optometric Association*, Vol. 29, 1958, 359–364.

______, and Albert Burg. "Effects of Underlining on the Readability of Highway Destination Signs," *Highway Research Board Proceedings*, Vol. 36, 1957, 561–574.

______, and Jinx Beers. "Wrong Way Driving Off Ramp Studies," Institute of Transportation and Traffic Engineering, University of California (Los Angeles), Dec. 1966, 1–16.

Hutchinson, John. "Planning for Highway Safety," *Research Review,* Vol. 9, No. 3, Sept. 1965, 83–86.

Hyde, W. Lewis, "Periscopes for Rear Vision," Paper No. 680403, Society of Automotive Engineers Mid Year Meeting, Detroit, May 20–24, 1968.

IES Lighting Handbook, Fifth Edition, Illuminating Engineering Society, 345 E. 47th St. New York, N. Y. 1992, Chapter 7.

"Illumination," *Traffic Control and Roadway Elements* Report of the Automotive Safety Foundation and the U.S. Bureau of Public Roads), 1963, 77–79.

Indiana State Police. *Indiana State Police Auto Crash Injury Research,* 3d ed., Indianapolis, Ind., 1957.

Industrial Medical Association. *Medical Aspects of Driver Licensing*, 1964.

Ingelstam, Erik, ed., *Lighting Problems in Highway Traffic,* Pergamon Press, London, 1963.

Institute for Perception. *Studies in Perception,* dedicated to M. A. Bouman, RVO TNO, National

Defense Research Organization, TNO, Soesterberg, The Netherlands, 1966.

Institute of Traffic Engineers. "Freeway Operations," Report of Freeway Operations Seminars.

Insurance Institute for Highway Safety. "Driver Behavior," Proceedings Second Annual Traffic Safety Research Symposium of the Automobile Insurance Industry (Suite 711, Watergate Office Bldg., 2600 Virginia Ave. NW, Washington, D.C. 20037), March 1968.

International Federation of Pedestrians. *Voice of the Pedestrian*, April 1968.

International Organization for Standardization. "Driver's Daylight Goggles, Draft Proposal," Institute Für Medizin Optik, Universitat München (Barbara Strasse, 16).

Irland, M. J. and V. L. Lindberg. "Control of Double Images in Automobile Glass," Paper No. 650536, Society of Automotive Engineers Mid Year Meeting, Chicago, May 1965.

Irvin, Robert. "Will Cars Ever Be Safer?" *Louisville Courier Journal Supplement,* March 6, 1966.

Jayle, Gaëtan E., et al. *Night Vision,* Charles C. Thomas, Springfield, Ill., Vol. 14, 1959.

Jellinek, E. M., and Ross A. McFarland. "Analysis of Psychological Experiments on the Effects of Alcohol," *Quarterly Journal of Studies on Alcohol*, Vol. 1, No. 2, 1940, 272–371.

Johansson, Gunnar, F. Backlund, and S. S. Bergstrom. *Studies in Motion Thresholds*, Psychological Laboratory, University of Uppsala, Sweden, Reports 1 and 2, Nov. 1957.

______, and F. Backlund. *An Eye Movement Recorder,* Psychological Laboratory, University of Uppsala, Sweden, Report 8, 1960.

______, et al. *Visible Distances During Night Driving,* Psychological Laboratory, University of Uppsala, Sweden, Report 9, Aug. 1961.

______, *Perception of Motion and Changing Form*, Psychological Laboratory, University of Uppsala, Sweden, Report 10 Oct. 163.

______, et al. *Drivers and Road Signs I,* Psychological Laboratory, University of Uppsala, Sweden, Report 11, Nov. 1963.

______, and Chris Ottander *Light Adaptation and Glare,* Psychological Laboratory, University of Uppsala, Sweden, Report 12, Nov. 1963.

______, and Kare Rumar. *Available Braking Distances in Night Driving,* Psychological Laboratory, University of Uppsala, Sweden, Report 13, Nov. 1963.

______, and ______. Silhouette *Effects in Night Driving,* Psychological Laboratory, University of Uppsala, Sweden, Report 19, Nov. 1964.

______, and ______. *Drivers' Brake Reaction Times,* Psychological Laboratory, University of Uppsala, Sweden, Report 26, March 1965.

______, and ______."Drivers and Road Signs: A Preliminary Investigation of the Capacity of Car Drivers to Get Information from Road Signs," *Ergonomics*, Vol. 9 , No. 1, 1966, 57.

______, and ______. "Visible Distances and Safe Approach Speeds for Night Driving," *Ergonomics,* Vol. 11, No. 3, 1968, 275–282.

______, and Frederik Backlund. *Drivers and Road Signs II,* Psychological Laboratory, University of Uppsala, Sweden, Report 50, April 1968.

Jost, F. "Tabakrauchen und Strassenverkehr" (Tobacco Smoking and Street Traffic), *Medizinische Welt,* No. 1, Jan. 1965, 30–35.

Judd, Deane B. "Facts of Color–Blindness," *J.O.S.A.*, Vol. 33, No. 6, June 1943, 294–307.

Karmeier, D. F., C. G. Herrington, and J. E. Baerwald. "Comprehensive Analysis of Motor Vehicle License Plates," *Highway Research Board Proceedings,* Vol. 39, 1960, 416–440.

Kearney, Paul W. *Drivers' Eye Tests: A Nation Wide Farce,* American Optometric Association, St. Louis, Mo., 1959.

______, *Highway Homicide,* Thomas Y. Crowell Co., New York, 1966.

Kerrick, J. C. "A Discussion of Current Driver Licensing Practices," *Journal of the American Optometric Association,* Vol. 32, 1960, 224–236.

King, J. N. "Measurement of Driver Visibility," *Optician*, Vol. 139, 1960, 110–112.

King, Lee Ellis, and Ernest C. Curwen. *Visibility of Colored Lights in Dense Fog,* delivered before 45th Annual Meeting, Highway Research Board, Washington, D.C., Jan. 1966.

______, and D. M. Finch. "Daytime Running Lights," *Highway Research Record 275*, 1969.

Kinney, J. A. S., E. J. Sweeny and A. P. Ryan. "A New Night Vision Sensitivity Test," *A.F. Medical Journal,* Vol. 11, 1960, 1020–1029.

______, and M. M. Connors. "Recovery of Foveal Dark Adaptation," *Highway Research Record* 70, 1965, 35.

Kite, C. R., and J. N. King. "Survey of the Factors Limiting the Visual Fields of Motor Vehicle Drivers in Relation to Minimum Visual Field and Visibility.

Standards," *British Journal of Physiological Optics,* Vol. 18, April 1961, 85–107.

Klein, Terry M., Burgess, Marilouise, "Alcohol Involvement in Fatal Traffic Crashes 1944," U. S, Department of Transportation, NHTSA Technical Report, DOT HS 808 343, Jan. 1996.

Knoll, H. A. "A Brief History of 'Nocturnal Myopia' and Related Phenomena," *American Journal of Optometry and Archives of American Academy of Optometry,* Vol. 29, No. 2, 1952, 69–81.

______, "Effect of Low Levels of Luminance and Freedom from Optical Stimulation of Accommodation Upon the Refractive State of the Eye," Armed Forces NRC Vision Committee, Minutes of 31st Meeting, Nov. 20–22, 1952.

Konig, A., and C. Dieterici. "Die Grundempfindungen in Normalen und Anomalen Farbensystemen und Ihre Intensitatsverteilung im Spectrum," *Zeitschrift für Psychologie,* Vol. 4, 1893, 241.

Korb, D. Preparing the Visually Handicapped Person for Motor Vehicle Operation. American Journal of Optometrist Physiological Optics 47(8) 1970, 619–628.

Kries, J. V. "Ueber Farbensysteme," *Zeitschrift für Psychologie*, Vol. 13, 1897, 239, 268, 315.

Kuziomko, Louise M., and Basil Y. Scott. "Upgrading Driver Licensing Vision Reexamination," *Traffic Digest and Review* (1804 Hinman Ave., Evanston, Ill., 60204), Vol. 16, No. 8, Aug. 1968, 14–19.

Lauer, A. R. "History and Development of the Driving Research Laboratory," *Optometric Weekly,* March 20, 1947.

______."What Visual Acuity Is Needed for Night Driving?" *Optometric Weekly,* Vol. 41, 1950, 485–488.

______."Certain Factors Influencing the Tolerance of Light and Visual Acuity," study carried out in the Engineering Experiment Station at Iowa State College, project of Committee on Motorists' Vision of the American Optometric Association.

______. *Psychology of Driving, Factors of Traffic Enforcement,* Charles C Thomas, Springfield, Ill., 1960, xxvii and 324. ______, and H. Kotvis. "Automotive Manipulation in Relation to Vision," *Journal of Applied Psychology,* Vol. 18, 1934, 422–431.

______, and Edwin H. Silver. "Survey of Research on Night Driving in Relation to Vision," a study made by the Engineering Experiment Station at Iowa State College in cooperation with the American Optometric Association.

Lavender, H. Jerry, Jr., and Raymond M. Ekstrom. "Red–Green Paradox," *Human Factors,* Vol. 10, No. 1, 1968, 63–66.

Lebensohn, James E. "Vision and Traffic Safety," *Sight–Saving Review*, Vol. 28, No. 3, 1958.

Lee, C. E. "Driver Eye Height and Related Highway Design Features," *Highway Research Board Proceedings,* Vol. 39, 1960, 46–60.

Lehmann, Konstantin. "Research into Causes of Road Accidents (Motorcycles and Automobiles)," *Australian Road Research,* Vol. 1, No. 4, Dec. 1962, 46–47. Leipper Dale F. *Fog Bibliography*, Scripps Institute of Oceanography, Fog Project Report No. 1, 1947.

Levine, Harry. *Automobile Driving: The Not So Simple Act,* Fall River, Mass., 1966.

Leygue, F., P. Duflot, and F. Hoffmann. "Investigation into the Influence on Accidents of the Age of the Driver, His Driving Experience, and the Age and Power of the Vehicle," *Highway Research Abstracts,* Vol. 36, No. 10, Oct. 1966, 3.

Lippman, Otto. "Eye Screening," *Archives of Ophthalmology,* Vol. 68, Nov. 1962, 692–706.

_____, Corn, A. L. and Lewis, M. C. "Bioptic Telescope Spectacles and Driving Performance: a study" in *Texas, Journal of Visual Impairment—Blind* 82, 1988, 182–187.

Lisper, Hans Olaf, et al. "Effects of Prolonged Driving upon a Subsidiary Serial Reaction Time," Department of Psychology, University of Uppsala, Sweden, Report 52, May 1968.

Lister, R. D., and R. N. Kemp. "Skid Prevention," *Automobile Engineer,* Vol. 48, No. 10 Oct. 1958, 382–391.

______, and Barbara M. Melsom. *Car Seat Belts: An Analysis of the Injuries Sustained by Car Occupants,* Road Research Laboratory, Department of Scientific and Industrial Research, Middlesex, England, 6–11.

Lit, Alfred. "Depth Discrimination Thresholds for Targets with Equal Retinal Illuminance Oscillating in a Frontal Plane," *American Journal of Optometry and Archives of American Academy of Optometry*, Vol. 43, No. 5, May 1966, 283–298.

______, William O. Sawyer, and Anthony J. Morandi. "Effect of Background Wavelengths on Stereoscopic Acuity at Scotopic and Photopic Illumination Levels," *American Journal of Optometry and Archives of American Academy of Optometry*, Vol. 45, No. 3, March 1968, 195–203.

Logan, H. L., and E. Berger. "Measurement of Visual Information Cues," *Illuminating Engineering,* Vol. 55, 1960, 507–508.

Luckiesh, M. "On 'Retiring' and 'Advancing' Colors," *American Journal of Psychology,* Vol.29, 1918, 186–192.

______. "Blue Light Undesirable for Blackouts," *Illuminating Engineering,* Vol. 37, No. 2, Feb. 1942, 113–114.

______. "Visual Acuity and Visual Tasks," *Illuminating Engineering,* Vol. 39, No. 7, July 1944, 429.

______, and Frank K. Moss. *The Science of Seeing,* D. Van Nostrand Co., New York, 1937.

______, and ______. "Contrast Sensitivity As a Criterion of Visual Efficiency at Low Brightness Levels," *American Journal of Ophthalmology,* Vol. 22, 1939, 274.

______, and ______. "New Method of Subjective Refraction Involving Identical Techniques in Static and in Dynamic Tests," *Archives of Ophthalmology*, Vol. 23, May 1940, 941–956.

______, and ______. "Characteristics of Sensitometric Refraction," *Archives of Ophthalmology*, Vol. 25, April 1941, 576–581.

______, and ______. "A New Method of Subjective Refraction at the Near–Point," *American Journal of Optometry and Archives of American Academy of Optometry,* Vol. 18, No. 6, June 1941, 249–257.

______, and ______. "Ability to See Low Contrasts at Night," *Journal of Aeronautical Sciences,* Vol. 9, No. 7, May 1942, 261.

______, and ______. "Comparison of a New Sensitometric Method with Usual Technique of Refraction," *Archives of Ophthalmology,* Vol. 30, Oct. 1943, 489–493.

______, and A. H. Taylor. "Visual Acuity at Low Brightness Levels," *American Journal of Ophthalmology,* Vol. 27, No. 1, Jan. 1944, 53–57.

______, and S. K. Guth. "Sensitometric Method of Refraction, Theory and Practice," *American Journal of Optometry and Archives of American Academy of Optometry,* No. 75, Sept. 1949.

Ludlam, William M. "Orthoptics Treatment of Strabismus," *American Journal of Optometry and Archives of American Academy of Optometry,* Vol. 38, 1961, 369–388.

Ludvigh, Elek. "Visual Acuity While One Is Viewing a Moving Object," *Archives of Ophthalmology,* Vol. 42, 1949, 14–22.

Ludvigh, E., and J. M. Miller. "Study of Visual Acuity During the Ocular Pursuit of Moving Test Objects," *Journal of the Optical Society of America,* Vol. 48, 1958, 799.

Lyle, W. M., and Henry W. Hofstetter. "Modification of the Bio–Photometer for Alterocular Fixation Control," *Highway Research Board Bulletin 336,* 336 1962 , 33–36.

Manheimer, Dean I, Glen D. Mellinger, and Helen M. Crossley. "Follow–up Study of Seat Belt Usage," *Research Review,* Vol. 10, No. 1, March 1966, 2–13.

"Man–made Highway Hazards That Kill," *Popular Science,* Vol. 186, No. 5, May 1965, 104–108ff.

Marcus, Konrad H. "Periscopic Rear Vision in Automobiles," Society of Automotive Engineers, Mid Year Meeting, Detroit, May 20–24, 1968.

Marsh, B. W. "Aging and Driving," *Traffic Engineering,* Nov. 1960.

Marsh, Charles R. "Highway Visibility in Fog," *Illuminating Engineering,* Vol. 52, 1957.

______. "Are Taillights Safe?" *Small World,* VW of America, Spring 1967, 20–22.

Masters, Dexter. "Our Chrome Plated Caskets," *Washington Post Book Week,* Jan. 23, 1966, 1–10.

Mayer, Albert J., and Thomas F. Hoult. *Motor Vehicle Inspection,* Wayne State University Public Relations Office, 1963.

McColcin, F. H. "Movement Thresholds in Peripheral Vision," *Journal of the Optical Society of America,* Vol. 50, 1960, 774.

McFarland, Ross A. "Psychological Effects of Oxygen Deprivation on Human Behavior," *Archives of Psychology* (Columbia University), No. 145, 1932.

______. "Anoxia: Its Effects on the Body," *Science*, Vol. 98, July 1943, 18–19.

______. "Human Factors in Highway Transportation Safety," paper delivered before annual meeting of American Mutual Alliance, Chicago, Ill., Oct. 30, 1951; *Highway Research Board Bulletin 60,* Jan. 1952.

______. "Human Variables in the Design and Operation of Highway Transport Equipment," *Society of Automotive Engineers Preprint No. 717,* Jan. 1952.

______. "Human Factors in Highway Transport Safety," *Harvard Public Health Alumni Bulletin,* May 1952, 11–16.

______. "Human Factors in Highway Safety," *Best's Fire and Casualty News,* Oct. 1952, 32–140.

______. "Human Engineering: A New Approach to Driver Efficiency and Transport Safety," *Society of Automotive Engineers Transactions,* Vol. 62, 1954, 335–345.

______. "Psycho–Physiological Problems of Aging in Air Transport Pilots," *Journal of Aviation Medicine,* Vol. 25, June 1954, 210–220.

______. "Medical Aspects of Traffic Accidents: An Epidemiological Approach to the Control of

Motor Vehicle Accidents," *Proceedings of the Montreal Conference,* H. Elliott, ed., Sun Life Assurance Company, 1955.

______. "Research in the Field of Accidental Trauma," *Military Medicine,* Vol. 116, No. 6, June 1955, 426–435.

______. Human and Environmental Factors of Automobile Safety," *Society of Automotive Engineers Transactions,* Vol. 64, 1956, 625–654.

______. "Human Factors in Highway Transport Safety," *Society of Automotive Engineers Transactions,* Vol. 64, 1956, 730–750.

______. "Psychological Aspect of Aging," *Bulletin of the New York Academy of Medicine* Vol. 32, No. 1, Jan. 1956, 14–32.

______, "Prevention of Accidents in Aviation Ground Operations," *Shell Aviation News*, June 1956, 14–17.

______. "Human Factors in Aircraft Safety," *Aviation Bulletin*, No. 160, July 1956.

______. "Human Limitations and Vehicle Design," *Ergonomics,* Vol, 1, No. 1, 1957, 5–20.

______. "Human Variables in Highway Safety," *International Road Safety Review,* Vol. 5, No. 3, 1957, 15–20.

______. "Motorist Injuries and Motorist Safety: Human Engineering and Automobile Safety," *Clinical Orthopedics*, No. 9, J. B. Lippincott Co., Philadelphia, Pa., 1957.

______. "Psychological and Psychiatric Aspects of Highway Safety," *Journal of the American Medical Association,* Vol. 168, Jan. 1957, 233–237.

______. "Role of Preventive Medicine in Highway Safety," *American Journal of Public Health,* Vol. 47, No. 3, March 1957, 288–296.

______. "Health and Safety in Transportation," *Public Health Reports*, Vol. 73, No. 7, Aug. 1958, 663–680.

______. "Current Research in Road Safety in the United States of America," *Practitioner,* Vol. 188, 1962, 457–466.

______. "Experimental Studies of Sensory Functions in Relation to Age," *Ergonomics,* Vol. 5, No. 1, 1962, 123–131.

______. "Epidemiology of Motor Vehicle Accidents," *Journal of the American Medical Association,* Vol. 180, April 1962, 189–300.

______. "Role of Human Engineering in Highway Safety," *Human Factors in Highway Safety,* Boston, Mass., 1963, 208–229.

______. "Critique of Accident Research," *Annals of the New York Academy of Sciences,* Vol. 107, No. 2, May 1963, 686–695.

______. "Experimental Evidence of the Relationship Between Aging and Oxygen Want; In Search of a Theory of Aging," *Ergonomics,* Vol. 6, No. 4, Oct. 1963.

______. "Human Factors Engineering," *American Society of Safety Engineers Journal,* Vol. 9, No. 2, Feb. 1964.

______, and A. L. Barach. "Relationship Between Alcoholic Intoxication and Anoxemia," *American Journal of Medical Sciences*, Vol. 192, No. 2, 1936, 186–198.

______, and W. H. Forbes. "Metabolism of Alcohol in Man at High Altitude," *Human Biology,* Vol. 8, No. 3, 1936, 387–398.

______, and ______. "Effects of Variations in the Concentration of Oxygen and of Glucose on Dark Adaptation," *Journal of General Physiology,* Vol. 24, No. 1, 1940, 69–98.

______. and J. N. Evans. "Alterations in Dark Adaptation Under Reduced Oxygen Tensions," *American Journal of Physiology,* Vol. 127, No. 1, 1939, 37–50.

______, and M. H. Halperin. "Relation Between Foveal Visual Acuity and Illumination Under Reduced Oxygen Tension," *Journal of General Physiology*, Vol. 23, No. 5, 1940, 613–630.

______, J. N. Evans, and M. H. Halperin. "Ophthalmic Aspects of Acute Oxygen Deficiency," *Archives of Ophthalmology,* Vol. 26, Nov. 1941, 886–913.

______, L. M. Hurvich, and M. H. Halperin. "Effect of Oxygen Deprivation on the Relation Between Stimulus Intensity and the Latency of Visual After Images," *American Journal of Physiology,* Vol. 140, No. 3, Dec. 1943, 354–366.

______, et al. "Effects of Carbon Monoxide and Altitude on Visual Thresholds," *Journal of Aviation Medicine,* Vol. 15, No. 6, Dec. 1944, 381–394.

______, M. H. Halperin, and J. I. Niven. "Visual Thresholds As an Index of Physiological Imbalance During Anoxia," *American Journal of Physiology,* Vol. 142, No. 3 Oct. 1944, 328–349.

______, ______, and ______. "Visual Thresholds As an Index of the Modification of the Effects of Anoxia by Glucose," *American Journal of Physiology,* Vol. 144, No. 3, Aug. 1945, 378–388.

______, ______, and ______. "Visual Thresholds As an Index of Physiological Imbalance During Insulin Hypoglycemia," *American Journal of Physiology,* Vol. 145, No.3, Jan. 1946, 299–313.

______, and A. L. Moseley. "Carbon Monoxide in Trucks and Buses, and Information from Other Areas of Research on Carbon Monoxide, Altitude, and Cigarette Smoking," *Health, Medical, and Drug Factors in Highway Safety,* Sept. 1954, 4.17–4.33.

______, A. L. Moseley, and M. B. Fisher. "Age and the Problems of Professional Truck Drivers in Highway Transportation," *Journal of Gerontology,* Vol. 9, No. 3, July 1954, 338–348.

______, and Bruce Fisher. "Alterations in Dark Adaptation As a Function of Age," *Journal of Gerontology,* Vol. 10, No. 4, Oct. 1955, 424–428.

______, Damon, and H. W. Stoudt. "Application of Human Body Size to Vehicular Design," *Special publication No. 142, of the Society of Automotive Engineers,* Nov. 1955.

______, ______, and ______. "Anthropometry in the Design of the Driver's Workspace," *American Journal of Physical Anthropology,* Vol. 16, No. 1, March 1958, 1–24.

______, R. C. Moore, and A. B. Warren. "Why Drivers Have Accidents," *Public Safety,* April 1956.

______, and R. C. Moore. "Human Factors in Highway Safety: A Review and Evaluation," *New England Journal of Medicine*, Vol. 256, April 25, May 2, May 9, 1957, 792– 799, 837–845, 890–897.

______, and Richard G. Domey. "Bio Technical Aspects of Driver Safety and Comfort," *Society of Automotive Engineers Transactions,* Vol. 66, 1958, 630–648.

______, and ______. "Experimental Studies of Night Vision As a Function of Age and Changes in Illumination," *Highway Research Board Bulletin 191*, 1958, 17–32.

______, and ______. "Human Factors in the Design of Passenger Cars, "*Highway Research Board Proceedings,* Vol. 39, 1960, 565–582.

______, ______, and A. Bertrand Warren. "Night Visibility: Dark Adaptation As a Function of Age and Tinted Windshield Glass," *Highway Research Board Bulletin 255,* 1960, 47–56.

______, A. Bertrand Warren, and C. Karis. "Alterations in Critical Flicker Frequency As a Function of Age and Light: Dark Ratio," *Journal of Experimental Psychology,* Vol. 56, No. 6, Dec. 1958, 529–538.

______, and Roland C. Moore. "Youth and the Automobile," *Values and Ideals of American Youth,* E. Ginzberg, ed., Columbia University Press, 1960.

______, and ______. "Accidents and Accident Prevention," *Annual Review of Medicine*, Los Angeles, Annual Reviews, Inc., 1962.

______, et al. "Dark Adaptation As a Function of Age, I," *Journal of Gerontology*, Vol. 15, No. 2, April 1960, 149–154.

______, and Howard W. Stoudt. "Human Body Size and Passenger Vehicle Design," *Special Publication No. 142A of Society of Automotive Engineers*, 1960.

______, and ______. "Ergonomics in Transport," *Medicine in Transport. Rail, Road, and Sea*, E. G. Norman, ed., Butterworths, London, 1964.

______, G. Sidney Tune, and Alan I. Wellford. "On the Driving of Automobiles by Older People," *Journal of Gerontology*, April 1964.

McKesson, Jon. "Autos Need Eight Big Changes to Make Them Visually Safe," *Indianapolis Star*, Jan. 23, 1966, 1.

McLaren, Donald S. "Nutritional Disease and the Eye," *Borden's Review of Nutritional Research*, Vol. 25, No. 1, Jan., March 1964.

"Medical Aspects of Driver Limitation," *Journal of the American Medical Association*, Vol. 187, Feb. 1964, 376.

Meldrum, J. F. "Automobile Driver Eye Position," *Highway Vehicle Safety*, Safety Committee of the SAE Passenger Car Activity, 848 pp.

Merck Index, Paul G. Stecher, ed., Merck & Company, Rahway, N.J., 1968.

Metcalf, R. A., and R. E. Horn. "Visual Recovery Times from High Intensity Flashes of Light," *American Journal of Optometry*, Vol. 36, 1960, 623–633.

Meyer, Robert L. "A Man Named Smith," *Traffic Safety*, Vol. 65, No. 11, Nov. 1965, 12–14 ff.

Michael, Leland D. and Merrill J. Allen. "Nutritional Supplementation, Electrical Stimulation and Age Related Macular Degeneration," *The Journal of Orthomolecular Medicine*, Vol. 8, No.3, Third Quarter, 1993, 168–171.

Michaels, Richard M. "Human Factors in Highway Safety," *Traffic Quarterly*, Oct. 1961, 586–598.

Michon, J. A. "The Problem of Perceptual Motor Load," *Studies in Perception*, Institute for Perception RVO–TNO, National Defense Research Organization TNO, Soesterberg, The Netherlands, 1966, 81–91.

Middleton, W. E. K. and G. W. Wyszecki. "Visual Thresholds in the Retinal Periphery for Red, Green, and White Signal Lights," *Journal of the Optical Society of America*, Vol. 51, 1960, 54–56.

Middleton, W. E. *Vision Through the Atmosphere*, University of Toronto Press, Canada, 1952; Reprint, Oxford University Press, London, 1958.

Miller, J. W. "Study of Visual Acuity During The Ocular Pursuit of Moving Test Objects, II," *Journal of the Optical Society of America*, Vol. 48, 1958, 803.

______, and E. Ludvigh. "Effect of Relative Motion on Visual Acuity," *Survey of Ophthalmology*, Vol. 7, 1962, 83.

Miller, H. Gene. "More About Small Cars," *United States Navy Medical News Letter*, Vol. 48, Oct. 1966, 23–24.

Minnesota Mining and Manufacturing Co. *This Could Save Your Life*, 3M Co., Reflective Products Division, St. Paul, Minn., 1964.

Mizoi, Y., S. Hishada, and Y. Maeba. "Diagnosis of Alcohol Intoxication by the Optokinetic Test," *Quarterly Journal of Studies on Alcohol*, Part A, Vol. 30, No. 1, March 1969.

Moore, George. "Three Colored Safety Taillights to be New Car Feature." *Indianapolis Star*,

Feb. 16, 1966.

Moore, R. L., "Forward Visibility From Vehicles," Department of Scientific and Industrial Research, Road Research Laboratory, England, October 1952 (mimeo.), 4.

______."Rear Lights of Motor Vehicles and Pedal Cycles," *Road Research Technical Paper No. 25,* Her Majesty's Stationery Office, London, 1952.

______, A. Crawford, and P. Odescalchi. "Driver Characteristics and Behavior Studies," *Highway Research Board Bulletin 25,* 1958, 104–120.

Moore, R. L., and H. P. R. Smith. "Visibility from the Driver's Seat: 'The Conspicuousness of Vehicles, Lights, and Signals," paper 6, *Ergonomics and Safety in Motor Car Design,* published by the Institution of Mechanical Engineers (1 Birdcage Walk, Westminster, London, SW1), Sept. 27, 1966.

______, and S. J. Older. "Pedestrians and Motor Vehicles Are Compatible in Today's World," *Traffic Engineering* (British), Sept. 1965.

Mortimer, R. G. "Psychological Considerations in the Design of an Automobile Rear Lighting System," *Traffic Safety Research Review*, Vol. 12, No. 1, 1968, 13–16.

______. "Dynamic Evaluation of Automobile Rear Lighting Configurations," *Research,* No. 4, Highway Safety Research Institute, University of Michigan, March 1969.

______. "Dynamic Evaluation of Automobile Rear Lighting Configurations," *Highway Research Record 275,* 1969.

______, and P. L. Olson. "Variables Influencing the Attention Getting Quality of Automobile Front Turn Signals," *Traffic Safety Research Review,* Vol., 10, No. 3, 1966, 83–88.

Moseley, Alfred L., et al. "Research on Fatal Highway Collisions," *Papers,* Harvard Medical School, Boston, 1961–62.

______, et al. "Research on Fatal Highway Collisions," *Papers,* Harvard Medical School, Boston, 1962–63.

"Motor Vehicle Accident Facts 1967," *Accident Facts,* 1968, 40–45.

"Motorcycle Accidents—An Epidemic," *Highway Research Abstracts*, Vol. 36, No. 12, Dec. 1966, 94.

Moynihan, Daniel P. "An Opinion about Traffic Accident Statistics," *Highway Research Abstracts,* Vol. 36, No. 6, June 1966, 2.

Muller, G. E. "Zur Theorie Des Stabchenapparates und der Zapfendblindheit," *Zeitschrift für Sinnesphysiologie*, Vol. 54, No. 9, 1922–23, 102.

Mullin, E. F. "The Part Visibility Could Play in Road Design," *Australian Road Research* Vol. 2, No. 9, Sept. 1966, 15–43.

Munker, H. "Experimentelle Untersuchungen zur Dynamischen Sehscharfe," Sonderabdruck aus, Bericht uber die 68, zusamnenkunft der Deutschen Ophthalmologischen Gesellschaft in Heidlelberg, 1967.

Nader, Ralph. *"Unsafe at Any Speed: The Designed in Dangers of the American. Automobile,* Grossman Publishers, New York, 1965.

Nadell, M. C., and H. A. Knoll, "Effect of Luminance, Target Configuration and Lenses Upon the Refractive State of the Eye, Part 1," *American Journal of Optometry and Archives of the American Academy of Optometry,* Vol. 23, 1956, 24–42.

Nathan, John, Geoffrey H. Henry and Barry, L. Cole. "Recognition of Colored Road Traffic Light Signals by Normal and Color Vision Defective Observers," *Journal of the Optical Society of America,* Vol. 54, No. 8, Aug. 1964, 1041–1045.

National Academy of Sciences. "Medical Guides Offered to Improve Design of 'Unsuitable

Ambulances,'" *News Report* (2101 Constitution Ave., Washington, D. C.), Vol. 9, No. 1, Jan. 1969.

National Commission on Safety Education. *Minimum Standards for School Buses*, National Conference on School Transportation, Washington, D.C., 1964.

______. *Selection, Instruction and Supervision School Bus Drivers*, Washington, D.C., 2nd ed., 1965.

National Safety Council. *Guide to Traffic Safety Literature*, Vol. 10, Chicago, 1955–1965.

______. *Accident Facts*, 1965, Chicago, 1966.

______.*Guidelines to Slow Moving Vehicle Emblem Legislation,* Chicago, 1966.

National Traffic Safety Act, H.R. 12548, House of Representatives of Eighty-ninth Congress, Second Session, Washington, D.C., 1966.

Nelson, Thomas M. "Efficiency of Two Dimensional Traffic Markers in Referring Command," *Human Factors,* Aug. 1964, 359–364.

New York Department of Motor Vehicles. *Feasibility Study of New York State Safety Car Program*, Albany, New York, 1966.

New York Department of Transportation. 1952 *Annual Report* (28–11 Bridge Plaza North, Long Island City, N. Y. 11101), 1952, 20–21.

"Night Vision Problems Studied at Michigan Traffic Center Seminar," *Traffic Safety*, Vol. 65, No. 8, Aug. 1965, 29.

Nowakowski, Rodney W., O.D., Ph.D., *Primary Low Vision Care,* Appleton and Lange, 1994, p. 276ff.

O Connell, Jeffrey, and Arthur Myers. *Safety Last, An Indictment of the Auto Industry,* Random House, New York, 1966.

O'Connor, Liam, "Wanted: Effective Traffic Signs," *Optometric Weekly,* June 5, 1958, 1076–1077.

"Ode to the Road," *Time,* Vol. 86, No. 11, Sept. 1965, 32–34.

Olenski, Z., and N. W. Goodden. *Clearness of View from Day Fighter Aircraft,* Farnborough (England) Royal Aircraft Establishment, Report No. Aero 1862, Oct. 1943.

"On/Off Sun Glasses," *New York Herald Tribune*, Jan. 23, 1966.

Ontario Medical Association. *A Guide for Physicians in Determining Fitness to Drive a Motor Vehicle,* Ontario, Canada, March 1964.

Oppenheimer, Jess. "Orientation Apparatus for Human Subjects," *Optometric Weekly,* October 24, 1968, 23–31.

"Optometrist and Safe Driving," *Journal of the American Optometric Association*, Vol. 31, 1960, 467–469.

Osmundsen, John A., "Science: Through a Glass Darkly," *New York Times*, Dec. 5, 1965.

Ott, John N. "Effects of Wavelengths of Light on Physiological Functions of Plants and Animals," *Illuminating Engineering,* Vol. 60, April 1965, 254–261.

______. "Some Observations on the Effect of Light on the Pigment Epithelial Cells of the Retina of a Rabbit's Eye," *Recent Progress in Photobiology,* E. J. Bowen, ed., Academic Press, New York, 1965, 395–396.

Ottander, Chris, and Hannes Eisler. *Hysteresis in the Continuum of Subjective Angular Velocity,* Psychological Laboratory, University of Uppsala, Sweden, Report 17, June 1964.

Pain, Richard. "Brightness and Brightness Ratio As Factors in the Attention Value of Highway Signs," *Highway Research Record 275*, 1969.

Park, W. L., J. Unatin and A. Herbert. "A Driving Program for the Visually Impaired," *Journal of American Optometric Association* 64, 1993, 54–59.

Parker, James F., Robert R. Gilbert and Richard F. Dillon. *Effectiveness of Three Visual Cues in the Detection of Rate of Closure at Night*, Biotechnology, Inc., 3219 Columbia Pike, Arlington, Va., March 1964.

Patrick, L. M., and R. P. Daniel. "Comparison of Standard and Experimental Windshields," *Research Review,* Vol. 9, No. 4, Dec. 1965, 99.

Peckham, R. H. "Effect of Exposure to Sunlight on Night Driving Visibility," *Highway Research Board Bulletin 56,* 1952, 17–24.

______, and W. M. Hart. "Association Between Retinal Sensitivity and the Glare Problem," *Highway Research Board Bulletin 255,* 1960, 57–60.

Phillips, A. J., and Alan Rutstein. "Amber Night Spectacles, a Further Study," *British Journal of Physiological Optics,* Vol. 24, No. 3, 1967, 161–205.

Pirenne, M. H. "Spectral Luminous Efficiency of Radiation," *The Eye,* Hugh Davson, ed., Academic Press, New York, Vol. 2, 1962, 65–91; see p. 67.

Pitts, D. G. "Transmission of the Visible Spectrum Through the Ocular Media of the Bovine Eye," *American Journal of Optometry,* Vol. 36, 1959, 289–298.

Platt, F. N. "Operation Analysis of Traffic Safety, IV, Proposed Fundamental Research on Driver Behavior," *Traffic Safety,* Vol. 4, No. 4, 1960, 4–7.

______. *Traffic Safety Research: A Unique Method of Measuring Road, Traffic, Vehicle and Driver Characteristics,* Ford Motor Co., Dearborn, Michigan, 1962.

Polk County (Iowa). 1959 Motor Vehicle Accident Study, Aug. 26, 1960.

Port of New York Authority. *Running Lights, Final Report,* Traffic Engineering Division (111 Eighth Ave. at 15th St., New York, N. Y. 10011), Oct. 1968.

Potter, Barrie. "Perception of Relative Movements of Illuminated Objects Along the Visual Axis," *British Journal of Physiological Optics,* Vol. 18, No. 2, April 1961, 117–124.

President's Committee for Traffic Safety. *Health, Medical Care and Transportation of the Injured (Driver Licensing and Alcohol and Drugs),* report distributed by Division of Accident Prevention, Public Health Service, 1960.

______. *Highway Safety Action Program,* Washington, D.C., 1966.

Prince, J. H., H. R. Blackwell and J. G. Ohmart. *Comparative Legibility of Highway and Advertising Signs Under Dynamic Conditions,* Ohio State University Institute for Research in Vision, Report on Project No. 886, 1963, 17.

Pritchard, B. S., and H. R. Blackwell. "Preliminary Studies of Visibility on the Highway in Fog," University of Michigan, Engineering Research Institute, Vision Research Laboratories, Final Report No. 2557–2–F, July 1957.

______, and ______. "Optical Properties of the Atmosphere and Highway Lighting in Fog," *Highway Research Board Bulletin 191*, National Academy of Sciences, National Research Council Publication 617, Washington, D.C., 1958, 7–16.

Proceedings of Joint Vehicular Signal System Committee Meeting, Columbus, Ohio, Aug. 18, 1965.

Projector, T. H., K. G. Cook and L. O. Peterson. *Analytic Assessment of Motor Vehicle Rear Signal System*, Century Research Corp., Contract No. F–11–6602, National Highway Safety Bureau, U. S. Department of Transportation, Jan. 1969.

"Provision of Safety Features for All Motor Vehicles Used in Interstate Commerce," *Congressional Record, Senate,* Feb. 23, 1965.

Rains, J. D. "Signal Luminance and Position Effect in Human Reaction Time," *Vision Research,* Vol. 3, 1963, 239.

Reading, R. W., and Henry W. Hofstetter. "Extrahoropteral Stereopsis in Vehicle Operator Orientation," *Highway Research News,* No. 17, Feb. 1965, 84.

Reese, John H. "Legal Nature of a Driver's License," *Highway Research Abstracts,* Vol. 36, July 1966, 5.

"Reflectorization—A Modern Safety Boon," *Fleet Owner,* Vol. 58, No. 4, April 1963, 98–99.

Rehling, C. J. "Drug Impaired Driver," *Highway Research Abstracts,* Vol. 37, No. 4, April 1967, 3.

Reid and Chanon. "Studies in Fundamentals of Highway Lighting," *Illuminating Engineering,* Vol. 31, 1936.

______. "Determination of Visibility on Lighted Highways," *Illuminating Engineering,* Vol. 32, 1937.

______. "Evaluation of Street Lighting," *Illuminating Engineering,* Vol. 34, 1939.

______. "A Street Lighting Evaluator," *Illuminating Engineering,* Vol. 35, 1940.

Reilly, Raymond E., et al. *The Translation of Visual Information Into Vehicular Control Actions,* Biotechnology, Inc. 3219 Columbia Pike, Arlington, Va., Report No. 65–2, Oct. 1965.

Reinecke, Robert D., and D. Miller. *Strabismus, A Programmed Text,* Appleton Century Crofts, N.Y., 1966.

Rex, Charles H. "Advancement in Roadway Lighting," *Highway Research Board Bulletin 255,* 1960, 158–189.

______. "Effectiveness Ratings for Roadway Lighting," *Illuminating Engineering*, July 1, 1963, 501–520.

______. *Light Distribution for the Motorist,* General Electric Company, Hendersonville, N. C., 1966.

______. "Visual Data on Roadway Lighting," *Highway Research Board Bulletin 336,* 1962, 61–75.

______, and J. S. Franklin. "Visual Comfort Evaluations of Roadway Lighting," *Highway Research Board Bulletin 255*, 1960, 101–116.

______, and ______. "Relative Visual Comfort Evaluations of Roadway Lighting," *Illuminating Engineering,* Vol. 55, 1960, 161–174.

Richards, Oscar W. "Vision at Levels of Night Road Illumination, I (Reviews and Bibliography), *Highway Research Board Bulletin 56,* 1952, 36–55.

______. "Vision at Levels of Night Road Illumination, II," *Highway Research Board Bulletin 146,* 1957, 58–66.

______. "Vision at Levels of Night Road Illumination, III, Literature, 1956–57," *Highway Research Board Bulletin* 191, 1958, 57–61.

______. "Night Driving Seeing Problems," *American Journal of Optometry and Archives of the American Academy of Optometry,* Vol. 35, No. 11, Nov. 1958, 22–28

______. Night Driving Seeing Problems," *Traffic Safety Research Review,* Vol. 3, No. 2, 1959, 22–28.

______. "Vision at Levels of Night Road Illumination, IV, Literature, 1957–58," *Highway Research Board Bulletin 226,* 1959, 56–61.

______. Vision at Levels of Night Road Illumination, V, Literature, 1959," *Highway Research Board Bulletin 255,* 1960, 190–195.

______. "Seeing for Night Driving," *Journal of the American Optometric Association..,* Vol. 32, 1960, 211–214.

______. "What the Well Dressed Deer Hunter Will Wear," *National Safety News,* Vol. 82, No. 5,

1960, 43–46, 104, 106, 108, 110, 112, 114, 124–127.

______. "Vision at Levels of Night Road Illumination, VI, Literature, 1960," *Highway Research Board RCS Circular 458,* 1961, 14 pp.

______. "Vision at Levels of Night Road Illumination, VII, Literature, 1961," *Highway Research Board Bulletin 336,* 1962, 12–21.

______. "Vision at Levels of Night Road Illumination, VIII, Literature, 1962," *Highway Research Board Record 25,* 1963, 76–82.

______. "Vision at Levels of Night Road Illumination, IX, Literature, 1963," *Highway Research Board Record 25,* 1963, 76–82.

______. "Do Yellow Glasses Impair Night Driving Vision?" *Optometric Weekly*, Feb. 27, 1964. 17–21.

______. "Vision at Levels of Night Road Illumination, X, Literature, 1964," *Highway Research Board Record 70,* 1965, 41–47.

______. "Motorist Vision and the Driver's License," *Traffic Quarterly*, Jan. 1966, 16–17.

______. "Vision at Levels of Night Road Illumination, XII, Changes of Acuity and Contrast Sensitivity with Age." *American Journal of Optometry and Archives of the American Academy of Optometry,* Vol. 43, May 1966, 313–319.

______. "Visual Needs and Possibilities for Night Driving," *Optician,* Parts 1–12, Vols. 154–155, Nos. 3999–4006, 4008, 4011, 4012, 4015, Nov. 17, 24, 1967; Dec. 1, 8, 22, 29, 1967; Jan. 5, 12–26, 1968; Feb. 16, 23, 1968; March 15, 1968.

______. "Night Myopia at Night Automobile Driving Luminances," *American Journal of Optometry and Archives of the American Academy of Optometry,* Vol. 44, No. 8, Aug. 1967, 517–523.

______. "Vision at Levels of Night Road Illumination, XI, Literature, 1965, *Highway Research Board Record 164,* 1967, 21–28.

______. "Vision at Levels of Night Road Illumination, XII, Literature, 1966," *Highway Research Board Record 179,* 1967, 61–67.

Riley, H. "Driving in Dark Glasses," *Optician*, Vol. 140, 1960, 22.

Ritter, P. *Planning for Man and Motor,* (Hamilton and Thurstone quoted), Macmillan Company, New York, 1964, 58.

Rivers, W. H. R. "Vision," in Schaefer's *Textbook of Physiology*, Vol. 2, London, 1900, 1091.

Rockwell, Thomas H. "Visual Factors in Automobile Driving," *Proceedings, Symposium on Visibility in the Driving Task,* sponsored by Highway Research Board, Illuminating Engineering Research Institute, and Texas A & M University, May 13–15, 1968, 17–43.

______, and Joseph Treiterer. *Sensing and Communication Between Vehicles,* National Cooperative Highway Research Program Report 51, Highway Research Board, National Academy of Sciences, National Academy of Engineering, 1968.

Roper, Val J. "Aiming for Better Headlighting." Preprint copies available from SAE Headquarters, 485 Lexington Ave., New York 17, N.Y.

______. "Nighttime Seeing through Heat Absorbing Windshields," *Highway Research Board Bulletin 68,* 1953, 16–17.

______. "Relation of Visual Acuity and Contrast Sensitivity Under Nighttime Driving Conditions," *Highway Research Board Bulletin 336,* 1962, 114.

______, and E. A. Howard. "Seeing with Motor Car Headlights," *Transactions of the Illuminating Engineering Society,* Vol. 33, No. 5, May 1938.

______, and K. D. Scott. "Silhouette Seeing with Motor Car Headlamps," Paper presented before the annual convention of the Illuminating Engineering Society, San Francisco, Aug. 21–25, 1939.

______, and ______. "Seeing with Polarized Headlamps," *Illuminating Engineering,* Vol. 36, No. 12, Dec. 1941, 1205–1218.

______, and G. E. Meese. "Seeing Against Headlamp Glare," *Illuminating Engineering,* Vol. 47, No.3, March 1952.

______, and ______. "More Light on the Headlighting Problem," *Highway Research Board Bulletin 70,* 1964.

Ross, H. L. "Recognition of Collision Course in Traffic Accidents," *National Safety Council Transactions,* Vol. 24.

Roth, W. J. and F. DeRose, Jr. "Interchange Ramp Color Delineation and Marking Study," Michigan Department of Highways, Dec. 1964, for presentation at Highway Research Board Annual Meeting, Washington, D. C., Jan. 1965.

Rouse, Kenneth A. "The Way to Go," Chicago, Ill., Kemper Insurance Group.

Rowan, Neilon J. "Tower Lighting Research," *Proceedings, Symposium on Visibility in the Driving Task,* sponsored by Highway Research Board, laminating Engineering Research Institute, and Texas A & M University, May 13–15, 1968, 124–129.

______, and Ned E. Walton. "Optimization of Roadway Lighting Systems," *Highway Research Record 216,* 1968, 34–47.

______, et al. *Impact Behavior of Sign Supports, II,* Texas Transportation Institute, College Station, Texas, 1965.

Ruedeman, A. D. "Foveal Coordination," *American Journal of Ophthalmology,* Vol. 36, 1953, 1220.

Rugaber, Walter. "U. S. Plans Strict Safety in 1968 Autos," Louisville (Ky.) *Courier Journal,* Feb. 17, 1966, 1.

Rumar, Kare. Visual Performance in Night Driving: *A Summary of Some Research Results,* Department of Psychology, University of Uppsala, Sweden, 1962.

______. "Night Driving Visibility," *Traffic Engineering and Control,* Feb. 1964, 611–613.

______. *Visible Distances in Night Driving with Misaligned Meeting Dipped Headlights,* Psychological Laboratory, University of Uppsala, Sweden, Report 28, Aug. 1965.

______. "Comparison of the Visibility and Readability between Conventional License Plates and License Plates with a Reflective Background," *International Police Chronicle,* No. 70, Jan–Feb. 1965, 21–44.

______. *Night Driving: Visibility of Pedestrians,* International Road Safety Congress reprint, 1966.

______. *Reflective Registration Plate,* paper delivered before Fifth World Meeting of International Road Federation, London, Sept. 1966.

Russell, A. "Psychological Investigation of Glare in Road Traffic," *Highway Research Abstracts,* Vol. 28, No. 6, 1958, 2–3.

Rutter, Richard. "Auto Industry Finds New Ways to Use Glass," *New York Times,* Jan. 3, 1966.

Ryan, James J. "Safe Car," *Minnesota Medicine,* Vol. 43, No. 12, Dec. 1960, 869–870.

______, and James R. Tobias. "Reduction in Crash Forces," *Proceedings of the Ninth Stapp Car Conference,* 1966, 413–419.

"Safety Experts Find Driver Behavior Prominent Cause of Accidents," *News Report,* Vol. 16, No. 4, April 1966, 5.

Said, F. S. and Robert A. Weale. "Variation with Age of the Spectral Transmissivity of the

Living Human Crystalline Lens," *Gerontologia* (London), 1959, 213–231.

Savin, L. H., H. C. Weston, and G. Grime. "Discussion of the Visual Problems of Night Driving," *Proceedings of the Royal Society of Medicine,* Vol. 50, 1957, 173–184.

"Scanning the News: Drinking Drivers," *AMA News,* March 28, 1966.

Schaller, Lyle E. "How Free Are the Freeways?" *Highway Research Abstracts,* Vol. 36, No. 6, June 1966, 4.

Schapero, Max, David Cline and Henry W. Hofstetter, eds., *Dictionary of Visual Science,* Chilton Book Co., Philadelphia, 1968.

Scheidt, Edward, D. J. Moffie and C. R. Milton. *North Carolina Vision Program,* North Carolina Department of Motor Vehicles, 1954.

Schmidt, I. "Are Meaningful Night Vision Tests for Drivers Feasible?" *American Journal of Optometry,* Vol. 38, June 1961, 295–348.

______, and Paul L. Connolly. *Visual Considerations of Man, the Vehicle and the Highway,* Society of Automotive Engineers, New York, N.Y., 1966.

Schober, Herbert. "Unfersuchungen uber die Blendungsfrage, im besondersen uber die Blendung bei Gelblicht," Sonderdruck aus dem Tagungsbericht des IV. Internationalen Kolloquiums der Hockschule für Elektrotechnik Ilmenau, 1959, Vorstand des Instituts für medizinische Optik der Universitat Munchen.

______. "Optische und Optometristische Probleme bei der Bekampfung der Blendung bei Nacht und im Strabenverkehr" (Optical and Optometrical Problems at Anti-Glare-Fight and Night Traffic), Sonderdruck aus Internationaler, Augenoptiker Kongreb, Kopenhagen, 1964.

______. "Role of Exact Eye Correction in Industrial Hygiene," *Sehanforderungen bei der Arbeit,* by Schmidtke and Schober, A. W. Gentner Verlag, Stuttgart, 1967, 96 pp.

______. "Reduction of Disability and Discomfort Glare in Traffic," *Prevention of Highway Injury.* Proceedings of April 19–21 Symposium, Highway Safety Research Institute, University of Michigan, 1967, 99–112.

______, and H. Munker. "Blendschutzbrillen Gelbrillen," Sonderdruck, aus der Fachzeitschrift der Augenoptiker, Dusseldorf, Heft, 6/1968.

______, ______, and Grimm. "Recognition of Moving Objects (Dynamic VA)," Klinische Monatsblatter für Augenheilkunde, 1967, 151, 399.

Schoppert, David W., and Dan W. Hoyt. "Factors Influencing Safety at Highway Rail Grade Crossings," National Cooperative Highway Research Program Report 50, Highway Research Board, National Academy of Sciences–National Academy of Engineering, 1968.

Schrenk, L. S. "Street Lighting and Safety," *Illuminating Engineering,* Vol. 33, 1938.

Schultz, Haskell B. *A Design for Safe Driving,* 3rd ed., Fort Wayne, Ind. 1963.

Schuster, D. H. "Prediction of Current Accident Board for Youthful Drivers," *Research Review,* Vol. 10, No. 1, March 1966, 22–25.

Sears, B. G. "Highways As Environmental Elements." Presented at 44th annual meeting of Highway Research Board, Jan. 1965.

"Seat Belts and Damages Collection," *Traffic Safety,* July 1967.

Seburn, T. J. "Street Lighting, Traffic Accidents, Crime," *Illuminating Engineering,* Vol. 46, 1951.

Seedorff, H. H. "Effect of Alcohol on the Motor Fusion Reserves and Stereopsis As Well As on the Tendency to Nystagmus," *Acta Ophthalmologica*, Vol. 34, 1956, 273–280.

Selzer, Melvin L., and Sue Weiss. "Alcoholism and Traffic Fatalities: Study in Futility," *Highway*

Research Abstracts, Vol. 36, No. 10, Oct. 1966, 4.

______, Paul Gikas and Donald Huelke, eds. *Prevention of Highway Injury,* University of Michigan, Highway Safety Research Institute, Ann Arbor, 1967.

Septon, Richard D. *Apparent Brightness Increases with Yellow Light,* Master's Thesis, Indiana University, Aug. 1968.

Severy, Derwyn M. "Facial Injuries, Causes and Prevention," *Seventh Stapp Car Crash Conference Proceedings,* Charles C Thomas, Springfield, Ill., 1965.

______. "Survival by Design, Head Protection," Seventh Stapp Car Crash Conference Proceedings, Charles C Thomas, Springfield, Ill., 1965.

Shaw, Lynette. "Practical Use of Protective Personality Tests As Accident Predictors," *Traffic Safety Research Review,* Vol. 9, No. 2, June 1965, 34–72.

Sheehe, G. H. "Importance of Driver Licensing Activities," *Optometric Weekly,* Vol. 51, 1960, 2566–2569.

Sherman, Reuel A. *Optometric Service in the Field of Automotive Driving,* Bausch and Lomb Optical Co., Rochester, N.Y., 1954.

Sherwood, Stephen L., ed. "Self–induced Epilepsy," *Archives of Neurology,* Vol. 6, 1962, 49–65.

Shipley, T. "Visual Efficiency in Monocular Driving," *Highway Research Board Bulletin 127,* 1955, 53–62.

Siebeck, R. "Praktische Bedeutung der Raumsinnstorung durch Anisokorie," *Klinische Monatsblätter für Augenheilkunde,* Vol. 123, 1953, 86.

Simmons, A. E. "Instrument for Assessment of Visibility Under Highway Lighting Conditions," *Highway Research Board Bulletin 336,* 1962, 76–94.

Sloan, L. L. "New Test Charts for the Measurement of Visual Acuity at Far and Near Distances," *American Journal of Ophthalmology,* Vol. 48, 1959, 807–813.

______, and S. M. Newhall. "Comparison of Cases of Atypical and Typical Achromatopsia," *American Journal of Ophthalmology,* Vol. 25, 1942, 945.

Smeed, R. J. "Some Factors Affecting Visibility from a Driver's Seat and Their Effect on Road Safety." *British Journal of Physiological Optics,* Vol. 10, No. 2, June 1953, 63–84.

______. "Proneness of Drivers to Road Accidents," *Nature,* Vol. 186, 1960, 273–275.

______. "Some Aspects of Pedestrian Safety," *Journal of Transport Economics* (London School of Economics and Political Science, Houghton St., Aldwych, London, WC 2), Vol. 2, No. 3, Sept. 1968, 255–279.

Smith, K. U., et al. "Application of a Real Time Computer System to the Clinical Treatment of Photosensitive Epilepsy," *Engineering in Medicine and Biology, Proceedings of the 19th Annual Conference,* 1966, Vol. 18, No. 4, 1966, 126.

"Smoke Dims Drivers' View," *Science News*, Vol. 90, Sept. 1966, 224.

Sneller, Robert C. "Introducing Special Session on Highway Safety," *Journal of the American Optometric Association,* Vol. 32, 1960, 210.

______. "Vision and Its Correct Use in Safe Driving," *Optometric Weekly,* Vol. 51, 1960, 2551–2555.

______. Vision and Driving, American Optometric Association, St. Louis, Mo., 1962.

Snyder, Harry L., and Charles P. Greening. *Effect of Direction and Velocity of Relative Motion Upon Dynamic Visual Acuity,* Washington, D.C., Department of Commerce, 1965.

Society of Automotive Engineers. *Lighting Equipment and Photometric Tests,* SAE, 485 Lexington Ave., New York, N. Y., May 1960.

______. *Design Aspects for Rear Vision in Motor Vehicles*, SAE, March 1964.

______. "Emblem for Identifying Slow–Moving Vehicles" (Corresponds to SAE J943) published by SAE, adopted by ASAE Dec. 1964.

______. *Proceedings of the Eighth Stapp Car Crash Conference*, Oct. 1964.

______. *Proceedings of the Ninth Stapp Car Crash Conference*, 1965.

______. *Proceedings of the Tenth Stapp Car Crash Conference*, Nov. 1966.

______. *Proceedings of the Eleventh Stapp Car Crash Conference*, Oct. 1967.

______. *Proceedings of the Twelfth Stapp Car Crash Conference*, 1968.

Solomon, David. *Accident Involvements on Main Rural Highways Related to Speed and Characteristics of Drivers and Vehicles,* U. S. Department of Commerce, Bureau of Public Roads, Washington, D.C., 1963.

______. *Accidents on Main Rural Highways Related to Speed, Driver, and Vehicle*, U. S. Department of Commerce, Bureau of Public Roads, Washington, D.C., 1964.

Sorsby, A., et al. "Vision, Visual Acuity and Ocular Refraction of Young Men," *British Medical Journal,* Vol. 183, 1960, 1394–1398.

Spencer, D. E., and S. C. Peek. "Adaptation on Runway and Turnpike," *Illuminating Engineering,* Vol. 55, 1960, 371–384.

Stalder, H. E., and A. R. Lauer. "Effect of Pattern Distribution on Perception of Relative Motion in Low Levels of Illumination," *Highway Research Board Bulletin 56,* 1952, 25–35.

Stanford Research Institute. "Literature Search and Evaluation of the Physics of Fog," Report No. 1, Feb. 16, 1953.

Starks, H. J. H. "Vehicle Design in Relation to Safety: Some Aspects of the Work of the Road Research Laboratory," *Medicine, Science, and the Law* (British), Oct. 1962, 469–481.

Stewart, Charles R. "Demonstration of the Effects of Alcohol on Vision," *Journal of the American Optometric Association,* Vol. 35, No. 4, 1964, 289–290.

Stiles, W. S., and C. Dunbar. "Evaluation of Glare from Motor Car Headlights." Technical Paper No. 16, Illumination Research Department of Scientific and Industrial Research, His Majesty's Stationery Office, England, 1935.

Stonex, K. A. "Review of Vehicle Dimensions and Performance Characteristics," *Highway Research Board Proceedings,* Vol. 39, 1960, 467–478.

______. "Roadside Design for Safety," *Traffic Safety Research Review,* Vol. 5, No. 4, 1961, 18–30.

______. "Vehicle Aspects of the Highway Safety Problem," *Traffic Safety Research Review,* Vol. 6, No. 2, 1962, 15–24.

______. "Relation of Cross Section Design and Highway Safety," *Traffic Safety Research Review,* Vol. 7, No. 4, 1963, 2–14.

Straub, A. L., and T. M. Allen. "Sign Brightness in Relation to Position, Distance, and Reflectorization," *Highway Research Board Bulletin 146,* 1957, 13–44.

Strickland, J. and B. Ward. "Some Observations of the Pulfrich Type Distortions while Driving," in preparation.

Strughold, H. "Human Time Factor in Flight," *Journal of Aviation Medicine,* Vol. 20, 1949, 300; Vol. 22, 1951, 100.

______. "Intermittent Light," *German Aviation Medicine, World War II,* Vol. 2, Dept. AF, Washington, D.C., April 1950, 972.

______. "Human Time Factor in Flight II. Chains of Latencies in Vision," *Journal of Aviation Medicine,* Vol. 22, 1951, 100.

Stuckey, W. E., and K. A. Harkness. *Pertinent Facts Regarding the Slow Moving Vehicle*

Emblem, Ohio State University.

"Studies, Trials and Resolutions concerning the Visibility and Legibility of License Plates," *International Police Chronicle, No. 70,* Jan–Feb. 1965, 52–61.

Sutro, P. J. "Windshield Visibility Clearance," *Traffic Safety Research Review,* Vol. 1, No. 1, 1957, 15–28.

Swearingen, John J. *Tolerances of the Human Face to Crash Impact,* Federal Aviation Agency, Oklahoma City, Okla., 1965.

Takayanagi, Yasuyo, M.D., et. al., "Situation of Restrictions Against Color Defective Applicants to Colleges," *Japan Clinical Ophthalmology* 1986; 40(7)780–781.

_____. "Easing Restrictions Against Color Defective Applicants to Colleges," *Journal of Japan Ophthalmologists Association* 1988, 59(2)123–124.

____. "Survey on the Restrication Against Color Defective People to Companies," *Journal of Japan Ophthalmologists Association* 1987, 58(9)801–814.

____. "Research on the Brightness Differentiation Perception of Color Defective People," *Journal of Japan Ophthalmologists Association* 1987, 58(7)517–524.

____. "Research on the Differentiating Ability of Color Defective People in Social Life," *Journal of Japan Ophthalmologists Association* 1989, 60(2)99–104.

____. "Questionnaires About Color Defectiveness," *Journal of Japan Ophthalmologists Association* 1988, 59(4)331–333.

____. "Handicapped by Doctors: The Color Blindness in Japan," Lecture, University of Mississippi, Medical Center, May 1995.

Taragin, A., and B. M. Rudy. "Traffic Operation As Related to Highway Illumination and Delineation," *Highway Research Board Bulletin 255*, 1960, 1–29.

Taylor, A. H. "Vision at Low Brightness Levels, I," *Illuminating Engineering,* Vol. 38, No. 2, Feb. 1943, 89–98.

Taylor, D. G. "Telescopic Spectacles for Driving: User Data Satisfaction, Preferences and Effects in Vocational, Educational, and Personal Tasks," *Journal of Visual Rehabilitation* 4(2)1990, 29–61.

Taylor, Stanford E. *Eye Movement Photography with the Reading Eye*, Educational Development Laboratories, Huntington, N.Y., 1960.

Thomas, Lewellyn. "Movements of the Eye," *Scientific American,* Vol. 219, No. 2, Aug. 1968, 88–95.

Thorndike, R. L. "Human Factor in Accidents with Special Reference to Aircraft Accidents," Report to School of Aviation Medicine, U. S. Air Force, Feb. 1951 (reprinted Jan. 1964 by U.S. Department of Health, Education and Welfare), 140.

"To Cut Crash Toll, AMA Advises Auto Design Changes, Stricter License Standards (excerpts)," *Journal of the American Medical Association,* Jan. 26–1957, excerpts printed in *Safety Standards.*

Todosiev, E. P. and R. E. Fenton. "Velocity Thresholds in Car Following." Presented at 43rd annual meeting of Highway Research Board, Jan. 1964.

Torf, Arthur S., and Lucien Duckstein. "Methodology for the Determination of Driver Perceptual Latency in Car Following," *Human Factors,* Oct. 1966, 441–447.

"Traffic Control and Roadway Elements; Their Relationship to Highway Safety," *Research Review,* Vol. 10, No. 4, Dec. 1966, 103.

Traffic Safety Act of 1966, S. 3005, Senate of the Eighty Ninth Congress, Second Session, Washington, D.C., 1966.

Travelers Insurance Company. *Deadly Reckoning: The Travelers 1961 Book of Street and*

Highway Accident Data, Hartford, Conn., 1961.

______. *Cowboys and Engines: The Travelers 1962 Book of Street and Highway Accident Data,* Hartford, Conn., 1962.

______. *Rushin' Roulette: The Travelers 1963 Book of Street and Highway Accident Data,* Hartford, Conn., 1963.

______. *The Casualty Count: The Travelers 1964 Book of Street and Highway Accident Data,* Hartford, Conn., 1964.

______. *A Tragedy of Errors: The Travelers 1965 Book of Street and Highway Accident Data,* Hartford, Conn., 1965, 29.

______. *You Bet Your Life: The Travelers 1966 Book of Street and Highway Accident Data,* Hartford, Conn., 1966.

______. *Was It Sudden? The Travelers 1967 Book of Street and Highway .Accident Data,* Hartford, Conn., 1967.

______. *Attitudes and Platitudes: The Travelers 1968 Book of Street and Highway Accident Data,* Hartford, Conn., 1968.

Turner, H. J. "Interaction Between Fixed Lighting and Vehicle Headlights," *Australian Road Research* Vol. 2, No. 3, March 1965, 13, 19.

Ungar, P. E., and J. Barnett. "Vision and the Driver," Highway Research Abstracts, Vol. 37, No. 4, April 1967, 4.

______, and ______. "Vision and the Driver," Aspects Techniques de la Securite Routiere, tiere *CIDITVA Bulletin,* Centre International de Documentation sur l'Inspection et la 'T'echnique des Vehicules Automobiles (14 rue du Gouvernment Provisoire, Brussels 1), No. 27, Drpy, 1966, 3.1–1.9.

"Uniformity Important in Lighting," *Traffic Safety*, March 1968, 25.

United Nations Conference on Road Traffic, Vienna, Oct. 7–Nov. 8, 1968, United Nations Publication, New York, 1969.

U. S. Department of Commerce. "Manual on Uniform Traffic Control Devices for Streets and Highway Signs," Bureau of Public Roads, June 1961.

______. *Standard Alphabets for Highway Signs,* Bureau of Public Roads, 1961.

U. S. Department of Health, Education, and Welfare. "Binocular Visual Acuity of Adults: United States, 1960–1962," Public Health Service Publication No. 1000, Series 11, No. 3, 1964.

______. *Alcohol and Accidental Injury Conference Proceedings,* U. S. Government Printing Office, Washington, D.C., 1965.

______. Accidents, U. S. Government Printing Office, Washington, D.C., Dec. 1964 – Jan. 1965.

U. S. Public Health Service. *Binocular Visual Acuity of Adults,* Publication No. 1000, Ser. 2, No. 3, Government Printing Office, Washington, D.C., 1964.

______. *Facts of Blindness,* Superintendent of Documents, Government Printing Office, Washington, D.C.

U. S. Department of Transportation. *Rail Highway Grade Crossing Accidents for the year ended Dec. 31, 1967*, Federal Railroad Administration, Bureau of Railroad Safety, 1968.

______. *Federal Motor Vehicle Safety Standards,* Federal Highway Administration, National Highway Safety Bureau, Aug. 6, 1968.

______. *National Traffic and Motor Vehicle Safety Act of 1966,* First Annual Report, U. S. Government Printing Office, Washington, D.C. 1968.

"Vehicle Safety Check News," 1968 National Vehicle Safety Check (2000 K Street, N. W.

Washington, D.C., 20006), sponsored by Auto Industries Highway Safety Committee with cooperation of Association of State and Provincial Safety Coordinators, Dec. 1968.

"Visual Acuity and Driving," *Traffic Safety,* March 1968, 24.

"Visual Acuity of Young Men," *Optician,* Vol. 139, 1960, 512–513.

"Visual Communication Between Motor Drivers," *Optician,* Vol. 139, 1960.

"Vision and Traffic Safety," *Journal of the California Optometric Association,* Vol. 27, 1959, 302–303.

"Visual Capabilities of the Automobile Driver: Effects of Glare," *Visual Factors in Automobile Driving,* Stanley S. Ballard and Henry A. Knoll, eds., Highway Research Board of the National Academy of Sciences, National Academy of Engineering, Washington, D.C., 1958, 11.

"Visual Requirements for Vehicle Driving," *Visual Factors in Automobile Driving,* Stanley S. Ballard and Henry A. Knoll, eds., Highway Research Board of the National Academy of Sciences, National Academy of Engineering, Washington, D.C., 1958, 5.

Voevodsky, John. "Inferences from Visual Perception and Reaction Time to Requisites for a Collision Preventing Cyberlite Stop Lamp," Proceedings of the National Academy of Sciences, Vol. 57, No. 3, March 1967, 688–695.

Vos, J. J. "Some New Aspects of Color Stereoscopy," *Journal of the Optical Society of America,* Vol. 50, 1960, 785–790.

______. "Letters to the Editors: The Color Stereoscopic Effect," *Vision Research,* Vol. 6, 1966, 105–106.

______. "Antagonistic Effect in Colour Stereoscopy," *Ophthalmologica,* Vol., 145, 1963, 442–445.

______. "Physiologic–Optical Aspects of Participation in Traffic," *Perspectives in Ophthalmology,* Report of the 1967 Post Graduate Courses held under the auspices of the Netherlands Ophthalmological Society and the Medical Faculty of Rotterdam, 223–229.

______, and J. Boogaard. "Contribution of the Cornea to Entoptic Scatter," *Journal of the Optical Society of America,* Vol. 53, No. 7, July 1963, 869–873.

______, and M. A. Bouman. "Disability Glare: Theory and Practice," *Proceedings of Commission Internationale de l'Eclairage,* Brussels, 1959, 298.

______, and ______. "Contribution of the Retina to Entoptic Scatter," *Journal of the Optical Society of America,* Vol. 54, No. 1, Jan. 1964, 95–100.

Wald, George. *Molecular and Fine Structures of the Retina: Recent Progress in Photobiology,* Academic Press, New York, 133–144.

Waldram, J. M., "Visual Problems in Streets and Motorways," *Illuminating Engineering*, Vol. 57, 1962, 361–375.

Walker, James T. "Slanting Disc Effect: A Kinetic Visual Stereophenomenon," *Optometric Weekly,* Nov. 14, 1968.

Waller, Julian. *Guide for the Identification, Evaluation and Regulation of Persons with Medical Handicaps to Driving,* American Association of Motor Vehicle Administrators, Washington, D.C., 1967.

Waller, Julius A., "Alcohol and Traffic Accidents: Can the Gordian Knot Be Broken?" *Traffic Research Review,* Vol. 10, No. 1, March 1966, 14–21.

Walraven, P. L. and H. L. Leebeek. "Recognition of Color Code by Normals and Color Defectives at Several Illumination Levels: An Evaluation Study of the HRR Plates," *American Journal of Optometry*, Vol. 37, 1960, 82–92.

Walton, W. G., and H. Kaplan. "Motorists' Vision and the Aging Patient," *Journal of the American Optometric Association,* Vol. 32, 1960, 215–216.

Wayne, E. "Alcohol and Road Traffic," *Proceedings of the 3rd International Conference* (London, 1962), B.M.A. House, London, 1963.

Weale, Robert A. "Retinal Illumination and Age," *Transactions of the Illuminating Engineering Society, (*London), Vol. 26, No. 2, 1961, 95–100.

______. *Aging Eye*, H. K. Lewis, London, 1963.

Weber, David. "Vehicle Lighting," *Fleet Owner,* Vol. 60, No. 7, July 1965, 86–93.

Weiss, N. J. "Adapting an Automobile for Driving with Hemianopsia," *Rehabilitative Optometry* 1984, 2(3)7.

Westheimer, G. "Eye Movement Responses to a Horizontally Moving Visual Stimulus," *Archives of Ophthalmology,* Vol. 52, 1954, 932.

Weston, H. C., and L. H. Savin. "Discussion on the Visual Problems of Night Driving," *Proceedings of the Royal Society of Medicine,* Vol. 50, No. 3, 1957, 173–179.

Whillans, Morley G., M.D. "Color Blindness: A Neglected Handicap," *British Columbia Medical Journal*, Vol. 37, No. 4, April 1995, 248–250.

Whiteside, T. C. D. *Heat Flash and Dazzle from Nuclear Weapons: The Principles of Aircrew Protection and Some Experimental Devices,* Ministry of Defense, Flying Personnel Research Committee, Farnborough, England, 1967.

Whittemore, Russell G. "Today's and Tomorrow's Automotive Glass," Society of Automotive Engineers Mid Year Meeting, Chicago, May 17–21, 1965.

______, J. C. Widman and J. D. Ryan. "Tomorrow's Automotive Glass A Dynamic Element in Car Design," *S.A.E. Journal,* Vol. 73, No. 9, Sept. 1965, 50–52.

Wilke, D. J. K. "Investigation of Visual Acuity of Drivers," *British Medical Journal,* No. 5174, 1960, 722–723.

Willett, T. C. "Criminal on the Road: A Study of Serious Motoring Offenses and Those Who Commit Them," *Highway Research Abstract,* Vol. 36, No. 3, March 1966.

Williams, Roger J. *Nutrition in a Nutshell,* Doubleday & Company, Garden City, N.Y., 1962.

Wohl, Michael G., and Robert S. Goodhart, eds. *Modern Nutrition in Health and Disease,* Lea Febiger, Philadelphia, 1964.

Wolf, Ernest. "Effects of Age on Peripheral Vision," *Highway Research Board Bulletin 336,* 1962, 26–32.

______. "Glare and Age," *Archives of Ophthalmology,* Vol. 64, 1960, 502–514.

______, and Michael. J. Zigler. WADC *Technical Report: Relationships of Glare and Target Perception,* U. S. Air Force, Wright–Patterson Air Force Base, Ohio, 1959.

______, ______, and H. B. Cowen-Solomons. "Variability of Dark Adaptation," *Journal of the Optical Society of America,* Vol. 50, 1960, 961–965.

______, Ross A. McFarland and Michael J. Zigler. "Influence of Tinted Windshield Glass on Five Visual Functions," *Highway Research Board Bulletin 255,* 1960, 30–46.

______, and Brenda McGowan "Effect of Light–Time: Dark–Time Ratio and Luminance on Peripheral Sensitivity to Flicker," *Archives of Ophthalmology,* Vol. 69, Feb. 1963, 241–250.

Wortman, Robert H. "Headlight Glare Related to Lateral Separation," *Proceedings, Symposium on Visibility in the Driving Task,* sponsored by Highway Research Board, Illuminating Engineering Research Institute, and Texas A & M University, May 13–15, 1968, 130–144.

Wright, H. L. "Atmospheric Opacity, A Study of Visibility Observations in the British Isles," *Quarterly Journal of the Royal Meteorological Society,* Vol. 65, 1939, 411–442.

Wright, K. A., and W. R. Blevin. "Night Time Luminance of White Roadlines," *Australian Road Research,* Vol. 2, June 1965, 3–11.

Wrigtit, W. D. Subjective Brightness and Contrast in Relation to the Visual Task in Night Driving," in Erik Ingelstam, ed., *Lighting Problems in Highway Traffic,* Pergamon Press, London, 1963, Vol. 2, 81–93.

Wulfeck, Joseph W., Alexander Weisz and Margaret Raben. *Vision in Military Aviation*, WADC Technical Report 58–399, ASTIA Document No. AD 207780.

______, et al. *Vision in Military Aviation*, WADC Technical Report 58–309, Wright Air Development Center, Wright Patterson Air Force Base, Ohio, Nov. 1958, 170.

______, D. F. Johanssen and P. L. McBride. "Studies on Dark Adaptation, III: Pre exposure Tolerances of the Human Fovea As Measured by Contrast Sensitivity," *Journal of the Optical Society of America,* Vol. 50, 1960, 556–558.

Wyatt and Lozance, "Effect of Street Lighting in the Night Traffic Accident Rate." *Illuminating Engineering*, Vol. 50, 1955.

"Yellow Headlights," *Ophthalmic Optician,* April 2, 1966, 363.

Zoli, M. T. "Bibliografia Sulla Miopia Notturna," *Atti Fond. Ronchi,* Vol. 14, 1959, 93–111.

About the Authors

Merrill J. Allen, O.D., Ph.D., Professor Emeritus of Optometry of Indiana University, School of Optometry, Bloomington, Indiana, has been involved in vision research and teaching since 1941. He has over 200 publications and has received 19 awards including the Research Medal Award from the British Optical Association (1970) and the Apollo Award from the American Optometric Association (1971).

He has served as an expert witness in over 600 law suits, providing opinions on the role of visual factors and alcohol in the cause of motor vehicle accidents. He has studied thousands of accident reports, done accident reconstruction and studied other data in order to render his opinions.

Dr. Allen has carried out government, industry and optometrically funded research projects and he considers that consulting on motor vehicle accidents is attorney subsidized research. Many of his research publications are directed at improving motor vehicle safety by eliminating the design errors that keep showing up in accidents.

High-mounted brake lights were a direct result of a research study he did on the Indianapolis Speedway. Daytime running lights resulted from his research funded by the *Indianapolis Star* newspaper. A railroad crossing accident in Kalamazoo Michigan, in which he testified, resulted in increasing the brightness of railroad signal lights across America.

He believes that simple changes of the visual features of motor vehicles and the driving environment can reduce our accidents 80 percent or more and save over 30,000 lives per year.

Bernard S. Abrams, O.D., is the founder of the Institute of Vehicular Safety. He received his B.S. in Visual Optics at Ohio State University. Dr. Abrams began pursuit of his lifelong interest in Traffic Safety in 1954 as a member of the Columbus Ohio Traffic Commission. Over the years, his interest in night vision and vehicular accidents was enhanced by his work in electro-physiological testing for the night vision of the aged. He has lectured about vision on three continents, has designed and built optical factories in several countries, and currently is Chairman of the Board of B.S.A. Industries. Dr. Abrams has authored numerous papers and articles dealing with driver visibility, object conspicuity, and nighttime discernibility. He has conducted research projects and also served on committees related to the vision requirements of the older driver. Dr. Abrams serves as a consultant to industries, attorneys, and governmental agencies. He is a nationally recognized expert witness in nighttime/daytime vehicular accidents.

Dr. Abrams is currently conducting classes at various universities, state patrols, and private institutions relating to the visibility aspects of vision in the courtroom.

Arthur P. Ginsburg, Ph.D., as founder and Director of the Aviation Vision Laboratory at Wright-Patterson Air Force Base, Vistech Consultants Inc. and currently as Director of Vision Sciences Research Corp., has worked extensively with pilots, astronauts and drivers under real and simulated visibility conditions to measure and demonstrate the effects of functional vision losses. Holding nine technology patents, Dr. Ginsburg has developed a filter model of vision, the VCTS and FACT contrast sensitivity clinical test systems, the MCT contrast and glare view-in vision tester, simulated night driving systems and the EyeView™ visual analysis software product.

Dr. Ginsburg provides expert witness services for visibility related air, auto and personal accidents for government, public and private agencies and has sixty published scientific book chapters, papers and reports.

Leslie Weintraub, O.D., is a graduate of Cornell University School of Business and the University of Houston College of Optometry. She is currently in private practice in Tucson, Arizona as a medical optometrist with an emphasis in pathology.

Index

B

C

D

E

F

G

H

M

P

T

Y

Low Speed Automobile Accidents: Accident Reconstruction and Occupant Kinematics, Dynamics and Biomechanics Second Edition, #5236

By Alan J. Watts, Ph.D., Dale R. Atkinson, B.S., Corey J. Hennessy, M.A. , Legal commentaries by Randall H. Kehl, J.D., Nicholas E. Vakula, Esq., Ripley B. Harwood, Esq., and Alan M. Immerman, D.C.; Accompanying videotape by Samantha N. Lapin, M.S.

This new book has been expanded to provide the accident reconstructionist with the necessary tools for correctly interpreting and reconstructing low-speed automobile accidents

Do you have clients who have been injured in a low speed collision? If so, then you understand the hassles such accidents can cause as the insurance companies refuse to cover injuries and the "experts" start arguing. Until now, little systematic study has been done for low speed impact cases, such as those which induce either zero or small (a few inches) crush damage to the vehicles. Yet these low speed cases are those frequently encountered in the well-known "whiplash" phenomenon, where one vehicle rear-ends another at differential speeds usually below 20 mph.

Written for the reconstructionist, attorney, automotive engineer, or other interested professional, this text details the often elusive science of reconstructing and analyzing the low-speed (0 to 20 mph) automobile accident. Topics include analysis of the accident with little or no vehicle damage, the "inexplicable" final position of a vehicle that would indicate speed much higher than the driver admits to, and potential injuries and threshold loads for injuries arising from low-speed impacts. The text will be readily understood by readers with only a basic understanding of accident reconstruction. However, full details and equation derivations are provided in appendices for the benefit of those with either higher technical education or a wish to more fully understand the issues.

Low Speed Automobile Accidents also contains a silent VHS videocassette tape, which includes film clips and animations to demonstrate the principles outlined in this book. This book provides a comprehensive guide to reconstruction and analysis of low-speed automobile accidents. It includes an overview of vehicle dynamics along with detailed analyses and description of vehicle and occupant responses. The scope is comprehensive, consistent with the state-of-the-art in low-speed accident analysis and reconstruction. The major topics covered in this book are Material and Vehicle Response (including crush response of vehicle materials and components, input vs. absorbed energy, post-impact speeds, critical damage speed, incomplete and side impacts, partial impacts, and induced rotations) and Occupant Kinematics (including whiplash, head injury and brain damage, chest and femur loadings, threshold loads for onset of injuries, and considerations for safe vehicle designs). No other textbook covers the subject of low speed automobile accident reconstruction as accurately and comprehensively.

New topics covered include energetics of collisions, bumper behavior, integrated hits and other effects interesting mechanical models, comparisons of CRASH3 and the POD model, proper solutions to various problems, statistics of injury causation, body bouncing and rotations, assorted biomechanical effects, Daubert/Kumho challenges, medical and biomechnical aspects of low-speed accidents, even more specific examples and animations, an enlarged appendix including related cases and affadavits. 6 $^1/_8$" x 9 $^1/_4$", hardbound, 688 pages (includes silent VHS videocassette tape), 1999.

Pedestrian Accident Reconstruction and Litigation Second Edition, #0977

By Jerry J. Eubanks and Paul F. Hill

Pedestrian accidents involving a motor vehicle vary in both nature and scope from accidents involving only passenger cars. Intensified collision damage and injuries frequently result, often due to the inherent disadvantages a pedestrian has in an accident. Reconstruction of these types of collisions pose a unique challenge for accident investigators, attorneys, and insurance professionals. The new *Pedestrian Accident Reconstruction* book and video set discusses, demonstrates, and teaches you the technical fundamentals and mechanics of collisions between motor vehicles and pedestrians; providing a single source of state-of-the-art research dealing with these types of collisions. This valuable set contains chapters on: history and statistics of motor vehicle/pedestrian collisions; pedestrian walking speeds and relative motion; vehicle speed and pedestrian collision formulas; human factors and conspicuity; photography of a motor vehicle/pedestrian collision; case discovery and preparation; and a workbook section covering the videotape of pedestrian accident investigation and reconstruction. 6 $^{1}/_{8}$" x 9 $^{1}/_{4}$", hardbound, 1008 pages (includes 120 min. VHS videotape), 1998.

Handbook of Charts and Tables for Vehicle Dynamics Analysis with CD-ROM, #5716

By Robert Swint, B.S., Barry Richard C.S.P., John Sweat B.S., and Marvin Larson

Quickly discover the accident information you need

Have you ever wanted to calculate how far a vehicle traveling at 47 miles per hour will have moved during perception reaction time? Or how about the distance a vehicle will traverse if it travels 20 miles per hour in 10 seconds? If you have been faced with questions like these in the past, you can now obtain the resource to find the answers quickly and reliably. The *Handbook of Charts and Tables for Vehicle Dynamics Analysis* is a complete reference tool that is a composite of engineering data expressed in formulas, charts, tables and graphs. It is the ideal resource for those initiated in the basics of accident reconstruction, specifically designed as a quick reference supplement to traditional textbooks. The formulas are those recognized by educational institutions and practitioners in the accident reconstruction arena. 8 $^{1}/_{2}$" x 11", 76 pages, 1999.

Pedestrian Formulas for Excel,® computer software, #5686

By C. Greg Russell

You will save many hours calculating vehicle speeds for pedestrian accidents using these pre-formatted spreadsheets. Pedestrian accident speeds can be analyzed with a comparatively large number of formulas. However, one disadvantage arises from the increasing numbers of pedestrian formulas because no one can definitively state that any given equation is the best one to use in a particular situation.

For that reason, this program will do just that. This program simultaneously calculates and displays the values of the equations, in both mph and fps. If an equation is not applicable due to the circumstances surrounding the accident or insufficient data, that equation will display a result of "N/A", and the reason why the equation was not completed will be displayed. Excel® 5.0 or higher, Windows 95® or higher, 1999. Software is non-returnable.

Boat Accident Reconstruction and Litigation, #5082

by Roy Scott Hickman, P.E.

The clearest guide to understanding accidents on and in the water. Your capability to reconstruct boating accidents can make the difference between successful and failed litigation. Yet even experienced engineers and attorneys are often unaccustomed with the myriad complexities of boating accidents which involve concepts and methods not present in other types of accidents. Now, whether you're a beginner or experienced litigator, you can access a wealth of information in this 496 page ground-breaking text. In fact, much of the information at hand here will save you hours of research time hunting through numerous books and on-line services.

You'll start with the basics of how boats function and progress to the way boats are designed which is a key element in the reconstruction of most boat accidents. You'll be introduced to fluid mechanics and the numerous formulae and methods normally used to analyze accidents. Of particular value is the extensive series of appendices which includes numerous Coast Guard regulations and rules controlling boating traffic and safety equipment. You can quickly access the most complete description of major boating accident case citations ever published. You'll be presented with chapters on safety equipment, transportation issues, boat descriptions and designs, and marina issues. All types of boats are covered including personal water craft, water-skiing and the sport of SCUBA diving. You'll also learn about the special problems of carbon monoxide poisoning with boats. 6" x 9", hardbound, 496 pages, 1996.

Basic Collision Analysis and Scene Documentation, Second Edition, #5821

By David A. Casteel and Steven D. Moss

The easy-to-understand-guide to automobile accidents

Point of possible perception? Point of actual perception? Point of response? Skid tire, scuff tire, metal marks or all three? Weather? Lighting? Trees and shrubs? Parked vehicles, fences, buildings, or other obstructions? Investigating any accident scene is no doubt a complex task. Determining the accurate answers to these questions from participants, and from non-participants as well, can be even harder. With this book, you will not have to spend fruitless hours re-creating the accident over and over again because of lack of notes, inadequate interviews, or blurry photographs. Instead, you will have everything organized from the start in a clear, cohesive story—fully documented with all the witness statements, notes, photographs, and reports ever needed. Discover how you can use this valuable guide to save time without sacrificing accuracy; it is, simply, the only book you will ever need to fully report any automobile accident scene. 8 $^1/_2$" x 11", wirebound, 186 pages, 2000.

Equations & Formulas for the Traffic Accident Investigator and Reconstructionist, #5694

By C. Greg Russell

This unique resource is a compilation of nearly every formula anyone who reconstructs accidents could need. Each equation is expressed in three formats: algebraic; modified long form; and spreadsheet format.

Equations are given for both metric and imperial units. Topics covered include: acceleration/deceleration factors, alcohol levels, bicycle equations, braking efficiency, dissipation of energy, distance equations, flips, impact speeds for head-on and rear end collisions, kinetic energy, linear momentum, pedestrian equations, quadrant linear momentum, rollover speed/propensity, speed equations, time equations, and velocity equations. 8 $^1/_2$" x 11", spiral-bound, 136 pages, 1999.

Emergency Vehicle Accidents, Prevention and Reconstruction, #5627

By Stephen S. Solomon, B.S., O.D.

Contributing authors: George L. Ellis, M.D., FACEP; James G. King;

Robert J. Simpson, Esq.; Steven Smyk, Esq.

If you are litigating accidents involving emergency vehicles, you know that many factors contribute to hazardous operations. In this well-documented volume, Stephen S. Solomon, firefighter, EMT, engine captain, fire commissioner, and optometrist shows how vision is an integral component in accidents, and in their prevention.

Whether fire truck, police car, or ambulance, an emergency vehicle's fast speed, bells, whistles, sirens, and flashing lights contribute to excitement-laden and potentially hazardous situations. For the attorney or investigator who must reconstruct events, it is important to understand how some of these supposed safety features actually cause rather than help prevent accidents.

The knowledge you will gain about the anatomy of the eyes will give you the edge in accident reconstruction. You will learn how inadequately trained emergency vehicle drivers make for a potentially lethal situation. Topics covered include: accident analysis and litigation, anatomy of the eyes, color vision, construction of emergency vehicles, emergency vehicle accident profiles, emergency vehicle accidents: Representing the innocent injured bystander, enforcement of law, fluorescent, phosphorescent and retroreflective materials and road flares, medical control, the police chase, and why fire vehicle color is an issue of safety. 6 $^1/_8$" x 9 $^1/_4$", hardbound, 304 pages, 1999.

Roadway Through the MUTCD: Vision and Other Human Factors in the Manual on Uniform Traffic Control Devices, #5511

By Archie C. Burnham Jr., P.E. and Bernard S. Abrams, O.D.

Essential for the Attorney and Reconstructionist in Understanding the MUTCD.

This book will guide you through the twists and turns of the MUTCD and show you how the National Committee is constituted, how it functions and how changes to the Manual are proposed and adopted. The Roadway Through the MUTCD diagrams every part of the MUTCD and shows how each part is related to the others.

The MUTCD is a compendium of uniform standards for design and use of traffic control devices by public authorities and officials having jurisdiction over traffic operations. It is compiled by the National Committee on Uniform Traffic Control Devices and published by the Federal Highway Administration. Roadway Through the MUTCD is intended to serve as a "navigational aid" for anyone having an interest in using the Manual to address questions or resolve disputes involving the design and use of traffic control devices.

After briefly describing the genesis, structure and composition of the National Committee, the authors present an overview of how it operates. They also describe the process through which it is revised and how it fits into the scheme of traffic regulations across the country. This book uses a human factors perspective because traffic control devices are meant to enhance public safety by affecting or channelling how we use our human faculties, especially vision, in traffic operations. The central importance of vision is reflected in the devotion of an entire chapter to a discussion of its fundamentals. From fundamentals and concepts of traffic control devices to detailed descriptions of how to use the manual, this book is your guide through a complex process. 8$^1/_2$" x 11", wirebound, 101 pages, 1998.

Motorcycle Accident Reconstruction and Litigation, 2nd Edition, #5031

By Kenneth S. Obenski, P.E. and Paul F. Hill, Esq.

Riding a motorcycle has been estimated as five times more complex as driving an automobile . . . and reconstructing an accident can be equally difficult. This text, written by a professional engineer who has investigated over 170 motorcycle accidents—and has safely ridden motorcycles for more than 35 years—gives you the detailed information you need to reconstruct and litigate accidents. In clear, jargon-free language the text sets out the basics of motorcycle operation, and the unique interactions between riders, passengers, machines, and other traffic. You'll understand why motorcycles frequently leave less evidence at the scene of an accident, and how a trained reconstructionist can observe and translate even scant evidence.

Of special significance is the section that explains what motorcycle operators can and cannot do, as well as what they should and should not do. Also included is training information published by the State of California, which is a basic source of motorcycle safe operating instruction. Your single source for motorcycle safety standards because its supplemental appendix contains the Department of Transportation (D.O.T.) Motorcycle Safety Standards as well as the preambles and superseded standards. With this detailed history you'll understand D.O.T.'s philosophy in arriving at each standard. 61/8" x 91/4", hardbound, 1128 pages, 1997.

Train Accident Reconstruction and FELA & Railroad Litigation Third Edition, #0969

By James R. Loumiet, BSME and William G. Jungbauer, Esq.

Train collisions usually result in serious injury or death to motorists and pedestrians, often resulting in litigation. Yet the railroad industry presents complexities not known to the average person, making it difficult for an attorney to prepare a successful case. Even experienced accident reconstructionists are usually unfamiliar with the operation of railroads and trains. Yet the ability to reconstruct train collisions is often vital to the successful conduct of railroad litigation.

This ground breaking reference text by Loumiet and Jungbauer is the first of its kind in the are of train accident reconstruction, FELA and railroad litigation. It explains how the railroads operate, the design and operation of trains, how to calculate train speed and successfully conduct FELA and railroad litigation. This text is for both the novice and experienced litigator and reconstructionist. It contains information and formulas that can be found nowhere else. $6^{1}/_{8}$" x $9^{1}/_{4}$", 686 pages, 1998.

Human Factors Engineering for Forensic and Safety Specialists, #5406

By Wesley E. Woodson

Your client's injury: Did a design flaw encourage misuse of a product?

This enlightening book calls upon the author's 50+ years of experience researching human factors engineering, and provides a wealth of information on the real world of machines, consumer products and operational environments. Human factors engineering is a ground-breaking area too often ignored or misunderstood by lawyers.

Often a designer's errors encourages mistakes or mis-use. Unfortunately, when trying these personal injury cases, legal professionals often pre-determine the "human factors" based on their own ability to use a product or operate in a particular environment. Since lawyers are human, they feel that they intuitively know about all human factors. The result? Many lawyers fail when trying personal injury cases, even though a thorough knowledge of human factors engineering could have meant a successful verdict. 81/2" x 11", hardbound, 275 pages, 1998.

Life and Worklife Expectancies, #5368

By Hugh Richards, M.S.

Contributing authors: Jon Abele, James Ciecka, Peter Ciecka, Tamorah Hunt, Joyce Pickers-Gill, Herbert Rutemiller, Frank Slesnick, and Robert Thornton.

Wouldn't you like to have all the information you need for determining life and worklife expectancies in one complete volume: smokers by education, many educational categories by race/Hispanic origin, persons with medical conditions, etc.? With *Life and Worklife Expectancies*, you can! Also, you will find an extensive treatment on how Hispanics, especially less educated Hispanics and those with little English language proficiency, challenge common sense conclusions about life and worklife expectancies. All this and more are shown with extensive tables and figures in easy to read format.

Part I contains an overview of the methodology and data sources used in life tables: differences between period and cohort life tables, properties of survival data, life expectancy by educational attainment and race/Hispanic origin and by cigarette use, relative mortality ratios for persons with medical risks, and much more.

Part II deals with all the main methods of determining duration of working life. Detailed tables for all methods and many educational, demographic, smoking status and occupational categories are provided. Biases in previous worklife estimates are corrected by including mortality rates by educational attainment, and the increment-decrement model is carefully analyzed for correction of other potential biases.

This is the first comprehensive overview of life and worklife expectancies for attorneys, insurance professionals, and forensic economists. In addition to correcting biases in older estimates, it discusses pros and cons of the various methods, for example worklife expectancies, Life-Participation-Employment (LPE) and Median Years to Retirement (MYR). This book is packed with extensive tables of life and worklife expectancies for many personal characteristics—race, smoking status, occupation etc. There is no other book like *Life and Worklife Expectancies*! 8 1/2" x 11", hardbound, 272 pages, 2000.

Civil Trial Practice: Winning Techniques of Successful Trial Attorneys, #5899

Edited by M.P. Papadakis, Esq.

It's easy to spot the winners! The best trial lawyers share their secrets for the 21st century.

Wish you could get some inside tips from the best? Inner circle members. Former national association presidents. Past presidents of state bar associations and trial lawyer associations. Now for the first time, this book gives you a privileged glimpse into the minds of the best trial lawyers in the country.

In today's market place, you know you need to distinguish yourself from the pack. The millennium will offer ever new challenges. This book offers a wealth of practical tips and shrewd observations about being a successful trial attorney from the best of the best. Get the competitive edge and save valuable time by reading the techniques of distinguished litigators gleaned from years of hands-on experience! 8 1/2" x 11", hardbound, 816 pages, 2000.

Elements of Trial Practice, #6060

by Peter D. Polchinski, Esq.

An invaluable guide for the new trial attorney

To win at trial, you must present your case clearly, simply, persuasively, and fairly, while you undermine your adversary's case in the same manner. Achieving excellence in trial advocacy is a lifelong pursuit. Nevertheless, trial skills and a basic understanding of this art can be learned quickly.

Short and persuasive—this book wastes no words. You'll discover how to select a favorable jury, prepare your witnesses, deliver powerful opening statements, conduct an effective direct examination, cross-examine any witness, introduce exhibits, impeach their witnesses, control consulting experts, and win the case on summation. *Elements of Trial Practice* will become your essential, instant-access reference for trial. Armed with its many valuable techniques, you will approach trial practice with new enthusiasm and confidence. 6" x 9", 113 pages, softbound, 2000.

Physical Evidence in Forensic Science, #5563, 5564

By Henry C. Lee, Ph.D. and Howard A. Harris, Ph.D., J.D.

This new classic by America's leading forensic scientists will give you an insider's grasp of physical evidence at the crime scene

Introducing a groundbreaking guide written by the nation's foremost forensic scientists! This easy-to-read reference will introduce you to the basics of crime scene evaluation. For forensic scientists and police investigators, this invaluable book is packed with numerous figures, tables, photographs and extensive lists. You'll learn how to collect, prepare, classify and analyze all types of crime scene evidence. Connect the victim(s) and suspect(s) to the crime scene and to the physical evidence left behind to provide convincing testimony based on scientific facts. Discover if the police and prosecution have done their jobs properly to process all crime scene materials.

Physical Evidence in Forensic Science will become your desktop reference! 6" x 9", available as softbound or hardbound, 297 pages, 2000.

Packaging Forensics—
Package Failure in the Courts, #5783

By Walter Stern, C.P.P.

Contributing authors: Martin K. Brigham, Patrick E. Carr, Peter Henningsen, Robert A. Luciano, Alfred H. McKinlay, Francis Patrick Murphy, Grantges J. Raymus, Paul Singh, Suzelle M. Smith, Eunice Trevor, Nancy A. Zettler

An in-depth reference for the products liability litigator

With the many variables to consider in any packaging forensics case, you'll first need to determine what type of expert to hire. A safety specialist? A mechanical engineer? Or an accident reconstructionist? Written by veteran packaging engineers, this essential resource will give you all the information you need to successfully litigate your case. Packaging forensics is a unique specialty incorporating transportation, distribution, packaging, and materials handling.

You'll learn how the proper documentation and photographic evidence of a manufacturer's operations in storage, loading, and ensuring the security of packages will convince the defense to settle a case before it goes to trial. Was weight distribution a factor in the accident? Were industry standards followed? Were written safety instructions read prior to the accident? Whether you're an attorney working for the defense or plaintiff, whether you're an industry executive or active professional engineer, you'll find that this book will be the most useful resource on this complex area of expertise. 6 $^{1}/_{8}$" x 9 $^{1}/_{4}$", hardbound, 352 pages, 2000.